KU-400-717

Legal Advisors
Library

WORDS AND PHRASES
legally defined

Volume 1: A–C

WORDS AND PHRASES
legally defined

THIRD EDITION

under the General Editorship of
John B Saunders
of Lincoln's Inn, Barrister

Volume 1: A–C

London
Butterworths
1988

United Kingdom	Butterworth & Co (Publishers) Ltd, 88 Kingsway, LONDON WC2B 6AB and 61A North Castle Street, EDINBURGH EH2 3LJ
Australia	Butterworths Pty Ltd, SYDNEY, MELBOURNE, BRISBANE, ADELAIDE, PERTH, CANBERRA and HOBART
Canada	Butterworths. A division of Reed Inc., TORONTO and VANCOUVER
New Zealand	Butterworths of New Zealand Ltd, WELLINGTON and AUCKLAND
Singapore	Butterworth & Co (Asia) Pte Ltd, SINGAPORE
USA	Butterworths Legal Publishers, ST PAUL, Minnesota, SEATTLE, Washington, BOSTON, Massachusetts, AUSTIN, Texas and D & S Publishers, CLEARWATER, Florida

© Butterworth & Co (Publishers) Ltd 1988

All rights reserved. No part of this publication may be reproduced or transmitted in any form or by any means, including photocopying and recording, without the written permission of the copyright holder, application for which should be addressed to the publisher. Such written permission must also be obtained before any part of this publication is stored in a retrieval system of any nature.

This book is sold subject to the Standard Conditions of Sale of Net Books and may not be re-sold in the UK below the net price fixed by Butterworths for the book in our current catalogue.

British Library Cataloguing in Publication Data

Words and phrases legally defined.—3rd ed/edited by John B Saunders
   1. Commonwealth countries. Common law countries. Law—Encyclopaedias
I., Saunders, John B (John Beecroft), *1911—*
342.009171'241

ISBN 0 406 08040 2 (set)
     0 406 08041 0 (vol 1)
     0 406 08042 9 (vol 2)
     0 406 08043 7 (vol 3)
     0 406 08044 5 (vol 4)

Typeset by Phoenix Photosetting, Chatham, Kent
Printed and bound in Great Britain by
Mackays of Chatham Ltd, Kent

OVERSEAS REVISING EDITORS

Australia
Arthur E Garcia   LLB(NSW), LLM(Syd)

Canada
Heather Probert   LLB
of the Ontario Bar

New Zealand
Anne Kiernan   BA (Hons), LLB

USA
Michael G Walsh
Assistant Professor in Business Law at the College of Commerce and Finance,
Villanova University, Villanova, Pennsylvania

EDITORIAL MANAGER

Margaret Cherry   LLB

The United Kingdom material in this volume states the law as at 31 December
1987. Material from jurisdictions outside the United Kingdom is up-to-date
to 30 September 1987.

PREFACE

WORDS AND PHRASES, first published nearly forty years ago, was, in its original form an anthology of judicial definitions. These comprised extracts from speeches made and judgments given in the House of Lords, the Judicial Committee of the Privy Council, and the various Divisions of the Supreme Court, and also of the superior courts of Australia, Canada and New Zealand. Save for occasional explanatory notes, every extract was reproduced in the words in which it was originally reported.

The second edition, published twenty years later, still remained largely a collection of judicial definitions. Its scope was broadened by the addition, to the UK material, of selections of statutory definitions and extracts from textbooks, notably the third edition of *Halsbury's Laws of England*. In addition, the material was regrouped so that it was possible to simplify the headings, which were limited to a single word or a short phrase of two or three words. This, in conjunction with the use of sub-headings, meant that it was possible in most cases to gather together groups of definitions which, under the former strictly alphabetical arrangement of phrases, would have fallen on different pages or even in different volumes. Such phrases as Private nuisance, Public nuisance, Statutory nuisance and Nuisance to the highway now fell logically under the main heading NUISANCE.

This third edition follows the style of the second edition. Many more judicial interpretations have been added, and references to the statutes and chosen statutory definitions have been updated. References to *Halsbury's Laws of England* have been amended to refer to the fourth edition of that work. Recognising that other jurisdictions frequently look to US materials for guidance, particularly in areas of commercial law, the scope of the work has been further broadened by the inclusion of selected extracts from the materials of leading states of the USA. A number of extracts from *Dictionary of Legal Words and Phrases*, published by Butterworths, South Africa, have also been added to the work.

It should be noted that a meaning which a number of expressions in common use are to bear when used in a United Kingdom statute, unless a contrary intention appears, are defined by the Interpretation Act 1978.

It is hoped that this edition will continue to serve as a useful companion to *Halsbury's Laws*.

J.B.S.
March 1988

A

ABANDON

'Whatever be the distinction between the terms "abandon" and "desert" when applied to a parent in connection with his child, both words imply in ordinary language a disregard of parental duty, and carry with them the idea of moral blame.' *Re O'Hara* [1900] 2 IR 232 at 252, CA, per Holmes LJ

'I do not think the facts in this case amount to abandonment or desertion. I think the words "abandoned or deserted the child" [in the Custody of Children Act 1891, s 1] point at the parent leaving the child to its fate. But in this case, although the petitioner did little for her child, she never really abandoned or deserted it, because she knew and approved of the steps which the respondent took for its maintenance.' *Mitchell v Wright* (1905) 7 F 568 at 574, per the Lord President

'By s 3(1)(a) of the Adoption Act 1950 [repealed; see now the Adoption Act 1976, s 16(2)(d)], it is provided that the court may dispense with the consent of a parent of an infant if the parent has abandoned, neglected or persistently ill-treated the infant . . . I am satisfied that the respondent has not abandoned the child as contemplated by s 3(1)(a) of the Act of 1950. She was not leaving the child to her fate; she was giving her over to people who desired to adopt her and in whom she had confidence, and, when one finds that s 3(1)(a) deals with abandonment, neglect or persistent ill-treatment, I think it is clear that abandonment means abandonment that would have rendered her liable to the criminal law.' *Watson v Nikolaisen* [1955] 2 All ER 427 at 430, 431, per cur.

Australia 'In my opinion the words [in an Ordinance] "abandoned, deserted or persistently neglected or ill treated the child" refer exclusively to morally reprehensible conduct. They are not apt to include the conduct of a mother who deliberately leaves her child in the care of a religious community when she knows that the child will be cared for by that community, with a view to its being handed over to the care of properly constituted adopters or guardians. . . .' *Re application for adoption of X and Re Adoption of Children Ordinance 1965* (ACT) (1984) 71 FLR 162 at 164, per Blackburn CJ

Canada 'The word "abandoned" is not given any definition in the Act [Wife's Protection Act, RSBC 1948, c 364 (repealed; see now RSBC 1960, c 407)] but the dictionary meaning of the word indicates that it has a connotation of finality. It means the relinquishment or extinguishment of a right, the giving up of something absolutely.' *Read v Read* [1950] 2 WWR 812 at 814, BCCA, per Sloan CJBC

ABANDONMENT

Of contract

Canada [The Mechanics and Wage-Earners Lien Act, RSO 1914, c 140, s 22(1) (repealed; see now Lien Act 1983 (Ont), c 6, s 31(1) provided that a claim for lien by a contractor or sub-contractor, in cases not otherwise provided for, might be registered before or during the performance of the contract or within thirty days after the completion or 'abandonment' thereof]. 'An abandonment of the contract contemplated by this section is, not leaving a work under the belief that the contract is completed, but, knowing or believing that the contract was not completed, declining to go on and complete it.' *Anderson v Fort William Commercial Chambers Ltd* (1915) 34 OLR 567 at 570, CA, per cur.

Of distress

The remedy by distress must not be used in an oppressive manner, and the general rule is that a landlord may not split one entire demand and distrain twice for the same rent when he might have taken enough on the first occasion. . . . The rule against a second distress applies where the landlord having distrained enough voluntarily abandons the distress, that is to say, where he surrenders or forbears to exercise his power of making the distress fruitful. Abandonment is a question of fact. (13 Halsbury's Laws (4th edn) paras 350, 352)

'Inasmuch as the goods were taken away without any intention whatever to abandon the distress, but with the knowledge that they would certainly be brought back again, when they were restored by the voluntary act of the person who took them away, they continued subject to the distress.' *Kerby v Harding* (1851) 6 Exch 234 at 241, per Parke B

'The quitting possession of goods, by the landlord, after he has distrained them, is not necessarily an abandonment of the distress.' *Bannister v Hyde* (1860) 2 E & E 627 at 631, per Wightman J

Of goods

Property, both in lands and moveables, being . . . originally acquired by the first taker, which taking amounts to a declaration that he intends to appropriate the thing to his own use, it remains in him, by the principles of universal law, till such time as he does some other act which shows an intention to abandon it: for then it becomes, naturally speaking, *publici juris* once more, and is liable to be again appropriated by the next occupant. So if one is possessed of a jewel, and casts it into the sea or a public highway, this is such an express dereliction, that a property will be vested in the first fortunate finder that will seise it to his own use. But if he hides it privately in the earth, or other secret place, and it is discovered, the finder acquires no property therein; for the owner hath not by this act declared any intention to abandon it, but rather the contrary: and if he loses or drops it by accident, it cannot be collected from thence, that he designed to quit the possession; and therefore in such case the property still remains in the loser, who may claim it again of the finder. And this, we may remember, is the doctrine of the law of England, with relation to treasure trove. (2 Bl Com 9)

Abandonment of goods takes place when possession of them is quitted voluntarily without any intention of transferring them to another. (35 Halsbury's Laws (4th edn) para 1126)

Of ship

'. . . whatever strictness of construction may have been applied to notices of abandonment in former times, it never could have been absolutely necessary to use the technical word "abandon"; any equivalent expressions which informed the Underwriters that it was the intention of the assured to give up to them the property insured upon the ground of its having been totally lost, must always have been sufficient.' *Currie & Co v Bombay Native Insurance Co* (1869) LR 3 PC 72 at 77–79, per cur.

'The word "abandon" is one in ordinary and common use, and in its natural sense well understood; but there is not a word in the English language used in a more highly artificial and technical sense than the word "abandon"; in reference to constructive total loss, it is defined to be a cession or transfer of the ship from the owner to the underwriter, and of all his property and interest in it, with all the claims that may arise from its ownership, and all the profits that may arise from it including the freight then being earned.' *Rankin v Potter* (1873) LR 6 HL 83 at 144, per Martin B

'There is no set form or sacrosanct ritual to constitute abandonment. . . . The question in each case must be whether the facts warrant the inference in law that the vessel was abandoned. For this purpose it must be steadily borne in mind also that abandonment here connotes the leaving of the vessel *sine spe revertendi*, made in good faith and to save life on the order of the master or person in charge.' *The Albionic* [1941] P 99 at 112, 113 per Langton J; affd [1942] P 81, CA

'The word "abandon" . . . has in the English legal use several different meanings. It is used in three different senses in the very group of sections [of the Marine Insurance Act 1906] which deal with constructive total loss. Indeed, it is used in two different senses in s 60(1). When the ship is spoken of as abandoned because of "its actual . . . loss appearing unavoidable," the word is used in nearly the same sense as when, according to the law of salvage, the ship is left by master and crew in such a way as to make it derelict, which condition confers on salvors a certain, but not complete, exclusiveness of possession, and a higher measure of compensation for salvage services. But to constitute the ship a derelict, it must have been left (a) with that intention (*animo derelinquendi*): See *The John and Jane* [(1802) 4 Ch Rob 216]; (b) with no intention of returning to her; and (c) with no hope of recovering her. Obviously that sense of the word is frequently inappropriate to the second case to which sub-s (1) applies, viz because it could not be preserved from total loss (i.e. an economic test) "without an expenditure greater than her value when the expenditure had been incurred".' *Court Line Ltd v R, The Lavington Court* [1945] 2 All ER 357 at 362, 363, CA, per Scott LJ

Of trademarks and tradenames

United States   A mark shall be deemed to be 'abandoned'—
(a) When its use has been discontinued with intent not to resume. Intent not to resume may be inferred from circumstances. Non-use for two consecutive years shall be prima facie abandonment.
(b) When any course of conduct of the registrant, including acts of omission as well as commission, causes the mark to lose its significance as an indication of origin.
(Lanham Act 1946, s 45)

ABATEMENT

Of legacy

'The rule is that in the case of a deficiency, all the annuities and legacies abate rateably, for since they cannot all be paid in full, they shall all abate rateably on the principle of the maxim "equality is equity" or "equity delighteth in equality". This rule is indeed subject to exceptions, for there are cases in which some annuities or legacies are to be paid in priority to others; but it is settled that the onus lies on the party seeking priority to make out that such priority was intended by the testator, and that the proof of this must be clear and conclusive. . . . . The onus is upon those who contend for a priority to show that the testator meant to give a preference to a particular legatee.' *Miller v Huddlestone* (1851) 3 Mac & G 513 at 523, 524, per Lord Truro LC

See, generally, 17 Halsbury's Laws (4th edn) para 1263.

Of nuisance

Abatement means the summary removal or remedy of a nuisance by the party injured without having recourse to legal proceedings. It is not a remedy which the law favours and is not usually advisable. Its exercise destroys any cause of action in respect of the nuisance except for damages in respect of harm sustained before the abatement. (34 Halsbury's Laws (4th edn) para 349)

ABDUCTION

South Africa   'The common law crime of abduction consists in the taking away of any female under the age of twenty-one years from the custody of her parents, guardians or those having charge of her, against her will. The object of the taking away need not necessarily be unlawful carnal connection; but of course it may be—and as a matter of fact it generally is. But under the common law, to take a girl away for the purpose of marrying her would be abduction.' *R v Roberts* 1908 TS 283 per Innes CJ

South Africa   'In a charge of abduction the taking, in my opinion, can happen in two ways: there can be a physical taking, as, for instance, in a vehicle, or there can be a taking by means of suggestion, inducement, persuasion. It is only where the taking is actually physical that there need be no suggestion, inducement, persuasion; but even if the taking be not physical and there be inducement, persuasion, suggestion on the part of the accused, then the willingness of the girl, the fact that she met the accused half-way, so to say, will not afford a defence.' *R v Ismail* 1943 CPD 420 per Davis J

ABET   *See* AID AND ABET

ABEYANCE

Of peerage

The doctrine of abeyance relates not to the extinction of a peerage, but to the state of suspense into which a peerage falls when co-heirship occurs in the succession. Hitherto the doctrine of abeyance has been accepted by the House of Lords only in respect of baronies in fee, that is, baronies created by writ of summons and sitting. Two claims have been made in respect of earldoms in fee, but no direct decision was given on the point of abeyance. Abeyance does not apply to Scottish peerages and is of recent origin, not being known before the seventeenth century, nor fully developed until the nineteenth century. When the owner of a fief died leaving no male issue but more than one daughter, his land fell to his daughters in equal shares, although for a landed barony it was held that the eldest daughter must have the chief residence where seisin was taken for the whole. A dignity being impartible and all the daughters having equal rights in it, the peerage right is held to be latent in all the co-heirs. (35 Halsbury's Laws (4th edn) para 840)

ABLE

Australia 'If a debtor is able to pay his debts but is recalcitrant, his creditors may resort to the remedies otherwise afforded by the law such as execution against his property and garnishee proceedings. The words "able to pay his debts" in s 52(2)(a) of the [Bankruptcy] Act 1966–1986 do not mean "willing and able" to do so.' *Sarina v Council of Shire of Wollondilly* (1980) 48 FLR 372 at 376, CA, per Bowen CJ

ABLE AND WILLING

[By a contract in writing, the owner of certain property instructed a firm of estate agents to procure for him a person 'able, ready and willing' to purchase the property.] 'These words do not mean a person ready, able and willing "to make an offer" or even "to enter into a contract"; they mean a person ready, able and willing "to purchase", that is, to complete the purchase. He must be a person who is "able" at the proper time to complete; that is, he must then have the necessary financial resources. He must also be "ready"; that is, he must have made all necessary preparations by having the cash or a banker's draft ready to hand over. He must also be willing; that is, he must be willing to hand over the money in return for the conveyance.' *Dennis Reed Ltd v Goody* [1950] 2 KB 277 at 287, CA, per Denning LJ

[A firm of estate agents were instructed to find a person 'able and willing' to purchase a business.] 'Was the purchaser here a person willing and able to purchase the business? Willing, certainly. Able? Counsel for the agents invited us to construe the word "able" as meaning financially able. . . . But it seems to me that "able" cannot be confined to financial ability. A purchaser must be able, in the case of a leasehold, to satisfy the lessor that he is a suitable tenant so that the lessor is willing to accept him as a tenant and to give his consent to the assignment. Otherwise he is not an "able" purchaser; for he is not able to complete the purchase. I think "able" means "able not only to sign a contract but also to go on and complete the purchase".' *Dellafiora v Lester, Lester v Adrian Barr & Co Ltd* [1962] 3 All ER 393 at 396, CA, per Lord Denning

ABLE-BODIED

A seaman shall not be entitled to the rating of AB, that is to say, of an able-bodied seaman, unless he has served at sea for three years before the mast, but the employment of fishermen in decked fishing vessels registered under the first part of this Act shall only count as sea service up to the period of two years of that employment; and the rating of AB shall only be granted after at least one year's sea service in a trading vessel in addition to two or more years' sea service on board of decked fishing vessels so registered. (Merchant Shipping Act 1894, s 126 (prospectively repealed by the Merchant Shipping Act 1970)

'The test of able-bodiedness is not whether a man can get work, but whether he can do work.' *Melrose Parish Council v Gordon Parish Council* 1924 SC 1034 at 1039, per Lord Alness (Lord Justice-Clerk)

ABLE TO EARN

New Zealand [The Workers' Compensation Act 1922 (NZ), s 5(6) (repealed; see now the Workers' Compensation Act 1956, s 14(4)), provided that, during any period of partial incapacity, the weekly payment was to be an amount equal to sixty-six and two-thirds per centum of the difference between the amount of the worker's weekly earnings at the time of the accident and the weekly amount which the worker was earning after the accident in any employment or business or was 'able to earn' in some suitable employment provided or found for him after the accident by the employer by whom he was employed at the time of the accident.] 'The fact is that the defendant county did provide a job for plaintiff and paid him his full pre-accident rate of pay, and that plaintiff left the job after working for some five weeks. He was able for five weeks to do what he was called upon to do. That is prima facie evidence that he could carry on the job. His reasons for knocking off—(i) that he could not take weight on his fingers, (ii) that the doctor told him to knock off—are not supported by his doctor. The fact that he decided not to work until his claim is settled must also be taken into consideration in deciding whether he could or could not have carried on the job. Having regard to these facts, I am unable to say that plaintiff has displaced the prima facie evidence that he could carry on the job. The fact that he was being paid full wages is not conclusive evidence that he is earning or able to earn those wages. The fact is the job was made to suit plaintiff.' *Lammas v Manawatu County* [1946] NZLR 232 at 235, per Ongley J; also reported [1940] GLR 117 at 118

ABNORMALITY OF MIND

[The Homicide Act 1957, s 2(1) provides that a person shall not be convicted of murder if he was suffering from such 'abnormality of mind' as substantially impaired his mental responsibility for his acts, etc.] '"Abnormality of mind", which has to be contrasted with the time-honoured expression in the M'Naghten Rules "defect of reason", means a state of mind so different from that of ordinary human beings that the reasonable man would term it abnormal. It appears to us to be wide enough to cover the mind's activities in all its aspects, not only the perception of physical acts and matters and the ability to form a rational judgment whether an act is right or wrong, but also the ability to exercise willpower to control physical acts in accordance with that rational judgment.' *R v Byrne* [1960] 3 All ER 1 at 4, CCA, per cur; also reported [1960] 2 QB 396 at 403

'There may be cases in which the abnormality of mind relied on cannot readily be related to any of the generally recognised types of "insanity". If, however, insanity is to be taken into consideration, as undoubtedly will usually be the case, the word must be used in its broad popular sense. It cannot too often be emphasised that there is no formula that can safely be used in every case—the direction to the jury must always be related to the particular evidence that has been given, and there may be cases where the words "border-line" and "insanity" may not be helpful. In the result, their Lordships are of opinion that the direction given to the jury by which they were told to assess the degree of abnormality of mind in terms of the border-line between legal insanity and legal sanity as laid down in the M'Naghten Rules was a serious and vital misdirection which would, no doubt, not have been given had the Chief Justice had the benefit of Lord Parker's judgment in *R v Byrne* [supra].' *Rose v R* [1961] 1 All ER 859 at 864, PC, per cur; also reported in [1961] AC 496 at 507, 508

ABODE   *See also* RESIDENCE

[A rule of court provided that the true place of abode of the deponent of an affidavit should be inserted in such affidavit.] 'The words "place of abode" did not necessarily mean the place where the deponent slept; . . . the object of the rule of court was to ascertain the place where the deponent was most usually to be found, which in the present case was the office at which he was employed during the greater part of the day, and not the place whither he retired merely for the purposes of rest.' *Haslope v Thorne* (1813) 1 M & S 103 at 104, per Lord Ellenborough CJ

'A man's residence, where he lives with his family and sleeps at night, is always his place of abode in the full sense of that expression.' *R v Hammond* (1852) 17 QB 772 at 780, 781, per Lord Campbell CJ

'A place of business is a "place of abode".' *Mason v Bibby* (1864) 2 H & C 881 at 888, DC, per Pollock CB

'A man may have two places of abode, one where he abides at night, and another where he abides by day.' Ibid, at 888, per Martin B

'In ordinary language I do not think one would speak of a place of business as a man's place of abode or residence—phrases which, I think, ordinarily mean the same thing; but when the words are used in a statute one must consider the purpose of the statute and the object to be effected by requiring the place of abode or residence to be described or visited.' *R v Braithwaite* [1918] 2 KB 319 at 330, CA, per Scrutton LJ

'The argument on behalf of the tenant is largely based on the provision of s 23 of the Landlord and Tenant Act 1927, and in particular on the words "last known place of abode in England and Wales". It is contended that "place of abode" in that phrase means the place where the tenant dwelt—his residence in the sense of the place where he slept at night, if nothing more. However, a large number of authorities show that, at any rate for certain purposes, "residence" or "place of abode" may include a place where the person in question works and has his business. The reason why those results have been reached in those cases really depends on the purposes for which the statutory provisions are intended, and if they are intended to make sure that proceedings or notice of proceedings and the like shall come to the knowledge of a certain person (as has been pointed out in these cases) it often may be far more likely that a person will receive due notice of the matters in question if the notice is sent to him at his usual place of business rather than the place where he happens to go home and sleep at night.' *Price v West London Investment Building Society* [1964] 2 All ER 318 at 321, CA, per Danckwerts J

[The Theft Act 1968, s 25(1) makes it an offence for a person, when not at his 'place of abode', to have with him any article for use in the course of or in connection with any burglary, theft or cheat. The appellant had been living rough in a car which was found to contain such articles.] 'We must construe the phrase in the context in which it appears in s 25(1) of the Theft Act 1968. In that context it is manifest that no offence is committed if a burglar keeps the implements of his criminal trade in his "place of abode". He only commits an offence when he takes them from his "place of abode". The phrase "place of abode", in our judgment, connotes, first of all, a site. That is the ordinary meaning of the word "place". It is a site at which the occupier intends to abide. So, there are two elements in the phrase "place of abode", the element of site and the element of intention. When the appellant took the motor car to a site with the intention of abiding there, then his motor car on that site could be said to be his "place of abode", but when he took it from that site to move it to another site where he intended to abide, the motor car could not be said to be his "place of abode" during transit.' *R v Bundy* [1977] 2 All ER 382 at 384, CA, per cur.

ABOLISH

'I cannot conceive myself but that the word "abolished" there [in a repealed Education Act] involves dissolution; it means that the school boards and school attendance committees shall be abolished, and it really is not denied that the effect of that section is that from the happening of "the appointed day" the school board and the committee would be incapable of doing anything.' *Oldham Corpn v Bank of England* [1904] 2 Ch 716 at 723, per Vaughan Williams LJ

ABOUT

Place

'The words "about a factory" [in the Workmen's Compensation Act 1897, s 7(1) (repealed)] . . . were evidently intended to meet the case of something being done in direct connection with the factory, though not exactly within it, as, for example, loading goods at a gate, or doing work in an annexe, though possibly separated from the principal yard by a street. It appears to me to be plain that this was the intention in inserting the word "about", and that it is not a word suitable to indicate that wherever a workman be sent to do work for his

master, he, as it were, carries the factory to that place, or establishes a factory for his employers at that place, so that he is doing work "about" the factory.' *Barclay, Curle & Co v M'Kinnon* (1901) 3 F 436 at 438, per the Lord Justice-Clerk

New Zealand 'The word "about" . . . is a geographical expression involving the idea of a certain physical contiguity, "but it also involves the idea of an employment connected with the business carried on at the place indicated": *Owens v Campbell Ltd* [[1904] 2 KB 60 at 64, CA, per Collins MR].' *Public Trustee v Gill* [1934] NZLR 832 at 837, per Reed J; also reported [1934] GLR 693 at 695

Quantity

'The question depends on the construction of the charterparty. By it, the defendant undertook to load a "full and complete cargo of iron ore, say about 1,100 tons". . . . The reasonable meaning seems to be that the shipowner undertakes, if the ship is of much greater capacity than 1,100 tons, to accept a cargo of about 1,100 tons as equivalent to a full cargo and thus effect is given to the words "say about", etc, as words of contract. . . . What, then, is the meaning of the word "about"? This is partly matter of fact and partly matter of law. I think the direction to the jury has always been that the deviation must not be very large. The difference must be such as people would ordinarily consider as included in the word "about". There can be no exact rule of law as to the percentage of difference allowed, but I have known juries often allow in practice 3 per cent.' *Morris v Levison* (1876) 1 CPD 155 at 156–158, per Brett J

ABOUT TO SAIL

'What do the words "now sailed or about to sail" represent to the charterers? To say that a ship "has sailed" is obviously to represent that she has done so. To say that she is "about to sail" is to represent either that she is loaded and just about to sail, or that, if she is not already loaded, she will be loaded in a day or two, and will then sail. Taken in connection with the first words "now sailed", it seems to me that the words "or about to sail" amount to a representation that the ship is just ready to sail.' *Bentsen v Taylor, Sons & Co (No 2)* [1893] 2 QB 274 at 278, CA, per Lord Esher MR

ABOVE   *See also* OVER

[The appellants had erected a girder across a river. The question was whether this contravened a local Act regulating erections 'above' the river.] 'I think . . . that the words "above the bed or waterway" mean, or at any rate include, "over" the bed or waterway.' *Burnley Co-operative Society v Pickles* (1898) 77 LT 803 at 807, 808, per Wright J

[The Building (Safety, Health and Welfare) Regulations 1948, reg 31(3) (revoked; see now the Construction (Working Places) Regulations 1966), laid down that suitable and sufficient ladders, etc, should be provided in cases where workmen, working on or near fragile roofs, had to pass over or work 'above' such roofs.] 'What does the word "above" mean? Does it mean above in the vertical plane of the fragile roof, or does it mean above merely in the sense of at a greater height? I think it means the former.' *Harris v Brights' Asphalt Contractors Ltd* [1953] 1 All ER 395 at 398, per Slade J; also reported in [1953] 1 QB 617 at 628

ABROAD

The expression 'abroad' means outside Great Britain and Ireland. (Children and Young Persons Act 1933, s 30)

Testamentary condition

'When the testator talks of the children being maintained in England, with regard to that I think there is no reasonable doubt. Then he says "and do not reside abroad except for a period not exceeding six weeks in each year". What does that mean? Is "abroad" contrasted with England, or has the word "abroad" the ordinary meaning in the English language? Mr Hart says that "abroad" means anywhere out of England. . . . I do not think that contention can be sound. . . . The word "abroad" can never be used by anybody in talking of a person who has gone to Scotland, nor I think of a person who has gone to Ireland *rebus sic stantibus*. There is, therefore, some little difficulty in deciding whether "abroad" means out of England, or means, as it ordinarily means, outside the British Islands. I think myself it must mean outside the British Islands.' *Re Boulter, Capital & Counties Bank v Boulter* [1922] 1 Ch 75 at 82, 83, per Sargant J

ABSENCE

Canada 'The expression "absence or inability to act" [of judge of Court of Sessions of Peace] should of course be given a construction at once reasonable and in harmony with the purpose of the statute. "Inability to act" may or may not involve "absence". It is usually accompanied by physical absence; and absence may be due to physical inability to be present. But, as used in the statute, "absence" clearly means something different from "inability to act". It connotes physical non-presence from whatever cause. The question is non-presence in what place or within what area? We are not concerned with the cause of absence.

"Absence", as used in this statute, must, I think, be taken to mean absence from the bench, or, at the utmost, absence from the court-room in which the trial takes place. That is a fact of which the replacing judge can be personally cognisant when the trial is beginning. Beyond that his actual knowledge ordinarily cannot extend.' *Brunet v R* (1918) 57 SCR 83 at 91, 92, SCC, per Anglin J

Canada [Under the Municipal Act, RSO 1937, c 266, s 213(2) (repealed), a majority of a municipal council could themselves call a meeting in the 'absence' of the mayor.] '[Counsel] urges . . . that "absence" . . . should be construed in its widest sense; that it requires no particular degree or amount of absence, viz. from the city or the Province, and that the applicants, going as they did, to the respondent's office in the City Hall and remaining from 9.30 to 11 am and finding the mayor not present, absence is established within the meaning of the section. . . . I cannot conclude that there was an absence here to warrant the applicants taking the steps they did. The respondent was in the city; he had been in his office the evening before; he would be in later in the day, and it was no doubt known that in the forenoon when the applicants called, he was on duty with the regiment to which he belonged.' *Cooper v Croll* [1940] 1 DLR 610 at 615, 616, Ont SC, per Gillanders J

ABSENT

'In the construction of an article like clause 97 of the articles of this bank it has been held that the expression "absents himself" means something more than the expression "is absent". . . . He [a director] could not be taken to have absented himself within the meaning of that article until there was a meeting which he ought to have attended. . . . I do not think that the period of absence began to run until then.' *Re London & Northern Bank, McConnell's Claim* [1901] 1 Ch 728 at 731, 732, per Wright J

New Zealand 'The rule of the New Zealand Code . . . which has come under discussion is r 53. . . . The material part of it is as follows:—"In actions founded on any contract made or entered into or wholly or in part to be performed within the colony, on proof that any defendant is absent from the colony at the time of the issuing of the writ, and that he is likely to continue absent . . . the Court may give leave to the plaintiff to issue a writ and proceed thereon without service". . . . The . . . contention related to the word "absent". . . . The appellant seeks to confine it to persons who at some previous time have been domiciled or resident in New Zealand. It is not easy to appreciate the reasons why such an artificial sense should be put upon the word; and during the argument their Lordships expressed agreement with the judges of the Court of Appeal, who held that the word is used in its ordinary sense, and describes persons who are not in New Zealand.' *Ashbury v Ellis* [1893] AC 339 at 341, 345, PC, per cur.

South Africa 'Not present in a given place at a given time.' *Jurlicke and Holdcroft v Currie* 27 NLR 154

Without leave

In this Act 'absent without leave' means absent from any hospital or other place and liable to be taken into custody and returned under this section, and related expressions shall be construed accordingly. (Mental Health Act 1983, s 18(6)

ABSOLUTE *See also* FEE SIMPLE
ABSOLUTE; TERM OF YEARS ABSOLUTE

[It was held that the obligation imposed by the Mines and Quarries Act 1954, s 81(1) (to maintain machinery, etc) was 'absolute'.] 'The word "absolute" in this connexion has become part of the dictionary of the law. Sometimes the word "continuing" is substituted for it. Either word means that, in effect, the employer warrants that the machine or other equipment which he is obliged to maintain will never be out of order.' *Hamilton v National Coal Board* [1960] 1 All ER 76 at 78, HL, per

Viscount Simonds; also reported in [1960] AC 633 at 639

Canada 'In my opinion the word "absolute" even when used in a technical sense in connection with the vesting of property may signify at least two different legal concepts. In one sense it may be used to denote the lack of limitation of the extent or duration of an interest in personal property while in another it may mean the freedom of the interest from dependence on other things or persons.' *Halley v Minister of National Revenue* [1963] Ex CR 372 at 375, Ex Ct, per Thurlow J; affd, without written reasons, 63 DTC 1359, SCC

ABSOLUTE AND INDEFEASIBLE

'Absolute and indefeasible means absolute and indefeasible against the whole world. Unless the enjoyment gives a title against all persons having any interest in the *locus in quo* it gives no title at all.' *Wheaton v Maple & Co* [1893] 3 Ch 48 at 68, CA, per Lopes LJ

ABSOLUTE ASSIGNMENT *See* ASSIGNMENT

ABSOLUTE INTEREST

A person shall [for the purpose of the interpretation of Part XV: Estates of deceased persons in course of administration] be deemed to have an 'absolute interest' in the residue of the estate of a deceased person, or in a part thereof, if and so long as the capital of the residue or of that part thereof, as the case may be, would, if the residue had been ascertained, be properly payable to him, or to another in his right, for his benefit, or is properly so payable, whether directly by the personal representatives or indirectly through a trustee or other person. (Income and Corporation Taxes Act 1970, s 432(2))

ABSOLUTELY

'What is the meaning of the word "absolutely"? If an independent meaning can be given to it, it must be "unconditionally".' *Re Pickworth, Snaith v Parkinson* [1899] 1 Ch 642 at 651, CA, per Rigby LJ

'I return to this simple will: "I give all my property to the person who, at the time of my death shall be or shall act as the abbess of the said convent absolutely". . . . The real difficulty in this case is the use of the word "absolutely". "Absolutely" means free of some fetter in some form. . . . I think that the word not only means that the recipient will retain the full ownership, for the purposes indicated, of that which is given, but also that she is to be free from any fetter or trust which would bind her to keep the fund intact for the purposes of the community.' *Re Ray's Will Trusts, Re Ray's Estate, Public Trustee v Barry* [1936] Ch 520 at 525, 526, per Clauson J

Australia 'Its [the word "absolutely"] ordinary meaning is "without condition or limitation". And in legal parlance it is commonly used with regard to vesting as meaning "indefeasibly".' *Re Thompson, Rhoden v Wicking* [1947] VLR 60 at 67, per Herring CJ

ABSTRACT OF TITLE

The abstract of title is a summary of the documents by which any dispositions of the property have been made during the period for which title has to be shown, and of all the facts, such as births, marriages, deaths, or other matters affecting the devolution of the title during the same period. As far as possible it is (as regards transactions dated since 1925) confined to dispositions of a legal estate. (42 Halsbury's Laws (4th edn) para 147)

'Now, I apprehend that an abstract is delivered whenever a number of sheets of paper, call it what you will, whenever a document is delivered to the purchaser, which contains, with sufficient clearness and sufficient fullness, the effect of every instrument which constitutes part of the title of the vendor, and that that is a delivery of the abstract, even though it takes place, as it must, I apprehend, in all cases take place, before the actual comparison of the abstract with the deeds themselves, which they purport to abstract.' *Oakden v Pike* (1865) 34 LJ Ch 620 at 622, per Kindersley V-C

ABSTRACTION

'Abstraction', in relation to water contained in any source of supply in a river authority area, means the doing of anything whereby any of that water is removed from that source of supply and either—
(a) ceases (either permanently or temporarily) to be comprised in the water resources of that area, or

(b) is transferred to another source of supply in that area, and 'abstract' shall be construed accordingly.
(Water Resources Act 1963, s 135)

ABUSE

'The information contains a charge of assaulting and abusing a certain woman; therefore, on the face of it, there is a complaint of something more than a mere assault. The expression "abusing" appears to me to import "assaulting" and something more. . . . I am not aware that the word "abuse" applied to a woman is ever used except with reference to sexual intercourse. Certainly, in more than one Act of Parliament the word "abuse" has had that meaning applied to it.' *Re Thompson* (1860) 6 H & N 193 at 200, per Pollock CB

'To my mind the word "abused" conveys no definite meaning: it is not a word of art; in popular language it means calling names— abusing by words. The only instance in which it is used as a term of art shows that it does not mean "ravish", because I find in the 9 Geo 4, c 31, s 18 [repealed by the Offences against the Person Act 1861], as to trials for the crimes of "rape and of carnally abusing girls" under the ages therein mentioned, the term "carnally abusing" is used as meaning something different from rape. The word "abusing" without the concomitant words "unlawfully and carnally" has no definite meaning. The expression "unlawfully assaulted and abused" alleges an assault, with a word which may mean that the prisoner did something else.' Ibid at 202, 203 per Bramwell B

ABUT   *See also* ADJACENT; ADJOIN

'I think . . . the language "with all the houses and grounds abutting on and upon the said road" . . . synonymous with the expression "bounded by the said road".' *R v Strand Board of Works* (1863) 4 B & S 526 at 549, per Cockburn CJ

'With reference to land to "abut" means to actually touch'. *Barnett v Covell* (1903) 68 JP 93 at 94, per Lord Alverstone CJ

[The Leicester Corporation Act 1897, s 31 provided (inter alia) that every hoarding 'in, abutting on, or adjoining' any street should be securely erected.] 'It seems to me that when there is an advertisement hoarding put up which becomes for the time being de facto the boundary of the street, so that if it is not strong enough it may possibly come down either into the street, or on to the people who are standing on the land adjoining the street, then within the meaning of this statute the hoarding is "in, abutting on, or adjoining the street".' *Rockleys Ltd v Pritchard* (1909) 101 LT 575 at 577, DC, per Lord Alverstone CJ

'Prima facie, at any rate, you ought to be careful to use the word [abut] in its proper sense; and "abut" in its proper and etymological sense, and as frequently used, means actual touch.' *R (on prosecution of Lewisham Borough Council) v South Eastern Rly Co* (1910) 74 JP 137 at 139, CA, per Kennedy LJ

Canada [An abutting owner had the right to purchase a stopped-up portion of a highway under Municipal Act, RSO 1960, c 249, s 477 (repealed; see now RSO 1980, c 302, s 316(1))] '. . . an abutting owner within the meaning of s 477 means an owner, the front, rear or side of whose property is contiguous to *a side of* a highway which is stopped up, but does not mean or include an owner whose property is contiguous to either terminus of a highway.' *Catkey Construction (Toronto) Ltd v Bankes* (1970) 15 DLR (3d) 13 at 14, Ont CA, per Jessup JA

ACCELERATION

'The doctrine of acceleration is that all interests which fail or are undisposed of are captured by a residuary gift or go on an intestacy, but that a testator is presumed to have intended an acceleration of subsequent interests where a life interest fails in consequence of the donee being prevented by law from taking.' *Re Kebty-Fletcher's Will Trusts, Public Trustee v Swan* [1967] 3 All ER 1076 at 1080, per Stamp J

ACCEPTANCE *See also* AGREEMENT

Of bill of exchange

'Acceptance' means an acceptance completed by delivery or notification. (Bills of Exchange Act 1882, s 2)

'That section [the Bills of Exchange Act 1882, s 19] provides "(1) An acceptance is either (a) general, or (b) qualified: (2) A general acceptance assents without qualification to the order of the drawer. A qualified acceptance in express terms varies the effect of the bill as drawn. In particular an acceptance is qualified

which is . . . (c) local, that is to say, an acceptance to pay only at a particular specified place. An acceptance to pay at a particular place is a general acceptance, unless it expressly states that the bill is to be paid there only and not elsewhere". The emphasis there is on the word "only", and it follows that, if an acceptor merely accepts a bill payable at a named place, it remains a general acceptance for the purpose of the section. It is only if he accepts expressly to pay at a specified place only and not elsewhere that it becomes a qualified acceptance.' *Banku Polskiego v Mülder (K J) & Co* [1941] 2 KB 266 at 267, 268, per Tucker J

New Zealand 'I am of opinion that the learned Magistrate has misconstrued the meaning of the acceptance of a bill on demand. The Bills of Exchange Act 1908, s 17, states: "The acceptance of a bill is the signification by the drawee of his assent to the order of the drawer". If the learned Magistrate's view is right, the words endorsed by the drawee here were meaningless. In my judgment, the words "will accept", when applied to a bill on demand, mean "will pay"; and this is the view taken by the late Mr Justice Byles, one of the greatest authorities on bills of exchange. In the case of *Smith v Vertue* [(1860) 30 LJCP 56] His Lordship said: "Any words which stipulate that the drawee means to pay is a sufficient acceptance; anything in writing to that effect and signed by the acceptor. The simple meaning of an acceptance is 'I will pay.'"' *Humphreys v Taylor* [1921] NZLR 343 at 344, per Stout CJ; [1921] GLR 123

See, generally, 4 Halsbury's Laws (4th edn) paras 362-65.

Of goods

The buyer is deemed to have accepted the goods when he intimates to the seller that he has accepted them, or (except where section 34 above otherwise provides) when the goods have been delivered to him, and he does any act in relation to them which is inconsistent with the ownership of the seller, or when after the lapse of a reasonable time he retains the goods without intimating to the seller that he has rejected them. (Sale of Goods Act 1979, s 35)

[Section 34 of the Act provides that a buyer is not deemed to have accepted the goods until he has had a reasonable opportunity of examining them in order to ascertain whether they are in conformity with the contract.]

United States (1) Acceptance of goods occurs when the buyer
(a) after a reasonable opportunity to inspect the goods signifies to the seller that the goods are conforming or that he will take or retain them in spite of their nonconformance; or
(b) fails to make an effective rejection (subsection (1) of Section 2–602), but such acceptance does not occur until the buyer has had a reasonable opportunity to inspect them; or
(c) does any act inconsistent with the seller's ownership; but if such act is wrongful as against the seller it is an acceptance only if ratified by him.
(2) Acceptance of a part of any commercial unit is acceptance of that entire unit. (Uniform Commercial Code 1978, s 2–606)

Of offer

An acceptance of an offer is an indication, express or implied, by the offeree made whilst the offer remains open and in the manner requested in that offer of the offeree's willingness to be bound unconditionally to a contract with the offeror on the terms stated in the offer. (9 Halsbury's Law (4th edn) para 245)

Of option

Canada '"Acceptance" of the option means the election of the plaintiff [the optionee] to buy the property on the terms specified, and . . . "exercising the option" means the same thing.' *Lawrance v Pringle* (1912) 17 BCR 250 at 255, BCCA, per Macdonald CJA

ACCESS

Means of access

'Means of access' includes any means of access, whether private or public, for vehicles or for foot passengers, and includes a street. (Town and Country Planning Act 1971, s 290(1))

Of light

'No doubt the Prescription Act [1832] says that "its provisions are to operate when the access and use of light to and for any dwelling-house, workshop or other building shall have been actually enjoyed therewith for the full period of 20 years, without interruption"; but does "use" in this clause mean user in the particular trade, business or occupation which may at the time of the controversy be carried on, or even

in any other requiring equivalent light? I cannot think so. It seems to me that the addition of "use" to "access", in the language of the statute, was to oblige that there should be actual admission of the light, not merely that the light should reach the building, which might have satisfied "access", and that there was no intention of prescribing that any particular user, either in kind or degree, should have existed. The object was to give title to relief, but not to define its extent.' *Mackey v Scottish Widows' Fund Life Assurance Society* (1877) IR 11 Eq 541 at 558, 559, CA, per Ball LC

'The material question in this case appears to me to turn on the 3rd section of the [Prescription Act 1832]. . . . I pause to observe that in my judgment the word "access" as used in that section, does not refer to the access through the orifice—through the aperture or window—but to the freedom of passage over the servient tenement, and I think some confusion has arisen from supposing that the access referred to there is the access through the window of the dominant tenement. Undoubtedly the two are closely connected together, because the right acquired under this section of the statute by the dominant tenement is governed and measured by the access to the dominant tenement, and therefore the aperture which lets the light into the dominant tenement defines in a manner familiar to us all the area which must be kept free over the servient tenement. The two things are closely connected together—the one is the measure of the other—but they are not the same thing.' *Scott v Pape* (1886) 31 Ch D 554 at 575, CA, per Fry LJ

'The claim of the plaintiffs is rested on s 3 of 2 & 3 Will 4, c 71 [Prescription Act 1832], which enacts that "when the access and use of light to and for any dwelling-house, workshop, or other building shall have been actually enjoyed therewith for the full period of twenty years without interruption, the right thereto shall be deemed absolute and indefeasible". . . . But the argument is that the plaintiffs have not enjoyed the use of light to these windows . . . within the meaning of the statute. That depends upon the signification of the words "actually enjoyed". Enjoying the use cannot mean shall have continuously used. If that had been the intention . . . some such word as "continuously" should be found in this section, and it might then be necessary to show that the plaintiffs had never closed their shutters for a day during twenty years next before the action.

I take "enjoyed" to mean "having had the amenity or advantage of using" the access of light; that is nearly equivalent to "having had the use", the intention being that the owner of a house may acquire the right to have the access of light over adjoining land to an opening which he has used in such manner as suited his convenience for the passage of light during twenty years.' *Cooper v Straker* (1888) 40 Ch D 21 at 26, 27, per Kay J

[The measure of light to which right is acquired under the Prescription Act 1832, s 3 is that which is required for the beneficial use of the building for any ordinary purpose to which it is adapted: *Allen v Greenwood* [1979] 1 All ER 819, CA.]

To and from highway

[Under the Private Street Works Act 1892, (repealed; see now the Highways Act 1980, s 207(3)(a)) an authority might apportion the expenses of works on an owner, notwithstanding that the premises did not front or abut on the works, if 'access' thereto from the part of the street upon which the repairs were to be executed was obtained through a court, passage, or otherwise.] '"Access by court, passage, or otherwise" does not necessarily mean access by a court, passage, or other means of access which is narrow because a passage is narrow; it means access by something which gives access to the street in the same way as a court or passage gives access to the street. . . . Access from a street to premises by means of another public street is not access within the meaning of s 10.' *Newquay Urban Council v Rickeard* [1911] 2 KB 846 at 853, DC, per Pickford J

ACCESSIBLE

'There was some discussion as to the meaning of the word "accessible" in this regulation [the Docks Regulations 1934, reg 37]. I think it is obvious that the word is not to be interpreted as meaning a place to which the workman is bound to go in the course of his duty or a place at which his work lies, and I think that it is sufficient for me to say for the purposes of this case that the word "accessible" means capable of access without any reasonable let or hindrance.' *Henaghan v Rederiet Forangirene* [1936] 2 All ER 1426 at 1433, per Lewis J

New Zealand [The question was as to the meaning of 'the nearest accessible pound' in the Impounding Act 1884, s 11 (repealed; see now the Impounding Act 1955, s 22).] 'A pound may be inaccessible from some temporary obstacle, or in some cases from permanent natural obstacles. "Accessible" must of course mean accessible in a reasonable sense by the animals which are included in the Act. I should be inclined to say that a pound which could only be reached by cattle by a journey, and under conditions which, from distance or other circumstances, would make such journey injurious or cruel (the impounder not being under any obligation by the Act to supply food or water in travelling), could not be said to be accessible to such cattle.' *Finlay v Barrett* (1897) 15 NZLR 436 at 440, 441, per Denniston J

ACCESSION

If any corporeal substance receives an accession by natural or artificial means, as by the growth of vegetables, the pregnancy of animals, or the embroidery of cloth, the original owner is entitled by his right of possession to the property in its improved state. Similarly, when the goods of one person are affixed to the land or chattel, for example a ship, of another, they may become part of it and so accrue to the owner of the principal thing. (35 Halsbury's Laws (4th edn) para 1138)

Secured transactions

United States A security interest in goods which attaches before they are installed in or affixed to other goods takes priority as to the goods installed or affixed (called in this section 'accessions') over the claims of all persons to the whole except as stated in subsection (3) and subject to Section 9–315(1) [priority when goods are commingled or processed]. (Uniform Commercial Code 1978, s 9–314(1))

ACCESSORY (Noun)   *See also*
ACCOMPLICE

'The law draws a distinction between principals in the first degree, principals in the second degree, and accessories—the latter being persons who aid or abet the principal offender in the commission of the offence, before or after.' *Stacey v Whitehurst* (1865) 18 CBNS 344 at 355, per Willes J

Australia 'Persuasion, advice, encouragement, suggestion or words of like import all fall into one important category of acts which will suffice to constitute the actor an accessory.' *R v Ready & Manning* [1942] VLR 85 at 88, per cur.

South Africa '(1) The less valuable of two things so joined together as to be inseparable. The more valuable, to which the accessory accedes, is called the principal. (2) An accessory is a secondary, additional or non-essential item of equipment.' *R v Silke* 1947 (4) SA 298(C)

After the fact

'The classic definition of an accessory after the fact is when a person, knowing a felony to have been committed, receives, relieves, comforts, or assists the felon; see 1 Hale, Pleas of the Crown 618; 4 Blackstone's Commentaries 37. These are all *active* acts of assistance from which it can be inferred that he assented to the felon going free, in contrast to misprision which consists of concealment only, from which no inference of assent need be drawn.' *Sykes v Director of Public Prosecutions* [1961] 3 All ER 33 at 40, HL, per Lord Denning

[All distinctions between felony and misdemeanour were abolished by the Criminal Law Act 1967, s 1(1). The former law relating to accessories after the fact was replaced by s 4 of the 1967 Act, which provides penalties for assisting any person who has committed an arrestable offence, with intent to impede his apprehension or prosecution.]

Before the fact

An accessory before, is he, that being absent at the time of the felony committed, doth yet procure, counsel, command, or abet another to commit a felony, and it is an offence greater than the accessory after. (1 Hale's PC 615)
[As to the abolition of the distinction between felony and misdemeanour, see supra.]

'An accessory before the fact must be absent at the time when the crime is committed, and the act must be done in consequence of some counsel or procurement of his.' *R v Brown* (1878) 14 Cox CC 144 at 144, per Lord Coleridge CJ

Australia 'The meaning of "accessory" particularly "accessory before the fact" may be important. . . . On the authority of *R v Taylor* (1875) LR 2 CCR 147, it is accurately stated, on p 149:—"There must be some active proceeding on his part. He must procure, incite or in some other way *encourage* the act done by the principal".' *R v Webbe & Brown* [1926] SASR 108 at 112, per cur.

ACCIDENT   *See also* INEVITABLE ACCIDENT

'I think the idea of something fortuitous and unexpected is involved in both words, "peril" or "accident".' *Hamilton, Fraser & Co v Pandorf & Co* (1887) 12 App Cas 518 at 524, per Lord Halsbury LC

'The word "accident" may be used in either of two ways. An accident may be spoken of as occurring to a person, or as occurring to a train, or vehicle, or bridge. In the latter case, though several persons were injured who were in the train, or vehicle, or on the bridge, it would be an accident to the train, or vehicle, or bridge. There might, however, be said to be several accidents to the several persons injured.' *South Staffordshire Tramways Co Ltd v Sickness & Accident Assurance Assocn Ltd* [1891] 1 QB 402 at 407, CA, per Bowen LJ

'The word "accident" is not a technical legal term with a clearly defined meaning. Speaking generally, but with reference to legal liabilities, an accident means any unintended and unexpected occurrence which produces hurt or loss. But it is often used to denote any unintended and unexpected loss or hurt apart from its cause; and if the cause is not known the loss or hurt itself would certainly be called an accident. The word "accident" is also often used to denote both the cause and the effect, no attempt being made to discriminate between them. The great majority of what are called accidents are occasioned by carelessness; but for legal purposes it is often important to distinguish careless from other unintended and unexpected events.' *Fenton v Thorley & Co Ltd* [1903] AC 443 at 453, per Lord Lindley

'A good deal was said about the word "accident". Etymologically, the word means something which happens—a rendering which is not very helpful. We are to construe it in the popular sense, as plain people would understand it, but we are also to construe it in its setting, in the context, and in the light of the purpose which appears from the Act [Workmen's Compensation Act 1906 (repealed)] itself. Now, there is no single rigid meaning in the common use of the word. Mankind have taken the liberty of using it, as they use so many other words, not in any exact sense but in a somewhat confused way, or rather in a variety of ways. We say that some one met a friend in the street quite by accident, as opposed to appointment, or omitted to mention something by accident, as opposed to intention, or that he is disabled by an accident, as opposed to disease, or made a discovery by accident, as opposed to research or reasoned experiment. When people use this word they are usually thinking of some definite event which is unexpected, but it is not so always, for you might say of a person that he is foolish as a rule and wise only by accident. Again, the same thing, when occurring to a man in one kind of employment, would not be called accident, but would be so described if it occurred to another not similarly employed. A soldier shot in battle is not killed by accident, in common parlance. An inhabitant trying to escape from the field might be shot by accident. It makes all the difference that the occupation of the two was different. In short, the common meaning of this word is ruled neither by logic nor by etymology, but by custom, and no formula will precisely express its usage for all cases.' *Trim Joint District School Board of Management v Kelly* [1914] AC 667 at 680, 681, HL, per Lord Loreburn

'It is necessary to emphasise the distinction between "accident" and "injury". . . . No doubt the more usual case of an "accident" is an event happening externally to a man. . . . But it is now established that apart from external accident there may be . . . internal accident. A man suffers from rupture, an aneurism bursts, the muscular action of the heart fails, while the man is doing his ordinary work. . . . In such cases it is hardly possible to distinguish in time between "accident" and "injury"; the rupture which is accident is at the same time injury from which follows at once or after a lapse of time death or incapacity. But the distinction between the two must be observed.' *Fife Coal Co v Young* [1940] AC 479 at 488, 489, per Lord Atkin

'In . . . ordinary language the word "accident" seems to me without any doubt to cover an act of God.' *J & J Makin Ltd v London & North Eastern Rly Co* [1943] 1 KB 467 at 474, 475, CA, per Lord Greene MR

'In the context of the statute [National Insurance (Industrial Injuries) Act 1965 (repealed; see now Part II (Chapter IV) of the Social Security Act 1975)] "accident" is used as descriptive of the first event in three chains of causation: (1) Accident—personal injury—incapability of work. (2) Accident—personal injury—loss of faculty—disablement. (3) Accident—personal injury—death. . . . In popular speech "accident", the first event in each chain, is used in a variety of meanings of which the common characteristics are unex-

pectedness and, generally, misfortune. As was pointed out by Lord MacNaghten in *Fenton v Thorley & Co Ltd* [supra] it embraces both an event which was not intended by the person who suffers the misfortune and an event which, although intended by the person who caused it to occur, resulted in a misfortune to him which he did not intend. An event which constitutes an "accident" with which the statute is concerned has two limiting characteristics: the misfortune which it causes must be "personal injury" to an insured person; and the event must be one which can be identified as arising out of and in the course of that person's employment.' *Jones v Secretary of State for Social Services* [1972] 1 All ER 145 at 184, HL, per Lord Diplock

[The Road Safety Act 1967, s 2(2) (repealed; see Road Traffic Act 1972, s 8(2), now substituted by the Transport Act 1981, s 25, Sch 8) provided that if an 'accident' occurred owing to the presence of a motor vehicle on a road or other public place, a constable in uniform might require the person driving or attempting to drive to take a breath test.] 'The court is of the opinion that the word "accident" in s 2(2) should as far as possible be given its ordinary rather than a technical meaning. The word "accident", unhappily, is well known in the context of road use and motor cars and we would deplore any technical meaning being attached to this simple, ordinary word in the context in which it appears. It is evident that the accident referred to in the subsection is something which can happen when a person is driving or attempting to drive a car, and furthermore that it must be an accident which occurs owing to the presence of a motor vehicle on a road. Several attempts at definitions of the word "accident" have been made in the course of argument. We have been referred in particular to the words of Lord Lindley in *Fenton v Thorley & Co Ltd* [supra], a case on the Workmen's Compensation Act 1897, in which the word "accident" was a prominent word. In that case Lord Lindley said: "The word 'accident' is not a technical legal term with a clearly defined meaning. Speaking generally, but with reference to legal liabilities, an accident means any unintended and unexpected occurrence which produces hurt or loss". Sachs LJ, in the course of the argument supplied an alternative, with which the other members of the court agree, in which he suggested that "accident" in the present context means an unintended occurrence which has an adverse physical result. . . . Such an occurrence is one in which prima facie at any rate the circumstance of the occurrence, and of the driver involved in it, deserve consideration by authority, and accordingly we think that the definition suggested by Sachs LJ, is one which fits the intention of Parliament and will not open the door unduly widely to the suggestion that random breath tests can be taken in purported consequence of it.' *R v Morris* [1972] 1 All ER 384 at 386, 387, CA, per cur.

'I hesitate to attempt a definition, lest my judgment should in future be quoted as if it were writing something into the 1972 [Road Traffic] Act. But it seems to me that "accident" in this context is perfectly capable of applying to an untoward occurrence which has adverse physical results, notwithstanding that one event in the chain of events which led to the untoward consequence was a deliberate act on the part of some mischievous person.' *Chief Constable of West Midlands Police v Billingham* [1979] 2 All ER 182 at 186, per Bridge LJ

Canada 'In common parlance when one hears someone relate that there has been an accident it does not . . . follow that there has been no negligence involved at all. For the word "accident" has in commonplace the significance of being opposed to a wilful and deliberate act, or, short of this, one which is of so obviously gross negligence [as to be] the obvious and natural result of a most imprudent and unreasonable act.' *McCollum (RD) Ltd v Economical Mutual Insurance Co* [1962] OR 850 at 858, Ont SC, per Lancheville J

New Zealand [The question was whether damage to a flat by subsidence was covered by an insurance against 'accidental damage'.] 'As to what is normally meant it is necessary to bear in mind Earl Loreburn's observation in *Trim Joint District School Board of Management v Kelly* [supra], that the meaning is "ruled neither by logic nor by etymology, but by custom, and no formula will precisely express its usage for all cases". As a general guide, however . . . it is traditional to take Lord Macnaghten's definition in *Fenton v Thorley & Co Ltd* [supra] "an unlooked-for mishap or an untoward event which is not expected or designed". Mr Hillyer cited another dictum, Mr Micawber's "Accidents will occur in the best-regulated families", thus effectively making the point that, in the ordinary sense, accidental results are very often produced by intended actions. It seems to me that both Lord Macnaghten's description and the usage in

Dickens fit the subsidence of the flat aptly. There is no finding, nor even any evidence, that when the flat was built the council or its officers expected it to subside, still less intended such a result. In retrospect the subsidence may be seen as inevitable, but that is often true of accidents caused by negligence. It is not profitable to essay precise rules or semantics in this field. Facts and risks vary too greatly. But in the end, in relation to the simple words "accidents" and "accidental damage to property" in this insurance policy, I doubt whether as a matter of law the court can go further than to say that those are helpful but not necessarily exhaustive tests.' *Mt Albert City v NZMC Insurance Co* [1983] NZLR 190 at 192, 193, 194, CA, per Cooke J

See, generally, 33 Halsbury's Laws (4th edn) para 486.

In bill of lading

'Looking at the proper meaning of the word "accident" I think it does not include injury to the cargo from the negligence of the master or crew.' *Lloyd v General Iron Screw Collier Co* (1864) 3 H & C 284 at 292, 293, per Bramwell B

'The exceptions in the bill of lading include ". . . or any other accidents of the seas". . . . It is to be borne in mind that the contract is for the carriage of the goods in a steamship, and the exceptions must relate to a contract of carriage by steamship. The learned judge has found, after stating that the ship was fit to carry the cargo, and that the cargo was properly stowed, that the damage was caused by heat proceeding from the bulkheads surrounding the engine and boiler space, and that this damage was the result of closing the ventilators during a period of seven days in a storm of exceptional severity and duration. . . . The ship being a fit ship, and the cargo being properly stowed, it is difficult to see what more the shipowner could do. . . . In my judgment, when once the meaning of these findings is realised, it becomes clear that this damage was the direct result of the accidents of the seas.' *The Thrunscoe* [1897] P 301 at 305, 306, per Gorell Barnes J

Canada 'The system of ventilation was sufficient for ordinary purposes, and . . . the heating of the maize . . . was caused by the stopping of ventilation, which, as a matter of good seamanship, was a matter of necessity imposed by the state of the weather. This brings the case within the exception "accidents

of the seas" contained in the bill of lading.'
Donkin, Creeden & Avery Ltd v The Chicago Maru (1917) 23 BCR 551 at 554, BCSC, per Martin LJA

In charterparty   *See also* DANGER

[A charterparty provided for the loading of a ship within a reasonable time except in case of riots, strikes or any other 'accidents' beyond the defendant's control. The loading was not completed because of a severe fall of snow.] 'An accident is not the same as an occurrence, but is something that happens out of the ordinary course of things. A fall of snow is one of the ordinary operations of nature, and is an incident rather than an accident, and, therefore, without going into the rule that general words are to be restricted to the same genus as the specific words which precede them, I think this natural occurrence did not come within the terms of the exception of the charterparty.' *Fenwick v Schmalz* (1868) LR 3 CP 313 at 316, DC, per Willes J

Industrial accident

For the purposes of this section (but subject to section 117(3) below), an accident whereby a person suffers personal injury shall be deemed, in relation to him, to be an industrial accident if—
(a) it arises out of and in the course of his employment;
(b) that employment is employed earners' employment for the purpose of Part II, Chapter IV [benefit for industrial injuries];
(c) payment of benefit is not under section 50(5) precluded because the accident happened while he was outside Great Britain.
(Social Security Act 1975, s 107(5))

[Section 117(3) of the Act makes additional provisions as to decisions relating to industrial injuries.]

In insurance policy

The event insured against may be indicated in the policy solely by reference to the phrase 'injury by accident' or the equivalent phrase 'accidental injury' or it may be indicated as 'injury caused by or resulting from an accident'. The word 'accident' or its adjective 'accidental' is no doubt used with the intention of excluding the operation of natural causes such as old age, congenital or insidious disease, or the natural progression of some constitutional physical or mental defect; but the ambit of what is included by the word is not entirely clear. It has been said that what is postulated is the intervention of some cause which is brought into operation by chance so as to be fairly describable as fortuitous. The idea of something haphazard is not necessarily inherent in the word; it covers any unlooked for mishap or an untoward event which is not expected or designed, or any unexpected personal injury resulting from any unlooked for mishap or occurrence. The test of what is unexpected is whether the ordinary reasonable man would not have expected the occurrence, it being irrelevant that a person with expert knowledge, for example of medicine, would have regarded it as inevitable. The standpoint is that of the victim, so that even wilful murder may be accidental as far as the victim is concerned. (25 Halsbury's Laws (4th edn) para 594)

'This was an action . . . on a policy of insurance effected by the deceased with the defendants, whereby he, being then about to proceed on a foreign voyage as master of a vessel, was insured to the extent of a reasonable compensation against any personal injury from or by reason of or in consequence of any accident which might happen to him upon any ocean, sea, river, or lake. . . . It is difficult to define the term "accident", as used in a policy of this nature, so as to draw with perfect accuracy a boundary line between injury or death from accident, and injury or death from natural causes; such as shall be of universal application. At the same time we think we may safely assume that, in the term "accident" as so used, some violence, casualty, or vis major, is necessarily involved. We cannot think disease produced by the action of a known cause can be considered as accidental. Thus disease or death engendered by exposure to heat, cold, damp, the vicissitudes of climate, or atmospheric influences, cannot, we think, properly be said to be accidental; unless, at all events, the exposure is itself brought about by circumstances which may give it the character of accident. Thus (by way of illustration), if, from the effects of ordinary exposure to the elements, such as is common in the course of navigation, a mariner should catch cold and die, such death would not be accidental; although if, being obliged by shipwreck or other disasters to quit the ship and take to the sea in an open boat, he remained exposed to wet and cold for some time, and death ensued therefrom, the death might properly be held to be the result of accident. It it true that, in one sense, disease or death through the direct effect of a known natural cause, such as we have referred to, may be said to be accidental, inasmuch as it is uncertain beforehand whether the effect will ensue in any particular case. Exposed to the same malaria or infection, one man escapes, another succumbs. Yet diseases thus arising have always been considered, not as accidental, but as proceeding from natural causes.' *Sinclair v Maritime Passengers Assurance Co* (1861) 3 E & E 478 at 484–486, per Cockburn CJ

Australia 'A man taking out what is known as an "accident" policy would think that he was insuring himself against fortuitous and unexpected injuries. If he suffers the injuries by his own design they are not fortuitous, but he would certainly think that injuries, although inflicted upon him by the design of another person, were fortuitous to himself. If the word "accidental" is ambiguous it should, I think, be construed *fortius contra preferentem*.' *Grant v Southern Cross Assurance Co Ltd* (1927) 30 WALR 65 at 68, per Draper J

Australia 'An injury is accidental when it is unforeseen or unexpected, but in order to show that an injury has been caused by accidental means there must be evidence that it was caused by some act of the insured which he had not intended and had not planned to do and which was an involuntary act on his part.' *Steinke v Australian Provincial Assurance Assocn Ltd* [1944] St R Qd 7 at 16, per Mansfield J

Australia 'As a matter of ordinary language in this country, an "accident" (from the Latin *accidens*) means very much what the etymologist would expect. It is something which happens without intention or design. When used with reference to something which causes injury, it means an unexpected and unintended mishap. In that context, the ordinary and natural meaning of the word still corresponds with Lord MacNaghten's definition in *Fenton v Thorley & Co Ltd* [supra] which . . . has commonly been accepted as applicable to the use of the word in public liability and other insurance policies: "an unlooked-for mishap or an untoward event which is not expected or designed".' *Australian Casualty Co Ltd v Federico* (1986) 66 ALR 99 at 108, per Wilson, Deane and Dawson JJ

Canada 'The word "accident" excludes the operation of natural causes, and implies the intervention of some cause which is brought into operation by chance, and which can there-

fore be described as fortuitous. . . . The fact that the particular consequence was not foreseen does not make it accidental, if it was in fact the natural consequence of a cause which is not accidental; there is no accident where a person with a weak heart injures it by running to catch a train.' *Sloboda v Continental Casualty Co* [1938] 2 WWR 237 at 239, Alta CA, per Harvey CJA

Canada 'I am disposed to accept the authority of Cornelius . . . on the proper interpretation of the words, "accidental means". When the insured received an injury by the intentional act of another, and the insured is not at fault and does nothing calculated to bring about the assault, such injury is effected by accidental means. Where the insured brings about an assault upon himself by his own wrongful act, or where he, under such circumstances that he would naturally be presumed to know that the injury is likely to be inflicted, voluntarily incurs an obvious hazard of this character, or places himself in a position that may be reasonably expected to bring about an assault upon him, an injury so received is not effected by accidental means.' *Travellers Insurance Co v Elder* [1940] 2 DLR 444 at 448, 449, Que KB, per Hall J

Canada 'In determining whether an accident had occurred within the terms of the policy or statute under advisement, the principal was long ago laid down, and has since been consistently followed, that the initial happening which set in motion the chain of events leading to the injury or death must govern, and is unaffected by the consequences flowing from the accident. The initial happening is the accident; the consequences are merely results flowing from the accident. Thus a mere pin prick fortuitously inflicted may become infected with fatal results. The infection would contribute to or cause the death but had it not been for the pin prick there would have been no infection. Similarly, if the happening reactivated a dormant illness or imposed itself upon a weakened body the happening would be the accident contemplated. . . . There must, of course, be a causal relationship between the accident and the consequences.' *Milashenko v Co-operative Fire & Casualty Co* (1967) 58 WWR 753 at 761–762, Sask QB, per Davis J; revsd (1968) 1 DLR (3d) 89, without affecting the definition; restored (1970) 72 WWR 228, 11 DLR (3d) 128, SCC

Canada [Insured claimed under products

liability policy for 'accident'.] 'Webster's New International Unabridged Dictionary defines an accident as "an event that takes place without one's foresight or expectation; an undesigned, sudden, and unexpected event." The word "accident" is not a technical legal term with a clearly defined meaning, and in the policy here it is to be read in its proper and ordinary sense. That sense is expressed in these definitions: "any unintended and unexpected occurrence that produces hurt or loss" and "an undesigned, sudden and unexpected event". Injuries are accidental or the opposite, for the purpose of indemnity, according to the quality of the results rather than the quality of the causes. An occurrence may be an accident even though it is the result of the fault of the insured, either slight or great, but it will not be an accident if it is due to an intentional act on the part of the insured, that is to say, an act intended to produce that result.' *Straits Towing Ltd v Washington Iron Works* (1973) 38 DLR (3d) 265 at 274, BCCA, per Robertson JA

Canada [Insurance policy excluded coverage for accident occurring outside Canada; insured based claim on acts of negligence in loading in Canada.] 'The "accident" was the shifting of the cargo which took place at sea beyond the territory of Canada and the United States but I am, with the greatest respect, unable to conclude that the accident at sea was so bound up with the negligence at the dockside as to transform the latter from being an originating cause into being the event of which it was causative. Such a construction appears to me to rob the word "accident" as used in the policy of its natural and ordinary meaning by interpreting it as connoting not the "accident" but the cause of the accident.' *Pickford Black Ltd v Canadian General Insurance Co* [1977] SCR 261 at 267, SCC, per Ritchie J

Canada [Claim was made in respect of accidental death under insurance policy.] 'It is the unexpectedness of the result that is the essence of what is meant by the term "accident or accidental" in policies of this sort. If a result of the type or kind that actually happens could be foreseen as a natural and probable result of the act engaged in, then the actor can be said to be courting the risk. What follows then ceases to be accidental even though it was hoped that a particular result would not follow.' *CNA Assurance Co v MacIsaac* (1979) 102 DLR (3d) 160 at 166, NSCA, per Hart JA

Canada [Insured claimed under vehicle policy for 'accidental' damage.] '. . . the element of unexpectedness is the principal and overriding element that must be present before one can say that there has been an accident and that the test to apply in determining whether an event was unexpected is whether or not it was the reasonably foreseeable consequence of the act of the person to whom it happens.' *Trynor Construction Co Ltd v Canadian Surety Co* (1970) 10 DLR (3d) 482 at 488, NSCA, per Cooper JA

Canada [Claim was made under accident insurance policy for death of intoxicated driver.] 'There is no comprehensive legal definition of the words "accident" or "accidental" and their meaning must be determined in each case from the wording of the policy and the circumstances giving rise to the claim. The authorities, nevertheless, provide guidance for determining whether any incident is an "accident". The basic rule that "accident" is a non-technical word to be understood in its popular and ordinary sense was set forth in *Fenton v J Thorley & Co Ltd* [1903] AC 443, where Lord Macnaghten said at p 448: ". . . the expression 'accident' is used in the popular and ordinary sense of the word as denoting an unlooked-for mishap or an untoward event which is not expected or designed." Rarely is an accident purely fortuitous. In most cases, some human act, usually of the insured, initiates the chain of circumstances from which the mishap results. The test of whether that mishap is an accident is the actual mental state of the actor at the time the act leading to it is performed.

Obviously, where the result is intended, as with suicide or an intentional tort, it is not an accident; but this is so even where the actor does not deliberately intend the specific result. It is sufficient if the actor, understanding the risk of that result, deliberately courts it by proceeding with a dangerous act. . . .' *Stats v Mutual of Omaha Insurance Co* (1976) 73 DLR (3d) 324 at 327, Ont CA, per Blair JA

ACCIDENTAL

Fire started accidentally

[Section 86 of the Fires Prevention (Metropolis) Act 1774 (repealed in part), enacts that a person in whose house or on whose estate a fire shall 'accidentally' begin shall not by reason therefor be liable to an action.] 'The question is upon the meaning and effect of the word "accidentally" . . . applied to fire. . . . It is true that in strictness, the word *accidental* may be employed in contradistinction to wilful, and so the same fire might both begin accidentally and be the result of negligence. But it may equally mean [as contended by the plaintiff] a fire produced by mere chance, or incapable of being traced to any cause, and so would stand opposed to the negligence of either servants or masters. . . . We think the plaintiff's construction much the more reasonable of the two.' *Filliter v Phippard* (1847) 11 QB 347 at 355, 357 per Lord Denman CJ

'The precise meaning to be attached to "accidentally" has not been determined, but it is clear . . . that where . . . fire is caused by negligence, it is not to be regarded as accidental.' *Balfour v Barty-King* [1957] 1 All ER 156 at 159, CA, per cur.; also reported in [1957] 1 QB 496 at 504

Canada 'The Statutes of Marlebridge and Gloucester [repealed] were followed by those of 6 Anne, c 31 [repealed], and 14 Geo 3, c 78 [repealed in part], which formed the basis of the Ontario statute now found as The Accidental Fires Act, RSO 1927, c 146 [see now RSO 1970, c 4]: "No action shall be brought against any person in whose house or building or on whose land any fire shall accidentally begin, nor shall any recompense be made by him for any damage suffered thereby; but no contract or agreement made between landlord and tenant shall be hereby defeated or made void." In the absence of any relevant stipulation between a landlord and tenant, the latter, by virtue of the provisions of this Act, would not be liable for any damage occasioned by a fire which should "accidentally begin". Many years ago it was decided that this expression did not include a fire caused by negligence —*Filliter v Phippard* [supra]—and this decision has been followed ever since. For two examples in this Court, see *Canada Southern Rly Co v Phelps* [(1884) 14 SCR 132] and *City of Port Coquitlam Corpn v Wilson* [[1923] SCR 235].' *United Motors Service Inc v Hutson* [1937] SCR 294 at 301, 302, per cur.

ACCIDENTAL SLIP OR OMISSION

In Arbitration Act 1950, s 17

'An accidental slip occurs when something is wrongly put in by accident, and an accidental omission occurs when something is left out by accident.' *Sutherland & Co v Hannevig Brothers Ltd* [1921] 1 KB 336, per Rowlatt J

ACCOMMODATION   *See also* SUITABLE ALTERNATIVE ACCOMMODATION; LIVING ACCOMMODATION

'I regard the word "accommodation" as used in this connection [accommodation for cattle in a market] as directed only to matters of the capacity of the pens provided, not to their fitness to hinder cattle from straying. The word "accommodation" is regularly used in connection with markets in the sense of space or room.' *Brackenborough v Spalding Urban District Council* [1942] AC 310 at 325, HL, per Lord Wright

[The Homeless Persons Act 1977, s 4(5) (repealed; see now the Housing Act 1985, s 65(2)) provided that housing authorities should make 'accommodation' available for homeless persons.] 'Nor is accommodation not accommodation because it might in certain circumstances be unfit for habitation for the purposes of Pt II of the Housing Act 1957 or might involve overcrowding within the meaning of Pt IV. What is properly to be regarded as accommodation is a question of fact to be decided by the local authority. There are no rules. Clearly some places in which a person might choose or be constrained to live could not properly be regarded as accommodation at all; it would be a misuse of language to describe Diogenes as having occupied accommodation within the meaning of the Act. What the local authority have to consider, in reaching a decision whether a person is homeless for the purposes of the Act, is whether he has what can properly be described as accommodation within the ordinary meaning of that word in the English language.

I do not, however, accept that overcrowding is a factor to be disregarded . . . But accommodation must, by definition, be capable of accommodating. If, therefore, a place is properly capable of being regarded as accommodation from an objective standpoint, but is so small a space that it is incapable of accommodating the applicant together with other persons who normally reside with him as members of his family, then on the facts of such a case the applicant would be homeless because he would have no accommodation in any relevant sense.' *Puhlhofer v Hillingdon London Borough Council* [1986] 1 All ER 467 at 474, HL, per Lord Brightman

Crew accommodation

In this section 'crew accommodation' includes sleeping rooms, mess rooms, sanitary accommodation, hospital accommodation, recreation accommodation, store rooms and catering accommodation provided for the use of seamen but does not include any accommodation which is also used by or provided for the use of passengers. (Merchant Shipping Act 1970, s 20(7))

ACCOMMODATION BILL

An accommodation party to a bill is a person who has signed a bill as drawer, acceptor, or indorser, without receiving value therefor, and for the purpose of lending his name to some other person.

Any person who thus signs a bill is liable thereon to a holder for value, whether the latter knew when he took the bill that such person was an accommodation party or not.

The intention of the parties in immediate relationship where one of them has signed for the accommodation of the other, is that that other should be at liberty to raise money by the negotiation of the bill, but should provide funds to meet the bill if called on at maturity. The relation is one of principal and surety.

Though an accommodation party may sign in any capacity the bill will, properly speaking, only be an accommodation bill when the accommodation party signs as acceptor thereof.

Where there is a fluctuating balance between the parties the bill is not to be deemed an accommodation bill, even if at the moment of drawing, acceptance, or payment the balance may be in favour of the acceptor. (4 Halsbury's Laws (4th edn) para 383)

ACCOMMODATION WORKS

And with respect to works for the accommodation of lands adjoining the railway, be it enacted as follows: The company shall make and at all times thereafter maintain the following works for the accommodation of the owners and occupiers of lands adjoining the railway; (that is to say),
Such and so many convenient gates, bridges, arches, culverts, and passages, over, under, or by the sides of or leading to or from the railway, as shall be necessary for the purpose of making good any interruptions caused by the railway to the use of the lands through which the railway shall be made; and such works shall be made forthwith after the part of the railway passing over such

lands shall have been laid out or formed, or during the formation thereof;
Also sufficient posts, rails, hedges, ditches, mounds, or other fences, for separating the land taken for the use of the railway from the adjoining lands not taken, and protecting such lands from trespass, or the cattle of the owners or occupiers thereof from straying thereout, by reason of the railway, together with all necessary gates, made to pen towards such adjoining lands, and not towards the railway, and all necessary stiles; and such posts, rails, and other fences shall be made forthwith after the taking of any such lands, if the owners thereof shall so require, and the said other works as soon as conveniently may be;
Also all necessary arches, tunnels, culverts, drains, or other passages, either over or under or by the sides of the railway, of such dimensions as will be sufficient at all times to convey the water as clearly from the lands lying near or affected by the railway as before the making of the railway, or as nearly so as may be; and such works shall be made from time to time as the railway works proceed;
Also proper watering places for cattle where by reason of the railway the cattle of any person occupying any lands lying near thereto shall be deprived of access to their former watering places; and such watering places shall be so made as to be at all times as sufficiently supplied with water as theretofore, and as if the railway had not been made, or as nearly so as may be; and the company shall make all necessary watercourses and drains for the purpose of conveying water to the said watering places:
Provided always, that the company shall not be required to make such accommodation works in such a manner as would prevent or obstruct the working or using of the railway, nor to make any accommodation works with respect to which the owners and occupiers of the lands shall have agreed to receive and shall have been paid compensation instead of the making of them.
(Railways Clauses Consolidation Act 1845, s 68)

ACCOMPLICE   *See also* ACCESSORY

'. . . persons are accomplices if they are participants in the offence charged, whether as principals, procurers, aiders or abettors. The following have also been held to be accomplices for this purpose: (1) handlers of stolen property have been held to be accomplices of the thieves from whom they received goods, on charges of larceny; and (2) persons who have been charged with particular offences and in respect of whom evidence of other similar offences has been admitted as showing system and intent and negative accident. (11 Halsbury's Laws (4th edn) para 457)

'There is no ground for saying that when the police have information that an offence is likely to be committed, and go to the place for the purpose of detecting it, they thereby become accomplices merely because they assent to the informer going there too, for the purpose of entrapping the offender.' *R v Heuser* (1910) 6 Cr App Rep 76 at 77, CCA, per Avory J

'We must first consider whether the second boy, whose age was under ten, was an accomplice. . . . The appellant took the two boys to a narrow place between two sheds, and there committed the offence on the elder, after telling the younger boy to keep watch. . . . The second boy was not an accomplice. There was, in our view, no evidence that he had a guilty knowledge fit to be left to the jury. . . . It is not disputed that to establish that he was an accomplice it must be proved that he had a guilty knowledge.' *R v Cratchley* (1913) 9 Cr App Rep 232 at 234, 235, CCA, per Isaacs CJ

'We do not think that . . . a narrow or precise definition of "accomplice" should be, or indeed can be, laid down. We think, however, that a person implicated either as principal or as accessory in the crime under investigation is an "accomplice" . . . though the degree and gravity of such complicity may vary.' *A-G v Linehan* [1929] IR 19 at 23, CCA, per Kennedy CJ

[In a criminal trial, where a person who was an 'accomplice' gives evidence on behalf of the prosecution, it is the duty of the judge to warn the jury that although they may convict on his evidence, it is dangerous to do so unless it is corroborated; this rule, although a rule of practice, now has the force of a rule of law.] 'What is an "accomplice" within the rule? . . . There is in the authorities no formal definition of the term "accomplice": and your Lordships are forced to deduce a meaning for the word from the cases in which X, Y and Z have been held to be, or held liable to be treated as, accomplices. On the cases it would appear that the following persons, if called as witnesses for the prosecution, have been treated as falling within the category:—(i) On any view, persons who are *participes criminis* in respect of the actual crime charged, whether as principals or accessories before or after the fact (in felonies) or persons committing, procuring or aiding and abetting in the case of misdemeanours. This is surely the natural and primary meaning of the term "accomplice". But in two cases, persons falling strictly outside the ambit of this category have, in particular decisions, been held to be accomplices for the purpose of the rule; viz. (ii) receivers have been held to be the accomplices of the thieves from whom they receive goods on a trial of the latter for larceny, . . . and (iii) when X has been charged with a specific offence on a particular occasion, and evidence is admissible, and has been admitted of his having committed crimes of this identical type on other occasions, as proving system and intent and negativing accident: in such cases the court has held that, in relation to such other similar offences, if evidence of them were given by parties to them, the evidence of such other parties should not be left to the jury without a warning that it is dangerous to accept it without corroboration.' *Davies v Director of Public Prosecutions* [1954] 1 All ER 507 at 513, HL, per Lord Simonds LC

Australia 'As to what an accomplice is, there is a singular dearth of legal authority. Foster describes him as any *particeps criminis* [Crown Law, p 341, cited by Poole J in *R v Young* [1923] SASR 35 at 69]. The definition given in the Century Dictionary is "any participator in an offence whether as principal or as accessory", and in the Encyclopædia Britannica, "one who is associated with another or others in the commission of a crime, whether as principal or accessory". Either of these definitions is, we think, sufficient.' *R v Webbe & Brown* [1926] SASR 108 at 111, 112, per cur.

Australia 'The only definition in the books of the word "accomplice" which counsel were able to cite to us was that pronounced by Denman J in *R v Cramp* [(1880) 14 Cox CC 390], who said that a witness would not be an accomplice unless she was privy to the criminal intent of the principal offender. In our opinion a person who knows nothing of the crime until it has been committed and is therefore not privy to it before its committal and then "receives, relieves, comforts or assists" the principal criminal does not fall within the reason of the rule which requires corroboration of the evidence of accomplices and unless required by authority to do so we should not think it proper to insist on such corroboration.' *R v Ready & Manning* [1942] VLR 85 at 93, per cur.

Australia 'A person is an accomplice in the crime charged if he took part in its commission, and was "privy to the criminal intent of the thing done": *R v Cramp* [(1880) 14 Cox CC 390], i.e. if he aided not only in the commission of what he knew to be a criminal act, but in the commission of what he knew to be, or to be likely to involve, the particular criminal act charged, so that what was done was in the course of carrying out a common purpose.' *R v Surridge, R v Harris* (1942) NSWSR 278 at 282, per Jordan CJ

ACCOMPLISH

[A ship's master subscribed to three bills of lading with the provision that 'the one of which bills being accomplished the others to stand void.'] 'Which I understand to mean that if upon one of them the shipowner acts in good faith he will have "accomplished" his contract, will have fulfilled it, and will not be liable or answerable upon any of the others.' *Glyn Mills & Co v East & West India Docks Co* (1882) 7 App Cas 591 at 599, per Lord Cairns

ACCORD AND SATISFACTION

Accord and satisfaction is the purchase of a release from an obligation, whether arising under contract or tort, by means of any valuable consideration, not being the performance of the obligation itself. The accord is the agreement by which the obligation is discharged. The satisfaction is the consideration which makes the agreement operative. (9 Halsbury's Laws (4th edn) para 585)

A release of a right of action made by deed is binding even though there is no consideration; but to constitute accord and satisfaction, the existence of which is a question of fact, there must be satisfaction as well as the agreement or accord, although the accord and satisfaction, duly constituted, are a discharge of the cause of action and may ordinarily be agreed orally. The benefit of a release by deed inter partes, or of accord and satisfaction, is available only as between the parties to it, apart from the special position where there are joint plaintiffs in respect of a joint interest. It may be vitiated by fraud. (45 Halsbury's Laws (4th edn) para 1270)

Accord is a satisfaction agreed upon between the party injuring and the party injured; which, when performed, is a bar of all actions upon this account. (3 Bl Com 16)

ACCOUNT

[A guarantee was in the words 'I hereby guarantee Mr John Jennings' account with you . . . to the amount of £100.'] 'I do not see how this can be considered as a prospective guarantee. . . . By "account", I understand the parties to mean some account contained in some ledger or book; and the case shows that there was such an account existing at that time. The natural construction of the guarantee therefore is, that it relates to that account.' *Allnutt v Ashenden* (1843) 5 Man & G 392 at 397, per Tindal CJ

Australia [It was held that certain solicitor's accounts, which only specified the general nature of work done together with a lump sum fee, were not 'accounts' within the meaning of the Family Law Rules, Ord 38, r 20.] 'In my view . . . an account for the purposes of Ord 38 r 20(1) must comply with certain requirements. Without necessarily being exhaustive, these do include the following.
(1) It must contain sufficient details to enable a taxation to take place.
(2) Its form must be such as to enable the parties to the taxation to define the issues, that is, the parts of the account which are in dispute.
(3) It must contain sufficient details to enable the client to make a conclusion as to what parts he wishes to dispute or as to which he wishes to seek advice and to crystallize the nature of the dispute, e.g. as to the work allegedly done.
(4) It must be such as not to place the client in a position of dilemma as to his possible liability for costs should he file a notice disputing account without being aware of the charges made in respect of the various items contained therein.'
Gillis v Rehfeld (1986) 10 Fam LR 1063 at 1066–1067, per Treyvaud J

Canada [Employer sought to enforce restrictive covenant against former employee, including prohibition from soliciting] '"any account within employee's territory". I looked at the legal dictionaries, Wharton & Strouds but I found no definition of "account" to help me so I turned to the old stand-by, the Random House College Dictionary, the latest edition, and the word "account" means, inter alia, "any customer or client". I also checked the word "solicit" and it means "to solicit orders or trade as for a business house".

I therefore take it that when the word "account" is used and if it is used in the usual business or commercial sense, it simply means "customer". That being the case, this clause deals with customers and if it deals with customers according to the cases the territory is of no consequence and therefore the definition of employee's territory, ambiguous and vague and obtuse as it is, is irrelevant. I therefore come to the conclusion that the non-solicitation clause refers to customers.' *W R Grace & Co of Canada Ltd v Sare* (1980) 111 DLR (3d) 204 at 212, 213, Ont SC, per Hollingworth J

For account of

[The phrase: 'War risk, if any required for charterers' account', appeared in a special clause in a charterparty.] 'Both sides adopt the view that that [the above phrase] means if, under the circumstances, any war risk insurance is reasonably requisite. What then does "for charterers' account" mean? Does it mean that the cost only of the insurance, the premium payable, is to be borne by the charterers, or does it mean that the charterers are both to provide and pay for the insurance—that is, that they are to effect the insurance and pay for it? In my opinion . . . the true construction of those words is that while the charterers have to bear the cost of the insurance, the actual insurance is to be effected by the owners, and not by the charterers.' *Holland Gulf Stoomvaart Maatschappij v Watson, Munro & Co* (1915) 85 LJKB 451 at 455, CA, per Swinfen Eady LJ

Bank deposits and collections

United States 'Account' means any account with a bank and includes a checking, time, interest or savings account. . . . (Uniform Commercial Code 1978, s 4–104(1)(a))

Secured transactions

United States 'Account' means any right to payment for goods sold or leased or for services rendered which is not evidenced by an instrument or chattel paper, whether or not it has been earned by performance. . . . All rights to payment earned or unearned under a charter or other contract involving the use or hire of a vessel and all rights incident to the charter or contract are accounts. (Uniform Commercial Code 1978, s 9–106)

Separate account

United States The term 'separate account' means an account established and maintained by an insurance company pursuant to the laws of any State or territory of the United States, the District of Columbia, or of Canada or any province thereof, under which income, gains and losses, whether or not realized, from assets allocated to such account, are, in accordance with the applicable contract, credited to or charged against such account without regard to other income, gains, or losses of the insurance company. (Securities Act of 1933, s 2(14))

ACCOUNT DEBTOR

Secured transactions

United States 'Account debtor' means the person who is obligated on an account, chattel paper or general intangible. (Uniform Commercial Code 1978, s 9–105(1)(a))

ACCOUNT PAYEE

'I do not think that they [the words "account payee"] indicate an intention that the cheque should not be transferable [within the meaning of the Bills of Exchange Act 1882, s 8(4)].' *National Bank v Silke* [1891] 1 QB 435 at 479, CA, per Lindley LJ

'The words "account AB" are a mere direction to the receiving bank as to how the money is to be dealt with after receipt.' *Akrokerri (Atlantic) Mines Ltd v Economic Bank* [1904] 2 KB 465 at 472, per Bigham J

'It [the marking "account of payees"] was a direction to the receiving banker that the drawer desired to pay the particular cheque into the bank which kept the account of the payee. To disregard a direction of that kind, if the banker had information which might lead him to think that the account into which he was paying the amount was not the payee's account, would . . . be negligence.' *Bevan v National Bank Ltd, Bevan v Capital & Counties Bank Ltd* (1906) 23 TLR 65 at 68, per Channell J

'The words "account payee" [on a cheque] . . . are a direction to the bankers collecting payment that the proceeds when collected are to be applied to the credit of the account of the payee designated on the face of the cheque.' *Morison v London County & Westminster*

Bank Ltd [1914] 3 KB 356 at 373, 374, CA, per Lord Reading CJ

'While this addition [of the words "account of payee"] does not affect the negotiability of an order or bearer cheque, I agree . . . that when such a cheque is paid into the account of a person who is not the payee the bank is put on inquiry, especially when he is the servant of the payee.' *Underwood (AL) Ltd v Bank of Liverpool, Underwood (AL) Ltd v Barclays Bank* [1924] 1 KB 775 at 793, 794, CA, per Scrutton LJ

'What is the meaning of a cheque marked, "Account payee only"? I do not know any better statement of it than that made by Bigham J, a very great authority on questions of commercial, and particularly of banking practice, in *Akrokerri (Atlantic) Mines v Economic Bank*, [supra], that "the paying bank has nothing to do with the application of the money after it has once been paid to the proper receiving banker. The words 'account AB' are a mere direction to the receiving bank as to how the money is to be dealt with after receipt".' *Importers Co Ltd v Westminster Bank Ltd* [1927] 2 KB 297 at 307, CA, per Atkin LJ

ACCOUNT STATED

'In common talk an account stated is treated as an admission of a debt due from the defendant to the plaintiff; but there is also a real account stated . . . when several items of claim are brought into account on either side, and, being set against one another, a balance was struck, and the consideration for the payment of the balance was the discharge on each side.' *Laycock v Pickles* (1863) 33 LJQB 43 at 47, per Blackburn J

'The essence of an account stated is not the character of the items on one side or the other, but the fact that there are cross items of account and that the parties mutually agree the several amounts of each and, by treating the items so agreed on the one side as discharging the items on the other side *pro tanto*, go on to agree that the balance only is payable. . . . There are mutual promises, the one side agreeing to accept the amount of the balance of the debt as true (because there must in such cases be, at least in the end, a creditor to whom the balance is due) and to pay it, the other side agreeing the entire debt as at a certain figure and then agreeing that it has been discharged to such and such an extent so that there will be

complete satisfaction on payment of the agreed balance.' *Firm Bishun Chand v Seth Girdhari Lal* (1934) 50 TLR 465 at 468, PC, per cur.

United States 'To establish an account stated, respondent must show that a balance was struck "in such circumstances as to import a promise of payment on the one side and acceptance on the other."' *United States v A S Kreider Co* (1940) 313 US 443 at 448, per Murphy J

ACCOUNTANT

'An accountant is a person who is paid for investigating accounts and certifying as to their accuracy.' *O'Connor & Ould v Ralston* [1920] 3 KB 451 at 456, per Darling J

United States '[A]ccountant' means accountant authorized under applicable law to practice public accounting, and includes professional accounting association, corporation, or partnership, if so authorized . . . (Bankruptcy Act 1978, s 101(1))

ACCOUNTING DATE

'Accounting date' means the date to which a company makes up its accounts, and 'period of account' means the period for which it does so. (Income and Corporation Taxes Act 1970, s 527)

ACCRETION   *See also* ALLUVION

'Accretion' means the gradual and imperceptible receding of the sea or inland water . . . (49 Halsbury's Laws (4th edn) para 294)

'In my judgment the land in question is an accretion within the meaning of the statute [Poor Law Amendment Act 1868, s 27 (repealed; see now Local Government Act 1972, s 72)]. It is an accretion from the sea, and . . . it is immaterial whether this accretion is natural or artificial. Before the Harbour Board had succeeded in excluding the sea it flowed over the site upon which the station and buildings now stand; thus the bed of the sea to the extent of some eleven acres has been reclaimed from the sea, and forms an accretion from the sea within the meaning of the Act.' *Barwick v SE & Chatham Rly Co* [1921] 1 KB 187 at 195, per Lord Reading CJ

Canada 'The act of accretion, when it is done

by alluvial deposit, contemplates the adding to existing land by the process of building up against that land. Accretion can occur in one of several ways: One is where tidal water recedes gradually and imperceptibly from the land; another is where land by alluvial deposit is added to the dry land or foreshore. In the latter case, if it is tidal water the addition must end up situate above the mean high-water mark of ordinary tides. If it is not tidal water, there is no need to worry about the movement of tides, as long as the land has lost the character of lake or river bottom. In either case the act of accretion means an adding to, a fixing on to the existing dry land. . . . If there is either a water channel or a strip of land or a ridge or other barrier between the upland and the newly created land, no accretion can be considered. It is not joined to that land, so it cannot become part of it.' *Re Bulman* (1966) 56 WWR 225 at 230, 231, BCSC, per Ruttan J

ACCRUAL BASIS

United States 'Keeping accounts and making returns on the accrual basis, as distinguished from the cash basis, import that it is the *right* to receive and not the actual receipt that determines the inclusion of the amount in gross income. When the right to receive an amount becomes fixed, the right accrues. When a merchandizing concern makes sales, its inventory is reduced and a claim for the purchase price arises.' *Spring City Foundry Co v Commissioner* (1933) 292 US 182 at 184–185, per Hughes CJ

ACCRUE   *See also* EXISTING AND
ACCRUING

Australia '"Accrued" suggests that the interest arises by way of an accession to or any advantage bestowed upon some other person.' *Trustees Executors & Agency Co Ltd v Federal Comr of Taxation* (1944) 69 CLR 270 at 287, per Starke J

Australia 'In the law of property and the law of trusts, the word "accrue" is used to denote the addition of further rights or interests to existing rights or interests. Generally, however, the word does not appear to be limited to the concept of addition, but is capable of meaning "to grow or occur as a natural result". The examples of its use, and particularly of the use of the participle "accruing",

given in the Oxford Dictionary, indicate that it is a word apt to describe a phenomenon or thing appearing for the first time as the natural result of some cause.' *Probate Duties Comr (Vic) v Wilson* (1979) 10 ATR 275 at 277, per cur.

Canada 'The words "all dividends accrued due" can surely only mean dividends which have become payable by the corporation to the shareholder, as the words "dividends accruing due" during any stated period can only mean dividends as they become payable by the corporation to the shareholder.' *Re Ganong, Ganong v Belyea* [1941] 1 DLR 433 at 440, SCC, per Crocket J; affd for other reasons, sub nom *Belyea v McBride* [1942] 3 DLR 785, PC

ACCUMULATION

'"Accumulation" implies some gradual accretion, a heaping up of matter, increasing from day to day; and "deposit" means something that is put down in some place and left there. Both these words involve the idea of a certain degree of permanency, and cannot, in our judgment, be held to touch the case of loading and unloading manure from the company's wagons for the purpose of its delivery to the farmers who come to take it.' *Great Northern Rly Co v Lurgan Town Comrs* [1897] 2 IR 340 at 351, per O'Brien CJ

[The Factories Act 1937, s 47(1) (repealed; see now the Factories Act 1961, s 63), made it obligatory for all practicable measures to be taken to prevent dust, fumes or other impurities from 'accumulating' in any workroom.] 'Counsel for the plaintiff relied on the . . . obligation . . . to take practicable measures to prevent the dust accumulating in any workroom. He submitted that in this case the dust accumulated in the air. I do not think that that is the meaning of accumulation within this section. I think that accumulation means accumulation of deposited dust. It has the same sort of meaning as is indicated by the use of the same term in s 1(a) of the Act of 1937 [see now s 1(1)(a) of the Act of 1961], which requires that "accumulations of dirt and refuse shall be removed daily by a suitable method from the floors and benches of workrooms . . .". Nor do I think it can be said, without an abuse of language, that the dust which settled on the plaintiff can be regarded as accumulating on him, and it was from the settlement of dust on him that he acquired the disease. One has only to test the matter by this simple question: How does one prevent the accumulation of dust? The answer, I think, is that, if one is old fashioned, one takes a duster and dusts it away, but no one would suggest that a settlement of dust on the skin of a workman was something which could be dusted away in that sense.' *Graham v Co-operative Wholesale Society Ltd* [1957] 1 All ER 654 at 661, per Devlin J

Of income

New Zealand '"Accumulation" ... must, we think, be the process of heaping up, of laying by, income, irrespective of whether it is reinvested as capital or not, and the term is to be applied to such income as is heaped up or laid aside unapplied, irrespective of whether it is or is not actually at the moment reinvested. The test is simply whether it is heaped up or not. Who can doubt that a specific direction to trustees to heap up income, leaving it uninvested and unproductive for fifty years, would be bad as a direction to "accumulate" for more than the allowed period? We do not find in any case, nor anywhere else than in s 40 of the Trustee Act, 1956, anything whatever that seems to us to support the argument that reinvestment is necessary before a sum can be said to be accumulated. Generally, of course, reinvestment is found sooner or later as a concomitant of accumulation; but this is because it is a trustee's duty promptly to reinvest all moneys held by him for a beneficiary. As soon as he has surplus income in his hands put by and not applied, of any substantial amount, his duty must be to reinvest it. But the duty to reinvest is a consequence of his having accumulated the funds; the surplus income does not become an "accumulation" as a consequence of reinvestment.' *Cameron v Inland Revenue Comr* [1965] NZLR 1017 at 1020, CA, per cur.

Of profits

Australia 'Accumulated profits are simply profits that are amassed or collected and not distributed, including, as the Act prescribes, amounts standing to the credit of the profit and loss account of the company.' *Federal Comr of Taxation v Miller Anderson Ltd* (1947) 73 CLR 341 at 369, per Starke J

ACCUSATION

Australia [The Extradition (Commonwealth Countries) Act 1966–86 (Cth), s 16 (as amended) provides that a court to which a person ordered to be extradited has applied for

a writ of habeas corpus may order that he be released if it is satisfied that by reason of the 'accusation' against the person not having been made in good faith or in the interests of justice it would be unjust, oppressive or too severe a punishment to surrender the person.] 'The "accusation" referred to is that made by the person who lays the information, or otherwise actually initiates the proceedings, and not the "accusation" made to the police or to the Director of Public Prosecutions. . . . It is clear that it is only when an information or other initiating process for his apprehension has been laid or issued that a person can be said to be "accused" in the relevant sense.' *Vyner v Keeper of HM Penitentiary (Malabar)* (1975) 6 ALR 105 at 109, per Yeldham J

ACCUSE

Canada 'To accuse, in ordinary parlance, in the form "to accuse (a person) of", means, to charge with the crime or fault of, etc. See Murray's Dictionary, *sub voce*. This may be done by laying an information against the person under s 558 of the Code [see now RSC 1970, s 553]. The person so charged is said to be the person *accused*.' *R v Kempel* (1900) 31 OLR 631 at 633, CA, per cur.

Canada 'Anyone who lays "an information in writing and under oath", before a magistrate, against any person, obviously "accuses" that person of the offence charged against him in such information.' Ibid at 634, per Meredith J

ACKNOWLEDGE

Australia 'Under s 57 of the [Mercantile] Act [1867 (Qld)] it is provided, inter alia, that a limited partnership shall not be deemed formed until the certificate required under s 55 "shall have been acknowledged by each partner before some justice of the peace". . . . In the Oxford English Dictionary the verb "acknowledge" is defined to mean inter alia "to own as genuine, or of legal force or validity; to own, avow or assent in legal form [to a document] so as to give it validity". The noun "acknowledgment" is defined in the same dictionary to mean inter alia "a formal declaration or avowal of an act or document so as to give it legal validity". . . . In my view, the intention of the legislature to be gleaned from the precise words used in s 57 of the Act is that each partner is required personally in effect to affirm or declare in a formal manner before a justice of the peace that the contents of the certificate which will eventually be registered are true.' *Re Cotton Crops Pty Ltd* [1986] 2 Qd R 328 at 338–340, per Ambrose J

ACQUAINTANCE

'A needy "acquaintance" of mine may appear to denote an individual whose existence I may acknowledge as occupying a position closer to me in association than a mere nodding recognition and less close than personal association on terms of friendship.' *Salvesen's Trustees v Wye* 1954 SLT 299 at 302, per Lord Russell

'Acquaintance seems to connote something more than bare recognition but falling short of the intimacy of friendship and still further short of ties of relationship by blood or affinity—a little less than kin and less than kind.' Ibid at 303, per the Lord President (Cooper)

ACQUIESCENCE   *See also* CONSENT

'There can only be acquiescence where there is knowledge. This Court never binds parties by acquiescence where there is no knowledge.' *Weldon v Dicks* (1878) 10 Ch D 247 at 262, per Malins V-C

'Mere inactivity on the part of a defendant is not to be construed as acquiescence in delay by the plaintiff. "Sleeping dogs, in the form of sleeping plaintiffs, need not be aroused by defendants from their slumbers" (per Roskill LJ in *Compagnie Française de Télévision v Thorn Consumer Electronics Ltd* [[1978] RPC 735 at 739]).' *Bremer Vulkan Schiffbau und Maschinenfabrik v South India Shipping Corpn* [1979] 3 All ER 194 at 198, per Donaldson J

'What is meant by acquiescence? It may involve no more than a merely passive attitude, doing nothing at all. It requires as an essential factor that there was knowledge of what was acquiesced in.' *Bell v Alfred Franks & Bartlett Co Ltd* [1980] 1 All ER 356 at 360, CA, per Shaw LJ

Compared with standing by

'The term "acquiescence" . . . does not accurately express any known legal defence, but if used at all it must have attached to it a very different signification according to whether the acquiescence alleged occurs while the act acquiesced in is in progress or only after it has been completed. If a person having a right, and seeing another person about to commit, or in the course of committing an act infringing upon that right stands by in such a manner as really to induce the person committing the act, and who might otherwise have abstained from it, to believe that he assents to its being committed, he cannot afterwards be heard to complain of the act. This, as Lord Cottenham said . . . is the proper sense of the term "acquiescence", and in that sense may be defined as quiescence under such circumstances as that assent may be reasonably inferred from it, and is no more than an instance of the law of estoppel by words or conduct. But when once the act is completed without any knowledge or assent upon the part of the person whose right is infringed the matter is to be determined on very different legal considerations. . . . Mere submission to the injury for any time short of the period limited by statute for the enforcement of the right of action cannot take away such right.' *De Bussche v Alt* (1878) 8 Ch D 286 at 314, CA, per Thesiger LJ

Infringement of patent right

'I will first take the question as to whether there had been any lying by, that is to say, any acquiescence in the proper sense of the word. In my opinion that cannot be held to be so. The right of the patentee does not depend on the defendant having notice that what he is doing is an infringement. If what he is doing is in fact an infringement, even although the defendant acts in the way which the counsel for the defendants said was bona fide or honest, he will not be protected from an injunction by that. It does not depend on notice. The right of monopoly has been granted to the patentee, and in order to raise an equity one must, as I understand, press this against the defendants. . . . It is necessary that the person who alleges this lying by should have been acting in ignorance of the title of the other man; that the other man should have known that and not mentioned his own title.' *Proctor v Bennis* (1887) 4 RPC 333 at 356, 357, CA, per Cotton LJ

When fraudulent

'The Court will not interfere with the exercise of a legal right, such as the defendant is seeking to exercise, unless he has so acquiesced as to render it fraudulent on his part to set up such a legal right. I will first inquire, what are the principal elements or ingredients of such fraudulent acquiescence? In the first place, the person seeking to avail himself of such acquiescence, whom I will call the plaintiff, must have made a mistake, in point of fact, as to his legal rights; for if he knew, he has no cause of complaint against anyone else. In the second place, the plaintiff must have expended money or done some act . . . on the faith of the mistaken belief. . . . In the next place, the defendant, who is the possessor of the legal right, must know that his own right is inconsistent with the acts of the plaintiff. . . . In the next place the defendant, the possessor of the legal right, must know the plaintiff's mistaken belief in his right. . . . And, lastly, the possessor of the legal right must encourage the person acting on the mistaken belief in laying out his money, or doing the other act, either by direct encouragement, or by abstaining from asserting his legal right.' *Willmott v Barber* (1880) 49 LJ Ch 792 at 793, per Fry J

ACQUIRE

The expression 'acquire' means buy, take in exchange, take in pawn or otherwise receive (whether apart from this section the receiving is lawful or not). (Army Act 1955, s 195(5); Air Force Act 1955, s 195(5); Naval Discipline Act 1957, s 98(3))

'Acquire' means hire, accept as a gift or borrow and 'acquisition' shall be construed accordingly. (Firearms Act 1968, s 57(4))

[The Finance Act 1936, s 18 (repealed; see now the Income and Corporation Taxes Act 1970, s 478) provided for the taxing of persons who, by means of transfers of assets, had 'acquired' the power to enjoy the income of a person resident or domiciled out of the United Kingdom.] 'We agree with the judge in the court below that the taxpayers' argument derives no support from the use of the word "acquired" in connection with the words "by means of" in sub-s (1) since, as he points out, "as used by lawyers the word 'acquired' has long covered transactions of a purely passive nature and means little more than receiving". Indeed, that is the second ordinary meaning given in the Shorter Oxford Dictionary. In addition, it would be contrary to the expressed object of the section if the word 'means', and 'acquired' were construed in the active sense for which the taxpayers contend. It would put back on the Revenue the burden of proving affirmatively that the benefits of the taxpayer, resulting to him in fact through transfers and associated operations, had all been brought about by his own activities whereas the section

is, in our opinion, plainly and successfully drafted with the intent of casting the burden of disproving tax avoidance on the taxpayer.' *Congreve v Inland Revenue Comrs* [1947] 1 All ER 168 at 173, CA, per Cohen LJ; affd [1948] 1 All ER 948

Canada 'It seems to me that "acquire" contemplates some positive action or step being taken, as contrasted with "accrue" which contemplates a result which flows, naturally from events which have occurred.' *Re Jago Plumbing & Heating Supplies Ltd* [1972] 1 OR 259 at 262, Ont SC, per Houlden J

ACQUISITION   *See also* DISPOSITION

Date of acquisition

'The date of acquisition' means—
(a) in the case of a compulsory acquisition, the date of the service of the notice to treat; and
(b) in the case of an acquisition by agreement, the date of the making of the agreement.
(Finance (No 2) Act 1945, s 57(6))

United States 'We need not go beyond the Clayton Act itself to conclude that "acquisition" as used in §7 of the Act means holding as well as obtaining assets. The Act provides that the F[ederal] T[rade] C[ommission], if it finds a violation of §7, can require a party to "divest itself of the stock, or other share capital, or assets, *held . . . contrary to the provisions of [§7]*." 15 USC §21(b). (Emphasis supplied.) Thus, the framers of the Act did not require the terms "acquire" and "acquisition" as unambiguously banning only the initial transaction of acquisition; rather, they read the ban against "acquisition" to include a ban against holding certain assets'. *United States v ITT Continental Baking Co* (1975) 420 US 223 at 240–241, per Brennan J

ACQUITTAL

'The word acquittal is also *verbum equivocum*, and may in ordinary language be used to express either the verdict of a jury or the formal judgment of the Court. . . . But there can be no doubt, if we bring the words to a strict legal test, that nothing would suffice to support a plea of *autrefois acquit* or *autrefois convict* but the production of the judgment.' *Burgess v Boetefeur* (1844) 13 LJMC 122 at 126, per Tindal CJ

ACROSS

Canada 'Subsection (2) [of s 373 of the Railway Act, RSC 1927, c 170 (repealed; see now RSC 1952, c 234, s 378(2), which has added the word 'under')] requires the legal consent of the municipality having jurisdiction over the highways, only when the telegraph line is to be constructed "upon, along or across any highway". No mention is made of a line to be constructed under the highway". . . . My view is that the word "across" does not include "under". "Across" means "over from side to side".' *Bell Telephone Co v Middlesex County* [1947] 1 DLR 248 at 255, 256, per Rinfret CJC

ACT

Discriminatory act

'Act' includes a deliberate omission. (Sex Discrimination Act 1975, s 82(1))

ACT IN EXECUTION

New Zealand 'The phrase "acting in the execution of this Act" [in the Police Force Act 1913 (NZ), s 31 (repealed; see now Summary Offences Act 1981, s 22)] . . . means the performance in accordance with law of the duties of a police constable. . . . When, for instance, a constable in the bona fide belief that an offence has been committed, takes into custody without warrant any disorderly person in pursuance of the power given him by s 65 of the Police Offences Act 1908 [NZ], he does so in the performance of that part of his contract with His Majesty which is referred to in s 11(2) of the Police Force Act 1913. He is therefore "acting in the execution of that Act", and he is accordingly entitled to the protection which s 31 gives him.' *Purua v Douglas* [1927] NZLR 255 at 259, 260, per Herdman J; also reported [1927] GLR 263 at 265

ACT OF GOD   *See also* ACCIDENT

In the legal sense of the term, an act of God may be defined as an extraordinary occurrence or circumstance which could not have been foreseen and which could not have been guarded against; or, more accurately, as an accident (1) due to natural causes, directly and exclusively without human intervention, and (2) which could not by any amount of ability have been foreseen, or, if foreseen, could not by any amount of human care and skill have been resisted. The occurrence need not be unique, nor need it be one that happens for the first time; it is enough that it is extraordinary, and such as could not reasonably have been anticipated. The mere fact that a phenomenon has happened once, when it does not carry with it or import any probability of a recurrence (when, in other words, it does not imply any law from which its recurrence can be inferred) does not prevent that phenomenon from being an act of God. It must, however, be something overwhelming, and not merely an ordinary accidental circumstance. (9 Halsbury's Laws (4th edn) para 458)

Where an injury results from natural causes which could not have been foreseen and could not have been avoided by any amount of foresight and care which could reasonably have been expected, it may be said to result from an act of God. Thus, in one sense, it is merely a type of inevitable accident, but its particular quality is that it affords a defence to common law torts involving strict liability whereas other categories of inevitable accident do not. (45 Halsbury's Laws (4th edn) para 1251)

'The act of God is natural necessity, as wind and storms, which arise from natural causes and is distinct from inevitable accident.' *Trent & Mersey Navigation Co v Wood* (1785) 4 Doug KB 287 at 290, per Lord Mansfield CJ

'That a storm at sea is included in the term "act of God", can admit of no doubt whatever. Storm and tempest have always been mentioned in dealing with this subject as among the instances of *vis major* coming under the denomination of "act of God". But it is equally true . . . that it is not under all circumstances that inevitable accident arising from the so-called act of God will, any more than inevitable accident in general by the Roman and continental law, afford immunity to the carrier. This must depend on his ability to avert the effects of the *vis major* and the degree of diligence which he is bound to apply to that end. . . . The rain which fertilises the earth and the wind which enables the ship to navigate the ocean are as much within the term "act of God" as the rainfall which causes a river to burst its banks and carry destruction over a whole district, or the cyclone that drives a ship against a rock or sends it to the bottom.' *Nugent v Smith* (1876) 1 CPD 423 at 435, 436 per cur.

'I do not think that the mere fact that a phenomenon has happened once, when it does not carry with it or import any probability of a recurrence—when, in other words, it does not imply any law from which its recurrence can be inferred—places that phenomenon out of the operation of the rule of law with regard to the act of God. In order that the phenomenon should fall within that rule it is not . . . necessary that it should be unique, that it should happen for the first time; it is enough that it is extraordinary, and such as could not reasonably be anticipated. . . . To say that a thing could not reasonably have been anticipated is to say that it is the act of God.' *Nitro-Phosphate & Odam's Chemical Manure Co v London & St Katharine Docks Co* (1878) 9 Ch D 503 at 515, 516, per Fry J

'I shall not now enter into a discussion, which at one time was rather rife, as to what was the exact meaning of the term the "act of God". In the older, simpler days I have myself never had any doubt but that it did not mean the act of God in the ecclesiastical and biblical sense, according to which almost everything is said to be the act of God, but that in a mercantile sense it meant an extraordinary circumstance which could not be foreseen, and which could not be guarded against.' *Pandorf v Hamilton* (1886) 17 QBD 670 at 675, per Lord Esher MR

'We are to assume that the storm which caused the flooding of the plaintiffs' premises was such as to bring it within the category of an act of God, that is to say, it was so unprecedented and unexpected that human agency would not reasonably anticipate it or be bound to take any steps to meet it.' *J & J Makin Ltd v London & North Eastern Rly Co* [1945] 1 KB 467 at 470, CA, per Lord Greene MR

Australia 'An "act of God" has been defined in various ways. In some definitions the idea appears that in order to be an act of God an event must be irresistible, for example, per Mellish LJ in *Nugent v Smith* [(1876) 1 CPD 423 at 441], but the more generally received definition is stated by James LJ [ibid, at 444] . . . where it is said that an event is an "act of God" where it is shown that "it is due to natural causes directly and exclusively, without human intervention, and that it could not have been prevented by any amount of foresight and pains and care reasonably to be expected". . . . The evidence in this case only shows that there was a very heavy and continuous fall of rain including, at a particular time, rainfall of great intensity. There was a tropical storm such as occurs from time to time in many parts of Australia. The particular

storm in question happened to be the most violent that had ever been experienced at York, but it cannot be said, in my opinion, to be such that it exceeded in amount that for which a reasonable man could have been expected to provide. . . . The contention that the rainfall amounted to an "act of God" has not been sustained.' *Railways Comr (WA) v Stewart* (1936) 56 CLR 520 at 528, 529, per Latham CJ

Canada 'Where the goods are lost, destroyed, or damaged by an operation of nature to which no man contributed, the loss is an act of God . . . climatic changes of temperature, decay, and deterioration from the inherent nature of the goods are operations of nature and acts of God as well as storms, lightning, and tempests.' *Pleet v Canadian Northern Quebec Rly Co* (1921) 50 OLR 223 at 230, Ont CA, per Ferguson JA; affd. [1923] 4 DLR 1112

Canada '[An act of God] must relate to an event which cannot be foreseen, or which if it can be foreseen cannot be guarded against.' *McQuillan v Ryan* (1921) 50 OLR 337 at 349, CA, per Middleton J

ACT OF GRACE

An Act of Grace, which is an Act for a general pardon, originates with the Crown. The bill is introduced into the House of Lords by a minister in obedience to a command of the Sovereign, and, as soon as it has been read a first time, a motion is made that it be humbly accepted and passed. This motion is agreed to *nemine contradicente*, and the bill is then sent to the House of Commons, where the same procedure is adopted. The bill receives the royal assent in the usual form and manner. (34 Halsbury's Laws (4th edn) para 1311)

ACT OF PARLIAMENT   *See* STATUTE

ACT OF STATE

'An act of state is essentially an exercise of sovereign power, and hence cannot be challenged, controlled, or interfered with by municipal Courts. Its sanction is not that of law, but that of sovereign power, and, whatever it be, municipal Courts must accept it, as it is, without question.' *Salaman v Secretary of State for India* [1906] 1 KB 613 at 639, CA, per Fletcher Moulton LJ

'The words "act of state" are used to denote different things at different times. *First:* When British troops act as the servants or agents of a foreign power, they are protected in our Courts by the defence of an act of state, i.e. that of a foreign state. . . . *Second:* When the British Government acquires property or territory by treaty, annexation or conquest, it cannot be made liable for the consequences. If anyone seeks to sue the British Government and has to rely on the treaty, annexation or conquest to found his cause of action, he fails on the simple ground that it is an act of state not cognisable in the municipal Courts. . . . *Third:* When British troops take or destroy the property of a foreigner in a territory outside Her Majesty's dominions, the foreigner cannot sue for damages in the English Courts. He must seek redress through his own government by diplomatic channels.' *Nissan v A-G* [1967] 2 All ER 1238 at 1242, CA, per Lord Denning MR

ACT OF VIOLENCE   *See* VIOLENCE

ACTING RANK

'Acting rank' means rank of any description (however called) such that under Queen's Regulations a commanding officer has power to order the holder to revert from the rank, 'acting warrant officer' and 'acting non-commissioned officer' shall be construed accordingly, and references to acting non-commissioned officers shall be construed as including references to lance-corporals and lance-bombardiers. (Army Act 1955, s 225(1); see also Air Force Act 1955, s 223(1))

ACTION   *See also* CAUSE; CONSOL-
IDATION

'Action' means any civil proceedings commenced by writ or in any other manner prescribed by rules of court. It has a wide signification as including any method prescribed by those rules of invoking the court's jurisdiction for the adjudication or determination of a lis or legal right or claim or any justiciable issue, question or contest arising between two or more persons or affecting the status of one of them. In its natural meaning 'action' refers to any proceeding in the nature of a litigation between a plaintiff and a defendant. It includes any civil proceedings in which there is a plaintiff who sues, and a defendant who is sued, in respect of

some cause of action, as contrasted with proceedings, such as statutory proceedings which are embraced in the word 'matter'. (37 Halsbury's Laws (4th edn) para 17)

Personal actions are such whereby a man claims a debt, or personal duty, or damages in lieu thereof; and likewise whereby a man claims a satisfaction in damages for some injury done to his person or property. The former are said to be founded on contracts, the latter upon *torts* or wrongs: and they are the same which the civil law calls "*actiones in personam, quae adversus eum intenduntur, qui ex contractu vel delicto obligatus est aliquid dare vel concedere.*" Of the former nature are all actions upon debt or promises; of the latter all actions for trespasses, nuisances, assaults, defamatory words, and the like. (3 Bl Com 117)

'Action' shall include every judicial proceeding instituted in any court, civil, criminal, or ecclesiastical. (British Law Ascertainment Act 1859, s 5)

'Action' includes counter claim and set off. (Bills of Exchange Act 1882, s 2)

'Action' includes a counterclaim, and any reference to the plaintiff in an action shall be construed accordingly. (Rights of Light Act 1959, s 7)

'Action' means any proceedings in a county court which may be commenced as prescribed by plaint. (County Courts Act 1984, s 147(1))

'Action' includes failure to act, and other expressions connoting action shall be construed accordingly. (Parliamentary Commissioner Act 1967, s 12)

In this Act, unless the context otherwise requires, 'action' means any civil proceedings commenced by writ or in any other manner prescribed by rules of court. (Supreme Court Act 1981, s 151(1))

'Actions may be personal as contradistinguished from real and mixed; the first being actions against the person only, for damages, the second for recovery of real estate, and the third for both. In this sense of the word "personal", there appears to be no question, but that an information of intrusion is a personal action, for its object is the recovery of damages, not the recovery of the estate, for the Crown has never in contemplation of law lost it. But the word "personal" may mean such actions as are for the recovery of debts or damages to the person or personal effects; and in this sense of the word, a writ of intrusion is not a personal action.' *A-G v Churchill (Lord)* (1841) 8 M & W 171 at 192, per cur.

'The word "action" is . . . a generic term, inclusive in its proper legal sense, of suits by the Crown.' *Bradlaugh v Clarke* (1883) 8 App Cas 354 at 361, per Lord Selborne LC

'In the popular use of words an information by the Attorney-General to recover a debt due to the Crown is spoken of as an information and not as an action, which in popular language would be taken to mean an action by a subject. But in legal phraseology "action" includes every suit, whether by a subject, or in the name of the Sovereign, or by an information by the Attorney-General on behalf of the Crown.' Ibid at 374, per Lord Blackburn

'The meaning of the word "action" is well known . . . ; and s 186 [of the County Courts Act 1888 (repealed; see now County Courts Act 1984, s 147)] says, "action shall include suit, and shall mean every proceeding in the Court which may be commenced as prescribed by plaint". That is as far as the Legislature has thought fit to enlarge the meaning of the word "action". It is said that it should be farther enlarged so as to include motion. You cannot do that.' *Re Locke, ex p Poppleton* (1890) 62 LT 942 at 943, per Smith J

'The term "action" is defined in s 100 of the Judicature Act 1873 [repealed; see now Supreme Court Act 1981, s 151(1)]. . . . It was intended to include in the term "action" any civil proceedings in which there is a plaintiff, who sues, and a defendant, who is sued, in respect of some cause of action, as contrasted with proceedings, such as statutory proceedings, which are embraced in the word "matter".' *Johnson v Refuge Assurance Co Ltd* [1913] 1 KB 259 at 262, 263, CA, per Buckley LJ

[The Administration of Justice Act 1920, s 15 (repealed; see now Supreme Court Act 1981, s 69(5)), provides that questions of foreign law in any action or other matter which is being tried by a judge with a jury in any Court in England and Wales shall be decided by the judge.] 'It was argued . . . that a criminal prosecution could not be included in the words "any action or other matter". . . . The words as used in s 15 are wide enough to include, and must be held to include, a criminal prosecution.' *R v Hammer* [1923] 2 KB 786 at 790, CCA, per Sankey J

'The primary sense of "action" as a term of

legal art is the invocation of the jurisdiction of a court by writ; "proceeding" the invocation of the jurisdiction of a court by process other than writ.' *Herbert Berry Associates Ltd v Inland Revenue Comrs* [1978] 1 All ER 161 at 170, HL, per Lord Simon of Glaisdale

Australia 'A proceeding by originating summons is manifestly a civil proceeding between parties which is commenced otherwise than by writ, but in a manner prescribed by Rules of Court. It is therefore an "action".' *Parkin & Cowper v James* (1905) 2 CLR 315 at 342, per cur.

Australia 'Whatever the popular signification of the word "action" may be, it is clear, as was pointed out by Bramwell and Lush LJJ in *Clarke v Bradlaugh* [(1881) 7 QBD 38 at 50, 57] and by the Earl of Selborne LC and Lord Blackburn in the same case on appeal to the House of Lords [supra] that in its proper legal sense it is a generic term of *nomen generale*, and includes every sort of legal proceeding. When used by the Legislature it must . . . be construed according to its true legal meaning unless it is apparent upon the face of the Act in which it is used that it is intended to bear a more restricted meaning.' *Re Carter Smith, ex p Taxation Comrs* (1908) 8 SRNSW 246 at 249, per Street J

Australia [The Law Reform (Miscellaneous Provisions) Act 1946–1986 (NSW), s 2(1) makes certain provisions that are to have effect in an 'action of tort'.] 'I consider that the words "action of tort" are equivalent to "action founded on tort". This latter, it has been held, means that a tort should be the gist of the action [*Keates v Woodward* [1902] 1 KB 542]. A tort cannot be described as the "gist of the action" when the action is partly founded in contract.' *Wright v Council of the Municipality of Port Macquarie* [1960] NSWR 210 at 214, per Jacobs J

New Zealand 'The plaintiff . . . filed a notice of motion under the Patents, Designs and Trade-Marks Act 1911 [repealed; see now Trade Marks Act 1953 (NZ)] . . . The notice of motion . . . involves two things: in the first place it is in the nature of a mandamus, as it asks for an officer to be directed to carry out his duty with regard to the registration of certain trade-marks; and, secondly, it asks for relief in the form of a correction to be effected in the Register of Trade-marks. . . . It is a civil proceeding commenced in a manner prescribed by rules. . . . I cannot limit the meaning of the term "action" as used in the rules by saying that it does not include the procedure in this case.' *Kiwi Polish Co Pty v Kempthorne, Prosser & Co's New Zealand Drug Co Ltd* [1922] NZLR 177 at 177, 179, per Stout CJ; also reported [1921] GLR 198 at 199

New Zealand [Rule 161 of the Code of Civil Procedure (NZ) confers the right to apply for an order for discovery upon any party to an 'action'.] 'An originating summons proceeding is 'an action' within the meaning of rule 161.' *Auckland Society for the New Church v Public Trustee* [1955] NZLR 561 at 562, per Shortland J

United States 'Action' in the sense of a judicial proceeding includes recoupment, counterclaim, set-off, suit in equity and any other proceedings in which rights are determined. (Uniform Commercial Code 1978, s 1–201(1))

ACTIVE HOSTILITIES *See* HOSTIL-
ITIES

ACTIVE SERVICE *See also* MILITARY
SERVICE

In this Act the expression 'on active service', in relation to a force, means that it is engaged in operations against an enemy or is engaged elsewhere than in the United Kingdom in operations for the protection of life or property (or subject to the provisions of this section) is in military occupation of a foreign country, and in relation to a person means that he is serving in or with a force which is on active service. (Army Act 1955, s 224(1); Air Force Act 1955, s 222(1) (both amended by the Armed Forces Act 1966, s 20(4))

[The further provisions of the above sections (which are in almost identical terms in the two Acts) provide that forces serving outside the United Kingdom may be 'deemed' to be, or not to be, on active service, in particular circumstances.]

For the purposes of this Act a force shall be deemed to be on active service when engaged in operations against an enemy, when situated in an area in which such operations are taking place, or when landed elsewhere than in the United Kingdom for the protection of life or property, and a person shall be deemed to be on active service when serving in or with a force which is on active service. (Naval Discipline Act 1957, s 134, as amended by the Armed Forces Act 1966, s 20(4)(c))

ACTIVITY

[The Redundancy Payments Act 1965, s 25(1) (repealed; see now the Employment Protection (Consolidation) Act 1978, s 153(1)) defines 'business' as including a trade or profession and as including any 'activity' carried on by a body of persons, whether corporate or unincorporate.] 'For my part, I do not think that "activity" in s 25(1) of the Act of 1965 has that dissected meaning which counsel has urged. I think that, read in the context of "business . . . trade or profession", it means the combination of operations undertaken by the corporate body, whether or not they amount to a business, trade or profession in the ordinary sense; they are there to cover such activities as charitable activities, schools, the National Trust or a statutory undertaking such as a water undertaking, which could not properly be described as a business or profession.' *Dallow Industrial Properties Ltd v Else* [1967] 2 All ER 30 at 33, per Diplock LJ

ACTUAL BODILY HARM

'It seems to me now that, if a person is caused hurt or injury resulting, not in any physical injury, but in an injury to the state of his mind for the time being, that is within the definition of "actual bodily harm".' *R v Miller* [1954] 2 All ER 529 at 534, per Lynskey J; see also [1954] 2 QB 282

ACTUAL FAULT OR PRIVITY

'Did what happened take place without the actual fault or privity of the owners? . . . My Lords, a corporation is an abstraction. It has no mind of its own any more than it has a body of its own; its active and directing will must consequently be sought in the person of somebody who for some purposes may be called an agent, but who is really the directing mind and will of the corporation, the very ego and centre of the personality of the corporation. . . . It must be upon the true construction of this section [the Merchant Shipping Act 1894, s 502] in such a case as the present one that the fault or privity is the fault or privity of somebody who is not merely the servant or agent for whom the company is liable upon the footing *respondeat superior*, but somebody for whom the company is liable because his action is the very action of the company itself.' *Lennard's Carrying Co Ltd v Asiatic Petroleum Co Ltd* [1915] AC 705 at 713, 714, per Lord Haldane LC

ACTUAL FINANCIAL LOSS

Canada 'We are told the chambers judge concluded that the insured services claim did not survive because it does not involve damages "that resulted in actual financial loss to the deceased or his estate". The right the deceased possessed was the right to recover the cost of insured services as "if he had been required to pay the whole cost of the hospital services". The defendants say that this is a deemed, or fictitious, as distinct from an actual loss.

In my view the object of s 5 is to distinguish between quantified economic loss in the nature of special damages and general damages. The term "actual" serves to exclude possible or contingent claims. By the Hospitals Act [RSA 1980, c H–11] the Legislature has chosen to deem the beneficiary to have suffered a loss and an object of a deeming provision is to obviate the need to go behind the deemed result. Since the beneficiary has the same right as if he had paid, we ought not to go behind that deemed result. In my view the claim is for a financial loss which is deemed to be an actual loss to the beneficiary, and is not excluded by s 5.' *James v Rentz* (1986) 27 DLR (4th) 724 at 726, Alta CA, per Stevenson JA

ACTUAL MILITARY SERVICE   *See* MILITARY SERVICE

ACTUAL OCCUPATION

New Zealand 'The word "actual" when used in conjunction with the word "occupation" is effective to exclude any constructive, legal, or notional occupation which might otherwise arise, and which does not completely correspond to the fact which it indicates. "Actual occupation" means occupation in fact as distinguished from constructive occupation.' *Brewer v Papatoetoe Town Board* [1934] NZLR 774 at 777, per Fair J; also reported [1934] GLR 737 at 738

ACTUAL TOTAL LOSS   *See* TOTAL LOSS

ACTUALLY

In possession

Australia [The Landlord and Tenant Act 1948 (Vic), s 57 (see now the Landlord and Tenant Act 1958–1986) dealt, inter alia, with cases where a lessee of prescribed premises died and a person (not being a lodger or boarder) who resided with him immediately prior to his death was 'actually in possession' of the premises immediately after his death.] 'Effect must be given to the word "actually" as a matter of construction. And it seems to us that the person the legislature must be taken to have intended to benefit by the use of the words "actually in possession" is one in actual occupation in contradistinction to a person with a legal right to possess but not in actual occupation.' *Walsh v Public Trustee* [1956] VLR 525 at 529, per Herring CJ and Gavan Duffy J

New Zealand 'I have . . . come to the conclusion that, having regard to the context in this case—the words of the bequest are "purse and all contents thereof and also all moneys actually in my possession at the time of my decease"— the bequest comprehends only moneys in the actual and physical possession and control of the testatrix at the time of her death. There may be circumstances in which under such a gift it might be held that money held in the house of the testatrix by, say, a servant or other person under her control was included, but in this case the testatrix died in Sydney, and the agent who held the cheques was in New Zealand. To hold that in such circumstances the cheques were "actually in the possession of the testatrix at the time of her death" would, in my view, be placing too great a strain upon the language of the bequest.' *Re Rowling, Ellis v Rowling* [1942] NZLR 88 at 106, per Myers CJ; also reported [1942] GLR 104 at 112

Vacant and unoccupied

New Zealand 'In the phrase "actually vacant and unoccupied" it [the word 'actually'] excludes a constructive vacancy or absence of occupation, whether that is due to the law or to the notional use of the latter words. In such a context its purpose and operation is to exclude a state of affairs denoted by the words "vacant and unoccupied" in their legal or constructive sense . . . it also operates to exclude the meaning of the words in their notional or secondary sense of "unoccupied for their usual or intended purposes." ' *Brewer v Papatoetoe Town Board* [1934] NZLR 774 at 777, per Fair J; also reported [1934] GLR 737 at 738

ACTUARIAL METHOD

United States 'Actuarial method' means the method, defined by rules adopted by the Administrator, of allocating payments made on a debt between principal or amount financed and loan finance charge or credit service charge pursuant to which a payment is applied first to the accumulated loan finance charge or credit service charge and the balance is applied to the unpaid principal or unpaid amount financed. (Uniform Consumer Credit Code 1969, s 1.301(1))

ACTUS REUS

'I desire to make an observation on the expression *actus reus*. . . . Strictly speaking, though in almost universal use, it derives, I believe, from a mistranslation of the Latin aphorism: *Actus non facit reum nisi mens sit rea.* Properly translated, this means, "An act does not make *a man* guilty of a crime, unless his mind be also guilty". It is thus not the *actus* which is *reus*, but the man and his mind respectively. Before the understanding of the Latin tongue has wholly died out of these islands, it is as well to record this as it has frequently led to confusion.' *Haughton v Smith* [1973] 3 All ER 1109 at 1113, 1114, HL, per Lord Hailsham of St Marylebone LC

'The question speaks of "actus reus". This expression is derived from Coke's brocard (3 Co Inst ch 1, fo 10), "*Actus non facit reum, nisi mens sit rea*", by converting incorrectly into an adjective the word reus which was there used correctly in the accusative case as a noun. As long ago as 1889 in *R v Tolson* [23 QBD 168 at 185–187, [1886–90] All ER Rep 26 at 36–37] Stephen J when dealing with a statutory offence . . . condemned the phrase as likely to mislead, though his criticism in that case was primarily directed to the use of the expression "mens rea". In the instant case . . . it is the use of the expression "actus reus" that is liable to mislead, since it suggests that some positive act on the part of the accused is needed to make him guilty of a crime and that a failure or

omission to act is insufficient to give rise to criminal liability unless some express provision in the statute that creates the offence so provides.

My Lords, it would I think be conducive to clarity of analysis of the ingredients of a crime that is created by statute, as are the great majority of criminal offences today, if we were to avoid bad Latin and instead to think and speak . . . about the conduct of the accused and his state of mind at the time of that conduct, instead of speaking of actus reus and mens rea.' *R v Miller* [1983] 1 All ER 978 at 979, 980, per Lord Diplock

ADAPT   *See also* CONSTRUCT

'The justices seem to have treated the word "adapted" [in the Customs and Inland Revenue Act 1888, s 4 (repealed)] as if it were synonymous with "suitable" or "apt", whereas it must be construed as meaning altered so as to make the vehicle apt for the conveyance of goods. The words are intended to cover the case of a vehicle which was not constructed solely for the purpose of conveying goods in the course of trade, but after its construction has been made apt for that purpose.' *French v Champkin* [1920] 1 KB 76 at 79, DC, per Lord Reading CJ

'It is necessary that the building in question should be a "building constructed or adapted to be used for human habitation" [within a repealed Housing Act]. . . . I think "adapted" is used to mean changed or altered or transformed.' *Davison v Birmingham Industrial Cooperative Society* (1920) 90 LJKB 206 at 208, per Lord Reading CJ

[The Road Traffic Act 1960, s 191(1) (repealed; see now the Road Traffic Act 1972, s 196(1)) defined goods vehicles as motor vehicles constructed or 'adapted' for use for the carriage of goods.] 'It was conceded on both sides, and, indeed, the decided cases so show, that "adapted" in this context means "altered so as to make fit".' *Flower Freight Co Ltd v Hammond* [1962] 3 All ER 950 at 951, per cur.; [1963] 1 QB 275 at 281

ADAPT FOR SALE

'I must confess that I can see no reason why, speaking generally, the process of sorting and segregating a mass of items that together contribute an "article" should not be capable of being an "adapting for sale", even though the items all remain physically unaltered when the process is completed.' *Valuation Comr v McAllister* [1954] NI 54 at 63, CA, per Lord MacDermott CJ

ADAPTATION

In this Act 'adaptation'—
(a) in relation to a literary or dramatic work, means any of the following, that is to say,—
  (i) in the case of a non-dramatic work, a version of the work (whether in its original language or a different language) in which it is converted into a dramatic work;
  (ii) in the case of a dramatic work a version of the work (whether in its original language or a different language) in which it is converted into a non-dramatic work;
  (iii) a translation of the work;
  (iv) a version of the work in which the story or action is conveyed wholly or mainly by means of pictures in a form suitable for reproduction in a book, or in a newspaper, magazine or similar periodical; and
(b) in relation to a musical work, means an arrangement or transcription of the work. (Copyright Act 1956, s 2(6))

ADDICTION

Canada 'The respondent brought a divorce action against the appellant alleging he was grossly addicted to alcohol. The word addicted is not defined in the Divorce Act 1967–68 (Can) c 24; the dictionary meaning is "to apply oneself habitually to the practice or use of". The Divorce Act contemplates something more than the habitual use of alcohol as a ground for divorce, otherwise a person could obtain a divorce from a spouse who habitually consumed one martini every night before dinner but never drank on any other occasion. Parliament must have intended the connotation of being dependent on alcohol in the sense we commonly speak of drug addiction.' *Lyman v Lyman* (1971) 20 DLR (3d) 549 at 549, NB, per Limerick JA

ADDITION   *See also* ALTERATION

'The question I have to determine on this summons is as to the true construction in s 13, sub-s (ii) of the Settled Land Act 1890 [repealed; see now Settled Land Act 1925, s 83 and Sch III, Part I, para xxiii], of the words "additions to or alterations in buildings". . . . A thing is none the less an addition, in the largest sense of the word, because it is not of the same quality as that to which it is added. But if the word in this section were understood in that sense there would fall within the word "additions" all such things as venetian blinds, outside sun-blinds, furniture put into an unfurnished house, a park added to a mansion-house which enjoyed no park, or a right of fishing or shooting added to a country house which had none such. All these are additions; but are they additions to buildings within the meaning of this sub-section? I think not. . . . An "addition" to buildings within this section does not, I think, include the addition of land to a house, or furniture to a house. The "addition" here means structural addition in some sense of the word. In such a context as this the addition must be of the same quality as the thing added to.' *Re Clarke's Settlement* [1902] 2 Ch 327 at 329, 330, per Buckley J

'The question is whether a tenant for life is entitled, out of capital moneys, to have paid for him the expense of an electric installation. . . . The plant is not any more than the furniture an addition of like to like, but is merely something that adds to the amenities of the building. Into what categories are you to divide the additions? You can only get three gradations—namely, loose chattels which are not attached at all, fixtures which are attached in a certain sense, and actual structural additions. Which of those is meant? It seems to me that it would be very difficult to divide off any possible alternative short of an actual structural addition. Prima facie it seems to me that the addition meant by the section is a structural addition to the building, and that it is not satisfied by putting wires into a building or putting an engine into an engine-house.' *Re Blagrave's Settled Estates* [1903] 1 Ch 560 at 561, 563, CA, per Collins MR

'The erection of a new building in place of an old building is not an addition to or alteration in that old building.' *Re Leveson-Gower's Settled Estate* [1905] 2 Ch 95 at 98, per Swinfen Eady J

[Extensive works were required to be done by the local authority to some old cottages, subject to a settlement. The question was whether the whole, including incidental work, such as plastering, should be regarded as of a capital nature.] 'I now come to the second question which is whether the words in the Settled Land Act 1925, Sch III, Part I, para xxiii, "additions to or alterations in buildings reasonably necessary or proper to enable the same to be let" are confined to structural additions or alterations. . . . I have to construe, not the Settled Land Act 1890, but the Settled Land Act 1925, and although, in construing it, I must have regard to the way in which the Court treated the words "additions to or alterations in buildings" in the earlier Act, those are not the decisions which bind me when I am dealing with another Act which contains different provisions . . . the conclusion to which I feel bound to come—and I think it is a proper conclusion—is that the word "structural" was omitted purposely when this Act was drawn, and that there is no justification for reading into this clause the word "structural", and that, therefore, "additions to or alterations in buildings reasonably necessary or proper to enable the same to be let" are not necessarily alterations and additions which are purely structural, but may include other additions and alterations as well.' *Re Lindsay's Settlement* (No 2) [1941] 1 All ER 143 at 147, 148, per Farwell J

ADDITIONAL

Canada 'The ordinary meaning of the word "additional" is "added to" or "other" and might very well [in a clause in a will respecting 'additional property'] include such property as had not been disposed of by the will or subsequently acquired property or both.' *Wurtz v Merritt* [1947] 1 WWR 44 at 45, Sask KB, per McNiven J

ADDRESS

Election address

'I certainly do not want to be supposed to define what an address [within Part II (3) of Sch 1 to the Corrupt Practices Act 1883 (repealed)] is, but I do think that anything which is in the nature of an appeal to a voter to vote for a particular candidate must be in the nature of an address . . . because candidates always appeal to the voters to vote for them, and they do it in different forms—sometimes in what I may call classical language, and sometimes it may be in football language, which very likely is not classical; but somehow or another it is an appeal to the voters to vote, and I think that must be an address.' *Exeter Borough Case,*

Duke v St. Maur (1911) 6 O'M & H 228 at 249, per Channell J

Place of residence

[By the Prison Act 1952, s 29 (repealed by the Criminal Justice Act 1961, s 21) persons specified thereunder were required to register their 'addresses' with the police. The appellant claimed that he had no fixed abode but had spent his time wandering about a town.] 'It seems to this court that "address", both in s 29 of the Act of 1952 and in Sch I, is not referring to an address in the ordinary sense of the word as a postal address. It denotes something less than that, and the court thinks that the obligation which arises on a deeming to reside in any "place of whatever description at which he spends a night" can be fulfilled, and should properly be fulfilled, by giving a reasonable identification of such a place, not necessarily a postal address but something which describes or identifies the place with reasonable certainty.' *R v Bishop* [1959] 2 All ER 787 at 791, CCA, per cur.

ADEMPTION   *See also* SATISFACTION

A total loss was said to have been 'adeemed' if the loss [under a policy of marine insurance] did not continue to be total at the commencement of the action. Thus, where the ship or goods had been captured, then even though due notice of abandonment was given, if the property was released so that the assured might reasonably be expected to take possession of it, he could only recover for a partial loss. On the other hand, the mere release or restitution of the insured property would not have this effect if the assured might eventually have to pay more for it than it was worth, and therefore could not reasonably be expected to take possession of it. (25 Halsbury's Laws (4th edn) para 329)

A testamentary gift may be adeemed or taken away from the donee: (1) by a subsequent disposition by the testator of the subject matter of the gift; (2) by a change in the ownership or nature of the property; and (3) by the presumption that the testator does not intend to provide double portions for his children or other persons to whom he stands *in loco parentis*. If, however, in a will there are gifts of two properties settled in trust, one by reference to the trusts of the other (for example where heirlooms are settled to follow the trusts of realty), the subsequent alteration of the trusts of one property by a deed executed by the testator in his lifetime does not affect earlier testamentary limitations relating to the other property. Apart from the presumption as to double portions, there can be no ademption of a residuary gift. (50 Halsbury's Laws (4th edn) para 342)

Australia '"Ademption" postulates the destruction of the subject matter, whether by physical dealing or by operation of rules of equity, while the word "conversion" postulates only a change in its character, so that one person cannot take it, while another can (Law Quarterly Review, Vol 49, at p 174).' *Fairweather v Fairweather* (1944) 69 CLR 121 at 139–140, per Rich J

South Africa 'The . . . revocation or recall of a legacy by some act of the testator other than testamentary revocation.' *Tutor Dative Dove's Minor Children v Estate Dove* 1937 NPD 407 per Carlisle J

ADEQUATE

Canada Applicant for citizenship was required to demonstrate 'adequate' knowledge of either official language.] 'The word "adequate" is defined in the Shorter Oxford English Dictionary as meaning "sufficient, suitable". That definition does not solve the problem because the question arises as to what standard of adequacy is applicable, that is, a subjective or an objective one. The word as used in the Act cannot be subjective because that would mean that the decision as to the adequate knowledge being that of an applicant who might well conclude that he has no need whatsoever for a knowledge of English or at the most a very limited knowledge. Rather I think the statute contemplates an objective test in the milieu of an English or French speaking community as the case may be. That, I think, means that the applicant should have the ability to communicate with reasonable ease with other members of an English-speaking community. She must be able to understand the language and to make herself understood in that language. I also think that consideration must be given to the applicant's status in the community, and the need that status imposes on the applicant to understand and make herself understood by others.' *Re Giancaterino* (1975) 60 DLR (3d) 380 at 382, Fed Ct TD, per Cattanach J

ADEQUATE STRENGTH

[The Factories Act 1937, s 23(1)(a) (repealed; see now the Factories Act 1961, s 26(1)(a)) provided that no chain, rope or lifting tackle should be used unless it was of good construction, sound material, 'adequate strength', and free from patent defect.] 'It may be that the "adequate strength" of a chain, rope, or lifting tackle must be in relation to its safe working load. Thus a chain or rope, when new, will have a prescribed safe working load. The effect of wear and tear may be to diminish strength. If strength ceases to be adequate, the chain or rope must no longer be used. In our judgment, however, it is not necessary to express any final view in these matters, for we cannot think that, where there is an obligation not to use a chain unless it is of adequate strength, a breach is established by proving that the strength was more than was necessary. It would be irrational to suppose that a rope or chain must be of a strength precisely equal to, but not a whit above, the strain imposed on it.' *Gledhill v Liverpool Abattoir Utility Co Ltd* [1957] 3 All ER 117 at 121, CA, per cur.

ADHERENT

To Church doctrine

[A testator by his will devised real property to the eldest son of F who should be a member of the Church of England and an 'adherent' to the doctrine of that church.] 'When he [the testator] uses the word "adherent", he is using a word that is commonly used as meaning "one who conforms to", or, "one who is attached to", and to say that it is impossible to know what the testator meant by the use of the word because no guidance is given to the degree of adherence, is, I think, . . . to import doubt that ought not to exist when the whole of the words used are given their ordinary meaning. I cannot subscribe to the view that it is impossible to say what is the doctrine of the Church of England. In my view, it is capable of reasonable formulation. I also think it is possible for a man to say: 'I conscientiously and sincerely agree with that doctrine, which is all that an adherent is required to do".' *Re Allen, Faith v Allen* [1953] 2 All ER 898 at 909; [1953] Ch 810 at 829 830, CA, per Birkett LJ

New Zealand 'The next condition [in a will] requires that J P W Gray shall adhere to the Protestant faith at the time of attaining twenty-five years of age. . . . What does the word "adhere" precisely signify? In my view, there must be grave doubt as to what particular course of conduct will constitute adherence. . . . In my view, the word "adhere" is too uncertain to be enforced. Would the condition be satisfied by a mere private adherence to the Protestant faith or would some public profession be required? Would outward adherence to the Protestant faith be sufficient whatever the private faith? Even if the Court could determine these matters, what degree of adherence would be required? How much Church attendance would be required? Would it be sufficient if J P W Gray answered, upon the taking of a census, that his religion was Protestant although he had no private faith, although he never went to Church, and merely relied upon a family connection with a Protestant church? These considerations show that the word "adhere" is too vague to be enforced and that this condition is void for uncertainty.' *Re Lockie, Guardian, Trust & Executive Company of New Zealand Ltd v Gray* [1945] NZLR 230 at 245, 246, per Smith J; also reported [1944] GLR 464 at 469

New Zealand [A testatrix by her will directed her trustee to stand possessed of her residuary estate upon trust for her grandson absolutely should he survive her and attain the age of twenty-five years and at the date of her death or the attainment by him of twenty-five years which ever last occurred be an 'adherent' of the Church of the Province of New Zealand otherwise known as the Church of England.] 'In *Clayton v Ramsden* [[1943] AC 320], and in *Re Lockie* [supra], the conditions were conditions subsequent, but it was not suggested in the argument of this summons, and in my opinion, there would be no warrant for suggesting that the standard of certainty required varies according as the condition be a condition precedent or a condition subsequent. I am therefore content to say that this condition is void if it is impossible to tell from reading it what the testatrix has required her grandson to do: *Clayton v Ramsden*, per Lord Romer. At the date of her death or when he attained the age of twenty-five years, he has to be "an adherent of the Church of England". What is such an adherent? In my opinion, it is impossible to say. . . . Portion of Smith J's judgment in *Re Lockie* is exactly in point, and I respectfully agree with it. . . . What Smith J says as to the verb "adhere" applies equally to the noun "adherent".' *Re Biggs, Public Trustee v Schneider* [1945] NZLR 303 at 307, 308, per Callan J; also reported [1945] GLR 70 at 71

To King's enemies

'If a man be adherent to the King's enemies in his realm by giving to them aid or comfort in his realm, or if he be adherent to the King's enemies elsewhere, that is by giving them aid or comfort elsewhere, he is equally adherent to the King's enemies, and if he is adherent to the King's enemies, then he commits the treason which the statute of Edward III [Treason Act 1351 (amended by the Criminal Law Act 1967, s 10, Sch 3)] . . . defines. . . . The subjects of the King owe him allegiance, and the allegiance follows the person of the subject. He is the King's liege wherever he may be, and he may violate his allegiance in a foreign country just as well as he may violate it in this country.' *R v Casement* [1917] 1 KB 98 at 137, CCA, per Darling J

ADJACENT   *See also* ABUT; ADJOIN; CONTIGUOUS; NEIGHBOURING

' "Adjacent" is not a word to which a precise and uniform meaning is attached by ordinary usage. It is not confined to places adjoining, and it includes places close to or near. What degree of proximity would justify the application of the word is entirely a question of circumstances.' *Wellington Corpn v Lower Hutt Corpn* [1904] AC 773 at 775, 776, PC, per cur.

' "Adjacent" means close to or nearby or lying by: its significance or application in point of distance depends on the circumstances in which the word is used.' *English Clays Lovering Pochin & Co Ltd v Plymouth Corpn* [1974] 2 All ER 239 at 243, CA, per cur.

Australia 'The question is, in relation to any particular street, what is meant by the phrase [in the Local Government Act (WA) 1960–1986, s 6] "land adjacent to the street". No doubt "adjacent" has a wider meaning than "adjoining" which is defined in s 6 of the Act to mean contiguous; it would include a street nearby or close to.' *Geneff v Shire of Perth* [1967] WAR 124 at 128, per Jackson J

New Zealand [A condition implied in a taxi-driver's licence was that the driver of a taxicab should not cause his taxicab to be drawn up on or 'adjacent' to a stand which was already occupied by the full number of vehicles the stand was intended to accommodate.] 'The meaning of the word "adjacent" is to be determined by having regard to the position of the taxi in relation to the stand, and not by having regard to the intentions of the driver. To hold otherwise would involve treating the word "adjacent" which connotes "propinquity" as having a varying meaning, according to the motive of the person charged' *Claney v Bland* [1958] NZLR 760 at 763, per North J

ADJOIN   *See also* ABUT; ADJACENT; CONTIGUOUS; NEIGHBOURING

'Ground cannot be properly said to adjoin a house unless it is absolutely contiguous.' *R v Hodges* (1829) Mood & M 341 at 343, per Parke J

'You cannot define "adjoin" as meaning benefit of access, or vice versa, but in considering whether houses adjoin which are placed in close proximity to the part of the street which is to be paved, it is a most important fact, and in many cases a dominant fact, to see whether there is substantial access and advantage which the houses enjoy from that portion of the street which is to be paved, and a substantial access and advantage of that kind, coupled with close proximity, may bring the case within the word "adjoin" though there is no actual touch.' *Lightbound v Higher Bebington Local Board* (1885) 16 QBD 577 at 584, per Bowen LJ

'What is the meaning of the phrase "Any of the premises adjoining or contiguous to the hereditaments hereby demised"? I think the word "contiguous" was used there by someone who did not fully understand its meaning. I do not think it was intended to have its strict meaning, viz "touching", because the phrase is "such adjoining or contiguous premises", and I think the two words, "adjoining" and "contiguous" were not intended to be merely synonymous, but were meant to be alternative, and that the meaning really was "such adjoining or neighbouring premises". But even if the word is construed strictly, still I think the plaintiff's and the defendant's premises are "adjoining or contiguous". They are situate on opposite sides of the street, and the words of the lease in the one case, and of the agreement in the other, are quite sufficient to pass the soil *ad medium filum viae.*' *Haynes v King* [1893] 3 Ch 439 at 448, per North J

'This case turns upon the construction of covenants in a lease. . . . It is said that the words "adjoining premises" extend not only to buildings which come in physical contact with the demised building, but also to any buildings which are situated near enough to the demised building for works done on the premises so situate to affect materially the demised premises. . . . I cannot agree to this construction. . . . It is plain from the use in other parts of the lease of the wider expression "adjoining or neighbouring" that the word "adjoining" cannot be used in this covenant in the sense of "neighbouring". A narrower meaning must be put on the word "adjoining". I believe that in this covenant "adjoining" is used in the sense of "in physical contact with".' *White v Harrow* (1902) 86 LT 4 at 5, 6, CA, per Williams LJ

'There are three words, "adjoining", "adjacent", and "contiguous", which lie not far apart in the meaning which they convey. But of no one of them can its meaning be stated with exactitude and without exception. As to "adjoining" the expression "next adjoining" or "immediately adjoining" is common and legitimate. This expression at once conveys that two things may adjoin which are not next to each other. "Adjacent" conveys that which lies "near to" rather than that which lies "next to". "Contiguous" is perhaps of all three the least exact. Any one of the three may by its context be shown to convey "neighbouring" without the necessity of physical contact.' *Cave v Horsell* [1912] 3 KB 533 at 544, CA, per Buckley LJ

'When used in conjunction with the word land, the word "adjoining" in its primary sense means that which lies near so as to touch in some part the land which it is said to adjoin.' *Re Ecclesiastical Comrs for England's Conveyance* [1936] Ch 430 at 440, per Luxmoore J

'I think that it is beyond doubt that the word "adjoins" [in the Highways Act 1959, s 295(1) (repealed; see now the Highways Act 1980, s 329(1))] or, indeed, the words "fronts" or "abuts", envisage actual contact between part of the premises and the street, not only contact but contact of the sort which will produce some frontage which can be measured.' *Buckinghamshire County Council v Trigg* [1963] 1 All ER 403 at 406, per Lord Parker CJ

Canada 'The word "adjoining" is different from the word "adjacent". "Adjoining", as its derivation implies, signifies being joint [sic] together; "adjacent" is simply lying near.' *Re Bowker & Richards* (1905) 1 WLR 194 at 196, BCSC, per Irving J

ADJOURN

[Commissioners appointed under the Election Commissioners Act 1852, s 4 (repealed) to make inquiry as to the existence of corrupt practices, had power to hold meetings and to 'adjourn' them from time to time.] 'The word "adjourn" must be construed with reference to the object of the context, and with reference to the object of the inquiry. What might in certain Acts of Parliament require a technical interpretation, where adjournments are well understood, as, for instance, relating to courts of justice, does not apply to inquiries of this nature. . . . When the power of holding those meetings is given . . . the word "adjourn" must be taken as used in the popular sense of deferring or postponing the inquiry to a future day.' *Fitzgerald's Case* (1869) LR 5 QB 1 at 10, per Mellor J

'The word "adjourn" is not used in its technical sense, as it is used when applied to proceedings of courts of justice, where the authority of holding a meeting is on a given day, but where the law implies an authority to create, as it were, a special extension of that period when it is needful for the purpose of completing the business for which the meeting is held. Where that is done, the whole period is regarded as being one day, and the meeting or sitting as one meeting. If in such a case the day has been suffered to expire without adjournment, then nothing can be done to keep alive the functions of the body, and their authority necessarily expires.' Ibid at 12, per Lush J

ADJUDGE

Canada 'In my opinion . . . the power of the Juvenile Court to adjudge guilt is equivalent to the power of an ordinary criminal Court to convict and I cannot see any essential difference between the power to adjudge a person guilty of an offence and the power to convict a person of the same offence.' *Morris v The Queen* (1978) 91 DLR (3d) 161 at 183, per Pratte J

ADJUDICATION   *See* DECISION

ADJUSTMENT

'The word "adjustment" is a word in common use. It is commonly applied to the settlement among various parties of their several shares in respect of claims, liabilities, or payments relating to a general average claim. That is not its only application; it is a word which is applied to other matters in the same manner in which it is commonly applied in marine insurance. When there are matters which require rearranging, regulating, or equalising so as to restore the true balance, the process of so rearranging, setting right, regulating or equalising may be described as "adjusting".' *Re Buckinghamshire CC & Hertfordshire CC* (1899) 68 LJQB 417 at 423, per Bruce J

ADMINISTER

In this Act 'administer' means administer to a human being or an animal, whether orally, by injection or by introduction into the body in any other way, or by external application, whether by direct contact with the body or not; and any reference in this Act to administering a substance or article is a reference to administering it either in its existing state or after it has been dissolved or dispersed in, or diluted or mixed with, some other substance used as a vehicle. (Medicines Act 1968, s 130(9))

'I am of opinion that, to constitute an administering [of poison, etc, contrary to 9 Geo 4, c 31 (repealed)] it is not necessary that there should be a delivery by the hand.' *R v Harley* (1830) 4 C & P 369 at 372, per Park J

ADMINISTRATION   *See also* MANAGEMENT

An administrator is a person appointed by a court of competent jurisdiction to administer the property of a deceased person. The office of administrator is said to be dative, because it derives from such a grant whereas the office of executor derives from the will of the deceased person. (17 Halsbury's Laws (4th edn) para 703)

'Administration' means, with reference to the real and personal estate of a deceased person, letters of administration, whether general or limited, or with the will annexed or otherwise. 'Administrator' means a person to whom administration is granted. (Administration of Estates Act 1925, s 55(1))

'Administration' includes all letters of administration of the effects of deceased persons, whether with or without a will annexed, and whether granted for general, special or limited purposes. (Supreme Court Act 1981, s 128)

ADMINISTRATION OF JUSTICE

Canada [Accused was charged with intent to interfere with administration of justice under s 157 of the Criminal Code (see now s 127 of the Criminal Code, RSC 1970, c C-34 'obstructing justice').] 'I am of opinion that the "administration of justice" mentioned in section 157 of the Criminal Code should not be restricted to what takes place after an information had been laid; but it includes the taking of necessary steps to have a person who has committed an offence brought before the proper tribunal, and punished for his offence. It is a very wide term covering the detection, prosecution and punishment of offenders.' *Kalick v The King* (1920) 61 SCR 175 at 186, SCC, per Brodeur J

ADMIRALTY

Jurisdiction

See now the Supreme Court Act 1981, ss 20–24.

ADMISSION

Of liability

New Zealand 'The first question for determination . . . depends upon the meaning of the expression "admission of liability" in the Motor-vehicles Insurance (Third-party Risks) Act 1928, s 11(3) [repealed; see now Transport Amendment Act 1972, s 22]. . . . The words are "admission of liability", and what they mean is "admission of liability to pay damages". I do not suggest that in order to come within the expression it is necessary that the admission should be in express terms an admission of liability to pay. The admission may be an admission of negligence couched in such terms as necessarily to imply an admission of liability to pay damages. . . . The admission in this case relied on by the insurance company is not an "admission of liability to pay damages". It is an admission of fault, but a person may be at fault without necessarily being legally responsible, and therefore liable to pay damages in respect of an accident. Consequently, an admission of fault is by no means necessarily an admission of liability to pay damages.' *SIMU Mutual Insurance Assocn v Minson's Ltd* [1938] NZLR 829 at 837-839, per Myers CJ; also reported [1938] GLR 534 at 536, 537

To benefice

'Admission' includes institution and induction, collation, licence, and any other process by which the cure of souls of a benefice and the right to its profits are given to an incumbent and 'admit' shall be construed accordingly. (Reorganisation Areas Measure 1944, s 53)

'Admission' includes institution and induction, collation, licence and any other process by which a person becomes the incumbent of a benefice or the holder of any other ecclesiastical preferment and "admit" shall be construed accordingly. (Overseas and Other Clergy (Ministry and Ordination) Measure 1967, s 6)

ADMITTED SET-OFF   *See* SET-OFF

ADMIXTURE

'The word "admixture" [in the Various Industries (Silicosis) Scheme, SR & O 1931, No 342 (revoked)] clearly means what it says; that is, not a chemical combination transferring the constituent parts of the new combination into something quite other than those of which the constituent parts are composed, but a physical or mechanical mixture in which each mixing part retains its own identity.' *Gledhall v Dalton Main Collieries Ltd* (1934) 27 BWCC 181 at 188, CA, per Slesser LJ

ADOPTION

Of child

At common law, the rights, liabilities and duties of parents are inalienable, and adoption, in the sense of the transfer of parental rights and duties in respect of a child to another person and their assumption by him, is unknown. In equity, however, it is possible for a relative or stranger to put himself *in loco parentis* towards a child by undertaking the office and duty of a father to make provision for the child, so as to assume a fiduciary position in respect of his relations with the child. . . . Since 1927, statutory provisions have made possible the legal adoption of children in England and Wales. (24 Halsbury's Laws (4th edn) paras 624, 625)

Of transaction

'By the Act [Sale of Goods Act 1893, s 18 (repealed; see now the Sale of Goods Act 1979, s 18, Rule 4(a))] the property is to pass to the buyer when "he signifies his approval or acceptance to the seller or does any other act adopting the transaction". . . . There must be some act which shews that he adopts the transaction; but any act which is consistent only with his being the purchaser is sufficient.' *Kirkham v Attenborough, Kirkham v Gill* [1897] 1 QB 201 at 203, CA, per Lord Esher MR

'The words of the Act [supra] are difficult to construe; but it seems to me that if the recipient of the goods retains them for an unreasonable time he does something inconsistent with the exercise of his option to return them, and thereby adopts the transaction. So if he does any other act inconsistent with their return, as if he sells them or pledges them, because if he pledges them he no longer has the free control over them so as to be in a position to return them.' Ibid at 204, per Lopes LJ

ADOPTION SOCIETY

'Adoption society' means a body of persons whose functions consist of or include the making of arrangements for the adoption of children. (Adoption Act 1976, s 72(1))

ADULTERATION

'When a simple article like tea has foreign ingredients added to it, like gypsum and Prussian blue, which are not required for the process of preparing and drying it, but are added for the purpose of making it look green, that is adulteration.' *Roberts v Egerton* (1874) LR 9 QB 494 at 500, per Blackburn J

See, generally, 18 Halsbury's Laws (4th edn) para 1066 et seq).

Canada [A regulation prohibited 'adulteration' of foods.] '. . . "adulteration" means the infusion of some foreign substance. It seems to me that a "foreign substance" would be wide enough to include any substance that one would not normally expect to be present in a food. In the context of the facts of this case, surely artificial sweeteners can be considered a "foreign substance" because in a can of peaches, for example, you would not normally expect to find an artificial chemically produced sweetener. In my view, the word "adulterated" cannot be restricted to only those substances which have been proven to be harmful. I consider the ordinary meaning of the word to be wide enough to encompass all

foreign substances, harmful or otherwise. Thus, I have the view that the addition of cyclamates to canned fruit results in the fruit being "adulterated" within the meaning of the Food and Drugs Act.' *Berryland Canning Co Ltd v The Queen* (1974) 44 DLR (3d) 568 at 578, Fed Ct T D, per Heald J

ADULTERY

For the purposes of relief in the matrimonial jurisdiction adultery means voluntary sexual intercourse between a married person and a person of the opposite sex, who is not the other spouse, during the subsistence of the marriage. (13 Halsbury's Laws (4th edn) para 562)

[Adultery is no longer, in itself, a ground for divorce; see now the Matrimonial Causes Act 1973, s 1 under which the sole ground for divorce is irretrievable 'breakdown of marriage'. Proof of breakdown, however, means that the petitioner must satisfy the court of one or more matters specified in the Act of 1973. One of these matters is that the respondent has committed adultery and the petitioner finds it intolerable to live with him.]

'I am not prepared to accede to the view that a husband can establish adultery against his former wife by proof that she has had sexual intercourse with a man without proving that that man was married at the material time.' *Chorlton v Chorlton* [1952] 1 All ER 611 at 612; [1952] P 169 at 171, per Lord Merriman P

'Adultery cannot be proved unless there be some penetration. It is not necessary that the complete act of sexual intercourse should take place. If there is penetration by the man of the woman, adultery may be found, but if there is no more than an attempt, I do not think that a finding of adultery would be right. In some recent editions of *Rayden on Divorce* there has been a definition of adultery. In the current edition there appears this passage [14th edn, at p 204]: "For purposes of relief in the Divorce Division, adultery may be defined as consensual sexual intercourse between a married person and a person of the opposite sex during the subsistence of the marriage'. In an earlier edition the passage (5th edn at p 89) was in the same form except that the word "voluntary" has been replaced in the current edition by "consensual". The evidence in the present case shows that both parties were ready and willing to have sexual intercourse the one with the other. On the commissioner's findings of fact there was no such sexual intercourse; there was no penetration. In my view there is no distinction to be drawn between the words "sexual intercourse" in the definition of "adultery" which I have read, and "carnal knowledge" in the criminal law. In regard to offences charged under the Criminal Law Amendment Act 1885, s 3 and s 5 [repealed; see now the Sexual Offences Act 1956, ss 4, 6 (s 6 amended by the Criminal Law Act 1967, Sch 2(14))] or on a charge of rape, it must be shown that there is some penetration.' *Dennis v Dennis* [1955] 2 All ER 51 at 55; [1955] P 153 at 160, CA, per Singleton LJ

[A girl aged twelve years who commits an act of sexual intercourse cannot be guilty of 'adultery'.] 'For the purpose of relief in the Divorce Division adultery may be defined as "consensual sexual intercourse between a married person and a person of the opposite sex during the subsistence of the marriage'. I take that definition from *Rayden on Divorce*, and for my purposes the most important word is "consensual" and "consensual" obviously means "by consent". The law throughout its development highly regards consent, and consent can only be given by those eligible to give it, that is to say, by people who are not legally disqualified by age from so doing.' *Barnett v Barnett* [1957] 1 All ER 389 at 389; [1951] P 78 at 81, per cur.

Australia 'We cannot doubt that any act of sexual gratification which actually leads to conception must amount in law to adultery. The result would be conclusive evidence of the nature and quality of the act by which it had been produced, but if it is conceded—as we think that it must be conceded—that the act is intercourse, in the circumstances suggested, we are unable to see why the same act should not be intercourse, whether or not conception ensues, or is in fact possible in the particular case. The nature and quality of the act is, as it were, inherent. It is not dependent upon conception or the possibility of conception, although conception has a probative value.' *McKinnon v McKinnon* [1942] SASR 107 at 108, per cur.

New Zealand 'There can be adultery which leaves the woman *virgo intacta*; there can be adultery without complete penetration in the full sense of the word.' *C v C* [1943] NZLR 45 at 48, per Callan J; also reported [1942] GLR 489 at 491

ADVANCE

Of money

'The words "advancing" and "lending" may each have a different signification; money may be "advanced" without being "lent"; the relation of borrower and lender does not exist in a great variety of the transactions which are distinctly authorised [in a memorandum of association].' *London Financial Assocn v Kelk* (1884) 26 Ch D 107 at 136, per Bacon V-C

'I cannot see any foundation for the argument that advances in this guarantee are restricted to mere overdrafts, and I am of opinion that they include payments made by the bank, whether directly out of the proper moneys of the bank or out of the proceeds of bills or notes discounted by the bank, which have been credited to the current account of the customer.' *Grahame v Grahame* (1887) 19 LR Ir 249 at 255, per Chatterton V-C

'The decision in this case turns upon the construction which is to be placed on the words used by the testator . . . and particularly on the word "advances". We are asked to read that word in the sense of the expression "advancement by portion" which is found in the marginal note to s 3 of the Statute of Distributions 1670 [repealed by Administration of Estates Act 1925, s 47(7)(iii) of which replaces s 3 of the 1670 Act]. . . . In my opinion the word is susceptible of that meaning. . . . That, however, is not the primary meaning: the word primarily refers to advances of money. An advance of money is commonly spoken of, and the expression is perfectly intelligible to everyone; but an advance of a house or a chattel would not be understood without explanation by anyone but a lawyer.' *Re Jaques, Hodgson v Braisby* [1903] 1 Ch 267 at 274, CA, per Stirling LJ

'I agree that the word "advances" is ambiguous and may either refer to prepayments of what will become due in future or be a polite euphemism for loans; but when "advances" are declared to be "repayable" (though only conditionally) they certainly lean to the side of loans.' *Lincolnshire Sugar Co Ltd v Smart* [1937] AC 697 at 703–705, per Lord Macmillan

'The learned judge [in the court below] set out his point of view very clearly in the following words: "It seems to me that 'advance' means: 'I will pay now what I may have to pay in the future. I am paying before due time. If, after the advance, some event in the future upon which payment becomes due does not occur, you can recover it back.' There are to be found cases where a tenant has paid rent in advance before due time to the landlord. That was held to be a loan by the tenant to the landlord. It was not rent because it was not due; it was in the nature of a loan. When someone says: 'I am going to make you an advance', I think they are saying: 'We will let you have it as a loan or on an implied understanding that if the event does not occur which makes it legally payable, we must have it back'." I accept the learned judge's very clear reasoning in his judgment.' *Bronester Ltd v Priddle* [1961] 3 All ER 471 at 475, CA, per Holroyd Pearce LJ

New Zealand 'The second point argued was whether this payment by the testator of the purchase-money was an "advance". What was it? It was not a gift. The money belonged to the testator, and he gave it to the son to buy a property, which the son bought, and entered into a mortgage with the father to secure the sum lent to the son. The fact that the money lent [in 1921] is not to be repaid till 1925 does not make it less an advance. . . . To advance money is to furnish money for a specified purpose. Here the money was advanced to buy the farm.' *Treadwell v Hitchings* [1925] NZLR 519 at 553, per Stout CJ; also reported [1924] GLR 551 at 553

South Africa 'The very use of the term "advanced' seems to me to indicate a payment to be given as prepayment of future earnings, for an advance is something paid before it is due.' *R v McKenzie* 1925 EDL 133 per van der Riet J

Of profession

'What is meant by the advance of some particular calling as a profession? If, for example, one says that in the last fifty years there has been a striking advance in the profession of accountancy, what idea is conveyed? Presumably this, that the profession has greatly increased in stature, importance, membership and general esteem, not simply that the fees have gone up, although that might be assumed as a consequence. How then is a profession to be "advanced" in this sense? The answer is, by service. Demands for more pay and better conditions for those engaged, however loud and persistent, and even successful, will not "advance" the profession in the sense that we have defined; but improvement in the quality and range of services rendered, and the spectacle of constant endeavour to do better, will certainly have that effect. If, then, one finds an organisation one of whose objects is to advance nursing as a profession, there is no great difficulty in interpreting this as meaning to improve

the quality and range of the services which nurses give and so to enhance the stature and importance of the nursing profession and the esteem in which it is held. It may well be, of course, that in order to improve nursing services more entrants must be attracted into the profession, and that this in time will mean improvements in pay and conditions; but such improvements will be means not ends.' *Royal College of Nursing v St Marylebone Corpn* [1958] 1 All ER 129 at 136, per cur; affd [1959] 3 All ER 663 at 667, 668, CA

ADVANCEMENT

The trust instrument may authorise the trustees to make advances out of the capital of any fund in which a minor or other person has a vested or presumptive or contingent interest. Apart from any such express authority conferred by the trust instrument, but subject to any contrary intention expressed in it, under a trust constituted or created after 1925 where the trust property consists of money or securities or property held on trust for sale trustees have statutory power [Trustee Act 1925, s 32] in their absolute discretion to pay or apply capital money subject to the trust for the advancement or benefit of any person entitled to the capital of the trust property or any share of it, not exceeding altogether in amount half the presumptive or vested share or interest of that person in the trust property, whether the person is entitled to the capital or a share of it absolutely or contingently on his attaining any specified age or on the occurrence of any other event or subject to a gift over on his death under any specified age or on the occurrence of any other event, and whether in possession or in remainder or reversion. Such an advance may be made notwithstanding that the interest of that person is liable to be defeated by the exercise of a power of appointment or revocation or to be diminished by the increase of the class to which he belongs. (48 Halsbury's Laws (4th edn) para 901)

[A settlement contained powers of advancement and appointment. The hotchpot clause was applicable to the former, but not to the latter. A child, having had a part of the trust fund paid over without its having been stated under which power, the decision was that the payment was prima facie attributable to the advancement clause.] 'An advancement has a definite meaning, distinct from an appointment. It means that a certain portion of the fund is actually taken out of the settlement altogether, and paid over to the object of the power. But an appointment deals only with the reversion of the fund, leaving the previous life interests untouched.' *Re Gosset's Settlement* (1854) 19 Beav 529 at 535, per Romilly MR

'I have always understood that an advancement by way of portion is something given by the parent to establish the child in life, or to make what is called a provision for him—not a mere casual payment. . . . I agree you may make the provision by marriage portion on the marriage of the child; you may make it on putting him into a profession or business in a variety of ways; you may pay for a commission; you may buy him the goodwill of a business, or give him stock in trade; all those things I understand; they are portions or provisions. . . . It is not every payment you make to the child which is to be regarded as advancement. It must be advanced by way of portion.' *Taylor v Taylor* (1875) 44 LJ Ch 718 at 719, per Jessel MR

'In my opinion, if a sum of money is paid by a father for the benefit of his son, it is an "advancement by portion". . . . If the father makes a will, saying that he wishes the son to have what he has given him in his lifetime over and above what he has given him by his will, the son will take it. But, if the father dies intestate, the law says, the right rule between children is equality, and, so far as is possible, there shall be equality among the children.' *Re Blockley, Blockley v Blockley* (1885) 29 Ch D 250 at 252, 253, per Pearson J

[The Trustee Act 1925, s 32 confers a power of 'advancement' for the benefit of any person entitled to the capital of a trust or any share thereof, whether absolutely or contingently.] 'The word "advancement" itself meant in this context the establishment in life of the beneficiary who was the object of the power or at any rate some step that would contribute to the furtherance of his establishment. Thus it was found in such phrases as "perferment or advancement" (*Lowther v Bentinck* (1874) LR 19 Eq 166), "business, profession or employment, or otherwise for the advancement or preferment in the world" (*Roper-Curzon v Roper-Curzon* (1871) LR 11 Eq 452), and "placing out or advancement in life" (*Re Breeds' Will* (1875) 1 Ch D 226). Typical instances of expenditure for such purposes under the social conditions of the nineteenth century were an apprenticeship or the purchase of a commission in the army or of an interest in business. In the case of a girl there could be advancement on marriage (*Lloyd v Cocker* (1860) 27 Beav 645). Advancement had, however, to some extent a limited range of meaning, since it was thought to convey the idea of some step in life of permanent significance, and accordingly, to prevent uncertainties about the permitted range of object for which moneys could be raised and made available, such words as "or otherwise for his or her benefit" were often added to the word "advancement". It was always recognised that these added words were "large words" (see Jessel MR in *Re Breeds' Will*) and indeed in another case, *Lowther v Bentinck*, the same judge spoke of preferment or advancement as being "both large words" but of "benefit" as being the "largest . . . of all". So too, Kay J in *Re Brittlebank, Coates v Brittlebank* [(1881) 30 WR 99]. Recent judges have spoken in the same terms—see Farwell J in *Re Halsted's Will Trusts, Halsted v Halsted* [[1937] 2 All ER 570], and Danckwerts J in *Re Moxon's Will Trusts, Downey v Moxon* [[1958] 1 All ER 386]. This wide construction of the range of the power, which evidently did not stand on niceties of distinction provided that the proposed application could fairly be regarded as for the benefit of the beneficiary who was the object of the power, must have been carried into the statutory power created by s 32, since it adopts without qualification the accustomed wording "for the advancement or benefit, in such manner as they may, in their absolute discretion, think fit. . . ." So much for "advancement", which I now use for brevity to cover the combined phrase "advancement or benefit". It means any use of the money which will improve the material situation of the beneficiary.' *Pilkington v Inland Revenue Comrs* [1962] 3 All ER 622 at 627, 628, HL, per Viscount Radcliffe

Australia ' "Advancement" is a word applicable to payments made in an early period of life and paid out of capital to secure a permanent benefit or advantage in life for the person "advanced". . . . An advancement is expenditure for the purpose of setting up an infant in life or conferring a special benefit of a permanent kind upon him. The word has been held to include the payment of money in order to enable an infant to emigrate.' *Re Dick, Dick v Dick* [1940] VLR 166 at 169, per O'Bryan J

Australia [The Testators' Family Maintenance and Guardianship of Infants Act, 1916–86, s 3(1) (NSW), provides, inter alia, that the Court shall, in the circumstances set out in the section, order that such provision as it thinks fit be made out of the estate of the testator for the maintenance, education or 'advancement' in life of the applicant widow or children of the testator as the case may be.] 'The presence of the words "advancement in life" in the New South Wales Act in addition to the words "maintenance and education" is not unimportant. These words appear in some but not all of the Territories of the Commonwealth. "Advancement" is a word of wide import. If found in a trust instrument it can often be confined by the context to the early period of the life of a beneficiary. But in the Testators' Family Maintenance and Guardianship of Infants Act no such limitation can be implied because the Act applies to children of any age.' *McCosker v McCosker* [1957] 97 CLR 566 at 575, per Dixon CJ and Williams J

See, generally, 21 Halsbury's Laws (4th edn) paras 384 et seq.

Of education

'I think that the advancement of education means the advancement of education for its own sake in order that the mind may be trained. It may be that it is unnecessary that that should be general education—I accept for the purposes of the present case that education in a particular subject is sufficient—but the main object must be the advancement of education in the sense of the training of the mind.' *Chartered Insurance Institute v London Corpn* [1957] 2 All ER 638 at 640, per Devlin J

'Take the word "advancement", as used in the phrase "advancement of education"? The word "advancement" connotes, to my mind, the concept of public benefit. When a man teaches his own children their lessons, he is not concerned with the "*advancement* of education" but solely with the "education" of his children. But when a schoolmaster teaches the boys in a public school, he is concerned— with their education truly—but also with the "advancement of education" generally. I would not, myself, confine the "advancement of education" to the advancement of education as an end in itself or for its own sake—if that means the advancement of the theory of education as taught in a training college for teachers—or even if it means the advancement of mind training. "Education" means, I think, simply the educating of people either in general subjects or in particular subjects. But the "advancement" of education connotes public, as distinct from private, benefit.' *National Deposit Friendly Society (Trustees) v Skegness*

Urban District Council [1958] 2 All ER 601 at 613, [1959] AC 293 at 322, HL, per Lord Denning

Of religion

'To advance religion means to promote it, to spread its message ever wider among mankind; to take some positive steps to sustain and increase religious belief.' *United Grand Lodge v Holborn Borough Council* [1957] 3 All ER 281 at 285, per cur.

'. . . The "advancement of religion" connotes the promotion of religion by spiritual teaching or by pastoral or missionary work among others outside one's own circle. When a man says his prayers in the privacy of his bedroom, he may truly be said to be concerned with religion but not with the "advancement of religion".' *National Deposit Friendly Society (Trustees) v Skegness Urban District Council* [1958] 2 All ER 601 at 613, 614, [1959] AC 293 at 322, HL, per Lord Denning

ADVANTAGE *See also* LIBERTY; TAX ADVANTAGE

The expression 'advantage' includes any office or dignity, and any forbearance to demand any money or money's worth or valuable thing, and includes any aid, vote, consent, or influence, or pretended aid, vote, consent, or influence, and also includes any promise or procurement of or agreement or endeavour to procure, or the holding out of any expectation of any gift, loan, fee, reward or advantage, as before defined. (Public Bodies Corrupt Practices Act 1889, s 7)

New Zealand 'I think it is necessary to say . . . that an advantage on the one hand and a profit on the other are not concepts that are necessarily synonymous. The former is a generic noun while the other is specific and embraced by it. To put the matter in another way, a profit is a particular kind of advantage which takes the form of a positive accretion to something as for example the gains received from a trade or dealing. While the more general concept of a pecuniary gain considered as an advantage can include such a benefit as receipts which do no more than keep down losses or produce a more favourable situation than otherwise would have been the case.' *Salvation Army v Canterbury Hotel Union* [1985] 2 NZLR 366 at 368, CA, per Woodhouse P

ADVENTURE *See* MARINE ADVENTURE

ADVERSE

Adverse occupation

New Zealand 'The "adverse occupation of a person rightfully entitled" [in the Land Transfer Act 1908, s 73 (repealed; see now Land Transfer Act 1952 (NZ), s 79)] does not mean what is ordinarily known as adverse possession. It means the occupation of a person who, but for the certificate of title would be rightfully entitled to the land.' *Zachariah v Morrow & Wilson* (1915) 34 NZLR 885 at 893, per Cooper J; also reported 17 GLR 655 at 658

Adverse party

Canada 'An "opposite party" has been held to mean a party on the other side of the record to the applicant, or a party on the same side between whom and the applicant there is some right to be adjusted in the action. A party to a cause or matter may be said to be adverse in interest to another party if he has a direct pecuniary or other substantial legal interest adverse to the legal interest of the other party, even although they may be upon the same side of the record and there is no issue on the record that the Court will be called upon to adjudicate between them.' *Rose & Laflamme Ltd v Campbell, Wilson & Strathdee Ltd* (1923) 17 SLR 332 at 340, 342, Sask CA, per Lamont JA

Adverse possession

No right of action to recover land accrues unless the land is in the possession of some person in whose favour the period of limitation can run. Such possession is called adverse possession. What constitutes such possession is a question of fact and degree; there is no general principle that, to establish possession of an area of land, the claimant must show that he made physical use of the whole of it. On the other hand, a claim to prescriptive rights to easements may be so extensive as to amount practically to a claim to the whole beneficial user of the servient tenement, in which case it can only succeed as a claim to adverse possession of the land itself. Occupation of land as a licensee is not adverse possession. (28 Halsbury's Laws (4th edn) para 768)

[The full statutory provision to which the above extract refers is as follows:
(1) No right of action to recover land shall be treated as accruing unless the land is in the possession of some person in whose favour the period of limitation can run (referred to below in this paragraph as 'adverse possession'), and where under the preceding provisions of this Schedule any right of action is treated as accruing on a certain date and no person is in adverse possession on that date, the right of action shall not be treated as accruing unless and until adverse possession is taken of the land.
(2) Where a right of action to recover land has accrued and after its accrual, before the right is barred, the land ceases to be in adverse possession, the right of action shall no longer be treated as having accrued and no fresh right of action shall be treated as accruing unless and until the land is again taken into adverse possession.
(3) For the purposes of this paragraph—
  (a) possession of any land subject to a rentcharge by a person (other than the person entitled to the rentcharge) who does not pay the rent shall be treated as adverse possession of the rentcharge; and
  (b) receipt of rent under a lease by a person wrongfully claiming to be entitled to the land in reversion immediately expectant on the determination of the lease shall be treated as adverse possession of the land.
(Limitation Act 1980, Sch 1, para 8)

Adverse witness

An adverse witness is one who shows a mind hostile to the party calling him and, by his manner of giving evidence, shows that he is not desirous of telling the truth. Whether he shows himself to be so hostile as to justify his cross-examination by the party calling him is a matter for the discretion of the judge, the exercise of which will rarely be interfered with by a higher court. This is so even where a party calls a witness who must of necessity wish to be unfavourable to him, for example, his opponent in the case. (17 Halsbury's Laws (4th edn) para 283)

[The Common Law Procedure Act 1854, s 22 (repealed; see now the Criminal Procedure Act 1865, s 3), enacted that a party might contradict his own witness or, by leave, prove that he had made inconsistent statements where, in the opinion of the judge, such witness proved 'adverse']. 'The question in this case is, whether, in construing the terms of the 22nd section . . . the word "adverse" ought to be understood as meaning merely "unfavourable'' or as meaning "hostile''. . . . I think the preferable construction is, that, in case the witness shall, in the opinion of the judge, prove "hostile'', the party producing him may not only contradict him by other witnesses, as he might heretofore have done, and may still do, if the witness is unfavourable, but may also, by leave of the judge, prove that he has made inconsistent statements.' *Greenough v Eccles* (1859) 5 CBNS 786 at 801, 804, per Williams J

Australia 'It can no longer be said that adverseness denotes a hostile demeanour and nothing else nor, I think, can it be right to say that an adverse or hostile witness is fully or sufficiently defined as one who is hostile or adverse to the party calling him. A person who is in fact hostile or adverse to the party calling him may indeed be also a hostile or an adverse witness within the meaning of the relevant rule. But there need not, I think, when one reflects on the matter, be shown to exist a sympathy for the other side, or a desire that the party calling the witness shall fail. The witness may have no precise desire or intention, or at all events the Court may not be prepared to find that he has any precise desire or intention, about the fate of the litigation; yet on the other hand it may appear clearly enough that the witness is determined not to tell the truth, or is desirous of not telling the truth, or at any rate the whole truth. . . . I think "adverse" must mean, in this field, unwilling, if called by a party who cannot ask him leading questions, to tell the truth and the whole truth in answer to non-leading questions—to tell the truth for the advancement of justice.' *R v Hayden* [1959] ALR 332 at 332, 333, per Sholl J

Canada ' "Adverse" [as applied to a witness] . . . means having exhibited such a hostile animus towards the party calling him as to reveal a desire not to tell the truth.' *R v Marceniuk* (1923) 20 Alta LR 53 at 54, Alta CA, per cur.

Canada 'The legislators manifestly sought after and used a term to depict a disposition of mind of the defaulting witness, which would have less extreme connotations than the word "hostile". But whether "adverse" portrays a mental attitude as moderate as that implied by the word "unfavourable" at the lower end of the scale or as inordinate as that indicated by the word "hostile" at the upper level or whether it denotes a condition of mind midway between these two extremes, the crucial question is whether the trial judge . . . should con-

sider as evidence relevant and material . . . the alleged inconsistent statement attributed to the witness.' *Boland v Globe and Mail Ltd* (1961) 29 DLR (2d) 401 at 422, 423, Ont CA, per Schroeder JA

ADVERSE CLAIM

Investment securities

United States 'Adverse claim' includes a claim that a transfer was or would be wrongful or that a particular adverse person is the owner or has an interest in the security. (Uniform Commercial Code 1978, s 8–302(2))

ADVERTISEMENT   *See also* INDECENT ADVERTISEMENT

'Advertisement' includes any notice, circular, label, wrapper, invoice or other document, and any public announcement made orally or by any means of producing or transmitting light or sound, and 'advertise' shall be construed accordingly. (Food Act 1984, s 132(1))

'Advertisement' means any word, letter, model, sign, placard, board, notice, device or representation, whether illuminated or not, in the nature of, and employed wholly or partly for the purposes of, advertisement, announcement or direction, and (without prejudice to the preceding provisions of this definition) includes any hoarding or similar structure used, or adapted for use, for the display of advertisements, and references to the display of advertisements shall be construed accordingly. (Town and Country Planning Act 1971, s 290(1))

'Advertisement' includes every form of advertising, whether in a publication or by the display of notices or by means of circulars or other documents or by an exhibition of photographs or a cinematograph film, or by way of sound broadcasting or television, and references to the issue of an advertisement shall be construed accordingly. (London Cab Act 1968, s 4(5))

(1) Subject to the following provisions of this section, in this Part [promotion of sales of medicinal products] of this Act 'advertisement' includes every form of advertising, whether in a publication, or by the display of any notice, or by means of any catalogue, price list, letter (whether circular or addressed to a particular person) or

other document, or by words described on any article, or by the exhibition of a photograph or a cinematograph film, or by way of sound recording, sound broadcasting or television, or by inclusion in a cable programme service or in any other way, and any reference to the issue of an advertisement shall be construed accordingly.

(2) Notwithstanding anything in the preceding subsection, in this Part of this Act 'advertisement' does not include spoken words except—

(a) words forming part of a sound recording or embodied in a sound-track associated with a cinematograph film, and

(b) words broadcast by way of sound broadcasting or television or included in a cable programme service.

(Medicines Act 1968, s 92 (amended by Cable and Broadcasting Act 1984, s 57(1), Sch 5, para 23(1)(2))

'Advertisement' includes a catalogue, a circular and a price list. (Trade Descriptions Act 1968, s 39(1))

'Advertisement' includes every form of advertising, whether in a publication, by television or radio, by display of notices, signs, labels, showcards or goods, by distribution of samples, circulars, catalogues, price lists or other material, by exhibition of pictures, models or films, or in any other way, and references to the publishing of advertisements shall be construed accordingly. (Consumer Credit Act 1974, s 189(1))

'Advertisement' includes every form of advertisement, whether to the public or not, and whether in a newspaper or other publication, by television or radio, by display of notices, signs, labels, showcards or goods, by distribution of samples, circulars, catalogues, price lists or other material, by exhibition of pictures, models or films, or in any other way, and references to the publishing of advertisements shall be construed accordingly. (Sex Discrimination Act 1975, s 82(1))

Australia [Section 29(1)(g) (see now s 29(2)(f)) of the Veterinary Surgeons Act 1923–86 (NSW), empowers the Governor to make regulations affecting the manner in which and the extent to which a veterinary surgeon is authorised to 'advertise'.] 'In our opinion, the word "advertise" in s 29(1)(g) should not be restricted as it would be if contrasted with "publish" or "print". There are various ways in which a professional man, if so minded, may "advertise" and the word in this context should not be confined to the positive acts which are commonly associated with the word. To give as did the applicant in this case an interview to a journalist on professional subjects and to permit photographs to be taken in a professional setting for publication constitute acts of advertising when done by a veterinary surgeon.' *Ex p Bowen, Re Blumer* [1962] NSWR 445 at 448, per cur.

Australia [The Town and Country Planning Act 1961 (Vic), Sch 3, para 5, empowers the planning scheme provisions prohibiting, restricting or regulating the construction, erection and use of advertising signs.] '[Counsel] referred me to the meaning in the New English Dictionary (Murray ed) of "advertisement" as "a public notice or announcement . . . usually in writing or print by placards or in a journal". The Macquarie Dictionary gives as the meaning for the noun "advertising": "The act or practice of bringing anything, as one's wants or one's business into public notice, especially by paid announcements in periodicals, or hoardings, etc, or by television." It has been held that the ordinary meaning of the word "advertise" is to make generally or publicly known, or to give public notice of something.' *Hersfield Development Corpn Pty Ltd v Melbourne & Metropolitan Board of Works* (1981) 46 LGRA 180 at 186, per McGarvie J

ADVERTISER

'Advertiser', in relation to an advertisement, means any person indicated by the advertisement as willing to enter into transactions to which the advertisement relates. (Consumer Credit Act 1974, s 189(1))

ADVICE

Canada 'The word "advice" in ordinary parlance means primarily the expression of counsel or opinion, favourable or unfavourable, as to action, but it may, chiefly in commercial usage, signify information or intelligence.' *J R Moodie Co Ltd v Minister of National Revenue* [1950] 2 DLR 145 at 148, SCC, per Rand J

ADVISED

Canada 'Those words ['until otherwise advised'] have a well-defined significance in legal parlance. They . . . mean until we are otherwise advised on our part, or, in other words, until we see reason for doing otherwise.' *Ledingham & Cooper v Me chants' Bank of Canada* (1917) 24 BCR 207 at 213 BCCA, per Macdonald CJA

ADVISEDLY

'The word "advisedly" may admit of two constructions. The first construction is "deliberately"—something said or done after "consideration", and as contrasted with something said or done inadvertently. . . . The second meaning is "intentionally".' *Heath v Burder* (1862) 15 Moo PCC 1 at 47, 48, per Lord Cranworth

Australia [Section 52 (see now s 52(2)) of the Criminal Code Act 1899–1986 (Qld), provides that any person who "advisedly" publishes seditious words is guilty of a misdemeanour.] 'The word "advisedly" is used somewhat curiously in s 52 of the Code, but it goes with the word "publishes", and it means, we think, no more than that the publication must be made deliberately in the sense that there is an intention to publish.' *Cooper v R* [1961] ALR 725 at 728, per cur.

ADVOCATE

South Africa 'The profession of an advocate consists in general in advising upon all legal questions; in settling and signing all petitions; in drawing the pleadings which must be filed of record by the attorney; in drawing and signing all documents; in pleading orally in court; and, moreover, in using all legal means by which the case of the client may best be furthered.' *Van der Linden Institute 3.2.4. See Ex p Masterson* 1974 (4) SA 321 (RA)

ADVOWSON

The initial right of a clerk to hold a church and benefice is acquired by presentation or, if the benefice is in the gift of the bishop of the diocese in which it is situate, by collation. The right to fill a church and benefice by presentation or collation is called an advowson or right of patronage, and the owner of it is called the patron. (14 Halsbury's Laws (4th edn) para 776)

Advowson is the right of presentation to a church, or ecclesiastical benefice. Advowson, *advocatio*, signifies *in clientelam recipere*, the taking into protection; and therefore is synonymous with patronage, *patronatus*. (2 Bl Com 21)

'An advowson, in modern times, and in ordinary language, has no doubt been confined to mean the perpetual right of presentation to a church or an ecclesiastical benefice. Lord Coke, however, in his First Institute [page 17b] defines it thus:—"Advowson—*Advocatio*, signifying an advowing or taking into protection, is as much as *jus patronatus*". The patronage or *jus patronatus* in this case, was not certainly to present to a church or an ecclesiastical benefice, but in every respect, other than that of having the cure of souls attached to the office, it exactly resembles, if it be not identical with, an ecclesiastical benefice. And, accordingly . . . the right of nomination to the guardianship of a hospital is called an advowson.' *A-G v Ewelme Hospital* (1853) 17 Beav 366 at 383, 384 per Romilly MR

'It seems to me, the words contained in this deed, "hereditaments situate in Doncaster", are not apt words to pass the advowson. . . . Prima facie, standing by themselves, they are not apt words to pass it. I think that follows, . . . from a simple consideration of what an advowson is. It is a hereditament, no doubt, but it is an unsubstantial and incorporeal thing; it is not the bodily possession of the church, but the right to give somebody else the bodily possession of it, and as such it is a right no doubt that concerns the land and concerns a certain place—a right collateral to the land, but not anything that has in itself a situation or spot on which it resides.' *Crompton v Jarratt* (1885) 30 Ch D 298 at 318, CA, per Bowen LJ

AERODROME

'Aerodrome' means any area of land or water designed, equipped, set apart or commonly used for affording facilities for the landing and departure of aircraft and includes any area or space, whether on the ground, on the roof of a building or elsewhere, which is designed, equipped or set apart for affording facilities for the landing and departure of aircraft capable of descending or climbing vertically. (Airports Authority Act 1975, s 23; Civil Aviation Act 1982, s 105(1))

'Aerodrome' means the aggregate of the land, buildings and works comprised in an aerodrome within the meaning of the Civil Aviation Act 1982 and (if and so far as not comprised in an aerodrome as defined in that Act) any land, building or works situated within the boundaries of an area designated, by an order made by the Secretary of State which is for the time being in force, as constituting the area of an aerodrome for the purposes of this Act. (Aviation Security Act 1982, s 38(1))

AERONAUTICS

Canada 'Nowhere can I find the word "aeronautics" used to describe, even remotely, a body of laws, rules or jurisprudence governing the right of a citizen to claim against an air carrier for negligence or pursuant to a contract of carriage.

The mere fact that in the Aeronautics Act such a power to make regulations concerning bills of lading is included among the numerous matters in the Act, all of which concern the control of air navigation and airports generally, is certainly not sufficient grounds to interpret the word "aeronautics" as used in s 23 of the Federal Court Act as including the jurisdiction to deal with claims between subjects arising out of an air bill. In order to justify such an extended interpretation, the effect of not interpreting the section in that manner would have to render it inoperative or, at least, very seriously and glaringly incomplete.' *Canadian Fur Co (NA) Ltd v KLM Royal Dutch Airlines* (1974) 52 DLR (3d) 128 at 133, 134, Fed Ct, per Addy J

AEROPLANE *See* AIRCRAFT

AFFAIRS

'For myself, I would think that, apart from some controlling consideration, contextual or other, the phrase "affairs of the company" comprises all its business affairs, interests or transactions, all its investment or other property interests, all its profits and losses or balance of profits or losses and its goodwill.' *R v Board of Trade, ex p St Martin Preserving Co Ltd* [1964] 2 All ER 561 at 568, [1965] 1 QB 603 at 618, per Winn J

AFFECT

[A restrictive covenant provided that no building should be erected on certain common land, nor should anything be done to or placed upon the land which should injure, prejudice, 'affect', etc, the land.] ' "Affect" following the word "prejudice" cannot, I think, mean "prejudicially affect" and must, therefore, mean "affect whether prejudicially or otherwise", that is to say, change or alter.' *National Trust for Places of Historic Interest or Natural Beauty v Midlands Electricity Board* [1952] 1 All ER 298 at 301, [1952] Ch 380 at 384, per Vaisey J

[Under the Inheritance (Family Provision) Act 1938, s 2(1A) (repealed) the court was empowered to extend the time for application under the Act, if satisfied that the time limit would operate unfairly, (a) if a further will were found, (b) if there were unresolved questions of construction, or (c) in consequence of some other circumstances 'affecting' the administration or distribution of the estate.] 'As I understand the word "affected" it means "influenced", "altered", "shaped". I find myself unable to share the view expressed by McTiernan J in the High Court of Australia in the case of *Shanks v Shanks* [infra] that: "in its ordinary usage 'affects' is a synonym for touching, or relating to, or concerning". That decision related to a provision as to appellate jurisdiction under a statute, and there were strong practical reasons for adopting a wide construction of the word.' *Re Bluston, Bluston v Davis* [1966] 3 All ER 220 at 225, 226, CA, per Winn LJ

[As to time limits for applications see now the Inheritance (Provision for Family and Dependants) Act 1975, s 4.]

Canada [The Town Planning Act RSNS 1954, c 292, s 16 deals with protests to rezoning by persons whose property would be 'affected'.] 'The word "affected" may mean "injuriously affected", and may apply to such properties as are adjoining or near the improvement, which may be physically affected or the value of which may be commercially affected, to a degree beyond such effect upon property in the city generally.' *Re Clarendon Development Ltd* (1965) 50 DLR (2d) 521 at 529, NSSC, per Currie J

AFFECTING COMMERCE *See* COMMERCE

AFFIDAVIT *See also* OATH

'Affidavit' includes affirmation, statutory or other declaration, acknowledgement, examination, and attestation or protestation of honour. (Commissioners for Oaths Act 1889, s 11)

AFFILIATE

Australia 'There is no definition of the rather vague word "affiliated", but in *Bridges v Wixon* (1945) 326 US 135 at p 143 the Supreme Court of the United States said of the word . . . that it imported less than membership and more than sympathy and that acts tending to show affiliation must be of a quality indicating adherence to or furtherance of the purposes of the proscribed body as distinguished from mere co-operation with it in lawful activities.' *Australian Communist Party v The Commonwealth* [1950–1951] 83 CLR 1 at 177, per Dixon J

Bankruptcy

United States '[A]ffiliate' means—
(A) entity that directly or indirectly owns, controls, or holds the power to vote, 20 percent or more of the outstanding voting securities of the debtor, other than an entity that holds such securities—
  (i) in a fiduciary or agency capacity without sole discretionary power to vote such securities; or
  (ii) solely to secure a debt, if such entity has not in fact exercised such power to vote;
(B) corporation 20 percent or more of whose outstanding voting securities are directly or indirectly owned, controlled, or held with power to vote, by the debtor, or by an entity that directly or indirectly owns, controls, or holds with power to vote, 20 percent or more of the outstanding voting securities of the debtor, other than an entity that holds such securities—
  (i) in a fiduciary or agency capacity without sole discretionary power to vote such securities; or
  (ii) solely to secure a debt, if such entity has not in fact exercised such power to vote;
(C) person whose business is operated under a lease or operating agreement by a debtor, or person substantially all of whose property is operated under an operating agreement with the debtor; or
(D) entity that operates the business or all or substantially all of the property of the debtor under a lease or operating agreement . . . .
(Bankruptcy Act 1978, s 101(2))

Petroleum marketing

United States The term 'affiliate' means any person who (other than by means of a franchise) controls, is controlled by, or is under common control with, any other person. (Petroleum Marketing Practices Act 1978, s 101(15))

AFFILIATION ORDER

In this Part of this Act [Part I: reciprocal enforcement of maintenance orders] 'affiliation order' means an order (however described) adjudging, finding or declaring a person to be the father of a child, whether or not it also provides for the maintenance of the child. (Maintenance Orders (Reciprocal Enforcement) Act 1972, s 21(1))

AFFIRMATION

'Counsel for the applicant submits that there are three requirements for a valid affirmation: (1) a solemn undertaking has to be given to the judicial authority; (2) it must be given prior to the giving of evidence to the court; (3) the undertaking ought to include some reference to a promise to tell the truth, however expressed. The right to affirm was introduced in 1838 for the benefit of Quakers and Moravians and the essential part of the declaration is still retained today, namely "I . . . do solemnly, sincerely, and truly declare and affirm". Although neither party suggests that this or any closely comparable formula has to be used, it is agreed that the mere signature to a document or the verbal acknowledgment that its contents are correct cannot amount to an affirmation. Where then is the line to be drawn? The answer cannot be precise: it must be a matter of fact and degree dependent on the particular circumstances of the case. I do not consider that the affirmation need take place prior to the making of the statement. What is required, where the statement has been made, is its adoption in circumstances which recognise the gravity and importance of the truth being told on the particular occasion.' *R v Governor of Pentonville Prison, ex p Singh* [1981] 3 All ER 23, per Ackner LJ

[Generally see also the Oaths Act 1978, ss 5, 6.]

'The primary and natural meaning of an "affirmation" in ordinary speech is a confirmation or declaration that something is true.' *Dowse v Government of Sweden* [1983] 2 All ER 123 at 127, HL, per Lord Diplock

AFFLUENCE

'As counsel for the administrator of the deceased daughter said, "affluence" does not mean extravagance or riotous living, but still something beyond ordinary comfort. . . . One must consider the testator to mean the words "comfort and affluence" to be construed with reference to his own position, and not with reference to the position of others.' *Re Moore's Trusts, Lewis v Moore* (1906) 96 LT 44 at 46, 47, per Kekewich J

AFFORESTATION

New Zealand [A testator by his will created a trust for the purpose of 'afforestation' or the making of domains or national parks in New Zealand.] 'As the testator has expressly dealt with the subject of parks both local and national, his intention was to use the term "afforestation" as referring to the production and care of timber for economic purposes—a view which is not affected by the circumstance that parts of the national parks might be made available for afforestation. . . . Nor can I agree that there is anything vague about the, term "afforestation". It may be that it is a wide term giving the trustees a wide field for their activities, and that it would include assisting a school of forestry, assisting local public bodies to establish forest areas, and a variety of other acts.' *Re Bruce, Simpson v Bruce & A-G* [1918] NZLR 16 at 27, 30, per Chapman J; also reported [1918] GLR 26 at 33

New Zealand 'In the modern sense . . . it means something more than merely covering tracts of land with timber. It includes the application of method and system by which the forests or plantations which exist or have been brought into being are maintained by renewal. The purpose to be served may be climatic; it may be to provide a sanctuary for birds or other animals; but the main object, especially where it is undertaken by the Government or on a large scale, is to ensure a concurrent and continuous supply of timber for the public

wants. . . . The essential point of afforestation is the permanent maintenance of a growth of forest trees by skilled or scientific methods of cultivation, treatment, and management.' Ibid at 31, per Hosking J

AFFRAY

[The essence of the common law offence of 'affray' is that two or more people (but see *Taylor v Director of Public Prosecutions*, infra) fight together to the terror of the Queen's subjects. It is not, as previously thought, a necessary ingredient of the offence that it should be committed in a public place.] 'In this House the appellants contended that until about the beginning of the nineteenth century there was no clear definition of an affray, but that since then it had always been held that it was a necessary ingredient of an affray that it should take place in public. . . . The respondent contended that the common law offence of an affray had been a recognised offence long before the beginning of the nineteenth century and consisted of two or more persons fighting together to the terror of the Queen's subjects and that it need not be committed in a public place. . . . We are much indebted to counsel whose arguments have involved research back into the centuries. In my opinion the respondent's argument is right. The essence of the offence is that two or more fight together to the terror of the Queen's subjects. Nowhere in the earlier writings is it suggested that the place where the fight occurs is a decisive matter. Lambard's Eirenarcha (1610 edn), c 3, p 125, under the side note "Affray and assault" said: "The words affray and assault be indifferently used of most men, and that also in some of our booke cases, but yet (in my opinion) there wanteth not a just difference between them. For affray is derived of the french effrayer which signifieth to terrifie, or bring feare". He described it (ibid) as a "common wrong". It is true that assault and affray were sometimes spoken of loosely as if they were interchangeable. This is perhaps not surprising since in each case the wrongful act is the same yet the mischief of the act falls on the victim in the offence of assault but on the bystander in the offence of affray.' *Button v Director of Public Prosecutions, Swain v Director of Public Prosecutions* [1965] 3 All ER 587 at 589, 590, HL, per Lord Gardiner LC

'The point of law certified in this case as being of general public importance is: "Whether a person commits the offence of affray if he alone is unlawfully fighting to the terror of other persons". That may seem to be a short and simple question but it cannot be answered without enquiring into the nature and history of the offence of affray. This offence has a long history going back at least 600 years. From the outset it has been clear that two elements are necessary. There must be violence done or immediately apprehended. And that violence must be such as to create terror. Until very recently there was practically no judicial authority but the offence is dealt with in every textbook, at least since 1593. The industry of counsel produced more than a dozen of some antiquity and authority. The earlier writers did not try to define the offence; they devoted more space to the rights and duties of constables and private citizens in dealing with an affray when it broke out. My impression is that any violent disturbance of the peace was regarded as an affray if it took place in such circumstances as to cause terror to the King's subjects. There was no need to confine the offence within narrower limits and I find nothing in the early books to suggest that the scope of the offence was more limited. For some reason which I have not discovered there were few prosecutions for this offence for a very long period before the middle of this century. But then the practical advantages to the prosecution of using this offence must have occurred to somebody. I understand that in recent years it has proved to be a valuable weapon for dealing with the rising tide of violent crime. Generally the offence was committed by several wrongdoers fighting each other in a street or other public place. So there crept into some of the textbooks suggestions that the offence could only be committed in a public place and could only be committed by two or more persons fighting together. No reasons for this were given. The first of these misapprehensions was corrected by this House in *Button v Director of Public Prosecutions* [supra]. We have now to deal with the second. One form of the offence consists of brandishing offensive weapons to the terror of the King's subjects. There is no suggestion that there need be more than one wrongdoer in that case. This form of the offence was dealt with in the Statute of Northampton 1328. That statute has now been repealed but it seems to be generally agreed that it did not supersede the common law and that the common law offence still survives. If this form of the offence may be committed by one person acting alone, one would expect to find some special reason to justify a conclusion that other forms of the

offence can only be committed by two or more persons. The only possible justification that I can see would be if the offence must be limited to two or more persons unlawfully fighting each other. There is no binding authority, requiring us so to limit the offence. Why should it be so limited? Such a limitation would exclude two cases both of which can be just as terrifying. In the first place, one of the combatants may be lawfully acting in self-defence. The fight may be just as real a fight and just as terrifying as if both combatants were wrongdoers. Onlookers will fear that if the unlawful assailant wins he will attack them. And secondly, one or more violent men may attack innocent and peaceful people and none of them may resist. Why are the assailants to escape punishment because their victims cannot or do not retaliate? Any such limitation would be quite illogical and I can see no justification for it.' *Taylor v Director of Public Prosecutions* [1973] 2 All ER 1108 at 1113, 1114, HL, per Lord Reid

'No doubt unlawful assembly differs from an affray, because, unlike affray, it implies a common purpose, and because, unlike affray, actual violence is unnecessary provided the public peace is endangered, but in my view it is analogous to affray in that (1) it need not be in a public place and (2) that the essential requisite in both is the presence or likely presence of innocent third parties, members of the public not participating in the illegal activities in question. It is their presence, or the likelihood of it, and the danger to their security in each case which constitutes the threat to public peace and the public element necessary to the commission of each offence.' *Kamara v Director of Public Prosecutions* [1973] 2 All ER 1242 at 1248, HL, per Lord Hailsham of St Marylebone LC

'In order to establish the offence of affray in a public place, the Crown must establish that: (i) there was unlawful fighting or unlawful violence used by one or more than one person against another or others, or there was an unlawful display of force by one or more than one person without actual violence, and (ii) the unlawful fighting, violence or display of force was such that a bystander of reasonable firmness and courage (whether or not present or likely to be present) might reasonably be expected to be terrified.' *A-G's Reference (No 3 of 1983)* [1985] 1 All ER 501 at 505, 506, per cur.

AFFREIGHTMENT *See* FREIGHT

AFTERNOON

'Afternoon has two senses. It may mean the whole time from noon to midnight; or it may mean the earlier part of that time as distinguished from the evening.' *R v Knapp* (1853) 2 E & B 447 at 451, per Erle J

United States 'Afternoon' means the period of a day between noon and midnight . . . (Uniform Commercial Code 1978, s 4–104(1)(b))

AGAINST

[The Criminal Evidence Act 1898, s (1)(f)(iii) (as amended by the Criminal Evidence Act 1979, s 1) provides that a person charged and called as a witness in pursuance of the Act shall not be asked, and if asked shall not be required to answer, any question tending to show that he has committed, etc, any offence unless he has given evidence 'against' any other person charged in the same proceedings.] 'The word "against" is one that is well understood. It is a clear and robust word. It has more decisiveness than is possessed by such phrases as "tending to show" or "such as to involve". It is a word that needs neither explanation nor translation. It calls for no synonym. The Act of 1898 does not call for any investigation as to the motives or wishes which may have prompted the giving of evidence against another person charged with the same offence. It is the nature of the evidence that must be considered. Its character does not change according as to whether it is the product of pained reluctance or of malevolent eagerness. If while ignoring anything trivial or casual the positive evidence given by the witness would rationally have to be included in any survey or summary of the evidence of the case which, if accepted, would warrant the conviction of the "other person charged with the same offence" then the witness would have given evidence against such other person.' *Murdoch v Taylor* [1965] 1 All ER 406 at 409, [1965] AC 574 at 583–4, HL, per Lord Morris of Borth-y-Gest

AGE *See* ATTAIN; FULL AGE

For the purposes of this Act, a person—
(a) is over or under a particular age if he has or, as the case may be, has not attained that age;

(b) is between two particular ages if he has attained the first but not the second.
(Social Security Act 1975, Sch 20)

AGED

'I find in the Statute of Elizabeth [Stat (1601) 43 Eliz c 4 (repealed)] that one of the classes of persons who are objects of charitable gifts are "aged persons". Without straining language, I cannot say that where there is a gift to persons not under fifty years of age those persons are not "aged" within the statute. I think they are. . . . I hold, therefore, that the gift is charitable.' *Re Wall, Pomeroy v Willway* (1889) 42 Ch D 510 at 512, per Kay J

AGENCY SHOP

United States '[Under] an "agency shop" arrangement, . . . every employee represented by a union—even though not a union member—must pay to the union, as a condition of employment, a service fee equal in amount to union dues.' *Abood v Detroit Board of Education* (1977) 431 US 209 at 211, per Stewart J

AGENT—AGENCY *See also* BRANCH OR AGENCY; CONSIGNEE; MERCANTILE AGENT

The terms 'agency' and 'agent' have in popular use a number of different meanings, but in law the word 'agency' is used to connote the relation which exists where one person has an authority or capacity to create legal relations between a person occupying the position of principal and third parties.

The relation of agency arises whenever one person, called 'the agent', has authority to act on behalf of another, called 'the principal' and consents so to act. . . . (1 Halsbury's Laws (4th edn) para 701)

'Agent' shall mean the solicitor, steward, or land agent of the seller. (Sale of Land by Auction Act 1867, s 3)

'Agent', when used in relation to the Crown, includes an independent contractor employed by the Crown. (Crown Proceedings Act 1947, s 38(2))

'Agent', in relation to the landlord of a dwelling—
(a) means a person who collects rent in respect

of the dwelling on behalf of the landlord, or is authorised by him to do so, and

(b) in the case of a dwelling occupied under a contract of employment under which the provision of the dwelling for his occupation forms part of the occupier's remuneration, includes a person who pays remuneration on behalf of the employer, or is authorised by him to do so.

(Housing Act 1985, s 343)

'No one can become the agent of another person except by the will of that other person. His will may be manifested in writing or orally, or simply by placing another in a situation in which, according to ordinary rules of law, or . . . the ordinary usages of mankind, that other is understood to represent and act for the person who has so placed him; but in every case it is only by the will of the employer that an agency can be created. This proposition, however, is not at variance with the doctrine, that where one has so acted as from his conduct to lead another to believe that he has appointed someone to act as his agent, and knows that that other person is about to act on that behalf, then, unless he interposes, he will, in general, be estopped from disputing the agency, though in fact no agency really existed.' *Pole v Leask* (1863) 33 LJ (Ch) 155 at 161, 162, per Lord Cranworth

[The Finance (No 2) Act 1939, s 12(2) defined the trades and businesses to which the section applied as all trades or businesses carried on in the United Kingdom, or carried on, whether personally or through an 'agent', by persons ordinarily resident in the United Kingdom.] '"Agent" there means agent, and a company whose shares are controlled by another company is not by mere existence of that control properly to be described as agent.' *English Sewing Cotton Co Ltd v Inland Revenue Comrs* [1947] 1 All ER 679 at 682, CA, per Lord Greene MR

Australia 'For almost a century, cases have appeared in the law reports illustrating the fact that the word "agent" is often used in business as meaning one who has no principal but who on his own account offers for sale some particular article having a special name. Agency is a word used in the law to connote an authority or capacity in one person to create legal relations between a person occupying the position of principal and third parties. But in the business world its significance is by no means thus restricted. As Lord Henschell said in a much quoted observation, "No word is more

commonly and constantly abused than the word 'agent'. A person may be spoken of as an 'agent' and no doubt in the popular sense may be said to be an 'agent', although when it is attempted to suggest that he is an agent under such circumstances as create the legal obligations attaching to agency, that use of the word is only misleading" [*Kennedy v de Trafford* [1897] AC 180].' *International Harverster Co of Australia Ltd v Carrigans Hazeldene Pastoral Co* [1958] 100 CLR 644 at 652, per cur.

Canada 'The word "agent" is one of wide signification and it may be said that in a general sense it applies to anyone who by authority performs an act for another, and it includes many classes of persons to which particular descriptive designations are given as e.g. factors, brokers, barristers and solicitors, cashiers of banks, clerks, consignees, etc. The outstanding feature of an agent's employment in a legal sense is that he is employed primarily to bring about business relations between the principal and third persons, and this characteristic is perhaps the most distinctive mark of the agent as contrasted with others not agents who act in representative capacities.' *Timmins (Town) v Brewers' Warehousing Co Ltd* [1962] OR 536 at 539, Ont CA, per Schroeder JA

New Zealand 'My view is that the terms "servant or employee or agent" together form a class of those aiding the carrier in the carrying out of his duties as a carrier and that all those so engaged by him for the handling of the goods gain the protection of the limit of liability provided by the Act [Carriers Act 1948, s 6, as amended by the Carriers Amendment Act 1962], and that the word "agent" is used following the words "servant or employee" deliberately by the Legislature in the wide sense of one who assists another in the carrying out of the business to be performed by him.' *Mason Bros (Mesco) Ltd v AGF Transport Ltd* [1969] NZLR 1 at 4, per Perry J

South Africa 'A person who has authority to act for and on behalf of another (called the principal) in contracting legal relations with third parties; the agent represents the principal and creates, alters or discharges legal obligations of a contractual nature between the latter and third parties.' *Mason v Vacuum Oil Co of SA Ltd* 1936 CPD 223

General agent

A general agent is one who has authority, arising out of and in the ordinary course of his business or profession, to do some act or acts on behalf of his principal in relation thereto, or one who is authorised to act on behalf of the principal generally in transactions of a particular kind or incidental to a particular business. (1 Halsbury's Laws (4th edn) para 711)

Of necessity

Agency of necessity is said to arise in a limited number of cases where, by reason of an emergency (1) the relation of principal and agent is deemed to exist between persons not otherwise in contractual relations or (2) authority to act on behalf of another is implied between persons already in contractual relations. (1 Halsbury's Laws (4th edn) para 724)

'One of the ways in which an agency of necessity can arise is where A is in possession of goods the property of B, and an emergency arises which places those goods in imminent jeopardy. If A cannot obtain instructions from B as to how he should act in such circumstances, A is bound to take without authority such action in relation to the goods as B, as a prudent owner, would himself have taken in the circumstances. The relationship between A and B is then known as an "agency of necessity", A being the agent and B the principal.' *China Pacific SA v Food Corpn of India, The Winston* [1981] 3 All ER 688 at 697, HL, per Lord Simon of Glaisdale

Signature 'as agent'

'The defence of the respondents is that they signed the charterparty "as agents" and did not incur thereunder any personal liability. The charterparty was signed as follows: 'For and on behalf of James McKelvie & Co (as agents).—J A McKelvie". The words "as agents" are, in my opinion, clearly words of qualification and not of description. They denote, in unambiguous language, that the respondents did not sign as principals, and did not intend to incur personal liability. The signature applies to the whole contract, and to every term in the contract. I think it would not be admissible to infer an implied term, or implied terms, in the contract inconsistent with the limitation of liability directly expressed in the qualification of the signature.' *Universal Steam Navigation Co v McKelvie (J) & Co* [1923] AC 492 at 503, 504, per Lord Parmoor

Special agent

A special agent is one who has authority to act for some special occasion or purpose which is not within the ordinary course of his business or profession. (1 Halsbury's Laws (4th edn) para 711)

AGGRAVATED

South Africa 'The term "wilful" affects the quality of the offence; the term "aggravated", I think, affects only the degree of seriousness of the offence.' *R v Nkonyana* 1939 NPD 154 per Feetham JP

AGGRAVATED ASSAULT

Australia [The Police Offences Act 1935–1986 (Tas), s 35(2) deals with cases of assault on children or females, and with assaults of an 'aggravated' nature.] 'I think the effect of the authorities may be stated in the following propositions:—(1) Aggravated assault means "aggravated *qua* assault", that is aggravated in respect of force or violence. (2) Conduct aggravating an assault within the meaning of proposition (1) may or may not be of an indecent character. It is none the less aggravating if it is indecent. (3) Mere indecency not having the effect set out in proposition (1) is not aggravation. . . . Where circumstances show an assault and indecency the fact that the seriousness of the defendant's whole conduct is rendered greater or "aggravated" by the presence of the indecency, will not justify a finding of aggravated assault unless the conduct aggravates the assault within the meaning of proposition (1). Highly indecent things may be done by conduct the very antithesis of violence—conduct which may be a technical assault but is more in the character of a caress. If it is the indecency which it is sought to punish, the charge should be indecent assault, for in such a case a finding of aggravated assault would not be permissible.' *Cure v Smith* [1951] Tas SR 5 at 11, per Morris CJ

AGGRAVATED BURGLARY *See* BURGLARY

AGGRAVATED DAMAGES *See* DAMAGES

AGGRAVATION

Of disease

Australia The Compensation (Commonwealth Government Employees) Act 1971–

1986, s 29 provides for compensation where an employee suffers an 'aggravation' of a disease.] 'Although it may be possible to attribute a meaning of growing worse to the term "aggravation" in the abstract, it is not possible to construe aggravation of a disease in s 29 as meaning a growing worse of a disease to which nothing but the natural progress of the disease has contributed. Something else must contribute an increased gravity to the employee's disease, a gravity over and beyond what the natural progress of the disease produces.' *Commonwealth v Johnston* (1980) 31 ALR 445 at 466, per Brennan J

AGGRIEVED PERSON   *See* PERSON
AGGRIEVED

AGISTMENT

A contract of agistment arises where one man, the agister, takes another man's cattle, horses or other animals to graze on his land for reward, usually at a certain rate per week, on the implied term that he will redeliver them to the owner on demand. Agistment is in the nature of a contract of bailment; it confers no interest in the land and therefore does not require to be evidenced in writing. (2 Halsbury's Laws (4th edn) para 214)

If a man takes in a horse, or other cattle to graze and depasture in his grounds, which the law calls agistment, he takes them upon an implied contract to return them safe to the owner. (2 Bl Com 452)

'The word "agistment" means, where cattle are in the land of another by his consent, or by some contract with the owner of the land.' *R v Croft (Inhabitants)* (1819) 3 B & Ald 171 at 177, per Best J

AGREE

'Anyone who has had experience of transactions in relation to the purchase of land can recall letters written by vendors saying that they agree to sell at a named price or that purchasers agree to purchase at a named price. The use of the word "agree" in such a context may or may not involve a contractual result. On the other hand, if you say that the price has been agreed when the contract is being negotiated, you do not use the word "agree" in the sense that any binding contract has been entered into. All you mean is that that parti-

cular element in the contract which you are negotiating has been decided. You are agreeing that that is the figure which will be put into the contract and then you go on to debate the other matters which fall for discussion. Therefore, words like "agree", "offer", "accept", when used in relation to price are not to be read necessarily as indicating an intention to make, then and there, a contract or an offer as the case may be. Whether they do or do not must depend entirely on the construction of the particular document.' *Clifton v Palumbo* [1944] 2 All ER 497 at 499, CA, per Lord Greene MR

AGREEMENT   *See also* CONDITIONAL
SALE AGREEMENT; HIRE-PURCHASE;
WRITTEN AGREEMENT

'In all cases where, by long habitual construction, the words of a statute have not received a peculiar interpretation, such as they will allow of, I am always inclined to give to them their natural ordinary signification. The clause in question in the Statute of Frauds [see also Law of Property Act 1925, s 40] has the word *agreement* ("unless the agreement upon which the action is brought . . . shall be in writing", etc). And the question is, whether that word is to be understood in the loose incorrect sense in which it may sometimes be used, as synonymous to *promise* or *undertaking*, or in its more proper and correct sense, as signifying a mutual contract on consideration between two or more parties? The latter appears to me to be the legal construction of the word, to which we are bound to give its proper effect.' *Wain v Warlters* (1804) 5 East 10 at 16, 17 per Lord Ellenborough CJ

'An agreement to buy imports a legal obligation to buy. If there was no such legal obligation, there cannot, in my opinion, properly be said to have been an agreement to buy.' *Helby v Matthews* [1895] AC 471 at 475, 476, per Lord Herschell LC

'I conclude that the "agreement" [within the Agricultural Holdings Act 1948, s 2(1) (repealed; see now the Agricultural Holdings Act 1986, s 2(1)–(3))] which it is to be postulated must, in every case to which the subsection applies, exist, means a contract enforceable at law, that is to say, a contract supported by valuable consideration flowing to the grantor from the grantee.' *Goldsack v Shore* [1950] 1 KB 708 at 713, CA, per Evershed MR

Australia ' "Agreement" . . . signifies primarily a contract, that is, a legally binding arrangement between two or more persons, by which rights are acquired by one or more to acts or forbearances on the part of the other or others. It also means "an agreement *de facto*" and includes an illegal arrangement [*Habel v Tiller* (1929) SASR 170 at 174].' *Re Symon, Public Trustee v Symon* (1944) SASR 102 at 110, per Mayo J

New Zealand 'Agreement is something more than having a common mind upon a matter, and there must, too, be something more than knowledge, on the part of each, of such common mind, or the communication each to the other of having such a mind: there must be the intention to form an agreement. That is vital. An agreement is constituted when both parties will the same thing, and each communicates his will to the other with a mutual engagement to carry it into effect.' *Ducker v Ducker* [1951] NZLR 583 at 590, 591; [1951] GLR 299 at 302, CA, per Gresson J

United States 'Agreement' means the bargain of the parties in fact as found in their language or by implication from other circumstances including course of dealing or usage of trade or course of performance as provided in this Act [Uniform Commercial Code] (Sections 1–205 and 2–208). Whether an agreement has legal consequences is determined by the provisions of this Act, if applicable; otherwise by the law of contracts (Section 1–103) (Compare 'Contract'.). (Uniform Commercial Code 1978, s 1–201(3))

United States 'Agreement' means the bargain of the parties in fact as found in their language or by implication from other circumstances including course of dealing or usage of trade or course of performance. (Uniform Consumer Credit Code 1969, s 1.301(3))

AGRICULTURAL BUILDINGS

In this section, the expression 'agricultural buildings'—
(a) means buildings (other than dwellings) occupied together with agricultural land or being or forming part of a market garden, and in either case used solely in connection with agricultural operations thereon; and
(b) includes a building which is used solely in connection with agricultural operations carried on on agricultural land and which is occupied either—

(i) by the occupiers of all that land; or
(ii) by individuals who are appointed by the said occupiers for the time being to manage the use of the building and of whom each is an occupier of some of the land or a member of the board of directors or other governing body of such an occupier who is a body corporate,

where the number of occupiers of all the said land does not exceed twenty-four (two or more persons occupying jointly being counted as one, but as a separate person from any of them who are occupying any of the land severally).
(General Rate Act 1967, s 26(4))

[The definition of 'agricultural buildings' in s 26 of the General Rate Act 1967 has been extended to include 'livestock buildings', 'buildings occupied in connection with bee keeping' and 'buildings occupied by bodies corporate and certain associations'; see the Rating Act 1971, Part I.]

AGRICULTURAL COTTAGE

'The ordinary meaning of "agricultural" as applied to a physical object or structure is in my view "used or designed for use in agriculture", as in agricultural implement, agricultural vehicle or agricultural building. If I were asked the short question: "What is an agricultural cottage?" I should answer: "It is a cottage occupied or designed for occupation by a person mainly engaged in agriculture". The adjective is apt to describe the purpose for which a cottage is used or intended to be used. As an architectural description, I find it meaningless.' *Wilson v West Sussex County Council* [1963] 1 All ER 751 at 760; [1963] 2 QB 764 at 782, CA, per Diplock LJ

AGRICULTURAL HOLDING

In this Act 'agricultural holding' means the aggregate of the land (whether agricultural land or not) comprised in a contract of tenancy which is a contract for an agricultural tenancy, not being a contract under which the land is let to the tenant during his continuance in any office, appointment or employment held under the landlord. (Agricultural Holdings Act 1986, s 1)

'I refuse to subscribe to the view that you cannot have an agricultural holding unless you have a tenant. There are undoubtedly many holdings which are not so held. The phrase is not a technical term or a term of art. In my judgment the words are used in their ordinary signification as meaning land which is used for agricultural purposes.' *Kemp v Ballachulish Estate Co Ltd* 1933 SC 478 at 488, per Alness (Lord Justice-Clerk)

See, generally, 1 Halsbury's Laws (4th edn) para 1001.

AGRICULTURAL LAND

The expression 'agricultural land' includes arable and meadow land and ground used for pastoral purposes or for market or nursery gardens, and plantations and woods and orchards, and also includes any fences on such land, but does not include any moorland or buildings. (Railway Fires Act 1905, s 4)

In this Act the expression 'agricultural land' means land used for agriculture which is so used for the purposes of a trade or business, or which is designated by the Minister for the purposes of this subsection, and includes any land so designated as land which in the opinion of the Minister ought to be brought into use for agriculture:
    Provided that no designation under this subsection shall extend—
(a) to land used as pleasure grounds, private gardens or allotment gardens, or
(b) to land kept or preserved mainly or exclusively for the purposes of sport or recreation, except where the Minister is satisfied that its use for agriculture would not be inconsistent with its use for the said purposes and it is so stated in the designation.
(Agriculture Act 1947, s 109).

'Agricultural land' means land used as arable, meadow or grazing land, or for the purpose of poultry farming, pig farming, market gardens, allotments, nursery grounds or orchards. (Dogs (Protection of Livestock) Act 1953, s 3)

In this section the expression 'agricultural land'—
(a) means any land used as arable, meadow or pasture ground only, land used for a plantation or a wood or for the growth of saleable underwood, land exceeding [0.10 hectare] used for the purposes of poultry farming, cottage gardens exceeding [0.10 hectare], market gardens, nursery grounds, orchards or allotments, including allotment gardens within the meaning of

the Allotments Act 1922 [i.e. allotments not exceeding forty poles in extent which are wholly or mainly cultivated by their occupiers for the production of vegetable or fruit crops for consumption by themselves or their families] but does not include land occupied together with a house as a park, gardens (other than as aforesaid), pleasure grounds, or land kept or preserved mainly or exclusively for purposes of sport or recreation, or land used as a race-course; and for the purposes of this paragraph the expression 'cottage garden' means a garden attached to a house occupied as a dwelling by a person of the labouring classes; and
(b) includes land occupied with, and used solely in connection with the use of, such a building as is mentioned in subsection (4)(b) of this section.
(General Rate Act 1967, s 26(3), as amended by SI 1978/318; for subsection (4)(b) see AGRICULTURAL BUILDING, supra).

[The definition 'agricultural land' in the General Rate Act 1967, s 26 has been extended to include land occupied with 'livestock buildings', 'buildings occupied in connection with bee keeping' and 'buildings occupied by bodies corporate and certain associations'; see the Rating Act 1971, Part I.]

In this Act 'agricultural land' means—
(a) land used for agriculture which is so used for the purposes of a trade or business, and
(b) any other land which, by virtue of a designation under section 109(1) of the Agriculture Act 1947 [supra], is agricultural land within the meaning of that Act.
(Agricultural Holdings Act 1986, s 1(4))

South Africa 'Arable, meadow or pasture land, market gardens, poultry farms, nursery gardens, plantations and orchards.' *Warmbaths Village Council v Reef Estates Ltd* 1941 TPD 264

AGRICULTURAL PRODUCE

'Agricultural produce' and 'fishery produce' include respectively all produce of agriculture or horticulture and of the fishing industry, all articles of food or drink wholly or partly manufactured or derived from any such produce as aforesaid, and fleeces and the skins of animals. (Agricultural Produce (Grading and Marking) Act 1928, s 7, substituted by the Agricultural Produce (Grading and Marking) Amendment Act 1931, s 2)

Australia [The defendant was the holder of a hawker's licence granted under the Hawkers and Pedlars Act 1958–1986 (Vic), s 32, which permitted him to sell 'agricultural produce'.] 'Reading the two words in conjunction, it appears to me that the combination of the meanings of the two words produces the result that agricultural produce means the products of agriculture, agriculture including the raising of livestock and birds such as poultry and products including offspring or progeny. Accordingly, the meanings of the two words making up the expression "agricultural produce", would, it appears to me, comprehend live poultry.' *Clifton v Masini* [1967] VR 718 at 721, per Menhennit J

AGRICULTURAL PRODUCT

'Agricultural product' includes—
(a) any product of agriculture or horticulture;
(b) any article of food or drink wholly or partly manufactured or derived from any such product; and
(c) fleeces (including all kinds of wool, whether from a living animal or from a dead animal or from the skin of a dead animal) and the skins of animals.
(Agricultural Marketing Act 1958, s 52(1))

United States 'Agricultural products' includes agricultural, horticultural, viticultural, and dairy products, livestock, wildlife, poultry, bees, forest products, fish and shellfish, and any products thereof, including processed and manufactured products, and any and all products raised or produced on farms and any processed or manufactured products thereof; cf the similar definition in the Truth in Lending Act 1968, s 103(s). (Uniform Consumer Credit Code 1969, s 1.301(4))

AGRICULTURAL PURPOSE

United States 'Agricultural purpose' means a purpose related to the production, harvest, exhibition, marketing, transportation, processing, or manufacture of agricultural products by a natural person who cultivates, plants, propogates, or nurtures the agricultural products. (Uniform Consumer Credit Code 1969, s 1.103(4); cf the similar definition in the Truth in Lending Act 1968, s 103(s))

AGRICULTURAL UNIT

In this Act the expression 'agricultural unit' means land which is occupied as a unit for agricultural purposes, including—

(a) any dwelling-house or other building occupied by the same person for the purpose of farming the land, and
(b) any other land falling within the definition in this Act of the expression 'agricultural land' which is in the occupation of the same person, being land as to which the Minister is satisfied that having regard to the character and situation thereof and other relevant circumstances it ought in the interests of full and efficient production to be farmed in conjunction with the agricultural unit, and directs accordingly:

Provided that the Minister shall not give a direction under this subsection as respects any land unless it is for the time being not in use for any purpose which appears to him to be substantial having regard to the use to which it might be put for agriculture. (Agriculture Act 1947, s 109)

AGRICULTURE

'Agriculture' and 'cultivation' shall include horticulture and the use of land for any purpose of husbandry inclusive of the keeping or breeding of livestock, poultry, or bees, and the growth of fruit, vegetables and the like. (Small Holdings and Allotments Act 1908, s 61; cf. Agricultural Credits Act 1928, s 5)

'Agriculture' includes dairy farming, livestock breeding, poultry farming, bee-keeping, fruit growing, vegetable growing and horticulture. (Agriculture (Miscellaneous Provisions) Act 1944, s 1)

'Agriculture' includes horticulture, fruit growing, seed growing, dairy farming and livestock breeding and keeping, the use of land as grazing land, meadow land, osier land, market gardens and nursery grounds, and the use of land for woodlands where that use is ancillary to the farming of land for other agricultural purposes, and 'agricultural' shall be construed accordingly. (Agriculture Act 1947, s 109; Agricultural Holdings Act 1986, s 96)

'Agriculture' includes dairy farming, the production of any consumable produce which is grown for sale or for consumption or other use for the purposes of a trade or business or of any other undertaking (whether carried on for profit or not), and the use of land as grazing, meadow or pasture land or orchard or osier land or woodland or for market gardens or nursery grounds. (Agricultural Wages Act 1948, s 17; Agriculture (Poisonous Substances) Act 1952, s 10; Agriculture (Safety,

Health and Welfare Provisions) Act 1956, s 24)

'Agriculture' includes horticulture, fruit growing, seed growing, dairy farming, the breeding and keeping of livestock (including any creature kept for the production of food, wool, skins or fur, or for the purpose of its use in the farming of land), the use of land as grazing land, meadow land, osier land, market gardens and nursery grounds, and the use of land for woodlands where the use is ancillary to the farming of land for other agricultural purposes, and 'agricultural' is to be construed accordingly. (Highways Act 1980, s 329(1); Town and Country Planning Act 1971, s 290; Water Resources Act 1963, s 135)

In this Act 'agriculture' includes—
(i)   dairy-farming and livestock keeping and breeding (whether those activities involve the use of land or not);
(ii)   the production of any consumable produce which is grown for sale or for consumption or other use for the purposes of a trade or business or of any other undertaking (whether carried on for profit or not);
(iii) the use of land as grazing, meadow or pasture land or orchard or osier land;
(iv)   the use of land for market gardens or nursery grounds; and
(v)   forestry.
(Rent (Agriculture) Act 1976, s 2(1))

'Persons are employed in agriculture and horticulture when employed upon any operations done about the production, preparation, or transfer of the products of farm or garden or orchard in the best saleable condition to a first buyer or to a salesman or agent for sale if one be employed, or to a distinct business under one proprietorship.' *Re Prior* (1927) 43 TLR 784 at 785, 786, per Roche J

'[Counsel] has made bold to contend before us that, for the purposes, at any rate, of this legislation [Agricultural Wages (Regulation) Act 1924, s 16 (repealed; see now Agricultural Wages Act 1948, s 17)], "agriculture" includes any use of land in connection with breeding or keeping any animal ordinarily found on a farm. I think that there is much to be said for that definition.' *Walters v Wright* [1938] 4 All ER 116 at 118, per Lord Hewart CJ

'Plainly not every rural or country activity is intended to be included in the definition of agriculture. Fishing, for example, is clearly excluded. The definition [in the Rent (Agri-

culture) Act 1976] is really directed towards including all operations involved in farming land for commercial purposes of which the one relevant to this appeal is the production of food.' *Lord Glendyne v Rapley* [1978] 2 All ER 110 at 112, CA, per cur.

[It was held that a gamekeeper employed to rear pheasants for sport was not employed in agriculture, and therefore he was not entitled to security of tenure of a cottage. See also *Earl Normanton v Giles* [1980] 1 All ER 106, HL.]

Australia   'In my view a proper definition of "agriculture" does not include forestry or sawmilling.' *Hill v Rothwell* [1954] Tas SR 49 at 50, per Green J

Australia   [The Workers' Compensation Act 1926–1986 (NSW) s 6(3) (see now s 6(3)(a)) refers, inter alia, to 'agricultural work'.] 'I do not think in Australia that grazing or depasturing sheep or cattle can be described as agricultural work. No doubt a great deal of mixed farming is done in Australia which combines a use of sheep, cattle, agriculture and perhaps includes almost any pursuit which can be described as rural. But the distinction between the pastoral industry and agricultural work is clear and traditional.' *Frauenfelder v Reid* (1963) 109 CLR 42 at 48, per Dixon CJ

Canada   [Validity of Farm Security Act 1944 (Sask) (now RSS 1978, c P9) depended on whether provisions were within provincial power to legislate in relation to agriculture.] 'The word "agriculture" must be interpreted in its widest meaning, and ought not to be confined to such a narrow definition, that would allow the province to enact legislation, pertaining only, as Morrison J said in *Brooks v Moore* [(1906) 4 WLR 110] "to those things that grow and derive their substance from the soil". I am strongly of opinion that legislation to relieve the farmers of financial difficulties, to lighten the burdens resulting from the uncertainties of farming operations, is legislation in relation to agriculture.' *Reference Re Validity of Section 6 of Farm Security Act 1944 of Saskatchewan* [1947] SCR 394 at 401, SCC, per Taschereau J

South Africa   'The science and art of cultivating the soil, including the gathering of crops, and the rearing of livestock.' *Thomson's Truck and Car Ltd v Odendaal* (1956) 1 SA 800

AID AND ABET

'To constitute an aider and abettor, some active steps must be taken by word or action, with the intent to instigate the principal or principals. Encouragement does not of necessity amount to aiding and abetting; it may be intentional or unintentional, a man may unwittingly encourage another in fact by his presence, by mis-interpreted words or gestures, or by his silence or non-interference, or he may encourage intentionally by expressions, gestures or actions, intended to signify approval. In the latter case he aids and abets; in the former he does not. It is no criminal offence to stand by a mere passive spectator of a crime, even of a murder. Non-interference to prevent a crime is not itself a crime. But the fact that a person was voluntarily and purposely present witnessing the commission of a crime, and offered no opposition to it, though he might reasonably be expected to prevent it and had the power so to do, or at least to express his dissent, might, under some circumstances, afford cogent evidence upon which a jury would be justified in finding that he wilfully encouraged, and so aided and abetted. But it would be purely a question for the jury whether he did so or not. So, if any number of persons arrange that a criminal offence shall take place, and it takes place accordingly, the mere presence of any of those who so arranged it would afford abundant evidence for the consideration of a jury of an aiding and abetting.' *R v Coney* (1882) 51 LJMC 66 at 78, CCR, per Hawkins J

'It is well known that the words "aid and abet" are apt to describe the action of a person who is present at the time of the commission of an offence and takes some part therein. He is then described as an aider and abettor, whereas the words "counsel and procure" are appropriate to a person who, though not present at the commission of the offence, is an accessory before the fact.' *Ferguson v Weaving* [1951] 1 All ER 412 at 413, per cur.

'I . . . repeat what I said, with the assent of the other members of the court, in *Johnson v Youden* [[1950] 1 All ER 300] "a person cannot be convicted of aiding and abetting the commission of an offence if he does not know of the essential matters which would constitute the offence". If a person shuts his eyes to the obvious, or perhaps, refrains from making any inquiry where a reasonably sensible man would make inquiry, I think the court can find that he was aiding and abetting.' *Davies, Turner & Co Ltd v Brodie* [1954] 3 All ER 283 at 286, per Lord Goddard CJ

'A person who supplies the instrument for a crime or anything essential to its commission aids in the commission of it; and if he does so knowingly and with intent to aid, he abets it as well and is therefore guilty of aiding and abetting.' *National Coal Board v Gamble* [1958] 3 All ER 203 at 207; [1959] 1 QB 11 at 20, per Devlin J

'The prosecution must prove that the act or omission on which they rely as constituting the alleged aiding and abetting was done or made with a view to assisting or encouraging the principal offender to commit the offence or, in other words, with the motive of endorsing the commission of the offence.' Ibid at 211, per Slade J

'Aiding and abetting almost inevitably involves a situation in which the secondary party and the main offender are together at some stage discussing the plans which they may be making in respect of the alleged offence, and are in contact so that each knows what is passing through the mind of the other.' *A–G's Reference (No 1 of 1975)* [1975] 2 All ER 684 at 686, CA, per cur.

Australia 'The words "aid, abet or procure" are not limited in their application to the employment of any particular means or kinds of means to bring about the commission of the particular felony charged.' *R v Ready & Manning* [1942] VLR 85 at 88, per cur.

See, generally, 11 Halsbury's Laws (4th edn) paras 42 et seq.

AIDED SCHOOL   *See* SCHOOL

AIRBILL   *See* BILL OF LADING

AIR NAVIGATION INSTALLATION

'Air navigation installation' means any building, works, apparatus or equipment used wholly or mainly for the purpose of assisting air traffic control or as an aid to air navigation, together with any land contiguous or adjacent to any such building, works, apparatus or equipment and used wholly or mainly for purposes connected therewith. (Aviation Security Act 1982, s 38(1))

AIR-RAID SHELTER

'Air-raid shelter' means protection, otherwise than by war-like means or by any article of apparel, from hostile attack from the air, and 'an air-raid shelter' means any premises, structure or excavation used or intended to be used to provide air-raid shelter. (Civil Defence Act 1939, s 90)

AIR SERVICE

New Zealand 'I am of the opinion that all these sections [the Air Services Licensing Act 1951, ss 18(2), 21 and 23] contain indications that a licence must be obtained if, and only if, a person is providing a *complete* air service, in the sense that there must come, from the same source, an aircraft and a pilot both ultimately engaged in a "flight" or a "journey" for "hire or reward".' *A–G (Ex rel James Aviation Ltd) v Makarau Co-operative Lime Society Ltd* [1973] 1 NZLR 207 at 213, per Moller J

AIR TRANSPORT SERVICE   *See also*
   TRANSPORT

'Air transport service' means a service for the carriage by air of passengers or cargo. (Civil Aviation Act 1982, s 105(1))

AIR WEAPON

This section [requirement of firearm certificate] applies to every firearm except . . . an air weapon (that is to say, an air rifle, air gun or air pistol not of a type declared by rules made by the Secretary of State . . . to be specially dangerous). (Firearms Act 1968, s 1(3))

'. . . we have no hesitation in arriving at the conclusion that we cannot give to the words "air weapon" any meaning other than their natural and ordinary meaning, that is a weapon where the propulsion is caused by or derived from the use of air.' *R v Thorpe* [1987] 2 All ER 108 at 111, per Kenneth Jones J

AIRCRAFT

'Aircraft' means any machine for flying, whether propelled by mechanical means or not, and includes any description of balloon. (Air Force Act 1955, s 223(1); Army Act 1955, s 225(1); Naval Discipline Act 1957, s 135(1))

British aircraft

'British aircraft' means an aircraft registered in—
(a) any part of Her Majesty's dominions;
(b) any country outside Her Majesty's dominions in which for the time being Her Majesty has jurisdiction;
(c) any country consisting partly of one or more colonies and partly of one or more such countries as are mentioned in the last foregoing sub-paragraph.
(Emergency Laws (Re-Enactments and Repeals) Act 1964, s 9)

Commander of aircraft

'Commander' in relation to an aircraft means the member of the crew designated as commander of that aircraft by the operator thereof, or, failing such a person, the person who is for the time being the pilot in command of the aircraft. (Civil Aviation Act 1982, s 94(7))

Military aircraft

'Military aircraft' means—
(a) an aircraft of the naval, military or air forces of any country; or
(b) any other aircraft in respect of which there is in force a certificate issued in accordance with any Order in Council in force under . . . this Act that the aircraft is to be treated for the purposes of that Order in Council as a military aircraft;
and a certificate of the Secretary of State that any aircraft is or is not a military aircraft for the purposes of this Act shall be conclusive evidence of the fact certified. (Civil Aviation Act 1982, s 92(5))

AIRCRAFT MATERIAL

'Aircraft material' includes—
(a) parts of, and components of or accessories for, aircraft, whether for the time being in aircraft or not;
(b) engines, armaments, ammunition and bombs and other missiles of any description in, or for use in, aircraft;
(c) any other gear, apparatus or instruments in, or for use in, aircraft;
(d) any apparatus used in connection with the taking-off or landing of aircraft or for detecting the movement of aircraft; and
(e) any fuel used for the propulsion of aircraft and any material used as a lubricant for aircraft or aircraft material.
(Naval Discipline Act 1957, s 135(1))

ALIBI

Canada '"Alibi" is a Latin adverb meaning "elsewhere or at another place" and if evidence for an accused that he was not present at a place at the time an offence was there committed is accepted by a jury, he is said to have established an alibi.' *R v Foll* (1957) 21 WWR 481 at 491, Man CA, per Montague JA

Evidence in support of

In this section 'evidence in support of an alibi' means evidence tending to show that by reason of the presence of the defendant at a particular place or in a particular area at a particular time he was not, or was unlikely to have been, at the place where the offence is alleged to have been committed at the time of its alleged commission. (Criminal Justice Act 1967, s 11(8))

ALIEN

A person who is not a British subject, that is to say a citizen of the United Kingdom and Colonies, a citizen of any of the specified Commonwealth countries, or a British subject without citizenship, or a British protected person, or a citizen of the Republic of Ireland, is an alien. . . . Aliens are divided into two classes, friends and enemies. An alien friend is one whose sovereign or state is at peace with the United Kingdom. The primary meaning of alien enemy is one whose sovereign or state is at war with the United Kingdom. In references to civil rights, however, the term 'alien enemy' is used in a different sense and denotes a person of whatever nationality, including British, who is carrying on business, or is voluntarily resident, in the enemy's country, or country occupied by the enemy. (4 Halsbury's Laws (4th edn) paras 948, 950)

'Alien' means a person who is not a British subject. (Status of Aliens Act 1914, s 27)

'Alien' means a person who is neither a Commonwealth citizen nor a British protected person nor a citizen of the Republic of Ireland. (British Nationality Act 1981, s 50(1))

'The word "alien" is a legal term. . . . It implies being born out of the liegeance of the King, and within the liegeance of some other state.' *Daubigny v Davallon* (1794) 2 Anst 462 at 468, per Macdonald CB

'The question of statelessness can have seldom arisen as an important or practical question. The division into subjects and aliens is clear and sufficient for the ordinary purposes of the common law; and the stateless person would be one of the aliens.' *Stoeck v Public Trustee* [1921] 2 Ch 67 at 80–81, per Russell J

Alien enemy

The primary meaning of 'alien enemy' is one whose sovereign or state is at war with the Sovereign of England. However, in reference to civil rights, 'alien enemy' is used by the United Kingdom courts in a different sense and means one who is voluntarily resident or who carries on business in an enemy or enemy-subjugated country, even though he is a natural-born British subject or a naturalised British subject, or the subject of a neutral state. A subject of an enemy state who is neither residing nor carrying on business in an enemy or enemy-subjugated country is not an alien enemy with reference to civil rights; and so may maintain an action in this country.

By residing and trading in an allied or neutral state, a subject of an enemy state may acquire a friendly or neutral commercial domicil, which will protect his goods if captured at sea from condemnation. A British born wife of an alien enemy separated from her husband and residing in a neutral or friendly country is not an alien enemy. To prove that a person is an alien enemy at the time of the commencement of an action, it is not enough to show that he was some time before domiciled in territory which has become hostile. (49 Halsbury's Laws (4th edn) para 146)

'It has been made clear by many decisions that "enemy alien" does not mean a person who is an enemy by birth or allegiance. Anyone who voluntarily resides in a hostile State, or who carries on business in a hostile State, is an enemy alien with regard to the State whose subject he was when war broke out. No authority has been cited to me to show that to meet the rule a man must be carrying on his own business and not that of another. If the residence is for "carrying on business" that is enough.' *Scotland v South African Territories Ltd* (1917) 33 TLR 255 at 256, per Darling J

'An "alien enemy" cannot sue in the King's courts or otherwise take up the position of an actor in British litigation save under royal licence. An alien enemy, in this connection, does not mean a subject of a state at war with this country, but a person, of whatever nationality, who is carrying on business in, or is voluntarily resident in, the enemy's country.' *Sovfracht (V/O) v Van Udens Scheepvaart en*

Agentuur Maatschappij (NV Gebr) [1943] AC 203 at 209, HL, per Lord Simon LC

ALIENATION

The most usual and universal method of acquiring a title to real estates is that of alienation, conveyance, or purchase in its limited sense: under which may be comprised any method wherein estates are voluntarily resigned by one man, and accepted by another; whether that be effected by sale, gift, marriage settlement, devise, or other transmission of property by the mutual consent of the parties. (2 Bl Com 287)

'Alienation implies a transaction by which property is given to another person.' *Re Gaskell & Walters' Contract* [1906] 2 Ch 1 at 10, per cur.

Australia ' "Alienation" denotes the act, or series of acts, of alienating, and takes place whenever the owner of land, or of an interest therein, so acts as to divest himself of his interest or some lesser interest, and to vest the same in another person [*Lang v Castle* [1924] SASR 255 at 263, 264]. Not every agreement that relates to property is necessarily an alienation or an undertaking to alienate. If all that is to be made over is a mere personal right, and not in the nature of property, there will, I apprehend, be no alienation.' *Re Symon, Public Trustee v Symon* [1944] SASR 102 at 108, per Mayo J

ALIKE

'The word "alike" is the same as the word "equally".' *Loveacres* d *Mudge v Blight* (1775) 1 Cowp 352 at 357, per Lord Mansfield CJ

ALIMONY   *See also* MAINTENANCE

'In the Ecclesiastical Courts the usual rate of alimony *pendente lite* in the normal case was something in the neighbourhood of one-fifth of the husband's income, and ordinarily something in the neighbourhood of a third of the husband's income where the decree had been made and the alimony was permanent. The statute which enabled this Court to make an order for reasonable alimony for a wife after judicial separation provided that the Court should take account of the former practice of the Ecclesiastical Courts. But those Courts had not made a hard and fast rule; and there never had been a hard and fast rule in this Court. The

Court has to make a reasonable provision.' *Dean v Dean* [1923] P 172 at 174, per Duke P

'Alimony is a phrase which is never used in the Divorce Division to cover payments by a husband to the wife after the decree absolute in divorce. It may be used as referring to "permanent alimony" where the marriage tie subsists and there is merely a decree of judicial separation, or it may be used as "alimony pending suit", which covers the period from the filing of the petition until the grant of the decree absolute.' *Gaisberg v Storr* [1950] 1 KB 107 at 112, CA, per Bucknill LJ

Australia 'Alimony is an allowance made to a wife out of her husband's estate for her support, and maintenance has a similar meaning, since an order for maintenance in respect of a wife is one which provides for the periodical payment of sums of money towards her maintenance by the husband against whom the order is made.' *Ex p Wearne, Re Stapleton* [1962] NSWR 1065 at 1066, per Richardson J; revd on other grounds [1963] NSWR 1131

Interim alimony

Canada 'The whole basis for granting costs and alimony to a wife in matrimonial causes in advance of a trial or decision on the merits is that the same are "necessaries". The costs are necessary to the employment of counsel and for paying witness fees, and otherwise making necessary preparation for a fair trial. The interim alimony is necessary for the wife's proper maintenance pending the final adjudication. This principle which admittedly governs in matrimonial causes when alimony is merely incidental, and which originally was the settled practice of the Ecclesiastical Courts, seems to me to be equally applicable where alimony alone is sought.' *McMain v McMain* [1924] 1 WWR 102 at 103, Sask KB, per Brown CJKB

ALIVE

Capable of being born alive

[A single woman, who was between 18 and 21 weeks pregnant, wished to terminate her pregnancy; the father sought an injunction restraining her from undergoing the termination. It was contended that as the fetus, if delivered, would demonstrate discernible signs of life, termination of the pregnancy would be an offence under the Infant Life (Preservation) Act 1929, s 1(1), which provides that it is an offence for any person, with intent to destroy the life of a child capable of being born alive, to cause it to die before it has an existence independent of its mother.] '[The doctors'] evidence is . . . necessarily directed at the stage in the development of a fetus which can normally be expected to have been reached by the 18th to 21st week. On this, as one would expect, they are in substantial agreement. At that stage the cardiac muscle is contracting and a primitive circulation is developing. Thus the fetus could be said to demonstrate real and discernible signs of life. On the other hand, the fetus, even if then delivered by hysterotomy, would be incapable ever of breathing either naturally or with the aid of a ventilator. It is not a case of the fetus requiring a stimulus or assistance. It cannot and will never be able to breathe. Where the doctors disagree is as to whether a fetus, at this stage of development, can properly be described as "a child capable of being borne alive" within the meaning of the 1929 Act. That essentially depends on the interpretation of the statute and is a matter for the courts.

We have no evidence of the state of the fetus . . . but, if it has reached the normal stage of development and so is incapable ever of breathing, it is not in our judgment "a child capable of being born alive" within the meaning of the 1929 Act and accordingly the termination of this pregnancy would not constitute an offence under that Act.' *C v S* [1987] 1 All ER 1230 at 1242, CA, per Sir John Donaldson MR

ALL

'I do not think it an exaggeration to say that the word "all" in a statute is extremely recalcitrant, and if the meaning is to be cut down so as to exclude certain things which might otherwise be included by it, that must be done in the clearest possible language. The proper way of construing a word like "all", is to say that it means "all", and does not mean "some", unless one finds a compelling context which forces one to place some limitation on the word.' *Re Wellsted's Will Trusts, Wellsted v Hanson* [1949] Ch 296 at 306, per Lord Greene MR

ALL RISKS

[A marine policy was printed in the form of an ordinary Lloyds' policy with the addition of clauses in type or writing. One such clause contained the provision: 'Including . . . all risks by land and by water. . . .'] 'The clause . . . finishes with the very general words "and all risks by land and by water by any conveyance until safely delivered". . . . It was said for the defendant that, if all risks were covered, why refer specifically to risks of robbery with or without violence, negligence, etc? On the other hand, it is very common to find in such contracts, although perfectly general words are made use of, including practically all risks, special reference to particular perils . . . *Jacob v Gaviller* [(1902) 7 Com Cas 116] is an illustration of this being done. I have to read this policy as I think it would be reasonably understood by any merchant or insurance broker, and doing so I come to the conclusion that the words "all risks by land and by water", etc, must be read literally as meaning all risks whatsoever. I think they are intended to cover all losses by any accidental cause of any kind occurring during the transit.' *Schloss Brothers v Stevens* [1906] 2 KB 665 at 673, per Walton J

'We are, of course, to give effect to the rule that the plaintiff must establish his case, that he must show that the loss comes within the terms of his policies; but where all risks are covered by the policy and not merely risks of a specified class or classes, the plaintiff discharges his special onus when he has proved that the loss was caused by some event covered by the general expression, and he is not bound to go further and prove the exact nature of the accident or casualty which, in fact, occasioned his loss.' *British & Foreign Marine Insurance Co v Gaunt* [1921] 2 AC 41 at 44–47, per Lord Birkenhead LC

'There are, of course, limits to "all risks". They are risks and risks insured against. Accordingly the expression does not cover inherent vice or mere wear and tear or British capture. It covers a risk, not a certainty; it is something which happens to the subject-matter from without, not the natural behaviour of that subject-matter, being what it is, in the circumstances under which it is carried. Nor is it a loss which the assured brings about by his own act, for then he has not merely exposed the goods to the chance of injury, he has injured them himself.' Ibid at 57, per Lord Sumner.

ALLEGE

In Gaming Act

[The Gaming Act 1845, s 18 provides inter alia that no suit shall be brought or maintained in any court of law and equity for recovering any sum of money or valuable thing 'alleged' to be won upon any wager.] 'I do not myself feel any real doubt as to the meaning of the word "alleged" in the section. The context in which it occurs is concerned with the bringing of a suit: and in such a context I should expect the word "alleged" to mean, alleged for the purposes of the suit, i.e., alleged in the declaration in which the claim is set forth.' *Hill v William Hill (Park Lane) Ltd* [1949] AC 530 at 558, HL, per Lord Greene

ALLEGIANCE

Allegiance is by statute due to the Sovereign, whether the rightful heir to the Crown or not, and the subjects are bound to serve in war against every rebellion, power, and might reared against the Sovereign, and are protected in so doing from attainder of high treason and from all forfeitures and penalties. The duty of allegiance is applicable to the Sovereign in both capacities, that is to say, as well in the natural as in the regal or political capacity. Allegiance has been distinguished as of three kinds, according to the persons from whom it is due, namely, natural, local and acquired. The practical effect of owing allegiance is to be liable for the offence of treason. (8 Halsbury's Laws (4th edn) para 862)

Allegiance, both express and implied, is . . . distinguished by the law into two sorts or species, the one natural, the other local; the former being also perpetual, the latter temporary. Natural allegiance is such as is due from all men born within the king's dominions immediately upon their birth. For, immediately upon their birth, they are under the king's protection; at a time too, when (during their infancy) they are incapable of protecting themselves. Natural allegiance is therefore a debt of gratitude; which cannot be forfeited, cancelled or altered, by any change of time, place, or circumstance, nor by any thing but the united concurrence of the legislature. An Englishman who removes to France, or to China, owes the same allegiance to the king of England there as at home, and twenty years hence as well as now. For it is a principle of universal law, that the natural-born subject of one prince cannot by any act of his own, no, not by swearing allegiance to another, put off or discharge his natural allegiance to the former: for this natural allegiance was intrinsic, and primitive, and antecedent to the other; and cannot be devested without the concurrent act of that prince to whom it was first due. Indeed the natural-born subject of one prince, to whom he owes allegiance, may be entangled by subjecting himself absolutely to another; but it is his own act that brings him into these straits and difficulties, of owing service to two masters; and it is unreasonable that, by such voluntary act of his own, he should be able at pleasure to unloose those bands, by which he is connected to his natural prince.

Local allegiance is such as is due from an alien, or stranger born, for so long time as he continues within the king's dominion and protection: and it ceases, the instant such stranger transfers himself from this kingdom to another. Natural allegiance is therefore perpetual, and local temporary only: and that for this reason, evidently founded upon the nature of government; that allegiance is a debt due from the subject, upon an implied contract with the prince, that so long as the one affords protection, so long the other will demean himself faithfully. As therefore the prince is always under a constant tie to protect his natural-born subjects, at all times and in all countries, for this reason their allegiance due to him is equally universal and permanent. But, on the other hand, as the prince affords his protection to an alien, only during his residence in this realm, the allegiance of an alien is confined (in point of time) to the duration of such his residence, and (in point of locality) to the dominions of the British empire. (1 Bl Com 357, 358)

'Allegiance is a thing to which there are two parties, the sovereign and the subject; it is, as Lord Coke says, *"Duplex et reciprocum ligamen"*, and again, *"merito igitur ligeantia dicitur a ligando quia continet in se duplex ligamen"*. And again, "Ligeance is the mutual bond and obligation between the King and his subjects, whereby subjects are called his liege subjects because they are bound to obey and serve him, and he is called their liege lord because he should maintain and defend them. Therefore it is truly said that *protectio trahit subjectionem et subjectio protectionem: Calvin's Case* (1608) 7 Co Rep 1a at 5a].' *Stepney Case, Isaacson v Durant* (1886) 17 QBD 54 at 62, per Lord Coleridge CJ

ALLOTMENT

Garden

'Allotment' includes a field garden. (Small Holdings and Allotments Act 1908, s 61)

In this section the expression 'allotment' means any parcel of land, whether attached to a cottage or not, of not more than two acres in extent, held by a tenant under a landlord and cultivated as a farm or a garden, or partly as a garden and partly as a farm. (Allotments Act 1922, s 3)

'Allotment garden' means an allotment not exceeding [0.10 hectare] in extent which is wholly or mainly cultivated by the occupier for the production of vegetable or fruit crops for consumption by himself or his family. (Agriculture Act 1947, s 109, as amended by the Agriculture (Amendment) Regulations 1978, SI 1978/446)

'Fuel or field garden allotment' means any allotment set out as a fuel allotment, or a field garden allotment, under an Inclosure Act. (New Towns Act 1981, s 80(1))

'Allotment' means any allotment set out as a fuel allotment or a field garden allotment under an Inclosure Act. (Housing Act 1985, s 581(4))

'We cannot hold as matter of law that this place was an allotment because it was less than two acres in extent and fruit or vegetables or flowers were grown in it. If the question were tried by a jury it would be necessary for the judge to give them a direction as to what constituted an allotment. . . . I think the proper direction in this case would be that if the piece of land was cultivated as a "garden" in the ordinary sense of being cultivated for food, or for pleasure, then it was an allotment . . ., but if it was a place used by a seedsman or market gardener in his business, then it was not such an allotment.' *Cooper v Pearse* [1896] 1 QB 562 at 566, 567, DC, per Collins J

See, generally, 2 Halsbury's Laws (4th edn) para 1.

Of shares

Allotment is an appropriation to some person or corporation of a certain number of shares, but not necessarily of any specific shares. (7 Halsbury's Laws (4th edn) para 366)

In relation to an allotment of shares in a company, the shares are taken for the purposes of this Act to be allotted when a person acquires the unconditional right to be included in the company's register of members in respect of those shares. (Companies Act 1985, s 738(1))

'In order to constitute a public allotment there must be an issue of shares to persons other than those who take shares in payment of wages or for work done or as a qualification for a seat on the board. Nothing turns on the use of the word "allotment". If the applications have been before the board and have been accepted and the applicants are found on the register, then there has been an allotment, even though the word allotment has never been used.' *Smith v Charing Cross, Euston & Hampstead Rly Co* (1903) 19 TLR 614 at 615, per Kekewich J

[The plaintiff lent £50 to the defendant to assist him in the promotion of a company. £100 was to be repaid within seven days of the company going to allotment.] 'I am asked to hold that the word "allotment" must mean an effective allotment, the execution of all necessary operations to bind the shareholders, to give them a complete title to their shares, and so forth; but I cannot read such provisions into the agreement. In my view, going to allotment took place as soon as the directors resolved to go to allotment and took the necessary steps to make their resolution effective, whatever the subsequent results might be.' *Ellett v Sternberg* (1910) 27 TLR 127 at 127, per Bankes J

Australia 'The words "allotment" and "issue" though used in relation to incorporated companies for more than a hundred years are not technical terms with precise meanings. Their application in particular circumstances often depends on the context. Their meaning was considered in *Re Florence Land and Public Works Co (Nichol's case)* [(1885) 29 Ch D 421]. In that case at first instance Chitty J said (at 426): ". . . What is termed 'allotment' is generally neither more nor less than the acceptance by the company of the offer to take shares. To take the common case, the offer is to take a certain number of shares, or such a less number of shares as may be allotted. That offer is accepted by the allotment either of the total number mentioned in the offer or a less number, to be taken by the person who made the offer. This constitutes a binding contract to take that number according to the offer and acceptance. To my mind there is no magic whatever in the term "allotment" as used in these circumstances. It is said that the allotment is an appropriation of a specific number of shares. It is an appropriation, not of specific shares, not of a certain number of shares. It does not, however, make the person who has thus agreed to take the shares a member from that moment; all that it does is simply this – it constitutes a binding contract under which the company is bound to make a complete allotment of the specified number of shares, and under which the person who has made the offer and is not bound by the acceptance is bound to take that particular number of shares. In most cases the act of placing the person who has agreed to become a member on the register is a mere matter of form, and may be described as a mere ministerial act; but it appears to me that in point of law all that is done by the process I have just indicated, and all that was done in this case, was to make a complete and binding contract." . . . In my opinion therefore the term "allotment" in the definition must be given the meaning which was suggested in argument by counsel for the companies as "complete allotment", an expression derived from Chitty J. Thus allotment and issue (including entry in the share register) constitute the process of creating the share, which must be complete before the property can be the subject of the disposition.' *Federal Taxation Comr v St Helens Farm (ACT) Pty Ltd* (1981) 11 ATR 544 at 604, 606 per Aickin J

Canada 'As applied to . . . a fixed number of shares, the word "allotment" can mean nothing more than to give, to assign, to set apart, to appropriate. The word has all these meanings . . . and I think "issue" and "allotment" taken together mean no more than some signification by the company of its assent that the defendant now was or had become the owner of the number of shares which he agreed to take.' *Nelson Coke & Gas Co v Pellatt* (1902) 4 OLR 481 at 489, Ont CA, per Maclennan JA

South Africa 'The appropriation to an applicant by resolution of directors of a certain number of shares in response to an application.' *Hocken v Union Trawling Co* 1959 (2) SA 255 (N)

ALLOW

'It seems to me that a man cannot be said to allow that of which he is unaware, or that which he cannot prevent.' *Crabtree v Fern Spinning Co Ltd* (1901) 85 LT 549 at 552, per Darling J

Australia 'Ordinarily speaking, before a person can be said to "allow" anything there must be something in the nature of actual knowledge or connivance, or in some cases extensive delegation of authority in circumstances where the defendant has delegated his power to prevent the act from being done. . . . Of course the meaning of the word "allow" may vary, having

regard to the circumstances and in some cases to the class of enactment in which it is found.' *Gilbert v Gulliver* [1918] VLR 185 at 189, 190, per Cussen J

Australia 'In *Crabtree v Fern Spinning Co Ltd* [(1901) 85 LT 549 at 552] Darling J is reported to have expressed the view that a man "cannot be said to allow that of which he is unaware". . . . But the question in that case was whether in a certain statute the prohibition of allowing something to occur was equivalent to requiring that it be prevented. It may be taken that "allow" is at least as wide as "permit", if not wider.' *De Kuyper v Crafter* [1942] SASR 238 at 243, per Richards J

New Zealand 'The short question I have to decide . . . is whether the neglect to take reasonable precautions to prevent billiard-playing during prohibited hours is in itself, in the absence of connivance, "allowing" such playing [within the Licensing Act 1881 (NZ) (repealed; cf. now the Sale of Liquor Act 1962)]. . . . No case has decided that pure carelessness on the part of a licensee or his servants will justify a finding that the licensee allowed gaming. . . . Failure to take reasonable steps amounts only to negligence or carelessness. If I were to hold that negligence or carelessness which is not in itself evidence of connivance, or has not been the means of giving a person in charge the opportunity to connive at a breach of the law, justifies a conviction for "allowing" gaming, I should . . . be extending the liability beyond the principle established by previous authority.' *Bailey v Pratt* (1902) 20 NZLR 758 at 760, 764–766, per Denniston J; also reported 4 GLR 195 at 197

South Africa '[The word "allow"] implies knowledge and consent on the part of the person concerned.' *Cape Town Council v Benning* 1917 AD 319 per Solomon JA

ALLOWANCE

Australia '"Allowance" in the relevant sense is defined in the Standard Dictionary as meaning:—"That which is allowed; a portion or amount granted for some purpose, as by military regulation, operation of law, or judicial decree: also a limited amount or portion, as of income or food; as, an allowance of rations; an allowance for costs; an allowance for tare or breakage; an extra allowance for services; to put one on an allowance of bread".

When the word is used in connection with the relation of employer and employee it means in my opinion a grant of something additional to ordinary wages for the purpose of meeting some particular requirement connected with the service rendered by the employee or as compensation for unusual conditions for that service. Expense allowances, travelling allowances, and entertainment allowances are payments additional to ordinary wages made for the purpose of meeting certain requirements of a service. Tropical allowances, overtime allowances, and extra pay by way of "dirt money" are allowances as compensation for unusual conditions of service.' *Mutual Acceptance Co Ltd v Federal Comr of Taxation* (1944) 69 CLR 389 at 396, 397, per Latham CJ

Canada 'A reference to standard dictionaries and legal dictionaries will confirm that the word "allowance" is a word of broad and various meanings. In its most common usage, it includes a payment to be made for a particular purpose which does not carry with it any liability to account. Examples of this use of the word might include the periodic "allowance" paid by a parent to a child, the "allowance" given to a ship's captain to feed his crew and, as the Order in Council, a living "allowance" of $25 per day. It is an amount determined arbitrarily and set as a top limit. And it is clearly to be distinguished from "reimbursement" which indicates a payment of a variable sum dependent on a precise accounting for the actual expenditure.' *R v Davis* (1978) 93 DLR (3d) 233 at 235, 237, BC Co Ct, per Anderson Co Ct J

South Africa 'When the word "allowance" is used in connection with the relation of employer and employee it means a grant of something additional to wages.' *R v Van Roogen* 1949 (3) SA 904 (0)

ALLUREMENT

'I think that this [the presence of broken glass on the defendant's land] was a trap rather than an allurement. I think that the word "allurement", as used in these cases, has been applied, or at any rate generally applied, to something . . . which would be attractive to children to play with . . . rather than to circumstances such as the present, where a local authority are in effect saying to children: "You can come and play on this land," the land containing pieces of glass and possibly other

objects such as tins which might be extremely dangerous if children fell down.' *Williams v Cardiff Corpn* [1950] 1 KB 514 at 517, CA, per Somervell LJ

'What is an allurement? I suppose that it is something attractive but dangerous, although not apparently so—something insidious. The capacity of an object to attract will, of course, vary with the age and experience of the person concerned. . . . Can a hole in the ground be an allurement? I think not. There is nothing insidious about a hole in the ground; its danger is not concealed. It was broad daylight at the time of the accident, the hole was quite obvious to a child, and the plaintiff knew that he ought not to go beyond the barrier. If a hole in a road is an allurement, what about dozens of objects met with in the daily life of children? What about a canal, an unfastened window, a flight of stairs? They are all dangers, but children know it. I cannot see anything alluring about a hole in the ground.' *Perry v Thomas Wrigley Ltd* [1955] 3 All ER 243 at 244, per Oliver J

Canada ' "Allurements" . . . have been relied upon in some cases to fasten liability upon a landowner in respect of an infant coming upon the land: and the cases show that, if the landowner place or leave upon his land anything that would naturally attract children to come upon his land without taking efficient means to keep them off, he may therefore be held to have invited or licensed them to come upon his property.' *Wallace v Pettit* (1923) 55 OLR 82 at 87, CA, per Riddell J

ALLUVION   *See also* ACCRETION

Where land is formed by alluvion, namely by the casting up of earth or sand on the shore of the sea, the additional increment belongs to the Crown where the casting up of the earth or sand takes place suddenly. However, where new land is formed by small accretions, and the additions or increments are so gradual as to be inappreciable, these belong to the owner of the adjacent land, whether the accretions are due to natural or to artificial causes, provided in the latter case the user of the land is lawful. (8 Halsbury's Laws (4th edn) para 1437)

As to lands gained from the sea, either by alluvion, by washing up of sand and earth, so as in time to make *terra firma*, or by dereliction, as when the sea shrinks back below the usual water mark; in these cases the law is held to be, that if this gain be by little and little, by small and imperceptible degrees, it shall go to the owner of the land adjoining. For *de minimis non curat lex*, and besides, these owners being often losers by the breaking in of the sea, or at charges to keep it out, this possible gain is therefore, a reciprocal consideration for such possible charge or loss; but if the alluvion or dereliction be sudden and considerable, in this case it belongs to the King, for as the King is lord of the sea, and so the owner of the soil while it is covered with water, it is but reasonable that he should have the soil when the water has left it dry. (2 Bl Com 262)

South Africa [Alluvial land is a deposit of earth upon the bank of a river so gradual that no one can perceive how much is added at any one moment of time; such deposit is inseparable from the native soil of the bank; and the owner of the latter acquires that latter by right of accession. Land reclaimed from the sea intentionally and by artificial means belongs to the Republic and cannot be claimed as an accession by alluvion by the owner of land adjoining that portion of the sea which has been so reclaimed. See *Colonial Government v Cape Town Council* 19 SC 97; *Van Niekerk v Carter* 1917 AD 374.]

ALMS   *See* BEG

ALMSHOUSE

[This case raised the point whether an institution was an almshouse, and so entitled to exemption in respect of income tax under the Income Tax Act 1842, s 61, Sch A, No VI (repealed; see now the Income and Corporation Taxes Act 1970, s 360.] 'I am justified in treating the word "almshouse" as being for all practical purposes equivalent to a "house provided for the reception or relief of poor persons". . . . To make a place an almshouse it is not necessary that the inmates should be entirely destitute, or that it should supply all their wants. I am satisfied that a large number of institutions popularly known as almshouses do not in point of fact supply the entire wants of their inmates, but include people who have some other means, and in many cases must have some other means in order to avail themselves of the benefits of the institution.' *Mary Clark Home Trustees v Anderson* [1904] 2 KB 645 at 651, 657, per Channell J

ALONGSIDE

'The charterparty provides that the ship is to proceed to ports in the Baltic and there load a cargo of timber, and that, being so loaded, she is to proceed therewith to the Surrey Commercial Docks, London, and there deliver the same; and it contains this clause: "The cargo to be brought to and taken from alongside the steamer at charterers' risk and expense, any custom of the port to the contrary notwithstanding'. . . . If the custom of the port is struck out, as, in my judgment, it must be, the obligation of the charterers is to take the cargo from alongside—that is, when offered to them over the ship's rail.' *Brenda SS Co v Green* (1900) 69 LJQB 445 at 446, CA, per AL Smith LJ

[Shipowners agreed to deliver timber at Great Yarmouth, cargo to be taken from 'alongside' the steamer at charterers' risk and expense as customary. The ship was unable to come nearer than 13 feet from defendants' quay, and by a custom of the port the cargo had to be landed not nearer than 10 feet from the edge of the quay: it therefore became necessary for the shipowners to erect a staging to discharge the vessel.] 'I am myself of opinion that the word "alongside", if it does not suggest actual contact, does at all events suggest close contiguity, and not the less so because the ordinary obligation of the shipowner is admittedly only to deliver to the consignee the cargo his ship carries at ship's rail.' *Palgrave, Brown & Son Ltd v SS Turid* [1922] 1 AC 397 at 404, per Lord Birkenhead LC

ALTAR

'The distinction between an "Altar" and a "Communion Table" is in itself essential and deeply founded in the most important difference in matters of faith between Protestants and Romanists; namely, in the different notions of the nature of the Lord's Supper which prevailed in the Roman Catholic Church at the time of the Reformation, and those which were introduced by the Reformers. By the former it was considered as a sacrifice of the body and blood of the Saviour. The Altar was the place on which the sacrifice was to be made. . . . The Reformers, on the other hand, considered the Holy Communion not as a sacrifice but as a feast, to be celebrated at the Lord's Table. . . . With respect to the question what is required to constitute a Roman Catholic Altar . . . the Altar is to be in the church; it is to be fixed and immoveable, . . . and it is required to be "*lapideum, et ab Episcopo consecratrum*". . . . Such then . . . is the Roman Catholic Altar. A stone structure fixed in the church, and immoveable, with a plane surface, or *mensa*, on which the unbloody sacrifice . . . may be offered; on which the Host and the Cup . . . may be placed with a crucifix, and two candlesticks, as essential adjuncts to it. . . . The Rubric of the present Prayer Book provides only that at the Communion time, the Table, having a fair white linen cloth upon it, shall stand in the body of the Church or Chancel. . . . The term "Altar" is never used to describe it [in the Prayer Book], and there is an express declaration at the close of the service against the doctrine of transubstantiation, with which the ideas of an Altar and sacrifice are closely connected.' *Liddell v Westerton* (1857) Brod & F 117 at 144–146, 150, PC, per cur.

ALTER

Canada 'On the basis of a number of dictionary definitions of the word "alter", he [the trial judge] found that "alter" comprehended a change or variation in something, a modification, a change in some elements or ingredients of the thing, but not a change in the whole, a total replacement. . . . The dictionary definitions to which he resorted amply support his conclusion that to replace or substitute one thing for another is not to alter the original. The original is gone and a new thing has taken its place.' *R v Parkway Chrysler Plymouth Ltd* (1976) 32 CCC (2d) 116 at 117, 118, Ont CA, per Wilson JA

New Zealand 'A person who without giving the matter any consideration has simply failed to act in a particular way cannot be said to have altered his position.' *Westpac Banking Corpn v Nangeela Properties Ltd* [1986] BCR 101 per Richardson J

ALTERATION   *See also* ADDITION

'Alteration' includes deterioration. (Merchant Shipping (Load Lines) Act 1967, s 32)

'Alterations', in relation to any school premises, includes improvements, extensions and additions, but does not include any significant enlargement of the school premises. (Education Act 1968, Sch 1(5)(a))

Australia 'As applied to a building . . . "alter" means to modify and change, and it

presupposes an existing building of which the fabric will remain substantially unchanged after the alterations have been completed.' *Re Church of St Jude* [1956] SASR 46 at 53, per Hannan J

Australia [The Family Law Act 1975 (Cth), s 79 specifically says that 'the court may make such order as it thinks fit "altering" the interests of the parties in the property, including an order for a settlement of property etc'.] 'If one wishes to indulge in semantics, (and it seems necessary to do so here) there would certainly appear to be a substantial difference between "affect" and "alter". The Shorter Oxford English Dictionary on Historical Principles defines "affect" as "to influence", but defines "alter" as "to make otherwise or different in some respect, without changing the thing itself; to modify. To become otherwise, or to undergo some change". In my view it is a question of degree in every case as to when a proprietary interest becomes so affected as to be altered.' *In the Marriage of Farr* (1976) 2 Fam LR 11,300 at 11,303 per Murray J

New Zealand 'It is, I think, apparent that the word "alteration" may well, in appropriate circumstances, refer to a repair or renewal incidental to the making of something "otherwise or different in some respect, without changing the thing itself". The circumstance that the dictionary meaning of "alter" comprehends that the thing itself is not changed is strongly suggestive, however, that the question of alteration must itself in every case be one of degree and that the test to be applied is whether the act done is in substance an alteration in part only or a replacement of substantially the whole.' *Auckland Trotting Club v Inland Revenue Comr* [1968] NZLR 193 at 200, per Moller J (quoting with approval the judgment of the Taxation Board of Review)

In valuation list

[The Valuation (Metropolis) Act 1869, s 44 (repealed; see now the General Rate Act 1967, ss 6(2), 69, 79) enacted that where in consequence of the decision on an appeal an 'alteration' in the valuation list was made which altered the amount of the assessment, the difference, if too much had been paid, should be repaid.] 'In the present case . . . there was an appeal to quarter sessions . . . on the ground that the plaintiff was not the occupier . . . and it was held that the plaintiff was not liable. That being so, the only question is whether the fact that he is held liable to no part of the rate is an alteration within the meaning of the section. . . . The question then is reduced to a very narrow one, whether an entire alteration of the rate is an alteration within the meaning of the statute, and I am of opinion that it is.' *Burton v Bloomsbury Vestry* [1901] 1 KB 650 at 654, per Mathew J

In will

'That section [Wills Act 1837, s 21] relates to obliteration, interlineation, or other alteration in the will after execution: all such are void, if not affirmed in the margin, or otherwise, by the signature of the testator, and attestation of witnesses. . . . It is not a mere difference of ink or handwriting, which would constitute any of the acts done according to the true meaning of the statute. . . . Blanks may be supplied, and in a different ink. . . . But the case is different when there is an erasure apparent on the face of the will, and when that erasure has been superinduced by other writing. In such a case there is an obliteration and something more which constitutes an alteration.' *Greville v Tylee* (1851) 7 Moo PCC 320 at 327, 328, per Dr Lushington

Of bill *See* APPARENT

Of picture

[Under the Fine Arts Copyright Act 1862, s 7 (repealed; see now Copyright Act 1956, s 43), the 'alteration' of a painting, drawing or photograph without the consent of the author or maker was an offence.] 'There is . . . a breach of the provisions of clause 4 of s 7 if a person knowingly publishes as or for the unaltered work of the artist a work which has been altered within the meaning of the enactment. "Alteration" is a word with a somewhat wide meaning, and in construing it one must always have regard to the maxim "*de minimis non curat lex*". It is quite possible that there may be some alterations which would not be alterations within the meaning of clause 4. For instance, I do not think that an alteration in the form of the artist's signature would come within the enactment. It would be an alteration not material to the object of the enactment. To come within the enactment an alteration must be a material alteration having regard to the object with which the enactment was passed; and that which would be material in that sense would be an alteration which might affect the credit and reputation of the artist. To my mind that is what is prohibited. I do not think that it

would be necessary to find in any particular case that the alteration had affected the character and reputation of the artist; it is sufficient if the alteration is of such a character that it might affect his character and reputation.' *Carlton Illustrators v Coleman & Co Ltd* [1911] 1 KB 771 at 779, 780, per Channell J

Of river bank

[The Metropolis Management (Thames River Prevention of Floods) Amendment Act 1879, s 23, imposed a penalty on any person who should make an 'alteration' to a bank so as to affect the security of premises from flooding.] 'We are dealing with a summons for a penalty under s 23 for altering a bank. . . . The word "repair" does not appear in s 23. . . . That has led me to the conviction that s 23, with a special penalty, was inserted for the purpose of dealing with the specific offence mentioned, namely, the alteration from the point of view of safety of a bank which had been previously sanctioned, that is to say, by making it lower than the height which had been previously ordered. In my opinion, s 23 has not touched, and was not intended to deal with, what I may call the temporary removal of a piece of the bank for the purpose of reconstruction.' *London County Council v London, Brighton & South Coast Rly Co* [1906] 2 KB 72 at 77, 78, per Lord Alverstone CJ

'It may be argued that the word "alteration" in s 23 of this Act must be read as having a wider meaning than it ordinarily has, and as including repairs. . . . I have come to the conclusion that the word is not used in that wide sense.' Ibid, at 79 per Ridley J

To premises

[A lease of premises, upon a part of which the business of a jeweller was to be carried on, contained a covenant that the lessee would not make or suffer to be made any 'alteration' to the premises without the written consent of the lessors.] 'The words "alteration to the said premises" apply only to alterations which would affect the form or structure of the premises.' *Bickmore v Dimmer* [1903] 1 Ch 158 at 167, CA, per Vaughan Williams J

ALTERNATIVE ACCOMMODATION
See SUITABLE ALTERNATIVE ACCOMMODATION

ALWAYS

In mortgage contract

'Prima facie a clause in a mortgage contract is limited to the duration of the mortgage relation between the contracting parties. In this clause we have the words "always hereafter"; but I observe that in two other clauses (the third and the fifth) a similar phrase, "at any time hereafter", is used and is limited by the context to the duration of the mortgage. I am disposed to say that the words "always hereafter", having regard to the nature and purport of the agreement, in like manner mean at any time hereafter during the currency of the loan.' *Bradley v Carritt* [1903] AC 253 at 269, per Lord Davey

In testamentary direction

[A testator directed that certain outgoings in respect of leasehold land settled by his will should 'always' be paid by his trustees out of the income of his residuary estate.] 'In the first place it is clear that the word "always" cannot mean for all time. The period during which the clause operates according to its tenor cannot extend beyond the existence of the leases. . . .' *Re Cassel, Public Trustee v Mountbatten* [1926] Ch 358 at 366, 367, per Russell J

AMALGAMATION

Of companies

Amalgamation is a blending of two or more existing undertakings into one undertaking, the shareholders of each blending company becoming substantially the shareholders in the company which is to carry on the blended undertakings. There may be amalgamation either by the transfer of two or more undertakings to a new company, or by the transfer of one or more undertakings to an existing company. (7 Halsbury's Laws (4th edn) para 1539)

'I do not find anywhere any technical definition of the term "amalgamate", and I have some difficulty in getting at its exact meaning; but whatever its definite meaning may be, it certainly does not imply an authority from a shareholder to his directors to execute on his behalf the deed of another company, and so to make him liable in respect of all the engagements of that other company.' *Re Bank of Hindustan, China, & Japan Ltd, Higgs' Case* (1865) 2 Hem & M 657 at 666, per Page Wood V-C

'Neither of these words, "reconstruction" and "amalgamation" has any definite *legal* meaning. Each is a commercial and not a legal term, and, even as a commercial term, bears no exact definite meaning. In each case one has to decide whether the transaction is such that, in the meaning of commercial men, it is one which is comprehended in the term "reconstruction" or "amalgamation". . . . Now what is an amalgamation? . . . There you must have the rolling, somehow or other, of two concerns into one. You must weld two things together and arrive at an amalgam—a blending of two undertakings. It does not necessarily follow that the whole of the two undertakings should pass—substantially they must pass—nor need all the corporators be parties, although substantially all must be parties. The difference between reconstruction and amalgamation is that in the latter is involved the blending of two concerns one with the other, but not merely the continuance of one concern. An amalgamation may take place . . . either by the transfer of undertakings A and B to a new corporation, C, or by the continuance of A and B by B upon terms that the shareholders of A shall become shareholders in B. It is not necessary that you should have a new company. You may have a continuance of one of the two companies upon the terms that the undertakings of both corporations shall substantially be merged in one corporation only.' *Re South African Supply & Cold Storage Co, Wild v South African Supply & Cold Storage Co* [1904] 2 Ch 268 at 281, 282, 287, per Buckley J

'I find some definition, if it be a definition, of "amalgamation" in Buckley on the Companies Acts [14th edn, p 678]. It is a definition which, so far as it is a definition, I should like to adopt as my own; it is there stated as follows: "The word 'amalgamation' has no definite legal meaning. It contemplates a state of things under which two companies are so joined as to form a third entity, or one company is absorbed into and blended with another company." ' *Re Walker's Settlement, Royal Exchange Assurance Corpn v Walker* [1935] Ch 567 at 583, CA, per Romer LJ

[Generally, see the Companies Act 1985, s 427.]

Australia 'Much has been said of the vague and indefinite meaning of the word "amalgamate" as a description of a transaction between companies. . . . The expression is figurative and is a commercial rather than a legal description. The general notion conveyed by "amalgamation" is the combination of separate things or separate collections of things into a single uniform or homogeneous whole. In spite of the commercial origin of the use of the terms "amalgamation", "reconstruction", and "reorganisation" as descriptions of company transactions, their meaning is not to be ascertained by considering the lay understanding of the expressions, but rather by referring to text writers upon company law, who are specially conversant with the subject. . . . Text writers concur in treating amalgamation as a description of transactions which, however carried out, result in the substitution of one corporation for the two or more uniting companies, and the conversion, in effect, of the separate sets of members of the *uniting* companies into a single set of members of the one corporation.' *Citizens & Graziers' Life Assurance Co Ltd v Commonwealth Life (Amalgamated) Assurances Ltd* (1934) 51 CLR 422 at 455, 456, per Dixon J

Canada 'Whether an amalgamation creates or extinguishes a corporate entity will, of course, depend upon the terms of the applicable statute, but as I read the Act [Canada Corporations Act, RSC 1970, c C-32] in particular s 137, and consider the purposes which an amalgamation is intended to serve, it would appear to me that upon an amalgamation under the Canada Corporations Act no "new" company is created and no "old" company is extinguished. . . . The French version of s 137(1), perhaps better than the English version, serves to express what has occurred, "Deux ou plus de deux compagnies, . . . peuvent fusionner et continuer comme une seule et même compagnie". The effect is that of blending and continuance as one and the self same company.' *R v Black & Decker Manufacturing Co Ltd* (1974) 13 CPR (2d) 97 at 101, 102, SCC, per Dickson J

Of land

'Amalgamation' means a transaction for securing that agricultural land which is comprised in a holding to which a notice to quit relates and which together with some other agricultural land could form an agricultural unit, shall be owned and occupied with that other land. (Agriculture (Miscellaneous Provisions) Act 1968, s 20)

AMBIGUITY

There be two sorts of ambiguities of words; the one is *ambiguitas patens* and the other *latens*.

Patens is that which appears to be ambiguous upon the deed or instrument; *latens* is that which seemeth certain and without ambiguity, for anything that appeareth upon the deed or instrument; but there is some collateral matter out of the deed that breedeth the ambiguity. (Bacon's Law Tracts 99)

In patent

'I wish to add that . . . I think this patent is bad for ambiguity in the specification. There seems to be some danger of the well-known rule of law against ambiguity being in practice invaded. Some of those who draft specifications and claims are apt to treat this industry as a trial of skill, in which the object is to make the claim very wide upon one interpretation of it, in order to prevent as many people as possible from competing with the patentee's business, and then to rely on carefully prepared sentences in the specification which, it is hoped, will be just enough to limit the claim within safe dimensions if it is attacked in Court. . . . It is a duty of the patentee to state clearly and distinctly, either in direct words or by clear and distinct reference, the nature and limits of what he claims. If he uses language which, when fairly read, is avoidably obscure or ambiguous, the patent is invalid, whether the defect be due to design, or to carelessness, or to want of skill.' *Natural Colour Kinematograph Co Ltd v Bioschemes Ltd* (1915) 32 RPC 256 at 266, per Lord Loreburn

'The defendant company in its defence alleges that the patent is invalid . . . on the usual grounds, namely . . . ambiguity. . . . Ambiguity is directed to the issue whether the invention is sufficiently described and ascertained so as to enable the public to understand the scope of the monopoly granted by the letters patent. There is necessarily overlapping with regard to those two issues [ambiguity and insufficiency].' *No-Fume Ltd v Pitchford (Frank) & Co Ltd* (1934) 52 RPC 28 at 34, per Luxmoore J

Latent ambiguity

A latent ambiguity [in a will] arises when the description in the will, considered in the light of the context, is on the face of it apt to describe and determine, without obscurity at the time when the subject is to be ascertained, any of two or more different subjects, either accurately, or subject to inaccuracies such as blanks left in the description, on words which have to be rejected as a false description not applying to any one, or which are otherwise negligible.

Where the donee is described by a christian name, and there are found two persons, one having that name only, and the other having that name with others, both are treated as answering the description in the will with sufficient accuracy, and a latent ambiguity arises. A latent ambiguity does not arise where part of the description applies to one subject and another part to another subject; or where from the context of the whole will or by the aid of any rule of construction applicable to the will, such as the presumption as to repeated words or as to legitimacy or from the circumstances of the case properly admissible in evidence, it can be gathered which of the different subjects was intended. (50 Halsbury's Laws (4th edn) para 403)

Patent ambiguity

A latent ambiguity must be distinguished from a patent ambiguity, which arises where the description is on the face of it indefinite and insufficiently clear to determine any subject, for example where there is a gift to 'one of the sons' of a named person who has more than one son. In construing the will of a testator who died before 1st January 1983, no evidence is admissible to resolve such an ambiguity. (50 Halsbury's Laws (4th edn) para 403)

AMELIORATING WASTE   *See* WASTE

AMEND

Australia   [The appellant served a notice of appeal, to the Supreme Court of Tasmania, from a traffic conviction. He did not set out in the notice any specific grounds of appeal. The Justices Procedure Act 1919, s 152(6) (repealed; see now the Justices Act 1959, (Tas), s 123(2)) provides that grounds of appeal may be 'amended']. 'Under subsection (6) of s 152 the grounds of appeal may be amended but I cannot construe the word "amended" other than to mean the perfecting or ameliorating of an existing thing—not supplying a vacuum with something that should be there.' *Risley v Gough* [1953] Tas SR 78 at 79, per Gibson J

AMENITIES

'Amenities', in relation to any place, includes any view of or from that place. (Petroleum (Consolidation) Act 1928, s 23)

The 'standard amenities' for the purposes of this Part [XV: Grants for Works of Improvement, Repair and Conversion] are those described in . . . the following Table. . . .
A fixed bath or shower
A hot and cold water supply at a fixed bath or shower
A wash-hand basin
A hot and cold water supply at a wash-hand basin
A sink
A hot and cold water supply at a sink
A water closet
(Housing Act 1985, s 508(1))

'The word "amenity" is obviously used very loosely [in the Housing, Town Planning, etc, Act 1909 s 59(2) (repealed)]; it is, I think, novel in an Act of Parliament, and appears to mean "pleasant circumstances or features, advantages". Wide streets and plenty of air and room between houses seem clearly to be amenities, and a provision securing them by setting back houses to a given line seems to me to be a provision with a view to securing amenity.' *Re Ellis & Ruislip-Northwood Urban District Council* [1920] 1 KB 343 at 370, CA, per Scrutton LJ (dissenting)

Australia   [An owner of land submitted plans of a hotel proposed to be erected on such land to the council for that area. The council opposed the erection of the hotel on the ground, inter alia, that it was likely to cause injury to an 'amenity' of the neighbourhood.] 'Amenity is defined in the Concise Oxford Dictionary as "pleasantness" and pleasantness in its turn is what is "agreeable to mind, feelings or senses". Modern planning usage has stretched the word "amenity"—perhaps rather unfortunately—to denote personal convenience, so that the convenient arrangement of different but interdependent uses of land (for example, shopping and housing) or the provision of a service such as a public lavatory is called an amenity. . . . The word may be taken to express that element in the appearance and lay-out of town and country which makes for a comfortable and pleasant life rather than a mere existence. It is the quality which a well-designed building estate or neighbourhood will have and which streets of solid but uninspired "by-law" housing conspicuously lack. . . . We are firmly of opinion that the erection of a building such as a modern hotel, which in the ordinary course of human affairs must attract to its site or locality a large number of parked motor cars, can injure the amenity of the neighbourhood.' *Ex p Tooth & Co Ltd, Re Parramatta City Council* (1955) 55 SR (NSW) 282 at 306, 308, per Maxwell J, Roper CJ in Eq, and Herron J

Australia 'In *Vacuum Oil Company Pty Ltd v Ashfield Municipal Council* (1956) 2 LGRA 8, 11, Sugarman J offered the following observations on the concept of "amenity" in town planning legislation: "Amenity is not confined to the negative factor of freedom from physical discomfort through the effects of noise, smell, and the other matters referred to in the proviso to clause 27 of the County of Cumberland Planning Scheme Ordinance. It relates also to the preservation of such characteristics of a neighbourhood as make it pleasing in appearance as well to the passer-by as to the resident, and as well to those across the road, who may be unaffected by noise etc, as to the adjoining and other occupiers on the same side, 'Amenity' may be taken to express that element in the appearance or layout of town and country which makes for a comfortable and pleasant life rather than a mere existence." See also *Humby v Woollahra Municipal Council* (1964) 10 LGRA 56, 65. There is no doubt that the concept of amenity is wide and flexible. In my view it may in a particular case embrace not only the effect of a place on the senses, but also the resident's subjective perception of his locality. Knowing the use to which a particular site is or may be put, may affect one's perception of amenity.' *Broad v Brisbane City Council and Baptist Union of Queensland* [1986] 2 Qd R 317 at 326, per de Jersey J

Canada 'I prefer to conclude that "loss of amenities" in no significant or material sense includes impotence, and should attract no damages under its banner for any loss of sexual power or pleasure.' *V v C* [1972] 2 OR 723 at 732, Ont SC, per Wright J

AMERCEMENT

To be amerced, or *a mercie*, is to be at the King's mercy with regard to the fine to be imposed. (3 Bl Com 376)

[A charter of Henry VI in 1448 granted to the burgesses of a town all 'amercements', ransoms and issues forfeited, and also all issues, fines and 'amercements' from whatsoever pledges and mainpernors of any person dwelling within the town]. 'That word "amercements" is . . . the only one with which we have substantially to deal. . . . The word

"amerced" is a very old word in English law. . . . When a man is said to be amerced . . . he is to be in mercy as being liable to such a punishment as may be inflicted upon him, mostly by fine, but not necessarily by fine alone.' *Re Nottingham Corpn* [1897] 2 QB 502 at 508, per Pollock B

AMICUS CURIAE

Canada '*Amicus curiae* . . . is one who as a bystander, where a judge is doubtful or mistaken in a matter of law, may inform the court. In its ordinary use the term implies the friendly intervention of counsel to remind the court of some matter of law which has escaped its notice and in regard of which it is in danger of going wrong.' *Grice v R* [1957] 11 DLR (2d) 699 at 702, Ont SC, per Ferguson J

South Africa 'The name given to a member of the bar, or other bystander, who advises the court regarding a point of law or fact upon which information is required.' *Grimshaw v Mica Mines Ltd* 1912 TPD 450

AMMUNITION

In this Act, the expression 'ammunition' means ammunition for any firearm and includes grenades, bombs and other like missiles, whether capable of use with a firearm or not, and also includes prohibited ammunition. (Firearms Act 1968, s 57(2))

['Prohibited' ammunition includes any ammunition containing, or designed or adapted to contain, any noxious liquid, gas or other thing; see the Firearms Act 1968, s 5(1), (2) and the Firearms Act 1982, s 1(4)(b).]

AMNESTY

Australia 'The word "amnesty" comes from the Greek *amnestia* (forgetfulness, oblivion). It is an act of a sovereign power granting forgiveness for an offence or neglect.' *Salemi v Minister for Immigration and Ethnic Affairs (No 2)* (1977) 14 ALR 1 at 47, per Murphy J

AMORTIZATION

Canada 'It has been submitted that there is no case on record which defines the legal meaning of the word "amortization", and I have been unable to find such a case. In that event I consider it the duty of this court to make a definite finding on same owing to the fact that the system of repayment of a debt by instalments of principal and interest at the same time, in order to extinguish the debt within a fixed period, is a common one in this country. . . . I interpret it to mean that the payments made are equal in amount and are applied in payment of the accrued interest and of a portion of the principal.' *Price v Green* [1951] 4 DLR 596 at 599, 600, Man CA, per McPherson CJ

AMOTION

Amotion means depriving a corporate officer of his office. A power of amotion is incident to a corporation, unless it has been taken away by statute. It is necessary to the good order and government of corporate bodies that there should be such a power, and a corporation may by its incidental power to make byelaws confer upon itself power to amove for just cause, although there is no express power by the charter or prescription to make such a byelaw. (9 Halsbury's Laws (4th edn) para 1266)

AMPLIFIER

'I think that the word "amplifier" would be, possibly, enough to include a megaphone or foghorn such as is used on a ship.' *Reynolds v John* [1956] 1 All ER 306 at 310, per Lord Goddard CJ

AMUSEMENT

'Some people will make a very serious thing out of quite a simple game; and the fact that some people take such things much more seriously than others does not prevent them from being a diversion, amusement or game.' *Customs & Excise Comrs v E Keil & Co Ltd* [1951] 1 KB 469 at 471, 472, per Croom-Johnson J

Amusement arcade

[A covenant in a conveyance prohibited land from being used as an 'amusement arcade'.] 'The learned judge [in the court below] came to the conclusion that on the true construction of the covenant, an amusement arcade, for the purposes of the covenant, is a building with free access to the public and containing coin-in-the-slot amusement machines, irrespective of

whether they are gaming machines or not, but he thought that the description "amusement arcade" excluded a place of entertainment which was only for very small children. . . . I think the learned judge was justified in treating an amusement arcade as not requiring gaming machines, or dependent on the age of the patrons.' *Shaw v Applegate* [1978] 1 All ER 123 at 127, CA, per Buckley LJ

Amusement parlour

Australia 'There is no definition of amusement parlour in the instrument of delegation and we are accordingly left to decide as best we can according to the ordinary understanding of English what is meant by "amusement parlour". It is not necessary to attempt a definition. It is sufficient to say that the 1972 Supplement to the Oxford English Dictionary shows s.v. "Amusement" that the word is frequently found in combination with such words as arcade, centre, hall, park. The combinations denote places to which people resort for the purposes of amusement. The mere installation of two coin-operated amusement machines cannot convert a fish and chip shop into a place to which people resort for the purposes of amusement. It is nothing to the point that one or two people may do so. Necessarily a question of degree is involved. If there be an undoubted amusement parlour it would not have its character altered by the installation of a pie stall in one corner of it.' *Blount v Gianevsky* [1980] VR 156 at 161, per cur.

ANALYSIS

'Analysis' includes micro-biological assay but no other form of biological assay and 'analyse' shall be construed accordingly. (Food Act 1984, s 132(1); see also the Medicines Act 1968, s 132(1))

ANCESTOR

'The word "ancestor" is properly assignable to the person who really preceded in the estate, although that person may not be the progenitor of the successor—he may be, as in this case, his uncle.' *Zetland (Earl) v Lord Advocate* (1878) 3 App Cas 505 at 518, per Lord Hatherley

'The inquiry into the history of the writ of mort d'ancestor . . . has thrown a light upon the history of the word "ancestor" itself. Etymologically . . . the word means "antecessor", one who goes before, and in this wider sense it has been replaced in modern times by the word "predecessor". I am tempted to take the view, from the etymological authorities to which I was referred, that the word was imported into this country as part of the Norman-French which the Norman conquerors brought with them, and I can well believe that in the early days of its use its primary meaning was to connote the idea of succession, the "ancestor" being the person prior in succession to the "heir". That is the meaning, I understand, which is attributable to the word in connection with the writ of mort d'ancestor. It is, of course, a technical meaning, and it is clear that for some purposes that technical meaning survived. . . . But it is equally clear that at some time in English history another, and new, meaning of the word "ancestor" grew up, namely, as being the equivalent of fore-father or lineal ascendant, and it is in that sense that it is in common use in ordinary language in modern times.' *Knowles v A-G* [1951] P 54 at 67, per Willmer J

ANCHORAGE

'The right of anchorage is usually, if not universally, incident to the proprietorship of a port: Hale, *De Portibus Maris*, Chap 6, in describing the several port duties which arise from the *jus domini* of property or franchise in port, says: "These are of two kinds, and as to the former, viz. such as are common and ordinary, and so almost incident to every ownership of a port", he mentions, first, "anchorage, or a pre-station or toll for every anchor cast there, and sometimes though there be no anchor"; and he adds, "This doth in truth properly and prima facie arise from or in respect of the propriety of the soil, and is an evidence of it. But yet it is not so always, but grows due in respect of the franchise". . . . That both a toll upon merchandise, and also an anchorage toll were taken by the lords of the manor of Whitstable is clear, when we come to modern times. In the deeds of conveyance of the fishery, and also in the Act for incorporating the Free Fishers, the payment and dues for the anchorage of any ships or vessels . . . are distinguished from the payments or dues of the landing of any goods or merchandise; showing that these two descriptions of toll belonged, separately and distinctly, to the lord of the manor.' *Foreman v Whitstable Free Fishers & Dredgers* (1869) LR 4 HL 266 at 284, 286, per Lord Chelmsford

ANCHORED *See* AT ANCHOR

ANCIENT LIGHT *See* LIGHT

ANCIENT MONUMENT

'Ancient monument' means—
(a) any scheduled monument; and
(b) any other monument which in the opinion of the Secretary of State is of public interest by reason of the historic, architectural, traditional, artistic or archaeological interest attaching to it.
(Ancient Monuments and Archaeological Areas Act 1979, s 61(12)

[As to scheduled monuments, see s 1 of the Act.]

'Ancient monument' means any structure, work, site, garden or area which in the [Historic Buildings and Monuments] Commission's opinion is of historic, architectural, traditional, artistic or archaeological interest. (National Heritage Act 1983, s 33(8))

ANCILLARY

'The right [to grant relief] which the county court has under s 89 of the Judicature Act [1873 (repealed; see now County Courts Act 1984, ss 38, 39)] is ancillary, that is to say, supplemental. It is an additional remedy, the making more effective a remedy for the one cause of action.' *Smith v Smith* [1925] 2 KB 144 at 149, CA, per Bankes LJ

['Counsel . . . while not attempting an exhaustive definition of the word "ancillary", has submitted that the phrase "as ancillary" connotes "assistance of a subordinate or subservient kind". Even accepting this submission for present purposes, any agreement which is ancillary to an earlier agreement in this sense may well involve some variation of that agreement and thus, in one sense, a measure of conflict with it. However, the fact that such variation may be thought in some respects to involve a departure from the terms of the earlier agreement, even on a point of principle, does not in my view inevitably prevent the subsequent agreement from being properly described as "ancillary" to the earlier agreement, according to the ordinary meaning of words. This, I think, must be a question of degree according to the particular facts of each case.' *R v HM Treasury, ex p Smedley* [1985] 1 All ER 589 at 599, CA, per Slade LJ

AND/OR

'There is really a clear understanding of what the words "and/or" mean. To take one of the simplest cases and an obvious case, where there is a charterparty by which a ship is to proceed to Rotterdam and/or Antwerp at charterer's option it means one of three things: the charterer may either send the vessel to Rotterdam alone, or he may send her to Antwerp alone, or he may send her to Rotterdam and Antwerp. Now that . . . [is] the ordinary business meaning of the words "and/or".' *Gurney v Grimmer* (1932) 38 Com Cas 7 at 13, CA, per Scrutton LJ

'The question which I have to decide is what is the effect of the gift of the testator's residuary estate to "Margaret Ann and/or John Richards". It may mean an absolute gift to Margaret Ann and if she does not survive the testator and the tenant for life, then to John Richards; or it may be a gift to the two of them as joint tenants, or as a third alternative it may be wholly void for uncertainty. . . . I have come to the conclusion that this gift is not void for uncertainty, and I think that what the testator meant was that the husband and wife, Margaret Ann Richards and John Richards should take as joint tenants, and that, if Margaret Ann Richards did not survive the testator and the tenant for life, then the property should go to John Richards as a substitutional gift, but as both the husband and wife are alive they take as joint tenants.' *Re Lewis, Goronwy v Richards* [1942] 2 All ER 364 at 365, per Farwell J

ANGARY

'The right of a belligerent to requisition the goods of neutrals found within its territory, or territory of which it is in military occupation is recognised by a number of writers on international law. . . . It is sometimes referred to as the right of angary; and is generally recognised as involving an obligation to make full compensation.' *The Zamora* [1916] 2 AC 77 at 101, PC, per cur.

'There is a well ascertained right of a belligerent Sovereign to take possession of the property of neutrals so found within his territory or territory occupied by his forces for the purposes of warfare. This is the right of angary. It appears to me to be well recognised by the conventions of civilised nations, which consti-tute the body of international law, and it is equally clear that it is only so recognised on the footing that the Sovereign so exercising this right makes full compensation for the property he so seizes.' *Commercial & Estates Co of Egypt v Board of Trade* [1925] 1 KB 271 at 293, CA, per Atkin LJ

ANGLING

[The question was as to the meaning of the word 'angling' in the Larceny Act 1861, s 25 (repealed).] 'Without myself expressing an opinion that a person cannot angle without a rod, I do not think they can angle without a hook. I doubt whether they can angle without a line, but whether they can angle or not without a line seems to me to be a more difficult question. My own opinion is that when a person sticks a short piece of stick in the ground, and at the other end of the stick is a weight, and then one or more hooks . . . are allowed to swim out from the stone, or string fastened to the stone, that is not angling.' *Barnard v Roberts* (1907) 96 LT 648 at 650, per Lord Alverstone CJ

'There is a real reason for the distinction drawn between the ordinary poacher and the man who, although he may be a poacher, is what we should commonly call an angler—that is, that he is a man who is using a rod, a line, and a hook, and the kind of tackle which a man using a rod and line and hook would commonly have.' Ibid at 650, per Darling J

'I think the hook and the line are the only necessities for angling; but I think there is all the distinction between angling where the human element comes in, where the tackle is not set once and for all, but moved from time to time, and what Isaac Walton calls "pike fishing with a ledger and a walking bait," where you use a ledger bait in the sense of a line bait.' Ibid at 650, per Phillimore J

[The Larceny Act 1861 was wholly repealed by the Theft Act 1968. See now Sch 1 to the 1968 Act, which deals with the offence of taking or destroying fish. Angling in the daytime (that is, in the period beginning one hour before sunrise and ending one hour after sunset) is not per se an offence; but angling in the daytime in water which is private property or in which there is any private right of fishery is an offence for which the angler is liable to a fine on the ·standard scale.]

ANIMAL *See also* CAPTIVE ANIMAL

In law the term 'animals' includes all creatures not belonging to the human race. . . . In law animals are divided into two classes, domestic and wild, and this classification affects the rights of property in them and also liability for their behaviour. . . . The term 'domestic animals' includes all those domestic or tame animals as by habit or training live in association with man. An animal which does not exist in a wild state anywhere in the world is in law a domestic animal. It is a question of law, not fact, whether an animal is within the class of domestic animals or wild animals. . . . The term 'wild' (ferae naturae) applied to animals includes not only those animals which are savage by nature but also those of a more mild or timid nature which cannot be classed as domestic or tame animals. (2 Halsbury's Laws (4th edn) paras 201, 202, 204)

The expression 'animal' means any domestic or captive animal. (Protection of Animals Act 1911, s 15)

'Animal' does not include invertebrates. (Performing Animals (Regulation) Act 1925, s 5)

'Animal' includes any description of vertebrate. (Pet Animals Act 1951, s 7)

'Animal' does not include bird or fish. (Food Act 1984, s 132(1))

In this section [which places on the driver of a motor vehicle the duty to stop where an accident occurs causing injury to an animal] 'animal' means any horse, cattle, ass, mule, sheep, pig, goat or dog. (Road Traffic Act 1972, s 25(3))

'Animal' means any mammal. (Animals (Cruel Poisons) Act 1962, s 3)

[The rules of the common law imposing a strict liability in tort for damage done by an animal on the ground that the animal is regarded as ferae naturae, or that its vicious or mischievous propensities are known or presumed to be known, were replaced the Animals Act 1971, ss 2–5. Those sections cover, respectively: liability for damage done by dangerous animals; liability for injury done by dogs to livestock; liability for damage and expenses due to trespassing livestock; and exceptions from liability.]

'Animal' includes any bird, fish or reptile. (Medicines Act 1968, s 132)

'Animal' does not include bird or fish. (Slaughterhouses Act 1974, s 34)

In this section and in Sch 1 to this Act the expression 'animal' includes:
(a) any kind of mammal, except man,
(b) any kind of four-footed beast which is not a mammal, and
(c) fish, reptiles, crustaceans and other cold-blooded creatures not falling within paragraph (a) or paragraph (b) above . . .
(Diseases of Animals Act 1975, s 1(4))

(1) In this Act, unless the context otherwise requires 'animals' means—
(a) cattle, sheep and goats, and
(b) all other ruminating animals and swine, subject to subsections (2) and (3) below.
(2) The Ministers may by order for all or any of the purposes of this Act extend the definition of 'animals' in subsection (1) above so that it shall for those or any of those purposes comprise—
(a) any kind of mammal except man; and
(b) any kind of four-footed beast which is not a mammal.
(3) [*Further empowers Ministers, by order, to extend the definition to fish, reptiles, crustaceans and other cold-blooded creatures*].
(Animal Health Act 1981, s 87)

'Animals' means animals of the classes Mammalia, Aves, Reptilia, Amphibia, Pisces and Insecta and any other multicellular organism that is not a plant or a fungus and 'wild animals' means animals not normally domesticated in Great Britain. (Zoo Licensing Act 1981, s 21(1))

'Animal' includes any bird or fish. (Agricultural Marketing Act 1983, s 8)

New Zealand 'The bye-law . . . prohibits the keeping in the borough of all animals . . . which are wild by nature. . . . It was contended . . . that the term "animals" as used in the bye-law ought to have its primary legal meaning, according to which it includes all beasts, birds, reptiles, fishes, and insects. . . . The general rule, however, is that in dealing with matters relating to the general public, statutes are presumed to use words in their popular sense . . . and the context supports the view that the word "animals" is not used in the bye-law in its primary legal meaning. If it be limited in this way the prohibition then would not extend to bees and fishes.' *Boyd v Onehunga Borough* [1916] NZLR 713 at 725, 726, per Sim J; also reported [1916] GLR 506 at 512

Dangerous species

A dangerous species is a species—
(a) which is not commonly domesticated in the British Islands; and
(b) whose fully grown animals normally have such characteristics that they are likely, unless restrained, to cause severe damage or that any damage they may cause is likely to be severe.
(Animals Act 1971, s 6(2))

Domestic animal

The expression 'domestic animal' means any horse, ass, mule, bull, sheep, pig, goat, dog, cat, or fowl, or any other animal of whatsoever kind or species, and whether a quadruped or not, which is tame or which has been or is being sufficiently tamed to serve some purpose for the use of man. (Protection of Animals Act 1911, s 15)

'The question . . . is whether these linnets [which were kept in captivity, and trained as decoy birds for bird-catching] come within the term "domestic animal". These words would include, I think, any pet bird, such as a parrot, canary, or linnet, and it seems to me that linnets kept as these were are clearly domestic animals.' *Colam v Pagett* (1883) 12 QBD 66 at 67, per Huddleston B

'These lions are not domestic animals within the meaning of the Acts [Cruelty to Animals Acts 1849, 1854 (repealed; see now Protection of Animals Act 1911)]. . . . You must at least show that the animal has been sufficiently tamed to serve some purpose for the use of man. The mere caging and keeping in captivity a wild animal is not enough to make it a domestic animal.' *Harper v Marcks* [1894] 2 QB 319 at 321, 322, per Cave J

'I agree with the argument . . . that animals, however wild by nature, may become domestic under some circumstances. I should think that leopards trained to hunt for their master, otters trained to catch fish, and elephants trained to assist in the capture of wild elephants, might be held to be domestic. . . . Domestic is not the same thing as domesticated, but I think that an animal ought to be regarded as a domestic animal which is of a kind ordinarily domesticated, and which is in fact itself domesticated.' Ibid at 323, per Wright J

'It was quite clearly established . . . in my view that camels do not exist anywhere in the world to-day as wild animals. There is no race of wild camels which could be captured and tamed like elephants. . . . Nowhere in the world are camels wild. In every country where they exist they are domestic animals used for carrying either people or loads on their backs, or for draught purposes.' *McQuaker v Goddard* [1940] 1 KB 687 at 694, 695, CA, per Scott LJ

See, generally, 2 Halsbury's Laws (4th edn) paras 201–203, 424–427.

Endangered species

For the purposes of this Act an individual of the family Hominidae (man) is not an animal. (Endangered Species (Import and Export) Act 1976, s 12(1))

Pedigree animal

'Pedigree animal' means an animal of any description which is by its breeding eligible for registration with a recognised club or society keeping a register of animals of that description. (Pet Animals Act 1951, s 7)

ANNATES

First fruits, primitiae, or annates were the first year's whole profits of the spiritual preferment according to a valuation determined in 1292. (14 Halsbury's Laws (4th edn) para 1223)

ANNEX

Canada   [A caveat recited that an owner was desirous of 'annexing' certain covenants and conditions in respect to the use of buildings.] 'I consider it relevant to consider the ordinary meaning of the word "annex". Black's Law Dictionary, 4th edn, at p 115, defines "annex" as: "Derived from the Latin *annectere*, meaning to tie or bind to. To attach, and often, specifically, to subjoin. . . . To add to; to unite. The word expresses the idea of joining a smaller or subordinate thing with another, larger, or of higher importance. . . . To make an integral part of something larger. "Webster's Dictionary includes in the definition of "annex" the phrases, "to add or affix, especially a smaller thing to a larger . . . that which is added . . . addition". It seems to me, concerning the use of the word "annexes" as mentioned above in the caveat, that the true construction of the document is that these conditions and/or covenants are "added to" or "affixed" to the lands themselves, and they are therefore not personal in nature.' *Seiffeddine v Governor & Company of Adventurers of*

England Trading into Hudsons Bay (1978) 8
Alta LR (2d) 253 at 257, Alta SC, per Hope J;
affd. 11 Alta LR (2d) 229, CA

ANNOYANCE   *See also* NUISANCE

' "Annoyance" is a wider term than nuisance,
and if you find a thing which reasonably
troubles the mind and pleasure, not of a fanciful person or of a skilled person who knows the
truth, but of the ordinary sensible English
inhabitant of a house—if you find there is anything which disturbs his reasonable peace of
mind, that seems to me to be an annoyance,
although it may not amount to physical detriment to comfort.' *Tod-Heatly v Benham* (1888)
40 Ch D 80 at 98, CA, per Bowen LJ

ANNUAL

' "Annual" must be taken to have, like interest
on money or an annuity, the quality of being
recurrent or being capable of recurrence.'
Moss' Empires Ltd v Inland Revenue Comrs
[1937] AC 785 at 795, per Lord Maugham

'The word annual must at least connote "in the
year" if it is to have any meaning at all, and that
it has this meaning was laid down in *Ryall v
Hoare* [[1923] 2 KB 447] and approved in *Martin v Lowry* [[1927] AC 312].' *Gold v Coast
Selection Trust Ltd v Humphrey (Inspector of
Taxes)* [1948] AC 459 at 474, per Lord Oaksey

'The word "annual" has not been found to
admit of any significant interpretation. To the
courts it means no more than "recurrent"—
see, eg *Moss' Empires Ltd v Inland Revenue
Comrs* [supra]—or even "capable of recurrence".' *Whitworth Park Coal Co Ltd v Inland
Revenue Comrs* [1959] 3 All ER 703 at 715,
HL, per Lord Radcliffe

ANNUAL MEETING   *See* MEETING

ANNUAL PAY   *See* PAY

ANNUAL PAYMENT

'It is admitted that there may be . . . an annual
payment payable as a personal debt by virtue
of a contract which is not an "annuity or annual
payment" within the meaning of s 40 [of the
Income Tax Act 1853 (repealed; see now
Income and Corporation Taxes Act 1970,
s 109(2)(a)]. If there is a sum of money owing

by a debtor to his creditor, and it is agreed
between them that the debt shall be paid by
annual instalments . . . the annual instalments
are not annual payments within the meaning of
the section; further . . . where the debt and the
obligation to pay the instalments are created by
the same instrument the same rule applies, and
the instalments are not annual payments within
s 40. It is obvious that there will be cases in
which it will be very difficult to distinguish
between an agreement to pay a debt by instalments, and an agreement for good consideration to make certain annual payments for a
fixed number of years. In the one case there is
an agreement for good consideration to pay a
fixed gross amount and to pay it by instalments;
in the other there is an agreement for good
consideration not to pay any fixed gross
amount, but to make a certain, or it may be an
uncertain, number of annual payments.' *Chadwick v Pearl Life Insurance Co* [1905] 2 KB 507
at 513, 514, per Walton J

'The first question is whether the payment [of
maintenance by order of the Court] is an
annual payment within Case III, 1(a), of Sch D
[of the Income Tax Act 1918 (repealed; see
supra]. I can see no reason why it is not. It is no
doubt payable weekly, but that fact does not
prevent it from being an annual payment if the
weekly payments may extend beyond a
year. . . . It was however argued that although
it might be an annual payment it was not taxable as profit against the appellant under Sch
D. No doubt the words profits and gains are not
the most suitable words to describe such a
payment, but it is clear that annuities and
annual payments are for some purposes profits
and gains within the meaning of the Schedule,
though probably, in ordinary language, those
words would not be used to describe them.
Unless therefore there is something in the
nature of this particular payment which leads
to an opposite conclusion it seems to me clearly
within the Schedule. It is a personal allowance
made by the husband to his wife under the
order of the Court. . . . The fact that it is inalienable does not seem to me to be important;
many inalienable payments are taxable, for
example, inalienable pensions, and I do not see
that the fact that it can be increased, reduced or
terminated by the Court makes it less a taxable
annual payment so long as it continues.' *Smith
v Smith* [1923] P 191 at 196–198, CA, per Lord
Sterndale MR

[The question was whether payments for five
years to the executors of a deceased partner for
the use of goodwill, etc, were 'annual

payments' for income tax or instalments of capital.] 'What they [the executors] have really done is this. When the partnership was dissolved the right to the use of the name, and the goodwill, and these established grade marks, whatever they may be, were all assets of the partnership and ought to have been valued. But these were left in the partnership. . . . You might say his [the late partner's] executors were obliged to sell them, but what really happened was that they released their right . . . to have these assets valued or included in the liquidation of the partnership. . . . I think it [the yearly payment in question] is a payment in the nature of income for the use of the firm name, the goodwill and rights, a payment concurrent with the enjoyment of the thing for which the payment is made, running on year after year and therefore prolonging the interest of the deceased partner in the income, although it is merely securing an income for a period of five years.' *Mackintosh v Inland Revenue Comrs* (1928) 14 Tax Cas 15 at 19, 20, per Rowlatt J

'An order was made by the learned magistrate . . . that the husband should pay to the chief clerk of the Court, on behalf of the wife, a sum of 30s a week and a further sum of 5s a week in respect of each of their three children, a total of 45s a week. The appellant duly paid the sums ordered to be paid until a date in July 1933, when a demand was made on him by the revenue authorities for payment of income tax on those payments. The demand was made on the ground that the payments were annual payments within the meaning of s 19(1) of the General Rules for all Schedules of the Income Tax Act 1918 [repealed; see now the Income and Corporation Taxes Act 1970, s 52(1)], and I am bound, on the authority of *Smith v Smith* [supra] to hold that these payments were annual payments within the rule.' *Clack v Clack* [1935] 2 KB 109 at 111, per Avory J

'The question is whether certain payments made by the appellants in fulfilment of an obligation undertaken by them in an agreement . . . were "annual payments charged with tax under Sch D" [within the meaning of the Income Tax Act 1918, Rules applicable to Schs A, B, C, D, and E, r 21 (repealed; see now the Income and Corporation Taxes Act 1970, ss 53, 108, 109]. . . . The fact that the payments were contingent and variable in amount does not affect the character of the payments as annual payments.' *Moss Empires Ltd v Inland Revenue Comrs* [1937] AC 785 at 790, 793, 794, per Lord Macmillan

[The appellant company entered into an agreement with another company that each year the profits and losses of the two companies should be added together and shared between them in an agreed proportion.] 'By r 21 of the All Schedules Rules [to the Income Tax Act 1918, Sch D, Case III (repealed; see now the Income and Corporation Taxes Act 1970, ss 53, 108, 109] it is provided that upon payment of "any interest of money, annuity, or other annual payment charged with tax under Sch D" which is not payable out of "profits or gains brought into charge" the person by whom such payment is made shall deduct tax thereout and deliver to the Commissioners of Inland Revenue an account of the payment and of the tax so deducted, and the Special Commissioners shall assess and charge the payment on that person. . . . It is not easy to define what is or what is not an "annual payment" within r 21, but it seems clear that such a payment must, like interest of money, or an annuity, have the "quality of recurrence" (*Moss Empires Ltd v Inland Revenue Comrs* [supra]). The payments to be made under cl 3 of the agreement have, no doubt, the quality of recurrence, since in every year during the currency of the agreement a payment must be made by one company or the other. The peculiarity of this case is that the company receiving the "annual payment" one year may have to make the "annual payment" in the next, and it seems to me doubtful whether such payments can be considered to be "annual payments" within the meaning of r 21. They plainly differ from the payments of "interest" or of an "annuity", where year by year the person making the payment and the person receiving the payment remain the same and never change places.' *Utol Ltd v Inland Revenue Comrs* [1944] 1 All ER 190 at 191, 192, per Macnaghten J

'Under Sch D, Case III [see now the Income and Corporation Taxes Act 1970, s 109(2)], the tax chargeable in respect of "annual profits or gains" is charged: ". . . in respect of profits of an uncertain value and of other income described in the rules applicable to this case". Sch D, Case III, r 1, provides: "the tax shall extend to (a) any . . . other annual payment . . . either as a charge on any property of the person paying the same by virtue of any deed or will or otherwise, or as a reservation thereout. . . ." In order to be "annual" within the meaning of the rule, the payment need not necessarily be recurrent year by year. To use the language of Lord Maugham [in *Moss Empires Ltd v Inland Reve-*

nue Comrs (supra)] it is sufficient if it has "the quality of being recurrent, or being capable of recurrence".' *Cunard's Trustees v Inland Revenue Comrs, McPheeters v Inland Revenue Comrs* [1946] 1 All ER 159 at 163, CA, per Lord Greene MR

ANNUAL PROFITS OR GAINS

'Are these commissions received as "annual profits or gains" under Case 6 [of Sch D in the Income Tax Act 1918 (repealed; see now the Income and Corporation Taxes Act 1970, ss 108, 125)]? Two kinds of emolument may be excluded from Case 6. First, anything in the nature of capital accretion is excluded as being outside the scope and meaning of these Acts confirmed by the usage of a century. For this reason, a casual profit made on an isolated purchase and sale, unless merged with similar transactions in the carrying on of a trade or business is not liable to tax. "Profits or gains" in Case 6 refer to the interest or fruit as opposed to the principal or root of the tree. The second class of cases to be excluded consists of gifts and receipts, whether the emolument is from a gift inter vivos, or by will, or from finding an article of value, or from winning a bet. All these cases must be ruled out because they are not profits or gains at all. Without giving an exhaustive definition, therefore, we may say that where an emolument accrues by virtue of service rendered whether by way of action or permission, such emoluments are included in "profits or gains".' *Ryall v Hoare, Ryall v Honeywill* [1923] 2 KB 447 at 453, 454, per Rowlatt J

'"Annual profit or gain" . . . to my mind must mean something which is of the nature of revenue or income, although I also think it is plain that it need not be repeated every year so as to be a continuous source of income. It may come in only as income or revenue in the one year, but still it has to be in the nature of annual profit or gain.' *Cooper v Stubbs* [1925] 2 KB 753 at 775, per Atkin LJ

'I held, rightly or wrongly, that that [a commission paid] was still an annual profit or gain—"annual" in the sense that it belonged to the year, although it was not recurring." *Lyons v Cowcher* (1926) 10 Tax Cas 438 at 441, per Rowlatt J

'The appellant . . . says that . . . these profits did not come within the description of "annual profits or gains" arising or accruing in respect of a trade—those words being quoted from the first paragraph under Sch D to the Income Tax Act 1918 [repealed; see now the Income and Corporation Taxes Act 1970, ss 108, 125]. He says they did not come within those words, because they were not recurrent profits or capable of recurrence from year to year. . . . There are, no doubt, passages in the Act in which the word "annual" or the word "yearly" has an implication of recurrence; but one must have regard to the context in which the words are found, and, having regard to the context, I do not think that there is any such implication in the words "annual profits or gains", as applying to the profits or gains arising in respect of a trade which are taxable under Sch D of the Act. It appears to me that in that context the words bear the construction put upon them by Rowlatt J in the case of *Ryall v Hoare*, [supra] where he said that the words meant "profits or gains in any one year or in any year as the succession of years comes round".' *Martin v Lowry, Martin v Inland Revenue Comrs* [1927] AC 312 at 315, per Lord Cave LC

'It is now settled that annual profits and gains taxable under Sch D may be satisfied by profits falling within the year of charge and accruing during a period of less than a year: see *Martin v Lowry* [supra] in which the opinion of Rowlatt J on this point in *Ryall v Hoare* [supra] was approved. In that case Rowlatt J said: "The word 'annual' here can only mean 'calculated in any one year', and 'annual profits or gains' mean 'profits or gains in any one year or in any year as the succession of years comes round'." While this is so, the isolated nature of a transaction, as opposed to a series of transactions of the same kind, will have a material bearing not only on the question as to whether it was a "trade, adventure or concern in the nature of trade", but also as to whether the profit arising therefrom was an accretion of capital or "profits or gains" within the meaning of the Income Tax Act, which connotes the idea of revenue or income.' *Jones v Leeming* [1930] AC 415 at 427, 428, 430, per Lord Thankerton

'"Annual" profits does not mean profits which are made year by year. It is satisfied by profits made in one year only.' *Scott v Ricketts* [1967] 2 All ER 1009 at 1011, CA, per Lord Denning MR

ANNUAL RENTAL

Of settled property

'Now s 13, sub-s (iv) of the Settled Land Act 1890 [repealed; see now Settled Land Act 1925, Sch III (xxv)], places a limit on the amount which may be expended in the rebuilding of the principal mansion house: the amount is not to exceed one-half of the "annual rental". This subsection would have strange results if the words "annual rental" are to be read only as including rent of land, and so excluding income derived from capital money invested. That, to my mind, would be a narrow and erroneous construction, as I cannot suppose that the Legislature intended that the amount to be applied in rebuilding under this subsection (iv) was to depend on the accidental circumstance whether the settled land, or a portion of it, was at the particular moment land or money. Bearing in mind the scope and intention and general provisions of these Acts, I think that the reasonable construction to be put on these words "annual rental" is, that the expression is intended to apply to the total income of all the settled property, land as well as capital money invested.' *Re De Teissier's Settled Estates, Re De Teissier's Trusts, De Teissier v De Teissier* [1893] 1 Ch 153 at 157, per Chitty J

'What is to be included in the amount of half the annual rental, the limit [under the Settled Land Act 1890, s 13 (repealed; see supra)] of the sum to be applied out of capital moneys in the settlement. I am of opinion that the annual rental meant does not include any allowance as a rental value of a mansion and park in the occupation of the tenant for life, nor does it include any sum in respect of a farm held by the tenant for life and farmed by himself; but that it would include the rent usually paid for a farm which happens to be unoccupied for the time, though usually let to a tenant.' *Re Walker's Settled Estate* [1894] 1 Ch 189 at 193, per North J

'By s 13, sub-s (iv) of the Settled Land Act 1890 [repealed; see supra], the rebuilding the principal mansion house on the settled land is included as one of the improvements authorised, but that is subject to this proviso: "that the sum to be applied under this subsection shall not exceed one-half of the annual rental of the settled land." . . . It seems to me that when the subsection speaks of "annual rental"—not gross rental or net rental, but simply annual rental—it means the sum of the rents paid by the several tenants with, of course, this modification, that if any part of the land is temporarily vacant then one is entitled, for the purpose of applying the subsection, to treat it as producing the rent which a tenant occupying it usually pays. I think, therefore, the mortgage interest, at all events ought not to be deducted before ascertaining the rental. I also think that there ought to be no deductions for tithes, land tax, drainage rates, or the rentcharge.' *Re Windham's Settled Estate* [1912] 2 Ch 75 at 80, 81, per Warrington J

'In ascertaining the annual rental of the settled land, property tax should not be deducted from it, because payment of the property tax is a payment *pro tanto* of the rent; the annual rental means the gross amount of the rents reserved as payable by the tenants.' *Re Fife's Settlement Trusts* [1922] 2 Ch 348 at 356, per Russell J

ANNUAL SALARY

'Where a person is paid £5 or £6 a week it is not possible to say that he is engaged at an annual salary, even though a free supply of electric light may be thrown in. . . . What is the salary? It is £5 or £6 a week, and . . . an annual salary is not fifty-two times a weekly salary. This is a weekly salary. They are two entirely different and distinct things. . . . You cannot say that a weekly salary paid fifty-two times a year, with one day over or two days over, is an annual salary. It is not.' *Naylor v Peacehaven Electric Light & Power Co Ltd* (1931) 47 TLR 535 at 537, per Rowlatt J

ANNUAL VALUE

'Annual value', in relation to land, means the rent at which the land might reasonably be expected to let from year to year, if the tenant undertook to pay all usual tenant's rates and taxes and the landlord undertook to bear the cost of repairs and insurance and the other expenses necessary to command that rent. (Landlord and Tenant (War Damage) Act 1939, s 24)

'The term "annual value of land" is not a term of art, but means in common parlance the rack rent or the value of the gross produce of the land minus all payments, expenses, interest, labour and charges on the land or on the tenant. This has been the mode in which it has been treated in legislation, and in the construction of Acts of Parliament.' *Re Elwes* (1858) 3 H & N 719 at 725, per Watson B

'The words "annual value", as they occur in the statutes which we have to construe [Parochial Assessments Act 1836, s 1 (repealed; see now General Rate Act 1967, s 19) and a private Act], signify annual net value, which I take to be the primary meaning of the words. I do not understand that the judgment of this House . . . goes beyond that, or decides that in every statute, no matter what is the context, these words must be read as meaning net value.' *Dobbs v Grand Junction Waterworks Co* (1883) 9 App Cas 49, per Lord Watson

ANNUAL VOLUNTARY CONTRIBUTIONS

[The London Library claimed to be entitled to exemption from rates under s 1 of the Scientific Societies Act 1843 (repealed by the Rating and Valuation Act 1961) as a society (inter alia) supported in part by 'annual voluntary contributions'.] 'Annual voluntary contributions are in our judgment voluntary contributions which the society may reasonably expect to receive year by year and on which it may reasonably rely wholly or in part for the provision of the necessary annual expenditure of the society.' *London Library v Cane (Valuation Officer)* [1959] 3 All ER 726 at 732, CA, per cur.

[The Royal College of Music was held to be entitled to exemption from rates under s 1 of the Scientific Societies Act 1843 (repealed; see supra), as a society supported wholly or in part by 'annual voluntary contributions'.] 'I turn to an examination of these three words and ask what are annual voluntary contributions. (*a*) *Annual*. Gifts qualify if from the point of view of the donee their recurrence year by year can be reasonably relied on, even though the donor be in every case different. In other words, whether a gift is annual does not depend on whether one donor only makes the gift, but on whether the donee annually receives such a regular flow of gifts as enables him to rely on them as a source of income. That was the opinion of this court in the *London Library* case [*London Library v Cane (Valuation Officer)* (supra)] with which I agree. (*b*) *Voluntary*. A contribution is voluntary if it be gratuitous. This is clearly the law as laid down by Lord Halsbury LC, in *Savoy Overseers v Art Union of London* [[1896] AC 296] and confirmed recently by Lord Radcliffe in *Institution of Mechanical Engineers v Cane* [[1960] 3 All

ER 715]. It is therefore idle to argue on this topic that a gift is not voluntary because it issues from a trust where the trustees are not free agents. Voluntary here is not the antithesis of compulsory, but is apt to exclude annual subscriptions even though made without compulsion such as those to the Zoo or a professional society, or the Art Union in Lord Halsbury's case, where the subscriber expects a return for his money, not indeed in cash but in prestige perhaps, or some other more material form. (*c*) *Contributions*. This comprises all gifts satisfying the first two conditions. Contributions are to be credited when the money or money's worth reaches the hands of the corporation or the hands of trustees for it.' *Cane (Valuation Officer) v Royal College of Music* [1916] 2 All ER 12 at 28, [1961] 2 QB 89 at 119, CA, per Harman LJ

ANNUITY   *See also* ANNUAL PAYMENT

An annuity is a certain sum of money payable yearly either as the grantor's personal obligation or out of property not consisting exclusively of land; it differs from a rentcharge in that a rentcharge issues out of land. (39 Halsbury's Laws (4th edn) para 1212)

'An annuity is a right to receive *de anno in annum* a certain sum; that may be given for life, or for a series of years; it may be given during any particular period, or in perpetuity; and there is also this singularity about annuities that although payable out of the personal assets, they are capable of being given, for the purposes of devolution, as real estate. They may be given to a man and his heirs and may go to the heir as real estate—so an annuity may be given to a man and the heirs of his body; that does not, it is true, constitute an estate tail; but that is by reason of the Statute de Donis, which contains only the word *tenements*, and an annuity, though a *hereditament*, is not a *tenement*.' *Bignold v Giles* (1859) 4 Drew 343 at 346, 347, per Kindersley V-C

'An annuity means generally the purchase of an income, and usually involves a change of capital into income, payable annually over a number of years.' *Scoble v Secretary of State in Council for India* [1903] 1 KB 494 at 504, CA, per Mathew LJ; affirmed sub nom *Secretary of State in Council of India v Scoble* [1903] AC 299

'The fine distinction between an annuity properly so called for tax purposes and an annual payment which is in truth a capital payment . . . has repeatedly been emphasised, and no sure, or simple test has or can be laid down for the solution of this problem. The only principle that I can deduce from the cases is that the Court must have regard to the true nature of the transaction from which the annual payment arises and ascertain whether or not it is the purchase of an annual income in return for the surrender of capital. . . . In the case of a whole life annuity the sum paid is not in truth a return of capital plus interest. The annual payment is calculated on the grantee's expectation of life. He is to receive during his life an annual sum considerably in excess of the normal interest that he would obtain on an investment, while the grantor takes the risk of the life being prolonged beyond a period which will yield a profit to him on the transaction. The grantee retains no interest in the capital when once it has been paid; it becomes the property of the grantor.' *Sothern-Smith v Clancy* [1941] 1 KB 276 at 293, CA, per Goddard LJ

'An "annuity" means an annual sum, and the period for which this annual sum has to be paid must be gathered, in the light of the relevant facts, from the language of the instrument conferring it. Where no period is fixed in the instrument itself during which the annual sum has to be paid, the court would without question hold that the period of such payment was limited to the life-time of the annuitant in all cases where the only alternative is a payment in perpetuity.' *Reid v Coggans (or Reid)* [1944] AC 91 at 94, HL, per Lord Simon LC

Australia ' "Annuity" is a common term, which was defined very long ago as "a yearly payment of a sum certain granted to another in fee for life or years charging the person of the grantor only", but it does not include annual instalments of a debt, or of the purchase price of property; and if one consults the more modern Oxford Dictionary he will find it defined as the grant of an annual sum for years or for life or in perpetuity chargeable on the grantor and his heirs, but not on land.' *Watkins v Deputy Comr of Taxation* (1947) 49 WALR 63 at 67, per Dwyer CJ

Canada 'An annuity is a fixed sum payable periodically and it is distinct from a gift of income, which is not a fixed or sum certain but produce or profits from property, which may be expected to vary in amount.' *Re Wilson's Will* (1954) 11 WWR(NS) 497 at 504, Man CA, per Coyne JA

South Africa 'The main characteristics of an annuity are: (1) that it is an annual payment (this would probably not be defeated if it were divided into instalments); (2) that it is repetitive—payable from year to year for, at any rate, some period; (3) that it is chargeable against some person.' *Income Tax Case No 558* 1946 1 PH T 27

See, generally, 23 Halsbury's Laws (4th edn) para 529, 531

Life annuity

For the purposes of this section, 'life annuity' means an annuity payable for a term ending with (or at a time ascertainable only by reference to) the end of a human life, whether or not there is provision for the annuity to end during the life on the expiration of a fixed term or on the happening of any event or otherwise, or to continue after the end of the life in particular circumstances. (Income and Corporation Taxes Act 1970, s 230(6))

Purchased life annuity

In this section 'purchased life annuity' means a life annuity granted for consideration in money or money's worth in the ordinary course of a business of granting annuities on human life. (Finance Act 1956, s 38(6); see also the Income and Corporation Taxes Act 1970, s 230(6))

ANONYMOUS WORK

Copyrights

United States An 'anonymous work' is a work on the copies or phonorecords of which no natural person is identified as author. (Copyright Act of 1976, s 101)

ANSWER

'We are to construe the language of an Act of Parliament in that sense which will best effectuate the obvious intention of the Legislature. Construing the words of [Corrupt Practices Prevention Act 1863, s 7 (repealed; see now Representation of the People Act 1983, s 141(3)), which gives a certificate of indemnity to a witness who shall 'answer' questions] . . . in that sense, I cannot entertain the slightest doubt that, wherever a reference is made to an answer to a question, the Legislature meant a true answer, an honest bona fide answer.' *R v Hulme* (1870) LR 5 QB 377 at 388, per Lush J

ANSWERABLE

'In my humble opinion the word "answerable" is merely an equivalent for "liable"; and I observe that their Lordships in the Court of Appeal deal with the expression as having that meaning.' *River Wear Comrs v Adamson* (1877) 2 App Cas 743 at 775, per Lord Gordon

'When the Act [now the Pilotage Act 1983, s 35] says that the owner shall be answerable for . . . faulty navigation, it has to be determined whether "answerable" means more than that the damage, whether done to or done by his ship, is his responsibility or is confined to damage done by the ship. Either view no doubt is theoretically possible but I do not think that read in its context the use of the word "answerable" would naturally convey the suggestion that, though the shipowner is liable for any damage done by the pilot's fault, yet he can recover his own damage in full. "Answerable", as I think, simply means responsible, and a shipowner who through a compulsory pilot is responsible for faulty navigation is responsible for damage to his own ship as well as for injury to the property of another.' *Workington Harbour & Dock Board v SS Towerfield* [1951] AC 112 at 133, 134, HL, per Lord Porter

ANTARCTICA

'Antarctica' means the area south of the sixtieth parallel of south latitude, excluding any part of the high seas but including all ice shelves south of that parallel. (Antarctic Treaty Act 1967, s 10)

ANTE-NUPTIAL   *See also* SETTLEMENT

'Mr Middleton's argument comes to this. He says that any settlement inter vivos made upon either of two people who at any subsequent date marry is a settlement which the Court can deal with under the section [s 192 of the Supreme Court of Judicature (Consolidation) Act 1925 (repealed; see now Matrimonial Causes Act 1973, s 24)], because it is ante-nuptial. . . . In my view that cannot be. This section is dealing with ante-nuptial . . . settlements, and it refers to marriage. It refers to it because what it is dealing with is what we commonly know as a marriage settlement, that is, a settlement made in contemplation of, or because of, marriage, and with reference to the interests of married people or their children.' *Hargreaves v Hargreaves* [1926] P 42 at 44, 45, per Hill J

'To bring the section [s 192 of the Supreme Court of Judicature (Consolidation) Act 1925 (repealed; see supra)] into operation there must be a "marriage" which is the subject of the decree of divorce, and it is in contemplation of this marriage and because of this marriage that the settlement must be made. I do not think the Legislature intended a spouse of an existing marriage to contemplate a second marriage so as to be able to execute a settlement which is "ante-nuptial" as regards such contemplated marriage although at the time being he or she is married and, therefore, incapable of entering into a second marriage.' *Burnett v Burnett* [1936] P 1 at 15, 16, per Bucknill J

ANTECEDENT DEBT OR LIABILITY

[The Bills of Exchange Act 1882, s 27(1), provides that valuable consideration for a bill may be constituted by . . . (b) an 'antecedent debt or liability']. 'I think for myself that the proper construction of the words in (b) "An antecedent debt or liability" is that they refer to an antecedent debt or liability of the promisor or drawer of the bill and are intended to get over what would otherwise have been prima facie the result that at common law the giving of a cheque for an amount for which you are already indebted imports no consideration, since the obligation is past and has been already incurred.' *Oliver v Davis* [1949] 2 KB 727 at 735, CA, per Evershed MR

ANTECEDENTS   *See also* CHARACTER

Australia [The Offenders Probation & Parole Act 1965–1986 (WA), s 37(2)(a) (as amended) provides that the court is not required to fix a minimum term if it considers that the nature of the offence and the 'antecedents' of the convicted person render the fixing of a minimum term inappropriate.] 'The word "antecedents" is as wide as can be conceived [*R v Vallett* [1951] 1 All ER 231 at 232, per Lord Goddard CJ]. As used in s 37(2)(a) of the Act, it "refers primarily to the offender's previous history and past record" [*Cobiac v Liddy* (1969) 43 ALJR 257 at 264].' *Garlett v R* [1975] WAR 129 at 131, per Burt J

ANTICIPATE

'The liking which many persons appear to have for the use of words having twice as many syllables as the more natural and proper word to use has, in fairly recent times, undoubtedly led to the use of the word "anticipate" when the correct word is "expect". It is known to all of us that in ordinary conversation the word "anticipate" is used as meaning "expect".' *Jarman v Lambert and Cooke (Contractors) Ltd* [1951] 2 KB 937 at 942, CA, per Evershed MR

ANTICIPATED EARNINGS

'It is necessary to determine exactly what was the subject-matter insured and valued by the policy [of marine insurance]. The relevant words are "Anticipated earnings and/or interest". "Anticipated" must, of course, mean anticipated by someone and that someone can only be the assured. The earnings in this case must mean earning by the ships insured. Therefore it is clear and is not open to argument that what is being insured is the anticipated earnings by these ships during the respective periods of their charters. As between an assured who holds a number of ships on charter and underwriters those words mean the earnings which the assured expects to make out of the ships during the rest of the charter periods. "Earnings" means, I think, the difference between the freight received and the freight to be paid by the assured.' *Continental Grain Co Inc v Twitchell* [1945] 1 All ER 357 at 360, 361, per Atkinson J; affd, [1945] 1 All ER 575 n, CA

Anticipated freight

'The expression "anticipated freight" is a new expression which is brought into this policy. . . . The parties are saying, I think, by the policy: "I, the shipper, have a profit-earning ship, a ship with which I can earn profit, and I want to insure that, if this ship is seized during the time the policy is current and effective, I shall recover a certain sum which is anticipated"—"anticipated freight" I think it means—"because it is anticipated that I shall be able to earn at least that sum, if not more, during the period".' *Papadimitriou v Henderson* (1939) 55 TLR 1035 at 1036, 1037, per Goddard LJ

Anticipatory breach

'The doctrine of anticipatory breach is but a species of the genus repudiation and applies only to fundamental breach. If one party to a contract states expressly or by implication to the other party in advance that he will not be able to perform a particular primary obligation on his part under the contract when the time for performance arrives, the question whether the other party may elect to treat the statement as a repudiation depends on whether the threatened non-performance would have the effect of depriving that other party of substantially the whole benefit which it was the intention of the parties that he should obtain from the primary obligations of the parties under the contract then remaining unperformed. If it would not have that effect there is no repudiation, and the other party cannot elect to put an end to such primary obligations remaining to be performed. The non-performance threatened must itself satisfy the criteria of a fundamental breach.' *Afovos Shipping Co SA v Pagnan* [1983] 1 All ER 499 at 455, HL, per Lord Diplock

ANTIQUE

[Justices dismissed two informations for having in possession firearms without the holding of a firearm certificate, on the ground that the weapons in question were 'antique' firearms within the Firearms Act 1968, s 58(2)] 'I find it impossible to say that the justices adopted a wrong approach, unless it can be said that an antique must be over 100 years old. I do not think it is possible to lay down any such rule. It must vary depending on the article. Primarily one would think that an antique is something that has peculiar value because of its age, in addition to its other attributes. But to lay down what that age should be I think is quite impossible.' *Richards v Curwen* [1977] 3 All ER 426 at 430, per Wien J

ANY

'"Any" is a word of very wide meaning, and prima facie the use of it excludes limitation.' *Clarke-Jervoise v Scutt* [1920] 1 Ch 382 at 387, 388, per Eve J

Australia '"Any" is a word which ordinarily excludes limitation or qualification and which should be given as wide a construction as possible. "Any goods" therefore includes all goods except where this wide construction is limited by the subject matter and context of a particular statute.' *Victorian Chamber of Manufacturers v Commonwealth* (1943) 67 CLR 335 at 346, per Williams J

South Africa 'In its natural and ordinary sense, "any"—unless restricted by the context—is an indefinite term which includes all of the things to which it relates. A qualification applied to "any" of a certain class must necessarily affect each and all of the class.' *Hayne & Co v Kaffrarian Steam Mill Co Ltd* 1914 AD 37 per Innes JA

'Any' not limited to one

'The demise is of a farm to the plaintiff, with the right to sport over it, and also over other lands of the defendant, in common with the defendant, his heirs and assigns, and any friend of his or them. This means that he may grant permission, not to any one, but to friends of his . . . It would have been easy, if it had been intended, to limit the right to a single friend at a time. . . . The words used would be commonly understood to mean a plurality of friends.' *Gardiner v Colyer* (1864) 10 LT 715 at 715, per Cockburn CJ

Any person

'The words "any person" are perfectly general, and unless restricted in some way must include an unascertained or an unborn person.' *Re Turner's Will Trusts, Bridgman v Turner* [1959] 2 All ER 689 at 692, per Danckwerts J

'Counsel for the insurers argues that "any person" means any person of the class required to be covered by the Act [Road Traffic Act 1930, s 36(2) (repealed; see now the Road Traffic Act 1972, s 154)]. Why should the court give such a limited construction to the meaning of the words "any person"? In my view, such a construction involves writing words into the statute that are not there. If the legislature had intended the payment mentioned in s 36(2) [a payment under a motor insurance policy] to be confined to persons of the class required to be covered by the Act, it could have expressed that intention in plain language. Indeed, where the legislature does intend to confine the operation of the Act to such liability as is required to be covered by the Act, it expresses that intention clearly. . . . In my judgment, the words "where any payment is made . . . by an unauthorised insurer under . . . a policy issued under this Part of this Act in respect of . . . bodily injury to any person" are as wide as they can be and I can see no reason for cutting down their meaning.' *Barnett Group Hospital Management Committee v Eagle Star Insurance Co Ltd* [1959] 3 All ER 210 at 213, per Salmon J

APOLOGY

[The defendant pleaded to an action for libel that he had subsequently inserted in the newspaper concerned a full 'apology'. The apology was inserted in small type amongst the notices to correspondents.] 'An apology means the insertion of something which may operate as an apology. Inserting an expression of regret in small type, suitable only to a notice to correspondents, amounts to this, that the defendant did not insert an apology.' *Lafone v Smith* (1858) 3 H & N 735 at 736, 737, per Pollock CB

'I am of the same opinion. Inserting an apology means effectually inserting it; not so that people would not be likely to see it; but in such a manner as to counteract as far as possible the mischief done by the libel.' Ibid at 737, per Bramwell B

South Africa 'Apology [for a published defamatory statement] should not only contain an unreserved withdrawal of all imputations made, but should also contain an expression of regret that they were ever made. A mere retraction cannot be called a full and free apology.' *Ward Jackson v Cape Times Ltd* 1910 WLD 257 at 263 per Curlewis J

APOTHECARY

An apothecary was formerly a person who carried on the business which is now and has been since about the end of the eighteenth century carried on by pharmacists, that is to say, the preparation and sale of drugs for medicinal purposes and the compounding and dispensing of medicines. Gradually the apothecary assumed the functions of the physician, and the right of apothecaries to attend patients and to diagnose and treat their diseases was recognised by the law, although the dispensing and compounding of medicines according to the prescriptions of others was and continued to be regarded as a most important branch of the duty of an apothecary.

At the time when the Apothecaries Act 1815 was passed, the apothecary occupied an intermediate position between the doctor and the chemist. In modern times it may be said with sufficient accuracy for all practical purposes that apothecaries as a class of practitioner to be distinguished from registered medical practitioners on the one hand and from pharmacists on the other hand have ceased to exist. In practice apothecaries do not seek to perform the functions of pharmacists, and qualification as an apothecary is regarded as one of the methods of becoming a registered medical practitioner. As a result of this change in the status and functions of the apothecary many of the provisions of the law relating to apothecaries have become or are becoming obsolete. (30 Halsbury's Laws (4th edn) paras 609, 610)

'An apothecary was one who, from having been in earlier times a mere vendor of drugs and compounder "in tatter'd weeds, with overwhelming brows culling of simples", had become a person who applied himself to the cure of diseases and was entitled to prescribe, prepare and sell drugs for that purpose and on the prescription of others.' *Wedick v Osmond & Son* [1935] IR 820 at 845, per Hanna J

Australia 'The word "apothecary" is a survival but the apothecary was authorised by law to prescribe for the sick and treat them with the drugs and medicaments he compounded or supplied.' *Unger v Mason* (1947) 74 CLR 557 at 570, per Dixon J

APPARATUS

'Apparatus' includes pipes plant apparatus and fittings of whatever description. (London County Council (General Powers) Act 1949, s 4)

'Apparatus' includes any structure constructed for the lodging therein of apparatus. (Public Utilities Street Works Act 1950, s 39)

'Apparatus' means sewers, drains, culverts, watercourses, mains, pipes, valves, tubes, cables, wires, transformers, and other apparatus laid down or used for or in connection with the carrying, conveying or supplying to any premises of a supply of water, water for hydraulic power, gas or electricity, and standards and brackets carrying street lamps. (Housing Act 1985, s 296(4)(b))

APPARENT

'The Statute of Wills [1837] gives no effect to obliterations, except so far as the original words shall not be apparent. And this has been decided to mean "apparent on an inspection of the instrument", not "apparent by extrinsic evidence".' *In the Goods of McCabe* (1873) LR 3 P & D 94 at 96, per Hannen P

'I think that the word "apparent" in the 21st section [of the Wills Act 1837] means apparent on the face of the instrument in the condition in which it was left by the testator, and that if he has had recourse to extraordinary means to obliterate what he had written, then this Court is not bound to take any steps to undo what he had done.' *In the Goods of Horsford* (1874) LR 3 P & D 221 at 216, per Hannen P

'Words beneath obliterations, erasures or alterations are "apparent" within the meaning of the Wills Act, if experts, using magnifying glasses when necessary, can decipher them and satisfy the Court that they have done so.' *Ffinch v Combe* [1894] P 191 at 201, per Jeune P

[Where a will or codicil has been altered after the execution thereof and the words or effect of the will before such alteration can only be ascertained by such scientific means as the photographing of the document by the use of infra-red rays such words or effect are not 'apparent' within the Wills Act 1837, s 21.] 'If the words of the document can be read by looking at the document itself, then I think that they are apparent within the meaning of the section, however elaborate may be the devices used to assist the eye and however skilled the eye which is being used; but if they can only be read by creating a new document, as in this case by producing a photograph of the original writing on the codicil, then I cannot find that the words are apparent. They may be discoverable; in this case they have been proved to be so; but that is not the word used in the section.' *Re Itter, Dedman v Godfrey* [1950] P 130 at 132, per Ormerod J

See, generally, 50 Halsbury's Laws (4th edn) para 273.

Apparent easement

'Two propositions may be stated as what I may call the general rules governing cases of this kind. The first of these rules is that on the grant by the owner of a tenement of part of that tenement as it is then used and enjoyed, there will pass to the grantee all those continuous and apparent easements (by which, of course, I mean *quasi* easements), or, in other words, all those easements which are necessary to the reasonable enjoyment of the property granted, and which have been and are at the time of the grant used by the owners of the entirety for the benefit of the part granted. The second proposition is that, if the grantor intends to reserve any right over the tenement granted, it is his duty to reserve it expressly in the grant.' *Wheeldon v Burrows* (1879) 12 Ch D 31 at 49, 50, CA, per Thesiger LJ

Apparent good order and condition

'It has been decided by Channell J in *Compañia Naviera Vasconzada v Churchill & Sim* [[1906] 1 KB 237], and affirmed by the Court of Appeal in *Brandt v Liverpool, Brazil & River Plate Steam Navigation Co Ltd* [[1924] 1 KB 575, CA], that the statement as to "apparent good order and condition" estops (as against the person taking the bill of lading for value or presenting it to get delivery of the goods) the shipowner from proving that the goods were not in apparent good order and condition when shipped and therefore from alleging that there were at shipment external defects in them which were apparent to reasonable inspection. . . . He [the shipowner] is to say what is "apparent", that is, visible by reasonable inspection to himself and his servants, and on the faith of that statement other people are to act and if it is wrong, act to the prejudice. . . . Apparent good order and condition was defined by Sir R Phillimore in *The Peter der Grosse* [(1875) 1 PD 414] as meaning that "apparently, and so far as met the eye, and externally, they were placed in good order on board this ship". . . . I cannot think that a shipowner who receives, say, a wooden case broken open at one corner or side can describe it as "in apparent good order and condition" and afterwards prove the opposite. And if the insufficiency of the packing is obvious, again I think it cannot be described as in "apparent good order and condition".' *Silver v Ocean Steamship Co Ltd* [1930] 1 KB 416 at 425–427, CA, per Scrutton LJ

'I doubt very much whether the statement "shipped in apparent good order and condition" has any reference to original defects of quality or type. The words seem to me to refer rather to acquired damage or defect in the goods rather than to original defects of quality or type. . . . I am inclined to think that the words are confined to deterioration or damage which has occurred to the goods of the quality and type delivered.' Ibid at 433, per Greer LJ

Apparent member of firm

[The Partnership Act 1890, s 36, provides that where a person deals with a firm after a change in its constitution he is entitled to treat all 'apparent' members of the old firm as still being members of the firm until he has notice of the change.] 'The whole point depends, in my view, upon what is the meaning in s 36, sub-s (1) of "apparent members"—Apparent to whom? Does it mean apparent to the whole world, or notorious, or does it mean apparent to the particular person with which the section is concerned? . . . In my reading of that subsection, "apparent members" means persons who are apparently members to the person who is dealing with the firm, and they may be apparent either by the fact that the customer has had dealings with them before, or because of the use of their names on the notepaper, or from some sign outside the door, or because the customer has had some indirect information about them.' *Tower Cabinet Co Ltd v Ingram* [1949] 2 KB 397 at 403, per Lynskey J

APPARENT POSSESSION *See* POSSESSION

APPARENTLY

New Zealand 'A dictionary definition of "apparently" is "(i) as judged by appearance; without passing on its reality; as far as can be told; seemingly: (ii) as clearly evident to the senses; clearly; plainly". It involves a direct appeal to the senses.' *Eccles v Richardson* [1916] NZLR 1090 at 1093, 1094, per Denniston J; also reported [1916] GLR 704 at 706

APPEAL

In this Act, unless the context otherwise requires . . . 'appeal', in the context of appeals to the civil division of the Court of Appeal, includes (a) an application for a new trial, and (b) an application to set aside a verdict, finding or judgment in any cause or matter in the High Court which has been tried, or in which any issue has been tried, by a jury. (Supreme Court Act 1981, s 151(1))

Australia 'The word "appeal" may be used in two connections. It may refer to an appeal from one judicial tribunal to another; such an appeal may be an appeal *stricto sensu* or an appeal by way of re-hearing, in which latter case the jurisdiction exercised by the appellate tribunal is in part original; or the word may refer to an appeal from an executive authority to some other executive authority or to a Court. If such an appeal is to a Court, the jurisdiction which it exercises is not appellate but original.' *Ex p Australian Sporting Club Ltd, Re Dash* (1947) 47 SR (NSW) 283 at 283, per Jordan CJ

South Africa 'An appeal, applicable to courts of law, means a complaint to, and a judicial examination by, a higher court of a decision of an inferior court. The higher court then approves, corrects or sets aside the judgment of the inferior court.' *Sita v Olivier* 1967 (2) SA 442 (A) at 447–448

APPEAR

Australia 'The word "appear" in its ordinary use in the English language means "to show oneself; to come forth into view", and obviously, in the common use of the word a person cannot "show" himself unless he is there present in person. But in legal proceedings "appearance" has a more special meaning. It may be no more than the mere filing of a document in court, and this amounts to an appearance for certain purposes. So also in the conduct of proceedings in court an appearance may be made either by the party appearing in person or appearing by counsel or solicitor. If counsel appears in court for a party then that party is taken to have appeared in the proceedings. *R v Gobert* [1958] SR (NSW) 114 at 116, 117, per Street CJ

APPERTAINING *See also* BELONGING TO

'The question in this case turns on the meaning of the words "appertaining" and "belonging". The messuage is conveyed, "together with all ways, roads, rights of road, paths and passages to the said hereby demised premises, or any part thereof, belonging or in anywise appertaining". The word "belonging", and the word "appertaining", I consider to be, as here used, synonymous.' *Barlow v Rhodes* (1833) 1 Cr & M 439 at 447, per Lord Lyndhurst CB

APPLICANT

For patents

United States Unless the contrary is indicated, the word 'applicant' when used in these sections refers to the inventor or joint inventors who are applying for a patent, or to the person mentioned in [37 CFR] §§ 1.42, 1.43, or § 1.47 who is applying for a patent in place of the inventor. (Title 37, Code of Federal Regulations s 1.41(b))

For trademark or tradename

United States The [term] 'applicant' . . . embrace[s] the legal representatives, predecessors, successors and assigns of such applicant or registrant. (Lanham Act 1946, s 45)

APPLICATION

[The Patents and Designs Act 1907, s 8A(2) (repealed; see now the Patents Act 1977, s 20) provided that if an 'application' was not in order within the allowable period, it should become void]. 'I agree that there are certain sections of the Acts in which the words "the application" appear to be used as referring to the application form. For example, I think the application form is referred to in s 1(3) of the Acts, which provides that "the application" must contain a certain declaration; again, when in s 3(2) it is provided that the Comptroller may require that "the application", specification, or drawings be "amended", it seems to me that the phrase "the application" refers to the piece of paper, the application form. No doubt instances could be multiplied where the words "the application" appear to refer to the form and not to the proceeding; but, in my view, in s 8A, sub-s 2 of the Act, what is referred to is not a piece of paper, but a legal proceeding.' *Re Kempe's Application* (1942) 59 RPC 72, per Morton J. Cf also the Patents Act 1977, ss 14–16.

APPLY

Australia [The Stamp Duties Act 1920-1986 (NSW) s 102(2)(b) states, inter alia, that references in the Act to gifts for the relief of poverty or the promotion of education include only gifts that have to be 'applied' in New South Wales.] 'The plain words . . . require that "gifts for the promotion of education be gifts that *have* to be applied in New South Wales". The emphasis is mine. The meaning which I consider should be given to the word "applied" in the paragraph is "appropriated", "put to use" or "disposed of": Shorter Oxford Dictionary, 3rd Ed.' *Flynn v Stamp Duties Comr* [1975] 1 NSWLR 208 at 210-211, per Sheppard J

To own use

Australia [The Sales Tax Assessment Act 1930-1986 (Cth), s 3 imposes tax in respect of goods supplied to a taxpayer who has 'applied'

those goods to his own use.] 'It may not be correct to say that all advertising material that is distributed is, by being distributed, brought within the description of goods applied by the distributor to his own use. But I think . . . that if free samples of goods be distributed in conjunction with a business carried on by their owner, distributed that is for his business purposes, they can be said to be applied by him to his own use. That is the use to which he puts them, the manner of use for which they were acquired by him. The fact that they would ultimately be used by somebody else is, as I see it, not a matter of critical importance. It cannot be said that a thing is not applied by a person to his own use because the use to which he puts it is to make it available to be used, according to its nature, by somebody else. A thing made available to be used by the owners, officers, servants or subcontractors might well be said to be thereby applied by him to his own use. Sometimes it must be so too if it be made available to be used by other persons such as customers for example when containers, paper bags, cardboard boxes are provided for the carrying away of goods.' *Deputy Taxation Comr v Taubmans (NSW) Pty Ltd* [1966] ALR 849 at 851, per Windeyer J

In Trade Descriptions Act

(1) A person applies a trade description to goods if he—
   (a) affixes or annexes it to or in any manner marks it on or incorporates it with—
      (i) the goods themselves, or
      (ii) anything in, on or with which the goods are supplied; or
   (b) places the goods in, on or with anything which the trade description has been affixed or annexed to, marked on or incorporated with, or places any such thing with the goods; or
   (c) uses the trade description in any manner likely to be taken as referring to the goods.
(2) An oral statement may amount to the use of a trade description.
(3) Where goods are supplied in pursuance of a request in which a trade description is used and the circumstances are such as to make it reasonable to infer that the goods are supplied as goods corresponding to that trade description, the person supplying the goods shall be deemed to have applied that trade description to the goods.
(Trade Descriptions Act 1968, s 4)

'Then the definition of the term "apply" in s 5 [Merchandise Marks Act 1887, repealed; see now Trade Descriptions Act 1968 (supra)] seems to suggest that it is not to be confined to a physical application for it provides that a person shall be deemed to apply a trade description to goods who (inter alia) "uses" it "in any manner calculated to lead to the belief that the goods in connection with which it is used are described by that trade description". No doubt the description must be used in connection with goods, but I think we should be cutting down the intention of the Act if we were to hold that the delivery of an invoice or other description of the goods, at the time of, or immediately after, the delivery of the goods themselves, was not a use in connection with the goods within the meaning of the section.' *Budd v Lucas* [1891] 1 QB 408 at 412, DC, per Pollock B

[The application of a false trade description need not be in physical relation to the goods for an offence to be committed.]

In settlement

Australia [A testator directed his trustee to pay and 'apply' the interest or income to or for the maintenance, education and benefit of a daughter during minority, then to pay her such income for life with a gift over of the capital on her death.] 'His intention was to make an absolute gift to the appellant throughout her life of the whole of the income. . . . During her minority that income was to be applied for her benefit. . . . The word "applied" does not import a power of selection; it simply means "devoted to" or "employed for the special purpose of". And the words maintenance, education and benefit are equivalent to "for the benefit of" (*Williams v Papworth* [[1900] AC 563 at 567, PC]). . . . There is no indication in the will that any unapplied part of the income should be accessory to the capital. . . . What is given is not so much of the interest and income as shall be necessary for maintenance, but the whole interest and income. The income became, as it fell due, the absolute property of the appellant.' *Davies v Perpetual Trustees Executors & Agency Co of Tasmania Ltd* (1935) 52 CLR 604 at 607, 608, per cur.

APPOINT

[A testatrix who was entitled to a special power of appointment gave legacies to persons who were not objects of the power. The will then proceeded: 'I give bequeath and appoint all the residue of my estate and effects whatsoever and wheresoever unto my husband absolutely.'] 'In the present case, the circumstances relied on as shewing an intention not to exercise the power are, first, that not one of the legatees is an object of the power; and, secondly, that all that is given to the husband is the residue of the testatrix's estate and effects. Still she does at the commencement of the will indicate an intention to exercise powers vested in her as well as dispose of her own estate, and by the use of the word "appoint" in addition to the words "give" and "bequeath", she seems to me to shew that this intention extended to what she describes as the residue of her estate and effects. On the whole . . . I am of opinion that the power has been exercised.' *Re Milner, Bray v Milner* [1899] 1 Ch 563 at 565, 566, per Stirling J

'The evidence shows that the testatrix had this one limited power and no other power at all. She uses the words "I appoint, devise, and bequeath." Now, the word "appoint" is a word of art, prima facie having reference to powers only. I do not of course say that if there were no other words of disposition the word "appoint" in itself would not pass all the testatrix's property. But here I have the three words, "appoint, devise, and bequeath," and the word "appoint" in this collocation necessarily refers to a power. . . . In the present case . . . "devise and bequeath" would be sufficient in themselves to execute a general power; so that I am only following the general rule of giving effect so far as possible to every word used by the testator if I say that the word "appoint" must necessarily refer to a special power.' *Re Mayhew, Spencer v Cutbush* [1901] 1 Ch 677 at 679, 680, per Farwell J

[A testator by his will devised his real estate and bequeathed all his personal estate and by virtue of the provisions contained in his marriage settlement he 'appointed' the funds subject to the trusts thereof unto his trustees upon certain trusts.] 'The word "appoint" is not here used in any narrow technical and restricted sense. . . . The result to my mind seems to be the same as if the testator had said in simple language "my mind and will is that all my real and personal property, including the fund subject to the trusts of my marriage settlement, which I can dispose of shall be held by my trustees upon trust after payment of my just debts".' *Re Griffiths' Settlement, Griffiths v Waghorne* [1911] 1 Ch 246 at 254, per Joyce J

[Failure in a will to use the word 'appoint' does not necessarily imply that a special power of appointment has not been exercised.] 'As to the omission of the word "appoint", this omission is undoubtedly an element which has to be taken into account when weighing up the considerations as a whole, but I do not think it is of any considerable importance in itself. It is not as though the words "I give" or "I bequeath" are altogether inapt or unsuitable when used in relation to property which is subject to a special power. All that can be said is that the words "I appoint" are more apt and more suitable and that the use of them would in some cases be decisive of an intention to exercise a power.' *Re Welford's Will Trusts, Davidson v Davidson* [1946] 1 All ER 23 at 26, per Romer J

Australia '[T]he meaning of the words "appoint" and "appointed" varies according to the context in which they are used. In some cases, the appointment of a person to fill a particular role or to perform a particular task will require nothing more than communication between appointor and prospective appointee. That is not ordinarily so in a case where one party to a contract is entitled or required to appoint a third person to do something with consequences that are contractually binding upon the other party or parties. In such a case and in the absence of contrary provision in the contract, the appointment will ordinarily be effective only when the prospective appointee has been clothed with the requisite authority by being identified by communication of his identity by the party or parties.' *Gollin and Co Ltd v Karenlee Nominees Pty Ltd* (1983) 153 CLR 455 at 470, per cur.

Canada 'The infinitive "to appoint" in ordinary usage means "to ordain or nominate a person to an office or to perform a function": see Oxford English Dictionary. Nevertheless it is often used in statutes in the sense of "to employ" or "to hire" depending upon the context.' *Re Faculty Association of University of St Thomas and St Thomas University* (1975) 60 DLR (3d) 176 at 181, NBCA, per Hughes CJ

New Zealand [The Municipal Corporations Act 1954 (repealed; see now the Local Government Act 1974, s 96(4)) gives the council of a municipal corporation power to 'appoint' one of its members to be deputy mayor.] 'The power of appointment is conferred by s 46 on the council as a whole. Basically it had to perform the normal functions of an election. . . . I am satisfied that in the context of s 46 the word "appoint" is synonymous with "elect".' *Wild v Maguire* [1970] NZLR 489 at 492, per Quilliam J

APPOINTMENT   *See also*
ADVANCEMENT

'An advancement has a definite meaning, distinct from an appointment. It means that a certain portion of the fund is actually taken out of the settlement altogether, and paid over to the object of the power. But an appointment deals only with the reversion of the fund, leaving the previous life interests untouched.' *Re Gosset's Settlement* (1854) 19 Beav 529 at 535, per Lord Romilly MR

See, generally, 24 Halsbury's Laws (4th edn) para 479.

Of arbitrator

'The section [the Arbitration Act 1889, s 5 (repealed; see now Arbitration Act 1950, s 10)] says that (among other cases) where a submission provides that the reference shall be to a single arbitrator, and all parties do not after differences have arisen concur in the appointment of an arbitrator, any party may serve the other parties with a written notice to appoint an arbitrator. . . . It is said that this notice is wrong because it is not a notice to appoint but only to concur in appointing an arbitrator. . . . In my opinion the word "appoint" in the section in such cases as this means "concur in appointing".' *Re Eyre & Leicester Corpn* [1892] 1 QB 136 at 142, CA, per Lord Esher MR

[The Agricultural Holdings (Scotland) Act 1949, s 68(4) provided for the 'appointment' of arbiters to settle disputes under the Act.] 'I cannot imagine that the legislature intended that a mere agreement to appoint a certain person arbiter, locked within the bosoms of the parties to the agreement and never communicated, would be a sufficient appointment. . . . Further, there is a paragraph in the Sixth Schedule which helps to convince me that mere agreement to appoint is not in itself an appointment of an arbiter in the sense of s 68(4). Para 4 of the Sixth Schedule says that "every appointment, notice, revocation and consent under the foregoing provision of this schedule must be in writing". An appointment "in writing" is, I think, something different from evidence of consent to an appointment contained in written correspondence between the parties. I think it indicates that there must be an express appointment in writing, not mere

written evidence of consent.' *Chalmers Property Investment Co Ltd v MacColl* 1951 SLT 50 at 53, 54, per Lord Keith

[A clause in a charterparty provided for disputes to be referred to two arbitrators, one to be 'appointed' by each party.] ' "Appoint" and "appointed" are words with meanings varying according to their contexts. When Dryden wrote: "Like pilgrims to th' appointed place we tend; The world's an inn, and death the journey's end" the first-line adjective did not necessarily connote any consensuality between the pilgrims and others regarding the place to which they were to tend. The same is true when one speaks of "Prayers appointed to be read in churches". But when one says of people that "They met at the appointed time", the implication is one of arrangement, which necessarily involves the concepts both of knowledge and of assent. It is indeed correct that "to appoint" embraces the idea of nomination, but in relation to *persons*, "appointment" is not generally a unilateral process. For example, my dictionary gives as instances of the nominatory aspect of the process, "to appoint a man ambassador; to appoint to a professorship". Is it conceivable that John Doe can wake up one morning to find that he has effectively become an ambassador, or that Richard Roe can suddenly learn that he has validly been elected to a university chair without either having previously been approached regarding his willingness to be appointed? An affirmative answer would be an absurdity.' *Tradax Export SA v Volkswagenwerk AG* [1970] 1 All ER 420, CA, per Edmund Davies LJ

APPORTION   *See* PART

APPRAISER   *See* VALUER

APPRECIATE

Canada [The defence of insanity under the Criminal Code, RSC 1970, c C-34, s 16 refers to 'appreciating' nature and quality of act.] 'In contrast to the position in England under the M'Naghten rules, where the words used are "knows the nature and quality of his act", s 16 of the Code uses the phrase "appreciating the nature and quality of an act or omission". The two are not synonymous. The draftsman of the Code, as originally enacted, made a deliberate change in language from the common law rule in order to broaden the legal and medical considerations bearing upon the mental state of the accused and to make it clear that cognition was not to be the sole criterion. Emotional, as well as intellectual, awareness of the significance of the conduct, is in issue. . . . To "know" the nature and quality of an act may mean merely to be aware of the physical act, while to "appreciate" may involve estimation and understanding of the consequences of that act.' *Cooper v R* [1980] 1 SCR 1149 at 1160, 1161, SCC, per Dickson J

Canada 'In the ordinary usage of . . . language . . . it would appear that to appreciate embraces the act of knowing but the converse is not necessarily true.' *R v Barnier* [1980] 1 SCR 1124 at 1136, 1137, SCC, per Estey J

APPREHENSION

'The applicant . . . was arrested on board a steamer at Queenstown harbour by an Irish constable, without any warrant, and was brought before a police magistrate there, who then issued a warrant ordering his detention in prison. . . . All the proceedings were strictly regular, with this exception, that the prisoner was originally arrested without any warrant, and the whole objection is this, that the Irish magistrate's warrant was not a warrant for the "apprehension" of the prisoner within the meaning of s 8 of the [Extradition] Act [1870]. It appears to me that this would be to give too narrow a meaning to the word "apprehension". The word strictly construed means the seizing or taking hold of the man, and literally and truly you can do that although he may be already in custody. It means the taking hold of him and detaining him with a view to his ultimate surrender. I am not inclined to limit the word "apprehension" to the taking hold of a man who is not already in custody. It would follow that if a man was already in lawful custody you could not take him at all under this Act; the word "apprehension" would not apply. You would be compelled to restore him to liberty before you could apprehend him. . . . This would not be a rational mode of construing the Act.' *R v Weil* (1882) 9 QBD 701 at 705, CA, per Jessel MR

APPRENTICE

At common law a contract of apprenticeship is something more than a contract of service. By a contract of apprenticeship a person is bound to another for the purpose of learning a trade or calling, the apprentice undertaking to serve the master for the purpose of being taught, and the master undertaking to teach the apprentice. It is common practice for the apprentice's parent or guardian to be made a party to the contract and to guarantee the performance by the apprentice of his obligations. Where teaching on the part of the master or learning on the part of the other person is not the primary but only an incidental object, the contract is one of employment rather than of apprenticeship. The payment of a premium is strong, although not conclusive, evidence that a contract of apprenticeship was contemplated. Modern statutes include apprenticeship with or in the definition of contracts of service. (16 Halsbury's Laws (4th edn) para 506)

'The term "apprentice" is taken from the French word *apprendre*—to learn.' *R v Laindon (Inhabitants)* (1799) 8 Term Rep 379 at 383, per Lord Kenyon CJ

' "An apprentice" is a person who by contract is to be taught a trade, in contradistinction from a person who engages to serve another person generally.' Ibid at 384, per Grose J

'The use of the term "apprentice" (albeit it is specially defined [in the Family Allowances Act 1945, s 2(1)(b) (repealed; see now the Family Allowances Act 1965, s 19] suggests ideas long familiar in many branches of industry and the professions, and indicates that the attachment of the apprentice to the field of the chosen occupation must be *quasi-*permanent in character, and directed to the acquisition of full qualifications in that occupation. From all this I conclude that full-time training as an apprentice for a trade, etc, connotes a course of training which is in a substantial sense systematic and progressive, and which aims at the ultimate production of competence for engaging in the selected work.' *Fraser v Minister of National Insurance* 1948 SLT 54 at 56, per the Lord President (Cooper)

Articled clerk distinguished

'The Legislature [in (1825) 6 Geo 4, c 16, s 49 (repealed)] clearly meant by the term "apprentice" a person serving another who was engaged in trade, craft, or mysteries, and I think, according to every fair rule of construction, you must draw a distinction between an apprentice and an articled clerk.' *Re Fussell, ex p Prideaux & Rush* (1838) 2 Jur 366 at 367, per Lord Cottenham LC

APPROACH

To bridge

'Approach', in relation to a bridge or tunnel, means the highway giving access thereto, that is to say, the surface of that highway together with any embankment, retaining wall or other work or substance supporting or protecting the surface. (Highways Act 1980, s 329(1))

[The Railways Clauses Consolidation Act 1845, s 46, obliges a railway company to maintain bridges and their 'immediate approaches'.] 'One knows that a railway company must maintain fences in a proper manner if the railway runs alongside a high road, and that there is an additional obligation on a railway company with regard to fencing bridges; but I think that the subsequent sections of the Act of 1845, namely, ss 52–56, are the sections which deal with roads. I do not think that s 46 has anything to do with roads; it is simply concerned with bridges, and I am not prepared to hold that the words "immediate approaches" mean anything except that part that is adjacent to the bridge.' *Monmouthshire County Council v British Transport Commission* [1957] 1 All ER 662 at 664, per Lord Goddard CJ; affd [1957] 3 All ER 384, CA

To privately maintainable bridge

'Approaches' in relation to a [privately maintainable] bridge, means approaches for the maintenance of which the owners of the bridge are responsible and which connect the bridge to the highway maintainable at the public expense. (Highways Act 1980, s 95(8))

To roof

[The Building (Safety, Health and Welfare) Regulations 1948, reg 31(3)(b) (revoked; see now the Construction (Working Places) Regulations 1966, reg 36(3)), provided that prominent notices stating that roof coverings are fragile were to be affixed at the 'approaches' thereto.] ' "Approach" can only mean something of such a character that, if a notice were affixed to it, it would give a warning to a person who was about to work on or near the roof.' *Harris v Bright's Asphalt Contractors Ltd* [1953] 1 All ER 395 at 399, per Slade J (also reported in [1953] 1 QB 617 at 628)

APPROBATE AND REPROBATE *See also* ESTOPPEL

'The doctrine of approbate and reprobate in Scotland and the doctrine of election in England are the very same thing under different names. They depend upon a principle, which in its comprehensiveness and simplicity was put by Lord Eldon in the House of Lords in the Scotch case of *Ker v Wauchope* [(1819) 1 Bli 1] thus: "It is equally settled in the law of Scotland and of England that no person can accept and reject the same instrument".' *Pitman v Crum Ewing* [1911] AC 217 at 233, per Lord Shaw

'My Lords, I think our first inquiry should be as to the meaning and proper application of the maxim that you may not both approbate and reprobate. The phrase comes to us from the northern side of the Tweed, and there it is of comparatively modern use. It is, however, to be found in Bell's Commentaries, 7th ed, Vol I, pp 141–142; and he treats "the Scottish doctrine of approbate and reprobate" as "approaching nearly to that of election in English jurisprudence". It is, I think, now settled by decisions in this House that there is no difference at all between the two doctrines. . . . In the light of these authorities it seems that the phrase "you may not approbate or reprobate", or the Latin *"quod approbo non reprobo"*, as used in England is no more than a picturesque synonym for the ancient equitable doctrine of election, originally derived from the civil law, which finds its place in our records as early as the reign of Queen Elizabeth.' *Lissenden v Bosch (CAV) Ltd* [1940] AC 412 at 417, 418, HL, per Lord Maugham

APPROPRIATION

Of benefice

'There existed at one time some confusion between "appropriation" and "impropriation", but "appropriation", when that word is properly used, refers to the attachment of an ecclesiastical benefice to the perpetual use of some religious house, or Dean and Chapter, or other spiritual person. "Impropriation", on the other hand, is correctly used to refer to the transfer of the property of an ecclesiastical benefice into the hands of a layman, and to the possession by a layman of the property so transferred. Such was the nature of the ownership by a layman of a benefice transferred to him by royal grant or the like at the time of the Reformation.' *Representative Body of the Church in Wales v Tithe Redemption Commission, Plymouth Estates Ltd v Tithe Redemption Commission* [1944] AC 228 at 241, HL, per Lord Simon LC

Of goods

'The word "appropriation" may be understood in different senses. It may mean a selection on the part of the vendor, where he has the right to choose the article which he has to supply in performance of his contract; and the contract will show when the word is used in that sense. Or the word may mean, that both parties have agreed that a certain article shall be delivered in pursuance of the contract. . . . "Appropriation" may also be used in another sense . . . viz, where both parties agree upon the specific article in which the property is to pass, and nothing remains to be done in order to pass it.' *Wait v Baker* (1848) 2 Exch 1 at 8, 9, per Parke B

'Property in unascertained goods passes to the buyer when there is an appropriation of goods to a contract—which need not be a pre-existing contract—by the buyer with the assent, express or implied, of the seller, or by the seller with the assent of the buyer. The appropriation may be, and often is, quite distinct from delivery. If a man enters a shop and seeing a bottle of gin, points to it and says: "Please sell me that bottle", and the shopman gives it to him, there is then a sale of a specific chattel. If he says— the gin being under the counter, or elsewhere—"Please let me have a bottle" and the shopman takes one out and hands it to him, and he accepts it, there is an appropriation from his stock with the buyer's express consent. If the buyer writes or telephones or sends his servant and says: "Please send me or let me have a bottle" he is leaving it to the shopman to appropriate a bottle out of his stock to the customer, and as soon as the shopman does so the sale is complete. The customer has, by his conduct, impliedly assented to the appropriation.' *Furby v Hoey* [1947] 1 All ER 236 at 238, per Lord Goddard CJ

Of payments

South Africa 'It is for the debtor, and failing him for the creditor, to indicate at the time of payment to which of more items than one such payment shall be imported, and it is only on failure of both that the law steps in to make the appropriation. The debtor and failing him the creditor must declare his intention before or at the time of payment, in order that it may still be open to the creditor not to accept it upon the debtor's terms. If the debtor's intention had been declared before payment and not withdrawn, the creditor would be quite justified in acting upon it, and if he did not so act upon it there would be no necessity for any declaration of his intention. If the course of dealing between the parties has been such that the creditor has been reasonably led to believe that any payment was intended to be imputed to a particular item, and has acted upon that belief, the debtor cannot afterwards claim that the law should step in to make the appropriation.' *Stiglingh v French* 9 SC 411 per De Villiers CJ

Of rights of owner

[The Theft Act 1968, s 1 provides that a person is guilty of theft if he dishonestly 'appropriates' property belonging to another with the intention of permanently depriving the other of it.] Any assumption by a person of the rights of an owner amounts to an appropriation, and this includes, where he has come by the property (innocently or not) without stealing it, any later assumption of a right to it by keeping or dealing with it as owner. (Theft Act 1968, s 3(1))

Of shipbuilding materials

[A contract for the building of a ship provided that all materials and things 'appropriated' for her should, subject to a lien for unpaid purchase money, become the absolute property of the purchasers.] 'The point we have to determine is this: whether certain material that was worked and lying in the yard or the building berth ready to be incorporated in the hull of the vessel and which had been approved by the purchasing company's surveyor became thereby the property of the purchasers. . . . The real way of dealing with this question is to read the word "appropriated" in its proper technical sense and as limited to goods which have been so dealt with that the builder could not use them except for the purposes of the ship and that the purchasers could not refuse to accept them as part of the ship, but the mere intention on the part of the builder to use them is not enough to transfer the property to the purchasers.' *Re Blyth Shipbuilding & Dry Docks Co, Forster v Blyth Shipbuilding & Dry Docks Co* [1926] Ch 494 at 516–518, CA, per Warrington LJ

APPROVE

Approval of agreement

'The document [a draft agreement] became a document signed by a gentleman who was signing clearly as one of the three persons named as partners in the agreement, and it was signed therefore necessarily upon their behalf; and, although the word "approved" is added, that is a word which in this case could not at all have the meaning which the word frequently has in drafts. Often when a draft is signed by a solicitor or a conveyancer as "approved", the word "approved" means nothing more than that the legal form and expression of the instrument is approved. Here the word "approved", signed by one of the partners, could have meant nothing else than this—that he approved of the terms of the agreement on behalf of the partners.' *Brogden v Metropolitan Rly Co* (1877) 2 App Cas 666 at 675, per Lord Cairns LC

Approved insurance policy

'The question I intend to decide is whether the respondents tendered an "approved insurance policy". . . . Here [where by a letter of credit a bank agreed to honour a seller's draft if accompanied by, inter alia, an approved insurance policy] the insurance policy must be one to which no reasonable objection could be made and which ought therefore to be approved. What was tendered was a document called an American certificate. . . . A certificate in this form which does not state the terms of insurance so that they can all be seen by the person to whom it is tendered is not an approved policy; it is one to which a reasonable objection can be made.' *Scott & Co Ltd v Barclay's Bank Ltd* [1923] KB 1 at 14, 15, CA, per Scrutton LJ

Approved loading places

[A charterparty provided that a ship should proceed to certain 'approved' loading places in Newfoundland, etc] 'This form of charter requires that the vessel "shall sail and proceed to not more than two approved loading places as ordered . . . or so near thereunto as she may safely get and there load. . .". It appears to me that "loading place" in this context is used instead of the word "port" by reason of the nature of the places at which the defendants collect pulpwood for transport to this country. The word "approved" must mean approved generally in the trade or business. To say that it

means no more than approved by the parties, or, in other words, agreed between them, has the effect of depriving the word of any meaning in this setting. The defendants have the right to nominate not more than two approved loading places *as ordered*. It is for the charterers, the defendants, to nominate an approved loading place. A loading place would not be approved in the trade unless it was satisfactory, and no loading place is satisfactory unless it is recognised as normally safe for a ship of the size for which it is nominated.' *Compania Naviera Maropan SA v Bowaters Lloyd Pulp & Paper Mills Ltd* [1955] 2 All ER 241 at 243, 244, CA, per Singleton LJ; see also [1955] 2 QB 68

APPROXIMATE

'I find myself unable to say that when a measurement of a rear garden is made to a purchaser asking for particulars, i.e. footage details, it is true if you only give him 36 feet when the stated measurement is 40 feet. I cannot believe that 36 feet is approximately 40 feet. I can understand 36 feet being approximately 35 feet.' *Bellotti v Chequers Developments Ltd* [1936] 1 All ER 89 at 92, per Hilbery J

Canada [The Highway Traffic Act, RSM, 1970, c H–60, s 119, provides that when two vehicles approach or enter an intersection at 'approximately' the same time, the driver of the vehicle on the left shall yield right of way.] 'The word "approximately" as used in the above subsection means "about" or "nearly" and is the direct opposite of "exactly" or "precisely".' *Scheving v Scott* (1960) 32 WWR 234 at 237, Man CA, per Schulz JA

APPURTENANCES

'Appurtenance', in relation to a dwelling, or to a school, college or other educational establishment, includes all land occupied therewith and used for the purposes thereof. (General Rate Act 1967, s 19)

'If the King granted a manor, by such words as are contained in the grant of this manor . . . "with the appurtenances in as full and ample a manner as he held the same" this would pass an advowson appendant to the manor, although not named or referred to in the grant.' *A-G v Ewelme Hospital* (1853) 17 Beav 366 at 386, per Romilly MR

'The word "appurtenances" has a distinct and

definite meaning, and though it may be enlarged by the context, yet the burthen of proof lies on those who so contend. Prima facie, it imports nothing more than what is strictly appertaining to the subject-matter of the devise or grant, and which would, in truth, pass without being specially mentioned.' *Evans v Angell* (1858) 26 Beav 202 at 205, per Romilly MR

'It is settled by the earliest authority, repeated without contradiction to the latest, that land cannot be appurtenant to land. The word "appurtenances" includes all the incorporeal hereditaments attached to the land granted or demised such as rights-of-way, of common, or piscary, and the like, but it does not include lands in addition to that granted.' *Lister v Pickford* (1865) 34 Beav 576 at 580, per Romilly MR

'Neither in a deed nor in a will does the word "appurtenances" include land, if the principal subject of gift is land or a messuage. But, if from the circumstances at the date of the will, and the whole context, it is clear that land is intended to pass as appurtenant, the word "appurtenant" is flexible enough to carry it.' *Cuthbert v Robinson* (1882) 51 LJ Ch 238 at 241, per Kay J

'No doubt the word "appurtenances" is not apt for the creation of a new right, and the word "appurtenant" is not apt to describe a right which had never previously existed; and therefore the mere grant of all appurtenances or of all ways appurtenant to the principal subject of the grant has been held in many cases not to create a new right of way where the right was not pre-existing at the date of the grant. But from as long ago as the fourth year of Philip and Mary [*Hill v Grange* (1556) 1 Plowd 164, 170] the word "appurtenances" has easily admitted of a secondary meaning and as equivalent in that case to "usually occupied".' *Thomas v Owen* (1887) 20 QBD 225 at 231, 232, CA, per Fry LJ

'This case raises a question with regard to the definition of "house" in the Housing Act 1936, s 188 [repealed; see now Housing Act 1985, s 457]. That word is there defined as including "any . . . appurtenances belonging thereto or usually enjoyed therewith". . . . That word has had applied to it, through a long series of cases, mostly dealing with the meaning of the word in demises, a certain limited meaning, and it is now beyond question that, broadly speaking, nothing will pass, under a demise, by the word "appurtenances" which would not

equally pass under a conveyance of the principal subject-matter without the addition of that word, that is to say . . . that the word "appurtenances" will pass the house, the orchard, yard, curtilage and gardens, but not the land. That view . . . has never been departed from except that in certain cases it has been held that the word "appurtenances" may also be competent to pass incorporeal hereditaments. Certainly, no case has been cited to us in which the word "appurtenance" has even been extended to include land as meaning a corporeal hereditament, which does not fall within the curtilage of the yard of the house itself, that is, not within the parcel of the demise of the house.' *Trim v Sturminster Rural District Council* [1938] 2 KB 508 at 514–516, CA, per Slesser LJ

'In the absence of some contrary indication the word "appurtenances", in a context which shows that it is used in a sense capable of extending to corporeal hereditaments, will not be understood to extend to any land which would not pass under a conveyance of the principal subject-matter without being specifically mentioned, that is to say, to extend only to land or buildings within the curtilage of the principal subject-matter.' *Methuen-Campbell v Walters* [1979] 1 All ER 606 at 620, CA, per Buckley LJ

Of ship

'It may not be a simple matter to define what is, and what is not, an appurtenance of a ship. There are some things that are *universally* so—things which must be appurtenant to every ship, *qua* ship. . . . The word "appurtenances" must not be construed with a mere reference to the abstract naked idea of a ship; for that which would be an encumbrance to a ship one way employed, would be an indispensable equipment in another, and it would be a preposterous abuse to consider them alike in such different positions. You must look to the relation, they bear to the actual service of the vessel.' *The Dundee* (1823) 1 Hag Adm 109 at 126, 127, per Lord Stowell

'It has been argued that "ship" is equivalent to "ship and its appurtenances", and to a certain extent that is doubtless so. It would include spare sails, duplicate anchors, anything in fact which it would not be prudent to send a ship to sea without.' *Re Salmon & Woods, ex p Gould* (1885) 2 Morr 137 at 141, per Wills J

APPURTENANT

[A will contained the following words: 'It shall be a condition appurtenant to the taking of the gift of my estate whether by the son or daughter or adopted son of the said Agnes Sara Bond or my said nieces or either of them that the person so taking shall take and continue to bear my surname.'] 'As to the word "appurtenant", I think it means annexed to or inseparably connected with, and if the testator had been asked whether he was creating a condition precedent or a condition subsequent he would probably have said that it was neither, but somehow concurrent. In my judgment, however, it must be regarded and treated as a condition subsequent.' *Re Fry, Reynolds v Denne* [1945] Ch 348 at 352, per Vaisey J

ARABLE

In this section 'arable land' does not include land in grass which, by the terms of a contract of tenancy, is to be retained in the same condition throughout the tenancy. (Agricultural Holdings Act 1986, s 15(7))

Australia 'In its derivation "arable" is of Latin origin. "Aro, arare" are parts of the root verb which can have one or other of several significations: (i) to plough or till ground; (ii) to dig it up, to dress and order it; and (iii) to reap or gather. The adjective "arabilis" means "that can be ploughed". According to dictionaries, "arable" means "ploughable, fit for, or hence, cultivated by ploughing or tillage.". . . . Primarily, so far as the countryside is in its native state, i.e. where timber, bushes and shrubs are undisturbed and the virgin condition remains, land, however promising its future, will not be classed as "arable".' *Kelly v Elliott* [1960] SASR 222 at 226, 227, per Mayo J

Canada 'To assist the witnesses, this court on the former appeal [(1924) 18 SLR 96] defined "arable land" as "land fit for cultivation and which will grow crops of grain".' *Mutual Life Assurance Co of Canada v Armstrong (No 2)* (1924) 19 SLR 90 at 91, Sask CA, per Lamont JA; affd. [1925] SCR 671

ARBITRARILY

'Now, it is said that a vendor is not to act capriciously. I rather prefer the word "arbitrarily" . . . which I take to mean "without any reasonable cause".' *Quinion v Horne* [1906] 1 Ch 596 at 603, 604, per Farwell J

'In my opinion the expressions "unreasonably", "wholly unreasonably", and "without reasonable cause" practically mean the same thing. Each of these expressions, I think, correctly defines the meaning of the word "arbitrarily" as used in the underlease." *Mills v Cannon Brewery Co* [1920] 2 Ch 38 at 45, per P O Lawrence J

South Africa 'Capricious or proceeding merely from will and not based on reason or principle.' *Buckingham v Boksburg LLB* 1931 TPD 280

ARBITRATION   *See also* ARBITRATION AGREEMENT; ARBITRATOR

An arbitration is the reference of a dispute or difference between not less than two parties for determination, after hearing both sides in a judicial manner, by a person or persons other than a court of competent jurisdiction.

Arbitrations properly so called arise either out of an agreement between the parties thereto or out of the terms of an Act of Parliament or some other instrument of statutory force. Where they are not otherwise defined by law, the subject matter of the reference and the arbitrator's authority in references arising out of an agreement between the parties derive from and are prescribed by the agreement of reference. (2 Halsbury's Laws (4th edn) paras 501, 507)

Arbitration is where the parties, injuring and injured, submit all matters in dispute, concerning any personal chattels or personal wrong, to the judgment of two or more *arbitrators*; who are to decide the controversy: and if they do not agree, it is usual to add, that another person be called in as *umpire, (imperator)* to whose sole judgment it is then referred: or frequently there is only one arbitrator originally appointed. This decision, in any of these cases, is called an *award*. And thereby the question is as fully determined, and the right transferred or settled, as it could have been by the agreement of the parties or the judgment of a court of justice. (3 Bl Com 16)

'An arbitration is a reference to the decision of one or more persons, either with or without an umpire, of some matter or matters in difference between the parties.' *Collins v Collins* (1858) 26 Beav 306 at 312, per Romilly MR

'If it appears from the terms of the agreement by which a matter is submitted to a person's decision, that the intention of the parties was that he should hold an inquiry in the nature of a judicial inquiry, and hear the respective cases of the parties, and decide upon evidence laid before him, then the case is one of an arbitration. The intention in such cases is that there shall be a judicial inquiry worked out in a judicial manner. On the other hand, there are cases in which a person is appointed to ascertain some matter for the purpose of preventing differences from arising, not of settling them when they have arisen, and where the case is not one of arbitration but of a mere valuation. There may be cases of an intermediate kind, where, though a person is appointed to settle disputes that have arisen, still it is not intended that he shall be bound to hear evidence or arguments. In such cases it may be often difficult to say whether he is intended to be an arbitrator or to exercise some function other than that of an arbitrator. Such cases must be determined each according to its particular circumstances.' *Re Carus-Wilson and Greene* (1886) 18 QBD 7 at 9, CA, per Lord Esher MR

Australia [The Commonwealth of Australia Constitution Act 1900, s 51 (xxxv), provides that: 'The Parliament shall, subject to this Constitution, have power to make laws for the peace, order, and good government of the Commonwealth with respect to . . . concili-ation and arbitration for the prevention and settlement of industrial disputes extending beyond the limits of any one State.'] 'The word "arbitration", . . .for present purposes is to be interpreted according to the way it is under-stood and was in 1900 understood in relation to industrial disputes. . . . In relation to indus-trial disputes, arbitration signifies a means of settling a question in dispute by reference to a third party or parties when the contendants themselves have failed to agree. But it is all-important to observe that *in industrial history that does not mean that the third party or parties must be unconnected with the disputants them-selves.* . . . It is also unquestionably evident that as used and understood in relation to industrial disputes from 1860 continuously to the present day, the ambit of the term "arbit-ration" is large enough to include decisions by persons selected either voluntarily or compul-sorily as arbitrators who represent the view-points of the disputants, and even if they are directly interested in the dispute itself as members or employees of the disputing

parties. *It is expected of them that they will act impartially. It is presumed that they will do so to the best of their ability*, and the course of industrial history on this point shows that it is often safer in the interests of industrial peace to trust to the members of the tribunal recognising not only the duty of conscientiously considering opposing views, but also the advantage of the parties with whose interests they are industrially connected or identified, not to persist in refusing what is reasonable. This, according to the authorities I refer to, has obviously been considered a more satisfactory method of arbitration than confining the term to the decision of persons whose personal ignorance of the conditions of the industry is a *sine qua non* of their eligibility as arbitrators.' *Australian Rlys Union v Victorian Rlys Comrs* (1930) 44 CLR 319 at 354, 355, 361, per Isaacs CJ

New Zealand 'It is essential, in order to constitute a "reference" or "submission" to arbitration, that there shall appear in the instrument, either expressly or by necessary implication, the intention of the parties that there shall be an inquiry in the nature of a judicial inquiry, and that their respective cases shall be heard and a decision arrived at upon the evidence adduced by the parties. It is not in every case where two parties intend to be concluded by the decision of a third that that third person is an arbitrator.' *Fraser v Hamilton Corpn* (1912) 32 NZLR 205 at 213, per Cooper J; also reported 15 GLR 176 at 180

ARBITRATION AGREEMENT

In this Part [Part 1] of this Act, unless the context otherwise requires, the expression 'arbitration agreement' means a written agreement to submit present or future differences to arbitration, whether an arbitrator is named therein or not. (Arbitration Act 1950, s 32)

'Arbitration agreement' means an agreement in writing (including an agreement contained in an exchange of letters or telegrams) to submit to arbitration present or future differences capable of settlement by arbitration. (Arbitration Act 1975, s 7(1))

ARBITRATOR   *See also* VALUER

'It is contended that the submission here does not provide that the reference shall be to a single arbitrator [within the Arbitration Act 1889, s 5(a) (repealed; see now the Arbitration Act 1950, s 10(1))], because the words are "arbitrator or umpire", and no doubt there is a technical meaning which is often applied to the word "umpire" when it is used to denote a person (often appointed by the arbitrators themselves) who is to settle any differences that may arise between two arbitrators; but that cannot always be the necessary meaning of the word, for where, as here, the word "arbitrator" is used in the singular, the word "umpire" in the sense to which I have referred, can have no application. I am, therefore, of opinion that in this contract the words "arbitrator" and "umpire" are used as synonymous terms, and if that is so, the submission provides for a reference to a single arbitrator.' *Re Eyre & Leicester Corpn* [1892] 1 QB 136 at 139, 140, CA, per Lord Coleridge CJ

See, generally, 2 Halsbury's Laws (4th edn) para 568 *et seq.*

ARCHAEOLOGICAL INVESTIGATION

For the purposes of this Act 'archaeological investigation' means any investigation of any land, objects or other material for the purpose of obtaining and recording any information of archaeological or historical interest and . . . includes in the case of an archaeological investigation of any land—
(a) any investigation for the purpose of discovering and revealing and (where appropriate) recovering and removing any objects or other material of archaeological or historical interest situated in, on or under the land; and
(b) examining, testing, treating, recording and preserving any such objects or material discovered during the course of any excavation or inspections carried out for the purposes of any such investigation.
(Ancient Monuments and Archaeological Areas Act 1979, s 61(4))

ARCHBISHOP

As superintendent of all ecclesiastical matters in his province an archbishop has, throughout the province at all times, metropolitical jurisdiction to correct and supply the defects of other bishops; and during the time of his metropolitical visitation he has jurisdiction as 'Ordinary', except in places and over persons exempt by law or custom. Each archbishop has his own diocese where he exercises episcopal jurisdiction.

Within his province an archbishop is the principal minister, and to him belong the rights of (1) confirming the election of every person to a bishopric; (2) being the chief consecrator at the consecration of every bishop; (3) receiving such appeals in his provincial court as may be provided by law; (4) holding metropolitical visitations at times or places limited by law or custom; and (5) presiding in the convocation of the province either in person or by such deputy as he may lawfully appoint. The two archbishops are Joint Presidents of the General Synod. (14 Halsbury's Laws (4th edn) para 430)

ARCHDEACON

An archdeacon is an ordained minister, having statutory jurisdiction under the Crown and next after the bishop over a portion of a diocese, called an archdeaconry, in matters ecclesiastical. Originally the office was, as the name ('chief deacon') implies, limited to deacons, but now a clergyman to hold it must not only be a priest, but must have been for six complete years in priest's orders. Thus, he must be thirty years of age at least. (14 Halsbury's Laws (4th edn) para 496)

ARCHITECT

An architect is one who possesses, with due regard to æsthetic as well as practical considerations, adequate skill and knowledge to enable him (1) to originate, (2) to design and plan, (3) to arrange for and supervise the erection of such buildings or other works calling for skill in design and planning as he might, in the course of his business, reasonably be asked to carry out or in respect of which he offers his services as a specialist. (4 Halsbury's Laws (4th edn) para 1301)

'There being no legal definition in the Act of Parliament [Architects Registration Act 1938] of the word "architect", one has recourse to the ordinary meaning of the word "architect". Using one's knowledge, and looking at the dictionary definitions of the word "architect", it is perfectly clear to my mind that the word "architect" connotes a certain amount of skill. In Murray's New English Dictionary, which counsel for the respondents cited to us yesterday, the first meaning of "architect" is:

"A skilled professor of the work of building, whose business it is to prepare the plans of edifices, and exercise a general superintendence over the course of their erection". Therefore, one has the fact, if that definition of the word "architect" in Murray's New English Dictionary is right, the word connotes "A skilled professor". If one looks at Webster's International Dictionary, the meaning of "architect" is given as "A person skilled in the art of building". In my opinion, the word "architect" must convey to anybody some degree of skill.' *R v Architects' Registration Tribunal, ex p Jaggar* [1945] 2 All ER 131 at 135, per Lewis J

ARCHITECTURAL INTEREST

[The question was whether certain buildings were of special 'architectural or historic interest' within the Town and Country Planning Act 1947, s 29(1) (repealed; see now the Town and Country Planning Act 1971, s 54)]. 'In my view the architectural interest of a building, in many cases, cannot be divorced from its surroundings, whether they be the surroundings of topography or of other adjacent buildings. An architect who ignored these factors would, I should have thought, have been a bad architect. I am far from saying that in every case a building becomes of architectural interest, or of special architectural interest, because of its relationship or propinquity to other buildings which are of architectural interest or of special architectural interest. I am, however, of opinion that, in considering the architectural interest of a particular building, it would be wrong to say that its architectural interest can in no circumstances be affected, and increased, by reason of neighbouring buildings. Thus, for example, if one considers a terrace of houses of architectural interest, it might well be that one of these houses, if it were to be artificially considered as though it were standing alone in isolation, would not be considered by the viewer to be of "special architectural interest". Where, however, that self-same house is viewed by the same viewer as it really is—that is, as a part of a terrace—the viewer might reasonably hold the opinion that the house, in that context (to use the minister's word), is of "special architectural interest".' *Iveagh (Earl) v Minister of Housing and Local Government* [1961] 3 All ER 98 at 103, per Megaw J

AREA

'Area' in relation to a building means the superficies of a horizontal section thereof made at the point of its greatest surface inclusive of the external walls and of such portions of the party walls as belong to the building. (London Building Act 1930, s 5)

[The respondents were charged under the Vagrancy Act 1824, s 4 with being found in an enclosed 'area' for an unlawful purpose. The place in question consisted of railway sidings fenced on every side except across the lines of rails.] 'There is, apparently, no authority as to the precise significance of the word "area" in the section, and we were informed that different meanings have been given to it in various parts of the country when charges have been preferred under the section. It appears to me that in 1824, when the Act was passed, the word "area" would not have been used in the context in which it appears in the section, to describe the large spaces surrounded by ring fences which at that time were frequently to be found all over the country. The words "yard" and "garden" which precede the word "area" in the section, are plainly words of a very limited scope. A garden might, at the most, include a small number of acres, but the railway company has urged that the word "area" can apply to an enclosed space however large it is. Having regard to the use of the words "yard" and "garden" immediately before the word in question here, and bearing in mind that this is a penal section, I think that the word "area" should be construed in the sense given to it by the justices. The use of the word "area" to denote that part of the basement of a house which is open to the air was formerly very familiar, and, indeed, is familiar to most people to-day. It is commonly used to denote the open space below the level of the ground which has been excavated for the purpose of building a house on the site, and the justices came to the conclusion that that was the sense in which the word is used in s 4 of the Vagrancy Act. I think that that interpretation is right, and I will only say that, if the view I have expressed is not the right one, either the use of the word "area" in the section is inapt, or the words "yard" or "garden" are unnecessary since it would have been sufficient to say: "in or upon any dwelling-house . . . or in any enclosed area".' *Knott v Blackburn* [1944] 1 KB 77 at 79, per Lord Caldecote CJ

New Zealand [The Police Offences Act 1927 (NZ), s 52(1)(i), is in the following terms:

'Every person shall be deemed a rogue and vagabond within the meaning of this Act, and be liable to imprisonment with hard labour for any term not exceeding one year. (i) Who is found by night without lawful excuse (the proof of which excuse shall be on him) in or on any building or in any enclosed yard, garden, or area, or in or on board any ship, launch, dredge, yacht, boat, or other vessel.' [Cf. s 4 of the Vagrancy Act 1824, supra.] 'In my opinion, the words "enclosed yard, garden, or area" in the section in our Act must be interpreted as applying and being limited to an enclosed yard, garden, or area appurtenant to a building.' *R v Letton* [1943] NZLR 687 at 692, CA, per Myers CJ; [1943] GLR 437 at 439.

ARISE

Canada ' "To arise" is an intransitive verb and connotes spontaneity or action without external influence, whereas "to raise" is a transitive verb and connotes some external force or influence acting on an object and so producing movement or emergence of an idea.' *Re Dalrymple, Hogg v Provincial Tax Commission* [1941] 2 WWR 302 at 303, 304, Sask KB, per MacDonald J

ARISE OUT OF EMPLOYMENT   *See* COURSE OF EMPLOYMENT

ARM

Of sea   *See* TIDAL RIVER

ARMED

[The prisoners were tried for felony under 57 Geo 3, c 90 (repealed; see now Game Act 1831, s 32, also partly repealed by the Wild Creatures and Forest Laws Act 1971) for entering a park, armed, with intent to kill game. The three prisoners and another man had two guns between them; O'Flanaghan had one, but it did not appear which of the other three men had the second gun.] 'Any one of the party being armed, was sufficient to bring the others within the statute.' *R v Smith, O'Flanaghan & Preston* (1818) Russ & Ry 368 at 369, per cur.

'If the instruments [guns, nets, engines, etc] were not taken out for offensive purposes the prisoners would not be "armed" [within the

Night Poaching Act 1828]. But if you are satisfied that they were taken out for poaching purposes, for carrying nets and *also* for resisting the keepers, the prisoners *would* be armed. It does not follow that because an instrument can be used for another purpose the person carrying it would not be armed.' *R v Sutton* (1877) 13 Cox CC 648 at 649, per Lindley J

'The expression "armed" is an ordinary English word. Normally, it will involve either physically carrying arms, or it will involve proof that, to his knowledge, a defendant knows that they are immediately available. In our judgment, it is not necessary to prove an intent to use those arms if the situation should require it, though clearly if a defendant does use them, or has used them, then that is an obvious indication that he is armed.' *R v Jones* [1987] 2 All ER 692 at 698, per Tucker J

Australia   'To be armed with a weapon means something more than to be in possession of it; the weapon must also be available for immediate use as a weapon. No doubt questions of fact and degree are involved. A man is armed with a pistol if he is wearing it in a holster, though perhaps not if it is in the boot of his car. It is not necessary for it to be in his hand for him to be armed with it.' *Miller v Hrvojevic* [1972] VR 305 at 306, per Lusher J

ARMS

Court of Chivalry

The Lord High Constable and the Earl Marshal are two great officers of state whose duties in the Middle Ages were largely connected with the army in the field. From about 1348 onwards they jointly held a court, known as the High Court of Chivalry or *Curia Militaris*, in which offences committed out of the realm and matters relating to arms not triable under the common law were tried. Since the beginning of the sixteenth century appointments to the office of Lord High Constable have only been made on special occasions, mostly coronations, but the Court of Chivalry has continued to be held before the Earl Marshal alone and in consequence it has often been known as the Earl Marshal's Court. Questions of right to arms, precedence, descent and other kindred matters of honour, which are not within the jurisdiction of the ordinary courts of law are decided there. A declaration of that jurisdiction, by Charles II in 1672 defined the Earl Marshal as next and immediate officer under the Sovereign for determining and ordering all matters touching arms, ensigns of nobility, honour, and chivalry. The court last sat in 1954, but until then had not sat for over 200 years. (35 Halsbury's Laws (4th edn) para 816)

Officers of arms

There are three ranks of officers of arms, namely Kings of Arms, Heralds and Pursuivants, often referred to indifferently as 'heralds'. There are three Kings of Arms, six Heralds, and four Pursuivants. They are appointed by the Sovereign by letters patent under the Great Seal, and are under the jurisdiction of the Earl Marshal.

The Kings of Arms are Garter, Clarenceux, and Norroy and Ulster. The office of Garter King of Arms was constituted at a chapter of the Order of the Garter held in 1415, at which he was declared to be an officer of the Order and sovereign within the office of arms over all other officers of arms of the kingdom of England.

The Heralds number six, and are known as Windsor, Chester, Lancaster, Somerset, York and Richmond. The Pursuivants are four in number, known as Rouge Croix, Rouge Dragon, Bluemantle and Portcullis. It is not the function of Heralds or Pursuivants to grant arms, though they act as agents for applicants for grants of arms.

The Kings of Arms, Heralds and Pursuivants were incorporated in 1556 by King Philip and Queen Mary, who gave them a mansion called Derby House, which stood on the site of the present building known as the College of Arms, or Heralds' College.

Heralds Extraordinary and Pursuivants Extraordinary are occasionally appointed. They are nominated by the Earl Marshal and appointed by royal warrant addressed to the Earl Marshal. They are not members of the College of Arms and have only ceremonial duties. (35 Halsbury's Laws (4th edn) paras 810-814)

ARMY CHAPLAIN

'Army chaplain' shall mean a commissioned chaplain to Her Majesty's military forces in holy orders of the said Church. (Army Chaplains Act 1868, s 2)

ARRANGEMENT   *See also* COMPROMISE

[The Companies Act 1929, s 251 (repealed; see now the Companies Act 1985, s 601) enacted that any 'arrangement' between a company about to be, or in the course of being, wound up and its creditors should, subject to a right of appeal, be binding on the company if sanctioned by extraordinary resolution, and on the creditors if acceded to by three-fourths in number and value of the creditors.] 'What does "arrangement" mean? . . . It seems prima facie that "arrangement" in s 251 was not intended to include a compromise, properly so-called, for the word "compromise" is deliberately omitted. . . . A composition by a company with its creditors, as a result of which the company will be solvent, is not an arrangement by a company about to be wound up within the meaning of s 251.' *Re Contal Radio Ltd* [1932] 2 Ch 66 at 68–70, per Maugham J

'There was some discussion of the use of the word "arrangement" [in the Variation of Trusts Act 1958, s 1]. . . . If I may respectfully say so, the language used by the learned judge [in the court below] seems to indicate that an arrangement must be in some sense inter partes, some kind of scheme which two or more people have worked out. I do not myself accept that. I think that the word "arrangement" is deliberately used in the widest possible sense so as to cover any proposal which any person may put forward for varying or revoking the trusts.' *Re Steeds Will Trusts, Sandford v Stevenson* [1960] 1 All ER 487 at 492, CA, per Lord Evershed MR

[By the Restrictive Trade Practices Act 1956, s 6(3) (repealed; see now the Restrictive Trade Practices Act 1976, s 43(1)) an 'agreement' includes any agreement or 'arrangement', whether or not it is or is intended to be enforceable by legal proceedings.] 'I think it is highly significant that Parliament did not see fit to include any definition of "arrangement". I infer from this that it was intended that the word should be construed in its ordinary or popular sense. Though it may not be easy to put it into words, everybody knows what is meant by an arrangement between two or more parties. If the arrangement is intended to be enforceable by legal proceedings, as in the case where it is made for good consideration, it may no doubt properly be described as an agreement. But the statute clearly contemplates that there may be arrangements which are not enforceable by legal proceedings, but which create only moral obligations or obligations binding in honour. . . . When each of two or more parties intentionally arouses in the others an expectation that he will act in a certain way, it seems to me that he incurs at least a moral obligation to do so. An arrangement as so defined is therefore something "whereby the parties to it accept mutual rights and obligations".' *Re British Basic Slag Ltd's Agreements* [1963] 2 All ER 807 at 814, CA, per Willmer LJ

'No necessary or useful purpose would be served by attempting an expanded and comprehensive definition of the word "arrangement" in s 6(3) [repealed; see supra] of the Act. Cross J, said: ". . . all that is required to constitute an arrangement not enforceable in law is that the parties to it shall have communicated with one another in some way and that as a result of the communication each has intentionally aroused in the other an expectation that he will act in a certain way." I think that I am only expressing the same concept in slightly different terms if I say without attempting an exhaustive definition, for there are many ways in which arrangements may be made, that it is sufficient to constitute an "arrangement" between A and B, if (i) A makes a representation as to his future conduct with the expectation and intention that such conduct on his part will operate as an inducement to B to act in a particular way; (ii) such representation is communicated to B, who has knowledge that A so expected and intended, and (iii) such representation or A's conduct in fulfilment of it operates as an inducement, whether among other inducements or not, to B to act in that particular way.' Ibid at 819, per Diplock LJ

[The Companies Act 1948, s 206 (repealed; see now the Companies Act 1985, s 425) makes provision for the ordering of a meeting of creditors or members of a company where it is proposed to make a compromise or 'arrangement'.] 'I think the word "arrangement" in this section implies some element of give and take. Confiscation is not my idea of an arrangement. A member whose rights are expropriated without any compensating advantage is not, in my view, having his rights rearranged in any legitimate sense of that expression.' *Re NFU Development Trust Ltd* [1973] 1 All ER 135, per Brightman J

Australia [The Income Tax Assessment Act 1936–1986, s 260, makes void any contract, agreement or 'arrangement' which has the purpose or effect of evading, etc, tax.] 'Their Lordships are of opinion that the word "arrangement" is apt to describe something less than a binding contract or agreement, something in the nature of an understanding

between two or more persons—a plan arranged between them which may not be enforceable at law. But it must in this section comprehend, not only the initial plan, but also all the transactions by which it is carried into effect—all the transactions, that is, which have the effect of avoiding taxation, be they conveyances, transfers or anything else.' *Newton v Taxation Comr of Commonwealth of Australia* [1958] 2 All ER 759 at 763, PC, per Lord Denning; also reported [1958] AC 450 at 465

Australia '"Arrangement" [in the Income Tax Assessment Act 1936, s 80B(5) (see now s 80 DA (8)(c)] includes an understanding or plan between two or more persons which may not be enforceable in law and comprehends the legally effective acts done in carrying it out.' *Taxation Comr v Porter (K) & Co Pty Ltd* (1973) 22 FLR 344

New Zealand 'The next question is "was there an arrangement"? An arrangement I take to be something less formal than a binding agreement. It is appropriately expressed by Tompkins J in *Katz v Jones* [1967] NZLR 861 and I am happy to accept his definition of an arrangement as a promise to lend on mortgage as a result of a request made—a promise not in vague terms but in ascertained terms leading to the reasonable expectation of completion.' *Dunsford v Tate* [1971] 1 NZCPR 600 at 601 per Speight J

ARRANGEMENT OR UNDERSTANDING

Australia 'An arrangement or understanding normally involves communication between the parties arousing expectations in each that the other will act in a particular way [*Re British Slag Ltd's Agreements,* supra. For my part I find it difficult to envisage circumstances where there would be an understanding involving a commitment by one party as to the way he should behave without some commitment by the other party. Unless there is reciprocity of commitment I do not readily see why the parties would come to an arrangement or understanding.' *Trade Practices Commission v Email Ltd* (1980) 31 ALR 53 at 65, 66, per Lockhart J

ARRANGER OF CREDIT

Truth in lending

United States 'Arranger of credit' means a person who regularly arranges for the extension of consumer credit by another person if:

(i) A finance charge may be imposed for that credit, or the credit is payable by written agreement in more than four installments (not including a downpayment); and

(ii) The person extending the credit is not a creditor.

The term does not include a person (such as a real estate broker) when arranging seller financing of a dwelling or real property. (Truth in Lending Regulations 1982, 12 CFR s 226.2(a)(3))

ARREARS *See also* IN ARREAR

' "Arrears" is not a term of art but a well-known word commonly used to describe sums overdue and payable in respect of periods of time—for example, unpaid annuities, unpaid interest, unpaid preference dividends.' *Queen Anne's Bounty v Tithe Redemption Commission* [1938] Ch 229 at 237, per Bennett J

Australia 'The word "arrears" presupposes a time fixed for payment of a sum of money and the lapse of time thereafter without payment.' *Paice v Ayton* [1941] VLR 63 at 68, per Mann CJ

Canada 'We take arrears [in a contract requiring payment of moneys] to mean something which is behind in payment, or which remains unpaid. . . . It implies a duty and a default.' *Corbett v Taylor* (1864) 23 UCR 454 at 455, Ont CA, per cur.

ARREST

Arrest consists of the actual seizure or touching of a person's body with a view to his detention. The mere pronouncing of words of arrest is not an arrest, unless the person sought to be arrested submits to the process and goes with the arresting officer. An arrest may be made either with or without a warrant. (11 Halsbury's Laws (4th edn) para 99)

Arrest . . . is the apprehending or restraining of one's person, in order to be forthcoming to answer an alleged or suspected crime. (4 Bl Com 286)

'It is laid down by Holt CJ, and the other judges, in *Genner v Sparks* [(1704) 6 Mod Rep 173], that a mere touch constitutes an arrest, though the party be not actually taken.' *Sandon v Jervis* (1859) EB & E 935 at 947, 948, Ex Ch, per Crowder J

'An arrest does not become wrongful merely because the constable arrests a man for one felony, say murder, and he is subsequently charged with another felony, say manslaughter. . . . It is clear that the constable has not been guilty of an illegal arrest, if he reasonably suspected that murder had been done. Again I think it is clear that there is no need for the constable to explain the reason of arrest, if the arrested man is caught red-handed and the crime is patent to high Heaven. Nor, obviously, is explanation a necessary prelude to arrest where it is important to secure a possibly violent criminal. Nor again, can it be wrongful to arrest and detain a man upon a charge, of which he is reasonably suspected, with a view to further investigation of a second charge upon which information is incomplete. In all such matters a wide measure of discretion must be left to those whose duty it is to preserve the peace and bring criminals to justice. These and similar considerations lead me to the view that it is not an essential condition of lawful arrest that the constable should at the time of arrest formulate any charge at all, much less the charge which may ultimately be found in the indictment. But this, and this only, is the qualification which I would impose upon the general proposition. It leaves untouched the principle, which lies at the heart of the matter, that the arrested man is entitled to be told what is the act for which he is arrested. The "charge" ultimately made will depend upon the view taken by the law of his act. In ninety-nine cases out of a hundred the same words may be used to define the charge or describe the act, nor is any technical precision necessary: for instance, if the act constituting the crime is the killing of another man, it will be immaterial that the arrest is for murder and at a later hour the charge of manslaughter is substituted. The arrested man is left in no doubt that the arrest is for that killing. This is I think, the fundamental principle, *viz*, that a man is entitled to know what . . . are "the facts which are said to constitute a crime on his part".' *Christie v Leachinsky* [1947] 1 All ER 567 at 575, HL, per Lord Simonds

'In the ordinary way, an arrest consists of the actual seizure or touching of the person's body, with a view to his detention, and the mere pronouncing of words of arrest is not an arrest unless the person sought to be arrested submits to the process.' *R v Jones, ex p Moore* [1965] Crim LR 222 at 222, per cur.

'It is accepted . . . that there was no formal arrest of the respondent. He was asked to come to the police station because it was a wet night.

No doubt if he had refused to come, the police officer in question might have thought it necessary to arrest him and then this difficulty may never have arisen at all. But because the respondent was reasonable and went there on his own accord, it is impossible to say he was arrested.' *Campbell v Tormey* [1969] 1 All ER 961 at 966, per Ashworth J

[See also *Alderson v Booth* [1969] 2 All ER 271: an arrest is constituted where any form of words is used which in the circumstances of the case were calculated to bring to the accused's notice, and did bring to his notice, that he was under compulsion and thereafter he submitted to that compulsion.]

'It all depends on the circumstances of any particular case whether in fact it has been shown that a man has been arrested, and the court considers it unwise to say that there should be any particular formula followed. No formula will suit every case and it may well be that different procedures might have to be followed with different persons depending on their age, ethnic origin, knowledge of English, intellectual qualities, physical or mental disabilities. There is no magic formula; only the obligation to make it plain to the suspect by what is said and done that he is no longer a free man.' *R v Inwood* [1973] 2 All ER 645 at 649, CA, per cur.

[The question was as to the powers of the police to 'arrest' a person under the Road Traffic Act 1972 s 9(1) (now substituted by the Transport Act 1981, s 25(3), Sch 8) for failure to provide a specimen for a breath test.] 'What does "arrested" mean when used in the Act? Counsel for the appellant demonstrated without difficulty that the term is frequently used in the cases and in textbooks to cover unlawful, as well as lawful, arrest. But, despite the frequency of such use and the exalted standing of many who so employ it, I remain unconvinced that "arrest" is *stricto sensu* an accurate term to use in respect of the wholly unlawful restraint of the person of another. It may, in general, be acceptable to say (as in Halsbury's Laws [supra]) that "arrest consists in the seizure or touching of a person's body with a view to his restraint . . ." and in most cases no confusion results therefrom. But, in my judgment, where a man has quite unlawfully been physically restrained and is (however temporarily) detained in a condition which automatically invests him with a right to sue for damages for the tort of false imprisonment, it is in strictness inaccurate to describe him as having "been arrested" or as being "under arrest".' *Spicer v Holt* [1976] 3 All ER 71 at 82, 83, HL, per Lord Edmund-Davies

'It must be clearly understood that neither customs officers, nor police officers have any right to detain somebody for the purposes of getting them to help with their enquiries. Police officers either arrest for an offence or they do not arrest at all. Customs either detain for an offence or they do not detain at all. The law is clear. Neither arrest nor detention can properly be carried out without the accused person being told the offence for which he is being arrested. There is no such offence as "helping police with their enquiries". This is a phrase which has crept into use, largely because of the need for the press to be careful about how they report what has happened when somebody has been arrested but not charged. If the idea is getting around amongst either customs and excise officers or police officers that they can arrest or detain people, as the case may be, for this particular purpose, the sooner they disabuse themselves of that idea the better.' *R v Lemsatef* [1977] 2 All ER 835 at 839, CA, per cur.

'The word "arrest" in s 2 [of the Criminal Law Act 1967] is a term of art. First, it should be noted that arrest is a continuing act: it starts with the arrester taking a person into his custody (*sc.* by action or words restraining him from moving anywhere beyond the arrester's control), and it continues until the person so restrained is either released from custody or, having been brought before a magistrate, is remanded in custody by the magistrate's judicial act. . . . Strictly speaking, the arrester may change from time to time during a continuous period of custody since the arrester is the person who at any particular time is preventing the arrested person from removing himself from custody; but, although this may be important in a case where the initial arrest has been made by a person who is not a constable (a "citizen's arrest"), it is without practical significance in the common case of arrest by a constable and detention in police custody at a police station, since s 48(1) of the Police Act 1964 makes the chief constable of the police area vicariously liable for torts committed by members of the force that he commands in the performance or purported performance of their duties as constables. Second, it should be noted that the mere act of taking a person into custody does not constitute an "arrest" unless that person knows, either at the time when he is first taken into custody or as soon thereafter as it is reasonably practicable to inform him, on what charge or on suspicion of what crime he is being arrested: see *Christie v Leachinsky* [1947] 1 All ER 567].' *Holgate-Mohammed v Duke* [1984] 1 All ER 1054 at 1056, HL, per Lord Diplock

Australia 'Obviously, "arrest" should have a consistency of meaning. An arrest consists in the seizure or the touching of a person's body with a view to his restraint; words may, however, amount to an arrest if, in the circumstances of the case, they are calculated to bring, and do bring, to a person's notice that he is under compulsion and he thereafter submits to the compulsion: see *Halsbury's Laws of England*, 4th edn, vol 11, para 99, at p 73 [see supra]. Similarly, in general, an arrested person must be informed of the true ground of his arrest, unless the circumstances are such that he must know the substance of the alleged offence; a person is entitled to know for what offence or on suspicion of what offence he has been seized and the person arresting him does not make a lawful arrest if he keeps the reason for it to himself or gives a reason which is not the true one: see *Christie v Leachinsky* [1947] AC 573 [supra]. See also *Donaldson v Broomby*, a decision of the Federal Court of Australia, per Deane J (1982) 40 ALR 525. Whilst it is a condition of lawful arrest that the party arrested should know on what charge or on suspicion of what charge he is arrested, it does not follow that a person who has been arrested on one charge cannot be detained in custody on another charge.' *Lewis v Norman* [1982] 2 NSWLR 649 at 655, per Enderby J

Of ship

'The arrest of a ship in an action *in rem* is the means whereby, among other things, a necessaries man obtains security for a debt of a special character without a judgment or order for payment of money. It is a right given to him by the legislature, a right the scope of which, in my view, has recently been extended by the Administration of Justice Act 1956, s 1(1)(m), and possibly also by s 1(1)(p) (repealed; see now the Supreme Court Act 1981, s 20). The special character of the debt, in my view, is that it is incurred by giving credit to the owners of vessels for the use of those vessels. It is to be regarded in this way: it is the advancing of goods on credit to a ship which, in the ordinary course of business, moves away from the port of supply, to which it may or may not return. The goods have been supplied for the neces-

sary use of the ship and for the purpose of the ship prosecuting its adventures, and, as I say, the ship may never return to that port again. . . . Arrest, as I see it, is the means given by law, whereby security is obtained for a debt of a special character, and, by so arresting, the necessaries man becomes a secured creditor.' *The Zafiro, John Carlborn & Co Ltd v Zafiro (Owners)* [1959] 2 All ER 537 at 544, per Hewson J

ARRESTS, RESTRAINTS AND DETAINMENTS

The words [in a policy of marine insurance] 'arrests, restraints, and detainments, of all kings, princes and people of what nation, condition or quality soever', refer to political or executive acts, and do not include a loss caused by riot or by ordinary judicial process; and by the word 'people' is meant not mobs or multitudes of men, but the ruling power of the country, whatever that may be. A restraint does not necessarily involve the use of actual physical force; any authoritative prohibition on the part of any governing power or the operation of any municipal law is sufficient. It is doubtful whether compliance with an *ultra vires* order of a government department unaccompanied by a threat of force is a loss by restraint of princes. (25 Halsbury's Laws (4th edn) para 161)

The term 'arrests, etc, of kings, princes, and people' refers to political or executive acts, and does not include a loss caused by riot or by ordinary judicial process. (Marine Insurance Act 1906, Sch 1)

ARRIVAL

Of ship

'Where the words "arrived at the port" are used evidence may always be given to shew when, by the usage of the port, the ship can be said to have arrived in the port. Examples were given in the cases referred to, and one is familiar with it in practice, that there are ports of very large area, and by the custom of the port arrival is considered to take place on the arrival of the ship at some particular place within that area, and any days that are to be dated in a shipping document "from arrival", are the days dated from arrival at that particular spot within the port, and not from the moment of her actual arrival within the area or ambit of the port. Such has been held with regard to the port of Liverpool, the port of Hull, the port of Antwerp, the port of St Louis, in the Mauritius, and many other large ports, where the port extends over a considerably large area of ground. Such is the case, of course, with regard to the port of Liverpool, which extends, I presume, down to the mouth of the Mersey, and no authority is wanted, nor was it denied before us, that if a dispute had arisen, it would have been perfectly legitimate to tender and receive evidence to shew that "arrival at the port of Liverpool" did not mean arrival at the mouth of the Mersey, but arrival at some place at or near Liverpool itself.' *Norden SS Co v Dempsey* (1876) 45 LJQB 764 at 766, 767, DC, per Lord Coleridge

'Now, the answer to the inquiry whether the ship can or cannot properly be described as an "arrived" ship obviously depends upon the point which the parties have chosen to designate in the charterparty as the destination. The degree of precision is purely a matter of agreement between them. In practice the destination is generally one of the following: (1) a port; (2) a specified area within a port, such, eg as a basin, a dock, or a certain distance or reach of shore on the sea coast or in a river; or (3) the still more limited and precise point where the physical act of loading is to take place, as, eg a particular quay, pier, wharf or spout, or (where the operation is to be performed by means of lighters, and the ship is not to be in a shore berth) a particular mooring. . . . If the stipulated point of destination is either (2) or (3), the answer to the question as to whether the ship is or is not an "arrived" ship . . . depends on an absolutely simple fact, viz her being or not being in the one case within the specified area, or, in the other case, at the narrower and more limited point of destination. . . . The limits of a port established by law or ancient custom may be very wide; or, again, in the case of a newly-established place of shipping traffic, the limits may be uncertain because not yet defined by any competent authority. . . . Lord Coleridge CJ, in the course of his judgment [in *Norden SS Co v Dempsey,* supra] said: "Principle and authority have alike decided that where the question is what particular part of an extensive port a vessel must have reached before she can be said to have arrived at her destination, evidence may be given as to the usage of the port in that respect.". . . In the absence of any proof of a custom of this kind . . . the commercial area of a port, arrival within which makes

the ship an arrived ship, and, as such, entitled to give notice of readiness to load, and at the expiration of the notice to begin to count lay days, ought, I think, to be that area of the named port of destination on arrival within which the master can effectively place his ship at the disposal of the charterer, the vessel herself being then, so far as she is concerned, ready to load, and as near as circumstances permit to the actual loading "spot" . . . be it quay or wharf, or pier, or mooring, and in a place where ships waiting for access to that spot usually lie, or, if there be more such loading spots than one, as near as circumstances permit to that one of such spots which the charterer prefers.' *Leonis SS Co Ltd v Rank Ltd* [1908] 1 KB 499 at 518, 519, 521–523, CA, per Kennedy LJ

'Before a ship can be treated as an arrived ship she must be within the port and at the immediate and effective disposition of the charterer and . . . her geographical position is of secondary importance. . . . It is so much easier to establish that, if the ship is at a usual waiting place within the port, it can generally be presumed that she is there fully at the charterer's disposal. I would therefore state what I would hope to be the true legal position in this way. Before a ship can be said to have arrived at a port she must, if she cannot proceed immediately to a berth, have reached a position within the port where she is at the immediate and effective disposition of the charterer. If she is at a place where waiting ships usually lie, she will be in such a position unless in some extraordinary circumstances proof of which would lie in the charterer. . . . If the ship is waiting at some other place in the port then it will be for the owner to prove that she is as fully at the disposition of the charterer as she would have been if in the vicinity of the berth for loading or discharge.' *The Johanna Oldendorff, EL Oldendorff & Co GmbH v Tradax Export SA* [1973] 3 All ER 148 at 157, HL, per Lord Reid

'While until *The Johanna Oldendorff* [supra] there may have been uncertainty under a port charter as to where within the named port a ship must be in order to complete the voyage stage, there was a legal certainty that neither in port nor berth charter was the voyage stage brought to an end by the arrival of the ship at any waiting place short of the limits of the named port.' *Federal Commerce and Navigation Co Ltd v Tradax Export SA* [1977] 2 All ER 849 at 857, HL, per Lord Diplock

ARSON

Arson, *ab ardendo*, is the malicious and wilful burning of the house or outhouses of another man. This is an offence of very great malignity, and much more pernicious to the public than simple theft: because, first, it is an offence against that right, of habitation, which is acquired by the law of nature as well as by the laws of society; next, because of the terror and confusion that necessarily attends it; and, lastly, because in simple theft the thing stolen only changes its master, but still remains *in esse* for the benefit of the public, whereas by burning the very substance is absolutely destroyed. It is also frequently more destructive than murder itself, of which too it is often the cause: since murder, atrocious as it is, seldom extends beyond the felonious act designed; whereas fire too frequently involves in the common calamity persons unknown to the incendiary, and not intended to be hurt by him, and friends as well as enemies. (4 Bl Com 220)

A person who without lawful excuse destroys or damages any property belonging to another intending to destroy or damage any such property or being reckless as to whether any such property would be destroyed or damaged is guilty of an offence. . . . A person who without lawful excuse destroys or damages any property, whether belonging to himself or another, intending to destroy or damage any property or being reckless as to whether any property would be destroyed or damaged, and intending by the destruction or damage to endanger the life of another or being reckless as to whether the life of another would be thereby endangered, is guilty of an offence. . . . The common law offence of arson has been abolished but if either of the offences above referred to is committed by destroying or damaging property by fire, it is charged as arson. A person guilty of arson is liable on conviction on indictment to imprisonment for life. (11 Halsbury's Laws (4th edn) para 1306)

'The crime of arson at common law consists in maliciously and voluntarily burning the house of *another*.' *R v Spalding* (1780) 1 Leach 218 at 219, per cur.

'Arson is the burning of the house of another . . .; it is an offence immediately against the *possession*, and . . . therefore if a person in possession of a house as tenant, however short his term may be, set fire to it, it is not arson.' *R v Breeme* (1780) 1 Leach 220 at 221, per cur.

[The common law offence of arson was abolished by the Criminal Damage Act 1971, s 11(1). It was made a statutory offence, with liability to imprisonment for life, under ss 1(3), 4(1) of that Act.]

ART *See* FINE ART

ARTICLE

'Articles' includes substances. (Supply Powers Act 1975, s 7)

'Article' includes any substance, whether in solid or liquid form or in the form of a gas or vapour. (Aviation Security Act 1982, s 38(1))

[A clause in the conditions of letting attached to a tenancy agreement provided that the landlord would not be responsible for (inter alia) the loss of 'articles' entrusted to him. A cabin trunk was deposited in a baggage room attached to the block of flats concerned, its loss being discovered two years later.] 'It is contended by the appellants that the cabin trunk was an "article" within the meaning of that clause. In my view, that clause has no concern with what I may call long term or semi-permanent deposits of luggage in a baggage room, maintained for the convenience of all tenants of the various flats, to enable them to keep bulky things in it for a considerable period of time. In the present case the baggage room was under the porter's office. That condition is addressed to purely temporary things; parcels delivered by trades-people, letters left by hand, telephone messages, and so on, to various members of the staff: it has nothing to say as to the proper care of baggage deposited in the care of the porter in the baggage room.' *Andrews v Home Flats Ltd* [1945] 2 All ER 698 at 699, CA, per Scott LJ

'It is necessary . . . to interpret cl 1 of a notice which was affixed to the door of the plaintiff's bedroom. . . . Clause 1 begins thus: "The proprietors will not hold themselves responsible for articles lost or stolen unless handed to the manageress for safe custody". The word "articles" is there used in connection with the notion of handing them to the manageress for safe custody. A packet of pins, a lead pencil, a pair of pyjamas, and numerous other things are articles, but one would not expect such things to be carried down every time a guest went out to shop and handed to the management. The clause proceeds: "Valuables should be deposited for safe custody in a sealed packet and a receipt obtained." Anything more ludicrous than to apply a phrase of that sort to the articles I have mentioned would be difficult to imagine. In my view, the clause must be read as a whole, and must refer to things like diamond neck-laces and not to the clothes one normally wears.' *Olley v Marlborough Court Ltd* [1948] 1 All ER 955 at 956, per Oliver J; affd. [1949] 1 KB 532

'The question whether premises are a factory depends on the nature of the process which is carried on there: the definition specifies various kinds of process but all are processes dealing with "articles". The respondents say that water is not an article and therefore dealing with it cannot make their premises a factory. They say that no one has ever main-tained that the Factories Act 1937, applies to any kind of waterworks. This case therefore raises an important new point. The word "article" has many different meanings or shades of meaning and therefore the context in which it occurs is of crucial importance. The respondents maintain that an article must be a solid article and that the word excludes liquids and gases, or alternatively they maintain that a natural substance or at least a natural liquid or gas is not an article: no one would call water in a stream or air in a room an article and it can make no difference that it is collected, impounded or confined in some way. There may have been a time when few liquids but alcohol and no gases were made or treated by industrial processes, but that time is long past and I find it impossible to suppose that as recently as 1937 Parliament intended to make so fundamental a distinction between solid articles and, say, petrol or coal gas as to deny the benefits of the Factories Act 1937, to workers in premises where only liquids or gases were being treated or manufactured. Many substances take solid, liquid or gaseous form according to temperature and pressure and it would be, to say the least odd, if in this context a substance is an article when solid, ceases to be an article when made liquid or gaseous, and becomes an article again when it solidifies. I need not consider whether water is an article before it has been impounded or reduced into possession. But if other liquids are articles I see no reason why the natural origin of water should make a difference. No doubt water is generally dealt with in larger quantities than other liquids, but it could not be that a small quantity of water is an article but a large quan-tity is not. It therefore appears to me that the water in the filter house is an article and that by

reason of its treatment there the premises are a factory within the meaning of the definition in s 151.' *Longhurst v Guildford Water Board* [1961] 3 All ER 545 at 546, 547, HL, per Lord Reid

Australia 'The word "article" according to the Shorter Oxford Dictionary bears the meaning "a piece of goods or property". The word would, I think, according to its normal and ordinary meaning include a carpet or cur-tain, a desk and a bookshelf.' *Taxation Comr v Faichney* (1973) 47 ALJR 35 at 38, per Mason J

Of food

[The Sale of Food and Drugs Act 1875, s 2 (repealed) enacted that 'the term "food" shall include every article used for food or drink by man other than drugs or water.' Section 3 en-acted that 'no person shall mix, or order, or permit any other person to mix any article of food with any ingredient or material so as to render the article injurious to health, with intent that the same may be sold in that state.'] 'We are asked by the case to say . . . whether the baking powder [composed of bicarbonate of soda, ground rice and alum] is an article of food within the meaning of the statute. . . . We are clearly of opinion that the baking pow-der in question is not an article of food, and that neither the sale of it, nor the admixture of it with an article of food, unless such article is intended for sale, is prohibited by the statute. . . . We do not . . . in anything we have said intend to convey it as our opinion that nothing can be deemed to be an article of food unless it be made up into an eatable or drinkable form and fit for immediate use, for we have no doubt that the substantial and requisite materials for making, and which are to form part of the unadulterated article when made—e.g. flour, butter, salt, mustard, pep-per, etc.—are articles of food; for though nobody would ordinarily dream of eating them alone, yet they are articles intended to form substantial components of articles of food, or to be eaten as adjuncts thereto. Such, however, is not the character of baking pow-der.' *James v Jones* [1894] 1 QB 304 at 307–309, per cur.

Of value

[An agreement in the form of a building lease contained a clause providing that every relic or 'article' of antiquity or 'value' found on the site should belong to the Corporation.] 'Although the matter is largely one of first impression, I can see no reason for departing from the general rule that words are to be taken to be used in their ordinary and natural sense, unless there is something in the instrument itself to show that the words are not used in that sense. Bank notes are, in their ordinary meaning, articles of value. Many relics, for example pieces of Roman pottery, have no corporeal value, if I understand the expression correctly, in themselves, but have a value dependent on extraneous factors, for example, age and historical association. Many articles of antiquity or rarity have a value to others than collectors, and have a value other than curiosity value. There are no words in the clause to confine articles of value to articles which have a value dependent on their antiquity or rarity. Again, it is to be observed that treasure trove, which is also mentioned in the clause, is not limited to articles of value to a collector or antique articles. . . . Furthermore, the phrase "shall be carefully and without avoidable damage removed", which was relied on as indicating that the words related to articles of a fragile nature by reason of their antiquity, would equally apply to modern bank notes which had been damaged by fire or water. A modern gold watch or a hoard of smuggled Swiss watches would, as I think, be within the plain intention of the clause, which is, in substance, to secure that any adventitious profit derived from the finding of articles, whether relics, antique or rare articles, or articles of value, should go to the Corporation. I see no reason for cutting down the generality of the words "articles of value".' *London Corpn v Appleyard* [1963] 2 All ER 834 at 840, per McNair J

Of vertu *See* VERTU

ARTICLES *See also* MEMORANDUM OF ASSOCIATION

Articles are clauses of a document, and hence the word 'articles' sometimes means the document itself. 'Marriage articles' commonly means a contract in consideration of marriage to settle property on terms intended to be embodied subsequently in a formal marriage settlement. (42 Halsbury's Laws (4th edn) para 628)

'Articles' means, in relation to a company, its articles of association, as originally framed or as altered by resolution, including (so far as applicable to the company) regulations contained in or annexed to any enactment relating to companies passed before this Act, as altered

by or under any such enactment. (Companies Act 1985, s 744)

[Generally, as to articles of association, see ss 7–9 of the Act of 1985. For form see Table C as set out in the Companies (Tables A–F) Regulations 1985, SI 1985/805.]

'Articles' means written articles of clerkship binding a person to serve a solicitor as an articled clerk. (Solicitors Act 1974, s 87(1))

ARTICLES OF INCORPORATION

United States 'Articles of incorporation' include amended and restated articles of incorporation and articles of merger. (Revised Model Business Corporation Act 1984, s 1.40(1))

ARTICULATED VEHICLE *See* VEHICLE

ARTIFICER

All workmen, labourers, and other persons in any manner engaged in the performance of any employment or operation, of what nature soever, in or about the hosiery manufacture shall be and be deemed to be 'artificers'. (Hosiery Manufacture (Wages) Act 1874, s 7)

'I cannot conceive that the term "artificer" [in s 3 of 4 Geo 4, c 34 (repealed) which gave to the justices jurisdiction over any servant in husbandry, 'artificer', etc, who was guilty of misconduct, etc] is applicable only where manual labour is used. This person [a pattern designer employed by calico printers] sets the whole establishment at work, and so he may fairly be considered an artificer, as contributing, and importantly, to the printing of calico.' *Re Ormerod* (1844) 1 New Sess Cas 38 at 40, per Williams J

ARTISTIC

'I think we must avoid philosophic or metaphysical argument about the nature of beauty, not only because there does not seem to be any consensus about this but also because those who are ignorant of philosophy are entitled to have opinions about what is artistic. I think that by common usage it is proper for a person to say that in his opinion a thing has an artistic character if he gets pleasure or satisfaction or it may be uplift from contemplating it. No doubt it is necessary to beware of those who get pleasure from looking at something which has cost them a great deal of money. But if unsophisticated people get pleasure from seeing something which they admire I do not see why we must say that it is not artistic because those who profess to be art experts think differently. After all there are great differences of opinion among those who can properly be called experts. It is I think of importance that the maker or designer of a thing should have intended that it should have an artistic appeal but I would not regard that as either necessary or conclusive. If any substantial section of the public genuinely admires and values a thing for its appearance and gets pleasure or satisfaction, whether emotional or intellectual, from looking at it, I would accept that it is artistic although many others may think it meaningless or common or vulgar.' *Hensher (George) Ltd v Restawile Upholstery (Lancs) Ltd* [1974] 2 All ER 420 at 423, 424, per Lord Reid

ARTISTIC WORK

In this Act 'artistic work' means a work of any of the following descriptions, that is to say,—
(a) the following, irrespective of artistic quality, namely paintings, sculptures, drawings, engravings and photographs;
(b) works of architecture, being either buildings or models for buildings;
(c) works of artistic craftsmanship, not falling within either of the preceding paragraphs.
(Copyright Act 1956, s 3(1))

New Zealand 'The product drawing [of a mould for production of toilet fittings] is a drawing within the definition of the term "artistic work" in s 2(1) of the Copyright Act 1962. By that definition it is not required that the drawing should have any artistic quality.' *P S Johnson & Associates Ltd v Bucko Enterprises Ltd* [1975] 1 NZLR 311 at 315, per Chilwell J

New Zealand 'The definition of artistic work is set out in s 2(1)(a) of the Copyright Act 1962. " 'Artistic work' means a work of any of the following descriptions, that is to say—(a) the following, irrespective of artistic quality, namely, paintings, sculptures, drawings, engravings, and photographs." A reading of the definition of "artistic work" in s 2(1)(a) of the Act indicates that the Act when it speaks of engraving primarily has in contemplation the

final prints made from an engraved plate rather than the plate itself. In deciding whether an engraved plate such as the mould or die is an engraving in terms of our New Zealand statute, it is important to know the process by which the mould or die was created. . . . We agree with the conclusion . . . that engraving embraces not only the image made from the engraved plate but the engraved plate itself. . . . It is the purpose of copyright to protect the original skill and labour of the author and there is a large degree of that skill and labour brought to bear in making the engraved plate. We do not believe that it was the intention of Parliament to deny copyright in the plate and yet allow it in the print taken from that plate.' *Wham-O MFG Co v Lincoln Industries* [1984] 1 NZLR 641 at 656, 657, 659, CA, per Davison CJ

AS AND WHEN

Canada 'The meaning to be placed upon the phrase in the contract "as and when required to fill export orders" is the chief question to be determined. I think the words "as and when" indicate that export orders will be forthcoming and deliveries would be asked for to fill these orders. These words refer to a future uncertain time and indicate, in my opinion, that export orders, will be received in future, and that delivery of the goods will be required. . . . The words "as and when" are not synonymous with the word "if".' *Wingold v Looser & Co* [1951] 1 DLR 429 at 434, Ont CA, per Hogg JA

AS FAR AS POSSIBLE

'The information is laid against the appellant under the 108th section of the Towns Improvement Clauses Act 1847 (repealed) for so negligently using his furnace as not to consume the smoke. . . . That section . . . is qualified by s 55 of the special Act, which provides that the words "consume the smoke" shall not mean in all cases "consume all the smoke", and remits the penalties, if the furnace is so constructed as to consume *as far as possible* all the smoke arising from it, and if the defendant has carefully attended to it, and has consumed the smoke *as far as possible*. . . . I apprehend these words mean, "as far as possible, consistently with carrying on the trade in an ordinary manner, and with a careful use and management of a properly constructed furnace".' *Cooper v Woolley* (1867) LR 2 Exch 88 at 90, 91, per Kelly CB

[The matter is now governed by the provisions of the Clean Air Act 1956, in which the phrase is 'as far as is practicable'.]

AS IS

Canada 'When used with reference to a sale, people generally take the term "as is" to mean that the product is bought and sold in the condition in which it then exists, for better or for worse, with altogether no warranties in relation to quality, durability, or fitness, and with the entire risk in those respects to be borne by the buyer.' *MacLeod v Ens* (1982) 135 DLR (3d) 365 at 367, Sask CA, per Cameron JA

AS IT STANDS

'I think that the intention of the parties to be gathered from the contract itself [a contract for the sale of a cargo "as it stands"] was, that the cargo should be taken by the purchaser for better for worse for less or for more. Both parties put faith in the correctness of the bill of lading. . . . On this footing the calculation of the price to be paid proceeds. The price was to be 30s. per quarter "the quantity to be taken from the bill of lading". . . . This shows that . . . the risk of the quantity turning out to be misrepresented in the bill of lading was thrown on the purchaser. If it had turned out to measure more he would have been the gainer; if it be less he must abide by the loss.' *Covas v Bingham* (1853) 23 LJQB 26 at 29, 30, per Lord Campbell CJ

AS NEARLY AS MAY BE

Australia [Rule 26(1) of the Rules made under the Workers Compensation Act 1926 (NSW) provides that the procedure of the hearing of an application shall conform 'as nearly as may be' to a district court action.] 'The words "as nearly as may be" means presumably "as nearly as possible" or, as I would prefer, "as nearly as reasonably practicable". *Schipp v Herford Pty Ltd* [1975] 1 NSWR 412 at 420, per Samuels JA

AS OF RIGHT

The enjoyment of a right claimed to exist under an alleged custom must be enjoyment 'as of right' . . . that is to say, all acts which it is alleged were committed under and by virtue of the custom in order to establish the custom must have been done without violence, without stealth or secrecy, and without leave or licence asked for and given, either expressly or impliedly, from time to time. (12 Halsbury's Laws (4th edn) para 423)

'There is only one way in which the public can enjoy a footway, and that is by walking over it. . . . Members of the public enjoy it "as a right", when, as Tomlin J said, in *Hue v Whiteley* [[1929] 1 Ch 440 at 445], they use it: believing themselves to be exercising a public right to pass from one highway to another. This seems to me the simplest and truest interpretation of the three words "as of right", as applied to public rights of way. It is doubtless correct to say that negatively they import the absence of any of the three characteristics of compulsion, secrecy or licence.' *Jones v Bates* [1938] 2 All ER 237 at 245, CA, per Scott LJ

New Zealand 'I do not think a way on private property used with the consent of, or at least without objection from, the owner or owners by such members of the public as desire to use it as a passage from saleyards to a hotel and a main road can properly be described as open to or used by the public "as of right".' *Taylor v Seymour* (1915) 34 NZLR 919 at 921, per Denniston J; also reported 17 GLR 382 at 383

AS SOON AS

'By the terms of the contract tendered to the plaintiffs' agent the hoops were to be furnished [by the manufacturer] "as soon as possible". . . . I think this contract means no more than a reasonable time, regard being had to the plaintiffs' facilities and extent of business, and to the contracts they already had in hand.' *Attwood v Emery* (1856) 1 CBNS 110 at 115, per Cresswell J

'To do a thing "as soon as possible" means to do it within a reasonable time, with an undertaking to do it in the shortest practicable time. . . . I quite agree that a manufacturer or tradesman is not bound to discard all other work for the occasion, in order to take in hand a thing which he promises to do "as soon as possible", for instance, a tailor, who accepts an order to make a coat "as soon as possible", need not put down a half-made vest in order to begin the coat; every customer knows at the time of giving the order that the manufacturer or tradesman may have other orders on hand.' *Hydraulic Engineering Co Ltd v McHaffie* (1878) 4 QBD 670 at 673, CA, per Bramwell LJ

'A mining lease contained a clause, whereby the lessees covenanted that they would immediately, or 'as soon as may be' after the demise, proceed to open the mines thereby demised.] 'I think that it is quite impossible to say that when a man covenants in regard to particular mines that he will proceed to open and get them "as soon as may be" after the date of the demise, that means that he may do so as soon as may be, having regard to his own convenience, and to his business interests in working other lands and other mines outside the demised mines altogether. I think that this would be making those words far more pregnant and giving them a far wider meaning than can in any legitimate way be attributed to them. If the appellants had wished to protect themselves in order that they might be able to work this mine entirely as an auxiliary to their other mines, they ought to have taken care to put their bargain in language which at all events would admit of the construction upon which they now seek to insist.' *Wigan Coal & Iron Co v Eckersley* (1910) 103 LT 468 at 470, HL, per Lord Loreburn LC

'It seems to me . . . that the expression "as soon as practicable" must mean in the ordinary course of navigation, and that it does not mean as soon as practicable for the convenience of the merchant's business. If the merchant has a steamer available to carry a cargo of oil and does not use her for that oil, but uses her to carry other oil to some other place, and so delays the transhipment of the particular cargo, it seems to me that he is not shipping it as soon as practicable.' *Anglo-American Oil Co Ltd v Port of London Authority* [1914] 1 KB 14 at 24, 25, per Pickford J

Canada 'To do a thing "as soon as possible" means to do it within a reasonable time, with an understanding to do it within the shortest possible time.' *King's Old Country Ltd v Liquid Carbonic Can Corpn Ltd* [1942] 2 WWR 603 at 606, Man KB, per Dysart J; affd [1943] 1 WWR 189, Man CA

AS THE CROW FLIES

'The phrase "as the crow flies" is a popular and picturesque expression, to denote a straight line, which I think is clearly the proper mode of measuring the distance from one given point to another.' *Stokes v Grissell* (1854) 14 CB 678 at 689, per Maule J

ASCERTAIN

New Zealand The Transport Act 1962, s 65(1) places an obligation on a motor vehicle driver who has been involved in an accident to stop and also to 'ascertain' whether any other person has been injured.] 'He [the driver] had admittedly merely glanced at the other vehicle just prior to the collision. It appeared to him, and indeed to his passengers, to be empty—as in fact it was—but he made no further investigation of that fact. He assumed from this glance that it was empty, that no person, therefore, had been injured, and the question is whether ascertainment means an assumption on such slight investigation or something more. I am quite clear in my mind that the duty to ascertain is the duty to make sure whether any person was injured or not. The word "ascertain" means that in ordinary parlance, and there is no reason to construe it in any other way.' *Laughton v Christchurch City* [1970] NZLR 1114 at 1115, per Wilson J

Ascertained goods

'I rule that "ascertained" [in the Sale of Goods Act 1893, s 52 (repealed; see now the Sale of Goods Act 1979, s 52) which, inter alia, deals with specific performance of contracts to deliver "ascertained goods"] means that the individuality of the goods must in some way be found out, and when it is, then the goods have been ascertained.' *Thames Sack & Bag Co Ltd v Knowles & Co Ltd* (1918) 88 LJKB 585 at 588, per Sankey J

'The claim of the claimants to specific performance in their arguments in the Courts below and before us was based solely on the provisions of s 52 of the Sale of Goods Act 1893, [repealed; see supra]. That section is a re-enactment in an amended form of s 2 of the Mercantile Law Amendment Act 1856, which gave the remedy in all actions and suits for breach of contract to deliver specific goods for a price in money. The present section gives the remedy "in any action for breach of contract to deliver specific or ascertained goods". . . . "Ascertained" probably means identified in accordance with the agreement after the time a contract of sale is made, and I shall assume that to be the meaning.' *Re Wait* [1927] 1 Ch 606 at 630, per Atkin LJ

See, generally, 41 Halsbury's Laws (4th edn) para 719.

ASCERTAINABLE

Canada [The Motor Vehicle Indemnity Act 1947 (Alta) c 11, s 9 (repealed; see now the Motor Vehicle Accident Claims Act RSA 1980, c M–21, s 9) provided recourse against a provincial insurance fund where the driver or owner of a motor vehicle causing an accident was not 'ascertainable'.] 'It seems to me that the word "ascertainable" in the section can at the most mean no more than ascertainable by such reasonable means as are available to the injured person, and that there is no obligation on him to perform a series of acts which are bound to be futile or which involve the expenditure of an unreasonable sum of money. In my view if the injured person or someone in his behalf reports in due course to the police, and the police, with all the means available to them, employ such methods as in their experience they deem reasonable, and these methods prove unsuccessful, then the injured person should be deemed to have used reasonable efforts to ascertain the identity of the driver and such identity is not "ascertainable" within the meaning of the section.' *Dowhaniuk v Superintendent of Insurance and Davies* [1955] 1 DLR 560 at 564, per Egbert J

Canada [Taxability of income from office depended on its being 'fixed or ascertainable'.] 'I take that word to mean that the amount to be paid is capable of being made certain, or capable of being determined but not that a definite sum be known by the office-holder at the commencement of holding office. The word has to have some meaning beyond "fixed" or else it is completely redundant.' *Merchant v R* [1984] 2 FCR 197 at 202, Fed Ct TD, per Reed J

ASSAULT   *See also* AFFRAY;
AGGRAVATED ASSAULT; BATTERY;
INDECENT ASSAULT

Assault . . . is an attempt or offer to beat another, without touching him: as if one lifts up his cane, or his fist, in a threatning manner at another; or strikes at him, but misses him; this is an assault, *insultus*, which Finch describes to be 'unlawful setting upon one's person'. This also is an inchoate violence, amounting considerably higher than bare threats; and therefore, though no actual suffering is proved, yet the party injured may have redress by action of *trespass vi et armis;* wherein he shall recover damages as a compensation for the injury. (3 Bl Com 120)

An assault is any act committed intentionally, or possibly recklessly, which causes another person to apprehend immediate and unlawful violence. If force is actually applied, directly or indirectly, unlawfully or without the consent of the person assaulted, the assault becomes a battery, however slight the force. A battery may or may not include an assault. Although an assault is an independent crime and should be treated as such, for practical purposes the term 'assault' is generally synonymous with 'battery' and is used to mean the actual intended use of unlawful force to another person without his consent.

There may be an assault without the application of force, but in such cases there must be some threatening act sufficient to raise in the mind of the person threatened a fear of immediate violence; if a threat is made to strike a person with the fist, at such a distance as to make it impossible for the blow to reach, there is no assault; similarly, where a firearm is aimed at a range to which the missile could not possibly carry. There seems no logical reason why mere words should not amount to an assault.

The mental element in the offence of battery is satisfied by proof that the defendant intentionally or recklessly applied force to the person of another. There must, however, be a positive act; no mere omission to act can amount to a battery. (11 Halsbury's Laws (4th edn) para 1210)

Assault is an intentional offer of force or violence to the person of another. There is an assault if there is a menace of violence, with a present ability to commit it. The menace must either be accompanied by an intention to commit the violence or must raise an actual fear of violence in the mind of the person threatened. Thus, it is an assault for one person within striking distance unlawfully to advance to another in a threatening attitude with the fist clenched and with the intention of striking him immediately; or to point or brandish a weapon at another with the intention of using it; or to present a firearm at another with a threat of shooting; or to ride after another in a threatening manner so as to compel him to run for shelter to avoid being beaten. (45 Halsbury's Laws (4th edn) para 1310)

'It may be material to consider what is the meaning of the expression "common assault". It appears to me that it means an assault not accompanied by any such aggravated circumstances as would give to the assault the character of a distinct offence recognised by the law as something more than an assault.' *Re Thompson* (1860) 30 LJMC 19 at 23, per Pollock CB

An assault can be constituted, without there being battery, for instance, by a threatening gesture or a threat to use violence against a person, but I do not know any authority which says that where one person invites another person to touch him that can be said to be an assault. The question of consent or non-consent only arises if there is something which can be called an assault and, without consent, would be an assault. If that which was done to this child was of an indecent nature and would have been an assault if done against her will, it would also be an assault if it was done with her consent because she could not consent to an indecent assault. Before we decide whether there has been an indecent assault we must decide whether there has been an assault, and I cannot hold that an invitation to somebody to touch the invitor can amount to an assault on the invitee.' *Fairclough v Whipp* [1951] 2 All ER 834 at 834, per Lord Goddard CJ

'An assault is any act which intentionally—or possibly recklessly—causes another person to apprehend immediate and unlawful personal violence. Although "assault" is an independent crime and is to be treated as such, for practical purposes today "assault" is generally synonymous with the term "battery", and is a term used to mean the actual intended use of unlawful force to another person without his consent. On the facts of the present case, the "assault" alleged involved a "battery". Where an assault involved a battery, it matters not, in our judgment, whether the battery is inflicted directly by the body of the offender or through the medium of some weapon or instrument controlled by the action of the offender. An assault may be committed by the laying of a hand on another, and the action does not cease to be an assault if it is a stick held in the hand and not the hand itself which is laid on the person of the victim'. *Fagan v Metropolitan Police Comr* [1968] 3 All ER 422 at 445, per James J

'For convenience we use the word "assault" as including "battery", and adopt the definition of James J in *Fagan v Metropolitan Police Comr* [supra] namely "the actual intended use of unlawful force to another person without his consent", to which we would respectfully add "or any other lawful excuse".' *Attorney-General's Reference (No 6 of 1980)* [1981] 2 All ER 1057 at 1058, CA, per cur.

'An assault is an act by which the defendant intentionally or recklessly causes the complainant to apprehend immediate, or to sustain, unlawful personal violence.' *R v Kimber* [1983] 3 All ER 316 at 319, CA, per Lawton LJ

New Zealand ' "Assault" is defined by s 207 of the Crimes Act 1908 [repealed; see now, the Crimes Act 1961, s 2] as follows: "An assault is the act of intentionally applying force to the person of another, directly or indirectly, or attempting or threatening by any act or gesture to apply such force to the person of another, if the person making the threat has, or causes the other to believe upon reasonable grounds that he has, present ability to effect his purpose". . . . In England, assault is a common-law offence. In New Zealand it is a statutory crime, and a perusal of the definition above quoted shows that our definition is intended to be an adoption of the result of the numerous cases exemplifying the English common law. Our definition expressly recognizes that there may be an assault although no physical force has been applied to the person of the person assaulted. It constitutes the *"attempting or threatening by any act or gesture to apply force"* an assault if the person making the threat has or causes the other to believe upon reasonable grounds that he has present ability to effect his purpose. . . . To constitute an assault within the meaning of the section, there must be the intentional application of force direct or indirect or an attempt or threat by some act or gesture to apply force.' *Fogden v Wade* [1945] NZLR 724 at 726, 728, per Blair J; also reported [1945] GLR 374 at 375, 376

New Zealand [The Crimes Act 1961, s 2, defines an 'assault' as 'the act of intentionally applying or attempting to apply force to the person of another, directly or indirectly, or threatening by any act or gesture to apply such force to the person of another, if the person making the threat has, or causes the other to believe on reasonable grounds that he has, present ability to effect his purpose.' The respondent had pointed a carving knife at a policeman and threatened to stab him if he approached.] 'In our opinion, if the other conditions of the definition were met—as they undoubtedly were—there is no reason why a conditional threat should not constitute an assault. A threat in its very nature usually provides the person threatened with an alternative, unpleasant though it may be.' *Police v Greaves* [1964] NZLR 295 at 298, CA, per cur.

ASSAY OFFICES

[The assay of metals is the testing of the fineness of precious metals and their alloys. The principal assay offices are (1) The Wardens and Commonalty of the Mystery of Goldsmiths of the City of London; (2) The Incorporation of Goldsmiths of the City of Edinburgh; (3) The Guardians of the Standard of Wrought Plate in Birmingham; (4) The Guardians of the Standard of Wrought Plate within the town of Sheffield. See the Hallmarking Act 1973, s 22(1). *See also* HALL-MARK.]

ASSEMBLE

'Assemble', in relation to a medicinal product, means enclosing the product (with or without other medicinal products of the same description) in a container which is labelled before the product is sold or supplied, or, where the product (with or without other medicinal products of the same description) is already enclosed in the container in which it is to be sold or supplied, labelling the container before the product is sold or supplied in it, and 'assembly' has a corresponding meaning. (Medicines Act 1968, s 132)

'Assembly is putting things together to make a whole and if various manufactured parts of, say, a motor car, are assembled on a conveyor belt in a factory, that is assembly pure and simple and involves no degree of installation.' *Engineering Industry Training Board v Foster Wheeler John Brown Boilers Ltd* [1970] 1 All ER 490 at 498, 499, per Bridge J; revd, [1970] 2 All ER 616, CA

ASSEMBLY *See* UNLAWFUL ASSEMBLY

ASSENT

Canada [The Bills of Exchange Act RSC 1906, c 119, s 145 (repealed; see now RSC 1970, c B-5, s 145) enacted that where a bill or acceptance was materially altered without the assent of all parties liable on the bill, the bill was voided, except as against a party who had himself made, authorised, or 'assented to' the alteration, and subsequent indorsers.] 'The words "assented to" are apt words to expressly cover not only the use or meaning of the words "consented to" which imply a privity to the act itself, but also the cases of ratification of an alteration made by an agent or one professing to act as an agent, in any innocent way.' *Hébert v Banque Nationale* (1908) 40 SCR 458 at 481, per Idington J

ASSESS

Water rate

'The word "assessed" means reckoned on the value. It is not accurate to say "assessed on the premises"; but it is not very far from accurate to say that a water rate is a rate assessed upon the lessees in respect of the house.' *Re Floyd, Floyd v Lyons (J) & Co* [1897] 1 Ch 633 at 640, CA, per Rigby LJ

ASSESSMENT

'The word "assessment" is used in our income tax code in more than one sense. Sometimes, by "assessment" is meant the fixing of the sum taken to represent the actual profit for the purpose of charging tax upon it but in another context the "assessment" may mean the actual sum in tax which the taxpayer is liable to pay on his profits. These two things are, of course, not the same, or, at any rate, will not become the same unless and until income tax is charged at the rate of 20s. in the pound.' *Income Tax Comrs for City of London v Gibbs* [1942] AC 402 at 406, HL, per Lord Simon LC

Australia '"Assessment" in the context of the Act [Land Tax Management Act 1956–1986 (NSW), s 16(4)] means no more than the ascertainment of the extent of a previously existing liability.' *Tooth & Co Ltd v Newcastle Developments Ltd* (1966) 116 CLR 167 at 170, per cur.

Australia [The Income Tax Assessment Act 1936 (Cth), s 177 provides that the production of a notice of assessment . . . under the hand of the Commissioner . . . shall be conclusive evidence of the due making of the assessment and (except in proceedings on appeal against the assessment) that the amount and all the particulars of the assessment are correct.] 'Isaacs J explained the character of "an assessment" for present purposes (*IR v DCT (SA)* (1926) 37 CLR 368 at 373): "An assessment is not a piece of paper: it is an official act or operation; it is the Commissioner's ascertainment, on consideration of all relevant circumstances, including sometimes his own opinion, of the amount of tax chargeable to a given taxpayer. When he has completed his ascertainment of the amount, he sends by post a notification thereof called 'a notice of assessment' . . . But neither the paper sent nor the notification it gives is the 'assessment'. That is and remains the act or operation of the Comissioner.'' *Re Deputy Comr of Taxation WA); ex p Briggs* (1986) 69 ALR 185 at 189, per cur.

ASSETS

'Asset' means any description of property or rights other than land or an interest in land. Income and Corporation Taxes Act 1970, s 492)

'In my opinion the assets or property of the company which are referred to in those sections [the Companies Act 1862, ss 98 and 133 (repealed; see now Companies Act 1985, s 502] must mean that portion of the capital which the directors have not actually dealt with before the winding-up commenced. . . . Property which is in mortgage is not, in my opinion, "assets" of the company, . . . namely, free assets, assets which can be dealt with by the company in payment of their debts without regard to those who have a mortgage on this portion of the property of the company.' *Re Pyle Works* (1890) 44 Ch D 534, CA, per Cotton LJ

'My opinion in this particular case goes on the word "assets". To my mind that must include uncalled capital. . . . What is the meaning of the word? We generally use it in reference to a winding-up or bankruptcy. That is its first meaning—that which is available for payment of debts on taking proper accounts in the liquidation. . . . But the word has a second sense equally good and familiar and I find the remarks I make justified by a reference to the Century Dictionary where this second meaning is put forward quite as on a par with the first. Even such a well established corporation as the Bank of England publishes a statement of its assets and liabilities, the assets including everything that is available to meet the liabilities. All property . . . set together against the liabilities is assets and in that sense uncalled capital assets.' *Page v International Trust Agency & Industrial Trust Ltd* (1893) 62 LJ Ch 610 at 612, 613, per Kekewich J

[The question was whether a company, by making contributions to a superannuation fund, had acquired an 'asset' within the Finance (No 2) Act 1939, Sch 7, Pt II, r 1.] 'The word "asset" is one which in this context has, I venture to think, some definite meaning in law as well as in business. If anyone were to ask: Do the assets of the company exceed its liabilities, and, if so, by how much? I do not think anyone would answer the question by taking into account payments of this description. . . . It frequently happens that a company secures for itself an advantage for which it pays without having anything definite to show for it. One example that occurred to me in the course of the argument was the case where a company, having land subject to a right of way, pays a sum of money in order to get rid of the right of way. It has secured an advantage, but the cash that is paid would never be put into a balance sheet as an asset. It might very well be that as the result of the extinction of the right of way the company's own land had become more valuable, and it might be justifiable to write up its value in the balance sheet by a corresponding amount, but that would not be because the company had acquired an asset: it would be because the company had got rid of a disadvantage, and by getting rid of that disadvantage had improved the value of an existing asset whose value before was adversely affected. It seems to me quite clear that the mere improvement of an existing asset by getting rid, for example, of a servitude which affects it is not the acquisition of an asset within the meaning of this schedule.' *Lever Brothers & Unilever Ltd v Inland Revenue Comrs* [1945] 1 All ER 145 at 150, CA, per Lord Greene, MR; affd [1946] 1 All ER 486 n, HL

See, generally, 2 Halsbury's Laws (4th edn) paras 637–639.

Family assets

'Counsel for the husband referred us to a passage in *Wachtel v Wachtel* [[1973] 1 All ER 829] which refers to family assets. The judgment in *Wachtel v Wachtel* quite rightly described that as a convenient shorthand phrase. Counsel for the husband tells us, however, that a great deal of energy is spent in the courts dealing with these matters debating whether or not a particular item is properly regarded as a family asset. I would only like to say once and for all that the phrase "family assets" does not occur in the 1973 Act and it has nothing to do at all with s 25 of that Act. Section 25 requires the court to have regard to the items set out in it and "family assets" is nothing to do with it. It is a convenient phrase that came into existence in the days before the courts had the wide jurisdiction provided originally by the Matrimonial Proceedings and Property Act 1970. In my judgment, it is not now a phrase of any particular use.' *P v P* [1978] 3 All ER 70 at 73, CA, per Ormrod LJ

Fixed assets

'I do not think . . . it is necessary for me to give any precise definition of the meaning of "fixed assets". . . . I think that for the purposes of this case "fixed assets" may be taken to mean the same thing as the "fixed capital" employed in the particular year to which the balance-sheet relates.' *Galloway v Schill, Seebohm & Co Ltd* [1912] 2 KB 354 at 359, per Lord Alverstone CJ

New Zealand 'Fixed assets are the assets of a company which are normally expected to be available to a company and remain "permanently" with the company for the purpose of carrying out the business of the undertaking. . . . "Fixed", in the company law sense is opposed to "current" or "circulating", not to "movable" or "unattached".' *Tudor Heights Ltd (in liquidation) v United Dominions Corpn Finance Ltd* [1977] 1 NZLR 532 at 534, SC, per Jeffries J

ASSIGN

'The word "assign" does not mean "heir", it means a person substituted for another by an act of some kind or other.' *Doe* d *Lewis v Lewis* (1842) 9 M & W 662 at 664, per Parke B

'The lease declares that the lessor, his heirs and assigns, may re-enter on breach of certain covenants, and the first point that arises is that the mortgagor is not an assign of the lessor. Assign in such case means legal assign, and a person who owns an equity of redemption does not come within that description.' *Matthews v Usher* [1900] 2 QB 535 at 537, CA, per A L Smith LJ

'It is said that the Public Trustee is neither the heir nor the executor nor administrator of the survivor of the trustees originally named in the will, nor is he an assign of the survivor, it being intended, upon the true construction of the will, in order to be included in the expression "my trustees" a person had to be able to say of himself he was an assign of the survivor of the four named persons. As a matter of construction I do not take that view. As a matter of construction I think an assign is a person to whom the property has been assigned, either by the four original named trustees or by any of

the survivors or by the survivor of them and the Public Trustee in my judgment falls within the definition.' *Re Symm's Will Trusts, Public Trustee v Shaw* [1936] 3 All ER 236 at 239, 240, per Bennett J

Canada 'The term "assign" has been interpreted widely. Blackstone's definition is "to make or set over to another, to transfer or to assign property or some interest therein". In *Sovereign Fire Insurance Co of Canada v Peters* (1886) 12 SCR 33 at 38, assign is defined as "to make over to another the right one has in any object as in an estate, chose in action or reversion". In *United States v Colorado* (1912) 225 USR 219, assign is defined as "one who becomes invested with the entryman's right in the land through the voluntary act of the latter". A donee has been held to be an assignee.' *Follis v Albermarle (Township)* [1941] OR 1 at 7, Ont, CA, per cur.

ASSIGNMENT

Assignment of choses in action takes place when the liabilities imposed or the rights acquired under a contract between A and B are transferred to C, who was not a party to the original contract. Such assignment may be made either by act of the parties or by operation of law. (9 Halsbury's Laws (4th edn) para 336)

'In strict legal phraseology, an instrument does not operate as an assignment unless the grantor parts with the whole of his interest, but in common parlance it is otherwise.' *Butler v Capel* (1823) 2 B & C 251 at 253, per cur.

'An assignment of a term differs from an underlease in that the former means parting with the whole and the latter with only a portion of the lessee's interest.' *South of England Dairies Ltd v Baker* [1906] 2 Ch 631 at 638, per Joyce J

Absolute assignment

[The Judicature Act 1873, s 25 (repealed; see now Law of Property Act 1925, s 136), enabled the owner of a legal debt or chose in action to assign his legal right to it.] 'Such assignment must be effected by the means indicated by the section. First, there must be an absolute assignment by writing under the hand of the assignor (not purporting to be by way of charge only) of the debt or other legal chose in action. . . . The question is whether the instrument now in question is an absolute assignment, not purporting to be by way of charge only. The instrument clearly purports, and is intended in point of form, to be an absolute assignment, because the word "absolutely" is used in it: and, although it is true that a trust is constituted by it in respect of moneys recovered under it by the assignee, nevertheless the intention of the parties clearly is that it shall be absolute in the sense that the assignee shall have all the rights given by the 6th subsection of the 25th section of the Judicature Act 1873. Therefore, not only is the instrument an absolute assignment in point of form; but the intention of the parties is that it shall operate as such. . . . It appears to me . . . that the plain intention of the parties was that the instrument should operate both in form and substance as an absolute assignment of the legal property in the debts, subject to a trust in respect of the moneys recovered; and I know no reason why it should not have effect accordingly.' *Comfort v Betts* [1891] 1 QB 737 at 740, 741, CA, per Fry LJ

'To bring a case within the subsection [6 of s 25 of the Judicature Act 1873 (repealed; see supra)] transferring the legal right to sue for the debt and empowering the assignee to give a good discharge for the debt there must be . . . an absolute assignment not purporting to be by way of charge only. . . . It is plain that every equitable assignment in the wide sense of the term as used in equity is not within the enactment. . . . Where there is an absolute assignment of the debt, but by way of security, equity would imply a right to a reassignment on redemption, and the subsection would apply to the case of such an absolute assignment. . . . A mortgage is not mentioned in the enactment; but where there is an absolute assignment of the debt, the limiting words as to a charge only are not sufficient to exclude a mortgage.' *Durham Brothers v Robertson* [1898] 1 QB 765 at 771, 772, per Chitty LJ

By operation of law

'An assignment "by act and operation of law" is clearly an assignment which the law itself effects in certain circumstances, as, for instance, in the case of bankruptcy.' *Foley v Galvin* [1932] IR 339 at 350, per Kennedy CJ

Equitable assignment

'To constitute a good equitable assignment of a debt, all that is necessary is that debtor should be given to understand that the debt has been made over by the creditor to some third person, and if debtor disregards such notice he does so at his peril. An equitable assignment does not always take the form of an assignment. It may be addressed to debtor, it may be couched in the language of command; it may be a courteous request; it may assume the form of mere permission. The language is immaterial if the meaning is plain. All that is necessary is that debtor should be given to understand that the debt has been made over by the creditor to some third person. If debtor ignores such a notice, he does so at his peril. If the assignment be for valuable consideration and communicated to the third person, it cannot be revoked by the creditor or safely disregarded by debtor.' *William Brandt's Sons & Co v Dunlop Rubber Co* [1905] AC 454 at 461, HL, per Lord Macnaghten

ASSIST

[The vendors of a quarry business covenanted (inter alia) that they would not 'assist' in carrying on the business of a quarry within a certain area.] 'The first phrase that requires attention is "assist in carrying on". I should have thought that those words were wide enough to cover a person who provides the necessary capital to enable a business to be carried on. It is not merely the equipment of a business which is brought about by the provision of capital, but its whole life. In other words, the provision of the capital which is necessary to set up a business gives the business life, and its effects continue after the installation is complete for the simple reason that the business as carried on owes its origin entirely to the provision of the capital. I can think of no more effective way of assisting a person in carrying on his business than to provide for him free of charge the necessary equipment to enable him to begin the business.' *Batts Combe Quarry Ltd v Ford* [1943] Ch 51 at 53, CA, per Lord Greene MR

[By an agreement the defendant, who was a qualified surgeon and physician, covenanted not to practise or cause or 'assist' any other person to practise in any department of medicine, surgery or midwifery nor accept nor fill any professional appointment within a radius of 10 miles from the partnership address for 5 years after the termination of his assistantship.] 'I find it extremely difficult to appreciate in what circumstances the defendant might be supposed to "cause" another to practise in medicine, surgery or midwifery, but the word "assist" cannot, I think, exclude financial assistance, so that the defendant is, for example, by his covenant prohibited from advancing money to a lady to enable her to establish a maternity home within the area.' *Routh v Jones* [1947] 1 All ER 179 at 182, per Evershed J; affd. [1947] 1 All ER 758

[The Theft Act 1968, s 22(1) provides that a person handles stolen goods if (otherwise than in the course of the stealing) . . . he dishonestly 'assists' in their retention by or for the benefit of another person.] 'In *R v Thornhill*, decided in this court on 15th May 1981, and in *R v Sanders*, decided in this court on 25th February 1982, both unreported, it was held that merely using stolen goods in the possession of another does not constitute the offence of assisting in their retention. To constitute the offence, something must be done by the offender, and done intentionally and dishonestly, for the purpose of enabling the goods to be retained. Examples of such conduct are concealing or helping to conceal the goods, or doing something to make them more difficult to find or to identify. Such conduct must be done knowing or believing the goods to be stolen and done dishonestly and for the benefit of another.' *R v Kanwar* [1982] 2 All ER 528 at 529, CA, per cur.

Canada 'The phrase "assisting in rape", if not in full and common usage in England in the late nineteenth century, was nevertheless an expression well-known in the law at the time of the drafting of the Draft Code and the enactment of the first Criminal Code of Canada [see now RSC 1970, c C–34]. It was an expression descriptive of participation in rape and could include, and in its use in the Criminal Code was intended to include, the crime of rape whether committed by one acting as ravisher or by one who participated by assisting. . . . The word "assisting" is capable of various meanings and one of the most significant involves the element of participation. Reference to standard and authoritative dictionaries will reveal such definitions as "to aid or help, to be present at, to second and support, to further and promote an action or result, and to participate in an activity.' *Bergstrom v R* [1981] 1 SCR 539 at 549, SCC, per Mc Intyre J

South Africa 'Everybody who, in the opinion of the Judge, does something to further the purpose of a criminal is a person who "assists" or helps at the crime. Even the person who keeps a look-out to see that the police do not interrupt the perpetration of a crime is punish-able according to our law.' *R v Parkham* 1906 TS 804 per Wessels J

[Earlier (ibid at 803) Wessels J said: 'Our law differs considerably from the English law in that respect. Our law is void of any technicality. It says that a person who "assists" at a crime is himself guilty of the offence.']

ASSISTANCE

Canada [Taxpayer was required to deduct from capital cost of an asset any amount received as 'assistance' from public authority.] 'The key word in this text, as it seems to me, is "assistance", which, in the context, clearly carries with it the colour of a grant or subsidy.' *R v Consumers' Gas Co Ltd* [1987] 2 FC 60 at 65, 66, Fed CA, per Hugessen J

New Zealand [The Transport Act 1949 (NZ), s 47(1) (repealed; see now the Transport Act 1962, s 65) provided that where an accident arising directly or indirectly from the use of a motor vehicle occurred to any person or to any horse and vehicle in charge of any person, the driver of the motor vehicle should stop, and should ascertain whether he had injured any person, in which event it should be his duty to render all 'practicable assistance' to the injured person.] 'In my opinion, the expression "all practicable assistance to the injured person" is wide enough to include, and must be construed as including, assistance to persons who are so injured that it may be difficult or impossible to say, either at the relevant time or subsequently, whether or not death had already occurred.' *Swift v Pine* [1959] NZLR 728 at 731, 732, per F B Adams J

Writ of assistance

In some cases, where the judgment or order is personal, and the remedy by writ of possession or writ of delivery or by ordinary process for contempt would probably be futile (for example, where the person in contempt has absconded) a writ of assistance may be directed to issue. This writ may also be resorted to when possession of documents or securities is desired and the person against whom an order for delivery has been made is out of the jurisdiction, or when sequestrators experience difficulty in obtaining possession of the chattels of the persons against whom sequestration has been granted.

The writ of assistance is a process for contempt, and is only issued after service of a duly endorsed order. The writ is obtained on *ex parte* application, supported by an affidavit which must show that the order was not complied with within the time limited in it. The writ is directed to the sheriff, and recites a contempt of court in disobedience to a judgment or order of the court, and the order for the issue of the writ, and commands the sheriff to put the applicant into possession of the chattels or property of which delivery is ordered, and to defend and keep him in quiet possession. (17 Halsbury's Laws (4th edn) para 521)

ASSISTANT   *See also* SHOP ASSISTANT

'It appears to us that according to the ordinary meaning of language a person may "join as assistant for the purpose of assisting to carry on professional business" without necessarily entering into the relationship of a servant to his master. A professional man may well "join" an "undertaking" on the terms that he is to be free to exercise his professional skill without being under the obligation to conform to any directions as to how he is to do his work.' *Faraday v Auctioneers' & Estate Agents' Institute of United Kingdom* [1936] 1 All ER 496 at 503, CA, per Greene LJ

ASSIZES

'*Assisa* properly commeth of the Latin word *assideo*, which is to associate or sit together; so as properly assise is an association or sitting together'. (Co Litt 153*b*)

[All courts of assize were abolished as from 1 January 1972, by the Courts Act 1971, ss 1, 59(2), Part II of which established the Crown Court as part of the Supreme Court.]

ASSOCIATE WITH

'The receiving a man's visits whenever he choses to call, is associating with him.' *Lord Dormer v Knight* (1809) 1 Taunt 417 at 418, per cur.

ASSOCIATED COMPANY   *See*
   COMPANY

ASSOCIATED OPERATIONS

For the purposes of this section, 'an associated operation' means, in relation to any transfer, an operation of any kind effected by any person in relation to any of the assets transferred or any assets representing, whether directly or indirectly, any of the assets transferred, or to the income arising from any such assets, or to any assets representing, whether directly or indirectly, the accumulations of income arising from any such assets. (Income and Corporation Taxes Act 1970, s 478(4))

ASSOCIATION

'An ordinary partnership is a partnership composed of definite individuals bound together by contract between themselves to continue combined for some joint object, either during pleasure or during a limited time, and is essentially composed of the persons originally entering into the contract with one another. A company or association (which I take to be synonymous terms) is the result of an arrangement by which parties intend to form a partnership which is constantly changing, a partnership to-day consisting of certain members and tomorrow consisting of some only of those members along with others who have come in, so that there will be a constant shifting of the partnership, a determination of the old and a creation of a new partnership, and with the intention that, so far as the partners can by agreement between themselves bring about such a result, the new partnership shall succeed to the assets and liabilities of the old partnership.' *Smith v Anderson* (1880) 15 Ch D 247 at 273, 274, CA, per James LJ

Australia 'In the modern idiom the term association has come to be regarded as attaching to a body of persons associated for a common purpose; the organization formed to effect their purpose; a society (Shorter Oxford Dictionary). It may be incorporated or unincorporated and, usually, this appellation is attached to a society of a non-trading or commercial type—whereas the term company is normally associated with a commercial, profit orientated, undertaking.' *Quinton v South Australian Psychological Board* (1985) 38 SASR 523 at 531, per Olsson J

ASSUME

'It is, I think, clear that the word "assume" in reference to a surname necessarily imports some degree of user.' *Re Murray, Martin's Bank Ltd v Dill* [1954] 3 All ER 129 at 133, per Evershed MR; see also [1955] Ch 69

ASSURANCE   See also INSURANCE

'Now a covenant is not strictly an assurance. The point has been much contested as to the meaning of that word in the Bills of Sale Act. An assurance is really something which operates as a transfer of property, and an assurance can hardly be a covenant.' *Re Ray* (1896) 65 LJ Ch 316 at 320, CA, per Kay LJ

ASYLUM

Since a state has a discretion as to whether or not to admit aliens into its territory, it follows that it has discretion whether or not to grant asylum to refugees. The so-called right of asylum belongs to the state which wishes to grant it and not to the refugee. The right to grant asylum may be limited or excluded altogether by a treaty obligation to return a fugitive criminal to another state, as in the case of an extradition treaty. Thus, asylum is in general only accorded for political offences. With respect to extra-territorial asylum, as where a state grants asylum to an individual in one of its embassies or consulates or in a warship, no such institution exists outside Latin America, although, in other cases, states do sometimes grant asylum to political refugees who are in immediate peril of persecution and where the dictates of humanity require it. (18 Halsbury's Laws (4th edn) para 1717)

'The word "asylum", according to its original derivation and in its widest meaning, simply signifies a refuge—a place of retreat and security. In its English acceptation, the word is most commonly used to denote an establishment for the detention and cure of persons suffering from mental disease and also a place for the reception and up-bringing of destitute orphans. . . . The word might be loosely applied to a night refuge for the homeless, or to any similar institution.' *Dilworth v Stamps Comr, Dilworth v Land & Income Tax Comr* [1899] AC 99 at 107, 108, PC, per cur.

[As regards establishments for the detention and cure of persons suffering from mental disorder, the term 'mental hospital' was substituted for the term 'asylum' by the Mental Treatment Act 1930. The Act of 1930 has in turn been repealed; see now the Mental Health Act 1959, also largely repealed by the Mental Health Act 1983, in which the term used is 'hospital'.]

AT

'The word *at* may, in one sense, be read *before*, but it cannot be read *after*. The expression may not always refer to time; for instance, in the words "judge at the trial", it does not refer to time, but is used to characterise the individual who is to give relief, viz. the judge presiding at the trial. . . . The words "*at* the commencement" here, clearly have reference to time, and can only mean before or at the time of commencing the suit.' *Doe* d *Ellis v Owens* (1842) 12 LJ Ex 53 at 56, per Lord Abinger CB

[A notice to quit was given by the defendant to Pettit, requiring him to leave 'at' Michaelmas Day 1858.] 'Pettit's interest expired on Michaelmas Day. . . . Still the defendant had the *whole* of that day to remove, the word "at" or "until" being *inclusive*.' *Archer v Sadler* (1859) 1 F & F 481 at 483, per Wightman J

[Ann Bennett Lowis, having a power of appointment over certain property comprised in her marriage settlement, by her will dated the 23rd of February, 1805, gave her real and personal estate to her husband, Charles Lowis, for his life, and at his death her estate, called Brynbedw, 'to my godson, Charles Legh Lowis, and at his death to his child or children; but, if he die without children, to Edward Thelwall', with remainder, in the event of Edward's dying without children, to Miles Thelwall in fee.] ' "At his death" is the same as "from and after his death"—pointing out the period from which the class to whom an interest is given by the former words are to take.' *Thelwall v Finney* [1868] WN 313 at 313, per Giffard V-C

'Now it is admitted the word "at" does not mean "upon" and the word "at" does not mean "within". . . . Although I agree that when we come to construe an Act of Parliament or an agreement it is dangerous merely to take the dictionary meaning, still the dictionaries do assist. . . . According to Richardson's Dictionary "at" is used to denote near approach, nearness or proximity, adjunction or conjunction, association or consociation, connection; and that would seem to be its natural or ordinary idiomatic use in the English language. It may sometimes be equivalent to "in" or "within", but not because the word itself includes the idea of inclusion within limits but by reason that inclusion involves association or consociation.' *Price v Bala & Festiniog Rly Co* (1884) 50 LT 787 at 789, per Chitty J

'When considering the validity of a notice to

quit given in time and expiring on the anniversary of the commencement of a tenancy, I can find no distinction ever drawn between tenancies commencing "at" a particular time or "on" a particular day and "from" the same day. "At", "on", "from", and "on and from" are for this purpose equivalent expressions.' *Sidebotham v Holland* [1895] 1 QB 378 at 384, CA, per Lindley LJ

[The Road Traffic Act 1972, s 8(2) (substituted by the Transport Act 1981, s 25, Sch 8) allows, in certain circumstances, a breath test to be taken from a person who is a patient 'at' a hospital. The question was as to the position of a patient who had received treatment but had then been permitted to leave.] 'I cannot see any reason to construe the phrase "at a hospital" in a limited way. I cannot see any reason at all for restricting it to exclude the car park. It may very well be in most cases the description "at a hospital" means in a ward, but that is not always so. There is nothing unreasonable in allowing a police officer to make a request for a sample of breath while the suspect is in the car park, provided of course the suspect is no longer present as a patient. . . . As far as I can see, the phrase "at a hospital" can be appropriate to anywhere within the precincts of a hospital.' *A-G's Reference (No 1 of 1976)* [1977] 3 All ER 557, CA, per cur.

South Africa 'The word "at" denotes a local or geographical point only, whereas the word "within" refers to a place included within a certain defined area.' *R v Kakateka* 1943 SWA 1 per Hoexter J

At death

'"At their death" cannot mean the contemporaneous death of all, but the deaths of each respectively.' *Wills v Wills* (1875) LR 20 Eq 342 at 345, per Jessel MR

AT ANCHOR

'For a vessel to be at anchor, it is not necessary that there should be an anchor down. For instance, a vessel made fast to moorings has no anchor down, and yet nobody would say that she was not at anchor. So again with fishing boats which are brought up by dropping overboard an exceedingly heavy piece of stone. They are "at anchor", though not attached to an anchor.' *The Dunelm* (1884) 51 LT 214 at 218, CA, per Brett MR

'Bye-law 5 provides definitions of the language used in the bye-laws generally, It directs (inter alia) that "In these bye-laws . . . unless there be something in the subject or context repugnant to such construction . . . the expression 'under way' when used in relation to a vessel means when she is not at anchor, or moored, or made fast to the shore, or aground, and includes a vessel dropping up or down the river with her anchor on the ground". . . . In *The Esk* [(1869) LR 2 A & E 350] Sir Robert Phillimore had to determine whether . . . the schooner *Esk* . . . was still at anchor. . . . The learned judge found that the *Esk* was not in fact holden by her anchor. "The true criterion", he said, as to the application of the regulation (that is as to the display of navigation lights), "must be, whether the vessel be actually holden by and under the control of her anchor, or not. The moment she ceases to be so, she is in the category of a vessel "under way", and must carry the appointed coloured lights".' *The Palembang* [1929] P 246 at 252, 253, per Lord Merrivale P

AT AND FROM

Where a ship is insured 'at and from' an island, the whole island is considered as one starting point, and the ship is not considered as having sailed on her voyage until she has cleared away from the island with the purpose of proceeding directly to the port of destination. (25 Halsbury's Laws (4th edn) para 57)

Where a ship is insured 'at and from' a particular place, and she is at that place in good safety when the contract is concluded, the risk attaches immediately.

If she be not at that place when the contract is concluded, the risk attaches as soon as she arrives there in good safety, and, unless the policy otherwise provides, it is immaterial that she is covered by another policy for a specified time after arrival.

Where chartered freight is insured 'at and from' a particular place, and the ship is at that place in good safety when the contract is concluded the risk attaches immediately. If she be not there when the contract is concluded, the risk attaches as soon as she arrives there in good safety.

Where freight, other than chartered freight, is payable without special conditions and is insured 'at and from' a particular place, the risk attaches pro rata as the goods or merchandise are shipped; provided that if there be cargo in readiness which belongs to the shipowner, or which some other person has contracted with him to ship, the risk attaches as soon as the ship is ready to receive such cargo. (Marine Insurance Act 1906, Sch 1, para 3)

AT ANY TIME

[Under the terms of a tenancy agreement, the tenant was given the right of option to purchase the freehold 'at any time' for an agreed sum. After the period of the tenancy had expired the tenant remained in possession as a statutory tenant under the Rent Restrictions Acts. He subsequently gave notice of his intention to exercise the option.] 'The words "at any time" cannot mean precisely what they say, and the question is what is the limitation that I ought to read into them here. It seems to me prima facie most unlikely, especially in these days of Rent Acts, that a landlord would agree in advance to a tenant having the right to purchase the reversion, at a price named in the agreement, throughout the quite uncertain period during which the tenant may continue to be his tenant by holding over. . . . On the whole . . . although the question is by no means an easy one . . . I consider that, on the true construction of this agreement, the right given to the tenant to purchase the freehold was a right to purchase it at any time during the currency of the agreement.' *Longmuir v Kew* [1960] 3 All ER 26 at 30, per Cross J

'Counsel for the wife submits that the effect of the Matrimonial Causes (Property and Maintenance) Act 1958, s 1 [repealed; see now the Matrimonial Causes Act 1973, s 23(1)] . . . is that there is now no limit to the number of applications which may be made by a wife for permanent maintenance or a secured provision. His argument goes, and must go, as far as saying that, if a wife has made, for example, fifteen applications for maintenance, each one of which has been dismissed, either on the figures or in the light of the circumstances and the conduct of the parties, she is nevertheless entitled to make thereafter a subsequent application with a view to re-litigating the question all over again. In effect, that would mean that the words "at any time thereafter" would be almost equivalent to "at any number of times thereafter". In my judgment, that is plainly wrong. The effect of the Act is to empower the court to make an order for maintenance on or at any time after the decree instead of, as formerly, on the decree.' *L v L* [1961] 3 All ER 834 at 841, CA, per Davies LJ; also reported [1962] P 101 at 121

AT THE INSTANCE OF

Canada 'As I read it [the Criminal Code, s 2, RSC 1970, c C–34], the intention of Parliament was to yield up to the provinces in a general way the conduct of criminal proceedings in this country, but at the same time to reserve unto the Attorney-General of Canada the right to prosecute certain cases in which Canada has a special interest. The definition begins "'Attorney-General' means the Attorney-General or Solicitor-General of a province" and continues ". . . and, with respect to . . . (b) proceedings instituted at the instance of the Government of Canada and conducted by or on behalf of that Government . . . means the Attorney-General of Canada". The meaning of the word "institute" ("instituted") is readily apparent—"to set on foot, initiate, start" (Shorter Oxford English Dictionary). Why follow "instituted" with "at the instance of"? Is this a mere circumlocution for "by"? I think not. Black's Law Dictionary, 4th edn defines "instance" thus: "In pleading and practice: Solicitation, properly of an earnest or urgent kind. An act is often done at a party's 'special instance and request'." If this interpretation is correct, the meaning then of the words "proceedings instituted at the instance of the Government of Canada" is precise and they are intended to apply to proceedings of a very special kind in which the Attorney-General for Canada has a very special interest. They allow him to act not only in respect to offences under other Acts of Parliament but in respect to Criminal Code offences, but always with the qualification that the proceedings are "instituted at the instance of the Government of Canada".' *R v Knechtel* [1975] 4 WWR 203 at 208, 209, BCSC, per McKenzie J

AT LARGE

[The appellant was walking in a thoroughfare with six or seven greyhounds on a master lead with small leads from it to which the dogs were attached, when one of the dogs sprang at a passer-by and bit him. On a later date, the appellant was again in a thoroughfare with five or six greyhounds, all of which were on leads, when one of the dogs leapt and bit a passer-by. The appellant was convicted of two offences under the Metropolitan Police Act 1839 s 54(2), namely, of suffering to be 'at large' an unmuzzled ferocious dog on each of the two occasions.] 'The justices in this case clearly, I think, came to the conclusion that, although a person might have control of a dog by some physical means such as a lead, yet if he did not control the dog, the dog was at large. They say—with regard, it is true, to only one of the offences charged, but I understand that the facts were the same in each case—that the dogs were all on leads, and that "The appellant did not try to control the dog", that is, the dog that jumped up and bit the passer-by. For my part I am quite satisfied that an offence is not committed under s 54(2) where a person has the physical means of controlling the dog but does not do so. I think that the subsection is aimed at the case where a person has no physical control of the dog at all. The case was put in argument of a person who had a dog on a lead so long that he could not exercise any physical control. It may well be that in such a case it could be said that the control was so minimal that the dog was to all intents and purposes a dog at large. However, that is not the present case. This is a case where a man could exercise control over the dog by means of the lead, but did not do so. In my judgment, the justices were wrong in convicting the appellant on these two charges and the appeal must be allowed.' *Ross v Evans* [1959] 2 All ER 222 at 223, per Lord Parker CJ; also reported [1959] 2 QB 79 at 81

New Zealand [The Dogs Registration Act 1955 (NZ), s 28(1) (repealed; see now the Dog Control and Hydatids Act 1982, s 60), provides that where complaint is made that a dog has been seen 'at large' among stock or poultry, a magistrate's court, if it is satisfied as to the grounds of complaint, may make an order directing the owner forthwith to cause the dog to be destroyed.] 'The words "at large", in reference to dogs, contained in s 12(2) of the Dog and Goat Act 1898 (NSW) were construed by Sir Kenneth Street CJ in *Jolliffe v Dean* [(1954) 54 SR (NSW) 157] wherein the learned Chief Justice said: "I think the meaning of the words 'at large' is free or at liberty. In the case of a dog the normal way in which it would be set at large would be to take it off the chain or release it from the pen in which it was confined". I respectfully adopt the same construction for the same words in s 28(1) of the Dogs Registration Act 1955. The words "among . . . stock or poultry", in my view, mean simply that the dog was so situate as to be in fact intermingled with stock or poultry. To bring the dog within the words of s 28(1) it must, in my opinion, (a) be seen, and (b) when seen be at large, or in other words free or at liberty, and (c) when seen at large be among, or in other words, intermingled with stock or poultry.

Each of the foregoing ingredients must, in my view be established as a matter of fact.' *Payze v Everitt* [1959] NZLR 423 at 425, 426, per Shortland J

AT LEAST

Canada 'Where an act is required by, statute to be done so many days "at least" before a given event, the time must be reckoned excluding both the day of the act and that of the event.' *Ashton v Powers* (1921) 51 OLR 309 at 311, Ont SC, per Middleton J

Canada [The Criminal Code s 237(1)(c), RSC 1970, c C–34, provides that on a charge of driving with a blood-alcohol level of over 80 milligrams per 100 millilitres of blood contrary to s 236 there is a presumption that the blood-alcohol level at the time of the breath tests is the same as at the time of the offence if there has been an interval of 'at least' 15 minutes between the times when the samples are taken.] 'I think judicial authority makes it clear when the term "at least" is used in reference to the days between two events, that means "clear days". Thus, in the determination of such days, both the day of the act and the day of the event are excluded. In my opinion, when the term "at least" is used in reference to the period between two events, whether that period is expressed in years, months, weeks, hours, or minutes, the same effect must be given to those words as is given to them when the period is expressed in days. There can be no basis for anything but a consistent interpretation of such words. Thus, in the present case, in determining whether or not there was an interval of at least 15 minutes between the times when the samples were taken, there must be excluded the minute in which the first sample was taken and the minute when the second sample was taken. There must be at least 15 clear minutes between such events.' *R v Davis* (1977) 35 CCC (2d) 224 at 227, Sask CA, per Culliton CJS

AT OR NEAR

Canada [Charter authorised construction of railroad to point 'at or near' Ottawa.] 'There is no inflexible rule that "at" is always to be construed as exclusive, and we have not to lay down any broad proposition as to its signification. What it means in this statute is all what we have to determine. That the words "to a point at the City of Ottawa" must in this charter be read as "to a point in the City of Ottawa" is to my mind the only reasonable construction to be given to those words under the circumstances. And the words "near" given as the alternative point where the terminus may be shows that "at" and "near" cannot be construed as meaning the same thing,' *City of Ottawa v Canada Atlantic Railway Co* (1903) 33 SCR 376 at 381, SCC, per Taschereau CJ

AT ONCE

'In order to ascertain what offence the prisoner has in fact committed . . . we must first ascertain what it was his duty as a servant to do. . . . Now it was not his duty to hand over to his employers the specific money he received, but he was "at once" (which means within a reasonable time) to remit the amount of all moneys he received.' *R v Rogers* (1877) 3 QB 28 at 33, per Field J

AT SEA

[While a ship was lying in the Thames loading a cargo of explosives for Australia and Manila, her captain wrote a letter on board her containing testamentary dispositions. The ship was afterwards lost with all hands. The captain's wife sought to treat the letter as a will for the purpose of a grant of administration *cum testamento annexo*, as permitted to seamen at sea by s 22 of the Statute of Frauds 1677, and Wills Act 1837, s 11.] 'I think you may take the grant. The deceased had gone on board, and the voyage had begun for the purposes of making this document the will of a seaman at sea.' *In the Goods of Patterson* (1898) 79 LT 123 at 124, per Barnes J

'In considering the true construction of the words "at sea" it will be observed that the words contained in s 11 [of the Wills Act 1837] are "seamen being at sea" not "on the sea". It is clear from the authorities which have been cited to me that the court has put a liberal interpretation on those words. For instance, it seems to me to be clearly established by authority that a seaman who is ashore on leave at a port during the course of a voyage and while ashore on such leave makes a will is a seaman "at sea".' *In the Estate of Newland* [1952] 1 All ER 841 at 843, per Havers J (also reported in [1952] P 71 at 74, 75)

Australia 'The question is whether the deceased was entitled to make a privileged

will, that is, whether he came within the provisions of s 10 of the Wills, Probate and Administration Act 1898–1986 (NSW). . . . There is no reported case . . . in which the meaning of "at sea" is extended to cover such a case as this, where the will was made on shore some years after the seaman had been interned in an enemy country. On principle, it appears to me that the voyage of the deceased having come to an end, and the will in fact being made on land, it cannot be the will of a "mariner or seaman being at sea". The capacity of a naval seaman or mariner to make a valid will, while he is a prisoner of war, and the formalities required, are dealt with in England by the Navy and Marine (Wills) Act 1865, and the form of that legislation indicates that naval seamen and marines were not considered to be "at sea" when they were prisoners of war. In my opinion, the deceased in this case, whose position was in some respects analogous to that of a prisoner of war, also cannot be considered to have been at sea when this will was made.' *Re Will of L H Bickley (decd)* (1949) 49 NSWSR 94 at 95, per Roper CJ (Eq)

ATOMIC ENERGY

'Atomic energy' means the energy released from atomic nuclei as a result of any process, including the fission process, but does not include energy released in any process of natural transmutation or radio-active decay which is not accelerated or influenced by external means. (Atomic Energy Act 1946, s 18)

AT THE TIME

[The Road Safety Act 1967, s 3(3)(a) (repealed; cf. the Road Traffic Act 1972, s 7; (substituted by the Transport Act 1981, s 25, Sch 8) provided that a person who failed to provide a specimen for a laboratory test should be guilty of an offence, if it were shown that 'at the relevant time' he was driving or attempting to drive a motor vehicle on a road or other public place.] 'To give s 3(3)(a) a reasonable interpretation in its context, the words "at the time" he was required to take a breath test must be given a broad interpretation as signifying the occasion rather than the moment of time when the request was made.' *Sakhuja v Allen* [1972] 2 All ER 311 at 330, HL, per Viscount Dilhorne

ATTACK

[The Piracy Act 1850, s 2 (repealed), enacted: 'Whenever any of His Majesty's ships . . . shall attack or be engaged with any persons alleged to be pirates afloat or ashore it shall be lawful for the High Court of Admiralty of England . . . to determine whether the persons . . . so attacked or engaged were pirates.'] 'There is, I apprehend, a clear difference in the meaning of these two words. I take an attack to be the use of, or the attempt to use, force or violence. I take it, it is not necessary to constitute an attack that there should be any resistance or any actual combat or any blood spilt. Engagement is a different word, and seems necessarily to imply that there was something of a combat or fight. . . . I think that bloodshed is not an indispensable ingredient to form an attack within the meaning of statute, and that the Legislature never intended that, in order to entitle themselves to reward, the captors must take away human life.' *The Megellan Pirates* (1853) 1 Ecc & Ad 81 at 87, per Dr Lushington

ATTAIN

Age

[By the Family Law Reform Act 1969, s 1 the age of majority was reduced from twenty-one years to eighteen years and all statutory references to minority and infancy are to be construed accordingly. Section 9 of the Act of 1969 further provides that the time at which a person attains a particular age expressed in years shall be the commencement of the relevant anniversary of the date of his birth. The old common law rule that a person was deemed to attain a particular age at the first moment of the day immediately preceding the relevant anniversary of his birth has thus been abolished.]

ATTAINDER

Although an Act of Attainder takes the form of a legislative enactment, it is an exercise of the jurisdiction of the entire Parliament because an individual for whose punishment such a bill is introduced is tried by both Houses of Parliament and can only be condemned with the assent of the Crown.

A Bill of Attainder is usually introduced in the House of Lords and the procedure upon it in both Houses is the same as upon an ordinary public bill, except that, as the measure is one of judicial character, the accused person is allowed to produce evidence and employ counsel.

The procedure upon a Bill of Pains and Penalties, which is also an exercise of the judicial power of Parliament in a legislative form, is the same as that upon a Bill of Attainder. (34 Halsbury's Laws (4th edn) para 1312)

ATTEMPT

If, with intent to commit an offence to which this section applies [offences triable on indictment in England and Wales] a person does an act which is more than merely preparatory to the commission of the offence, he is guilty of attempting to commit the offence. (Criminal Attempts Act 1981, s 1(1))

[See generally the full section and the notes thereto in 12 Halsbury's Statutes (4th edn) 846–848.]

'There is, no doubt, a difference between the preparation antecedent to an offence, and the actual attempt. But if the actual transaction has commenced which would have ended in the crime if not interrupted, there is clearly an attempt to commit the crime.' *R v Cheeseman* (1862) Le & Ca 140 at 148, per Blackburn J

'What amounts to an attempt has been described variously in the authorities, and, for my part, I prefer to adopt the definition given in Stephen's Digest of Criminal Law (5th edn, 1894), art 50, where it says that: "An attempt to commit a crime is an act done with intent to commit that crime, and forming part of a series of acts which would constitute its actual commission if it were not interrupted". As a general statement that seems to me to be right, though it does not help to define the point of time at which the series of acts begins. That, as Stephen said, depends on the facts of each case. A helpful definition is given in para 4104 in Archbold's Pleading, Evidence and Practice (36th edn), where it is stated in this form: "It is submitted that the *actus reus* necessary to constitute an attempt is complete if the prisoner does an act which is a step towards the commission of the specific crime, which is immediately and not merely remotely connected with the commission of it, and the doing of which cannot reasonably be regarded as having any other purpose than the commission of the specific crime".' *Davey v Lee* [1967] 2 All ER 423 at 425, per Lord Parker CJ

'An attempt to commit crime is itself an

offence. Often it is a grave offence. Often it is as morally culpable as the completed offence which is attempted but not in fact committed. Nevertheless it falls within the class of conduct which is preparatory to the commission of a crime and is one step removed from the offence which is attempted. The court must not strain to bring within the offence of attempt conduct which does not fall within the well-established bounds of the offence. On the contrary, the court must safeguard against extension of those bounds save by the authority of Parliament. The bounds are presently set requiring proof of specific intent, a decision to bring about, insofar as it lies within the accused's power, the commission of the offence which it is alleged the accused attempted to commit, no matter whether the accused desired that consequence of his act or not.' *R v Mohan* [1975] 2 All ER 193 at 200, CA, per cur.

'There is a great deal of authority relating to what does and what does not constitute an attempt to commit an offence. It is, however, necessary only to refer to *R v Eagleton* [(1855) Dears CC 575] in which Parke B in a celebrated passage lays down the guiding principle in deciding whether or not an attempt has been made. "The mere intention to commit a misdemeanour is not criminal, some act is required; and we do not think that all acts towards committing a misdemeanour are indictable. Acts remotely leading towards the commission of the offence are not to be considered as attempts to commit it; but acts immediately connected with it are . . ." It follows that mere preparatory steps towards committing a crime do not constitute an attempt. An attempt consists in addition to a guilty intention, of an overt act or series of acts which if not interrupted would have constituted the actual commission of the complete offence.' *Director of Public Prosecutions v Stonehouse* [1977] 2 All ER 909 at 925, HL, per Lord Salmon

[In *Anderton v Ryan* [1985] 2 All ER 355, HL, the House of Lords had to determine the true construction of the Criminal Attempts Act 1981, s 1. Lord Roskill observed that 'the language used in the statute is such as to make the attainment of common sense and the avoidance of asininity at one and the same time almost impossible of achievement.']

Australia 'It seems to me hardly necessary but by way of emphasis I point out that "attempt" in the Shorter Oxford English Dictionary . . . means "to make an effort or endeavour to do or accomplish some action". This is consistent with meaning by action to achieve a particular result rather than simply to contemplate the possibility or even the likelihood of such a result by such action. The seeking to achieve a result involved in an attempt simply must involve an intention to achieve it. I can think of no practical use of the word which does not involve an intent.' *R v Leavitt* [1985] 1 Qd R 343 at 345, per Andrews SPJ

Canada 'Section 244(b) [of the Criminal Code, RSC 1970, c C-34] in referring to "attempt", in my view, quite obviously means some aggressive act on the part of the appellant and not merely a request that the other person act.' *R v Baney* [1972] 2 OR 34 at 35, 36, Ont CA, per Brooke JA

New Zealand 'He who sets out to commit a crime may in the event fall short of the complete commission of that crime for any one of a number of reasons. *First*, he may, of course, simply change his mind before committing any act sufficiently overt to amount to an attempt. *Second*, he may change his mind, but too late to deny that he had got so far as an attempt. *Third*, he may be prevented by some outside agency from doing some act necessary to complete commission of the crime—as when a police officer interrupts him while he is endeavouring to force the window open, but before he has broken into the premises. *Fourth*, he may suffer no such outside interference, but may fail to complete the commission of the crime through ineptitude, inefficiency or insufficient means. The jemmy which he has brought with him may not be strong enough to force the window open. *Fifth*, he may find that what he is proposing to do is after all impossible—not because of insufficiency of means, but because it is for some reason physically not possible, whatever means be adopted. He who walks into a room intending to steal, say a specific diamond ring, and finds that the ring is no longer there but has been removed by the owner to the bank, is thus prevented from committing the crime which he intended, and which, but for the supervening physical impossibility imposed by events he would have committed. *Sixth*, he may without interruption efficiently do every act which he set out to do, but may be saved from criminal liability by the fact that what he has done, contrary to his own belief at the time, does not after all amount in law to a crime.' *R v Donnelly* [1970] NZLR 980 at 990, 991, CA, per Turner J

New Zealand 'In order to constitute an attempt within the meaning of s 93 of the Crimes Act [1908 (repealed; see now Crimes Act 1961 (NZ), s 72)] there must be . . . some overt act immediately connected with the proposed crime . . . and indicating an intention to commit that crime.' *R v Barker* [1924] NZLR 865 at 870, per Sim J; also reported [1924] GLR 393 at 395

'In order to constitute an attempt the acts of the accused must be such as to clearly and unequivocally indicate, of themselves, the intention to commit the offence.' Ibid at 871, per Stringer J

'An act done with intent to commit a crime is not a criminal attempt unless it is of such a nature as to be in itself sufficient evidence of the criminal intent with which it is done. A criminal attempt is an act which shows criminal intent on the face of it. . . . An act . . . which is in its own nature and on the face of it innocent . . . cannot be brought within the scope of criminal attempt by evidence *aliunde* as to the criminal purpose with which it is done.' Ibid at 874, 875, per Salmond J

South Africa 'The fact that an accused's criminal purpose cannot be achieved, whether because the means are, in the existing or all conceivable circumstances, inadequate, or because the object is, in the existing or in all conceivable circumstances, unattainable, does not prevent his endeavour from amounting to an "attempt". Two cautionary observations must be made: (1) if what the accused was aiming to achieve was not a crime, an endeavour to achieve it could not, because by a mistake of law he thought that his act was criminal, constitute an attempt to commit a crime; (2) statutory crimes may require special consideration, for the language of statutes may convey a wide variety of legislative intentions.' *R v Davies* 1956 (3) SA 64(A) per Shreiner JA

ATTEND

'It does appear to me . . . that the words "attend school" do not mean merely sending the child to the school door with the certainty of its being sent away but sending it to the school door under such circumstances as that the person who sends the child can have reasonable ground to suppose that he is doing his duty within the Act [Education Act 1876 (repealed; see now Education Act 1944, ss 36–40].' *Saunders v Richardson* (1881) 7 QBD 388 at 393, 394, per Denman J

New Zealand 'When a person has paid for admission to a dance and has entered and joined in the dancing, and comes out while the dance is in progress, and is found consuming liquor in close proximity to the hall where the dance is still going on, in my opinion that person is "attending the dance" within the meaning of s 59(3) of the Statutes Amendment Act 1939 [repealed; see now Sale of Liquor Act 1962, s 265] notwithstanding that he may decide when accosted by the Police that he will not return to the hall, and even notwithstanding that he had decided not to return when he left the hall, for the liquor might cause him to alter his decision and return. If he were found consuming liquor at some considerable distance from the hall, thus showing that he had left the vicinity for good, it might be a different matter, for his actions would have given a clear indication that his decision was final, and that he had ceased to attend the dance; but while he is drinking liquor close by the hall, I think it can be said in popular language that he was still attending the dance.' *Blake v Graham* [1942] NZLR 15 at 17, per Ostler J; also reported [1941] GLR 647 at 648

ATTENDANCE

[The Increase of Rent and Mortgage Interest (Restrictions) Act 1920, s 12(2)(i) (repealed), provided that the Act should not apply to a dwelling-house bona fide let at a rent which includes payments in respect of board, 'attendance', or use of furniture.] 'One of the . . . things which was in consideration of the rent was the covenant by the landlord "To keep the entrance hall and the general staircase and other common parts of the said building . . . clean and in good order, and to remove such house refuse as cannot be burnt from the said flat and carry the lessee's coals thereto once in every week day free of charge to the lessee." . . . Were the taking up of the coals and the bringing down of the refuse "attendance" within the meaning of the above subsection? . . . I am absolutely clear in my own mind that a man who does the work which is necessary upon the flat itself, taking up coals and taking away refuse, is rendering attendance in respect of the demised premises, and that therefore this case is within the proviso.' *Nye v Davis* [1922] 2 KB 56 at 58, 59, per Horridge J

'He [counsel] said that the landlord here covenanted to provide and supply a good and sufficient supply of hot water for the demised premises at all times, and he invited me to hold that that constitutes "attendance" within the meaning of the proviso [Increase of Rent and Mortgage Interest (Restrictions) Act 1920, s 12(2)(i) (repealed)]. In my view it is not attendance. . . . I think the word "attendance" in the proviso refers to actual personal attendance by the landlord's servants or agents having actual corporeal existence. This view is supported by the meaning given to the word in Dr Johnson's Dictionary and in the Imperial Dictionary, and there is nothing in the definition of the word "Attendant" in Termes de la Ley to destroy the conclusion at which I have arrived.' *Wood v Carwardine* [1923] 2 KB 185 at 190, per McCardie J

'I do not think that an undertaking to maintain a system of electric bells, an undertaking to maintain a gas cooker, and an undertaking to maintain a dustbin at the rear of the house can properly be described as "attendance" within the meaning of the section.' *Engvall v Ideal Flats Ltd* [1945] KB 205, as reported in [1945] 1 All ER 230 at 233, CA, per Lord Greene MR

'What is attendance? It means service personal to the tenant performed by an attendant provided by the landlord in accordance with his covenant for the benefit or convenience of the individual tenant in his use or enjoyment of the demised premises. "Service" is a wider word than attendance. Attendance, being personal in its nature, may be dispensed with by an individual tenant at his pleasure, though it is not on that account excluded from what the tenant pays for when the landlord has covenanted to supply it. But services common to others (eg the heating of a communal water supply, or the cleaning of passages, halls, etc, outside the demised premises) will not constitute attendance. It follows from the above that a landlord's covenant to supply someone to carry up coals to a flat or to carry down refuse from the flat is a covenant to provide attendance. Similarly, the provision of a housemaid or valet to discharge duties in connection with the flat would be the provision of attendance, but a covenant by the landlord to provide a resident porter or house-keeper for a block of flats would not.' *Palser v Grinling; Property Holding Co Ltd v Mischeff* [1948] AC 291 at 310, 311, per Viscount Simon

[The Increase of Rent and Mortgage Interest (Restrictions) Act 1920, s 12(2)(i) and the Rent and Mortgage Interest Restrictions Act 1939, s 3(2)(b) have both been repealed. See now the Rent Act 1977, s 7(1) which provides that a tenancy is not a protected tenancy if under the tenancy a dwelling house is bona fide let at a rent which includes payments in respect of board or 'attendance'.]

ATTENTION *See* CARE

ATTEST

'To "attest" is to bear witness to a fact. Take a common example: a notary public attests a protest; he bears witness, not to the statements in that protest, but to the fact of the making of those statements; so I conceive the witnesses in a will bear witness to all that the statute [s 9 of the Wills Act 1837] requires attesting witnesses to attest, namely, that the signature was made or acknowledged in their presence. The statute does say "that no form of attestation shall be necessary"; still the witnesses must attest, although the outward work of attestation may be subscription only. If more be wanted to explain the meaning of the word "attest", the old form of attestation clause will show that it comprehended more than bare subscription of the will itself.' *Hudson v Parker* (1844) 1 Rob Eccl 14 at 26, per Dr Lushington

'Attest [as used in s 9 of the Wills Act 1837] means the persons shall be present and see what passes and shall, when required, bear witness to the facts.' *Bryan v White* (1850) 2 Rob Eccl 315 at 317, per Dr Lushington

' "Attestation" in its primary meaning, as the dictionaries show, involves witnessing, and witnessing only, but when it is applied to documents the dictionaries show, and the authorities also that it involves writing.' *Re Selby-Bigge* [1950] 1 All ER 1009 at 1011, per Hodson J

See, generally, 50 Halsbury's Laws (4th edn) paras 261 et seq.

ATTORNEY

'Attorney' signifies anyone who acts in the turn or place of another, and the power to authorise an attorney in the general sense, for example to execute a deed, has existed from a very remote period. (44 Halsbury's Laws (4th edn) para 1)

ATTORNMENT

A person in occupation of property may establish the relationship of landlord and tenant between himself and another person by attornment, that is by acknowledging that he is tenant to that other person. (27 Halsbury's Laws (4th edn) para 3)

ATTRIBUTABLE

[The question was whether the plaintiff's loss of employment was 'attributable' to the provisions of the Local Government Act 1972.] 'The fundamental problem is whether Mr Walsh's loss of employment was "attributable to" any provision of the 1972 Act, ie the April 1974 reorganisation. These words have been considered in a number of cases and I do not wish to add to the explanations and definitions which have been given. Counsel for Mr Walsh submits that it is a wider concept than "directly caused by", or "caused by or resulting from", but he accepts that it involves some nexus between the effect and the alleged cause. He suggests that "owing to" or "a material contributory cause" or "a material cause in some way contributing to the effect" may be synonyms. Lord Reid in *Central Asbestos Co v Dodd* [[1972] 2 All ER 1135] said: ". . . 'attributable'. That means capable of being attributed. 'Attribute' has a number of cognate meanings; you can attribute a quality to a person or thing, you can attribute a product to a source or author, you can attribute an effect to a cause. The essential element is connection of some kind." Suffice it to say that these are plain English words involving some causal connection between the loss of employment and that to which the loss is said to be attributable. However, this connection need not be that of a sole, dominant, direct or proximate cause and effect. A contributory causal connection is quite sufficient.' *Walsh v Rother District Council* [1978] 1 All ER 510 at 514, per Donaldson J

New Zealand 'The word "attributable" means owing to or produced by.' *Hartley v Hartley* 4 NZFLR (1986) 201 per Somers J

AUCTION   *See also* WITHOUT RESERVE

An auction is a manner of selling or letting property by bids, usually to the highest bidder by public competition. (2 Halsbury's Laws (4th edn) para 701)

Mock auction

Subject to the following provisions of this section, for the purposes of this Act a sale of goods by way of competitive bidding shall be taken to be a mock auction if, (but only if, during the course of the sale—
(a) any lot to which this Act applies is sold to a person bidding for it, and either it is sold to him at a price lower than the amount of his highest bid for that lot, or part of the price at which it is sold to him is repaid or credited to him or is stated to be so repaid or credited, or
(b) the right to bid for any lot to which this Act applies is restricted, or is stated to be restricted, to persons who have bought or agreed to buy one or more articles, or
(c) any articles are given away or offered as gifts.
A sale of goods shall not be taken to be a mock auction by virtue of paragraph (a) of the last preceding subsection, if it is proved that the reduction in price, or the repayment or credit, as the case may be,—
(a) was on account of a defect discovered after the highest bid in question had been made, being a defect of which the person conducting the sale was unaware when that bid was made, or
(b) was on account of damage sustained after that bid was made.
(Mock Auctions Act 1961, s 1(3), (4))

AUCTIONEER

An auctioneer is an agent who is employed to sell at a public auction. He may be agent for both seller and buyer and may or may not be entrusted with possession of the goods or property to be sold or of the documents of title thereto. (1 Halsbury's Laws (4th edn) para 713)

AUDIOVISUAL WORKS

Copyright

United States 'Audiovisual works' are works that consist of a series of related images which are intrinsically intended to be shown by the use of machines or devices such as projectors, viewers, or electronic equipment, together with accompanying sounds, if any, regardless of the nature of the material objects, such as films or tapes, in which the works are embodied. (Copyright Act of 1976, s 101)

AUDITOR

'I think that the term "auditor" is unfortunate; it leads the mind to the idea of a company's auditor, whose business is to ascertain and state the true financial position of the company at the time of the audit and nothing more. . . . But the auditors of the [metropolitan borough] council are appointed by the Local Government Board, not by the council, nor are they elective, as are the auditors under the Municipal Corporations Act. They are outside officials appointed by a government office to perform the duties set forth in s 247 of the Public Health Act [1875 (repealed; see now, as to the accounts and audit of present-day local authorities, the Local Government Finance Act 1982, Pt III)].' *R v Roberts* [1908] 1 KB 407 at 437, 438, per Farwell LJ

AUTHOR

'Author', in relation to a sound recording or a cinematograph film, means the maker of the recording or film. (Copyright Act 1956, s 35(5))

'Adaptation is not of course so fine an art as original work, but I cannot see why a man should not be the "author" of a dramatic piece because the foundation of it is taken from some other drama.' *Tree v Bowkett* (1896) 74 LT 77 at 78, per Kekewich J

South Africa 'The word "author" is not comprehensively defined in s 1 [of the Copyright Act No 36 of 1965], and must consequently be given its popular and conventional meaning which, according to the dictionary, denotes the maker or creator of a work concerned. . . . The work must therefore be original in the sense that it was not copied from another work, but originated from the author.' *Pan African Engineers v Hydro Tube* 1972 (1) SA 470 (W) per Boshoff J

See, generally, 9 Halsbury's Laws (4th edn) paras 858 et seq.

Joint author

In this Act 'work of joint authorship' means a work produced by the collaboration of two or more authors in which the contribution of each author is not separate from the contribution of the other author or authors. (Copyright Act 1956, s 11(3))

Of compilation

'It seems to me that where a book of this sort [Who's Who] is being compiled and the compiler invites information, the information given, whether it be given verbally or in writing, is not given otherwise than as material available for use by the compiler, and that, if it happens to be written, the man who writes it is not the author of something in which he has a copyright in any sense contemplated by the Copyright Act [Copyright Act 1911, ss 5, 6, 7, repealed; see now Copyright Act 1956, ss 4, 17, 18].' *Black (A & C) Ltd v Claude Stacey Ltd* [1929] 1 Ch 177 at 179, per Tomlin J

Of photograph

'Author', in relation to a photograph, means the person who at the time when the photograph is taken, is the owner of the material on which it is taken. (Copyright Act 1956, s 48(1))

'I confess I cannot be very clear about it [ie who is the "author" of a photograph where persons combine to take and develop it], all I can do is to see who is the nearest person—the nearest like the author of a painting or the author of a drawing. Certainly it is not the man who simply gives the idea of a picture, because the proprietor may say "Go and draw that lady with a dog at her feet, and in one hand holding a flower". He may have the idea, but still he is not there. He may be 100 miles from the place, and he may have given the instructions by letter. The nearest I can come to is that it is the person who effectively is, as near as he can be, the cause of the picture which is produced—that is the person who has superintended the arrangement, who has actually formed the picture by putting the people into position and arranging the place in which the people are to be.' *Nottage v Jackson* (1883) 11 QBD 627 at 632, CA, per Brett MR

Of report

'A mere copyist of written matter is not an author within the [Copyright] Act [of 1842 (repealed); see now Copyright Act 1956]. . . . A person to whom words are dictated for the purpose of being written down is not an "author". . . . But an author may come into existence without producing any original matter of his own. . . . The compilation of a street directory, the reports of proceedings in courts of law . . . have been held to bring the producers within the word "author"; and yet in one sense no original matter can be found in such publications. Still there was something apart from originality on the one hand and mere mechanical transcribing on the other which entitled those who gave these words to the world to be regarded as their authors. Now, what is it that a reporter [in reporting the speech of a leading statesman] does? Is he a mere scribe? Does he produce original matter or does he produce the something I have mentioned which entitles him to be regarded as an "author" within the Act? I think that from a general point of view a reporter's art represents more than mere transcribing or writing from dictation. . . . I have, after some doubt, come to the conclusion that a reporter of a speech under the conditions existing in this case is the meritorious producer of the something necessary to constitute him an "author" within the meaning of the Copyright Act of 1842.' *Walter v Lane* [1900] AC 539 at 554, 555, per Lord James of Hereford

AUTHORISE

Australia 'The word "authorise" should be read in its ordinary sense of sanction, approve or countenance.' *Winstone v Wurlitzer Automatic Phonograph Co of Aus Pty Ltd* [1946] ALR 422 at 426, per Herring CJ

Australia 'The word "authorise", according to its natural meaning, signifies the conferring upon a person of a right to do something which, apart from the authorisation, he does not possess. . . . But the word, like any other word, may be controlled by its context.' *Ex p Johnson, Re MacMillan* (1947) 47 NSWSR 16 at 18, per Jordan CJ

Australia 'The word "authorise" in legislation of similar intendment to s 36(1) [Copyright Act 1968–1986 (Cth)] has been held judicially to have its dictionary meaning of "sanction, approve, countenance". It can also mean "permit", and in *Adelaide Corporation v Australasian Performing Right Association Ltd* [40 CLR 481], "authorise" and "permit" appear to have been treated as synonymous. A person cannot be said to authorise an infringement of copyright unless he has some power to prevent it. Express or formal permission or sanction, or active conduct indicating approval, is not essential to constitute an authorisation: "Inactivity or indifference, exhibited by acts of commission or omission, may reach the degree from which an authorisation or permission may be inferred". However, the word "authorise" connotes a mental element and it could not be inferred that a person had, by mere inactivity, authorised something to be done if he neither knew nor had reason to suspect that the act might be done.' *Moorhouse & Angus &*

Robertson (Publishers) Pty Ltd v University of New South Wales [1976] RPC 151 at 158, 159, per Gibbs J

Course of vessel

Article 28 of the Regulations for Preventing Collisions at Sea 1897, provides that when vessels are in sight of one another, a steam vessel under way, in taking any course 'authorised' or required by these rules, shall indicate that course, by certain signals on her whistle or siren.] 'It has been sought to put a rather narrow interpretation upon the rule . . . the word "required" is clear enough. . . . The word "authorised" is, however, very much larger, and I am inclined to think that a large interpretation ought to be given to it; and that it includes any course which, for the safety of the vessels, good seamanship requires to be taken with reference to the other vessel then in sight—although it is quite true that there are certain cases where you may say a more distinct authorisation arises.' *The Uskmoor* [1902] P 250 at 254, per Jeune P

Printing and publishing

'It has been ingeniously argued in the subsection [the Copyright Act 1911, s 1(2) (repealed; see now Copyright Act 1956, s 1(1))] "to authorise any such acts" means to sanction their being done by the servant or agent of the person affecting to give the authority on his behalf, and that there is no infringement of a copyright when that person to whom authority is given is not the servant or agent of the person affecting to give it. In my judgment this is to put too narrow a meaning on the word, which is defined in the Oxford Dictionary as meaning in connection with the authorisation of acts "to give formal approval to, to sanction, approve, countenance", and it is to be observed that where a man sold the rights in relation to an MS to another with the view to its production, and it was in fact produced, both the English language and common sense required him to hold that this man had "authorised" the printing and publication.' *Evans v Hulton (E) & Co Ltd* (1924) 131 LT 534 at 535, per Tomlin J

AUTHORITY

Australia 'The word "authority" has long been used to describe a body or person exercising power or command. No doubt this has come about by a transfer of meaning from the abstract conception of power or command to the body or person possessing it. But in relation to such a public affair as public transport the use of the word "authority" as a description of a person or body implies he or it is an agency or instrument set up to exercise control or execute a function in the public interest whether as an emanation of the general government or as an adjunct of local government or as a specially constituted officer or body.' *Federal Comr of Taxation v Silverton Tramway Co Ltd* [1953] 88 CLR 559 at 565–566, per Dixon CJ

AUTHORITY OF STATE

Australia 'The expression "authority of a State" refers to a body which exercises power derived from or delegated by the State, but the fact that a body is established under State law and possesses power conferred upon it by State law will not necessarily mean that the body is an authority of a State. For example, a private company, such as a gas supply company, which provides a public service for profit, may be set up under the company laws of a State, and may be given special statutory powers to enable it to carry on its undertaking, but it does not thereby become an authority of a State. The words "authority of a State" naturally mean a body which is given by the State the power to direct or control the affairs of others on behalf of the State.' *Committee of Direction of Fruit Marketing v Australian Postal Commission* (1980) 30 ALR 599 at 602, per Gibbs J

AUTOMATISM

'Automatism was defined by the Court of Criminal Appeal [of Northern Ireland] in this case as connoting the state of a person who, though capable of action, "is not conscious of what he is doing. . . . It means unconscious involuntary action, and it is a defence because the mind does not go with what is being done". This is very like the words of the learned President of the Court of Appeal of New Zealand in *R v Cottle* [infra] where he said: "With respect, I would myself prefer to explain automatism simply as action without any knowledge of acting, or action with no consciousness of doing what was being done".' *Bratty v A-G for Northern Ireland* [1961] 3 All ER 523 at 527, HL, per Viscount Kilmuir LC

[A motorist who took drugs for diabetes and who was charged with driving while under the influence of a drug, pleaded that he had been reduced to a state of 'automatism'.] 'Whether or not any given state of evidence in any case provides a foundation for a finding of automatism is a question of law; compare *Bratty v A-G for Northern Ireland* [supra]. Such a foundation was laid in this case by the medical evidence, and the justices were, therefore, bound to determine whether the prosecution had excluded automatism beyond reasonable doubt with respect to at least a part of the driving. It is equally a question of law what constitutes a state of automatism. It is salutary to recall that this expression is no more than a modern catchphrase which the courts have not accepted as connoting any movement of the body or limbs of a person.' *Watmore v Jenkins* [1962] 2 All ER 868 at 874, per cur.; also reported in [1962] 2 QB 572 at 585

New Zealand 'It would appear that automatism raised as a defence to a criminal charge may be something quite different and distinct from insanity. In a particular case, it may be that the automatism relied on is due to some "disease of the mind" but it is not necessarily so. Automatism, which strictly means action without conscious volition, has been adopted in criminal law as a term to denote conduct of which the doer is not conscious—in short, doing something without knowledge of it, and without memory afterwards of having done it—a temporary eclipse of consciousness that nevertheless leaves the person so affected able to exercise bodily movements. In such a case, the action is one which the mind, in its normal functioning, does not control. This may be due to some "disease of the mind" or it may not; it may happen with a perfectly healthy mind (eg in somnambulism, which may be unaccompanied by any abnormality of mind), or it may occur where the mind is temporarily affected as the result of a blow, or by the influence of a drug or other intoxication. It may, on the other hand, be caused by an abnormal condition of the mind capable of being designated a mental disease.' *R v Cottle* [1958] NZLR 999 at 1007, CA, per Gresson P

South Africa 'It is a good defence to any criminal charge that the accused, when committing the act complained of, was in an unconscious state having neither judgment, will, purpose nor reasoning.' *R v Ahmed* 1959 (3) SA 776 (W) per Marais J

AUTREFOIS ACQUIT

The plea of *autrefois acquit*, or a former acquittal, is grounded on this universal maxim of the common law of England, that no man is to be brought into jeopardy of his life more than once for the same offence. (4 Bl Com 329)

'The plea of *autrefois acquit* was rightly rejected. The principle on which this plea depends has often been stated. It is this, that the law does not permit a man to be twice in peril of being convicted of the same offence. If, therefore, he has been acquitted, ie found to be not guilty of the offence, by a Court competent to try him, such acquittal is a bar to a second indictment for the same offence. This rule applies not only to the offence actually charged in the first indictment, but to any offence to which he could have been properly convicted on the trial of the first indictment. Thus any acquittal on a charge of murder is a bar to a subsequent indictment for manslaughter, as the jury could have convicted of manslaughter.' *R v Barron* [1914] 2 KB 570 at 574, CCA, per cur.

[After the quashing of his conviction on a charge of murder, the appellant was proceeded against on a second indictment for robbery.] 'For the doctrine of *autrefois* to apply it is necessary that the accused should have been put in peril of conviction for the same offence as that with which he is then charged. The word "offence" embraces both the facts which constitute the crime and the legal characteristics which make it an offence. For the doctrine to apply it must be the same offence both in fact and in law. Robbery is not in law the same offence as murder (or as manslaughter, of which the accused could also have been convicted in the first indictment), and so the doctrine does not apply in the present case.' *Connelly v Director of Public Prosecutions* [1964] 2 All ER 401 at 433, HL, per Lord Devlin; also reported [1964] AC 1254

AUTREFOIS CONVICT

The plea of *autrefois convict*, or a former conviction for the same identical crime, though no judgment was ever given, or perhaps will be . . . is a good plea in bar to an indictment. (4 Bl Com 330)

The pleas of *autrefois convict* or *autrefois acquit* aver respectively that the defendant has been previously convicted or acquitted on a charge for the same offence as that in respect of which he is arraigned. (11 Halsbury's Laws (4th edn) para 241)

'It has been argued before us on this appeal that upon the second trial these two men ought

to have been acquitted—that the matter should not have been left to the jury on the ground that both had been lawfully convicted of the same offence, or practically the same offence, at the Central Criminal Court in January last. That plea, which was raised before the Recorder and which was left to the jury practically with the direction that they could decide it only in one way, raises a question of law, namely, what it is necessary to prove, in order that an accused person may rely on the plea of *autrefois convict*. It is quite clear that, to enable an accused person to rely on that plea, the offence with which he is charged on the second occasion must be the same offence, or practically the same offence, as that with which he was charged on the first occasion. It is not enough to say that the evidence tendered on the second charge was the same evidence as that offered to prove the first charge.' *R v Kendrick & Smith* (1931) 23 Cr App Rep 1 at 4, 5, CCA, per Swift J

New Zealand 'It is well established that the same act or omission may constitute two or more different offences, and that a person may be convicted of two distinct offences arising out of the same act or the same facts. . . . The test is not whether the facts relied upon by the Crown are the same in respect of the two charges, but whether the offence in respect of which the accused has been convicted or acquitted, as the case may be, on the first charge is the same, or practically or in substance the same, as that with which he is subsequently charged.' *R v Burton* [1941] NZLR 519 at 529, CA, per cur.; also reported [1941] GLR 309 at 312

AUTOMOBILE   *See* MOTOR CAR

AVAILABLE

'We do not understand "available balance in hand" merely to mean money in the coffers of the defendant society, but money which without undue loss or undue delay they could realise, as, for example, money invested in Consols or in any other security capable of being readily realised.' *Brett v Monarch Investment Building Society* [1894] 1 QB 367 at 371, 372, CA, per Lopes LJ

[The question was whether safety-belts were 'available' within reg 97 of the Building (Safety, Health and Welfare) Regulations 1948 (revoked; see the Construction (Working Places) Regulations 1966).] 'The learned judge came to the conclusion that having safety belts at the main office was not a compliance with the regulation. The words that he used about that were these: "Now what is meant by 'making available'? 'Making available' to my mind must mean to make reasonably available to the men who elect to use them. Quite clearly if a man desires to elect to use a safety belt it is no good telling him that those belts are situated some half a mile or three-quarters of a mile away. That is not, in my judgment, 'available' within the meaning of these regulations. In my judgment, that duty entails an obligation on the employers to have available on the site where a man who, in special circumstances perhaps, makes up his mind that he desires to use a belt, may get one and get it reasonably quickly". I agree with the learned judge on that matter.' *Roberts v Dorman Long & Co Ltd* [1953] 2 All ER 428 at 434, 435, CA, per Birkett LJ

[The Education Act 1944, s 39(5) defines 'walking distance' from school by reference to the nearest 'available' route.] 'Counsel for the appellant contended that the meaning of the word "available" in the Education Act 1944, s 39(5), is that there is no sound reason why that route should not be used by children. I am bound to say that I cannot read that meaning into the word. The "nearest available route" means the method by which the two miles [three miles if aged 8 or over] are to be measured from the child's house to the school in order to ascertain whether or not it is a walking distance.' *Shaxted v Ward* [1954] 1 All ER 336 at 338, per Lord Goddard CJ

[*Shaxted v Ward* was distinguished in *Rogers v Essex County Council* [1985] 2 All ER 39 where it was held that a route which is unsafe to the extent that a responsible parent would not permit his child to use it is not an 'available' route within the meaning of s 39(5).]

Canada [A policy of insurance provided that at the end of the third or any subsequent year during which full premiums had been paid or within thirty days thereafter, the surrender value in cash should become 'available' to the assured.] ' "Available" does not mean "existing". It means "in such a condition as that it can be taken advantage of".' *Devitt v Mutual Life Insurance Co of Canada* (1915) 33 OLR 473 at 478, Ont CA, per Riddell J

New Zealand [The Transport Act 1949 (NZ), s 96 (repealed; see now Transport Act 1962, s 109) provided that the carriage of any goods from one place to another by a heavy motor-vehicle that was designed exclusively or principally for the carriage of goods was to be deemed to be a goods service if there was between those two places an 'available' route for the carriage of goods that included not less than thirty miles of open Government railway.] 'The word "available" as used in s 96 inherently means "capable of use in fact" or "open and usable". It is to the characteristic of the road from the point of view of fitness for use that the word "reasonably", if introduced, would relate. In other words, I am not disposed to think that the word "available" in the subsection has any relation to the economic incidents of user of a road. If this were not so, then whether routes were available or not might have to be determined in the light of question of extra cost involved in their use by reason of their steepness or other characteristics involving increased running costs. Nothing of that sort was, I am satisfied, intended by the Legislature which, when it used the word "available", meant no more than "susceptible of use".' *Hanna v Garland* [1954] NZLR 945 at 946, 947, per Finlay J

AVAILABLE MARKET

[The Sale of Goods Act 1893, s 50(3) (repealed; see now the Sale of Goods Act 1979, s 50(3)) deals with the ascertainment of the measure of damages for non-acceptance and non-payment where there is an 'available market' for goods.] 'Had the matter been *res integra*, I think I should have found that an "available market" merely means that the situation in the particular trade in the particular area was such that the particular goods could freely be sold, and that there was a demand sufficient to absorb readily all the goods that were thrust on it, so that if a purchaser defaulted the goods in question could readily be disposed of.' *Thompson (WL) Ltd v Robinson (R) (Gunmakers) Ltd* [1955] 1 All ER 154 at 159, per Upjohn J

AVERAGE

'Average' includes certain charges which are to be borne partly by the ship and partly by the cargo, such as the expense of towing or beaconage. These and similar charges were also sometimes known as 'petty average'. The word has many different meanings in the shipping world. (43 Halsbury's Laws (4th edn) 736)

During the performance of a contract of carriage by sea there are, in general three separate interests which are exposed to the risks incidental to a maritime adventure, namely the interest in the ship, the interest in the freight and the interest in the cargo. In the ordinary course, any loss which may be sustained by any of these interests falls upon the particular interest affected, in which case the loss, if not total, is called a 'particular average loss'. Where, however, the loss arises in consequence of extraordinary sacrifices made or expenditure incurred for the preservation of the several interests involved, it no longer falls on the particular interest exclusively, but must be borne in due proportion by all. The loss is then called a 'general average loss'; the sacrifices or expenditure which give rise to it are known as 'general average sacrifices' and 'general average expenditure', whilst the amount to be contributed towards the loss by the respective interests is called a 'general average contribution'. (43 Halsbury's Laws (4th edn) para 742)

'The word "average", far from being a term of art (except in so far as, according to the evidence, usage may have limited its meaning to loss or damage to the goods themselves), or a word with a rigid or unchanging signification, necessarily including expenses in the defence or safeguard of the subject-matter insured, is a word used in a great variety of phrases, as applicable to different subject-matters, and not with any fixed or settled application.' *Kidston v Empire Marine Insurance Co Ltd* (1866) 35 LJCP 250 at 256, per Willes J

Australia 'The word "average" (apart from its technical usage in maritime law) is not, when used in every-day language, a scientific term or a term of art but one which, as can be seen from well-known and authoritative dictionaries, has meanings which vary according to the context in which it is found. The expression "the average man" means the ordinary or typical man. The primary meaning of "average" is synonymous with equalling an arithmetical mean or, less strictly, approximating an arithmetical mean, a process which usually involves a division of unequal sums or quantities.' *Flinders Shire Council v Smiles* [1970] Qd R 364 at 369, per cur.

Australia 'The primary meaning of "average" is synonomous with equalling an arithmetical mean or, less strictly, approximating an arithmetical mean, a process which usually involves a division of unequal sums or quantities. But a person is not infrequently heard to say: "My average speed from A to B was 40 mph", although the time taken to travel that distance may have been less than an hour. Because the word, in ordinary usage, is capable of more than one meaning it must be construed by reference to the tenor of the regulations as a whole, and all parts of the regulations must be construed together: *George Pearce Pty Ltd v O'Flynn* [(1962) 79 WN (NSW) 328].' *Flinders Shire Council v Smiles* (1982) 42 LGRA 92 at 95, per W B Campbell J

Free from average

'This is an insurance on goods "warranted free from particular average",—in effect an insurance against a total loss.' *Great Indian Peninsula Rly Co v Saunders* (1862) 2 B & S 266 at 272, 273, per Erle CJ

'"Average", as used in this connection [a policy of marine insurance], is clearly a technical expression and it has a well-established mercantile signification. It means a partial as distinguished from a total loss. If there is a total loss of the whole of the things mentioned, or of the whole of any one of them, or a total loss of any part which is so put on board as that there can be a total loss of that part, the clause will not apply to that loss. Taking "average" then to mean average or partial loss, the meaning is that certain articles mentioned are warranted free from partial loss or partial loss under certain percentage, unless it be a general average loss, that is to say, a loss voluntarily occasioned for the safety and benefit of the common enterprise.' *Price & Co v Al Ships' Small Damage Insurance Assocn Ltd* (1889) 22 QBD 580 at 584–586, per Lord Esher MR

[A contract for the sale of a ship provided that the sellers should deliver the ship 'free of average'.] 'I take the view, as a matter of construction, that, in this context, "free from average" does not mean "free from damage to the ship", but does mean "free from claims against the ship".' *Kelman v Livanos* [1955] 2 All ER 236 at 240, per McNair J

Free of all average

'I can see no reason whatever for not giving the words "warranted free of all average" [in a policy of marine insurance] their customary meaning, which, of course, is that the policy does not cover a partial loss but only a total loss of the anticipated earnings insured and, of course, that total loss must be occasioned by a total loss of the ship or a constructive total loss of the ship, or though it is irrelevant in this case, an arranged loss.' *Continental Grain Co (Inc) v Twitchell* [1945] 1 All ER 357 at 359, per Atkinson J

General average

A general average loss is a loss caused by or directly consequential on a general average act. It includes a general average expenditure as well as a general average sacrifice. There is a general average act where any extraordinary sacrifice or expenditure is voluntarily and reasonably made or incurred in time of peril for the purpose of preserving the property imperilled in the common adventure. Where there is a general average loss, the party on whom it falls is entitled, subject to the conditions imposed by maritime law, to a rateable contribution from the other parties interested, and such a contribution is called a general average contribution. (25 Halsbury's Laws (4th edn) para 249)

'This claim for average contribution, at all events, is part of the law of the sea . . . the captain . . . makes the sacrifice on behalf of one principal, whose agent of necessity he is, on the implied terms, if you like to call it so, that that principal shall be indemnified afterwards by the rest . . . those who wish to make exceptions in their own favour, and by which they are to be relieved from the ordinary laws of the sea, ought to do so in clear words.' *Burton v English* (1883) 12 QBD 218 at 223, 224, CA, per Bowen LJ

'To make a general average act, there must be a common peril, and there is no general average contribution without a general average act, or an act consequential upon a general average act, and so intimately connected with it as to make with it in substance one continuous act done to release the whole venture from a common peril.' *Hamel v Peninsular & Oriental Steam Navigation Co* [1908] 2 KB 298 at 305, per Lord Alverstone CJ

'The sacrifice or expenditure must be extraordinary, it must be made or incurred intentionally, and made or incurred reasonably for the common safety for the specific purpose referred to, namely, preserving upon peril the property involved in a common maritime adventure. If any of this language is inapplicable to the facts of a particular case then that case is not one involving a general average act.'

Athel Line Ltd v Liverpool & London War Risks Insurance Assocn Ltd [1944] KB 87 at 93, per Tucker J

Australia 'A "general average act", that is, an act which gives rise to the necessity for adjustment by general average, is an act done by virtue of an agency of necessity.' *Gillespie Bros Pty Ltd v Burns Philp & Co Ltd* (1947) NSWSR 122 at 131, per Jordan CJ

Canada ' "General average" is a term used to describe a procedure to be followed when by reason of some maritime misfortune both the ship and her whole cargo are in danger. In such cases, if the master deliberately and reasonably takes action for the benefit of all concerned which has a direct consequence of damaging the ship or cargo, the loss becomes a "general average loss", and is adjusted between all the parties to the marine adventure.

The most obvious and perhaps the earliest recorded example of this is a case where tempestuous seas make it necessary to lighten ship and part of the cargo is jettisoned to save the ship and the remaining cargo. General average may, however, apply to any sacrifice or expense intentionally and reasonably incurred for the benefit of all in the face of an emergency.' *Federal Commerce and Navigation Co Ltd v Eisenerz GmbH* [1974] SCR 1225 at 1234, SCC, per Ritchie J

Particular average

A particular average loss is a partial loss of the subject matter insured, caused by a peril insured against, and which is not a general average loss. Thus, if part of the goods is lost, or if the ship is damaged, by a peril insured against, that loss or damage, where not caused by a general average act so as to constitute a general average loss, is a particular average loss. 'Particular average' does not include expenses incurred by or on behalf of the assured for the safety or preservation of the subject matter insured. Such expenses are either general average or salvage charges, or they are 'particular charges'. (25 Halsbury's Laws (4th edn) para 262)

'Simple or particular average is not a very accurate expression; for it means damage incurred by or for one part of the concern, which that part must bear alone; so that in fact it is no average at all, but still the expression is sufficiently understood, and received into familiar use. The loss of an anchor or cable, the starting of a plank, are matters of simple or particular average, for which the ship alone is liable. Should a cargo of wine turn sour on the voyage, it would be a matter of simple average, which the goods alone must bear; and there might be a simple average for which each would be severally liable under a misfortune happening to both ship and cargo at the same time, and from a common cause; as if a waterspout should fall on a cargo of sugars, and a plank from the same violence should start at the same time.' *The Copenhagen* (1799) 1 Ch Rob 289 at 293, 294, per Sir W Scott

'Subject to average'

'The question turns upon the meaning of the words in Lloyd's policy "subject to average". According to the evidence given before me these words "subject to average" or the words "subject to the conditions of average" have a clearly defined meaning in a Lloyd's policy. It is expressed in a slip which is frequently attached to a Lloyd's policy, which runs in the following form: "Average clause—Whenever a sum insured is declared to be subject to average, if the property covered thereby shall at the breaking out of any fire be collectively of greater value than such sum insured, then the assured shall be considered as being his own insurer for the difference, and shall bear a rateable share of the loss accordingly".' *Acme Wood Flooring Co Ltd v Marten* (1904) 90 LT 313 at 314, per Bruce J

AVERMENT

Australia 'The word "averment" has no very definite meaning. It may include both allegations of law and allegations of fact, but under this particular section [the Income Tax Assessment Act 1936, s 243 (see now Taxation Administration Act 1953–1987 (Cth) s 8ZL)] the averment is taken to be prima facie evidence "of the fact only".' *Brady v Thornton* (1947) 75 CLR 140 at 146, per Starke J

AVIATION INSURANCE *See*
INSURANCE

AVOID

[By the Finance Act 1936, s 18 (repealed; see now the Income and Corporation Taxes Act 1970, s 478), provision was made for the prevention of the 'avoiding' by individuals ordinarily resident in the United Kingdom of liability to income tax by means of transfers of assets by virtue of which income became payable to persons resident abroad.] 'We have . . . to look for an individual who is ordinarily resident in the United Kingdom and avoiding liability to income tax. There cannot be two opinions as to what "avoiding" means. Where what is to be avoided is a liability, it must mean to evade or to keep out of the way of, whether it be as in Richard III, "The censures of the carping world", or anything else unpleasant that might befall a man such as a tax.' *Congreve & Congreve v Inland Revenue Comrs* [1946] 2 All ER 170 at 181, per Wrottesley J; revd. [1947] 1 All ER 168, CA

Australia [The Income Tax Assessment Act 1936 (Cth), s 260, provides that every contract, agreement or arrangement made or entered into for the purpose of (inter alia) defeating, evading or 'avoiding' any duty or liability imposed on any person by the Act shall be absolutely void, as against the Commissioner, or in regard to any proceeding under the Act, but without prejudice to such validity as it may have in any other respect or for any other purpose.] 'Their Lordships . . . are clearly of opinion that the word "avoid" is used in its ordinary sense—in the sense in which a person is said to avoid something which is about to happen to him. He takes steps to get out of the way of it. It is this meaning of "avoid" which gives the clue to the meaning of "liability imposed". To "avoid a liability imposed" on you means to take steps to get out of the reach of a liability which is about to fall on you.' *Newton v Federal Taxation Comr* (1959) 98 CLR 2 at 7, PC, per Lord Denning; also reported [1958] AC 450 at 464

AVOIDABLE *See* UNAVOIDABLE

AWARD

'What is the nature of an award? An award is a decree made by a judge or judges, deriving authority from the choice of the parties. The power of such judge or judges to decide, and the duty incumbent on the parties to obey the decision, arise solely from the contract of submission. In order, therefore, to support an action on an award, the contract of submission must be proved. The award itself is no evidence of contract, but, when made in pursuance of a proper submission, then the parties may be said to have contracted to pay that, which the arbitrators, so empowered, have by the award directed to be paid.' *Winter v White* (1819) 1 Brod & Bing 350 at 357, per Richardson J

B

BACKWARDATION *See* CONTANGO

BAD CHARACTER *See* CHARACTER

BAGGAGE

[The Administration of Justice Act 1956, s 1(1)(g) (repealed; see Supreme Court Act 1981) provided that the Admiralty jurisdiction of the High Court should include jurisdiction to hear claims for loss of or damage to goods carried in a ship. Section 8(1) of the Act provided that 'goods' was to include 'baggage.'] 'I was referred to dictionary definitions of the word "baggage", which tend to show that it means the belongings of a passenger or traveller. Bearing in mind those definitions, and the context in which the word is here used, I have come to the conclusion that para (g) should be construed as covering passengers or travellers' baggage only, and not as extending to the belongings of those who are on board a ship, not as passengers or travellers, but as employees of the shipowners in order to man and operate her.' *The Eschersheim* [1974] 3 All ER 307, per Brandon J

BAILIWICK

The area for which an under-sheriff acts is known as a bailiwick, each bailiwick being the same area as that for which an under-sheriff acted prior to the reorganisation of local government in 1974. One of the effects of the reorganisation was that some of the old counties, together with a number of cities and towns which had been counties in themselves, for which high sheriffs and therefore under-sheriffs had been appointed, disappeared. Thus, many of the bailiwicks do not have the same boundaries as the new counties for which high sheriffs are appointed, with the result that in many cases there are two or more bailiwicks within a county and a bailiwick may be situated in more than one county. Where a bailiwick is situated in two or more counties, the duty of appointing the under-sheriff for that area must be discharged by the high sheriff of the county containing the greater part of that area, after consulting any other high sheriff concerned. (42 Halsbury's Laws (4th edn) para 1111)

BAILMENT

A bailment, properly so called, is a delivery of personal chattels on trust, usually on a contract, express or implied, that the trust shall be duly executed, and the chattels redelivered in either their original or an altered form, as soon as the time or use for, or condition on, which they were bailed shall have elapsed or been performed. The legal relationship of bailor and bailee can exist independently of any contract, and is created by the voluntary taking into custody of goods which are the property of another, as in cases of sub-bailment or of bailment by finding. The element common to all types of bailment is the imposition of an obligation, because the taking of possession in the circumstances involves an assumption of responsibility for the safe keeping of the goods. An action against a bailee can be regarded as an action on its own, sui generis, arising out of the possession had by the bailee of the goods.

A bailment is distinguishable from a sale, which is effected wherever chattels are delivered on a contract for an equivalent in money or money's worth, and not for the return of the identical chattels in their original or an altered form. The relationship of bailor and bailee is also to be distinguished from the relationship of licensor and licensee which, in the absence of special contractual provisions, carries no obligation on the part of the licensor towards the licensee in relation to the chattel subject to the licence. . . .In the leading case of *Coggs v Bernard* [(1703) 2 Ld Raym 909] Holt CJ divided bailment into six classes, which Sir William Jones rearranged into five classes, as follows:

(1) the gratuitous deposit of a chattel with the bailee, who is simply to keep it for the bailor;

(2) the delivery of a chattel to the bailee, who is to do something without reward for the bailee to or with the chattel;

(3) the gratuitous loan of a chattel by the bailor to the bailee for the bailee to use;

(4) the pawn or pledge of a chattel by the bailor to the bailee, who is to hold it as a security for a loan or debt or the fulfilment of an obligation; and

(5) the hire of a chattel or services by the bailor to the bailee for reward.

(2 Halsbury's Laws (4th edn) paras 1501, 1502)

New Zealand 'When one person delivers to another any movable thing in order that it may be used, gratuitously or otherwise, by the person to whom delivery is made, the act of delivery is the "bailment", the person making the delivery is the "bailor", and the person to whom it is made is the "bailee".' *Booth Macdonald & Co Ltd v Hallmond (Official Assignee of)* (1913) 33 NZLR 110 at 118, per Cooper J; also reported 16 GLR 103 at 107

BAKEHOUSE

'Bakehouse' means any place in which bread, biscuits or confectionary is or are baked by way of trade or for purposes of gain. (Factories Act 1961, s 176)

BALANCE

'I am not sure that there is much difference between "balance" and "surplus", but each of those words presupposes a primary expenditure which is first to be brought into account before ever a balance or a surplus can be ascertained.' *Re Herbert, Herbert v Lord Bicester* [1946] 1 All ER 421 at 423, per Vaisey J

Australia 'In this case [where a testator after making certain specific devises, gave 'all the balance of my real and personal property that being house and land', and followed this by an enumeration which included all his real estate and omitted some personal estate] I have no doubt that, on the proper construction of the will, I should hold that the gift of "all the balance of my real and personal property" is a gift of all the real and personal estate of the testator not otherwise disposed of, and that the words which follow, beginning "that being house and land", are words of enumeration merely, and not words which limit the prior residuary gift.' *Re Duffell, Equity Trustees, Executors & Agency Co Ltd v Duffell* [1926] VLR 489 at 491, per Macfarlan J

Australia 'What does "outstanding balance" mean? In many contexts I suppose it means the amount of a debt due unpaid on a certain date but in another sense it can reasonably mean I think the amount shown in some particular account or book of account as the balance outstanding. The word "balance" in some contexts may mean an amount shown in a formal document of account as the balance of liability over assets or debits over credits or vice versa. A balance sheet is an account in which the surplus or deficiency as the case may be is added on the other side of the account so as to produce the balance. In a literal sense a balance stands out when it is put down on paper and called "outstanding balance".' *Re An Appeal from the Credit Tribunal by John Martin & Co Ltd* (1974) 8 SASR 237 at 241, per Bray CJ

New Zealand [A testator by his will gave his residuary estate upon trust to divide the 'balance' thereof after certain payments amongst his brothers and sisters.] 'The word used in this will is not "residue" or "remainder" but "balance". I do not think, however, that there is any real difference between these words in this context. It is true that the word "balance" is more properly used to indicate the excess of one thing over another when two are compared. It is, however, frequently used in the sense of residue or remainder, which is its sense here.' *Re Andrew, Andrew v Andrew* [1934] NZLR 526 at 531, per Kennedy J; also reported [1934] GLR 529 at 531

BALLAST   *See also* IN BALLAST

'Ballast' means any of the following materials, that is to say—
(a) sand, gravel, shingle, ashes and clinker of any description;
(b) broken slag, slag chippings, granite chippings, limestone chippings, slate chippings and other stone chippings (including such materials which have been coated with tar, bitumen or cement);
(c) any other material commonly used in the building and civil engineering industries as a hardcore or an aggregate; and
(d) any other material commonly known in those industries as ballast.

(Weights and Measures Act 1985, Sch 4)

BALLOT   *See also* LOT

[Article 85 of the articles of a company provided that, if the directors could not agree amongst themselves which of them were to retire, the matter should be determined by 'ballot'.] 'The word "ballot" clearly may cover a case in which the decision depends on chance or is made by lot. . . . But the word "ballot" has undoubtedly been used in other circumstances to indicate a secret vote. When I look at the language of art 85 in this case and consider the circumstances, the view at which I arrive is that the proper construction of the words "by ballot" is "by lot".' *Eyre v Milton Proprietary Ltd* [1936] Ch 244 at 252, CA, per Lord Wright MR

BANK—BANKING

A 'banker' is an individual, partnership or corporation, whose sole or predominating business is banking, that is the receipt of money on current or deposit account and the payment of cheques drawn by and the collection of cheques paid in by a customer. . . . The judicial recognition of the banker's lien implies the inclusion in banking business of the making of advances or the granting of overdrafts to customers. (3 Halsbury's Laws (4th edn) para 38)

In this Act the expressions 'bank' and 'banker' mean—
(a) a recognised bank, licensed institution or municipal bank, within the meaning of the Banking Act 1987;
(b) . . .
(c) the National Savings Bank; and
(d) the Post Office, in the exercise of its powers to provide banking services.
(Bankers' Books Evidence Act 1879, s 9 (amended by the Banking Act 1987, s 108(1), Sch 6 and the Trustee Savings Bank Act 1985, s 4(3), Sch 4)

'In 1921 Atkin LJ gave a modern picture of a characteristic banking account in *Joachimson v Swiss Bank Corpn* [[1921] 3 KB 110]: "The bank undertakes to receive money and to collect bills for its customer's account. The proceeds so received are not to be held in trust for the customer, but the bank borrows the proceeds and undertakes to repay them. The promise to repay is to repay at the branch of the bank where the account is kept, and during banking hours. It includes a promise to repay any part of the amount due against the written order of the customer addressed to the bank at the branch . . . bankers never do make a payment to a customer in respect of a current account except upon demand". This was followed in 1948 by the *Bank of Chettinad Ltd of Colombo v Income Tax Comr, Colombo* [[1948] AC 378], where the Privy Council accepted the Ceylon description of a "banking company" as "a company which carries on as its principal business the accepting of deposits of money on current account or otherwise, subject to withdrawal of cheque, draft or order". And now the Shorter Oxford Dictionary gives the meaning of a "bank" in modern use as: "An establishment for the custody of money received from, or on behalf of, its customers. Its essential duty is to pay their drafts on it: its profits arise from the use of money left unemployed by them." There are, therefore, two characteristics usually found in bankers today: (i) they accept money from, and collect cheques for, their customers and place them to their credit; (ii) they honour cheques or orders drawn on them by their customers when presented for payment and debit their customers accordingly. These two characteristics carry with them also a third, namely, (iii) they keep current accounts, or something of that nature, in their books in which the credits and debits are entered.' *United Dominions Trust Ltd v Kirkwood* [1966] 1 All ER 968 at 975, CA, per Lord Denning MR

'What I think is common to all modern definitions and essential to the carrying on of the business of banking is that the banker should accept from his customers loans of money on "deposit", that is to say, loans for an indefinite period on running account, repayable as to the whole or any part thereof on demand by the customer either without notice or on an agreed period of notice. Some verbal confusion and perhaps some misunderstanding of the less recent judgments may arise from the fact that an account kept by a banker of his customer's loans made without interest and repayable on demand, is nowadays generally called a "current account", while the account kept of his customer's loans made at interest and repayable only on notice is generally known as a "deposit account". Accounts of both these types, however, possess the essential characteristics of running accounts of "deposits" of money by the customer. Accordingly it is, in my view, essential to the business of banking that a banker should accept money from his customers on a running account into which sums of money are from time to time paid by the customer and from time to time withdrawn by him by cheque, draft or order. I am inclined to agree with Lord Denning MR, and the author of the current edition of Paget on Banking [10th edn, 1987] that to constitute the business of banking today the banker must also undertake to pay cheques drawn on himself (the banker) by his customers in favour of third parties up to the amount standing to their credit in their "current accounts" and to collect cheques for his customers and credit the proceeds to their current accounts.' Ibid at 986, 987, per Diplock LJ

Australia 'These authorities emphasise what no doubt for most people is the main function of a bank, namely, the honouring of customers' cheques to the extent of the credits in their accounts. It was the absence of this function which led to Griffith CJ's dissenting judgment in *The Commissioners of the State Savings Bank of Victoria v Permewan Wright & Co Ltd* [(1915) 19 CLR 457]. In that case the majority, consisting of Isaacs, Gavan Duffy, Powers and Rich JJ, held that the essential characteristics of the business of banking (for the purposes of the application of the Bills of Exchange Act 1909 (Cth)) were the collection of money by receiving deposits on loan, repayable as agreed upon, and the utilisation of the money so collected by lending it again in such sums as are required. (See per Isaacs J at 470). I am satisfied that this decision is decisive of the present question, inasmuch as it lays down as an essential requisite of the business of banking, the lending of customers' money to other people.' *Re Adelaide Co-operative Society Ltd* [1964] SASR 266 at 277, per Chamberlain J

United States 'Bank' means any person engaged in the business of banking. (Uniform Commercial Code 1978, s 1–201(4))

United States The term 'bank' means (A) a banking institution organized under the laws of the United States, (B) a member bank of the Federal Reserve System, (C) any other banking institution, whether incorporated or not, doing business under the laws of any State or of the United States, a substantial portion of the business of which consists of receiving deposits or exercising fiduciary powers similar to those permitted to national banks under section 11(k) of the Federal Reserve Act, as amended, and which is supervised and examined by State or Federal authority having supervision over banks, and which is not operated for the purpose of evading the provisions of this chapter, and (D) a receiver, conservator, or other liquidating agent of any institution or firm included in clauses (A), (B), or (C) of this paragraph. (Securities Exchange Act of 1934, s 3(a)(6))

Advising bank

United States An 'advising bank' is a bank which gives notification of the issuance of a [letter of] credit by another bank. (Uniform Commercial Code 1978, s 5–103(1)(e))

Bankers' books

Expressions in this Act relating to 'bankers' books' include ledgers, day books, cash books, account books and other records used in the ordinary business of the bank, whether those records are in written form or are kept on microfilm, magnetic tape or any other form of mechanical or electronic data retrieval mechanism. (Bankers' Books Evidence Act 1879, s 9, substituted by the Banking Act 1979, s 51(1), Sch 6)

Banking days

Canada 'The plain ordinary meaning of "banking days" when used in a context that signifies some business in which there will be a transfer of currency, cheques or bank-notes, must be those days on which the banks are ordinarily open to do business with the public.' *McDiarmid v Bearss* (1975) 7 OR (2d) 370 at 374, Ont SC, per Grant J; affd, ibid, at 375, Ont CA

United States 'Banking day' means that part of any day on which a bank is open to the public for carrying on substantially all of its banking functions. . . . (Uniform Commercial Code 1978, s 4–104(1)(c)

Collecting bank

United States 'Collecting bank' means any bank handling the item for collection except the payor bank. . . . (Uniform Commercial Code 1978, s 4–105(d))

Confirming bank

United States A 'confirming bank' is a bank which engages either that it will itself honor a [letter of] credit already issued by another bank or that such a [letter of] credit will be honored by the issuer of a third bank. (Uniform Commercial Code 1978, s 5–103(1)(f))

Custodian bank   *See* CUSTODIAN BANK

Depositary bank

United States 'Depositary bank' means the first bank to which an item is transferred for collection even though it is also the payor bank. . . . (Uniform Commercial Code 1978, s 4–105(a))

Intermediary bank

United States 'Intermediary bank' means any bank to which an item is transferred in course of collection except the depositary or payor bank. . . . (Uniform Commercial Code 1978, s 4–105(c))

BANK (Embankment)

The expression 'bank' and the expression 'dam' includes any bank, wall, fence, wharf, dock, lock, gate, sluice, dam, or defence, or appliance, whether of a moveable, temporary, fixed, or permanent character, for the protection of lands within the limits of this Act from floods or inundations caused by the overflow of the River Thames. (Metropolis Management (Thames River Prevention of Floods) Amendment Act 1879, s 2)

'Banks' means banks, walls, or embankments adjoining or confining, or constructed for the purposes of or in connection with, any channel or sea front, and includes all land between the bank and low-water mark. (Land Drainage Act 1976, s 116(1))

'When you speak of the banks of a canal you mean the land on either side of the canal which confines the water. There are banks of the canal therefore on both sides of it, and when you speak of the banks you mean the substantial soil which confines the water.' *Monmouthshire Canal & Rly Co v Hill* (1859) 28 LJ Ex 283 at 285, per Martin B

'It seems to me to be impossible on this definition [see now the Land Drainage Act 1976, s 116(1), supra] to hold that the Barrier Bank, which is in some places as much as three-quarters of a mile distant from the channel of the River Welland, is a bank "adjoining" that channel. It certainly does not in any ordinary sense of the word "confine" the waters of the River Welland. This word is apt to describe the function of the natural or Fisherman's Bank. . . . The meaning of the definition becomes clearer when its last words are considered, . . . for it would appear to be an abuse of language to define as a bank the flat tract of land comprising many hundreds of acres . . . and lying between the river and an artificial bank erected at a distance in some places of more than three-quarters of a mile from it.' *North Level Comrs v River Welland Catchment Board* [1938] Ch 379 at 393, 394, per Luxmoore J

'So far as it is possible to decide a question of this sort save in the light of all the relevant facts, in the particular case under consideration I would . . . hold that the expression "banks" in s 38(1) [of the Land Drainage Act 1930 (repealed; see now the Land Drainage Act 1976, s 33(2))] means so much of the land adjoining or near to a river as performs or contributes to the performance of the function of containing the river. I think that is as good a definition as it is possible to provide *in vacuo*; but I emphasise that its application in any particular case must depend to a great extent on the particular facts of the case—the character of the river, the character of its surroundings, and, no doubt, other considerations as well.' *Jones v Mersey River Board* [1957] 3 All ER 375 at 380, CA, per Jenkins LJ; [1958] 1 QB 143 at 153

BANK HOLIDAY

'Bank holiday' includes any public holiday or day of public rejoicing or mourning. (Shops Act 1950, s 74)

[Bank holidays in England and Wales are Easter Monday; the last Monday in May; the last Monday in August; 26th December, if not a Sunday; and 27th December in a year in which the 25th or 26th December is on a Sunday (Banking and Financial Dealings Act 1971). From 1974, New Year's Day has been appointed a bank holiday by Royal proclamation in the *London Gazette*, under s 1(3) of the Act of 1971. Similarly, since 1978, the first Monday in May has been declared a bank holiday by proclamation.

Bank holidays in Scotland are New Year's Day and the following day (if either falls on a Sunday, then 3rd January); Good Friday; the first Monday in May; the first Monday in August, and Christmas Day (if on a Sunday, 26th December). See also the Act of 1971.]

BANK HOLIDAY BREAK   *See also* HOLIDAY

'Bank holiday break' means any bank holiday not included in the Christmas break (q.v.) or the Easter break (q.v.) and the period beginning with the last week day before that bank holiday and ending with the next week day which is not a bank holiday. (Local Government Act 1972, s 270(1); Representation of the People Act 1983, s 40)

BANK NOTE *See also* CURRENCY NOTE

Bank of England notes' shall extend and apply to the promissory notes of . . . the Bank of England payable to bearer on demand. (Bank Charter Act 1844, s 28; as amended by SLR Act 1891)

Banknotes' means notes of the Bank [of England] payable to bearer on demand. (Currency Act 1983, s 4(2)

The Forgery Act 1830, s 18 (repealed; see now the Forgery and Counterfeiting Act 1981, s 18), made it an offence to engrave upon a plate any bill of exchange or promissory note or the payment of money, or part of the bill or note' of any persons carrying on the business of bankers (other than and except the Bank of England) without the authority of such persons.] 'I have no doubt that the conviction was right, and that this case comes not only within the intention, but within the precise words of the statute. Extrinsic evidence was properly resorted to in order to ascertain whether the engraving resembled the genuine note, and indeed one cannot ascertain what a thing purports to be without having recourse to extrinsic evidence, and this applies equally whether the engraving purports to be part of a note or an entire note. By part of a note is meant any of those *indicia* appearing on a genuine note by which it is known; and it is quite clear that two of those *indicia* appear upon the plate which the prisoner caused to be engraved.' *R v Keith* (1855) Dears CC 486 at 493, per Crowder J

BANK RATE

['Bank rate' meant the minimum rate at which the Bank of England would lend to discount houses. Later known as the minimum lending rate, it was suspended from 20 August 1981.]

BANKRUPTCY

Bankruptcy is a proceeding by which the State takes possession of the property of a debtor by an officer appointed for the purpose, and such property is realised and, subject to certain priorities, distributed rateably amongst the persons to whom the debtor owes money or has incurred pecuniary liabilities. (2 Bl Com 472)

'Bankrupt' includes any person whose estate is vested in a trustee or assignee under the law for the time being in force relating to bankruptcy. (Bills of Exchange Act 1882, s 2)

'Bankruptcy' includes liquidation by arrange-

ment; also in relation to a corporation means the winding up thereof. (Law of Property Act 1925, s 205)

'That section [the Bankruptcy Act 1869, s 72 (repealed; see now the Insolvency Act 1986, s 363)] enacts that "Every Court having jurisdiction in bankruptcy under this Act shall have full power to decide all questions of priorities and all other questions whatsoever, whether of law or fact, arising in any case of bankruptcy coming within the cognizance of such Court, or which the Court may deem it expedient or necessary to decide for the purpose of doing complete justice" under the provisions of the Act. It appears to me very clear that "bankruptcy" does in this section include "composition." The word "bankruptcy" is a general term, and is used to include all the three modes of settling the debts of a debtor with his creditors which are included in the Act; and the words, "Every Court having jurisdiction in bankruptcy," include, surely, every court having jurisdiction in a composition. In my opinion, therefore, bankruptcy does clearly include composition.' *Re Thorpe, ex p Hartel* (1873) 8 Ch App 743 at 745, per Mellish LJ

[By a codicil to a will a testator bequeathed a sum of money, upon trust to pay the income thereof to his son 'during his life, or until he shall become bankrupt'.] 'He has become bankrupt according to the law of Scotland. . . . In default of evidence I shall assume that bankruptcy in Scotland is a bankruptcy within the meaning of the words "shall become a bankrupt". . . . We all know what a bankruptcy means. It means shortly a *cessio bonorum* for the benefit of all the creditors of the person who makes that *cesser,* and unless it were proved to me that by the municipal law of a particular country there was some such unfairness or some such departure from what is sometimes called "natural law" that I ought not to regard it as a bankruptcy within our law, and within the meaning of this clause, I should certainly regard bankruptcy according to the law of any civilised country as a bankruptcy within the meaning of the instrument before me.' *Re James, Clutterbuck v James* (1890) 62 LT 454 at 455, per Kekewich J

Canada 'Bankruptcy is a well understood procedure by which an insolvent debtor's property is coercively brought under a judicial administration in the interests primarily of the creditors. To this proceeding not only a personal stigma may attach but restrictions on freedom in future business activity may result. The relief to the debtor consists in the cancellation of debts which, otherwise, might effectually prevent him from rehabilitating himself economically and socially. . . . Insolvency, on the other hand, seems to be a broader term that contemplates measures of dealing with the property of debtors unable to pay their debts in other modes or arrangements as well. There is the composition and the voluntary assignment, devices which, in appropriate circumstances, may avoid technical bankruptcy without too great prejudice to creditors and hardships to debtors. These means of salvage from the ravages of misfortune are of the essence of insolvency legislation, and they are incorporated in the Bankruptcy Act.' *Canadian Bankers Assocn and Dominion Mortgage & Investments Assocn v A-G of Saskatchewan* [1956] SCR 31 at 46, SCC, per Rand J

BAR

'Bar' includes any place exclusively or mainly used for the sale and consumption of intoxicating liquor. (Licensing Act 1964, s 201)

'The bar of a public house is, as we know, strictly speaking, the counter over which liquor is served, and it has come to be extended to the space in front of it where the people stand.' *Donaghue v M'Intyre* 1911 SC (J) 61, per Lord Ardwall

'A public bar is a bar open to members of the public, without discrimination, who desire to purchase and to be served with refreshment.' *Howman v Doyle* 1921 SC (J) 49 at 53, per the Lord Justice-General (Lord Clyde)

'Sometimes a room is called a bar, for instance, a saloon bar or a lounge bar. . . . Ordinarily a saloon bar will have a counter in it over which drinks are supplied, but the definition in s 201 [of the Licensing Act 1964] extends the meaning of "bar" to include any place exclusively or mainly used for the sale and consumption of intoxicating liquor. So, for the purposes of s 76(5), a place can be a bar even though it has not within it any bar counter.' *Carter v Bradbeer* [1975] 3 All ER 158 at 168, HL, per Viscount Dilhorne

Australia 'The prima facie meaning of an hotel "bar" is a room set apart for the sale of liquor to customers, stocked with liquor of various kinds, and fitted up for the convenience of customers, who drink then and there the liquor with which they are supplied.' *Mel-*

drum v Hotels Arcadia Ltd (1917) 17 NSWSR 648 at 651, per Harvey J

South Africa 'The crisp question which this court has to determine is whether any portion of a bottle store, more particularly that portion to which the public in general has admission for purposes of transacting business, is commonly known as . . . a bar. Speaking for myself, I have no hesitation in finding that in ordinary English usage no part of a bottle store . . . is commonly known as the bar. In common usage the word bar, in my opinion, refers to a place where food or drink is served.' *R v Isaacson* 1947 (2) SA 348 (T) per Dowling AJ

BARBED WIRE

'Barbed wire' means wire with spikes or jagged projections, and barbed wire is to be deemed to be a nuisance to a highway if it is likely to be injurious to persons or animals lawfully using the highway. (Highways Act 1980, s 164(1)(b))

BARE LICENSEE *See* LICENSEE

BARE TRUSTEE *See* TRUSTEE

BARGAIN *See also* CONTRACT; UNCONSCIONABLE BARGAIN

'The word bargain means the terms upon which parties contract.' *Kenworthy v Schofield* (1824) 2 B & C 945 at 947, per Bayley J

'A "bargain" is only another name for a contract which may exist upon the slightest valuable consideration.' *Crossman v R* (1886) 56 LJQB 241 at 245, 246, per Hawkins J

BARGE *See also* CANAL BOAT; DUMB BARGE

'Barge' includes a lighter or any similar vessel. (Prevention of Oil Pollution Act 1971, s 29)

'The whole point is whether the barge, being a sailing barge, is a barge within the words "all barges" in s 11(2)(f) of the [Port of London] Act of 1908 [see now Port of London Act 1962, s 9]. Hamilton J has held that she is. In my opinion that decision is right.' *Smeed, Dean & Co v Port of London Authority* [1913] 1 KB 226 at 232, CA, per Buckley LJ

'The term "barge" in ordinary parlance,

whether in regard to the carriage of goods, or other purposes for which one knows barges were used in times past, does not connote the absence of sails; it never has done so, as far as I know.' Ibid at 240, per Kennedy LJ

BARONET　*See also* PEERAGE

The hereditary dignity of baronet was first instituted by James I in 1611, to be granted to those persons who should contribute to the expenses of the Plantation of Ulster. In 1625 it was decided to encourage the Plantation of Nova Scotia in the same manner. There are now five classes of baronets, namely, (1) baronets of England, created between 1611 and 1707; (2) baronets of Ireland, created between 1618 and 1801; (3) baronets of Nova Scotia, created between 1625 and 1707; (4) baronets of Great Britain, created between 1707 and 1801; and (5) baronets of the United Kingdom, created since 1801. The dignity is created by letters patent under the Great Seal. (35 Halsbury's Laws (4th edn) para 863)

BARRATRY

In the Lloyd's policy 'barratry' includes every wrongful act wilfully committed by the master or crew to the prejudice of the owner, or, as the case may be, the charterer, and this is so whether the master's act is induced by motive of benefit to himself, malice to the owners, or a disregard of those laws which it was his duty to obey and upon his observance of which his owners relied.

Sailing out of port without paying port dues or in breach of an embargo, or wilful breach of blockade, in consequence of which the ship is seized or other loss is sustained, may be barratry. If the ship is fraudulently run away with by the master or by members of the crew, this is barratry on their part. Deviation for a fraudulent or criminal purpose may be barratrous, but the commission of a crime is not an essential feature of barratry.

Deviation, if barratrous, does not avoid the policy, for the underwriters are liable under it for loss by barratry.

Loss arising from the master's ignorance or incompetence, through a mistake as to the meaning of his instructions, or as to the best mode of carrying them into effect, does not amount to barratry. (25 Halsbury's Laws (4th edn) para 165)

The term 'barratry' includes every wrongful act wilfully committed by the master or crew to the prejudice of the owner, or, as the case may be, the charterer. (Marine Insurance Act 1906, Sch 1, para 11)

'What is meant by barratry of the master? I take the word to have been originally introduced by the Italians, who were the first great traders of the modern world. In the Italian dictionary the word "Barratrare" means to cheat, and whatsoever is by the master a cheat, a fraud, a cozening or a trick is barratry in him.' *Vallejo v Wheeler* (1774) 1 Cowp 143 at 154, per Lord Mansfield CJ

'A fraudulent breach of duty by the master, in respect to his owners, or, in other words, a breach of duty in respect to his owners, with a criminal intent, or *ex maleficio*, is barratry. And with respect to the owner of the ship or goods, whose interest is to be protected by the policy, it can make no difference in the reason of the thing whether the prejudice he suffers be owing to an act of the master, induced by motives of advantage to himself, malice to the owner, or a disregard to those laws which it was the master's duty to obey, and which (or it would not be barratry) his owners relied upon his observing. It has been strongly contended . . . that if the conduct of the master, although criminal in respect of the State, were in his opinion likely to advance his owner's interest, and intended by him to do so, it will not be barratry. But to this we cannot assent. . . . We do not feel any apprehension that simple deviations will be turned into barratry, to the prejudice of the underwriters; for unless they be accompanied with fraud, or crime, no case of deviation will fall within the true definition of barratry, as above laid down.' *Earle v Rowcroft* (1806) 8 East 126 at 138, 139, per Lord Ellenborough CJ

BARTER　*See* SALE

BASE FEE

A base fee is a fee which is limited in duration and admits of an absolute fee existing by way of remainder upon it; but during its continuance it was until 1926 descendible, like an absolute fee, to the heirs general, and now devolves on the personal representatives of the deceased owner. It cannot be created by limitation, but arises from a disposition by a tenant in tail, which, though purporting to create an absolute fee, is ineffectual to bar either the remainders only, or both the issue in tail and the remainders. (39 Halsbury's Laws (4th edn) para 449)

The expression 'base fee' shall mean exclusively that estate in fee simple into which an estate tail is converted where the issue in tail are barred, but persons claiming estates by way of remainder or otherwise are not barred. (Fines and Recoveries Act 1833, s 1)

BASE METAL

In this paragraph [para 6 of Part III to the Schedule] 'base metal' means any metal other than gold, silver or platinum of at least the minimum fineness therefor. (Hallmarking Act 1973, Sch 2)

BASEMENT STOREY

'Basement storey' means any storey of a building which is under the ground storey. (London Building Act 1930, s 5)

BASIC WAGE   *See* WAGES

BASIS

' "Basis" is defined in the Imperial Dictionary as "the foundation of a thing; that on which a thing stands or lies"; and similar definitions are to be found elsewhere. The basis of a thing is that upon which it stands, and on the failure of which it falls; and when a document consisting partly of statements of fact and partly of undertakings for the future is made the basis of a contract of insurance, this must . . . mean that the document is to be the very foundation of the contract, so that if the statements of fact are untrue or the promissory statements are not carried out the risk does not attach.' *Dawsons Ltd v Bonnin* [1922] 2 AC 413 at 431, 432, per Lord Cave

BASTARD

Bastards, by our law, are such children as are not born either in lawful wedlock, or within a competent time after its determination. (2 Bl Com 247)

BATTERY   *See also* ASSAULT

Battery . . . is the unlawful beating of another. The least touching of another's person wilfully, or in anger, is a battery; for the law cannot draw the line between different degrees of violence, and therefore totally prohibits the first and lowest stage of it: every man's person being sacred, and no other having a right to meddle with it, in any the slightest manner. And therefore upon a similar principle the Cornelian law *de injuriis* prohibited *pulsation* as well as *verberation*; distinguishing verberation, which was accompanied with pain, from pulsation which was attended with none. But battery is, in some cases, justifiable or lawful; as where one who hath authority, a parent or master, gives moderate correction to his child, his scholar, or his apprentice. So also on the principle of self-defence: for if one strikes me first, or even only assaults me, I may strike in my own defence. (3 Bl Com 120)

An assault is any act committed intentionally, or possibly recklessly, which causes another person to apprehend immediate and unlawful violence. If force is actually applied, directly or indirectly, unlawfully without the consent of the person assaulted, the assault becomes a battery, however slight the force. A battery may or may not include an assault. Although an assault is an independent crime and should be treated as such, for practical purposes the term 'assault' is generally synonymous with 'battery' and is used to mean the actual intended use of unlawful force to another person without his consent. . . . The mental element in the offence of battery is satisfied by proof that the defendant intentionally or recklessly applied force to the person of another. There must, however, be a positive act; no mere omission to act can amount to a battery. (11 Halsbury's Laws (4th edn) para 1210)

'The least touching of another in anger is a battery.' *Cole v Turner* (1704) 6 Mod Rep 149 at 149, per Holt CJ

'We are here concerned primarily with battery. The fundamental principle, plain and incontestable, is that every person's body is inviolate. It has long been established that any touching of another person, however slight, may amount to a battery. So Holt CJ held in 1704 that "the least touching of another in anger is a battery": see *Cole v Turner* [(1704) 6 Mod Rep 149, 90 ER 958]. The breadth of the principle reflects the fundamental nature of the interest so protected; as Blackstone wrote in his Commentaries, "the law cannot draw the line between different degrees of violence, and therefore totally prohibits the first and lowest stage of it; every man's person being sacred, and no other having a right to meddle with it, in any the slightest manner" (see 3 Bl Com 120). The effect is that everybody is protected not only against physical injury but against any form of physical molestation. But so widely drawn a principle must inevitably be subject to exceptions. For example, children may be subjected to reasonable punishment; people may be subjected to the lawful exercise of the power of arrest; and reasonable force may be used in self-defence or for the prevention of crime. But, apart from these special instances where the control or constraint is lawful, a broader exception has been created to allow for the exigencies of everyday life. Generally speaking, consent is a defence to battery; and most of the physical contacts of ordinary life are not actionable because they are impliedly consented to by all who move in society and so expose themselves to the risk of bodily contact. So nobody can complain of the jostling which is inevitable from his presence in, for example, a supermarket, an underground station or a busy street; nor can a person who attends a party complain if his hand is seized in friendship, or even if his back is (within reason) slapped (see *Tuberville v Savage* [(1669) 1 Mod Rep 3, 86 ER 684]). Although such cases are regarded as examples of implied consent, it is more common nowadays to treat them as falling within a general exception embracing all physical contact which is generally acceptable in the ordinary conduct of daily life.' *Collins v Wilcock* [1984] 3 All ER 374 at 378, per cur.

BAWDY HOUSE *See* BROTHEL

BAZAAR

South Africa 'When you permit a person to trade within an area, unless you specifically limit his customers, you mean that he is entitled to set up a shop and to sell to anybody who is prepared to buy from him. And that is indeed the general meaning of the word "bazaar".' *Lalu Baba v Boksburg Municipality* 1922 TPD 89 per Wessels JP.

BEACH *See* SEASHORE

BEACON *See* BUOY

BEAR

'The words "bearing even date" in the Act of the 55 Geo 3, c 184, Schedule [Stamp Act 1815, Sch, Pt I (repealed in part; see now Stamp Act 1891, Sch I)] . . . are plain and clear. They tie down the operation of that clause of the Schedule to the date written on the instrument. Here the bond does not bear the same date as the instrument on which the stamp denoting the payment of the *ad valorem* duty is impressed. The bond, therefore, is not within the words of that part of the Schedule.' *Wood v Norton* (1829) 9 B & C 885 at 887, per Lord Tenterden CJ

Condition of testamentary gift

'There was a direct descendant of the brother . . . who bore the name of Roberts-Gawen, but who was not born with that name, and the appellant contends that we are not to take the expression "bear the name" in its literal sense, but treat it as denoting only persons acquiring the name by descent. I can see no reason for not reading it literally. The clause for forfeiture on abandoning the name tends strongly to show that the testatrix, by the words "bear the name" meant "use the name". Looking at the state of the family, I think she meant this, because the name was not her family name but one which her brother had assumed.' *Re Roberts, Repington v Roberts-Gawen* (1881) 19 Ch D 520 at 531, CA, per Jessel MR

BEARER

'Bearer' means the person in possession of a bill or note which is payable to bearer. (Bills of Exchange Act 1882, s 2)

'The term ['bearer' in the Bills of Exchange Act 1882] applies only to the person in possession of a bill or note payable to bearer.' *Day v Longhurst* (1893) 62 LJ Ch 334 at 335, 336, per Stirling J

United States 'Bearer' means the person in possession of an instrument, document of title, or certificated security payable to bearer or indorsed in blank. (Uniform Commercial Code 1978, s 1–201(5))

BEARER CERTIFICATE

'Bearer certificate' means a certificate of title to securities by the delivery of which (with or without endorsement) the title to the securities is transferable. (Exchange Control Act 1947, s 42)

BEARER CHEQUE   See CHEQUE

BEASTS OF CHASE   See CHASE

BEASTS OF WARREN   See WARREN

BEAT

South Africa '"Beat" means to strike repeatedly. One would not ordinarily apply the term "beat" or beating to the striking of one blow.' *R v Tom* 1939 OPD 3 per Fischer J

BECOME

'Then there is the word "entitled". According to its ordinary sense, that means having some right or title; but the words are "become entitled". What is the effect of the word "become"? The ordinary construction, and I think its correct construction is, according to Johnson's definition, "to enter into some state or condition by a change from some other"; becoming entitled means, therefore, entering into the state of being entitled from the state of not being entitled. In other words to "become entitled" means to acquire a right or title. In *Blythe v Granville* [(1842), 13 Sim 195] the Vice-Chancellor of England correctly I think observed that the words "become entitled" mean "become entitled either in possession or in reversion"; and certainly a remainderman does, on the death of the tenant for life become entitled to the estate in possession as a change of condition from being entitled in remainder.' *Wilcox v Smith* (1857) 4 Drew 40 at 50, 51, per Kindersley V-C

'The word "become" in its usual and proper acceptation imports a change of condition, that is the entering into a new state or condition by a change from some former state or condition.' *Archer v Kelly* (1860) 1 Drew & Sm 300 at 304, per Kindersley V-C

'I have not heard any argument upon the question whether the words "in case my said nephew should . . . become bankrupt" . . . can be applied to an insolvency before the date of the will. My present impression is that the words contemplate only a future contingency.'

Re Draper (1888) 57 LJ Ch 942 at 943, per Kekewich J

BED

Of minerals

In a legal document, the context may show that the word 'bed' or 'seam', instead of bearing its normal meaning of a layer or member of a series of stratified rocks, is used to designate what is actually a deposit consisting of two or more strata of mineral separated by thin layers of other rock, for example, shale, as distinguished from any one layer of mineral; in such a case, the word 'vein' is sometimes applied to each of the layers of minerals comprised in the seam. (31 Halsbury's Laws (4th edn) para 12)

Of river

'I will cite a passage from the judgment in an American case, namely, that of the *State of Alabama v State of Georgia* [(1859) 64 US 515] . . . for it exactly conveys what I understand by the meaning of the phrase "bed of a river". It is thus: "The bed of the river is that portion of its soil which is alternately covered and left bare, as there may be an increase or diminution in the supply of water, and which is adequate to contain it at its average and mean stage during the entire year, without reference to the extraordinary freshets of the winter and spring, or the extreme droughts of the summer or autumn". This, when applied to a tidal river, means without reference to extraordinary tides at any time of year.' *Thames Conservators v Smeed Dean & Co* [1897] 2 QB 334 at 338, CA, per A L Smith LJ

'What is the proper meaning of the term "bed" when applied to such a river as the Thames, which from its source as far as Teddington Lock is a non-tidal river, and from Teddington Lock downwards is a tidal river? In my opinion the bed of the Thames means, and includes, the soil or ground which is covered by water in the ordinary course of nature—the ground over which the water flows or on which it lies.' Ibid at 353, per Chitty LJ

New Zealand 'The shingle from bank to bank is within what may properly be called the "bed" of the river, although the water of the river does not in the dry weather ordinarily flow over such shingle.' *Kingdon v Hutt River Board* (1905) 25 NZLR 145 at 158, per cur.; also reported 7 GLR 634 at 636

BEDDING

'The word "bedding" is used more often than not as describing something which does not include a bedstead. But the question is, in what sense is the word "bedding" used in the Act [Law of Distress Amendment Act 1888, s 4, which refers to s 96 of the County Courts Act 1846 (repealed; see now the County Courts Act 1984, s 89)]? . . . What is the meaning of *"the* bedding" of the person in question? We are justified . . . in reading those words as meaning whatever he has for the purposes of sleeping accommodation. If he sleeps on a mattress laid on the floor, the mattress is his "bedding". If he has a bedstead and mattress, they are his "bedding"; and if his mattress has gone and he sleeps upon the bedstead, that is his "bedding" within the meaning of the Act.' *Davis v Harris* [1900] 1 QB 729 at 731, 732, DC, per Channell J

BEER

'Beer' includes ale, porter, stout and any other description of beer, and any liquor which is made or sold as a description of beer or as a substitute for beer and which on analysis of a sample thereof at any time is found to be of a strength exceeding [1.2 per cent.], but does not include—
(a) black beer the worts whereof before fermentation were of a specific gravity of 1200° or more; or
(b) liquor made elsewhere than upon the licensed premises of a brewer for sale which on analysis of a sample at any time is found to be of an original gravity not exceeding 1016° and to be of a strength not exceeding [1.2 per cent.].
(Alcoholic Liquor Duties Act 1979, s 1(3))
[The words in square brackets were substituted by the Alcoholic Liquors (Amendment of Enactments Relating to Strength and to Units of Measurement) Order 1979, SI 1979/241. 'Worts' may be described as liquor which is unfermented or in the course of fermentation.]

Black beer

In this Act . . . 'black beer' means beer of the description called or similar to black beer, mum, spruce beer or Berlin white beer, and any other preparation (whether fermented or not) of a similar character. (Alcoholic Liquor Duties Act 1979, s 4(1))

BEERHOUSE

'It is conceded that a beerhouse cannot mean a place where beer is sold in any quantities, but that there must be some limitation to the meaning of the word. The question then is, what was the meaning of the parties to the deed, and what was the ordinary meaning of the term "beerhouse" at the time when it was executed (1860)? Now, a person minded to ascertain the legal meaning of the word would naturally resort to Burn's *Justice of the Peace* which was the book in constant use by magistrates who had to decide upon granting or refusing licences. In the edition of 1845, current at that time, it was defined as a house in which beer, etc, "is sold by retail to be drunk or consumed on the premises".' *London & North Western Rly Co v Garnett* (1869) LR 9 Eq 26 at 26, 27, per James V-C

'I put this question to myself, should I, in ordinary usage and ordinary parlance, call a grocer's shop at which beer is sold, either by wholesale or by retail, a beerhouse, when the principal business carried on in that shop is that of a grocer, and when the business of the sale of beer is merely ancillary to that business of a grocer: and I answer that I should not myself do so.' *Holt & Co v Collyer* (1881) 16 Ch D 718 at 722, per Fry J

[As to applications for old beerhouse licences, see now the Licensing Act 1964, s 12, infra.]

Old beerhouse licence

'Old beerhouse licence' means an old onlicence for the sale of beer or cider, with or without wine, granted by way of renewal from time to time of a licence for premises for which a corresponding excise licence was in force on 1st May 1869. (Licensing Act 1964, s 12)

BEFORE

'Section 7(3) of the Workmen's Compensation Act 1925 [repealed] . . . provides that, on the bankruptcy of an employer, a workman's claim in respect of compensation or liability for compensation due by the employer which has accrued before the date of "a receiving order" shall be given a preferable ranking. . . . "Before" must, in my view, be read as equivalent to "not after". Such a construction is open if the context and sense of the enactment so require—Denman CJ in *R v Arkwright* [(1848) 12 QB 960 at 970].' *Thornton's Executrix v Angus & Son's Trustee* 1934 SC 279 at 289, 290, per Lord Murray

Canada 'In their Lordships' opinion, "before and at the beginning of the voyage" [in Art III, r 1 of the Schedule to the Water Carriage of Goods Act 1936 (see now Carriage of Goods by Water Act, RSC 1970, c C-15, Art III, r 1)] means the period from at least the beginning of the loading until the vessel starts on her voyage. The word "before" cannot, in their opinion, be read as meaning "at the commencement of the loading".' *Maxine Footwear Co Ltd v Canadian Government Merchant Marine Ltd* [1959] 2 All ER 740 at 744, PC, per Lord Somervell of Harrow; also reported [1959] AC 589 at 603

New Zealand [The Matrimonial Property Act 1976, s 2(4) provides for the classification of certain matrimonial property, depending on the use to which it was being put by the parties 'before' they ceased to live together as husband and wife.] 'In its statutory context the expression "before" bears its ordinary and natural meaning of "previously to the time when" or "up to the time when".' *Evers v Evers* [1985] 2 NZLR 209 at 211

In the sight of

'Their Lordships are of opinion that the words "before the people" [in the rubric], coupled with the direction as to the manual acts, are meant to be equivalent to "in the sight of the people". They have no doubt that the rubric requires the manual acts to be so done, that, in a reasonable and practical sense, the communicants, especially if they are conveniently placed for receiving of the Holy Sacrament, as is presupposed in the office, may be witnesses of, that is, may see them.' *Ridsdale v Clifton* (1877) 2 PD 276 at 342, 343, PC, per cur.

BEG

'The offence created by s 3 of the Vagrancy Act 1824 applies to every person wandering abroad or placing himself or herself in any public place to beg or gather alms. . . . No offence is committed if in fact the person is collecting money bona fide for a specific charitable purpose. In that case he cannot be said to be begging or gathering alms within the meaning of the statute. The offence consists of wandering abroad or placing himself in a public place to beg, and I think that, inasmuch as that purpose has to be shown, the case of a person who is merely found casually begging would be excluded.' *Mathers v Penfold* [1915] 1 KB 514 at 525, DC, per Atkin J

Australia [The defendant was charged with having gone from house to house begging and gathering alms, contrary to the Police Offences Act 1953–1982 (SA), s 12] . . . ' "[B]egging" is the crucial word. One may beg without gathering anything; the gathering of alms will, in the context of this section, normally be the result of the begging. What distinguishes begging from non begging is a whole complex of factors including the relationship between the asker and the potential giver, and the nature and the occasion of the approach. The act of asking for food may be begging in some circumstances and if done from house to house, may constitute the offence charged. But the person approaching the neighbour for milk, sugar, tea, etc and going if necessary to the other side neighbour, is not begging and not going from house to house begging; possibly it might constitute begging if practised on a sufficient scale and for a sufficient period. Society recognises that it is "neighbourly" to help one's neighbours; that one's neighbours can presume where a complete stranger may not; and that on another day the boot may be on the other foot. The relationship of neighbours affects the character of the transaction. The Oxford Dictionary gives the first meaning of "beg" as "to ask in alms". "Alms" is defined as "charitable relief of the poor". The second meaning of "beg" is given as "to ask as a favour; hence to ask humbly, supplicatingly". . . . It may often be the touchstone, but not always. The explanation is to be found in the absence of any social relationship which I earlier spoke of and which requires or is deemed by the person seeking assistance to require a supplicating approach. Section 12 as a whole reflects this aspect of begging.' *Begg v Daire* (1986) 40 SASR 375 at 387, per Johnston J

BEGET

To be begotten

'Then come the words, "lawfully to be begotten", which would give rise to a material question if it had not been settled by a series of authorities, and impeached by none, that "to be begotten" mean the same as "begotten", embracing all those whom the parent shall have begotten during his life, *quos procreaverit*.' *Doe* d *James v Hallett* (1813) 1 M & S 124 at 135, per Lord Ellenborough CJ

'If there is a bequest to the children of A, begotten and to be begotten, it has been generally held that the words "to be begotten" show only that the testator contemplated children to be born after the date of his will and before his death.' *Butler v Lowe* (1839) 10 Sim 317 at 325, per Shadwell V-C

'I now come to the cases which deal with the rule of law with reference to the meaning of the words "to be begotten". The rule is a very old one; it is laid down in Coke on Littleton [20 b] in these terms: 'As *procreatis* shall extend to the issues begotten afterwards, so *procreandis* shall extend to the issue begotten before". And in the note of the editor it is stated that it was adjudged accordingly in a case cited from Hale's MSS.' *Locke v Dunlop* (1888) 39 Ch D 387 at 398, CA, per Stirling J

BEHALF   *See* ON BEHALF OF

BEHAVIOUR

[The Divorce Reform Act 1969, s 2(1) (repealed; see now the Matrimonial Causes Act 1973, s 1(2)(b)) provided that a marriage should not be held to have broken down irretrievably unless (inter alia) the court was satisfied that the respondent had 'behaved' in such a way that the petitioner could not reasonably be expected to live with the respondent.] 'Behaviour is something more than a mere state of affairs or a state of mind, such as for example, a repugnance to sexual intercourse, or a feeling that the wife is not reciprocating his love, or not being as demonstrative as he thinks she should be. Behaviour in this context is action or conduct by the one which affects the other. Such conduct may take either acts or the form of an act of omission or may be a course of conduct and, in my view, it must have some reference to the marriage.' *Katz v Katz* [1972] 3 All ER 219 at 223, per Baker P

BELIEVE

'It is objected that this is only an affidavit of the *best of the belief* of the maker. I think, however, that a man who makes such a statement imports that he is entitled to entertain the belief he expresses, and that we must not take him to mean that the "best" of his belief is no belief at all.' *Roe v Bradshaw* (1866) LR 1 Exch 106 at 108, per Pollock CB

Canada   'A suspicion *or* belief may be entertained, but a suspicion *and* belief cannot exist together. Suspicion is much less than belief; belief includes or absorbs suspicion.' *Gifford v Kelson* (1943) 51 Man R 120 at 124, Man KB, per Dysart J

BELONG

[The Merchant Shipping Act 1894, s 686(1) provides that a British subject may be tried for an offence committed on a foreign ship to which he does not 'belong'.] 'In the context of this section, it is our view that those persons "belong to" a vessel who have some reasonably permanent attachment to it. Understood in this sense, the phrase is wide enough to include not only the master and crew but persons who are on the ship for a substantial period of time for some other purpose, for example, scientists or engineers engaged in exploration or survey. The words do not, however, include persons who are passengers on a passenger ferry and are only on the ship for the duration of a short voyage.' *R v Kelly* [1981] 1 All ER 370 at 374, CA, per cur.

BELONGING TO   *See also*
APPERTAINING

[The Theft Act 1968, s 1 provides that a person is guilty of theft if he dishonestly appropriates property 'belonging to' another with the intention of permanently depriving the other of it.]
(1) Property shall be regarded as belonging to any person having possession or control of it, or having in it any proprietary right or interest (not being an equitable interest arising only from an agreement to transfer or grant an interest).
(2) Where property is subject to a trust, the persons to whom it belongs shall be regarded as including any person having a right to enforce the trust, and an intention to defeat the trust shall be regarded accordingly as an intention to deprive of the property any person having that right.
(3) Where a person receives property from or on account of another, and is under an obligation to the other to retain and deal with that property or its proceeds in a particular way, the property or proceeds shall be regarded (as against him) as belonging to the other.
(4) Where a person gets property by another's mistake, and is under an obligation to make restoration (in whole or in part) of

the property or its proceeds or of the value thereof, then to the extent of that obligation the property or proceeds shall be regarded (as against him) as belonging to the person entitled to restoration, and an intention not to make restoration shall be regarded accordingly as an intention to deprive that person of the property or proceeds.

(5) Property of a corporation sole shall be regarded as belonging to the corporation notwithstanding a vacancy in the corporation.

(Theft Act 1968, s 5)

Australia 'When we speak of physical objects as belonging to a person, without any qualifying expressions, the primary natural meaning is that they are his own absolute property, and not that he has, instead of the objects themselves a mere option which he may never exercise or a mere contractual right to own them on conditions which he may yet elect not to undertake. This is stated in unequivocal language by Lord Macnaghten in *Heritable Reversionary Co v Millar* [[1892] AC 598 at 621]'. *Myerson v Collard & the Commonwealth* (1918) 25 CLR 154, per Isaacs and Rich JJ

New Zealand 'The premises in respect of which a liquor licence could be granted were to include not only the principal building from which ales and spirits were to be sold but also, if I may paraphrase the legislation, all buildings and places ancillary thereto. . . . There is nothing in the previous definitions to suggest that the ancillary buildings or places must be contiguous with the principal building. The test whether such other buildings or places form part of the premises has always been whether they "belong to" or in any manner "appertain to" the principal building. The phrase "belonging to" has reference to the building, and nothing but the building. . . . In my opinion, a building or place "belongs to" a principal building when the use or occupation of that building or place is for all practical purposes part of the use or occupation of the principal building. . . . In other words the phrase "belonging to" relates both to a case where the building and place ancillary to the principal building is on the same site as the principal building, and where it is adjacent to that principal building though not contiguous therewith, or sufficiently close to it that it may be said that the use or occupation of the ancillary building or place is associated with or part of the use or occupation of the principal

building itself. Then there is the phrase "appertaining to". This phrase seems to me to have been used by the legislature in a technical sense. In popular parlance it is only a variant of the phrase "belonging to" and is probably synonymous, but the word "appertain" has always had a settled legal meaning. . . . The phrase "appertaining to" must not be construed by reference to the modern contraction of that phrase which emerges as "pertaining to" which only means "in some way related to" whether actually or figuratively. The statutory phrase must still retain, in my opinion, its original legal meaning based on the necessity for close definition of what is comprised in premises proposed to be licensed, and I think that in that sense the phrase "appertaining to" may mean a building or place which is contiguous with the principal building. But even if that is the correct meaning of the phrase, the other phrase "belonging to" is not in my opinion restricted in that way. I can see no reason why a building or place may not "belong to" a principal building even though the principal building is on other land or on the other side of the street.' *Re Red Lyon Inn Ltd* (1979) 2 NZLR 668 at 671, per Mahon J

BELONGINGS

'Now the word "belongings" is wide enough to cover a testatrix's personal estate, and has been held by Eve J in *Re Bradfield, Bradfield v Bradfield* [[1914] WN 423] to have the primary meaning of property. So, unless there is sufficient in this will to afford a context restricting the meaning of the term "belongings", it should be interpreted as meaning property.' *Re Mills' Will Trusts, Marriott v Mills* [1937] 1 All ER 142 at 144, per Bennett J

'Counsel for the plaintiff has cited a number of authorities. I think they are of assistance because they show that, whatever might be thought to be the dictionary meaning properly to be given to the word "belongings", the court has construed the word as meaning "that which belonged to the giver"—certainly all property of a personal character which belonged to the giver. . . . I think the cases show further (if authority is necessary) that where you get general words such as "belongings" or "effects" they must not be cut down by applying the *ejusdem generis* rule in circumstances in which so to do would be to deprive a residuary gift of full effect and leave some of the residue undisposed of.' *Re Hynes, Knapp v Hynes* [1950] 2 All ER 879 at 880, per Evershed MR

Australia 'The testator made a short will, in which he made gifts of personal estate to various persons, and also devised two pieces of land, one by name. It turns out now that there is a third piece of land which has not been expressly dealt with, and the question is whether the last clause in the will is wide enough to cover that, or whether there is an intestacy in regard to it. After stating that he "gives devises and bequeaths", the words in question are, "James George Hall my house and 136 acres of land also about 100 sheep together with horse waggon and harness and all my belongings remaining". . . . . I think "all my belongings remaining" must mean everything left undisposed of, and I answer the question by saying that there is no intestacy.' *Re Hall, Bentick v Hall* [1918] VLR 448 at 449, 450, per Hood J

BENEFICE

'Benefice' has in common practice been confined to (1) rectories (or parsonages) with cure of souls; (2) vicarages; (3) perpetual curacies; (4) chapelries or districts belonging or reputed to belong, or annexed or reputed to be annexed, to any church or chapel, and districts formed for ecclesiastical purposes under statutory authority; (5) independent churches or chapels without districts; and (6) sinecure rectories.

Formerly charges on a benefice to secure the payment of money or for any other purpose were unlawful and void by statute, but there is apparently no law now prohibiting an incumbent from charging his benefice. An incumbent has certain powers of mortgaging his benefice which are discussed subsequently. (14 Halsbury's Laws (4th edn) para 768)

In the construction of this Act the word 'benefice' shall be deemed, construed, and taken to extend to and comprise all rectories with cure of souls, vicarages, perpetual curacies, and chapelries, the incumbents of which respectively in right thereof shall be corporations sole. (Parsonages Act 1838, s 16)

The expression 'benefice' comprehends all rectories with cure of souls, vicarages, perpetual curacies, endowed public chapels, and parochial chapelries, and chapelries or districts belonging or reputed to belong, or annexed or reputed to be annexed, to any church or chapel, and districts formed for ecclesiastical purposes by virtue of statutory authority, and includes benefices in the patronage of the Crown or of the Duchy of Cornwall, but does not extend to any of Her Majesty's Royal Chapels, or to any Royal peculiar, nor to any cathedral or capitular preferment or dignity, nor to any chapel belonging to any college, school, hospital, inns of court, asylum, or public or charitable institution, nor to any private chapel. (Benefices Act 1898, s 13)

'Benefice' means a benefice with cure of souls, and includes perpetual curacies, endowed public chapels, parochial chapelries, chapelries and districts belonging or annexed, or reputed to belong or to be annexed, to any church and districts formed by ecclesiastical purposes by virtue of statutory authority. (Reorganisation Areas Measure 1944, s 53)

'Benefice' means a benefice with cure of souls and includes all rectories and vicarages with cure of souls. (Ecclesiastical Offices (Age Limit) Measure 1975, s 6)

Without prejudice to section 6(2) of this Measure, in this Measure 'benefice' means the office of rector or vicar, with cure of souls, including the office of vicar in a team ministry established under the Pastoral Measure 1968 but does not include any office in a Royal Peculiar nor the office of dean or provost of a parish church cathedral within the meaning of the Cathedrals Measure 1963. (Incumbents (Vacation of Benefices) Measures 1977, s 19)

[Section 6(2) excepts certain incumbents from enquiries into disability.]

'Benefice' means the office of rector or vicar of a parish or parishes, with cure of souls, but not including (except in section 85) the office of a vicar in a team ministry. (Pastoral Measure 1983, s 86(1)

[Section 85 of the Measure relates to pluralities, and in respect of this section only, benefice does include the office of a vicar in a team ministry.]

Ancillary benefice

'Ancillary benefice' means a benefice the right of patronage of which is so vested in the incumbent of a principal benefice; and the word 'ancillary' shall be construed accordingly. (Benefices (Purchase of Rights of Patronage) Measure 1933, s 1)

Principal benefice

'Principal benefice' means a benefice in the incumbent of which is vested by virtue of his office a right of patronage of another benefice.

(Benefices (Purchase of Rights of Patronage) Measure 1933, s 1)

United benefice

'United benefice' means a benefice formed by the union of two or more benefices, either with or without the addition thereto of a parish, or part of a parish, of any other benefice, and 'union of benefices' shall be construed accordingly. (Reorganisation Areas Measure 1944, s 53)

BENEFICIAL

'It cannot be argued that "beneficially" must always be taken to mean "in possession". . . . "Beneficially entitled" [in a covenant by a wife to settle after-acquired property to which she should become beneficially entitled] is opposed to "entitled in trust", everything else is included.' *Re Jackson's Will* (1879) 49 LJ Ch 82 at 85, per Jessel MR

'To my mind the use of the word "beneficial" in our language is exceedingly inaccurate, and I think it is as frequently used in the active as in the reflective sense. We are just as much accustomed to talk of a man exercising his power, or using his wealth in a "beneficial" way meaning in a way to benefit others, as of his doing so in a way to benefit himself. When, therefore, I have to construe the words "over which at the time of my decease I shall have any beneficial disposing power by this my will", I can only say that I do not think I am obliged to confine the word "beneficial" to powers by which the testator could benefit himself or his estate. Moreover, I think the word is less likely to be used in a will, which a man knows will not take effect until after his death, in that sense rather than in the sense of his being able to benefit others by what he is doing.' *Von Brockdorff v Malcolm* (1885) 30 Ch D 172 at 180, 181, per Pearson J

BENEFICIAL ENJOYMENT

'Beneficial enjoyment means no more than [enjoyment] in his own right, and for his own benefit, not as trustee for another.' *A-G v Sefton (Earl)* (1865) 11 HL Cas 257 at 271, per Lord Wensleydale

BENEFICIAL INTEREST

'There has been considerable argument what that phrase [in the Administration of Estates Act 1925, s 51] "any beneficial interest in real estate" properly describes, but it cannot be doubted, I think, that least in some contexts a share in the proceeds of sale of realty would be covered by it.' *Re Bradshaw, Bradshaw v Bradshaw* [1950] Ch 582 at 592, CA, per Evershed MR

BENEFICIAL OCCUPATION

'The question of beneficial occupation . . . has been frequently before the Court. . . . We will . . . again observe that "beneficial" and "profitable", in the ordinary sense of the word are not convertible terms; that a party holding property in its nature rateable is not discharged from his legal liability because he does it at a loss.' *R v Vange (Inhabitants)* (1842) 3 QB 242 at 254, 255, per cur.

'I shall deal first with the question whether the occupation by the plaintiffs of the premises was beneficial during the year of assessment. It is now clear law that "beneficial" in this connection does not connote pecuniary profit. It is enough in the case of a public body, such as the plaintiffs, that the occupation is of benefit or advantage to them in the performance of their public duties.' *London County Council v Hackney Borough Council* [1928] 2 KB 588 at 593, per Wright J

'It was at one time considered that in order to create a *liability* for rates, occupation must be shown to be "beneficial" in the sense of being "profitable". This doctrine, . . . severely questioned in *Jones v Mersey Docks* [(1865) 11 HLC 443], was finally disposed of in subsequent cases, including the decisions of the House of Lords in *London County Council v Erith and West Ham* [[1893] AC 562], and *West Kent Main Sewerage Board v Dartford Union* [[1911] AC 171]. It is now well established that "beneficial occupation" does not connote pecuniary profit.' *Macdonald v Comr of Valuation for Northern Ireland* [1943] NI 14 at 22, 23, per Andrews CJ

'It is, I think, the law of Scotland as well as that of England that "beneficial" in this connection does not connote pecuniary profit.' *Greenock Corpn v Arbuckle Smith & Co Ltd* 1960 SLT 49 at 54, per Lord Mackintosh; revsd. [1960] 1 All ER 568

BENEFIT

'The section [the Settled Land Act 1925, s 1] provides that any instrument by virtue of which any land after the commencement of the Act stands for the time being (sub-s (1)(v)) charged "with the payment of any rentcharge for the life of any person, or any less period, or of any capital, annual or periodical sums, for the portions, advancement, maintenance, or otherwise for the benefit of any persons . . . creates . . . a settlement". . . . It was suggested that a restricted sense must be attributed to the word "benefit" in that clause, that "benefit" there means something *ejusdem generis* with portions, advancement and maintenance, and accordingly that the word "benefit" must be construed in some restricted sense. I do not see any reason for construing it in a restricted sense.' *Re Bird, Watson v Nunes* [1927] 1 Ch 210 at 215, per Clauson J

'Where a testator gives a sum . . . for the benefit of the choir he intends an impersonal gift, namely, a gift for the advancement and improvement of the musical services in the church by means of a choir.' *Re Royce, Turner v Wormald* [1940] Ch 514 at 518, per Simonds J

Australia 'In my opinion, in order that a payment be for the benefit of a beneficiary it must be made for a particular examinable purpose, which on examination appears to be beneficial, and the mere enlargement of the estate of the beneficiary is not such a purpose.' *Wyatt v Gaskell* (1949) 49 NSWSR 27 at 30, per Roper CJ (Eq)

Direct benefit

Canada 'Counsel for the plaintiff contend . . . that while the erection of a building under a building lease may not be "for the direct benefit" of the landlord the drilling of an oil well under an oil lease is "for the direct benefit" of the landlord since he gets one barrel of oil out of eight. It is clear that both the building and the oil well are for the advantage of the landlord but I am not able to see that the oil well is more for the direct benefit of the landlord than the increased rent and security which the landlord receives under a building lease.' *Morgan v Sunray Petroleum Corpn* [1941] 2 WWR 517 at 523, Alta SC, per O'Connor J

Of doubt

South Africa 'Before an accused can be accused of a crime, the prosecution must prove its case beyond reasonable doubt. If there is a reasonable doubt about the guilt of the accused

he is entitled to the benefit of that doubt and be acquitted.' *R v Britz* 1949 (3) SA 293 (A) at 302

BENEVOLENT   *See also* CHARITY— CHARITABLE; PHILANTHROPIC

New Zealand 'In accordance with a well-established series of authorities . . . a gift for benevolent purposes is bad, because such purposes go beyond the legal definition of charities. . . . There remains the consideration of the true meaning to be attached . . . to the word "benevolent" owing to the fact that it is used in a New Zealand will by a testator having a New Zealand domicil. It is, of course, quite possible that an English word might be used in New Zealand with a meaning different from that which it possesses here, and it may well be that "benevolent institutions and organisations" are . . . charitable institutions in New Zealand according to the strict meaning of the phrase. . . . But, even upon this assumption, the appellant's difficulties are not removed, for this reasoning would not endow the word "benevolent" with the same signification when it is . . . attached to the word "objects" and their Lordships cannot accept the appellant's argument that if benevolent institutions and benevolent associations in New Zealand are properly regarded as charitable this involves the conclusion that benevolent objects, where the adjective has no such local limitation of meaning are necessarily charitable also.' *A-G for New Zealand v Brown* [1917] AC 393 at 395–398 PC, per cur.

New Zealand 'In the present bequest the fatal word "benevolent" occurs on which so many testamentary dispositions have been shipwrecked, but it is urged that the bequest is salved by the fact that it is not in favour of benevolent purposes at large to be selected by the trustee but is in favour of institutions, societies or objects in or about Auckland for benevolent purposes. . . . It is probably the case that the addition of a local qualification may in certain circumstances render sufficiently definite what would otherwise be too wide a class, but in the present instance the want of precision is inherent in the word "benevolent" itself. Consequently, however circumscribed the local area and assuming that only existing organisations are intended, it still remains that to predicate of an institution, society or object in or about Auckland that it must be "benevolent" is not to identify it with the requisite precision.' *A-G of New Zealand v New Zea-*

land Insurance Co Ltd [1936] 3 All ER 888 at 890, PC, per cur.

See, generally, 5 Halsbury's Laws (4th edn) para 556.

Benevolent institution

[A testator gave his residuary estate to trustees upon trust to apply the same and the income thereof in providing or endowing any hospital wards, beds, or cots for, at, or in connection with, any hospital or convalescent home or other charitable or 'benevolent institution'.] 'It is true that in this will the testator used the words "benevolent institution". Those words, I think, must be construed in this case as *ejusdem generis* with "hospital", because the testator intended that at, or in connection with, any benevolent institution there should be provided or endowed hospital wards, or hospital beds, or hospital cots.' *Re Baron Ludlow, Bence-Jones v A-G* (1923) 93 LJ Ch 30 at 31, per Lawrence J; affd (1923) 93 LJ Ch 31, CA

BEQUEATH

'He [the testator] says, "the trustees shall stand possessed of and interested in the residue or surplus of the trust moneys, stocks, funds and securities thereby to them bequeathed, in trust, upon trust to apply and appropriate the same", etc, etc. I am unable to follow the argument that, as a matter of strict interpretation, this must be confined to personal estate, and not extended to real estate, by force of the word "bequeath", which was properly applicable to personal, and not to real, estate. I think the word "bequeath" is large enough to carry real estate if distinctly applied to it.' *Whicker v Hume* (1851) 14 Beav 500 at 518, per Romilly MR

'I was surprised that any doubt could be entertained, that a testator, who after disposing of his personal estate, makes a gift in the form: "I bequeath all the residue of my estate and effects" does by these words pass realty as well as personalty. . . . The use of the word "bequeath" affords no solid argument to exclude the realty, the general words being of the largest possible kind.' *Gyett v Williams* (1862) 2 John & H 429, per Page Wood V-C

'The ordinary accepted meaning and interpretation of the word "bequeathed" confines it to property derived under a testamentary instrument.' *Re Armstrong, Marescaux v Armstrong* (1879) 49 LJ Ch 53, per Hall V-C

'The words "devise" and "bequeath" are terms of known use in our law, the former from Glanville's time and earlier. In their ordinary sense they signify the declaration of a man's will concerning the succession to his own property after his death. Such a devise or bequest operates (on the subjects which either by common or by statute law, or by custom, can be so disposed of) by virtue of the will, and of that alone. . . . It follows . . . that the words "devise" or "bequest" when used in the Wills Act [1837] without any indication of an intention that they should apply to appointments under powers, ought, prima facie, to be understood in their ordinary sense, viz. as referring to a gift by will of the testator's own property and nothing else.' *Holyland v Lewin* (1884) 26 Ch D 266 at 271, 272, CA, per Lord Selborne LC

Australia   [By his will a testator gave, devised and bequeathed certain real and personal property to his son E with a direction that in the event of E dying 'without lawful issue the property bequeathed to him shall be equally divided.'] 'In this case it seems to me that the word "bequeathed" must refer to and include the real estate devised to the plaintif as well as to the [personal estate]. . . . The testator has, in the present case, used the words "bequeathed" and "devised" as synonymous and has, in fact, given his own interpretation to the word "bequeathed" and I think that the decision in *Whicker v Hume* [supra] is in point.' *Re Galligan, Galligan v Galligan* (1913) 13 NSWSR 291 at 293, 294, per Harvey J

Canada   'There is no question that in our common usage a "gift bequeathed" means a "gift by will". No doubt the use of "bequeath" was at one time less restricted. Counsel quoted Shakespeare to prove it. The more modern Oxford English Dictionary says, however, that "to leave by will" is now "the only surviving sense of the word".' *Re Snowball* [1941] OR 269 at 272, Ont CA, per cur; affd, [1942] SCR 202, SCC.

BEQUEST

The terms 'legacy' and 'bequest' in their ordinary sense are used of a gift of money or a chattel, but with a proper controlling context are capable of meaning a devise of land. (50 Halsbury's Laws (4th ·dn) para 469)

BERWICK-ON-TWEED   *See* ENGLAND

BEST EDITION

Copyrights

United States The 'best edition' of a work is the edition, published in the United States at any time before the date of deposit, that the Library of Congress determines to be most suitable for its purposes. (Copyright Act of 1976, s 101)

BEST EVIDENCE   *See* EVIDENCE

BESTOW

'The 1962 Act [Education Act 1962], in s 1 [substituted by the Education Act 1980, s 19, Sch 5] provides for bestowing awards on certain persons. "Bestow" is an unusual word to find in an Act of Parliament and carries a special connotation. It is commonly used in connection with words such as "bounty" or "favours" or some similar charitable or quasi-charitable act.' *R v London Borough of Barnet, ex p Shah* [1980] 3 All ER 679 at 682, per Ormrod LJ

BET   *See also* FIXED ODDS

. . . various attempts have been made by statute to define 'bet' with more precision. For the purposes of the Betting, Gaming and Lotteries Act 1963, a bet does not include any bet made or stake hazarded in the course of, or incidental to, any gaming. For the purposes of the statutes relating to betting, the word 'bet' is now virtually confined to (1) a wager, (2) a bet of any kind on a horse race or dog race, including a transaction with a totalisator, or (3) a bet made with a registered pool promoter, as in a football pool. (4 Halsbury's laws (4th edn) para 1)

'Bet' does not include any bet made or stake hazarded in the course of, or incidentally to, any gaming. (Betting, Gaming and Lotteries Act 1963, s 55(1), inserted by the Gaming Act 1968, s 53, Sch 11, Part I)

'Betting is one thing, and paying the bet is another. The words of the statute [Betting Act 1853, s 1 (repealed; see now Betting, Gaming and Lotteries Act 1963, s 1)] are "for the purpose of" certain classes of persons "betting with persons resorting to" a house, room, etc. The payment of a bet made and lost is not "betting". The betting has been done before.' *Bradford v Dawson* [1897] 1 QB 307 at 311, per Wills J

'In my opinion the respondent loitered in the streets . . . for the purpose of betting, by which I mean that he was doing that which was a substantial part of the business of betting, namely, giving a man who was invited to bet information as to the terms upon which Morton [a bookmaker] would bet and as to the means by which the bet could be negotiated.' *Dunning v Swetman* [1909] 1 KB 774 at 776, 777, DC, per Lord Alverstone CJ

'The essence of a bet is that on the determination of an event in one way, the first party wins and the second loses.' *A-G v Luncheon & Sports Club Ltd* [1929] AC 400 at 406, per Lord Dunedin

[The question was whether the insertion of a coin into a gaming machine was the making of a 'bet'.] 'I would . . . say that the action of inserting a coin, taken by itself, cannot properly be described as the making of a bet by the person inserting it. He is not forecasting an event or series of events; he is not backing his estimate of any outcome; he is simply hoping that some paying combination may turn up; he is gambling, but not in any ordinary sense of the word betting.' *Seay v Eastwood* [1976] 3 All ER 153 at 158, HL, per Lord Russell of Killowen

Australia 'A bet within the meaning of s 42(1) of the Gaming and Betting Act (NSW) 1912–1986, can exist even if both the parties interested take part, or one of them takes part, in attempting to bring about the event which is to decide it.' *Grigg v Bell* [1966] 2 NSWR 170 at 173, per Sugerman J

Canada 'Murray's New English Dictionary defines the substantive "bet" as the backing of a forecast by offering to forfeit in the case of an adverse issue a sum of money or article of value to one who maintains the opposite and backs his opinion by a corresponding stipulation; the staking of money or other value on the event of a doubtful issue. The most usual form of betting is that between non-participants in the event which is the subject of the bet, but this does not preclude the possibility of betting by one or more of the participants. I do not know of any instance in which the payment of money for the right or privilege of participating in an event, in the hope of winning a prize, even where the entry moneys form a part of the prize, has been held to be a bet. To do so would be to apply to the word "bet" a meaning foreign to its ordinary accepted meaning.' *R v Lebansky* [1941] 2 DLR 380 at 381, Man CA, per cur.

New Zealand 'In ordinary understanding a bet is made when one person stakes money or some other valuable thing against money or other valuable thing staked by another person upon the condition that the person whose prediction as to the result of a future uncertain event proves incorrect forfeits his stake to him whose prediction proves correct.' *Police v Thomas* [1966] NZLR 1008 at 1010, per Wilson J

South Africa 'A racing bet with a bookmaker is a promise to pay money to the bookmaker if a certain horse loses and a promise on the part of the bookmaker to pay if the horse wins. The promises are mutual and the one promise is the quid pro quo for the other.' *Est Wage v Strauss* 1932 AD 82–83, per Wessels ACJ

South Africa 'The ordinary meaning of a bet, which was accepted in *R v Bernstein* [1927 TPD 491], is a contract by which two persons agree that dependent upon a future uncertain event, one shall win from the other, and the other shall pay a sum of money or other stake, neither party having any other interest in the contract than the stake he will win or lose.' *R v Cunningham* 1946 TPD 243

Betting transaction

'Betting transaction' includes the collection or payment of winnings on a bet and any transaction in which one or more of the parties is acting as a bookmaker. (Betting, Gaming and Lotteries Act 1963, s 55)

Coupon betting

For the purposes of this Part [Part I: betting duties] of this Act, bets shall be deemed to be made by way of coupon betting where they are made in pursuance of an invitation which offers stated odds for a choice of bets, being bets of a description not commonly made without such an invitation, unless made by way of pool betting, and not of a description commonly made by means of a totalisator. (Betting and Gaming Duties Act 1981, s 11)

Dutiable betting

'Dutiable betting' means betting by way of pool betting or coupon betting. (Betting and Gaming Duties Act 1981, s 8(3))

On-course bet

In this Part [Part I: betting duties] of this Act . . . 'on-course bet' means a bet made in the course of a meeting, either by means of a totalisator situated on premises forming part of the track or with a bookmaker present at the meeting, where—
(a) the person making the bet (that is to say, the person originating the bet and not any agent or intermediary) is present at the meeting, or
(b) the bet is made by a person carrying on a bookmaking business acting as principal (and not acting as agent for, or on behalf of, some other person).
(Betting and Gaming Duties Act 1981, s 12(4))

Pool betting

For the purposes of this Act, any bet shall be deemed to be made by way of pool betting unless it is a bet at fixed odds, and, in particular, bets shall be held to be made by way of pool betting wherever a number of persons make bets—
(a) on terms that the winnings of such of those persons as are winners shall be, or be a share of, or be determined by reference to, the stake money paid or agreed to be paid by those persons, whether the bets are made by means of a totalisator, or by filling up the returning coupons or other printed or written forms, or otherwise howsoever; or
(b) on terms that the winnings of such of those persons as are winners shall be, or shall include, an amount (not determined by reference to the stake money paid or agreed to be paid by those persons) which is divisible in any proportions among such of those persons as are winners; or
(c) on the basis that the winners or their winnings shall, to any extent, be at the discretion of the promoter or some other person.
(Betting and Gaming Duties Act 1981, s 10(1))

Starting price betting

In this subsection [which defines bets at fixed odds] 'starting prices' means, in relation to any event, the odds ruling at the scene of the event immediately before the start. (Betting and Gaming Duties Act 1981, s 10(2))

'Betting on horse-racing falls under one or other of two heads: It may be effected in cash on the course, in which case it is spoken of as "on the course" betting, or it may be transacted away from the course with commission agents who conduct their business on a credit basis with known clients and settle bets by the official starting price made on the racecourse. This type of betting is known as "starting price" or "off the course" betting, and its volume preponderates largely over "on the course" betting.' *A-G v Racecourse Betting Control Board* [1935] Ch 34 at 39, CA, per Eve J

BETWEEN   *See also* DIVIDE BETWEEN

'In *Re Walbran* [*Milner v Walbran* [1906] 1 Ch 64], Joyce J founded himself substantially on his view that, etymologically, the word "between' indicated division into two. In *Re Harper* [*Plowman v Harper* [1914] 1 Ch 70], Sargant J did not accept that strict view and said that, whatever its etymology, the word in popular usage no longer indicated division into two, as against any other number of parts. In *Re Prosser* [*Prosser v Griffith* [1929] WN 85], Clauson J substantially followed *In re Walbran* because the language of the wills in the two cases was almost identical. In *Re Cossentine* [*Philip v Wesleyan Methodist Local Preachers' Mutual Aid Assocn Trustee* [1933] Ch 119] attention was for the first time closely directed to the proper inference to be drawn from the use of the word "between". Maugham J examined the article in the Oxford Dictionary on the word and pointed out that, today, with reference to a division and particularly to an equal division, the word "between" was not only the natural word to use, but was just as proper as the word "among". I say "just as proper", but, where equal distribution is emphasised, it might well be said to be more proper. In my view, *In re Cossentine* really destroys the foundation of much of the argument in favour of a division into moieties, which prevailed in *In re Walbran*. In my judgment it is not true, in 1945, that any inference in favour of division into two can be drawn from the use of the word "between" in a context such as that now before me. I respectfully adopt and follow the opinion of Maugham J in *In re Cossentine*, that "an ordinary man directing a sum to be divided between the children of his sister and, say, his nephew Jack, would . . . be intending a division *per capita*". That is supported, I think, by the fact that Hawkins on Wills, 3rd ed, at p 148, Jarman on Wills, 7th ed, vol iii, at p 1687, and Theobald on Wills, 9th ed, at p 264, all take the view that, prima

facie, a direction to divide between A and the children of B imports a division *per capita* among the whole class consisting of A plus all the children of B. That rule must, of course, yield in particular cases to the proper inference to be drawn from particular instruments.' *Re Alcock, Bonser v Alcock* [1945] 1 Ch 264 at 268, 269, per Evershed J

Australia 'I do not think that the word "between" does in strictness imply division into two parts rather than more. The etymological or original meaning is not necessarily the strict meaning of the word, if by strict is meant the meaning that should prima facie be applied to it. . . . I do not think that in the ordinary use of the word, which is not a word of art, a division into two parts rather than more is imported.' *Re Ninnes* [1920] SALR 480 at 490, per Poole J

New Zealand ' "Between" is . . . in legal English, a good equivalent for "among", "as used in case of distributive discrimination".' *Evans v Turner* (1904) 23 NZLR 825 at 828, per Denniston J; also reported 7 GLR 8 at 10

BIAS

'By "bias" I understand a real likelihood of an operative prejudice, whether conscious or unconscious.' *R (De Vesci) v Queen's County JJ* [1908] IR at 294, per Lord O'Brien

BICYCLE   *See* CARRIAGE; CYCLE

'Bicycle' includes a motor scooter, a bicycle with an attachment for propelling it by mechanical power and a bicycle to which a side-car is attached. (Vehicles (Excise) Act 1971, Sch 1)

BID   *See also* COMPETITIVE BIDDING

'It is competent for a bidder to make his bids [at an auction] by signals but he can only make an effective bid by communicating it to the auctioneer, and if his signal fails to register through no fault of the auctioneer he has, I think, simply failed to make a bid in any relevant sense. There is clearly a wide scope for doubt in particular circumstances: for example, whether an auctioneer has in fact seen the signal, or again whether it was the auctioneer's fault that he missed it.' *Richards v Phillips* [1967] 3 All ER 876 at 881, per Pennycuick J

BIGAMY

Whosoever, being married, shall marry any other person during the life of the former husband or wife, whether the second marriage shall have taken place in England or Ireland or elsewhere, shall be guilty of felony. . . . Provided, that nothing in this section contained shall extend to any second marriage contracted elsewhere than in England and Ireland by any other than a subject of Her Majesty, or to any person marrying a second time whose husband or wife shall have been continually absent from such person for the space of seven years then last past, and shall not have been known by such person to be living within that time, or shall extend to any person who, at the time of such second marriage, shall have been divorced from the bond of the first marriage, or to any person whose former marriage shall have been declared void by the sentence of any court of competent jurisdiction. (Offences Against the Person Act 1861, s 57)

[The distinction between felony and misdemeanor was abolished by the Criminal Law Act 1967, s 1(1).]

South Africa 'By our law a person, whether husband or wife, is not punishable as for bigamy if he or she reasonably and bona fide believed that his or her spouse was dead at the time of the subsequent marriage. Whether the belief is reasonable and entertained in good faith is a question for the jury, but as a general rule it may be broadly stated that such belief is neither unreasonable nor male fide if the spouse has been absent for seven years or more and, notwithstanding due inquiries, has not been heard of or from during that period.' *Re Booysen*, Foord 190 per Villiers CJ

BILL

Bills submitted to Parliament are divided into two classes and are described either as public or private bills. A public bill may be introduced by a member of either House, but a private bill may only be laid before Parliament upon a petition presented by the parties interested. With certain exceptions each House has the right to originate and pass any public bill.

As a general rule, it may be laid down that any measure the object of which is to alter the general law or which deals in any way with the public revenue, with the general administration of justice, or with the constitution or election of local governing bodies, should be

introduced as a public bill; whereas any measure which confers particular powers or benefits on any person or body of persons, including individuals, local authorities, statutory companies or private corporations, in excess of or in conflict with the general law, should be introduced as a private bill. (34 Halsbury's Laws (4th edn) paras 1222, 1223)

Hybrid bill

Bills which, although introduced into Parliament as public bills, are found to affect private interests are subject partly to the rules of procedure which govern private bills and partly to those which govern public bills, and are known as hybrid bills. A bill relating to Crown property, or a bill introduced by the government, even if it affects private interests, must be introduced as a public bill and not as a private bill because the Crown cannot petition itself in Parliament! Such a bill is treated as a hybrid bill. (34 Halsbury's Laws (4th edn) para 1224)

BILL OF EXCHANGE *See also*
ACCEPTANCE; CHEQUE; DRAFT

A bill of exchange is an unconditional order in writing, addressed by one person to another, signed by the person giving it, requiring the person to whom it is addressed to pay on demand or at a fixed or determinable future time a sum certain in money to or to the order of a specified person, or to bearer. (Bills of Exchange Act 1882, s 3)

BILL OF LADING

A bill of lading is a receipt for goods delivered to and received by a ship, signed by the person who contracts to carry them, or his agent, and evidencing the terms of the contract of carriage under which the goods have been so delivered and received. During the period of transit and voyage the bill of lading is recognised by the law merchant as the symbol of the goods described in it, and the endorsement and delivery of the bill of lading operates as a symbolic delivery of the goods. (41 Halsbury's Laws (4th edn) para 946)

A bill of lading is a document signed by the shipowner, or by the master or other agent of the shipowner, which states that certain specified goods have been shipped in a particular ship, and which purports to set out the terms on which the goods have been delivered to and received by the ship. After signature, it is handed to the shipper, who may either retain it or transfer it to a third person. This person may be named in the bill of lading as the person to whom delivery of the goods is to be made on arrival at their destination, in which case he is known as the consignee; if he is not named in the bill of lading, he is usually known as the holder or indorsee of the bill of lading. A bill of lading issued by the shipowner's agent in the absence of any contract of carriage is a nullity. The effect of a bill of lading depends upon the circumstances of the particular case, of which the most important is the position of the shipper and of the holder. There is no stamp duty on a bill of lading. . . .

A bill of lading is usually expressed in a printed document, containing blank spaces for the insertion of the necessary details. It states that the goods specified in it have been shipped in good order and condition by the shipper in and upon a certain ship then lying in the port of loading and bound for a particular port, and are to be delivered in like good order and condition at their destination to, or to the order of, a specified person or his assigns, or to bearer, upon payment of freight. Under the usual form the ship is given liberty to deviate, certain perils are excepted, and there is a negligence clause. The charterparty, if any, is usually incorporated to a greater or less extent, and provision is made for the payment of general average. In some cases the bill of lading contains a large number of stipulations, which deal fully with the respective rights and duties of the parties. (43 Halsbury's Laws (4th edn) paras 490, 498)

'In Article 3 of Scrutton on Charterparties [17th edn pp 8, 9] is a definition which says: "A bill of lading is a receipt for goods shipped on board a ship, signed by the person who contracts to carry them, or his agent, and stating the terms on which the goods were delivered to and received by the ship". . . . From the earliest times a bill of lading was a document which acknowledged actual shipment on board a particular ship.' *Diamond Alkali Export Corpn v Fl Bourgeois* [1921] 3 KB 443 at 449, per McCardie J

'The liberty to tranship is ancient and well established, and does not derogate from the nature of a bill of lading.' *Marlborough Hill (Ship) v Cowan & Sons* [1921] 1 AC 444 at 451, 452, PC, per cur.

South Africa 'According to English law a bill of lading, which is included in the class of documents known as documents of title . . . is an acknowledgment by a shipowner, a master or other agent that certain goods have actually been delivered on board a definite vessel. This definition is not peculiar to English law.' *Standard Bank of SA Ltd v Efroiken and Newman* 1924 AD 189, per de Villiers JA

United States 'Bill of lading' means a document evidencing the receipt of goods for shipment issued by a person engaged in the business of transporting or forwarding goods, and includes an airbill. "Airbill" means a document serving for air transportation as a bill of lading does for marine or rail transportation, and includes an air consignment note or air waybill. (Uniform Commercial Code 1978, s 1–201(6))

Clean bill of lading

'There is a very clear statement as to the meaning of the phrase "clean bill of lading" to be found [in Maude and Pollock's Law of Merchant Shipping (4th edn (1881))] and there it is said that a clean bill of lading is a bill of lading which contains nothing in the margin, qualifying the words in the bill of lading itself, "Shipped in good order and well-conditioned; goods of certain character, or a certain weight or quality or what not." But where, for instance, you insert in the margin of the bill of lading the weight or quantity or quality unknown, that is not a clean bill of lading, because that contains a qualification. Where, on the other hand, there is no such qualification inserted in the margin, there the bill of lading is a clean one.' *Restitution SS Co v Sir John Pirie & Co* (1889) 61 LT 330 at 333, per Cave J

'A "clean bill of lading" has never been exhaustively defined, and I certainly do not propose to attempt that task now. I incline to the view, however, that a clean bill of lading is one that does not contain any reservation as to the apparent good order or condition of the goods or the packing.' *British Imex Industries Ltd v Midland Bank Ltd* [1958] 1 All ER 264 at 268, per Salmon J; also reported [1958] 1 QB 542 at 551

[In *Golodetz (M) & Co v Czarnikow-Rionda Co Inc* [1980] 1 All ER 501, it was held that a bill of lading was 'clean' because (i) there was nothing in it to qualify the admission that at the time of shipment the goods were in apparent good order and condition, and (ii) there was no evidence that it was not a document which would ordinarily and properly have been accepted in the trade as being an appropriate document.]

BILL OF SALE

A bill of sale may be described as an instrument in writing whereby one person transfers to another the property he has in goods or chattels, or as a document given with respect to the transfer of goods or chattels, used in cases where possession is not intended to be given. (4 Halsbury's Laws (4th edn) para 601)

The expression 'bill of sale' shall include bills of sale, assignments, transfers, declarations of trust without transfer, inventories of goods with receipt thereto attached, or receipts for purchase moneys of goods, and other assurances of personal chattels, and also powers of attorney, authorities, or licenses to take possession of personal chattels as security for any debt, and also any agreement, whether intended or not to be followed by the execution of any other instrument, by which a right in equity to any personal chattels, or to any charge or security thereon, shall be conferred, but shall not include the following documents; that is to say, assignments for the benefit of the creditors of the person making or giving the same, marriage settlements, transfers or assignments of any ship or vessel or any share thereof, transfers of goods in the ordinary course of business of any trade or calling, bills of sale of goods in foreign parts or at sea, bills of lading, India warrants, warehouse-keepers' certificates, warrants or others for the delivery of goods, or any other documents used in the ordinary course of business as proof of the possession or control of goods, or authorising or purporting to authorise, either by indorsement or by delivery, the possessor of such document to transfer or receive goods thereby represented. (Bills of Sale Act 1878, s 4)

'I am satisfied on the construction of the Bills of Sale Acts that they do not include letters of hypothecation accompanying a deposit of goods by merchants or factors, or pawn tickets given by pawnbrokers, or in fact any case where the object and effect of the transaction are immediately to transfer the possession from the grantor to the grantee.' *Re Hall, ex p Close* (1884) 14 QBD 386 at 393, per Cave J

'If a document is intended by the parties to it to be a part of the bargain to pass the property in the goods, then, whatever the form of the document may be, even if it be only a simple receipt for the purchase money, it is by s 4 [of the Bills of Sale Act 1878] to be deemed to be a bill of sale, though it is not so in fact. But, if the document is not intended to be part of the bargain to pass the property in the goods—if the bargain is complete without it, so that the property passes independently of it—then it is not to be deemed to be that which it is not in fact—a bill of sale.' *Ramsay v Margrett* [1894] 2 QB 18 at 23, 24, CA, per Lord Esher MR

BINDING

'I can see no difference at all between enacting that certain words shall be valid and obligatory and saying that the agreement is to be confirmed and made binding on the several parties.' *R v Midland Rly Co* (1887) 19 QBD 540 at 547, per Stephen J

'I am going to assume that the contract between the parties in this case is as stated by the commission note and that the commission was payable if the plaintiffs produced a person ready, willing and able to enter into a binding contract. The first thing which I have to consider is: What is the meaning of the words "binding contract"? I have to give a meaning to the word "binding". I think that it means a contract that is enforceable. Every contract that is entered into freely between two persons, provided that it is not one of those contracts which is void, as, for instance, a contract entered into by an infant or a contract entered into for some immoral or illegal purpose, is a binding contract. . . . I think that the words "binding contract" mean, in a case of this sort a contract which can be enforced by the vendor against the purchaser. . . . "Binding", I think, means binding in law.' *Peter Long and Partners v Burns* [1956] 2 All ER 25 at 26, 27, per Lord Goddard CJ; affd. [1956] 3 All ER 207, HL

Australia 'It should not be forgotten that the word "binding" is used in more than one connection and that it is not a word limited to the description of obligations created by judicial action. A man is "bound" by a statute which applies to him; he is "bound" by a contract which he makes; he is "bound" by an award of an arbitrator pursuant to a submission to him; he is "bound" by an industrial award which applies to him.' *Rola Co (Aus) Pty Ltd v Commonwealth* (1944) 69 CLR 185 at 197, per Latham CJ

Legally binding contract

' "Legally binding" means legally binding. Not every contract which is legally binding is enforceable by an order for specific performance. There must be many cases of contracts for the sale of land, as well as contracts for the sale of goods, in which the court, in the exercise of its discretion, will not order specific performance or specific delivery but will make an award of damages. Although I agree . . . that obligations and remedies belong to separate departments of the law of contract, I think it is reasonable to say that a contract must be legally binding if a breach of it gives rise to a right of action for damages.' *Sheggia v Gradwell* [1963] 3 All ER 114 at 123, CA, per Pearson LJ

BIRD   *See also* WILD BIRD

Game bird

'I entertain no doubt whatever but that the words "birds of game" in stat 1 & 2 Will 4, c 32, s 4 [Game Act 1831, s 4 (amended and repealed in part)] include live birds. The words must have the same meaning throughout the section, and the reference in its second clause to "birds of game kept in a mew or breeding place" shows plainly that the Legislature had live birds in view.' *Loome v Baily* (1860) 3 E & E 444 at 449, per Wightman J

Of warren

[Under the old forest laws, franchises could be granted of either 'chase', park or warren. The latter acquired the meaning of game reserve, in which the rights of taking animals or birds of warren were strictly protected.

The franchises themselves were abolished by the Wild Creatures and Forest Laws Act 1971.]

'Now there is not any one book in the law which has mentioned grouse as a bird of warren. Manwood confines his description to two species, pheasants and partridges. . . . Perhaps it may not be easy at this distance of time to say why one species should be a bird of warren and not another. One reason why grouse were not so considered may be, that grouse were not birds that could be taken by any of the ordinary modes of sport in use at the time when this franchise had its origin. Another may be, that those birds were known only in some parts of England.' *Duke of Devonshire v Lodge* (1827) 7 B & C 36 at 40, per Lord Tenterden CJ

'I am not at all satisfied that a wild duck is not a bird of warren. Sir Edward Coke refers to mallards as birds of warren—1 Inst 233 *a*;—and though Manwood (4th edn, 1717) p 362, refers only to the pheasant and the partridge, I do not think it was decided in *Devonshire (Duke) v Lodge* [supra] that birds of warren were confined to the pheasant and the partridge, but merely that a grouse was not a bird of warren. Manwood, in the same passage, seems to consider that birds of warren are such as are taken by long-winged hawks. Certainly herons were in ancient times taken by long-winged hawks, and Manwood does not mention them as birds of warren, though Sir Edward Coke does. I find on reference to Mr Turner's introduction to the Selden Society's volume Select Pleas of the Forest, pp cxxix, cxxxi, that there is authority for including quails, plover, or even larks as birds of warren. . . . In my opinion . . . Sir Edward Coke was right, and wild duck are birds of warren.' *Fitzhardinge (Lord) v Purcell* [1908] 2 Ch 139 at 163, 164, per Parker J

BIRTH   *See* BORN

BISHOP

The bishop of a diocese is a legally ordained minister appointed by the Crown, who, under the supremacy of the Crown and the supervision of the archbishop, is 'chief in superintendency' in matters ecclesiastical within the diocese. He is also called 'Ordinary' in some enactments 'as having ordinary jurisdiction in causes ecclesiastical', 'immediate to the King'.

The bishop is a corporation sole, with perpetual succession and a seal. He may use a seal other than that of his office for letters of institution, as the seal is not material. (14 Halsbury's Laws (4th edn) para 458)

'Bishop' in relation to any church, parish, district or other area or place means the bishop of the diocese in which the church, parish, district or other area or place is situated, or if the parish, district, area or place is situated partly in one diocese and partly in another, the bishop of each such diocese. (New Parishes Measure 1943, s 29)

Overseas bishop

'Overseas bishop' means a bishop of the Church of England or a Church in Communion with the Church of England having a diocese or office elsewhere than in the province of Canterbury, the province of York, Ireland, Wales or Scotland, and 'overseas diocese' means the diocese of an overseas bishop. (Overseas and Other Clergy (Ministry and Ordination) Measure 1967, s 6)

Suffragan bishop

Strictly speaking all the bishops of a province are suffragans or helpers to the archbishop, but the term 'suffragan' is now only applied to bishops who assist the diocesan bishop. (14 Halsbury's Laws (4th edn) para 493)

BLACK BEER *See* BEER

BLACKLEG

'The word "blackleg", in my opinion, has been used long enough to be known and to be as well understood by persons not accustomed to slang, as those who are. If so, it is for the judge to explain the meaning of it as a word in the English language. I have always understood it to mean a person who gets his living by frequenting race-courses and practising games of chance and skill, constantly betting with the best odds he can obtain in his favour, giving the least odds he possibly can, doing this with the view of making money, but not necessarily dishonest in so doing, or cheating in the sense in which the word is used in the common or statute law. And that being so, I think it is not actionable to call a man a blackleg any more than to call him a "cheat", or a "swindler", or a "villain", which clearly is not actionable, though all these terms plainly impute dishonesty. They do not necessarily imply the commission of any crime punishable by law. It is notorious that there are many expressions which if applied to a man would have a tendency to drive him from society and hold him up to odium, but which are not actionable, because not conveying a charge of crime legally punishable, unless followed by special damage. And I think the word "blackleg" is of that class. The dictionary does not give it a more criminal sense than that of a person who is a professed gamester.' *Barnett v Allen* (1858) 27 LJ Ex 412 at 414, per Pollock CB

'I do not think that the word "blackleg" has any precise signification in our language. In itself it clearly does not import any crime, and it must be by its use only that it has such a meaning. It may mean only that a man is a professed gambler. It might mean that he cheated at cards. It may mean both. But the word itself does not appear to import necessarily an indictable offence.' Ibid at 415, per Watson B

[Watson B agreed with Pollock CB, but Martin and Bramwell BB held that 'blackleg' implied cheating. The Court was thus evenly divided. Since *Barnett v Allen*, 'blackleg' has acquired an additional meaning in connection with trade disputes and that meaning has not yet been the subject of reported litigation.]

BLACKMAIL *See also* MENACE

(1) A person is guilty of blackmail if, with a view to gain for himself or another or with intent to cause loss to another, he makes any unwarranted demand with menaces; and for this purpose a demand with menaces is unwarranted unless the person making it does so in the belief—
  (a) that he has reasonable grounds for making the demand; and
  (b) that the use of the menaces is a proper means of reinforcing the demand.
(2) The nature of the act or omission demanded is immaterial, and it is also immaterial whether the menaces relate to action to be taken by the person making the demand.
(Theft Act 1968, s 21(1), (2))

South Africa 'The word "blackmailer" has been extended to include any one who, by threats of exposure or disclosure or adverse criticism, endeavours to extort money from another.' *Kernick v Fitzpatrick* 1907 TS 391 per Innes CJ

BLAMEWORTHINESS

South Africa 'Blameworthiness . . . is the deflection from an ideal standard of conduct, that of the *diligens paterfamilias*, the average reasonable man, conceived as acting in the same circumstances as the person whose conduct is in question. Like moral concepts this standard is not static or uniform; it is influenced by the generally accepted notions and the social conscience of this community and this age.' *Meskin v Anglo-American Corpn of SA Ltd* 1968 (4) SA at 800 per Van den Heever J

BLASPHEMY

Blasphemy is an indictable offence at common law consisting in the publication of words attacking the Christian religion or the Bible so violent, scurrilous or ribald as to pass the limits of decent controversy and tend to lead to a breach of the peace. It is immaterial whether the words are spoken or written; if written they constitute a blasphemous libel. The offence is punishable by fine and imprisonment at the discretion of the court. (11 Halsbury's Laws (4th edn) para 1009)

South Africa 'Now the definition of "blasphemy" in our law is to be found in Moorman and Van der Linden. "Blasphemy" according to these writers consists either in the denial of the existence of God or in slandering God.' *R v Webb* 1934 AD 496 per Wessels CJ

['Blasphemy' consists in unlawfully, intentionally, and publicly acting contemptuously towards God: Hunt, SA Criminal Law, Vol II.]

Blasphemous libel

'The mere denial of the truth of the Christian religion, or of the Scriptures, is not enough, *per se*, to constitute a writing a blasphemous libel, so as to render the writer or publisher indictable. But indecent and offensive attacks on Christianity or the Scriptures, or sacred persons or objects, calculated to outrage the feelings of the general body of the community, do constitute the offence of blasphemy, and render writers or publishers liable at common law to criminal prosecution.' *R v Ramsay* (1883) 15 Cos CC 231 at 232, per Lord Coleridge CJ

'In my opinion, to constitute blasphemy at common law there must be an element of vilification, ridicule or irreverence as would be likely to exasperate the feelings of others and so lead to a breach of the peace.' *Bowman v Secular Society Ltd* [1917] AC 406 at 445, 446, HL, per Lord Parker of Waddington

'I do not subscribe to the view that the common law offence of blasphemous libel serves no useful purpose in the modern law. On the contrary, I think there is a case for legislation extending it to protect the religious beliefs and feelings of non-Christians. The offence belongs to a group of criminal offences designed to safeguard the internal tranquility of the kingdom. In an increasingly plural society such as that of modern Britain it is necessary not only to respect the differing religious beliefs, feelings and practices of all but also to protect them from scurrility, vilification, ridicule and contempt. . . . The *actus reus* of the offence of blasphemy consists of the publication of words spoken or written. In the 17th century words challenging or questioning the doctrines of the established church were regarded as blasphemy: for "Christianity is parcel of the laws of England; and therefore to reproach the Christian religion is to speak in subversion of the law", as Hale CJ put it in *R v Taylor* [(1676) 1 Vent 293]. His view was accepted in 1729 in *R v Woolston* [(1729) 1 Barn KB 162], though Raymond CJ did add: ". . . we do not meddle with any differences in opinion and . . . we interpose only when the very root of Christianity is struck at . . .". Nevertheless in almost all the reported cases the words complained of were scurrilous, insulting or offensive; indeed Keble reports Hale CJ as saying expressly that "contumelious reproaches of the established religion are punishable here". And in one famous case, that of *R v Shipley* [(1784) 4 Doug KB 73], in which there was no element of scurrility, the defendant was ultimately acquitted. The watershed between the old and the modern law comes with the cases of *R v Hetherington* [(1841) 4 State Tr NS 563] and *R v Ramsay and Foote* [supra]. . . . Since *Ramsay and Foote's* case, the modern law has been settled and in 1917 received the accolade of this House's approval. "What the law censures or resists is not the mere expression of anti-Christian opinion", said Lord Sumner in *Bowman v Secular Society Ltd* [supra]. The words must constitute, as it is put by Odgers on *Libel and Slander*, an interference with our religious feelings, creating a sense of insult and outrage "by wanton and unnecessary profanity".' *R v Lemon, R v Gay News Ltd* [1979] All ER 898 at 921, 923, 924, HL, per Lord Scarman

[Lord Scarman went on to say that in his judgment the modern law of blasphemy was correctly stated in Stephen's *Digest of the Criminal Law* (9th edn, 1950), as follows: 'Every publication is said to be blasphemous which contains any contemptuous, reviling, scurrilous or ludicrous matter relating to God, Jesus Christ, or the Bible, or the formularies of the Church of England as by law established. It is not blasphemous to speak or publish opinions hostile to the Christian religion, or to deny the existence of God, if the publication is couched in decent and temperate language. The test to be applied is as to the manner in which the doctrines are advocated and not as to the substance of the doctrines themselves. Everyone who publishes any blasphemous document is guilty of the [offence] of publishing a blasphemous libel. Everyone who speaks blasphemous words is guilty of the [offence] of blasphemy.']

BLENDED

Canada [The Interest Act, RSC 1970, c I-18, refers to principal money or interest secured by mortgage of real estate being made payable by the mortgagee on any plan under which the payments of principal money and interest are 'blended'.] 'The Supreme Court of Canada in the *Kilgoran* case [*Kilgoran Hotels Ltd v Samek* [1968] SCR 3] approved of the definition of "blended" as meaning "mixed so as to be inseparable and indistinguishable". This definition, however, does not mean utterly incapable of separation or distinction. No doubt any payment which includes both principal and interest can be separated or distinguished in some way. In my opinion, the payment must be distinguishable or separable on the face of the mortgage without reference to implied terms.' *Re McGoran and Cowan* [1973] 3 OR 557 at 559, Ont HCJ, per Zuber J

BLIND PERSON

'Blind person' means a person so blind as to be unable to perform any work for which eyesight is essential. (National Assistance Act 1948, s 64)

BLOCK

South Africa 'It is a matter of some difficulty to define a block, but the use of concrete blocks for buildings is well known. Such blocks are so shaped that they remain in equilibrium on whatever side they rest and they are used for building purposes in a similar manner to bricks or dressed stones. It seems to me that to constitute a block the thickness of the concrete article must not be so very much less than either the length or height.' *R v Becker* 1940 AD 25 per de Wett CJ

BLOCK OF FLATS *See* FLAT

BLOCKADE *See also* RESTRAINT OF PRINCES

The object of a blockade is completely to prevent access to or egress from the enemy's coasts or ports. In order to be binding the blockade must be effective, and a neutral is affected with notice of the blockade, either actual or constructive. (37 Halsbury's Laws (4th edn) para 1314)

'A blockade may be more or less rigorous either for the single purpose of watching the military operations of the enemy, and preventing the egress of their fleet . . . or on a more extended scale, to cut off all access of neutral vessels to that interdicted place; which is strictly and properly a blockade, for the other is in truth no blockade at all, as far as neutrals are concerned. It is an undoubted right of belligerents to impose such a blockade, though a severe right, and as such not to be extended by construction; it may operate as a grievance of neutrals, but it is one to which, by the law of nations, they are bound to submit. . . . A temporary and forced secession of the blockading force, from the accidents of winds and storms, would not be sufficient to constitute a legal relaxation . . . but . . . no force was applied for the purpose of enforcing the blockade. . . . What is a blockade, but to prevent access by force? If the ships stationed on the spot to keep up the blockade will not use their force for that purpose, it is impossible for a court of justice to say there was a blockade actually existing at that time.' *The Juffrow Maria Schroeder* (1800) 3 Ch Rob 147 at 154, 156, per Sir W Scott

'Of the war clauses which were attached to the charterparty clause 1 was as follows: "The master shall not be required or bound to sign bills of lading for any blockaded port or for any port which the master or owners in his or their discretion consider dangerous or impossible to enter or reach." By clause 2 (A): "If any port of discharge . . . be blockaded, or (B) if owing to any war, hostilities, warlike operations, civil war, civil commotions, revolutions, or the operation of international law entry to any such port . . . be considered by the master or owners in his or their discretion dangerous or impossible for the vessel to reach such discharging port, the cargo . . . shall be discharged at any other safe port in the vicinity . . . as may be ordered by the charterers.". . . The "blockade" declared by General Franco never was a blockade—it was not recognised by the British Government, and in fact there was no greater danger to British shipping, or no greater risk of interference with British shipping, after the declaration than before. . . . [Counsel] also argued . . . that a reference to a blockaded port in the clauses did not mean blockade in its strict legal sense. . . . He suggested that the word "blockade" in this charterparty could not mean, and was not intended to mean, such a state of affairs as, for example, the learned author of Arnould on Marine Insurance (Vol II, section 767) lays down as being requisite to constitute a blockade [s 767 of Arnould states that one requisite of blockade is that the port must be invested by a number of vessels 'sufficiently near the port to make the entry evidently dangerous']. I am quite unable to accept that argument, and the juxtaposition in the clauses of such words as "blockaded port", and "a port dangerous or impossible to enter or reach", and, in particular the terms of clauses 2 (A) and (B) make it clear, to my mind, that "blockaded" means what it says—that is to say "blockaded" in its strict legal sense.' *Spanish Government v North of England SS Co Ltd* (1938) 54 TLR 852 at 854, 856, per Lewis J

BLOOD RELATIONS   *See* RELATIONS

BLOOD TEST

'Blood tests' means blood tests carried out under this Part [Part III: provisions for use of blood tests in determining paternity] of this Act and includes any test made with the object of ascertaining the inheritable characteristics of blood. (Family Law Reform Act 1969, s 25)

BLOODSTOCK

'I think myself that the conclusion from the evidence is that among those interested in thoroughbred horses the word "bloodstock", used in connection with an owner, has a meaning which, without being precise, covers, or in many ordinary contexts is used as covering, a share in a horse as distinct from full ownership.' *Re Gillson, Ellis v Leader* [1948] 2 All ER 990 at 993, CA, per Somervell LJ

BOARD

[The Increase of Rent and Mortgage Interest (Restrictions) Act 1920, s 12(2) (repealed) excluded from the operation of the Act a dwelling-house bona fide let at a rent which included payments in respect of 'board', atten-

dance or use of furniture.] 'The statute does not indicate whether full or partial board . . . is aimed at . . . It uses the [word] quite generally, and in my opinion any amount of board . . . will satisfy this . . . test, which is not ruled out of consideration by the application of the rule *de minimis non curat lex. . . .* Where the amount of board . . . included in the rent is so small as to be negligible, that would go far to dispose of the question of the bona fides of the letting.' *Wilkes v Goodwin* [1923] 2 KB 86 at 93, 94, CA, per Bankes LJ

'"Board" . . . is defined . . . in the Oxford Dictionary as "daily meals provided in a lodging or boarding house according to stipulation; the supply of daily provisions". The word without suffix or affix suggests to my mind sufficiency. . . . The natural interpretation of the word as we find it in this exception involves the conception of a provision by the landlord of such food as in the case of a particular tenancy would ordinarily be consumed at daily meals and would be obtained and prepared by a tenant for himself, if it were not provided for by somebody else.' Ibid at 110, per Younger LJ (dissenting)

[See now the Rent Act 1977, s 7(1), which provides that a tenancy is not a protected tenancy if under the tenancy a dwelling house is bona fide let at a rent which includes payments in respect of 'board' or attendance.]

BOARD OF DIRECTORS

[The articles of association of a company provided that the board of directors should consist of not less than three directors, but all but two of the directors had resigned.] 'When . . . the articles provide for the filling up of a vacancy by "the board", I think a properly constituted board is meant, and not merely two directors, who do not and cannot form a board, though they could, if a legally constituted board were in existence, but competent (if no greater number thought fit to attend) to form a quorum sufficient to transact business.' *Faure Electric Accumulator Co Ltd v Phillipart* (1888) 58 LT 525 at 528, per Hawkins J

BOARDING HOUSE

The keeper of a boarding-house may for some purposes be regarded as a hotel keeper, although he is not liable as an innkeeper. At a boarding-house a guest may have the use of certain rooms in common with others, his own bedroom, his board, and the attendance of servants in exchange for an agreed periodical payment, but this does not make the boarding-house a hotel within the statutory definition [in the Hotel Proprietors Act 1956, s 1]. (24 Halsbury's Laws (4th edn) para 1210)

New Zealand 'In the case of a "boarding house" the emphasis is on communal or institutional occupation, where there would for example be a common dining room where "board" was part of the service provided.' *Godfrey v Christchurch City Council* (1985) 10 NZTPA 417 at 419, per Roper J

BOAT *See also* BRITISH OWNED; CANAL BOAT; FISHING BOAT; SHIP; VESSEL; WATERMAN

'Boat' means every vessel not a ship as above defined [vessels used in sea navigation] which is used in navigation in any inland water or any harbour, whether propelled by oars or otherwise. (Explosives Act 1875, s 108)

'Boat' includes any hover vehicle or craft being a vehicle or craft designed to be supported on a cushion of air and which is used on or over water. (Countryside Act 1968, s 49(2))

BODILY FUNCTIONS

[The Social Security Act 1975, s 35(1) provides that if a person is so severely disabled physically or mentally that, by day, he requires from another person frequent attention throughout the day in connection with his 'bodily functions', he shall be entitled to an attendance allowance.] 'If I have to break down and attempt to analyse the language, I would emphasise three points. First, the disablement must be severe. Second, the phrase "bodily functions" is a restricted and precise one, narrower than, for example, "bodily needs". Third, the phrase "attention . . . in connection with his bodily functions", which must, I think, be read as a whole, connotes a high degree of physical intimacy between the person giving and the person receiving the attention. . . . At the end of the day I doubt if the construction of the relevant words can be more accurately or more concisely expressed than in the passage from the decision of Mr Commissioner Monroe in 1974 [decision CA 60/74], cited by Dunn LJ [[1981] 2 All ER 738 at 744]: "I consider that the words of the section refer to a person who needs the relevant degree of attention in connection with the performance of his bodily

functions and that they are directed primarily to those functions which the fit man normally performs for himself." This criterion has the great merit of being clear and easily applied.' *Woodling v Secretary of State for Social Services* [1984] 1 All ER 593 at 596, per Lord Bridge of Harwich

BODILY HARM *See* ACTUAL BODILY HARM; GRIEVOUS BODILY HARM

BODY

Corpse

What constitutes a body has not been judicially defined. There must have been independent life; a non-viable fetus expelled at a stage of pregnancy at which separate existence is impossible does not fall within the coroner's jurisdiction. Similarly, inquiry into still-birth is not a matter for the coroner unless there is doubt as to whether or not separate existence has been achieved. (9 Halsbury's Laws (4th edn) para 1055)

Of note

'What is the meaning of "in the body of" the note [in s 87(1) of the Bills of Exchange Act 1882]? I am in agreement with the observation made by Greer LJ, . . . that "in the body of" the note must mean in the terms of the actual contract to pay which is contained in the note. You may have some additional matter or a memorandum added to the note. But if it is to be in the body of the note, it must be part of the actual terms of the contract made by the maker of it.' *Re British Trade Corpn Ltd* [1932] 2 Ch 1 at 9, CA, per Lord Hanworth

See, generally, 4 Halsbury's Laws (4th edn) para 422.

Of persons

'Body of persons' means any body politic, corporate or collegiate, and any company, fraternity, fellowship and society of persons, whether corporate or not corporate. (Income and Corporation Taxes Act 1970, s 526(5))

BOLT *See* QUIT

BONA FIDES *See also* GOOD FAITH

'There are three things to be considered [in an action about a fraudulent deed] fraud, consideration and bona fide; now the bona fide is opposite to fraud.' *Teynham (Lord) v Mullins* (1674) 1 Mod Rep 119 at 119, per Hale CJ

'The term "bona fide traveller" [in the Revenue Act 1867, s 17 (repealed; see now Customs and Excise Management Act 1979, s 106(3)(b))] . . . is a term of trade well known to mean a man who does in fact travel about the country soliciting orders which he sends up to his employer for execution.' *Killick v Graham, Lintern v Bruchell* [1896] 2 QB 196 at 201, per Grantham J

'What is the meaning of the phrase "bona fide let at a rent which includes payments in respect of board, attendance or use of furniture"? In my opinion "bona fide" in this phrase governs the whole of the words which follow. The words amount to a stipulation that the rent to be paid genuinely includes payments in respect of board, attendance or use of furniture.' *Palser v Grinling, Property Holding Co Ltd v Mischeff* [1948] AC 291 at 310, HL, per Viscount Simon

[The Trade Marks Act 1938, s 8, provides that no registration of a trade mark shall interfere with any bona fide use by a person of his own name, etc.] 'The . . . point which was discussed before us was as to the meaning of "bona fide use" in s 8. Danckwerts J said [in the court below] that he understood that "bona fide" normally ". . . means the honest use by the person of his own name, without any intention to deceive anybody or without any intention to make use of the goodwill which has been acquired by another trader": and in that sense he acquitted the defendants of any want of bona fides in the present case. We agree with the learned judge's definition of the term "bona fide" and we see no reason to attribute a different or special meaning to the phrase in its context in s 8. The mere fact in itself that a trader is using his own name which too closely resembles a registered trade name of which he is aware does not prevent the user from being "bona fide", provided that the trader honestly thought that no confusion would arise and if he had no intention of wrongfully diverting business to himself by using the name. The truth is that a man is either honest or dishonest in his motives; there is no such thing, so far as we are aware, as constructive dishonesty. In our judgment, if a trader is honestly using his own name, then no action will lie for infringement of trade mark and any rival trader who thinks himself aggrieved must sue, if at all, for passing off.' *Baume & Co Ltd v Moore (A H) Ltd*

[1958] 2 All ER 113 at 123, CA, per cur.; also reported [1958] Ch 907 at 921

Australia [The Landlord and Tenant (Amendment) Act 1948–1986 (NSW), s 62(5)(p)(ii), deals with cases where a lessee has ceased to be a 'bona fide' occupant of premises.] 'The words "bona fide" stress the substantial and genuine nature of the occupation required.' *Morgan v Davis* [1962] NSWR 1013 at 1017, per Wallace J

Canada [The Mechanics' Lien Act 1956, s 7(1) (repealed; see now RSBC 1979, c 40, s 7(1)), provided that a registered mortgage should have priority over a lien to the extent of the mortgage-moneys bona fide secured prior to the filing of the claim of lien, etc.] 'In this case the mortgage-moneys were secured prior to the filing of the plaintiff's claim of lien, and so, if they were "bona fide secured," the mortgage has priority over the plaintiff's lien. In my view the expression "bona fide secured" in its context here means "in good faith, not as a sham or a mere paper transaction, not collusively or as part of a scheme to defraud anybody, but being in fact what it is in form, a genuine transaction" [see *A-G v Richmond (Duke) (No 2)* [1908] 2 KB 729 at 741, per Cozens-Hardy MR].' *Casson v Dunsmuir Construction Ltd* (1961) 35 WWR 521 at 524, BCCA, per Tysoe J

Canada 'Section 3 of the Fraudulent Conveyances Act [RSO 1980, c 176, whereby conveyances to defeat creditors are void] excepts transactions where there has been good consideration and where the transfer was made bona fide. In my view, the phrase bona fide in this context ought to be taken to mean a sale to a real purchaser and not merely a nominee or put another way, the transaction must be more than a form of purchase. The phrase bona fide signifies something done in good faith without fraud or deceit or collusion. There must be honesty in fact. There must be complete frankness.' *Re Dougmor Realty Holdings Ltd, Fisher v Wilgorn Investments Ltd* [1967] 1 OR 66 at 85, per Lieff J; revsd [1968] 1 OR 61, without affecting definition.

Canada [Estate tax exemption in Estate Tax Act 1958 (Can), c 29, s 4(1) (now RSC 1970, c E–9) referred to bona fide purchase from deceased.] '. . . the words "bona fide" qualify the word "purchase". Unless they are interpreted as indicating the kind of purchase to which the subsection applies, they become mere surplusage. Obviously such a result is as undesirable as reading into the section words that are not there. Whether a "purchase" is "bona fide" it seems to me, requires a determination of the purchaser's intentions as disclosed by its actions. Otherwise the word "purchase" would bear only its ordinary meaning and would not require the qualification provided by the words "bona fide".' *Smith v Minister of National Revenue* (1975) 60 DLR (3d) 723 at 732, 733, Fed CA, per Urie J

United States A 'bona fide purchaser' is a purchaser for value in good faith and without notice of any adverse claim:
(a) who takes delivery of a certificated security in bearer form or in registered form, issued or indorsed to him or in blank;
(b) to whom the transfer, pledge, or release of an uncertificated security is registered on the books of the issuer;
(c) to whom a security is transferred under the provisions of paragraph (c), (d)(i), or (g) of Section 8–313(1).
(Uniform Commercial Code 1978, s 8–302(1))

BONA VACANTIA

The term 'bona vacantia' is applied to things in which no one can claim a property, and includes the residuary estate of persons dying intestate and without husband and wife or near relatives, wreck, treasure trove, waifs and estrays, and all property and rights of a dissolved corporation, but not goods lost or designedly abandoned, the property in which is vested in the first finder and is good against all, except the true owner in the case of goods lost. Bona vacantia extends to an equity of redemption of leaseholds. The property in bona vacantia is vested in the Crown to prevent the strife and contention to which title by occupancy might otherwise give rise. (8 Halsbury's Laws (4th edn) para 1503)

If no person takes an absolute interest the Crown or the Duchy of Lancaster or the Duke of Cornwall for the time being, as the case may be, takes the intestate's residuary estate as bona vacantia, and in lieu of any right to escheat, and does so by statutory and not by prerogative right. Power is reserved to the Crown or the duchy or the Duke to provide for the intestate's dependants, whether kindred or not, and other persons for whom the intestate might reasonably have been expected to make provision, according to the existing practice. (17 Halsbury's Laws (4th edn) para 1398)

'The law as it regards the succession to intestates, dying without kindred, is stated with perfect clearness by Lyndwood, who wrote in the reign of Henry the Sixth. . . . In the case of a clerk, he states that, with certain exceptions, the Church succeeds; in case of a layman, the Crown. . . . It is the right of the Crown to "*bona vacantia*"; to property which has no other owner.' *Dyke v Walford* (1848) 5 Moo PCC 434 at 494–496, per cur.

BOND   *See also* OBLIGATION; POST OBIT

A bond is a document under seal whereby a third party guarantees the fulfilment by the contractor of the contract. (4 Halsbury's Laws (4th edn) para 1106)

An obligation, or bond, is a deed whereby the obligor obliges himself, his heir, executors, and administrators, to pay a certain sum of money to another at a day appointed. (2 Bl Com 340)

'I really have no materials for holding that in construing this English will I ought to apply to the word "bonds" . . . any other meaning than that which would be applied to the use of the word in a will made in the English language. Accordingly, I must hold that it does not include stocks the certificates of which are not under seal.' *Re Manners, Manners v Manners* [1923] 1 Ch 220 at 225, per Eve J

BOND WASHING   *See also* DIVIDEND-STRIPPING

The rules relating to sales cum-dividend . . . give rise to the device for tax avoidance popularly known as 'bond-washing'. This is countered by legislation as follows. Where the owner of securities (including stocks and shares) sells them and at the same time agrees to buy back those (or similar) securities, and as a consequence some other person receives any dividend, that dividend is deemed to be the income of the original seller, and if the dividend is paid without deduction, he may be assessed in respect thereof under Schedule D Case VI [of the Income and Corporation Taxes Act 1970, s 469]. Where a right to receive interest is sold, without the securities, the interest is deemed to be the income of the owner of the securities (whether or not chargeable to tax in the hands of the person purchasing the right) and of no other person, and if it is paid without deduction the owner may be assessed under Schedule D Case VI [of the

Income and Corporation Taxes Act 1970,
s 470]. (Simon's Taxes E1. 434)

BONUS *See also* DIVIDEND

[Trustees of a settlement were directed to pay
interest, dividends and yearly proceeds of
shares to a tenant for life, but any 'bonuses'
were to be treated as capital.] 'It is hard to lay
down any general rule as to what bonus is; but I
think, that whatever comes from an accumulated fund, which has either become too large
or else unnecessary, is a bonus; but what is
usually called so, being merely an extra dividend, is not so in reality.' *Hollis v Allan* (1866)
12 Jur NS 638 at 639, per Kindersley V-C

'I adopt the definition of "bonus" given in the
New English Dictionary, viz.: "a boon or gift
over and above what is normally due as
remuneration to the receiver, and which is
therefore, something wholly to the good".' *Re
Eddystone Marine Insurance Co* [1894] WN 30
at 30, per Stirling J

'The sole question in this case is whether or not
a bonus agreed to be paid to a seaman as
recorded in the ship's articles is to be treated as
wages, or whether it can be regarded as something apart from wages. . . . "Bonus" in such a
case as the present one is in truth nothing else
but a euphemism for "addition to wages".'
Shelford v Mosey [1917] 1 KB 154 at 158, 159,
CA, per Lord Reading CJ

'I have no doubt that the war bonuses were part
of the civilian's pay. For good and sufficient
reasons that part of pay which was intended to
remain permanently was distinguished from
that part which was granted only for a period
and was to cease when the need which occasioned it had disappeared; but it was none the
less pay. He was entitled to be paid for the time
being for his services the total amount of permanent pay and war bonuses. The term
"bonus" may, of course, be properly used to
describe payments made of grace and not as of
right. But it nevertheless may also include as
here, payments made because legally due, but
which the parties contemplate will not continue indefinitely.' *Sutton v A-G* (1923) 39 TLR
294 at 297, HL, per Lord Birkenhead

'The testator says: "I bequeath to my trustees
three hundred ordinary shares in the Lancaster
Steam Coal Collieries Ltd, upon trust to pay
the dividends, bonuses and income thereof to
the said Robert Speir of Roebank, Largs,
aforesaid and Jane Speir his wife during their
lives and during the life of the survivor". What

do those words mean, "dividends, bonuses and
income". Are they confined solely to income,
or is the use of the word "bonuses" introduced
as meaning to include a distribution of capital
as bonus? . . . Applying the rule of *ejusdem
generis*, I think the three words relate to what I
will call the income or produce of the shares. It
may be that the word "income" might be sufficient by itself, but I think the word "bonuses"
was intended by the testatrix to refer to cash
bonuses which might be distributed, as had
been done before, in addition to dividends, all
of which point to something which is in the
nature of income, and not of capital; and it is
the income or produce of the share which is
given to the tenants for life. If there be a distribution of shares as capital, then it is not
within the words of the bequest.' *Re Speir, Holt
v Speir* [1924] 1 Ch 359 at 366, 367, CA, per
Pollock MR

'This war bonus appears to me to be in every
true sense a wage. It was a flat rate and applicable to all grades for the simple reason that the
rise in the cost of living affected all grades. It
was put into a separate category of nomencla-
ture because it was regarded as something
which was not necessarily permanent, but
something which, if the war came to an end
within a reasonable time, might be expected to
disappear. Those circumstances do not appear
to me to make any difference to the true nature
of this payment. I may take an analogy, not
because it is an analogy which ought to be
followed, but because I think it helps to explain
the reasoning that appeals to me. Suppose a
company which is in the habit of maintaining,
let me say, a five per cent. dividend, earns in
one year, or perhaps in two or three years,
some exceptional profits and then proceeds to
declare a dividend of five per cent. and a bonus
of, let me say, two per cent., that bonus is just
as much a dividend as the five per cent. The
reason why the directors choose to call it a
bonus is that they want to mark it as something
which is regarded not as the company's normal
rate of dividend, but as something which may
or may not be continued on a future occasion.
Very much in the same way the parties concerned chose to treat this war bonus as something to be labelled in a particular way to show
its special character in not necessarily being
permanent.' *Picken v Balfour of Burleigh
(Lord)* [1945] 1 Ch 90 at 98, CA, per Lord
Greene MR

Canada 'A bonus may be a mere gift or gratuity as a gesture of goodwill, and not enforce-

able, or it may be something which an employee is entitled to on the happening of a condition precedent and is enforceable when the condition is fulfilled. But in both cases it is something in addition to or in excess of that which is ordinarily received.' *Great Western Garment Co Ltd v Minister of National Revenue* [1947] Ex CR 458 at 467, Ex Ct, per O'Connor J

New Zealand [The Income Tax Act 1976, s 68(2), provides for reduced rates of taxation, in certain circumstances, where any payment is made in a lump sum by way of a 'bonus', gratuity, or retiring allowance.] 'A bonus may be a gratuity or it may be something which an employee is entitled to on the happening of a condition precedent and which is enforceable when the condition is fulfilled (*Sutton v A-G* (1923) 39 TLR 294; *Great Western Garment Co v Minister of National Revenue* [1947] Ex CR 458, 467.) In either case it is an addition to regular salary or wages. It is a payment above the normal and is often, but not always, paid for extraordinary work or service. Its special character is that it is an additional amount, not part of the regular permanent remuneration.' *Inland Revenue Comrs v Smythe* [1981] 1 NZLR 673 at 676, per Richardson J

South Africa 'A bonus is after all what its name implies, a gift. It is nothing which the servant has a contractual right to obtain; it is given ex gratia in consideration of a temporary stress of circumstances, and it is intended that at most it shall not be continued longer than the circumstances remain exceptional.' *Crossley v Union Government* 1921 NPD 123

BOOK   *See also* VOLUME

'First, it is said that a stamp album is a "book", and that the loose cards are scarcely distinguishable from "books". An album probably is a book, but the question is whether the album and cards pass, with the stamps contained in them, under the bequest of "books". . . . In my opinion, the collection of stamps does not pass under the gift "books". The album in which the stamps are contained is altogether an accessory to the stamps, being merely the receptacle in which the stamps are kept. An album is a convenience for arranging and preserving the stamps; but it is the stamps which are valuable, and the album is merely the case or cover containing what is of value.' *Re Masson, Morton v Masson* (1917) 86 LJ Ch 753 at 754, CA, per Swinfen Eady LJ

[A number of original manuscript letters had been inlaid in sheets of paper, which had been bound up into three volumes.] 'I have come to the conclusion that these three volumes are books. The factors leading me to that conclusion are these: the volumes are in book form; to the outward eye they look like books, and in the ordinary course they can be, and are, handled like books. Next, I observe, that they can be used like books, in the sense that, as one turns over the sheets one can, if able to decipher the handwriting, read the various letters as a collection of letters bound up in the books. I observe further that they are not detachable letters in the ordinary sense, but have been so inserted in the sheets that they are in substance permanent parts of the volumes, unless, indeed, they should be cut out or removed by some forcible effort. On these grounds I think that I am justified in holding that the volumes do pass, under the description of books in the gift [in a will].' *Re Tomline's Will Trusts, Pretyman v Pretyman* [1931] 1 Ch 521 at 528, per Maugham J

'The minute book of the plaintiff company consists of a number of loose leaves fastened together in two covers in such a physical condition that, at any moment, if anyone wishes to do so he can take any number of leaves out and substitute any number of other leaves. It is a thing with which anyone disposed to be dishonest can easily tamper, and the question is whether such a thing is a book within the meaning of s 120 of the Companies Act 1929 [repealed; see now the Companies Act 1985, ss 382, 383]. There appears to be no authority on that point. I propose to hold that it is not, because I consider that it is most undesirable that something from which a part may be taken out or into which something else may be put should be used in evidence without the sanction of an oath as to its accuracy and without the party against whom the evidence is to be used being able to test its accuracy by cross-examination.' *Hearts of Oak Assurance Co Ltd v James Flower & Sons* [1936] 1 Ch 76 at 77, per Bennett J

(See now, however, the Companies Act 1985, s 722, under which any register, index, minute book or accounting records, may be kept, subject to reasonable safeguards being employed.]

Canada 'It becomes important . . . to decide whether the transfer books kept by [the transfer agent and registrar of an Ontario company's capital stock at Toronto and the registrar of the company's stock at Toronto] . . . and the register of shareholders kept by [the registrar at Toronto and the company's additional registrar and transfer agent at Buffalo] . . . are legally the books of the company. I am unable to see any objection to the proposition. It is part of the transfer agents' and registrars' job to keep these books. They get paid for keeping them by the company, and they are surely the company's books in just the same way as a book of account kept by a salaried accountant is a book of the company.' *Williams v R* [1940] 3 DLR 73 at 76, Ont CA, per McTague JA; affd [1942] AC 541

BOOK DEBTS

'By "book debts", the Legislature [in the Bankruptcy Act 1861, s 137 (repealed; see now the Insolvency Act 1986, s 344)] doubtless intended to describe debts in some way connected with the trade of the bankrupt. . . . "Book debts" of the bankrupt . . . mean all debts contracted with him in the course of his trade. . . . To constitute the debt a "book debt", it cannot to my mind be necessary that the transaction should be entered in a book.' *Shipley v Marshall* (1863) 14 CBNS 566 at 570, 571, per Erle CJ

'They must be such debts as are commonly entered in books.' Ibid at 573, per Byles J

'The expression "all book debts owing to me" [used by a testator in a bequest] . . . may be argued to include the bank balance, but those words really appear to mean debts which are due to the business and which, in the ordinary course of business, would pass through the business ledgers.' *Re Haighs' Estate, Haigh v Haigh* (1907) 51 Sol Jo 343 at 343, per Parker J

'*Shipley v Marshall* [supra], I think, establishes that, if it can be said of a debt arising in the course of a business and due or growing due to the proprietor of that business that such a debt would or could in the ordinary course of such a business be entered in well-kept books relating to that business, that debt can properly be called a book debt whether it is in fact entered in the books of the business or not.' *Independent Automatic Sales Ltd v Knowles and Foster* [1962] 3 All ER 27 at 34, per Buckley J

Australia 'It [ie the phrase "book debts" in a definition "chattels shall include book debts"] points to debts owing to a business, of a kind usually entered in books of account of the business and in fact so entered." *Robertson v Grigg* (1932) 47 CLR 257 at 266, per Gavan Duffy CJ and Starke J

New Zealand [The owner of a business agreed to sell it, together with the stock, 'book debts', and goodwill thereof.] 'Book debts include all such as are entered, or even usually entered, in the account books of the vendor. . . . The phrase "book or other debts" is a usual phrase in assignments of businesses . . . because "book debts" have a limited signification. The phrase would not include "cash at bankers". . . . A bill left at a banker's, not actually discounted, may be treated as a book debt.' *Stanley Stamp Co v Brodie* (1914) 34 NZLR 129 at 148, 149, per Stout CJ; also reported 17 GLR 328 at 332

New Zealand 'In my view it is at least established on the common authority of *Independent Automatic Sales* [*v Knowles & Foster*, supra] and *Paul & Frank Ltd* [*v Discount Bank (Overseas) Ltd* [1966] 2 All ER 922] that any debt in existence at the time of the creation of a charge is properly classified as a "book debt", even though it may not be due and payable at the date of the charge.' *Contemporary Cottages v Margin Traders* [1981] 2 NZLR 114 at 129, per Thorp J

BOOK OF COMMON PRAYER

. . . 'the Book of Common Prayer' means the Book annexed to the Act of Uniformity 1662 and entitled 'The Book of Common Prayer and Administration of the Sacraments and other Rites and Ceremonies of the Church according to the use of the Church of England together with the Psalter or Psalms of David pointed as they are to be sung or said in Churches and the Form and Manner of Making Ordaining and Consecrating Bishops, Priests and Deacons' as altered by any enactment passed before the passing of this Measure. (Prayer Book (Versions of the Bible) Measure 1965, s 1(4))

BOOKMAKER

'Bookmaker' means any person other than the Totalisator Board who—
(a) whether on his own account or as servant or agent to any other person, carries on, whether occasionally or regularly, the business of receiving or negotiating bets or conducting pool betting operations; or
(b) by way of business in any manner holds himself out, or permits himself to be held

out, as a person who receives or negotiates bets or conducts such operations,
so, however, that a person shall not be deemed to be a bookmaker by reason only of the fact—
(i) that he carries on, or is employed in, sponsored pool betting business; or
(ii) that he operates, or is employed in operating a totalisator;
and the expression 'bookmaking' shall be construed accordingly. (Betting, Gaming and Lotteries Act 1963, s 55)

'Those who back horses are for the most part members of the general public; those with whom the horses are backed, that is, those who lay the odds against the different horses, are known as "bookmakers", and no doubt attend at all race-meetings with the primary object of carrying on their business of betting.' *Powell v Kempton Park Racecourse Co Ltd* [1899] AC 143 at 195, per Lord James of Hereford

'A bookmaker is a person who carries on the business of receiving or negotiating bets. It matters not whether he carries on that business on his own account or as servant or agent to any other person, and it matters not whether he carries on that business in any of those capacities occasionally or regularly. He is in any of those events a bookmaker.' *Lake v Cronin, Hunt v Cronin* [1929] 1 KB 31 at 36, per Lord Hewart CJ

New Zealand 'The acts constituting the offence are admitted, but they only constitute an offence when done by a bookmaker. By s 2 of the Gaming Act 1908, a person who acts as a bookmaker is within the definition. Here the appellant, when he made the bets, made an entry in a book. That is of itself a significant circumstance, but it is not the only circumstance. The Magistrate was entitled to group together all the facts in order to determine whether what may be called the status of bookmaker was made out. The fact of a stranger asking the appellant for so much on each of the named horses, just as he might ask a trader for some known commodity, shows that he assumed that he was dealing with a person who treated betting as a matter of business, and the fact that this was at once agreed to at least tended to confirm this assumption or belief. To ask for "10s on Square Deal and 10s on Retana" is not the form in which friends make proposals for casual bets, or in which a stranger usually approaches another man even if he wants to bet with him. Then the appellant took the £1, and Doull paid it to him as a matter of course. That is usual in such cases, but by no

means usual where private bets are made, in which case, if one shows less trust than the other, the stake is deposited with a third party. The mere fact that Doull was able to conclude two distinct bets in one transaction gives that transaction an air of business. Further, there is the significant conversation in which appellant said that "he was not paying out that day". "Paying out" means something slightly different from paying in the simple case, and is a term appropriate to such a business as this.' *Weston v Cummings* [1916] NZLR 460 at 462, per Chapman J; also reported [1916] GLR 362 at 363

Northern Ireland 'Bookmaker' means any person who, whether on his own account or as servant or agent of any other person, carries on, whether occasionally or regularly, the business of receiving or negotiating bets, or who in any manner holds himself out, or permits himself to be held out in any manner, as a person carrying on such business, and the expression 'bookmaking' shall be construed accordingly. (Betting and Lotteries Act (Northern Ireland) 1957, s 20)

BOOTY

Prize differs from booty in that prize is taken by a maritime force and booty by a land force. There is, however, a species of booty which consists of goods belonging to the enemy state or to a public trading company of the enemy exercising powers of government which are taken in a fortress or possession on land. Booty may also be a ship taken in waters defended by or belonging to a fortress or possession. In respect of these things a British prize court has jurisdiction as if they were captured at sea. (37 Halsbury's Laws (4th edn) para 1305

BORN   See also ALIVE; LIVING

'Inasmuch as it is adopted as a rule of construction that a child *en ventre sa mere* is within the intention of a gift to children living at the death of a testator, because plainly within the reason and motive of the gift; so a child *en ventre sa mere* is to be considered within the intention of a gift to children born in the life-time of a testator, because it is equally within the reason and motive of the gift.' *Trower v Butts* (1823) 1 Sim & St 181 at 184, 185 per Leach V-C

'With respect to the birth, the being born must mean that the whole body is brought into the world; and it is not sufficient that the child respires in the progress of the birth. Whether the child was born alive or not depends mainly upon the evidence of the medical men. None of them say that the child was born alive; they only say that it had breathed.' *R v Poulton* (1832) 5 C & P 329 at 330, per Littledale J

'I think that no greater force can be given to the words "already or hereafter to be born" than to the words "born or hereafter to be born" (without the word "already"), or to other like expressions which from the time of Lord Coke to this day have been held to mean children living at the testator's death to the exclusion of such as may have previously died.' *Woodhouse v Herrick* (1855) 1 K & J 352 at 360, per Page Wood V-C

'The fiction or indulgence of the law which treats the unborn child as actually born applies only for the purpose of enabling the unborn child to take a benefit which, if born, it would be entitled to. . . . Reference is made by the testatrix to the time when the youngest of the children of her three nephews and nieces who shall have been born and living at the time of her decease, shall arrive at the age of twenty-one years; and this reference is made for the purpose of putting an end on that event to a trust for accumulation, and the words, therefore, are descriptive only of a natural event, that is, the coming of age of the youngest of the children who were born and living at the death of the testatrix, in which description the word "born" must have its natural, and not its fictitious legal interpretation. . . . Inasmuch therefore as the words in question are used for the purpose only of ascertaining a period of time, and are *not* a description of children as objects of a bequest or trust, I am of opinion that the words "born and living at the time of my decease" do not include children *in utero*.' *Blasson v Blasson* (1864) 2 De G J & Sm 665 at 670, 671, per Lord Westbury LC

'It can scarcely be contended that the words "born in my lifetime" are terms of art, or that the word "born" does not in its natural and common import mean "brought forth".' *Villar v Gilbey* [1907] AC 139 at 147, per Lord Atkinson

'Whatever may be the meaning of the word "born" in ordinary parlance, a rule of construction has been established which was stated forty-four years ago by Mr Vaughan Hawkins, in my opinion with absolute accuracy, in his admirable treatise on wills, in these terms (p 79): "Rule, A devise or bequest to children 'born' or to children 'living' at a given period,

includes a child *en ventre* at that period and born afterward".' *Re Salaman, De Pass v Sonnenthal* [1908] 1 Ch 4 at 8, CA, per Farwell LJ

BORROW

'Borrowing necessarily implies repayment at some time and under some circumstances.' *Re Southern Brazilian Rio Grande Do Sul Rly Co Ltd* [1905] 2 Ch 78 at 83, per Buckley J

'The words "borrow" and "lend" are not words of narrow legal meaning. They represent a transaction well known to business people which has taken its place in the law as a result of commercial transactions among the merchants of this country, and when the law, under the Bills of Exchange Act or elsewhere, has to deal with matters of this kind, it is dealing with commercial transactions.' *Inland Revenue Comrs v Rowntree & Co Ltd* [1948] 1 All ER 482 at 486, CA, per Tucker LJ

'It seems to me that this case brings out very well that there are two ways at least (there may be more) of raising money. One is by borrowing it and the other is by discounting a bill of exchange. They are both quite well known methods. One is borrowing and the other is discounting a bill. The fact that in many cases they produce the same result of providing financial resources for carrying on a business does not mean that the words which are apt to describe one must be construed as covering the other.' Ibid at 487, per Somervell LJ

BORROWER

Australia 'The words "the borrower" are, in my view, apt and intended to describe or denote the party to whom . . . money is lent, whether that party consists of one person or several persons. They mean, I think, the person or persons, as the case may be, who borrow. In the case of a loan to one person, that person, and in the case of a loan to several persons, those persons. Each of those persons may be said to be "a borrower", but "the borrower" is all of them. Accordingly, in my opinion, where a loan is made to several, the note or memorandum of the contract is not signed by the borrower and the contract for repayment is unenforceable unless it is signed by each of those persons.' *Deposit & Investment Co Ltd v Greenaway* [1969] VR 714 at 718, per Little J

BOTTLE

'Bottle' means a bottle jar or other similar container. (London County Council (General Powers) Act 1957, s 81(7)).

Australia ' "Bottle" is an ordinary English word. Reference to a dictionary (Standard Dictionary) shows that it means a vessel for holding, carrying and pouring liquids, having a neck and narrow mouth that can be stopped. There is no difficulty in ascertaining the meaning of the common word "bottle". . . . The meaning of the word, as already stated, is clear enough, but there may be difficulties in applying it. There are vessels such as demijohns and other vessels with necks or spouts as to which there might be doubt and room for argument whether they should be regarded, as bottles.' *Bendixen v Coleman, Scott and Croft* (1943) 68 CLR 401 at 416, per Latham CJ

BOTTOMRY

The master has authority in circumstances of unforeseen necessity or distress to pledge the ship and freight to raise the necessary funds for the voyage by a contract called 'bottomry', the bottom or keel of the ship being figuratively used to express the whole body of the ship.

There is no settled form for the bottomry contract. It has usually taken the form of a bond by which the master states the occasion for resorting to bottomry and pledges himself, the ship and freight, and sometimes the cargo, for the repayment of the principal and interest on the safe arrival of the ship at the end of her voyage on such conditions as to risk as may be agreed upon. Where the cargo alone is hypothecated, the instrument is called a respondentia bond. Bottomry and respondentia are obsolete in practice. (43 Halsbury's Laws (4th edn) para 198)

'To have a good contract of bottomry you must have a loan with repayment conditional upon safe arrival—ie you must have a voyage the sea risk of which is to be run by the lender. Lord Stowell in *The Atlas* [(1827) 2 Hag Adm 48 at 58] said: "The definition of bottomry bonds which I find in all the writers that have adverted to the subject, are contracts in the nature of mortgages of a ship on which the owner borrows money to enable him to fit out the ship, or to purchase a cargo for a voyage proposed, and pledges the keel or bottom of the ship, *pars pro toto*, as a security for repayment. It is moreover stipulated, that if the ship is lost

in the course of the voyage, by any of the perils enumerated in the contract, the lender also shall lose his money".' *The James W Elwell* [1921] P 351 at 366, per Hill J

BOUNDARY

A boundary is an imaginary line which marks the confines or line of division of two contiguous parcels of land. The term is also used to denote the physical objects by reference to which the line of division is described as well as the line of division itself. In this sense boundaries may be classified as natural and artificial, according to whether or not such physical objects are man-made.

For the purposes of the Building Regulations 1972 'boundary' is specially defined so that in relation to a building the term means the boundary of the land belonging to the building and such land is deemed to include any abutting part of any street, canal or river, but only up to the centre line thereof.

Boundaries are fixed either (1) by proved acts of the respective owners, or (2) by statutes or by orders of the authorities having jurisdiction, or (3), in the absence of such acts, statutes, or orders, by legal presumption. (4 Halsbury's Laws (4th edn) para 831)

BOYCOTT

Australia 'The word "boycott" has acquired a signification which is now generally recognised in common speech. It connotes a concerted withdrawal of intercourse of some kind. Manifestly no exhaustive definition can be formulated, but, without attempting that, it may be said that the intercourse withdrawn may be of a social, commercial, professional or industrial nature, and may be with reference to a person or his property or his employees or any of his interests. A boycott does not connote a pre-existing contractual relation: it means withdrawal from such intercourse as would naturally and reasonably be expected to take place between the parties concerned as members of the com.nunity in normal circumstances.' *R v Archdall & Roskruge, ex p Carrigan & Brown* (1928) 41 CLR 128 at 136, per Knox CJ and Isaacs, Gavan Duffy and Powers JJ

BRAND

'I do not think a brand is something that is to be burnt into . . . goods. I do not think a brand is omething that is to be stamped on goods. I see no reason why a brand should not be woven nto the goods just as much as stamped on to hem or burnt into them.' *Pirie (Alexander) & Sons v Goodall* [1892] 1 Ch 35 at 41, per Vaughan Williams J

BREACH OF CONTRACT

'Breach of contract occurs where that which is complained of is a breach of duty arising out of the obligations undertaken by the contract.' *Jarvis v Moy, Davies, Smith, Vandervell & Co* [1936] 1 KB 399 at 404, 405, CA, per Greer LJ

BREACH OF DUTY

[The Law Reform (Limitation of Actions, etc) Act 1954, s 2(1) (repealed; see now the Limitation Act 1980, s 11) reduced to three years the period of limitation for actions for damages for negligence, nuisance or 'breach of duty'.] 'The tort of "negligence" is firmly established. So is the tort of "nuisance". These are given by the legislature as signposts. Then these are followed by words of the most comprehensive description: "Actions for breach of duty (whether the duty exists by virtue of a contract or of a provision made by or under a statute or independently of any contract or any such provision)." Those words seem to me to cover not only a breach of a contractual duty, or a statutory duty, but also a breach of any duty under the law of tort. Our whole law of tort today proceeds on the footing that there is a duty owed by every man not to injure his neighbour in a way forbidden by law. Negligence is a breach of such a duty. So is nuisance. So is trespass to the person. So is false imprisonment, malicious prosecution or defamation of character. Professor Winfield indeed defined "tortious liability" by saying that it "arises from the breach of a duty primarily fixed by law; this duty is towards persons generally and its breach is redressable by an action of unliquidated damages"; see Winfield on Tort [(8th edn) p 2]. In my judgment, therefore, the words "breach of duty" are wide enough to comprehend the cause of action for trespass to the person as well as negligence.' *Letang v Cooper* [1964] 2 All ER 929 at 933, CA, per Lord Denning MR; also reported [1965] 1 QB 232

BREACH OF THE PEACE

'Breach of the peace consists in such acts as will reasonably produce alarm in the minds of the lieges—not necessarily alarm in the sense of personal fear, but such alarm as causes them to believe that what is being done causes or will cause real disturbance to the community and the breaking-up of the peace of the neighbourhood.' *Ferguson v Carnochan* (1889) 2 White 278 at 281, per the Lord Justice-Clerk (Macdonald)

'There is a breach of the peace whenever a person who is lawfully carrying out his work is unlawfully and physically prevented by another from doing it.' *R v Chief Constable of Devon & Cornwall Constabulary, ex p Central Electricity Generating Board* [1981] 3 All ER 826 at 832, per Lord Denning MR

'A comprehensive definition of the term "breach of the peace" has very rarely been formulated so far as we have been able . . . to discover from cases which go as far back as the eighteenth century. The older cases are of considerable interest but they are not a sure guide to what the term is understood to mean today, since keeping the peace in this country in the latter half of the twentieth century presents formidable problems which bear on the evolving process of the development of this branch of the common law. Nevertheless, even in these days when affrays, riotous behaviour and other disturbances happen all too frequently, we cannot accept that there can be a breach of the peace unless there has been an act done or threatened to be done which either actually harms a person, or in his presence his property, or is likely to cause such harm, or which puts someone in fear of such harm being done. There is nothing more likely to arouse resentment and anger in him, and a desire to take instant revenge, than attacks or threatened attacks on a person's body or property. In 11 Halsbury's Laws (4th edn) para 108, it is stated: "For the purpose of the common law powers of arrest without warrant, a breach of the peace arises where there is an actual assault, or where public alarm and excitement are caused by a person's wrongful act. Mere annoyance and disturbance or insults to a person or abusive language, or great heat and fury without personal violence, are not generally sufficient". . . . The statement in Halsbury's Laws of England is in parts, we think, inaccurate because of its failure to relate all the kinds of behaviour there mentioned to violence. Furthermore, we think the word "disturbance" when used in isolation cannot constitute a breach of the peace. We are emboldened to say that there is a breach of the peace whenever harm is actually done or is likely to be done to a person or in his presence to his property or a person is in fear of being so harmed through an assault, an affray, a riot, an unlawful assembly or other disturbance. It is for this breach of the peace when done in his presence or the reasonable apprehension of it taking place that a constable, or anyone else, may arrest an offender without warrant.' *R v Howell* [1981] 3 All ER 383 at 388, 389, CA, per cur.

BREAK   *See also* BURGLARY; FORCIBLE ENTRY

New Zealand   [The accused was convicted of 'breaking' and entering a shop by opening a casement window hinged at the top and fitted with a casement stay which enabled the window to be latched in a number of fixed positions. He had inserted his hand through the partially-opened window and unlatched the stay and then opened the window sufficiently to enable him to enter.] 'We are of opinion that the words "to break any part internal or external of a building", which appear in the first part of the statutory definition of the words "to break" [in the Crimes Act 1908, s 271 (repealed); see now Crimes Act 1961 (NZ), s 240] are to be construed as including any act which would have constituted an actual breaking at common law. . . . In our opinion, there is no sensible or logical distinction between a latched window which has a hole in the glass and a window held in a near-closed position by a fastening leaving a small opening. In both cases the aperture was one which allowed the entering of the hand to undo the fastening or unlatch the stay. Herein lay the breaking. The act of unlatching is itself within the concept of breaking as known to the common law. . . . We are of the clear opinion that if a door were held in a partially open position by a hook (such as is commonly done in the case of the door of a ship's cabin) the unlatching of the door by lifting the hook from its eye would be as much a breaking in law as would the unlatching of the same door from its fully closed position. Similarly, the unlatching of the window in the present case, in our opinion, must constitute a breaking. It is the unlatching of the hook or latch which constitutes the breaking and brings the operation within the first part of the statutory definition.' *R v Parry* [1957] NZLR 847 at 847–849, CA, per cur.

BREAKAGE

'If these words [in a plate-glass policy] "breakage during removal" be read as meaning any breakage during the time of removal, then any damage done by anyone during that time would be within the exception. I think, however, that that is not the ordinary or grammatical construction of the words, and I think that they should be read as meaning breakage by some accident from, or incident to, the removal.' *Marsden v City & County Assurance Co* (1865) 35 LJCP 60 at 64, per Willes J

BREAKDOWN

'Article 12 [of a charterparty] . . . prescribes that the hire is to cease when, inter alia, there is a breakdown of machinery. . . . I entirely agree with the Lord Ordinary in holding that the words "a breakdown of machinery" must be construed in a popular and reasonable sense, and that in such sense the vessel broke down when a defect was discovered which rendered it necessary in the opinion of a prudent navigator that she should proceed to a harbour for repairs. This does not mean . . . that the question of when there is a breakdown is made to depend entirely upon the opinion of the master. The master's opinion is, of course, of great value as a piece of evidence, but should it turn out that that opinion was wrong, it may be corrected by other evidence in any particular case.' *Giertsen v Turnbull & Co* 1908 SC 1101 at 1110, 1111, per Lord Ardwall

Australia   [A machinery insurance policy indemnified the insured against damage to an ore crushing mill resulting from 'breakdown'. 'Breakdown' was defined to mean the 'actual breaking' of any part of a machine whilst the machine was in use from either mechanical or electrical defects in the machine causing sudden stoppage of the functions thereof and necessitating repair or replacement before it could resume working.] 'Counsel for the plaintiffs drew a distinction between something which was cracked and something which was broken and relied heavily on the use in the definition of the word "actual" before the word "breaking" as emphasising the need for there to be a fracture. . . . In my opinion "actual breaking" includes a fracturing of the part in fact as opposed to an absence of fracturing.' *Sun Alliance & London Insurance Group v NW Iron Co Ltd* [1974] 2 NSWLR 625 at 628, 629, NSWSC, per Sheppard J

BREAKDOWN OF MARRIAGE

The court hearing a petition for divorce shall not hold the marriage to have broken down irretrievably unless the petitioner satisfies the court of one or more of the following facts, that is to say (a) that the respondent has committed adultery and the petitioner finds it intolerable to live with the respondent; (b) that the respondent has behaved in such a way that the petitioner cannot reasonably be expected to live with the respondent; (c) that the respondent has deserted the petitioner for a continuous period of at least two years immediately preceding the presentation of the petition; (d) that the parties to the marriage have lived apart for a continuous period of at least two years immediately preceding the presentation of the petition . . . and the respondent consents to a decree being granted; (e) that the parties to the marriage have lived apart for a continuous period of at least five years immediately preceding the presentation of the petition. (Matrimonial Causes Act 1973, s 1(2))

BREATH TEST

'Breath test' means a preliminary test for the purpose of obtaining, by means of a device of a type approved by the Secretary of State, an indication whether the proportion of alcohol in a person's breath or blood is likely to exceed the prescribed limit. (Road Traffic Act 1972, s 12(1), substituted by the Transport Act 1981, s 25, Sch 8)

'It does not follow that a test carried out for the purpose stated in the definition [in the Road Safety Act 1967, s 7(1) (repealed; see supra)] and with a device of the approved type will fail to be a "breath test" within the meaning of the Act merely because there is not perfect compliance with the instructions. The more rational view is that such a test is a "breath test" although carried out imperfectly. There may well be an implication that the test must be carried out with reasonable competence, or with such accuracy as is reasonably attainable in the circumstances. For practical purposes that differs very little from the requirement, which can be derived directly from the words of the definition, that the test must be carried out by the constable genuinely for the purpose of obtaining a true indication. A test which is carried out negligently may well be rejected as not constituting a "breath test" within the meaning of the Act. . . . My opinion is that

there is not in this Act any absolute requirement, express or implied, that a test in order to be a "breath test" within the meaning of the Act must be carried out in perfect compliance with the maker's instructions. There is an express requirement that the test must be carried out for the purpose of obtaining an indication of the proportion of alcohol in the blood, and it follows that the police officer must be trying to use the device correctly in order to obtain a true indication. I think also that there probably is an implied requirement (not adding much for practical purposes to the express requirement) that the test must be carried out with such accuracy as is reasonably attainable in the circumstances.' *Director of Public Prosecutions v Carey* [1969] 3 All ER 1662 at 1673, 1674, HL, per Lord Pearson

BRIBE

New Zealand 'It seems to us that the words [in sub-s 117(b) of the Crimes Act 1961] "attempts to influence by . . . bribes" must be read, in the context which the other subsections furnish, as including the offer of a bribe. What was done in this case—the unsuccessful offer of a bribe—seems to us to have been one of the very things which this subsection was intended to penalise.' *Munro v R* [1971] NZLR 122 at 124, CA, per Turner J

BRIBERY

A bribe or secret commission is a profit or benefit received by the agent from the third person with whom the agent is dealing on his principal's behalf without the knowledge or consent of the principal, or which was not contemplated by the principal at the creation of the agency. (1 Halsbury's Laws (4th edn) para 791)

Bribery at a parliamentary or local election was, and still is, an offence at common law as well as a statutory offence, and as such punishable on indictment by fine or imprisonment. Wherever a person is bound by law to act without any view to his own private emolument, and another by a corrupt contract engages him on condition of the payment or promise of money or other lucrative consideration to act in a manner which he is to prescribe, both parties are by such contract guilty of bribery at common law. (15 Halsbury's Laws (4th edn) para 767)

(1) A person shall be guilty of a corrupt practice if he is guilty of bribery.

(2) A person shall be guilty of bribery if he, directly or indirectly, by himself or by any other person on his behalf—

(a) gives any money or procures any office to or for any voter or to or for any other person on behalf of any voter or to or for any other person in order to induce any voter to vote or refrain from voting, or

(b) corruptly does any such act as mentioned above on account of any voter having voted or refrained from voting, or

(c) makes any such gift or procurement as mentioned above to or for any person in order to induce that person to procure, or endeavour to procure, the return of any person at an election or the vote of any voter,

or if upon or in consequence of any such gift or procurement as mentioned above he procures or engages, promises or endeavours to procure the return of any person at an election or the vote of any voter.

For the purposes of this subsection—

(i) references to giving money include references to giving, lending, agreeing to give or lend, offering, promising, or promising to procure or endeavour to procure any money or valuable consideration; and

(ii) references to procuring any office include references to giving, procuring, agreeing to give or procure, offering, promising, or promising to procure or to endeavour to procure any office, place or employment.

(3) A person shall be guilty of bribery if he advances or pays or causes to be paid any money to or for the use of any other person with the intent that that money or any part of it shall be expended in bribery at any election or knowingly pays or causes to be paid any money to any person in discharge or repayment of any money wholly or in part expended in bribery at any election.

(4) The foregoing provisions of this section shall not extend or be construed to extend to any money paid or agreed to be paid for or on account of any legal expenses incurred in good faith at or concerning an election.

(5) A voter shall be guilty of bribery if before or during an election he directly or indirectly by himself or by any other person on his behalf receives, agrees, or contracts for any money, gift, loan or valuable consideration, office, place or employment for himself or for any other person for voting or agreeing to vote or for refraining or agreeing to refrain from voting.

(6) A person shall be guilty of bribery if after an election he directly or indirectly by himself or by any other person on his behalf receives any money or valuable consideration on account of any person having voted or refrained from voting or having induced any other person to vote or refrain from voting.

(7) In this section the expression 'voter' includes any person who has or claims to have a right to vote.

(Representation of the People Act 1983, s 113)

'Bribery is the giving of money . . . for a vote. . . . There is nothing about corruption in it. It does not apply to the mind of the man who offers or the mind of the man who takes. It condescends upon the fact of giving money to the man to vote.' *Bradford Case (No 2), Storey & Garnett v Forster* (1869) 19 LT 723 at 726, per Martin B

'There are two ways in which a candidate, or his agent, may be guilty of bribery in the distribution of charitable tickets: First, by the giving of them to individuals, coupled with a request for their vote, in which case the offence falls within the same principle as any other direct bribery which is procured by the giving of money, or anything else which is valuable to the recipient. . . . Another . . . mode of bribing by the distribution of charitable tickets is by giving them dishonestly and colourably on a large scale, and without due consideration of the need of the persons to whom they are given, so that the proper inference to be drawn from the conduct of the giver is that his motive was not that of true charity, but of corrupting the minds of the recipients and inducing them to support him in his election; and this might well be so, although there was no selection of voters only, and even if a large proportion of those to whom the tickets were given were non-voters. . . . Indeed, such a course of conduct would amount to bribery at common law, apart from the recent statutes, and is probably more mischievous and invidious than the buying of a vote by money.' *St. George's Division, Tower Hamlets Case, Benn v Marks* (1896) 5 O'M & H 89 at 93, per Pollock B

'Without attempting an exhaustive definition I

may say that the following is one statement of what constitutes a bribe. If a gift be made to a confidential agent with the view of inducing the agent to act in favour of the donor in relation to transactions between the donor and the agent's principal and that gift is secret as between the donor and the agent—that is to say, without the knowledge and consent of the principal—then the gift is a bribe in the view of the law.' *Hovenden & Sons v Millhoff* (1900) 83 LT 41 at 43, per Romer LJ

'There is a clear distinction between bribery and treating. In cases of bribery there is always something in the nature of a contract. "If you give me a sovereign I will give you a vote", or some such understanding, but treating is an entirely different matter. In treating it is not necessary that the person treated should belong to the opposite party, whereas it is of no use to give money to a man who is going to vote for you already, the money must be given to the other side in order to draw another vote.' *Bodmin Division, Cornwall Case, Tom & Duff v Agar-Robartes* (1906) 5 O'M & H 225 at 231, per Lawrance J

'For the purposes of the civil law a bribe means the payment of a secret commission, which only means (i) that the person making the payment makes it to the agent of the other person with whom he is dealing; (ii) that he makes it to that person knowing that that person is acting as the agent of the other person with whom he is dealing; and (iii) that he fails to disclose to the other person with whom he is dealing that he has made that payment to the person whom he knows to be the other person's agent. Those three are the only elements necessary to constitute the payment of a secret commission or bribe for civil purposes.' *Industries & General Mortgage Co Ltd v Lewis* [1949] 2 All ER 573 at 575, per Slade J

South Africa 'Bribery . . . is the unlawful and intentional taking or giving, or procuring the taking or giving, of any money or valuable consideration; or office, place or employment; or gift, loan or promise of such, or of an advance of money; for the performance or non-performance of any public duty, or for false judgment or evidence, or for the performance of some unjust or illegal act.' *State v Aaron H 146*; 10 CLJ 238

South Africa 'Bribery implies a voluntary gift; extortion implies at least a transfer of property induced by illegitimate pressure upon

the transferor.' *R v Muller* 1934 NPD at 146 per Matthews AJP

BRIDGE *See also* ROAD

'Bridge' includes the abutments of a bridge and any land adjacent to a bridge or the abutments thereof which is held by the Council or the corporation (as the case may be) either alone or jointly with any other person for purposes connected with the management maintenance repair or renewal of that bridge. (London County Council (General Powers) Act 1949, s 31)

'Bridge' does not include a culvert, but, save as aforesaid, means a bridge or viaduct which is part of a highway, and includes the abutments and any other part of a bridge but not the highway carried thereby. (Highways Act 1980, s 329(1))

'The want of parapets does not prevent a structure from being a bridge, nor does the mere fact of an arch passing over a stream necessarily make it a bridge.' *R v Whitney (Inhabitants)* (1835) 3 Ad & El 69 at 71, per Lord Denman CJ

'The apparatus in question [a floating bridge] conveys passengers over the river instead of the river being passed over by them: it is more in the nature of a steam ferry boat than a bridge. It does not afford a continuous means of transit for passengers across the river; the passage is only made after certain intervals of time. and during those intervals passengers must be content to wait. There is a broad distinction between such a means of transit and a bridge, which is a permanent structure and may be traversed at all times.' *Ward v Gray* (1865) 6 B & S 345 at 351, per Cockburn CJ

Canada 'In early times a bridge was probably thought of as a structure crossing water but it now seems clear that the meaning is much broader. . . . In these times, particularly in large cities and densely populated areas, it has become necessary to carry highways or other roadways over railway lines, streets and even buildings.' *Re Colhoun and East Kildonan (City)* (1959) 27 WWR 529 at 541, Man QB, per Williams CJQB; affd, 29 WWR 71, Man CA

Whether approaches part of bridge

'The . . . point . . . is whether the duty of widening a bridge imposed . . . upon a railway company by s 51 of the Railway Clauses Act 1845 [repealed], relates to the entire structure erected to carry a road over a railway, or relates only to that part of it which actually crosses the railway line. . . . The word "bridge" in s 51 means that part of the structure within the points of crossing or intersection.' *Rhondda Urban Council v Taff Vale Rly Co* [1909] AC 253 at 258, 260, per Lord Loreburn LC

'The word "bridge" as used in this section [of a private Act], includes the approaches of the bridge on either side thereof.' *A-G & Derbyshire County Council v Midland Rly Co* (1908) 99 LT 961 at 964, per Parker J; affd (1909) 100 LT 866, CA

Whether roadway over bridge is part

'The appellants . . . admit their continuing liability to repair and maintain both approaches and bridge. . . . They seek, however, to discriminate between the road or the surface of the road and the approaches and bridge. . . . I can see no ground for such a discrimination. . . . The railway company would not be maintaining the bridge in the true sense of that word if the substructure were sound but the road were to be so founderous as to be impassable. . . . I find in the speech of Lord Herschell [in *Lancashire & Yorkshire Rly Co v Bury Corpn* (1889) 14 App Cas 417] very strong confirmation of the view that a road over a bridge is naturally spoken of and considered as part of the bridge and that an obligation to maintain a bridge contained in such an Act as we are now considering [Great North of England Railway Act 1837], whether it is express or implied, would naturally extend to the road without which the bridge itself would be useless.' *London & North Eastern Rly Co v North Riding of Yorkshire County Council* [1936] AC 365 at 383, per Lord Maugham

Whether supporting piers part

'I cannot follow why, when one is talking of a "bridge", one shall put out of the definition the piers which carry the bridge. When the Public Health Act 1875 [s 4; repealed], includes a bridge within the definition of "street", it seems to me that the piers which support the surface of the highway over which the public pass and repass are as much a part of the bridge and as much included in the word "bridge" as the surface over which the public pass.' *Regent's Canal & Docks Co v Gibbons* [1925] 1 KB 81 at 85, per Swift J

BRIDLEWAY

'Bridleway' means a way over which the public have the following, but no other, rights of way, that is to say, a right of way on foot and a right of way on horseback or leading a horse, with or without a right to drive animals of any description along the way. (Road Traffic Act 1972, s 196(1); Road Traffic Regulation Act 1984, s 142(1))

[A similar definition, using the word 'highway' instead of 'way', is to be found in the Highways Act 1980, s 329(1).]

BRINE PUMPER

'Brine pumper' means a person or company who pumps or raises brine from shafts, wells, springs, or mines. (Brine Pumping (Compensation for Subsidence) Act 1891, s 52)

BRITANNIA   *See* STERLING

BRING

New Zealand   'I think it is apparent that the bringing of an appeal is a process which involves more than just the lodging of the notice of motion referred to in s 72(1) [of the Magistrates' Courts Act 1947 (repealed; see now the District Courts Act 1947, s 72)]. The appellant is required also to serve a duplicate upon other parties affected (sub-s (3)), and to lodge a further duplicate with the Registrar of the court appealed from (sub-s (6)). Each of these latter requirements is to be complied with "either before or immediately after the notice of motion is lodged". These words suggest strongly that compliance with those requirements is an integral part of the process of bringing an appeal. Not until they have all been complied with can the appeal be said to have been "brought".' *Clouston v Motor Sales (Dunedin) Ltd* [1973] 1 NZLR 542 at 543, per Quilliam J

BRITISH ISLANDS

'British Islands' means the United Kingdom, the Channel Islands, and the Isle of Man. (Interpretation Act 1978, Sch 1)

BRITISH OWNED

'British-owned', in relation to a fishing boat, means owned by a person who is (within the meaning of the Merchant Shipping Act 1894) a person qualified to own a British ship, or owned by two or more persons any one of whom is (within the meaning of that Act) a person so qualified. (Sea Fish (Conservation) Act 1967, s 22(1))

BRITISH POSSESSION

'British possession' means any colony, plantation, island, territory, or settlement within Her Majesty's dominions, and not within the United Kingdom, the Channel Islands, and Isle of Man; and all colonies, plantations, islands, territories, and settlements under one legislature, as herein-after defined, are deemed to be one British possession (Extradition Act 1870, s 26)

'British possession' means any part of Her Majesty's dominions outside the United Kingdom, and where parts of such dominions are under both a central and a local legislature, all parts under the central legislature are deemed, for the purposes of this definition, to be one British possession. (Interpretation Act 1978, Sch 1)

. . . 'British possession' means any part of His Majesty's dominions exclusive of the United Kingdom, and, where parts of those dominions are under both a central and a local legislature, shall include both all parts under the central legislature and each part under a local Legislature. (Evidence (Colonial Statutes) Act 1907, s 1(3))

New Zealand 'The Commonwealth of Australia is a British possession for the purposes of Part II of the Fugitive Offenders Act 1881 (Imp).' *Godwin v Walker* [1938] NZLR 712 at 743, CA, per Kennedy J; also reported [1938] GLR 405 at 417

BRITISH SHIP

'By this Order in Council [dated April 15, 1854] it is declared . . . "no British vessel shall . . . be permitted to enter any port . . . in the possession or occupation of her Majesty's enemies". . . . What is the definition or true meaning of the words "British vessels"? First, all vessels properly so called according to our municipal law. Secondly, all vessels under the British flag, though perhaps not strictly entitled thereto, because, by the Law of Nations, the carrying the British flag stamps on them, as to other nations, the British national character. And thirdly, such words may mean,

though this is a much more doubtful point, vessels under neutral flags but owned by British subjects.' *The Ionian Ships* (1855) 2 Ecc & Ad 212 at 224, per Dr Lushington

'The point . . . is this—was the ship British or not? I agree that its sailing under the British flag, coupled with the fact that the owner resided in London, amounted to prima facie evidence that the ship was British. Here, however, there is proof that the owner was an alien; and the mere fact that an alien is resident in London does not make him a British subject. Such a person merely owes a temporary allegiance to the British Crown so long as he remains in this country; and it would be absurd to say that the temporary residence of an alien in this country made his ship a part of the British territory.' *R v Bjornsen* (1865) Le & Ca 545 at 566, CCR, per Blackburn J

'The whole backbone of Mr Carter's argument proceeded upon the proposition that it had been laid down by judges in passages which have been quoted, that a British ship on the high seas was part of the United Kingdom. I do not think, for the reasons that have been given, that those judges intended to lay down any such proposition. I think that what they said was only meant as a picturesque illustration of the principle that the jurisdiction of our courts does apply to British ships on the high seas. In this connection it might be just as well to refer to an opinion of the great Lord Stowell, which is quoted in a footnote on page 304 of Hall's International Law, 8th edn, cited to us by the Solicitor-General, in which these words occur: "the great and fundamental principle of British maritime jurisprudence is, that ships upon the high seas compose no part of the territory of a state. The surrender of this principle would be a vital surrender of the belligerent rights of this country". I need not go into the question whether principles of international law march side by side with those of criminal law, but that certainly is a very striking statement from one of the greatest men who ever declared the law in this country, and does not encourage one in the view that any judge has ever intended to lay down that a British ship on the high seas was a piece of England.' *R v Gordon-Finlayson, ex p An Officer* [1941] 1 KB 171 at 189, 190, per Oliver J

See, generally, 43 Halsbury's Laws (4th edn) para 119.

BRITISH STANDARD TIME   *See* TIME

BROADCAST *See also* TELEVISION
BROADCAST

In this Act 'broadcasting by means of wireless telegraphy' means publication for general reception by means of wireless telegraphy within the meaning of the Wireless Telegraphy Act 1949, and 'broadcast by means of wireless telegraphy' shall be construed accordingly. (Defamation Act 1952, s 16)

'Broadcast' means broadcast by wireless telegraphy (within the meaning of the Wireless Telegraphy Act 1949), whether by way of sound broadcasting or of television. (Dramatic and Musical Performers' Protection Act 1958, s 8(1))

'Broadcast' means a broadcast by wireless telegraphy of sounds or visual images intended for general reception (whether the sounds or images are actually received by any person or not), but does not include a broadcast consisting in a message or signal sent in connection with navigation or for the purpose of securing safety. (Marine, &c, Broadcasting (Offences) Act 1967, s 9)

In this section 'broadcast' means broadcast by wireless telegraphy sounds or visual images intended for general reception. (Magistrates' Courts Act 1980, s 8(10))

BROADCAST RELAY STATION

'Broadcast relay station' means a station for the re-transmission by cable or wire, to the customers of the persons maintaining the station, of broadcast programmes which those persons receive either by cable or wire or by wireless from the persons who broadcast the programmes. (Broadcasting Act 1981, s 63(1))

BROKER *See also* FACTOR

A broker is a mercantile agent who in the ordinary course of his business is employed to make contracts for the purchase or sale of property or goods of which he is not entrusted with the possession or documents of title. (1 Halsbury's Laws (4th edn) para 712)

A broker for sale is an agent whose business it is to find buyers for those who wish to sell, and sellers for those who wish to buy, and to negotiate and superintend the making of the bargain between them. His duty is to establish privity of contract between the seller and the buyer. (41 Halsbury's Laws (4th edn) para 647)

'Broker' means a member of The Stock Exchange who carries on his business in the United Kingdom and is not a jobber. (Income and Corporation Taxes Act 1970, s 477(6), substituted by the Finance Act 1973, s 54, Sch 21, para 8)

'A factor, who has the possession of goods, differs materially from a broker. The former is a person to whom goods are sent or consigned, and he has not only the possession, but, in consequence of its being usual to advance money upon them, has also a special property in them, and a general lien upon them. When, therefore, he sells in his own name, it is within the scope of his authority; and it may be right therefore that the principal should be bound by the consequences of such sale; amongst which, the right of setting off a debt due from the factor is one. But the case of a broker is different; he has not the possession of the goods, and so the vendee cannot be deceived by that circumstance; and besides, the employing of a person to sell goods as a broker does not authorise him to sell in his own name. If therefore he sells in his own name, he acts beyond the scope of his authority, and his principal is not bound. But it is said, that by these means, the broker would be enabled by his principal to deceive innocent persons. The answer, however, is obvious, that that cannot be so unless the principal delivers over to him the possession and indicia of property.' *Baring v Corrie* (1818) 2 B & Ald 137 at 148, per Holroyd J

'The Law Dictionary defines brokers to be "those that contrive, make, and conclude bargains and contracts between merchants and tradesmen, for which they have a fee or reward".' *Milford v Hughes* (1846) 16 M & W 174 at 177, per Alderson B

'To make it a case of brokerage, it must relate to goods and money, and not merely to personal contracts for work and labour.' Ibid at 177, per Rolfe B

'There is no doubt a broker cannot sue; he has no authority to sell in his own name, or to receive the money, and has nothing to do with the goods. This is so laid down in Story on Agency, ss 28–34, 109:—"To use the brief but expressive language of an eminent judge, 'a broker is one who makes a bargain for another and receives a commission for so doing'. Properly speaking, a broker is a mere negotiator between the other parties, and he never acts in his own name, but in the names of those who employ him. When he is employed to buy or sell goods, he is not entrusted with the custody or possession of them, and is not authorised to buy or to sell them in his own name" (s 28). "So, a broker has ordinarily no authority *virtute officii*, to receive payment for property sold by him" (s 109).' *Fairlie v Fenton* (1870) LR 5 Exch 169 at 172, per Cleasby B

United States 'Broker' means a person engaged for all or part of his time in the business of buying and selling securities, who in the transaction concerned acts for, buys a security from, or sells a security to, a customer. (Uniform Commercial Code 1978, s 8–303)

United States The term 'broker' means any person engaged in the business of effecting transactions in securities for the account of others, but does not include a bank. (Securities Exchange Act of 1934, s 3(a)(4))

BROTHEL   *See also* DISORDERLY HOUSE

'A brothel is the same thing as a "bawdy house"—a term which has a well-known meaning as used by lawyers and in Acts of Parliament. In its legal acceptation it applies to a place resorted to by persons of both sexes for the purpose of prostitution. It is certainly not applicable to . . . this case, where one woman receives a number of men.' *Singleton v Ellison* [1895] 1 QB 607 at 608, per Wills J

'It is clear that premises cannot be regarded as a brothel if they are used by only one woman.' *Strath v Foxon* [1955] 3 All ER 398 at 400, per cur.; see also [1956] 1 QB 67

'At common law, a brothel was the same thing as a bawdy house. The further definition of what is involved in a bawdy house or a brothel has been variously stated in the cases. Sometimes it is stated as a place to which persons of both sexes resort for the purpose of prostitution; sometimes it is referred to as a place used by persons of both sexes for the purposes of prostitution. The form of indictment for keeping a bawdy house was referred to by Avory J in *Caldwell v Leech* [[1911–13] All ER Rep 703], where he said this: "It is only necessary to look at the form of indictment against a person for keeping a bawdy house, which has been in force from time immemorial, where we find the words: 'Did keep and maintain a certain house and in the said house for filthy lucre and gain divers evil-disposed persons, women as well as men, upon the times and days aforesaid as well as in the night as in the day

unlawfully and wickedly did receive and entertain', etc." It certainly contemplates there that women, in the plural, will use the premises. In 1930, in *Winter v Woolfe* [[1931] 1 KB 549], Avory J was again dealing with the word "brothel", and he there approved a definition given by Grove J in *R v Holland, Lincolnshire JJ* [(1882) 46 JP 312]. In *Winter v Woolfe*, Avory J said: "I am content to accept the definition of a brothel given by Grove J and Lopes J in *R v Holland, Lincolnshire JJ*. Grove J said: 'The sole question is whether there was any evidence to support this conviction before the justices for permitting these licensed premises to be a brothel. . . . I do not think that the matter of nuisance is of any importance, for it is too well known that these places are often kept in such a way as to be no nuisance at all, but kept perfectly private. But what needs only to be proved is this, namely, that the premises were kept knowingly for the purpose of people having illicit sexual connexion there'." Lopes J said: "Now the sole question before the justices was whether the applicant permitted his premises to be a brothel. What is the meaning of permitting the premises to be a brothel? I think my brother Grove has given a very apt definition, namely, that it is permitting people of opposite sexes to come there and have illicit sexual intercourse. That is a very complete and satisfactory definition of the whole matter." Accordingly, it would seem clear that, before premises can be said to be a brothel, people of both sexes, in the plural, must go there.' *Gorman v Standen* [1963] 3 All ER 627 at 630, 631, per Lord Parker CJ; also reported in [1964] 1 QB 294 at 301

'When premises . . . are being used by more than one prostitute for the purposes of her trade, the question whether those premises or part thereof are being used as a brothel is in each case of course a question of fact to be deduced from the circumstances as a whole. The mere fact that individual rooms in that house or in the relevant part of it were originally let under separate tenancies and let to separate women with their own Yale keys, does not of itself preclude a court from holding that the whole or part of the house is a brothel. Nor does the mere fact that the original lettings of those rooms were independently effected itself preclude the court from so finding on the aggregate of facts before it; nor before such a finding can be made is it necessary in every case to establish that the original independent lettings were effected as a subterfuge to escape the consequences of the relevant section. . . .

There is indeed a class of separate independent tenancies in which I go further, when, as here, considering cases arising under the second part of s 34 [of the Sexual Offences Act 1956]. I have in mind the class where in a single house individual rooms occupied by common prostitutes and used by them for their trade are sufficiently close to each other to constitute in effect what might be called a nest of prostitutes, be that nest large or small. In that particular class of case, the fact that the rooms were originally the subject of independent lettings for exclusive occupation may be of no weight at all, though in other types of cases the fact that there were independent lettings may be of considerable weight. In what might be called the "nest" type of cases, the result may well be the same whether technically the prostitute is occupying the room as a lodger, as a tenant or without making any payment at all.' *Donovan v Gavin* [1965] 2 All ER 611 at 612, per Sachs J

'A brothel is . . . constituted where the women (for there must be more than one woman) do not charge for sexual intercourse. . . . It is not essential that there be evidence that normal sexual intercourse is provided in the premises. It is sufficient to prove that more than one woman offers herself as a participant in physical acts of indecency for the sexual gratification of men.' *Kelly v Purvis* [1983] 1 All ER 525 at 528, 529, per cur.

Australia 'Premises to which women and men resort for the purpose of arranging intercourse for money elsewhere constitute a brothel, because that resorting is for the purpose of prostitution according to the generally accepted meaning of that word. It matters not that some of the men who resorted to the premises of the respondent went there only to obtain company for an evening.' *Samuels v Bosch* [1972–73] ALR 595 at 598, per Menzies J

New Zealand 'The Crown's case is that the use of the appellant's premises for prostitution was habitual. To prove that, it is not necessary to show that every room was used for the illicit purpose or that the same room or set of rooms had been used continuously. It is sufficient to prove such user of the premises or any part of them for the purposes of prostitution as to justify the inference that the premises or the part thereof in question were used habitually for such purpose.' *Wright v Brady* [1943] NZLR 38 at 40, per Smith J; also reported [1942] GLR 463 at 464

South Africa 'The ordinary and accepted meaning of the term brothel includes a place kept or used for the purposes of prostitution; a place where people of opposite sex are permitted to come habitually for the purpose of illicit sexual intercourse. Before it can be said that a person keeps a brothel it is essential to find that the keeper of the place had knowledge of the prostitution being practised there.' *R v de Bruyn* 1957(4) SA 411 C, per Rosenow AJ

BROTHER

'Brother' includes a brother of the half blood. (Marriage Act 1949, s 78)

'Now the words "children" and "brother" and other words indicating relationship, when used in a will, refer prima facie to a relationship traced through a legitimate tie. There are, however, numerous authorities to be found in the books, so well known that I need not refer to them by name, in which a testator has shown in his will with sufficient clearness that by such a word as "children" or other words denoting relationship, he means to indicate or include persons claiming through other than a legitimate tie. If in the present case Lady Cullum [the testatrix] knew that William Hanford Flood was her illegitimate brother, it is clear that she has used the word "brother" in other than its prima facie meaning.' *Re Cullum, Mercer v Flood* [1924] 1 Ch 540 at 544, per Romer J

BUILDING   *See also* AGRICULTURAL BUILDING; COMMERCIAL BUILDING; CONSTRUCTION; INDUSTRIAL BUILDING OR STRUCTURE

The expression 'building' includes any temporary or movable building. (Open Spaces Act 1906, s 20)

The expression 'building' means any building erection structure or hoarding (whether permanent or temporary) other than a boundary wall or fence. (Green Belt (London and Home Counties) Act 1938, s 2)

'Building' includes any structure or erection and any part of a building as so defined, but does not include plant or machinery comprised in a building. (Land Compensation Act 1961, s 39; Town and Country Planning Act 1971, s 290(1))

'Building' includes a wall. (Highways Act 1980, s 188(9))

The word 'building' for the purposes of (a) Part

I [building regulations] of this Act, and (b) any other enactment (whether or not contained in this Act) that relates to building regulations or that mentions 'buildings' or 'a building' in a context from which it appears that those expressions are there intended to have the same meaning as in Part I of this Act, means any permanent or temporary building, and, unless the context otherwise requires, it includes any other structure or erection of whatever kind or nature (whether permanent or temporary). (Building Act 1984, s 121(1))

'Building' includes any part of a building. (Agricultural Holdings Act 1986, s 96)

'What is a "building"? Now, the verb "to build" is often used in a wider sense than the substantive "building". Thus, a ship or a barge-builder is said to build a ship or a barge, a coach-builder is said to build a carriage; so, birds are said to build nests; but neither of these when constructed can be called a "building". . . . The imperfection of human language renders it not only difficult, but absolutely impossible, to define the word "building" with any approach to accuracy. One may say of this or that structure, this or that is not a building; but no general definition can be given; and our lexicographers do not attempt it. Without, therefore, presuming to do what others have failed to do, I may venture to suggest, that, by a "building" is usually understood a structure of considerable size, and intended to be permanent, or at least to endure for a considerable time. A church, whether constructed of iron or wood, undoubtedly is a building. So, a "cow-house" or "stable" has been held to be a building the occupation of which as tenant entitles the party to be registered as a voter. . . . On the other hand, it is equally clear that a bird-cage is not a building, neither is a wig-box, or a dog-kennel, or a hen-coop—the very value of these things being their portability.' *Stevens v Gourley* (1859) 7 CBNS 99 at 112, 113, per Byles J

'A small kennel for a lap dog could not be called a building. But it is a question of degree, and in this case we come to a structure 9 feet long, 7 feet high, 3 feet wide, erected some 30 feet in front of the line of street, and roofed in and fastened securely to the ground, intended to be used by a person inside, and not easily carried away. . . . A structure like that may properly be called a building.' *Brown v Leicester Corpn* (1892) 57 JP 70 at 71, per Pollock B

'In s 3 of the [Disused Burial Grounds] Act of 1884 the erection of any buildings upon a disused burial ground is forbidden except for the purpose of enlarging a church. I think the word "buildings" there means erections which would cover some part of the ground, as the enlargement of a church would do. It does not refer to something in the nature of a fence or barrier to prevent the acquisition of prescriptive rights to light.' *Boyce v Paddington Borough Council* [1903] 1 Ch 109 at 116, 117, per Buckley, J; reversed on appeal [1903] 2 Ch 556 CA; restored on appeal *sub nom. Paddington Corpn v A-G* [1906] AC 1

'I by no means affirm that in every contract a hoarding is a building, but this hoarding [which was of a permanent nature, 156 feet long and 15 feet high] is, I think, a building within these conditions [not to erect any building for the carrying on of, inter alia, any offensive trade]. It is a building erected for the purpose of the trade of bill-posting.' *Nussey v Provincial Bill Posting Co & Eddison* [1909] 1 Ch 734 at 738, CA, per Buckley LJ

'Here we have a work of an artificial character [a subway] constructed by man and constituting the result of the putting together of bricks and mortar, steel, and concrete, available for a variety of uses including use as a passage from one side of the road to the other. I cannot entertain any doubt that this is a building.' *Schweder v Worthing Gas Light & Coke Co* [1912] 1 Ch 83 at 88, 89, per Eve J

'No doubt, a building is something different from that which is ordinarily called a house, but . . . can anybody say that this canal is a building which, though not a house in the ordinary sense, is in the nature of a house? It is perfectly true that the undertaking as a whole comprises a number of structures which may be "buildings" according to the true construction of the Act of Parliament; but is the undertaking of the canal one "building" within the meaning of the Act? In my opinion it is nothing of the kind.' *Regent's Canal and Dock Co v London County Council* [1912] 1 Ch 583 at 590, per Warrington J

[The Housing of the Working Classes Act 1890, s 38 (repealed; see now Housing Act 1985, s 284) enabled local authorities to demolish any 'building', although not in itself unfit for human habitation, if it was so situate as to be an obstructive building.] 'Counsel for the plaintiffs relies strongly on the parenthetical phrase at the beginning of the section, "although not in itself unfit for human habitation", as an indication that the words "any building" ought not to be read in their widest sense, but ought to be limited to buildings capable of being used for human habitation, that is to say, as equivalent to the words "any dwelling-house". . . . The expression "any building" is wide enough to cover buildings of all descriptions, dwelling-houses, manufactories, places of worship, and even statues and monuments, and in my opinion all these come within the section.' *Jackson v Knutsford Urban Council* [1914] 2 Ch 686 at 692, 695, per Eve J

'I think that the word "buildings" in relation to a farm means in s 25(2) of the Finance (1909–10) Act 1910 [repealed], what one would ordinarily call farm buildings. If one were to say "this farm has very excellent buildings upon it", nobody conversant with farming language would suppose that one was talking about the stone walls which we have to consider in the present case, which run over the country to divide the fields, and also to shelter the sheep. I therefore do not think they are buildings. . . . These walls cannot be said to be either appurtenant to farm buildings or used in connection with them merely because the sheep shelter by them.' *Morrison v Inland Revenue Comrs* [1915] 1 KB 716, at 722–724, per Rowlatt J

[A private Act provided that a municipal corporation, should not use any 'building' for the performance of variety entertainments.] 'Luxmoore J was wrong . . . in holding that the bandstand, where variety entertainments were provided, was not a "building". This structure was undoubtedly a building.' *A-G v Eastbourne Corpn* (1934) 78 Sol Jo 633 at 633, CA, per Lord Hanworth MR

[The occupier of a piece of land constructed thereon a model village, a toy railway, a miniature racecourse, and other features.] 'On the question whether these model houses are buildings, I do not feel any doubt. By s 119(1) of the [Town and Country Planning] Act of 1947 [repealed; see now the Town and Country Planning Act 1971, s 290(1)] the expression "building" includes a structure or erection. As these models are constructed of stone and brick on concrete bases, I cannot say that they are not structures merely because they are small. . . . If a small building, or a little model house of brick or stone, is put up, it is none the less a building whether it is two feet high and one foot wide or four feet high and two feet wide. Similarly, I cannot see how it can make any difference if it is made of wood, provided it is there as a fixture and is intended to be part of

the exhibition.' *Buckinghamshire County Council v Callingham* [1951] 2 All ER 822 at 828, per Lord Goddard CJ; affd. [1952] 1 All ER 1166, CA

[A coal hopper and conveyor were erected by a coal merchant. Both were on wheels and neither was attached to the ground. Enforcement notices, requiring the removal of the equipment were served by the local planning authority under the Town and Country Planning Act 1947, s 23 (repealed).] 'Counsel for the planning authority has said that, owing to the very wide definition of "building" in s 119(1) of the Town and Country Planning Act 1947 [repealed; see supra] each of these pieces of equipment constitutes a building, and, if that is right, I should have thought that it would be abundantly clear that their erection would be a building operation. However, approaching the matter as I do, it seems to me that when the Act defines a building as including "any structure or erection and any part of a building so defined", the Act is referring to any structure or erection which can be said to form part of the realty, and to change the physical character of the land.' *Cheshire County Council v Woodward* [1962] 1 All ER 517 at 519, per Lord Parker CJ

Australia [The Criminal Law Consolidation Act 1935–1986 (SA), s 170(2) provides that in charges of breaking and entering any building, 'building' includes any dwelling house.] 'There can be no doubt that a flat, portion of a building, is, when separately occupied, a dwelling house. Whether a structure whilst in course of erection is a "building" within the meaning of the section is a question of fact. See *R v Manning* [(1871) LR 1 CCR 338 at 341] in which the legislation was similar, Lush J said: "A building need not necessarily be a completed structure".' *R v Andrews* [1943] SASR 44 at 46, per cur.

Australia [Under a covenant, no 'building' of whatever nature was to be erected. A tennis court with a fence was here held not to be a 'building' within the meaning of the covenant.] 'I shall deal first with the ordinary meaning of the word "building". Although popularly it refers to a house, its ordinary meaning, I think, is wider than this; but I think that in its ordinary meaning, it at least involves the concept of a structure with a roof and a support for that roof. It is true to say that the word is defined in the Shorter Oxford Dictionary as a structure or edifice, but I do not think that it can thereby be suggested that every structure is a building, although obviously every building is a structure. The second word in the definition, namely "edifice", refers, of course, to a large or formal building and every building is not such an edifice. I do not think that a single word as a synonym for the word "building" is available in the language, and it is necessary therefore to regard the word in terms of the concept. To me the ordinary concept is, as I have said, a structure of which the main feature is probably the existence of some form of roof. I do not think that a bridge is ordinarily described as a building, nor a built-up road, despite the use in that context of the past tense of the verb "to build". I do not think that a telegraph post or a wireless aerial would ordinarily be described as a building, nor do I think that a fence would ordinarily be so described.' *Hilderbrandt v Stephen* [1964] NSWR 740 at 742, 743, per Jacobs J

Canada 'A building is a structure which is designed for use as a habitation or other purposes of occupation, or for the storage of commodities. While the definition given in the Century Dictionary refers to user of the structure in general terms, it seems to the Commission that the author did not intend the scope of that definition to be extended to include machinery or equipment. In none of the judicial decisions affecting the word "building" has it been suggested that the meaning of the word can be extended in this fashion. . . . Dryers and kilns used in the manufacture of bricks . . . are not buildings.' *Re Dominion Fire Brick & Clay Products Ltd & Elmsthorpe Rural Muncipality* [1940] 3 WWR 139 at 143, per Assessment Commission.

Canada [The issue was whether a structure 'built' around a noisy shredder to muffle sound was exempt from municipal taxes under the Assessment Act, RSO 1980, c 31, s 3, para 17, as being machinery.] 'We start with two words in the Act, "building" and "machinery". The task of the tribunal is to decide, in the light of all of the circumstances of the case, whether the item comes within one word or the other. Admittedly "machinery" in today's scientific and technocratic world can properly be applied to things undreamed of when the word first entered the Assessment Act. "Building", however, is an ordinary English word, and in this statute should be given the meaning an ordinary person would attribute to it. What we have in this case *looks* like a building. It is

almost identical to its neighbouring structure, which is admittedly a building. It is *built* like a building. It is *used* like a building. Nothing takes place in it or on it of a mechanical or chemical nature independently of and distinct from the various machines that it encloses. The only reasonable conclusion, in my view, is that it *is* a building. It is therefore real property and not exempt from taxation.' *Metals & Alloys Co Ltd v Regional Assessment Commissioner, Region No 11* (1985) 49 OR (2d) 289 at 306, Ont CA, per Arnup JA

New Zealand 'What is a building must always be a question of fact and degree. Modern building practice suggests that a great variety of shapes, designs and types of structure may be regarded as buildings. Single dwelling-houses may be at one end of the scale, and large multi-storey structures containing a great number of flats at the other. In between them are semi-detached units and terraced houses in which individual units share common walls although separated from each other by fences, garages or in some other way.' *Spencer v Soljan* (1984) 10 NZPTA 289 at 291, per McMullin J

South Africa 'A building may not require masonry, but the word implies some degree of trouble, skill and elaboration in fixing or removing the structure.' *Ex p Greef* 24 SC 524 per Villiers CJ

In bye-laws

'The word "building" prima facie means every structure that could in any sense be called a building, even if erected for a mere temporary purpose.' *Fielding v Rhyl Improvement Comrs* (1878) 3 CPD 272 at 278, per Denman J

In Income Tax Acts

[The question was whether paddocks, lawns and enclosures attached to a racecourse came within the Income Tax Act 1918, Sch B, r 1 (repealed), which enacted that there should not be charged under Sch B any 'building' occupied for the purpose of carrying on a trade or profession.] 'I think the most that could be said would be that "building" must cover adjuncts, that is to say, a courtyard or something necessarily used in connection with the building. . . . The Commissioners, I think, failed to observe, that anything outside the four walls of the building that was to come within the exemption, must be an adjunct to the building. . . . Here I think one has only to look at the facts to see at once that the lawns and enclosures cannot possibly be regarded as adjuncts of the buildings.' *Smith v York Race Committee* [1934] 1 KB 517 at 523, per Finlay J

In Prescription Act 1832

'Obviously a timber yard is not a building, though the timber yard may be used for the storing of timber, for the exhibition of timber for sale, and for the sale thereof. . . . The structure of the plaintiffs is something more than a mere timber yard. It is a structure, but every structure obviously is not a building. . . . Its construction may be generally stated in this way; there are large upright baulks of timber and there are cross-beams. There are besides, floors, above that, in some parts at any rate, there are coverings which serve as a roof. . . . In this place the timber is stacked, is stored, is dried, exhibited for sale and sold. . . . It appears to me to be an important matter for consideration in this case that the structure is not enclosed. . . . There are no windows in the common and ordinary acceptation of the term. . . . There is no glass. That again is not decisive. The structure is not of stone, nor of brick. That again to my mind is not decisive, because I should, as at present advised, not, hesitate to say that a structure of iron, wood and glass completely enclosed, or for the great part enclosed, would be within the Act. . . . A structure like the Crystal Palace would, I think, be a building within this Act. . . . I have come to the conclusion that this is a structure, but not a building within s 3 of the Prescription Act.' *Harris v De Pinna* (1886) 33 Ch D 238 at 246, 249, per Chitty J; affirmed on appeal on another point.

[The Prescription Act 1832, s 3 enacts that where the access and use of light to and for any dwelling-house, workshop, or other 'building' has been actually enjoyed therewith for twenty (now twenty-seven) years without interruption, the right thereto will be deemed absolute unless the same was enjoyed by consent or agreement.] 'Is . . . a greenhouse a "building" within the Prescription Act, that is to say, a building requiring access of light for the ordinary purposes for which light is required. You require light for a dwelling-house, workshop or other building. You require it equally for a studio or picture-gallery, that is to say, for a building not being a dwelling-house or workshop. What Chitty J's judgment in *Harris v De Pinna* [supra] shows is that when a building is of such a character that access of light is of importance to it, it is in fact a "building", and that therefore the Legislature

intended that there should be protection for that light if it has been enjoyed for an uninterrupted period of twenty years. . . . Now here we have a greenhouse. If it were a studio—either an ordinary studio, or a photographic studio, or a picture-gallery—detached from the house, it would be a "building". If it were a conservatory attached to the house, it would be part of a building. It is difficult to say more than that this is a building. . . . The question of what constitutes a building within the Prescription Act came before me in *A-G v Queen Anne Garden and Mansions Co* [(1889) 60 LT 759], the case of the Guards' Chapel. I had to consider whether a chapel was such a "building": and I had no doubt in my mind that a chapel was a "building" within the Act. So, in my opinion, would be any erection which was being used for an assemblage of individuals, though not for sleeping and living there, such as a lecture room.' *Clifford v Holt* [1899] 1 Ch 698 at 702, per Kekewich J

In restrictive covenant

'I think it is quite impossible, prima facie at least, to say that a viaduct is not a building, and the covenant [by a railway company not to erect any building exceeding a specified height] extends to any building; therefore, independently of any context in the deed controlling the effect of the word "building", it would be clear that there is a breach of the covenant.' *Lloyd v London, Chatham & Dover Rly Co* (1865) 2 De GJ & Sm 568 at 575, per Turner LJ

'The question I have to consider is, whether in building a wall the defendant has committed a breach of the covenant . . . that "no buildings except dwelling-houses to front . . . shall be erected or built on" the property. Now the word "buildings" is perhaps an ambiguous expression, and certainly in its ordinary way it does not signify a wall. I certainly think that the repairing or reinstating of buildings would include the repairing or reinstating of a garden wall, or of a wall enclosing or defining some portion of a field. . . . I observe that in *Child v Douglas* [(1854) Kay 560] the word "building" was held to apply to the erection of a very high wall rising to some fifteen feet. . . . In this case . . . the lower portion of the wall is 8 ft 6 in high which is not an unusual or improper height. . . . I am of opinion that such a wall as this, built bona fide as a boundary of a garden, is quite . . . proper and justifiable.' *Bowes v Law* (1870) LR 9 Eq 636 at 641, 642, per James V-C

Obstructive building

In this Part [which gives local authorities power to order demolition of obstructive buildings] the expression 'obstructive building' means a building which, by reason only of its contact with, or proximity to, other buildings, is dangerous or injurious to health. (Housing Act 1985, s 283(1))

Public building

[A local Act provided for the rating and assessment of halls, chapels, meeting houses, etc, and other 'public buildings'.] 'I cannot help thinking that the true construction of the words "public buildings" is "not private buildings", because public buildings are to be assessed upon a different scale from private buildings. . . . An hospital is as much a public building as a public school, which no one has a right to enter but the scholars, governors, and those who have the privilege of sending scholars. So also, with respect to almshouses, it is not the whole world who are permitted to enter, but only the occupants, and those who subscribe to the charity. It is clear, however, that the statute treats almshouses as public buildings, for it excepts from the rate thereby imposed certain almshouses, which would therefore have to be assessed as private buildings.' *Bedford Infirmary (Governors) v Bedford Comrs* (1852) 7 Exch 768 at 774, 775, per Alderson B

School buildings

In this Act the expression 'school buildings', in relation to any school, means any building or part of a building forming part of the school premises, except that it does not include any building or part of a building required only (a) as a caretaker's dwelling; (b) for use in connection with playing fields; (c) for affording facilities for enabling the Secretary of State to carry out the functions conferred on him by paragraph (a) of section 5(1) of the National Health Service Act 1977 and Schedule 1 to that Act; or (d) for affording facilities for providing milk, meals or other refreshment for pupils in attendance at the school . . . (Education Act 1946, s 4, as amended)

BUILDING CONTRACT

'A building contract means a contract for the building of anything—not necessarily a house, but any other physical construction.' *Carlisle Rural Council v Carlisle Corpn* [1909] 1 KB 471 at 483, CA, per Buckley LJ

BUILDING LEASE   *See* LEASE

BUILDING OPERATION

'Building operation' means the construction, structural alteration, repair or maintenance of a building (including re-pointing, redecoration and external cleaning of the structure), the demolition of a building, and the preparation for, and laying the foundation of, an intended building, but does not include any operation which is a work of engineering construction within the meaning of this Act. (Factories Act 1961, s 176)

'Building operations' includes rebuilding operations, structural alterations of or additions to buildings, and other operations normally undertaken by a person carrying on business as a builder. (Town and Country Planning Act 1971, s 290(1))

[The Town and Country Planning Act 1971, s 45(4) provides times within which a planning permission can be revoked where the permission either relates to the carrying out of building or other 'operations', or where it relates to a change of use.] 'It seems to me that . . . "operations" comprises activities which result in some physical alteration to the land, which has some degree of permanence to the land itself, whereas . . . "use" comprises activities which are done in, alongside or on the land but do not interfere with the actual physical characteristics of the land.' *Parkes v Secretary of State for the Environment* [1979] 1 All ER 211 at 213, CA, per Lord Denning MR

BUILDING PURPOSES

[The Lands Clauses Consolidation Act 1845, s 128, provides that before the promoters of the undertaking dispose of any superfluous lands they shall, unless such lands be situate within a town, or be lands built upon or used for 'building purposes', first offer to sell the same to the person then entitled to the lands (if any) from which the same were originally severed.] 'When we read the two phrases together, "land built on", "or used for building purposes", it must be clear that the words "used for building purposes" do not mean what is ordinarily called "building land" . . . it is not because you think that certain land might be applicable for building purposes, and may be very suitable for those purposes, and may be sold for those purposes, that it comes within either the meaning or the spirit of the words "land used for building purposes", by which, I apprehend, is meant land actually used for building purposes; not land contemplated to be used for building purposes, or intended to be used for building purposes, or thoroughly suitable for building purposes.' *London & South Western Rly Co (Directors, etc) v Blackmore* (1870) LR 4 HL 610 at 616, 617, per Lord Hatherley LC

BUILDING SOCIETY

A society may be established under this Act if its purpose or principal purpose is that of raising, primarily by the subscriptions of the members, a stock or fund for making to them advances secured on land for their residential use. (Building Societies Act 1986, s 5(1))

[By the Building Societies Act 1986, s 119(1) a 'building society' is a building society incorporated (or deemed to be incorporated) under the Act.]

'Every man entering into a society of this description knows that its primary purpose is to enable all those who are at the time, or may become, subscribers, to raise a fund out of which they shall be able to make purchases of land and buildings; and that the mode of doing this is by means of advantageous investments on which they are empowered to lay out the money subscribed, principally with their own members.' *Armitage v Walker* (1855) 2 K & J 211 at 220, 221, per Page Wood V-C

'There is in my opinion a great distinction between a freehold land society and a benefit building society. A freehold land society buys land with the funds contributed by the members of the society, and then divides it amongst them; but a benefit building society advances to its borrowing members money derived from the subscriptions, and which the borrowing members themselves lay out in the purchase of lands or buildings, and then mortgage them to the society.' *Grimes v Harrison* (1859) 26 Beav 435 at 441, per Romilly MR

BULK

'In my view, the ordinary meaning of the words "the bulk" is "the greater part" and I see no reason for giving them any other meaning in this will. Nor do I see any reason to doubt that, in the context in which they occur, they mean the greater part in value. If the testatrix had been referring to land and nothing but land, there might have been some doubt whether she

meant the greater part in acreage or the greater part in value, but she is referring to an estate which may be "in any manner altered in the way of addition substitution diminution or otherwise", so that the subject-matter may consist partly of land, partly of money or investments, and partly of chattels settled to devolve as heirlooms. When the phrase "the bulk" is applied to such a subject-matter, I can give it no other meaning than "the greater part in value".' *Bromley v Tryon* [1951] 2 All ER 1058 at 1067, 1068, HL, per Lord Morton of Henryton

BULL

'Bull' includes any cow, bullock, heifer, calf, steer or ox. (Protection of Animals Act 1911, s 15)

BUNGALOW

'The only question I have to determine is what is the meaning of the word "bungalow". . . . It is not an ordinary English word. It is an Indian word, or rather a word of Indian derivation, and is obviously used in this conveyance as indicating a building which has some particular architectural features. It is a word of art; and I must find out its meaning from the evidence of persons acquainted with that art. . . . The defendant's experts have . . . given a definition which I accept—namely that a bungalow is a building of which the walls, with the exception of any gables, are no higher than the ground floor, and of which the roof starts at a point substantially not higher than the top of the wall of the ground floor, and that it does not matter in what way the space in the roof of the building so constructed is used.' *Ward v Paterson* [1929] 2 Ch 396 at 397–399, per Romer J

BUOY

'Buoys and beacons' includes all other marks and signs of the sea. (Merchant Shipping Act 1894, s 742)

BURDEN

'For the purpose of restricting the speed of certain vehicles the Road Traffic Act 1930, Sch 1 [see now Road Traffic Regulation Act 1984, Sch 6], divides vehicles into three large classes, each of which has its own special divisions. This vehicle [built in the form of a van and containing a sound-recording apparatus, which could not be disconnected from the vehicle, and a block of batteries which were never removed from the vehicle except for recharging] was said to be a goods vehicle within that schedule: that is to say, it came within the class of vehicles constructed or adapted to the conveyance of goods or burden of any description. Was not this vehicle carrying a burden of some description? It obviously was. When one comes to the ascertainment of the *quantum* of the load for other purposes, s 2(4)(b) says that where there is an apparatus essentially of a permanent character, that apparatus is not to be treated as part of the load. But it does not follow that it is not a burden. It manifestly is a burden. The vehicle was constructed to carry not passengers but a burden.' *Birmingham v Lindsell* [1936] 2 All ER 159 at 160, per Lord Hewart CJ

United States 'Burden of establishing' a fact means the burden of persuading the triers of fact that the existence of the fact is more probable than its non-existence. (Uniform Commercial Code 1978, s 1–201(8))

BURDEN OF PROOF

Australia 'The expression "burden" or "onus" of proof, "As applied to judicial proceedings . . . has two distinct and frequently confused meanings: (1) the burden of proof as a matter of law and pleading—the burden, as it has been called, of *establishing a case*, whether by preponderance of evidence, or beyond a reasonable doubt; and (2) the burden of proof in the sense of *introducing evidence*" [Phipson on Evidence (10th edn) paragraph 92]. This is a proposition which has been frequently acknowledged: see e.g. *Fitzpatrick v Walter E. Cooper Pty Ltd* [(1935) 54 CLR 200 at 218; [1936] ALR 29] and *Mummery v Irvings Pty Ltd* [(1956) 96 CLR 99 at 118 *et seq.*; [1956] ALR 795]. The position is, we think, correctly stated by the learned author of the work to which we have referred when he says: ". . . the burden of proof in the first sense is always stable, the burden of proof in the second sense may shift constantly, according as one scale of evidence or the other preponderates" (ibid, paragraph 95).' *Purkess v Crittenden* [1966] ALR 98 at 100, per cur.

BURGESS   *See* MUNICIPAL CORPORATION

BURGLARY

(1) A person is guilty of burglary if—
   (a) he enters any building or part of a building as a trespasser and with intent to commit any such offence as is mentioned in subsection (2) below; or
   (b) having entered any building or part of a building as a trespasser he steals or attempts to steal anything in the building or that part of it or inflicts or attempts to inflict on any person therein any grievous bodily harm.
(2) The offences referred to in subsection (1)(a) above are offences of stealing anything in the building or part of a building in question, of inflicting on any person therein any grievous bodily harm or raping any woman therein, and of doing unlawful damage to the building or anything therein.
(3) References in subsections (1) and (2) above to a building shall apply also to an inhabited vehicle or vessel, and shall apply to any such vehicle or vessel at times when the person having a habitation in it is not there as well as at times when he is.
(Theft Act 1968, s 9(1)–(3))

Aggravated burglary

A person is guilty of aggravated burglary if he commits any burglary and at the time has with him any firearm or imitation firearm, any weapon of offence, or any explosive; and for this purpose—
(a) 'firearm' includes an airgun or air pistol, and "imitation firearm" means anything which has the appearance of being a firearm, whether capable of being discharged or not; and
(b) 'weapon of offence' means any article made or adapted for use for causing injury to or incapacitating a person, or intended by the person having it with him for such use; and
(c) 'explosive' means any article manufactured for the purpose of producing a practical effect by explosion, or intended by the person having it with him for that purpose.
(Theft Act 1968, s 10(1))

BURIAL GROUND

In this section [use of certain churchyards and burial grounds] 'burial ground' means any land set apart and consecrated for the purpose of burials whether or not burials have taken place therein. (Pastoral Measure 1983, s 30(6)

BURN

[A clause in a Lloyd's policy was as follows: 'And all other goods, also the ship and freight, are warranted free from average under three pounds per cent, unless general, or the ship is stranded, sunk, or burnt.'] 'We must look at this word "burnt" in reference to the context: it is part of a phrase "unless the ship is stranded, sunk, or burnt". What does that mean? I take it the context shows that what is meant is that the ship as a whole must be . . . burnt, and I cannot accept the construction . . . that any fire on board a ship, doing a little structural damage to the ship itself, is a burning in ordinary language. It appears to me it is not so.' *The Glenlivet* [1894] P 48 at 52, CA, per Lindley LJ

'If this case had been tried before a jury in the ordinary way . . . the learned judge would have had to direct the jury . . . that a partial burning of the ship did not necessarily constitute a "burnt" ship. . . . He would also have said that it might do so, but that it would depend upon the character and nature of the partial burning of the ship.' Ibid at 55, per A L Smith LJ

BUSINESS   *See also* CARRY ON BUSINESS; ORDINARY COURSE OF BUSINESS; RETAIL TRADE

'Business' is a wider term than 'trade', and not synonymous with it, and means almost anything which is an occupation as distinguished from a pleasure. However, the term must be construed according to its context. (47 Halsbury's Laws (4th edn) para 2)

'Business' includes a professional practice and includes any activity carried on by a body of persons, whether corporate or unincorporate. (Medicines Act 1968, s 132(1))

'Business' includes a profession and the activities of any government department (including a Northern Ireland department) or local or public authority. (Sale of Goods Act 1979, s 61(1))

'Business' includes a professional practice and includes any other undertaking which is carried on for gain or reward or which is an undertaking in the course of which goods or services are supplied otherwise than free of charge. (Fair Trading Act 1973, s 137(2); applied by the Competition Act 1980, s 33)

'Business' includes a profession and the activities of any government department or local or public authority, (Unfair Contract Terms Act 1977, s 14)

'Business' includes a trade or profession and includes any activity carried on by a body of persons, whether corporate or unincorporate. (Employment Protection Act 1975, s 126(1); Employment Protection (Consolidation) Act 1978, s 153(1))

'Business' includes the undertaking of a canteen, club, school, hospital or institution, whether carried on for profit or not, and any undertaking or activity carried on by a public or local authority. (Food Act 1984, s 132(1))

'When a person habitually does a thing which is capable of producing a profit, for the purpose of producing a profit, he is carrying on a business.' *Smith v Anderson* (1880) 15 Ch D 247 at 258, per Jessel MR

'The word "business" . . . means almost anything which is an occupation, as distinguished from a pleasure—anything which is an occupation or duty which requires attention is a business.' *Rolls v Miller* (1884) 27 Ch D 71 at 88, CA, per Lindley LJ

'Whether one or two transactions make a business depends upon the circumstances of each case. I take the test to be this: if an isolated transaction, which if repeated would be a transaction in business, is proved to have been undertaken with the intent that it should be the first of several transactions, that is, with the intent of carrying on a business, then it is a first transaction in an existing business. The business exists from the time of the commencement of that transaction with the intent that it should be one of a series.' *Re Griffin, ex p Board of Trade* (1890) 60 LJQB 235 at 237, CA, per Lord Esher MR

'My present view is . . . that a solicitor's practice, at any rate in London, is a pursuit upon lines sufficiently commercial to bring it within the term "business" as distinguished from an occupation such as that of a schoolmaster which is not organised and conducted upon commercial lines.' *Re Wilkinson* [1922] 1 KB 584 at 587, per Roche J

'Colonel Ogilby contends that the intestate carried on the breeding of cattle not as a business, because she consistently made a loss, but as a hobby. I am wholly unable to follow that argument. According to the ordinary use of the English language, the intestate carried on the business of a farm at Westwood Park and on the adjoining small holding, known as Spring

Farm, and the live and the dead stock which she used for that purpose she used for the business of farming. It seems to me to be impossible to say that, in those circumstances, the live stock, including the cattle in question, and the dead stock, were not used for business purposes by her at her death, within the meaning of the Administration of Estates Act 1925.' *Re Ogilby, Ogilby v Wentworth-Stanley* [1942] Ch 288 at 289, per Simonds J

'I turn to the meaning of the word "business", and it seems to me that it is plain, on the meanings found attributed to the word in the dictionaries and in the authorities, that "business" is capable of including the practice of a profession. The Oxford English Dictionary gives, among others, this meaning: "Habitual occupation; profession; trade". That plainly includes the profession of a doctor.' *Re Williams' Will Trusts, Chartered Bank of India, Australia and China v Williams* [1953] 1 All ER 536 at 537, per Danckwerts J (also reported in [1953] Ch 138 at 141)

'Many different forms of spare-time activity are to be found, some more "active" than others. By and large, it seems to me that what a man does with his spare time in his home is most unlikely to qualify for the description "business" unless it has some direct commercial involvement in it, whether it be a hobby or a recreation or the performance of a social duty. . . . On the face of it these are matters which are not "business" matters at all; they go to a man's private life in his domestic surroundings.' *Abernethie v Kleiman Ltd* [1969] 2 All ER 790, CA, per Widgery LJ

'It seems easier to say what is not "business" than what is. Purely domestic activities are not "business". Purely recreational activities are not in my opinion "business", unless, maybe, when carried on by a body of persons. Nor, I think, are purely cultural pursuits, distinct from a business of providing education. A commercial element may not be essential, but on the other hand a philanthropic activity may not constitute a business if it be a gratuitous pursuit of a spare-time activity. But a serious undertaking earnestly pursued for the purpose of fulfilling a social obligation may constitute a business, even if not undertaken for profit. It seems to be to a great extent a question of degree and to depend largely on the character of the particular activity. The Queen's government undoubtedly carries on the business of government, and each department or ministry or executive agency of the government can be said without inaccuracy to carry on a part of that business; but . . . generally speaking the conduct of a branch of government business should not, in my opinion, be regarded as the carrying on of "a business" [within a statutory instrument controlling business rents].' *Town Investments Ltd v Department of the Environment* [1976] 3 All ER 479, per Buckley LJ at 496; on appeal, [1978] AC 359 HL

'The carrying on of "business", no doubt, usually calls for some activity on the part of whoever carries it on, though, depending on the nature of the business, the activity may be intermittent with long intervals of quiescence in between.' *American Leaf Blending Co v Director-General of Inland Revenue* [1978] 3 All ER 1185 at 1189, PC, per Lord Diplock

'The primary meaning of all these words [within the Finance Act 1972, s 2(2)(b)], "business, trade, profession and vocation", is an occupation by which a person earns a living. It is clear that all ordinary businesses, trades, professions and vocations can be carried on with differences from this standard and norm in regularity or seriousness of application, in the pursuit or disregard of profit or earnings, and in the use or neglect of ordinary commercial principles of organisation. As the decision in the *Morrison's Academy* case [*Customs & Excise Comrs v Morrison's Academy Boarding Houses Association* [1978] STC 1] has shown, the absence of one common attribute of ordinary businesses, trades, professions or vocations, such as the pursuit of profit or earnings, does not necessarily mean that the activity is not a business or trade etc if in other respects the activity is plainly a "business". Many people, however, carry on activities which are clearly "business" but which have little to do with ordinary businesses or trades; thus a man may be a professional sportsman or make a business of his hobby, or make a trade of domestic hospitality. In this area, as it seems to me, the essential difference between what is "business" or "trade" and what is an activity for pleasure and social enjoyment may on occasions be difficult to discern or to prove, but no man, I believe, has any doubt that that essential difference is a real difference, and, in my judgment, that essential difference survives in the true construction in law of this word in this statute.' *Customs & Excise Comrs v Lord Fisher* [1981] 2 All ER 147 at 157, per Gibson J

Australia 'The line between "trade" and "business" is not hard and fast and it is to be observed that in the Oxford English Dictionary one meaning of the word "trade" is: "The practice of some occupation, business, or profession habitually carried on, especially when practised as a means of livelihood or gain". In the same way, a meaning of the word "business" that is given is: "Stated occupation, profession, or trade". It is not, I think, a departure from ordinary usage when in the Income Tax Assessment Acts the word "business" is defined to include "trade".' *Cooney v Council of Municipality of Ku-ring-gai* [1963] 114 CLR 582 at 602, per Menzies J

Canada 'As used in various statutes it [the word "business"] involves at least three elements: (1) the occupation of time, attention and labour; (2) the incurring of liabilities to other persons; and (3) the purpose of a livelihood or profit. A person who devotes no time or attention or labour, by himself or by servants or employees, to the working or conduct of the affairs of an enterprise does not carry on the business of such enterprise. He might, for instance, be only financially interested. But to carry on business he must give attention, or perform labour, for the maintenance or furtherance of the undertaking, and devote time to the accomplishment of its objects.' *Re Pszon* [1946] 2 DLR 507 at 511, Ont CA, per Laidlaw JA

Canada 'I am of opinion upon the whole of the evidence that the preponderant purpose of the applicant credit union was to provide loans to its members at the lowest possible cost, rather than to earn profits, and that this being so the applicant is not a "business" or "financial business' within the meaning of s 9 of the Assessment Act [RSO 1960, c 23]. Upon the cases cited, I take the law to be this, that in order for an organisation to be liable to business assessment under s 9 its dominant or preponderating object must be profit, gain or livelihood.' *Re St Mary's Parish (Kitchener) Credit Union Ltd & City of Kitchener* [1968] 2 OR 226 at 234, Ont SC, per Haines J; affd [1968] 2 OR 820, Ont CA

Canada '"Business" is a word of large and indefinite import but (as used here) [for the purposes of business assessment] its evident and reasonable meaning is, to adopt the language of the Master of the Rolls in *Smith v Anderson* (1880) 15 Ch D 247 at 258, "something which is followed and which occupies time and attention and labour for profit": Osler JA in *Rideau Club v Corp of City of Ottawa* (1907) 15 OLR 118 at p 122. In the

same case, at p 124, Maclaren JA, after speaking of the many definitions offered for the word "business" in the dictionaries, and that its meaning in each case must depend largely on the context, observed that the most comprehensive meaning to be drawn from the American and English reported cases is "That which occupies the time, attention and labour of man for the purpose of a livelihood or profit", a definition followed in many cases since.' *Re Condon and City of Winnipeg* (1975) 65 DLR (3d) 568 at 571, Man QB, per Wilson J

New Zealand '"Business" includes any undertaking carried on for pecuniary profit. It is not necessary that such a profit should be made, but it is essential, even if not sufficient, that at least an intention to gain pecuniary profit from the activities should be proved before the undertaking can be termed a business.' *Inland Revenue Comr v Watson* [1960] NZLR 259 at 262, per Henry J cited with approval by North P in *Harley v Inland Revenue Comr* [1971] NZLR 482 at 487

New Zealand 'In common usage "business" has and has long had a wide and flexible meaning. In the sense in which it is used in legislation imposing a charge for tax in respect of revenue earning activities The Oxford English Dictionary definitions "a pursuit or occupation demanding time and attention; a serious employment as distinct from a pastime . . .; trade; commercial transactions or engagements" and Webster's Third New International Dictionary definitions "a usually commercial or mercantile activity customarily engaged in as a means of livelihood and typically involving some independence of judgment and power of decision . . . a commercial or industrial enterprise" reflect the underlying notion. . . . While there are obvious shades of difference, and while each of the words "profession, trade, manufacture or undertaking" [in the Land and Income Tax Act 1954, s 2] has a wide meaning, I cannot readily postulate any activity which they comprehend which is not also included in the general concept of "business" in ordinary usage. The second aspect of the definition is the element of intention. . . . Underlying each of the words in the definition in s 2 and the term "business" itself when used in the context of a taxation statute is the fundamental notion of the exercise of an activity in an organised and coherent way and one which is directed to an end result. And the definition itself proceeds to identify its concern that the enterprise be one carried on "for pecuniary profit". . . . I think it is necessarily implicit in the statutory definition that the qualifying words "for pecuniary profit" were regarded as applicable to all ventures to be recognised as business for income tax purposes.' *Grieve v Inland Revenue Comr* [1984] 1 NZLR 101 at 101, 106, 107, CA, per Richardson J

New Zealand 'Underlying each of the words in the definition in s 2 [supra] and the term "business" itself when used in the context of a taxation statute, is the fundamental notion of the exercise of an activity in an organised and coherent way and one which is directed to an end result. The decision whether or not a taxpayer is in business involves a two-fold inquiry: as to the nature of the activities actually carried on—including the period over which they are engaged in, the scale of operations and the volume of transactions, the commitment of time, money and effort, the pattern of activity and the financial results— and as to the intention of the taxpayer in engaging in those activities.' *Calkin v Inland Revenue Comr* [1984] 1 NZLR 440 at 443, 446, CA, per Cooke and Richardson JJ

United States 'Business' includes every trade, occupation, or profession. (Uniform Partnership Act 1914, s 2)

In agreement

Dubowski v Goldstein [[1896] 1 QB 478, CA] . . . shows that where a large and indeterminate word like "business" is used in an agreement . . . it will not be so construed as to include business which was wholly outside the contemplation of either of the parties at that time. . . . I think the learned judge was right when he said that "requirements for the purposes of its business" must be confined to the business which was in contemplation by the parties at the time of making the agreement.' *Kensington & Knightsbridge Electric Lighting Co v Notting Hill Electric Lighting Co* (1918) 87 LJKB 1076 at 1079, 1081, CA, per Pickford LJ

In Partnership Act

The expression 'business' includes every trade, occupation, or profession. (Partnership Act 1890, s 45)

'If I am right in construing the word "business" in the Partnership Act of 1890, as relating not merely to a life-long or a universal business or a long undertaking, but to any separate commercial adventure in which people may embark, this [a complicated transaction] was a contract which came within s 2(3)(d) of the Act. . . . It has been suggested to me that "business" does not mean an isolated adventure, but that it means the regular trade of people even though they may have two or three separate trades. I see no reason for construing it in this way.' *Re Abenheim, ex p Abenheim,* (1913) 109 LT 219 at 220, per Phillimore J

In restrictive covenant

[A lease contained a covenant that the lessee would not carry on on the premises any trade or 'business' without the lessor's consent.] 'I cannot read the two words "trade" and "business" as synonymous. . . . It is not essential that there should be payment in order to constitute a business. And the mere fact that there is payment under certain circumstances, does not necessarily make a thing a business which if there was no payment would not be a business.' *Rolls v Miller* (1884) 27 Ch D 71 at 85, CA, per Cotton LJ

Place of business

[The Bankruptcy Act 1883 s 6(1)(d) (repealed) provided that a creditor should not be entitled to present a bankruptcy petition against a debtor unless (inter alia) the debtor, within a year before the date of the presentation of the petition, had had a 'place of business' in England.] 'If a man has a room in a hotel where he keeps samples of his goods and sees his customers, I should think it would be a place of business. But if all a man did was to negotiate paper contracts at a room in a hotel, I should hesitate to say it was a place of business. Certainly, if he did it first at one hotel and then at another, it would not. In the present case there is not sufficient proof that the room in the hotel was his place of business.' *Re Norris, ex p Reynolds* (1888) 4 TLR 452 at 452, CA, per Lord Esher MR

Profit not essential

'If I were to define the business carried on I should say that it is the business of providing for, maintaining, and training pauper children, and that is none the less a business because it is carried on, not for profit, but, on the contrary, at a large expense.' *South-West Suburban Water Co v St Marylebone Guardians* [1904] 2 KB 174 at 180, per Buckley J

BUSINESS AND PLEASURE

Australia [The schedule to a policy of insurance of a motor car stated 'the purposes for which the motor vehicle is used' to be 'business and pleasure.'] 'The words "business and pleasure" set out as the purposes for which a motor car is to be used, mean that it is to be used for the purposes of business or for any purpose other than business for which it may please the owner to use it.' *Ortner v Automobile Insurance Co of Australia Ltd* [1930] VLR 194 at 202, per Irvine CJ

BUSINESS PREMISES

'The property was put up for sale as business premises, and upon that . . . the purchaser would be entitled to have property conveyed to him on which he could carry on any business, subject only to the restrictions imposed by the general law of the land—for example, so as not to create a nuisance—and subject also to the statutory restrictions in force with regard to any particular trade where such restrictions exist. . . . As the purchaser bought the premises as business premises, and it is shown . . . that the property is held subject to a covenant imposing a serious restriction upon its use as business premises, he is entitled to a declaration that the title is not such that he ought to be compelled to accept.' *Re Davis & Cavey* (1888) 40 Ch D 601 at 605, 609, per Stirling J

BUT

Australia '"But" is adversative in sense; it is not complementary or explanatory. It introduces a reference to circumstances which limit or prevent the application of some prior proposition.' *Dey v Victorian Railway Comrs* [1949] ALR 333 at 341, per Latham CJ

BUT SO THAT

'The words "but so that", and the words "and so that" seem to me quite indistinguishable from such words as "provided always that" and "and provided further that". They are suitable words to introduce the engrafting of trusts upon a gift which is in terms absolute.' *Re Litt, Parry v Cooper* [1946] Ch 154 at 161, per Morton LJ

BUY

United States 'Buying' may be for cash or by exchange of other property or on secured or unsecured credit and includes receiving goods or documents of title under a pre-existing contract for sale but does not include a transfer in bulk or as security for or in total or partial satisfaction of a money debt. (Uniform Commercial Code 1978, s 1–201(9))

BUYER

'Buyer' means a person who buys or agrees to buy goods. (Sale of Goods Act 1979, s 61(1))

United States 'Buyer in ordinary course of business' means a person who in good faith and without knowledge that the sale to him is in violation of the ownership rights or security interest of a third party in the goods buys in ordinary course from a person in the business of selling goods of that kind but does not include a pawnbroker. All persons who sell minerals or the like (including oil and glass) at wellhead or minehead shall be deemed to be persons in the business of selling goods of that kind. (Uniform Commercial Code 1978, s 1–201(9))

BY

'The question . . . is whether the contracts have been made by or through an agent within the meaning of the rule [RSC Ord XI, r 1(e) (see now RSC 1965, Ord. 11 r 1)]. A clear distinction has here been drawn between "by" and "through" an agent, but there is no indication what the distinction is intended to be. . . . I think that the only possible distinction is that where a contract is made by an agent, the latter purports to bind his principal, but where the contract is made through an agent, the meaning is that the terms of the contract are arranged through the mediation of the agent.' *National Mortgage & Agency Co of New Zealand Ltd v Gosselin* (1922) 38 TLR 832 at 833, CA, per Warrington LJ

'To return to the rule [Companies (Winding-up) Rules 1949, r. 163], it begins: "No member of a committee of inspection shall, except under and with the sanction of the court, directly or indirectly, by himself, or any employer, partner, clerk, agent, or servant, be entitled to derive any profit from any transaction arising out of the winding-up . . . ." The prior sanction of the court was admittedly not obtained in the present case. As has been stated by counsel for the Official Receiver, at first sight the presence in that list of persons of the employer is somewhat strange, but I think that when the character of the other persons mentioned is considered and it is appreciated that the phrase is introduced by the preposition "by" and not by the preposition "through", the proper way of construing the phrase is to treat the word "by" as equivalent to the phrase "in the person of", and the rule, therefore, is satisfied if through the activities of the member of the committee in question his employer makes a profit.' *Re Hawkins (FT) & Co Ltd* [1952] 2 All ER 467 at 469, per Wynn-Parry J (also reported in [1952] Ch 881 at 885)

[A notice to quit required a tenant to vacate premises 'by' 31 March 1954. It was contended, on behalf of the tenant, that the notice was bad, as it purported to cut off the last day of the tenancy by making it necessary for the tenant to have already vacated 'by' 31 March, ie by the time that day first began.] 'As a matter of definition . . . I should be inclined to think that "by the date" ought to mean "on or before the date". . . . When the writer . . . speaks of "vacating the office by the date (i.e. 31 March 1954)", I must confess that it seems to me beyond all reasonable doubt that he is stating that he is giving notice to determine the tenancy on the date when it was liable to be determined, viz., 31st of March.' *Eastaugh v Macpherson* [1954] 3 All ER 214 at 215, CA, per Evershed MR

Canada 'I cannot read the expression "by 31st of July" to mean at the expiration of that day. In some cases, it is true, it might mean before 31st of July, but in the relevant circumstances I am of the view it must mean on that day or before the end of that day; that is to say, during that day. If A promises to pay B $10 by 31st of July, there is no doubt, payment is to be made during that day; that is to say, up to and inclusive of midnight, but not after midnight.' *Munro (J H) Ltd v Vancouver Properties Ltd* [1940] 3 WWR 26 at 29, BCCA, per O'Halloran JA

BYE-LAW

A bye-law has been said to be an ordinance affecting the public, or some portion of the public, imposed by some authority clothed with statutory powers, ordering something to be done or not to be done, and accompanied by some sanction or penalty for its non-

observance. Further, it involves the consequence that, if validly made, it has the force of law within the sphere of its legitimate operation. (28 Halsbury's Laws (4th edn) para 1323)

'A bye-law, though made by, and applicable to, a particular body, is still a law, and differs in its nature from a provision made on or limited to particular occasions; it is a rule made prospectively, and to be applied whenever the circumstances arise for which it is intended to provide.' *Gosling v Veley* (1847) 7 QB 406 at 451, per Lord Denman CJ

'A bye-law is not an agreement, but a law binding on all persons to whom it applies, whether they agree to be bound by it or not. All regulations made by a corporate body, and intended to bind not only themselves and their officers and servants, but members of the public who come within the sphere of their operation, may be properly called "bye-laws", whether they be valid or invalid in point of law; for the term "bye-law" is not restricted to that which is valid in point of view.' *London Assocn of Shipowners & Brokers v London & India Docks Joint Committee* [1892] 3 Ch 242 at 252, CA, per Lindley LJ

'Looking to the character of the body legislating under the delegated authority of Parliament, to the subject-matter of such legislation, and to the nature and extent of the authority given to deal with matters which concern them, and in the manner which to them shall seem meet, I think courts of justice ought to be slow to condemn as invalid any bye-law, so made under such conditions, on the ground of supposed unreasonableness. . . . I do not mean to say that there may not be cases in which it would be the duty of the court to condemn bye-laws, made under such authority as these were made [bye-laws made by a county council], as invalid because unreasonable. But unreasonable in what sense? If, for instance, they were found to be partial and unequal in their operation, as between different classes; if they were manifestly unjust; if they disclosed bad faith; if they involved such oppressive or gratuitous interference with the rights of those subject to them as could find no justification in the minds of reasonable men, the court might well say, "Parliament has never intended to give authority to make such rules; they are unreasonable and *ultra vires*".' *Kruse v Johnson* [1898] 2 QB 91 at 99, 100, DC, per Lord Russell CJ

BY-PASS

'By-pass', in relation to a cattle-grid provided for a highway, means a way, over land not comprised within the limits of the highway, for the traffic for which the by-pass is provided, with a public right of way thereover—
(a) for that traffic; or
(b) if any part of the by-pass is provided along an existing highway, for the said traffic and for any other traffic entitled to use the highway before the by-pass was provided,
subject in either case to the limitation that there may be placed thereon any such gate or other works as may be necessary for the proper control of all or any of such traffic and the efficient operation of the cattle-grid for use in connection with which the by-pass is provided. (Highways Act 1980, s 82(6))

C

C & F *See* C.I.F.

C.I.F.

C.i.f. (cost, insurance, freight) contracts [are contracts] where the goods are sold at a price which includes their cost, freight and destination, and the premium on a policy of insurance covering the transit; the buyer's duty is to pay the price upon delivery not of the goods, but of documents covering them, which typically include the bill of lading, policy of insurance, and invoice. (41 Halsbury's Laws (4th edn) para 612)

Under a c.i.f. contract, the duty of the seller, so far as physical handing over of the goods themselves is concerned, is accomplished when the goods are put on board the ship or other specified place or vehicle for the purpose of the transit. In addition, he is under an obligation to make a contract of carriage with the carrier under which the goods will be taken to their contractual destination and there delivered, to effect an insurance available for the buyer, and to forward the bill of lading, policy of insurance and invoice to the buyer. Against tender of these documents the buyer's liability to pay the price arises. The contract is thus, in a commercial sense, an agreement for the sale of goods to be performed by delivery of documents, the seller having obligations in law in relation to both the goods and the documents covering them. (41 Halsbury's Laws (4th edn) para 909)

'It is an ordinary contract for the sale of goods upon cost, insurance, freight, or more shortly, c.i.f. terms. Under such a contract . . . the seller undertakes various obligations. He is bound in the first place to ship goods of the contract description on board a ship bound to the contract destination. He is bound in the second place to tender to the purchaser within a reasonable time after shipment the shipping documents, e.g. the bill or bills of lading and a policy of insurance reasonably covering the value of the goods.' *Johnson v Taylor Brothers & Co Ltd* [1920] AC 144 at 149, per Lord Birkenhead LC

'I think that when a vendor and purchaser of goods . . . enter into a c.i.f. contract . . . the vendor in the absence of any special provision to the contrary is bound by his contract to do [the following] . . . things. First, to make out an invoice of the goods sold. Second, to ship at the port of shipment goods of the description contained in the contract. Third, to procure a contract of affreightment under which the goods will be delivered at the destination contemplated by the contract. Fourth, to arrange for an insurance upon the terms current in the trade which will be available for the benefit of the buyer. Fifthly, with all reasonable despatch to send forward and tender to the buyer these shipping documents, namely the invoice, bill of lading and policy of assurance, delivery of which to the buyer is symbolical of delivery of the goods purchased, placing the same at the buyer's risk and entitling the seller to payment of their price. . . . If no place be named in the c.i.f. contract for the tender of the shipping documents they must prima facie be tendered at the residence or place of business of the buyer.' Ibid at 155, 156, per Lord Atkinson

'The price under a c.i.f. contract would ordinarily include the cost of the goods, the cost of the carriage from the named port to the named port on ordinary terms in the trade, and the cost of insuring the goods on that voyage against the risks usual in the trade . . . and what would ordinarily follow in a c.i.f. contract would be that, assuming goods in accordance with the contract were shipped, the seller would comply with the contract by tendering to the buyer documents which would enable the buyer to get delivery of the goods on arrival at the port of discharge or, if they did not arrive, or arrived damaged, to sue either the shipowner on the contract of carriage, or the underwriter on the policy of insurance.' *Re Denbigh Cowan & Co & Alcherley (R) & Co* (1921) 90 LJKB 836 at 840, CA, per Scrutton LJ

United States (1) The term C.I.F. means that the price includes in a lump sum the cost of the goods and the insurance and freight to the named destination. The term C. & F. or C.F. means that the price so includes cost and freight to the named destination.
(2) Unless otherwise agreed and even though used only in connection with the stated price and destination, the term C.I.F. destination or its equivalent requires the seller at his own expense and risk to
  (a) put the goods into the possession of a carrier at the port for shipment and obtain a negotiable bill or bills of lading covering the entire transportation to the named destination; and
  (b) load the goods and obtain a receipt from the carrier (which may be contained in the bill of lading) showing that the freight has been paid or provided for; and
  (c) obtain a policy or certificate of insurance, including any war risk insurance, of a kind and on terms then current at the port of shipment in the usual amount, in the currency of the contract, shown to cover the same goods covered by the bill of lading and providing for payment of loss to the order of the buyer or for the account of whom it may concern; but the seller may add to the price the amount of the premium for any such war risk insurance; and
  (d) prepare an invoice of the goods and procure any other documents required to effect shipment or to comply with the contract; and
  (e) forward and tender with commercial promptness all the documents in due form and with any indorsement necessary to perfect the buyer's rights.
(3) Unless otherwise agreed the term C. & F. or its equivalent has the same effect and imposes upon the seller the same obligations and risks as a C.I.F. term except the obligation as to insurance.
(4) Under the term C.I.F. or C. & F. unless otherwise agreed the buyer must make payment against tender of the required documents and the seller may not tender nor the buyer demand delivery of the goods in substitution for the documents.
(Uniform Commercial Code 1978, s 2–320)

C/O

Canada 'In the will as presented, the two children aged six and four years respectively are the sole legatees and the legacy takes the following form: "I bequeath my personal estate . . . unto Masters Ian Forbes, and Douglas Roderick McLennan (Boys) c/o George McMillan, Rural Route No 3 North Battleford, Saskatchewan, Can., absolutely". . . . The symbol "c/o" . . . is an abbreviation of the expression "in care of" used in relation to the two young infants. The strict and primary sense of this expression indicates that the two infants are or are to be in the care or custody or control of the party whose name follows. In another sense the symbol may only signify an address or a location. With this possibility of dual meaning and the obscurity resulting from it, it is open to the Court to look at extrinsic evidence in order to arrive at the true meaning. . . . I hold that the symbol "c/o" as used in the will was an abbreviation by which the testator intended to use the words "in care of". . . . I therefore hold that the testator intended to appoint and did in the said will appoint George McMillan of North Battleford to be the testamentary guardian of Ian Forbes McLennan and Douglas Roderick McLennan.' *Re McLennan Estate* [1940] 1 WWR 465 at 469, 470, 472, 473, Sask Surr Ct, per Bryant SCJ

CABIN PASSENGER *See* STEERAGE PASSENGER

CALCULATED

Australia [The Electoral Act 1929–1986 (SA), s 148(c) provides that a person is guilty of undue influence if he publishes certain untrue or defamatory material 'calculated' to influence the vote of any elector.] 'I do not understand the word "calculated" to mean "intended" but to mean "likely".' *Crafter v*

Webster (1980) 23 SASR 321 at 337, per Mitchell J

New Zealand [The Defamation Act 1954, s 5(1) provides that in an action for slander of title, slander of goods, or other malicious falsehood, it shall not be necessary to allege or prove special damage if the words upon which the action is founded are 'calculated' to cause pecuniary damage to the plaintiff.] 'The word "calculated" in this context is equivalent to "likely".' *Customglass Boats Ltd v Salthouse Bros Ltd* [1976] 1 NZLR 36 at 49, SC, per Mahon J

South Africa [A by-law provided that no person should in any street or public place use words or gestures 'calculated' to cause insult, nuisance or annoyance to other persons lawfully in or upon such street or public place.] 'The natural meaning of "calculated" in a context like the present one is clearly "likely", without reference to the state of mind of the person using the language or gestures.' *Amoils v Johannesburg City Council* 1943 TPD 389 per Schreiner J

CALL

At port

'To "call at a port" is a well-known sea-term; it means to call for the purposes of business, generally to take in or unload cargo, or to receive orders; it must mean that the vessel may stop at the port of call for a time, or else the liberty to call would be idle. I believe the term has always been interpreted to mean that the ship may call at such ports as would naturally and usually be ports of call on the voyage named. If the stipulation were only that she might call at any ports, the invariable construction has been that she would only be entitled to call at such ports in their geographical order; and therefore the words "in any order" are frequently added, but in any case it appears to me that the ports must be ports substantially on the course of the voyage.' *Leduc v Ward* (1888) 20 QBD 475 at 482, CA, per Lord Esher MR

[A contract for the carriage of goods from Valencia to Liverpool was contained in a bill of lading, which was given with liberty to 'call' at any port or ports in any rotation.] 'On the true construction of the bill of lading the defendants' only right was to call at ports which were substantially in the course of the voyage, as a sea voyage from Valencia to Liverpool. By the

course of the voyage I do not, of course, mean a straight track, neither do I mean the trade track, but I mean the navigation track.' *White v Granada SS Co Ltd* (1896) 13 TLR 1 at 1, CA, per Lord Esher MR

On shares

A call is a demand for payment of the amount or part of the amount which has not been paid or satisfied on a share, made by the company through its governing body upon its members prior to winding up, or by its liquidator when it is in course of winding up. (7 Halsbury's Laws (4th edn) para 328)

'The word "call" [in relation to shares] is capable of three meanings. It may either mean the resolution, or its notification, or the time when it becomes payable.' *Ambergate, Nottingham & Boston & Eastern Junction Rly Co v Mitchell* (1849) 4 Exch 540 at 543, 544, per Parke B

'On considering the statute [Companies Clauses Consolidation Act 1845, s 16], and the cases bearing on the subject, it appears that a call may mean either the resolution formally come to, by those who have the power to determine, that those who are bound to contribute, i.e. the shareholders, shall pay a certain instalment; or it may be that resolution, together with notice to the persons called on of such resolution having been come to; or the combination of facts making the parties called on liable to an action for non-payment of the money called for.' *R v Londonderry & Coleraine Rly Co* (1849) 13 QB 998 at 1005, per cur.

CALL IN QUESTION

Australia [The Industrial Arbitration Act 1940–1986 (NSW) s 84(1)(a) provides that any decision of the Commission in court session or of any member of the Commission sitting alone shall be final, and no award and no order, proceeding or contract determination of the Commission in court session or of any such member shall be vitiated by reason only of any informality or want of form or be liable to be challenged, appealed against, reviewed, quashed or 'called in question' by any court of judicature.] 'It is to be observed that the section, in using the expressions "challenged, appealed against, reviewed, quashed", is plainly referring to circumstances in which some court in fact scrutinises the decision of the Commission and passes judgment upon it or makes some adverse ruling in respect of it.

In my view, the expression "called in question" has a similar intention and contemplates some positive action or step taken by a court in relation to the final decision of the Commission, by which action or step the court asserts the invalidity in law of the Commission's decision and declines to act upon that decision. One such instance might be where a court rejected a tender of an award on the ground that it considered it invalid or defective for some reason, or allowed evidence to be allowed to establish error in it. This view accords with the dictionary definition of the expression "called in question". The Shorter Oxford English Dictionary defines it to mean: "To examine judicially, bring to trial; to take to task, to question the validity or status of; to raise objections to". The New Oxford English Dictionary defines it to mean: "To summon for trial or examination; to impeach; to challenge, impugn, dispute, cast doubt upon; formerly also to examine, make inquisition into".' *Young v Public Service Board* (1982) 2 NSWLR 456 at 468, per Lee J

CALLING

Canada 'I think it is clear that the words "trade, calling or profession" [in the Exemptions Act, RSS 1953 s 2(1) (repealed; see now RSS 1978, c E-14, s 2(1)] are words which are susceptible of analogous meaning. . . . Admittedly, "calling" is a more general term than "trade" or "profession", but when used together with these words, as it is in the legislation under review, its meaning must be restricted to a sense analogous to "trade" or "profession".' *Hayos v Patrick and Wonitowy* (1961) 36 WWR 562 at 564, Sask CA, per Culliton J

South Africa [The question was as to the meaning of 'calling' of a medical practitioner.] 'The only reasonable explanation is that the legislature must have had certain functions in mind, not the ethical urge which induced the man to become a doctor.' *R v Steenkamp* 1942 OPD 131 per van den Heever J

CALLOUS DISREGARD

Australia [The Traffic Act 1949 (Qld), s 31(1)(a) provides that the driver of any vehicle involved in a road incident resulting in injury or death of any person shall immediately stop such vehicle and remain at the scene until he has fulfilled the requirements of s 31(2) of the Act, one of which is that he shall 'render all reasonable assistance to that person'. If the offender has shown a 'callous disregard' for the dead or injured person the court shall impose an additional sentence.] 'Knowingly to flee the scene of an accident and leave a victim substantially injured and presumably suffering would in most persons' view ordinarily constitute "callous disregard".' *Crack v Post, ex p Crack* [1984] 2 Qld R 311 at 323, per Macrossan J

CANAL

'Canal' includes any river, inland navigation or lake, and any other waters situated wholly or partly within a county, whether those waters are or are not within the ebb and flow of the tide. (Public Health (Control of Disease) Act 1984, s 53)

CANAL BOAT

'Canal boat' means any vessel, however propelled, which is used for the conveyance of goods along a canal, not being—
(a) a sailing barge which belongs to the class generally known as 'Thames sailing barge' and is registered under the Merchant Shipping Acts 1894 to 1983, either in the Port of London or elsewhere, or
(b) a sea-going ship so registered, or
(c) a vessel used for pleasure purposes only. (Public Health (Control of Disease) Act 1984, s 53)

CANAL COMPANY

'Canal company' means any person or body of persons, corporate or unincorporate, being owner or lessee or owners or lessees of, or working, or entitled to charge tolls for the use of any canal in the United Kingdom, constructed or carried on under the powers of any Act of Parliament, or intrusted with the duty of conserving, maintaining, or improving the navigation of any inland water, and every such canal and inland water under the control of a canal company as above defined, and any wharf, dock, pier, jetty, and work in or at which barges do or can ship or unship goods or passengers, and other area, whether land or water, which belong to or are under the control of such canal company, are in the other portions of this Act included in the expression 'canal'. (Explosives Act 1875, s 108)

CANCEL

'Cancellation does not primarily import the destruction of a document.' *R v Linthwaite (Inhabitants)* (1849) 13 LTOS 116 at 116, per Erle J

'What is the ordinary business meaning of the word "cancel" in the English language? If there is no stipulation in the contract with reference to cancellation, neither party alone can cancel the contract; it can only be cancelled by mutual consent of both parties. In some cases charters contain what is known as a cancelling clause. In such cases both parties agree beforehand that that shall be part of the contract; but from a business point of view it would be said that the effect of it is that, if the ship does not arrive at the port of loading by a certain date, the charterer, without any further consent of the shipowner, although the latter be desirous of having the ship loaded, may cancel the charter. . . . In such a case, if the ship is so delayed, whether by a peril of the sea or by any other cause, that she does not reach the loading port by the date specified, the charterer is at liberty to cancel the charter, but is not bound to do so.' *Re Jamieson & Newcastle Steamship Freight Insurance Assocn* [1895] 2 QB 90 at 94, CA, per Lord Esher MR

Australia ' "Cancel" in its original derivation had some such meaning [i.e. importing dealing with in some physical way], but it is not true nowadays that it must have some physical connotation. Tearing up or putting lines through a document are merely examples of cancellation.' *Re Standard Insurance Co Ltd & Macfarlan's Arbitration* [1940] VLR 74 at 80, per Gavan Duffy J

New Zealand 'A policy . . . contained . . . the following words: ". . . This insurance may be terminated at any time at the request of the insured. . . . The company shall at any time, by giving seven days' notice in writing to the insured . . . be at liberty to cancel and determine this policy.". . . . The words "terminated" and "cancelled" are not terms of art, and their equivalent in legal terminology is "rescission". The word "terminated" connotes the rescission of the contract by the consent or agreement of both parties. . . . The word "cancelled" in the context in which it is used means the determination of the contract by the unilateral act of the company under and in pursuance of the power in that behalf expressed in the condition.' *Willcocks v New Zealand Insurance Co* [1926] NZLR 805 at 810,

811, per Stringer J; also reported [1926] GLR 530 at 533

United States 'Cancellation' occurs when either party puts an end to the contract for breach by the other and its effect is the same as that of 'termination' except that the cancelling party also retains any remedy for breach of the whole contract or any unperformed balance. (Uniform Commercial Code 1978, s 2–106(4))

CANCELLATION CLAUSE

Canada 'The "cancellation clause" . . . is the only clause of the agreement that refers to forfeiture in any way. . . . Like most clauses of the kind, this one provides that, upon default, entire or partial, by the purchasers, the agreement may be cancelled and terminated by notice, from the vendor, fixing a period of thirty days within which the default might be cured, and declaring that if the default be not so cured, the agreement shall then *ipso facto* be cancelled and foreclosed and all money paid thereunder shall be "forfeited" to the vendor. . . . The inclusion of such a clause in an agreement cannot mean that the forfeiture contemplated by it can be worked in any way other than that stipulated in the clause.' *Rudd v Balaz & Balaz* (1940) 48 Man LR 65 at 74, Man CA, per Dysart J

CANDIDATE

'Candidate'—

(a) in relation to a parliamentary election, means a person who is elected to serve in Parliament at the election or a person who is nominated as a candidate at the election, or is declared by himself or by others to be a candidate on or after the day of the issue of the writ for the election, or after the dissolution or vacancy in consequence of which the writ was issued;

(b) in relation to an election under the local government Act, means a person elected or having been nominated or having declared himself a candidate for election, to the office to be filled at the election.

(Representation of the People Act 1983, s 118)

'The Legislature [by stat 51 Geo 3, c 126 (repealed)] has directed that convenient booths shall be erected . . . for holding the election; and . . . they assumed that upon every occasion of an election there would be found a candidate or candidates in the ordinary ense of that word, that is, persons offering themselves to the suffrages of the electors. That I take it is, strictly speaking, the correct sense of the word candidate. Therefore a person cannot be in that sense of the word a candidate by the mere act of others, who propose him without his assent. The Legislature, indeed, assumed that it would always be the case of every person who should be proposed, that he would be so far assenting as to answer the description of a candidate.' *Morris v Burdett* (1813) 2 M & S 212 at 216, 217, per Lord Ellenborough CJ

Australia [The Legal Practitioners Act 1898–1986 (NSW) s 9 provides that no 'candidate' however qualified in other respects shall be admitted as a barrister unless the Board is satisfied that he is a person of good fame and character.] ' "Candidate" in s 9 has been held by this Court to mean "persons who seek to become barristers by the method of examination", that is, as distinct from solicitors of five years' standing who seek admission under s 11 of the Legal Practitioners Act [*Ex p Rofe* 1939) 39 SR (NSW) 124].' *Ex p Davis* [1963] SR (NSW) 54 at 61, per Sugerman J

CANNABIS

Cannabis' (except in the expression 'cannabis resin') means any plant of the genus *Cannabis* or any part of any such plant (by whatever name designated) except that it does not include cannabis resin or any of the following products after separation from the rest of the plant, namely—

(a) mature stalk of any such plant,
(b) fibre produced from mature stalk of any such plant, and
(c) seed of any such plant.

(Misuse of Drugs Act 1971, s 37, substituted by the Criminal Law Act 1977, s 52)

CANON

The description 'canon' was originally confined to persons, other than the dean, who were residentiary members of the chapter of a cathedral or collegiate church, but in more recent times the term has acquired a more extended meaning, being applied also to non-residentiary canons. In the Cathedrals Measure 1963 the term is defined as including a non-residentiary canon or prebendary, but not a minor canon or any person not in holy orders. Much of the older law is applicable only to the limited class of residentiary canons, and certain provisions of the Cathedrals Measure 1963 have a similarly restricted application. Non-residentiary canons are commonly identified with honorary canons; in strictness, however, it seems that the terms should not be regarded as interchangeable, since the law allows for the possibility of a stipendiary canon who is a person other than a residentiary canon, whereas an honorary canon has, as such, no emoluments. (14 Halsbury's Laws (4th edn) para 643)

In the construction of this Act the term 'canon' shall be construed to mean only every residentiary member of chapter, except the dean, heretofore styled either prebendary canon, canon residentiary, or residentiary. (Ecclesiastical Commissioners Act 1840, s 93)

'Canonry' includes any canonry, whether or not any remuneration is payable in connection therewith, the holder of which is entitled by virtue of his office to membership of the chapter of a cathedral church. (Ecclesiastical Fees Measure 1962, s 7)

'Canon' includes a non-residentiary canon or prebendary but not a minor canon or any person not in Holy Orders. (Cathedrals Measure 1963, s 52)

Minor canon

'Minor canon' shall be construed to extend to and include every vicar, vicar choral, priest vicar, and senior vicar, being a member of the choir in any cathedral or collegiate church. (Ecclesiastical Commissioners Act 1840, s 93)

'Minor canonry' includes any office by whatever name known the holder of which performs the duties of a minor canon in a cathedral church. (Ecclesiastical Fees Measure 1962, s 7)

CANON LAW

There existed from the very early times in Western Europe collections of canons of an unsystematic and incomplete character drawn up mainly to meet local and temporary needs. Except as to purely local matters these local canons were superseded in the English ecclesiastical courts by the codification of the canon law in the Corpus Juris Canonici, which was the foundation of the jus commune. After the time of Gratian, such canons as were made in England were made simply for the purpose of emphasising the rules of the Corpus Juris

Canonici and of applying them to local needs, and devising new means of enforcing them.

Historically speaking the canon law of papal Rome was applied, subject to modifications by local custom, within the realm of England and was enforced by a separate system of courts Christian. The canon law has never, however, as a body of laws, formed part of the law of England.

At the Reformation such of the canon law as applied in England and was not 'repugnant, contrariant or derogatory' to the laws or statutes of the realm, nor to the prerogatives of the Crown, received statutory recognition. The ecclesiastical law, including such of the canon law as was embraced at the Reformation, is thus now part of the law of the realm. Its authority, however, depends not upon its statutory recognition but upon its incorporation as such into the laws of the land at the Reformation.

Since the Reformation common lawyers have explained the application of the canon law of papal Rome within England on the basis of its reception. For this reason, in order to show that any directive, rule or usage of pre-Reformation canon law is now binding, it must be pleaded and proved to have been recognised, continued and acted upon in England since the Reformation.

The canons now in force are the Revised Canons Ecclesiastical of 1964 and 1969 as subsequently added to and amended. These are in part, like earlier post-Reformation canons, directives for the guidance of the Church in ecclesiastical matters and in part subsidiary legislation made under the direction of the Crown, originally in the Convocations of Canterbury and York and now, since 1970, by the General Synod. The Queen's assent and licence is necessary before canons can be promulged, and no canon may be made which is contrary or repugnant to the Queen's royal prerogative or the customs, laws or statutes of the realm.

The Revised Canons are, like those of 1603, binding on the clergy in ecclesiastical matters. As regards their application to the laity in general, it is still the position that the canons are not of their own force binding upon them, but they may, it seems, form the basis of legal obligation in the case of lay persons who have accepted office in the Church.

Insofar as any of the canons may be a reiteration or declaration of ancient usages and laws of the Church which had previously been received into common law they obtained no additional force by their incorporation into the post-Reformation canons. Insofar as any canon embodies provisions of, or is authorised by, an Act of Parliament or Measure, reference must be made to that Act or Measure in order to ascertain the force of those provisions.

The Revised Canons Ecclesiastical do not provide a complete statement of the law of the Church of England. They are a revision of the Code of Canons issued in 1603 and cover roughly the same areas of church life, but like that code they presuppose both the common and statute law of England and the general pre-Reformation canon law of the western Church, except where the canon law has been affected by contrary statute or custom in England. In this they differ to some extent from the much more comprehensive code of the Roman Catholic Church, and they follow the English secular legal tradition in their dislike of complete codification. (14 Halsbury's Laws (4th edn) paras 305, 306, 307, 308)

CANVASSER

A canvasser is a person who solicits and persuades individual voters, although not necessarily one by one separately, to vote for a candidate. (15 Halsbury's Laws (4th edn) para 700)

Australia 'Their Lordships are of the opinion that the term "insurance canvasser" . . . naturally conveys the idea of one who operates by the door-to-door method, and is not apt to describe one who solicits insurance business by other methods.' *General Accident Fire and Life Assurance Corpn Ltd v Pay-Roll Tax Comr (NSW)* (1982) 13 ATR 372 at 376, PC

CAPABLE

Of being sued

Australia [The State Housing Acts 1945–1986 (Qld), s 9, provides, inter alia, that a Commission representing the Crown under the name and style of the Queensland Housing Commission shall be 'capable in law of suing and being sued'.] 'I have no doubt that the words "capable in law of suing and being sued" have a wide meaning and are not to be restricted to a "suit" in the technical sense. Without attempting an exhaustive definition of them, I think they are wide enough to cover proceedings initiated, as these were, by notice of motion. But I do not think that it follows that he creation of the capability of being sued renders the property of the Commission, which t holds as agent for the Crown, and not otherwise, liable to seizure in an execution, or renders the Commission liable to attachment.' *Sundell v Queensland Housing Commission (No 5)* [1955] St R Qd 162 at 171, per Townley J

CAPITAL

'A man's business is to make boots and shoes. He has £10,000 which he takes into that business as his capital. He makes boots and shoes, and spends the whole of his £10,000 in doing it, and he sells and gets back from his customers a certain sum on the sale. He compares then, assuming he has sold all, what he has got back with his expenditure in producing the boots and shoes, and putting them on the market, and if he finds he has his £10,000 (I am treating it apart from any question of debts outstanding, supposing it is a good solid sale) then his capital is intact, and the rest, if there is a rest remaining in his hands, is profit. On the other hand, if he has only £9,000, his capital is not intact, and he has lost. It is exactly the same principle that has to be applied to a trading company under the Companies Act, and the capital that has to be regarded for the purpose of the Act of Parliament is the capital according to the Act and not the things, whether houses, goods, boots and shoes, or hats, or whatever it may be for the time being representing the capital, in the sense of being things in which the capital has been laid out.' *Lubbock v British Bank of South America* [1892] 2 Ch 198 at 201, 202, per Chitty J

'There is no hard and fast rule by which the Court can determine what is capital and what is profit. "The mode and manner in which a business is carried on, and what is usual or the reverse, may have a considerable influence in determining the question": per Earl of Halsbury LC in *Dovey v Cory* [[1901] AC 477 at 486]. "It may be safely said that what losses can be properly charged to capital, and what to income, is a matter for business men to determine, and it is often a matter on which the opinions of honest and competent men will differ: see *Gregory v Patchett* [(1864) 33 Beav 595]. . . . It is however necessary to bear in mind that the two propositions—(1) that dividends must not be paid out of capital, and (2) that dividends may only be paid out of profits—are not identical but diverse. . . . A company which has a balance to the credit of its profit and loss account is not bound at once to

apply that sum in making good an estimated deficiency in value of its capital assets. It may carry it to a suspense account or to reserve, and if the assets subsequently increase in value the amount neither has been nor will be part of the capital. If, therefore, a part of that balance is used in paying a dividend, that dividend is not paid out of capital, because the sum has never become capital, although it still remains a question whether it has been paid out of profits or not.' *Bond v Barrow Haematite Steel Co* [1902] 1 Ch 353 at 364, 365, per Farwell J

'The distinction which is to be drawn for the purposes of the Income Tax Acts between payments of an income character and payments of a capital nature is sometimes a very fine and rather artificial one. It may—in fact, it does—depend upon the precise character of the transaction. To take a simple case, if the true bargain is that a capital sum shall be paid, the fact that the method of the payment which is adopted in the document is that of payment by instalments will not have the effect of giving to those instalments the character of income. . . . On the other hand . . . where there is no undertaking to pay a capital sum and no capital obligation in existence, and all that exists is an undertaking to pay annual sums, those may, in the absence of other considerations, be annual payments of an income nature for the purposes of the Income Tax Acts.' *Inland Revenue Comrs v Mallaby-Deeley* [1938] 4 All ER 818 at 823, 824, CA, per Greene MR

Australia 'It is impossible to say that "capital" has a single technical meaning which prima facie should be attributed to the word in any statutory provision. The Companies Act distinguishes between nominal, issued, and paid-up capital, and the significance of the word in a particular case depends upon the context in which it is used.' *Incorporated Interests Pty Ltd v Federal Comr of Taxation* (1943) 67 CLR 508 at 515, per Latham CJ

Australia 'Although the categories of capital and income expenditure are distinct and easily ascertainable in obvious cases that lie far from the boundary, the line of distinction is often hard to draw in border line cases; and conflicting considerations may produce a situation where the answer turns on questions of emphasis and degree. That answer "depends on what the expenditure is calculated to effect from a practical and business point of view rather than upon the juristic classification of the legal rights, if any, secured, employed or exhausted in the process" [per Dixon J in *Hallstrom's Pty Ltd v Federal Commissioner of Taxation* (1946) 72 CLR 634 at 648; [1946] ALR 434]. As each new case comes to be argued felicitous phrases from earlier judgments are used in argument by one side and the other. But those phrases are not the deciding factor, nor are they of unlimited application. They merely crystallise particular factors which may incline the scale in a particular case after a balance of all the considerations has been taken.' *BP Australia Ltd v Federal Comr of Taxation* [1966] ALR 274 at 281, 282, PC

Australia 'Capital is not in truth a technical term. For the purpose of economics capital has been defined as produced wealth as distinguished from land and other natural resources used productively for gain. But in a business or mercantile sense . . . it is simply the means with which business is carried on, and it may consist of money or property convertible into money.' *Incorporated Interests Pty Ltd v Federal Comr of Taxation* (1943) 67 CLR 508 at 520, per Starke J

Canada [A will directed executors to pay debts and duties out of 'capital'.] 'The only indication of the source of fund is to be found in the word "capital". If by "capital", the testator meant the residue unfortunately he did not say so. The word "capital" is used in contradistinction to income, not residue. The whole estate here is capital. I do not think in using that word the testator indicates anything more as the source from which the duties are payable than he does when he directs payment out of the estate.' *Cave and Saunders v Day* [1945] 3 WWR 481 at 484, BCSC, per MacFarlane J

Capital expenditure

' "Capital expenditure" is not expenditure of money taken from capital, but the laying out of money which, upon its being laid out, becomes in itself capital. That is irrespective of the source from which the money comes.' *R v Wraith, ex p Kent County Council* [1907] 2 KB 756 at 762, 763, DC, per Darling J

Capital value

Australia [The Landlord and Tenant (Control) Act 1957 (Vict), s 24 (see now Landlord and Tenant Act 1958–1986, s 64(1)), provides that the Fair Rents Board, in determining the fair rent of prescribed premises shall, inter alia, have regard to the appropriate 'capital value'

of the premises.] 'In requiring the Board to have regard to the capital value of the premises and to the rate of interest charged upon overdrafts by the Commonwealth Bank of Australia, the Legislature doubtless had in mind the amount of capital which the landlord presumably had invested in the premises. This can best be ascertained by looking at the "market value" of the premises. This was assumed to be so by Sholl J in *Sandhurst and Northern District Trustees Executors and Agency Co Ltd v Auldrige* [[1952] VLR 448]. As Sholl J there pointed out an auction sale of the very property whose value is being considered at or about the time in question, if the auction was properly advertised and conducted, is the best possible evidence of market value. Opinion evidence of market value is commonly supported by evidence of the sale of comparable properties at or about the relevant date.' *Hume Investments Pty Ltd v Zucker* [1959] ALR 60 at 61, 62, per O'Bryan J

Circulating capital

Circulating capital is that part of the subscribed capital of a company used or intended to be used by being temporarily parted with and circulated in business in the form of money, goods or other assets, and which, or the proceeds of which, is intended to return to the company with increment and to be used again and to return again with some accretion. (7 Halsbury's Laws (4th edn) para 601)

'What is circulating capital? It is a portion of the subscribed capital of the company intended to be used by being temporarily parted with and circulated in business, in the form of money, goods or other assets, and which, or the proceeds of which, are intended to return to the company with an increment, and are intended to be used again and again, and to always return with some accretion. Thus the capital with which a trader buys goods circulates; he parts with it, and with the goods bought by it, intending to receive it back again with profit arising from the resale of the goods. . . . It must not, however, be assumed that the division into which capital thus falls is permanent. . . . The terms "fixed" and "circulating" are merely terms convenient for describing the purpose to which the capital is for the time being devoted when considering its position in respect to the profits available for dividend.' *Ammonia Soda Co v Chamberlain* [1918] 1 Ch 266 at 286, 287, CA, per Swinfen Eady LJ

If I understand the cases correctly, "circulating capital" is simply an expression used to denote capital expended in the course of the trade with a view to disposal at a profit of the assets produced or acquired by means of such expenditure, and represented at different stages of its career by cash, assets into which the cash has been converted, and debts owing from customers to whom those assets have been sold.' *Reynolds v Crompton* [1950] 2 All ER 502 at 511, CA, per Jenkins LJ; affd. sub nom. *Crompton v Reynolds & Gibson* [1952] 1 All ER 888, HL

Fixed capital

Part of the capital of a company may consist of fixed capital and part of circulating capital. Fixed capital means that capital which a company retains in the shape of assets upon which the subscribed capital has been expended and which assets either themselves produce income independently of any further action by the company, or, being retained by the company, are made use of to produce income or gain profits. (7 Halsbury's Laws (4th edn) para 600)

'What is fixed capital? That which a company retains, in the shape of assets upon which the subscribed capital has been expended, and which assets either themselves produce income, independent of any further action by the company, or being retained by the company are made use of to produce income or gain profits.' *Ammonia Soda Co v Chamberlain* [1918] 1 Ch 266 at 286, CA, per Swinfen Eady LJ

Issued and unissued capital

The nominal capital stated in the memorandum or articles . . . or in the resolution of the company for increase, is at first, and may for the most part always be, 'unpaid' capital; but some of it, namely the shares subscribed for by the signatories to the memorandum of association, is at once 'issued' capital. Shares registered in anyone's name, or in respect of which a share certificate has been issued, are part of the 'issued' capital. Shares, too, which are properly allotted stand in the same position. The residue of the 'nominal capital', or at any rate such of it as has not been agreed to be taken by any person, is 'unissued' capital. (7 Halsbury's Laws (4th edn) para 135)

Nominal capital

The word 'capital', as used in the Companies Act 1948 [repealed; see now the Companies Act 1985] and the statutes which it replaces, always means share capital in contradistinction to borrowed money, which is sometimes referred to as loan capital. It sometimes means the 'nominal' capital of the company, namely, that which is stated in the memorandum of association of any company, limited by shares or by guarantee with a share capital, or in the articles of an unlimited company which has a capital divided into shares, and any increase of that nominal capital which has been made in the manner required by statute. This 'nominal' capital does not at the outset, or necessarily at any time, represent money in the coffers of the company, or assets of any kind, but the amount of nominal capital at any given time limits the power of the company to limit shares. (7 Halsbury's Laws (4th edn) para 135)

Paid up capital

The Companies Act 1948 [repealed; see supra] limits the liability of the members of a company limited by shares to the amount, if any, unpaid on the shares respectively held by them. This means that the liability continues so long as anything remains unpaid upon a share, and can only be put an end to by payment in full. When that payment in full is made, the amount paid represents 'paid up' capital. (7 Halsbury's Laws (4th edn) para 137)

Registered capital   *See* REGISTER

Reserve capital

'Reserve' capital is the capital which is not capable of being called up except in the event and for the purposes of the company being wound up. (7 Halsbury's Laws (4th edn) para 139)

CAPITALISE

'The effect of an agreement to pay compound interest or to "capitalise" interest is stated with perfect clarity by Lord Sterndale MR in *Re Morris* [*Mayhew v Halton* [1922] 1 Ch 126], a statement with which I entirely concur. Such an agreement merely means that the interest at the stipulated rate as it falls due if it remains unpaid is added to the borrower's indebtedness and itself yields interest at the stipulated rate.' *Inland Revenue Comrs v Oswald* [1945] AC 360 at 372, HL, per Lord Macmillan

CAPITULAR BODY

'Capitular body' means, in the case of a dean and chapter cathedral, the dean and chapter, and, in the case of a parish church cathedral, the cathedral chapter. (Cathedrals Measure 1963, s 52)

CAPTAIN

'Captain', in relation to a hovercraft, means the person who is designated by the operator to be in charge of it during any journey, or, failing such designation, the person who is for the time being lawfully in charge of it. (Dumping at Sea Act 1974, s 12(1))

'Captain' means master (of a ship) or commander (of an aircraft). (Prevention of Terrorism (Temporary Provisions) Act 1984, s 14(1))

CAPTIVE ANIMAL

The expression 'captive animal' means any animal (not being a domestic animal) of whatsoever kind or species, and whether a quadruped or not, including any bird, fish, or reptile, which is in captivity, or confinement, or which is maimed, pinioned, or subjected to any appliance or contrivance for the purpose of hindering or preventing its escape from captivity or confinement. (Protection of Animals Act 1911, s 15)

CAPTURE   *See also* SEIZURE

Capture is a taking by an enemy as prize in time of war with intent to deprive the owner of all property in the thing taken. (25 Halsbury's Laws (4th edn) para 157)

The essential distinction between capture and arrest is that capture is the forcible taking of the subject matter of insurance in time of war with a view to taking it as prize, whereas arrest is a temporary detention only, with a view of ultimately releasing it or repaying its value. (25 Halsbury's Laws (4th edn) para 161)

In insurance policy

[A ship insured against loss by 'capture' was driven by a gale on the coast of an enemy and captured there by the enemy. The ship did not receive any damage from the gale.] 'This is clearly a loss by "capture" [and not by the perils of the sea], for had the ship been driven on any other coast but that of an enemy, she

would have been in perfect safety.' *Green v Elmslie* (1794) Peake 278 at 279, per Lord Kenyon CJ

'The general terms of insurance against "capture" are to be understood as virtually containing an exception of such captures as might eventually be made by His Majesty and his subjects, and against which a British subject could not consistently with his public duty insure in direct terms.' *Brandon v Curling* (1803) 4 East 410 at 417, per cur.

[Goods insured by a policy of insurance were warranted free from 'capture'.] '"Capture", in the warranty, is not confined to lawful capture, but includes any capture in consequence whereof the ship is lost to the insured.' *Powell v Hyde* (1855) 5 E & B 607 at 611, per Lord Campbell CJ

[Goods insured by a policy of insurance were warranted free from 'capture'.] 'I have not found any reason to change the opinion I ventured to express in *Sanday's* case [*British & Foreign Marine Insurance Co Ltd v Sanday (Samuel) & Co* [1916] 1 AC 650 at 665] to the effect that the old cases of *Hadkinson v Robinson* [(1803) 3 Bos & P 388] and *Lubbock v Rowcroft* [(1803) 5 Esp 50] established the principle which has since then been consistently applied in this country, that what is insured against . . . is the peril of actual capture, not the mere apprehensions of capture.' *Becker, Gray & Co v London Assurance Corpn* [1918] AC 101 at 109, per Lord Atkinson

In prize

'Capture consists in compelling the vessel captured to conform to the captor's will. When that is done *deditio* is complete, even though there may be on the part of the prize an intention to seize an opportunity of escape, should it present itself. Submission must be judged by action or by abstention from action; it cannot depend on mere intention, though proof of actual intention to evade capture may be evidence that acts in themselves presenting an appearance of submission were ambiguous and did not result in a completed capture. The conduct necessary to establish the fact of capture may take many forms. No particular formality is necessary: *The Esperanza* [(1822) 1 Hag Adm 85]. A ship may be truly captured, though she is neither fired on nor boarded (*The Edward and Mary* [(1801) 3 Ch Rob 305]), if, for example, she is constrained to lead the way for the capturing vessel under orders, or to follow her lead, or direct her course to a port or ther destination, as commanded. . . . It was contended . . . that hauling down the flag was conclusive . . . or at least was conclusive when taken in conjunction with stopping the engines as ordered. It was said to be an unequivocal act of submission, as eloquent as the words "I surrender" could have been. . . . This is to press *The Rebeckah* [(1799) 1 Ch Rob 227] beyond what it will bear, for there the facts showed that, after the act of formal submission by striking colours, there was no discontinuance of that submission . . . whereas Sir William Scott intimates that, if any attempt had been made to defeat the surrender, he would not have treated the *deditio* as complete till possession was actually taken. When ships are engaged in combat, striking the colours is an accepted sign of surrender. . . . In the case of a merchantman . . . the hauling down of the flag, like any other sign or act of submission, is to be tested by inquiring whether the prize has submitted to the captor's will. What a combatant seeks to intimate by acts signifying surrender is first and foremost that he ceases to fight and submits to be taken prisoner; what a merchantman intimates is that she means to do as she is told, and that the chattel property may be captured in prize though the seamen in charge of it are not made prisoners or placed under personal restraint.' *The Pellworm* [1922] 1 AC 292 at 302, 303, PC, per cur.

Assuming that there must be a capture as a condition precedent to jurisdiction in prize . . . the forcible bringing in of a vessel under an armed guard for purposes of search amounts to such a capture.' *Netherlands American Steam Navigation Co v Procurator-General* [1926] 1 KB 84 at 100, CA, per Atkin LJ

CAR   *See* MOTOR CAR

CARAT

(1) A description indicating that an article, or the metal in an article, is of so many carats is to be presumed to be an indication that the article of metal is of gold, and that its fineness is that specified in the following table for that number of carats.

(2) This paragraph shall not apply if (as in a case where the article is a precious stone) the word 'carat' is used as a measure of weight for precious stones, and not as a measure of fineness.

TABLE
indicates gold of a

Number of carats	standard of fineness of
9	375 parts per thousand
12	500 parts per thousand
14	585 parts per thousand
15	625 parts per thousand
18	750 parts per thousand
22	916.6 parts per thousand

and so in proportion for any other number of carats.
(Hallmarking Act 1973, Sch 1, Part III, para 2)

'The old standard of "nine carats of fine gold in every pound weight troy" is the same as the modern standard of "nine carats", the only difference being that in the old phrase "carat" is used to denote a weight, and in the modern one a proportion. The standard of nine carats means that, in every twenty-four parts, nine parts are of fine gold and fifteen parts of other metal.' *Westwood v Cann* [1952] 2 All ER 349 at 354, CA, per Denning LJ (also reported in [1952] 2 QB 887 at 899, 900)

CARAVAN

'Caravan' means any structure designed or adapted for human habitation which is capable of being moved from one place to another (whether by being towed, or by being transported on a motor vehicle or trailer) and any motor vehicle so designed or adapted, but does not include—
(a) any railway rolling stock which is for the time being on rails forming part of a railway system; or
(b) any tent.
(Caravan Sites and Control of Development Act 1960, s 29(1))

CARAVAN SITE

In this section [home loss payments for certain caravan dwellers] 'caravan site' means land on which a caravan is stationed for the purpose of human habitation and land which is used in conjunction with land on which a caravan is so stationed. (Land Compensation Act 1973, s 33(7))

CARCASE

'Carcase' means whole carcases of livestock, and sides, quarters and other wholesale cuts of carcases. (Agriculture Act 1967, s 25)

'Carcase' means the carcase of an animal and

includes part of a carcase, and the meat, bones, hide, skin, hooves, offal or other part of an animal, separately or otherwise, or any portion thereof. (Animal Health Act 1981, s 89)

CARD ISSUER

United States The term 'card issuer' means any person who issues a credit card, or the agent of such person with respect to such card. (Truth in Lending Act 1968, s 103(n))

CARDHOLDER

United States The term 'cardholder' means any person to whom a credit card is issued or any person who has agreed with the card issuer to pay obligations arising from the issuance of a credit card to another person. (Truth in Lending Act 1968, s 103(m))

CARE   *See also* REASONABLE CARE

' "Care" applies not only to the physical well-being of a child, his meals and his comfort at home, but also to his proper education. Otherwise he is not being properly cared for.' *Re DJMS (a minor)* [1977] 3 All ER 582 at 588, 589, CA, per Lord Denning MR

Australia [The Traffic Act 1949–1986 (Qld), s 17, provides, inter alia, that any person who drives a motor vehicle on a road without 'due care and attention' or without reasonable consideration for other persons using the road shall be guilty of an offence.] 'In *Simpson v Peat* [[1952] 1 All ER, at p. 449] the court interpreted the words "due care and attention" to mean that the question for the justices was— "Was the defendant exercising that degree of care and attention that a reasonable and prudent driver would exercise in the circumstances?" In my opinion it must not be forgotten that the relevant circumstances are in part created by the defendant driver; and that lack of "due care and attention" may not have amounted to negligence towards another person but may have been a failure to exercise that degree of care and attention that a reasonable and prudent driver would have exercised in looking after his own safety.' *Johannesen v Zeller, ex p Zeller* [1958] Qd R 366 at 371, per Stanley J

Canada [The Criminal Code (Can), s 285(4) (now RSC 1970, c C–34, s 235) provides that everyone who, while intoxicated, has the 'care or control of a motor vehicle, whether in motion or not, is guilty of an offence.] ' "Care" is intended to cover such a case as an intoxicated driver placing his vehicle, without applying the brakes, in such a situation that it may run away and occasion danger to the public. It is probably intended to cover the possible omission, because of intoxication, of such acts of care as would or might occasion harm, such acts, in short, as would render any person liable in damages for negligence. "Control" does not need definition. The man who is in a car and has within his reach the means of operating it is in control of it.' *R v Thomson* [1941] 1 DLR 516 at 518, 519, NBCA, per Baxter CJ

Canada 'It is my opinion that the words "care", "custody" and "control", as used in para (g) [of a clause in a policy of liability insurance referring to property in the care, custody or control of the insured] involve actual possession of the property that was the subject of damage. "Care" in the sense in which it is used in the paragraph is synonymous with "safekeeping"; "custody" imparts some authority over the property; "control" supposes physical possession of property over which control may be exercised.' *Excel Cleaning Service v Indemnity Insurance Co of North America* [1952] OR 9 at 13, Ont CA, per Laidlaw JA; affd. [1954] SCR 169

CARE OR CONTROL

It is hereby declared that, in the expression 'care or control', 'care' includes protection and guidance and 'control' includes discipline. (Children and Young Persons Act 1969, s 70(1))

CARE, CUSTODY OR CONTROL

Canada 'One cannot have "care" of something that is locked away from that person. To care for something means simply to preserve it or look after it. A person cannot care or preserve something he does not have access to. In my view, one cannot care or preserve something if he does not have physical possession or "custody" of it. The two words "care and custody" go together in that in order to have care or custody of something one must have actual physical possession of it. "Control", too, supposes physical possession of something. One cannot have care, custody or control without access.' *Neil's Trailer and Equipment Ltd v Butler, Maveety & Meldrum Ltd* (1977) 75 DLR (3d) 151 at 154, Alta SC, per Moore J

CARELESS DRIVING *See* DRIVE; DRIVER

CARGO *See also* SHIP

'Cargo' includes anything carried or to be carried in a ship or other vessel. (Dock Workers (Regulation of Employment) Act 1946, s 6)

'The words "cargo" and "freight" do, prima facie, and in their natural and ordinary meaning, refer to goods only; and where, in the same document, occur the words "cabin passengers" and "passage-money", and a contract is made between the same parties as to such latter mentioned subject-matter, the inference is almost irresistible, that the former words were not intended, within the meaning of the contracting parties, to comprise passengers and passage-money of any description; the parties showing themselves capable of making a contract as to passengers by their proper and specific name.' *Lewis v Marshall* (1844) 7 Man & G 729 at 744, 745, per cur.

'What . . . does the word "cargo" mean? It means the cargo of the ship, that is what is put on board the ship, or what the ship carries. . . . I find in Webster's Dictionary cargo defined as "the lading of freight of a ship, the goods, merchandise, or whatever is conveyed in a ship or other merchant vessel"; and Richardson gives its meaning as "the freight or lading of a ship". The question as to the meaning of the same word arose also in the case of *Sargent v Reed* [(1745) 2 Stra 1228]. . . . It was there argued that the word was uncertain and might mean only a small parcel of goods on board, but the court said that the word "cargo", as referred to a ship, was very intelligible, and must mean the whole loading. . . . This case was referred to in *Houghton v Gilbart* [(1836) 7 C & P 701], where the question as to the meaning of the word was left to the jury; but that was an action on a policy of insurance on cargo, which would not necessarily be on the whole, and it would therefore be a question for the jury what part of the cargo was insured. . . . Here, however, on my own reading of the word, and upon authority, I

think it means the whole cargo.' *Kreuger v Blanck* (1870) LR 5 Exch 179 at 183, 184, per Cleasby B

'An agreement to sell a cargo is, according to the plain and natural meaning of the words, an agreement to sell the entire quantity of goods loaded on board a vessel on freight for a particular voyage. By the terms of the contract the seller engages to deliver to the buyer a cargo of petroleum from 2,500 to 3,000 barrels at seller's option. . . . Effect must be given to the term "cargo", as distinguished from the specified quantity, as, if the parties had intended otherwise, it would have been enough to specify the quantity without introducing the term "cargo" at all. Now, generally speaking, the term "cargo", unless there is something in the context to give it a different signification, means the entire load of the ship which carries it, and it may fairly be assumed that when one man undertakes to sell and another to buy a cargo, the subject-matter of the contract is to be the entire load of the ship. . . . Such must have been the sense in which the term "cargo" is used in this contract.' *Borrowman v Drayton* (1876) 2 Ex D 15 at 19, CA, per cur.

'What . . . is a cargo? That is a question of fact. A very small quantity of goods in proportion to the carrying capacity of the ship could not be called a cargo. It must, to some extent, approach the carrying capacity.' *Miller v Borner & Co* [1900] 1 QB 691 at 692, 693, per Channell J

'The charterparty . . . provides that the steamer shall load "a cargo of beans not less than 6,500 tons but not exceeding 7,000 tons net intake weight of beans in bags as usual which the . . . charterers bind themselves to ship not exceeding what she can reasonably stow and carry". . . . I think . . . that a cargo of beans in this contract means in itself the entire lading of the vessel; that the words "not less than 6,500 tons" are a warranty to the charterers that she can take so much cargo; and that the words "but not exceeding 7,000 tons" are a term binding the shipowner not to ask for more than 7,000 tons, but entitling him to receive that amount if she can take it.' *Jardine, Matheson & Co v Clyde Shipping Co* [1910] 1 KB 627 at 629, 630, per Hamilton J

'In my opinion, goods which had been brought in a ship to a port would still be properly described and referred to as cargo while being unloaded, moved and, if the goods are stored after being unloaded, while being stored.'

National Dock Labour Board v John Bland & Co Ltd [1971] 2 All ER 779 at 789, HL, per Viscount Dilhorne

Deck cargo

[The Merchant Shipping Act 1894, s 85(1) enacts that if any ship, British or foreign, other than a home trade ship as defined by the Act, carries as 'deck cargo', that is to say, in any uncovered space upon deck, or in any covered space not included in the cubical contents forming the ship's registered tonnage, timber, stores, or other goods, all dues payable on the ship's tonnage shall be payable as if there were added to the ship's registered tonnage the tonnage of the space occupied by those goods at the time at which the dues become payable.] ' "Deck cargo" is to be understood as including anything carried on deck in some space not already included in the measurement of the ship's cargo-carrying capacity.' *Cairn Line of Steamships Ltd v Trinity House Corpn* [1908] 1 KB 528 at 532, CA, per Lord Alverstone CJ

See, generally, 43 Halsbury's Laws (4th edn) para 586

Discharge with customary despatch

'The question arises on the construction of a few words of the charterparty. They are as follows, viz., "to be discharged with all dispatch as customary". It has been held in *Dunlop & Sons v Balfour, Williamson & Co* [[1892] 1 QB 507, CA] and in other cases that the words "as customary" in such expressions as this are equivalent to "in the customary manner". They, therefore, primarily refer to manner of discharge, and secondarily only to time. They are not entirely disconnected with time, because the dispatch is to be in the customary manner, and that manner may be one which expedites or delays the discharge of the cargo. I read the words as meaning that the cargo is "to be discharged in the customary manner and with all reasonable dispatch"— that is to say, all dispatch which is reasonable having regard to the actual circumstances of the case, the custom of the port being one of such circumstances.' *Castlegate SS Co v Dempsey* [1892] 1 QB 854 at 861, CA, per Fry LJ

'The first question we have to consider is as to the meaning of the not uncommon provision in a charterparty as to the ship being discharged "with all despatch as customary". I think it is now settled that such a provision means that the discharge shall take place with all reasonable despatch, and that in considering what is reasonable you must have regard, not to a hypothetical state of things (that is, to what would be reasonable in an ordinary state of circumstances), but to the actual state of things at the time of discharge, and, in particular, to the customs of the port of discharge. So that a charterer is not liable for delay if he has (under the circumstances) used all reasonable diligence in procuring the discharge, and in considering what is reasonable diligence you must have regard (inter alia) to the appliances for discharge customary at the port.' *Lyle Shipping Co Ltd v Cardiff Corpn* [1900] 2 QB 638 at 647, CA, per Romer LJ

'Prima facie the receiver is bound to receive the cargo as fast as the steamer can deliver; but his obligation is usually qualified by words, such as "customary steamship despatch" or "ordinary custom of the port", which mean . . . the user of those facilities which the customary method of discharge at the port give for the particular kind of cargo. . . . The facilities of the port must be used by the receivers so as to give the ship as quick a discharge as possible, but . . . if there is a failure in the supply of facilities of the port . . . the charterer is not to blame where the words "custom of the port" are used in the charter party.' *Fawcett & Co v Baird & Co* (1900) 16 TLR 198 at 198, 199, per Kennedy J

'The charterparty provides that the cargo is to be "discharged with customary steamship despatch as fast as the steamer can . . . deliver during the ordinary working hours" of the port of discharge, "but according to the custom" of the port, "Sundays, general or local holidays (unless used), excepted". The question is, what is the meaning of this provision? Is it tantamount to fixing a certain definite number of days or hours as the period within which the discharge of the vessel is to be accomplished? Taking the words by themselves, apart from all authority, I should say certainly not. The words used do not specify, or even, I think, point to a definite period of time. What they do point to is the discharge of the cargo with the utmost despatch practicable, having regard to the custom of the port, the facilities for delivery possessed by the particular vessel under contract of affreightment, and all other circumstances in existence at the time not being circumstances brought about by the person whose duty it is to take delivery or circumstances within his control.' *Hulthen v Stewart & Co* [1903] AC 389 at 392, per Lord Macnaghten

'One must distinguish between the operation of discharge and the disposal of the cargo, when discharged by the consignee. Discharge begins and ends as from the ship on to the quay, or on to such appliances—wagons, lighters, or sheds—as are customary at the port of discharge. The actual discharge is an operation in which both shipowner and charterer are concerned, and have their respective duties. The subsequent destination or disposal of the cargo concerns the charterer alone.' *Dampskibsselskabet Svendborg v Love & Stewart Ltd* 1915 SC 543 at 551, per Lord Dundas; affirmed on appeal on another point 1916 SC 187, HL

'The extent of the obligation to discharge "as customary" is well settled; the obligation is to do what is reasonable in the circumstances.' *Bargate Steam Shipping Co v Penlee & St Ives Stone Quarries Ltd* (1921) 90 LJKB 572 at 573, per Roche J

Full and complete cargo

'The well-known and familiar expression "to ship a full and complete cargo" must have relation to the article which is to be shipped. If the parties want to have a contract which shall involve that every nook and cranny of the ship is to be filled with something, they must provide for it by some stipulation as to the amount of tonnage that is to be on board, or what not. . . . I look at the language of the charterparty, . . . and I find that the article specified there, "wet wood pulp", was tendered, and that article was loaded, and so loaded that the ship would hold no more. . . . It is not true to say that the merchant did not load "a full and complete cargo"; he did load a full and complete cargo of the thing which was contemplated to be loaded by the charterparty.' *Isis SS Co v Bahr* [1900] AC 340 at 342, 344, per Lord Halsbury LC

CARRIAGE   *See also* CONTRACT
CARRIAGE; EXPRESS CARRIAGE; HACKNEY CARRIAGE; INVALID CARRIAGE; STAGE CARRIAGE

'Carriage or vehicle' includes a bicycle. (Offences Against the Person Act 1861, s 35)

'Carriage' includes any carriage, waggon, cart, truck, vehicle, or other means of conveying goods or passengers by land, in whatever manner the same may be propelled. (Explosives Act 1875, s 108)

'I think the word "carriage" is large enough to include a machine such as a bicycle.' *Taylor v Goodwin* (1879) 4 QBD 228 at 229, DC, per Mellor J

'Any mechanical contrivance, which carries people or weights over the ground, carrying the weights or taking the people off their own feet, so that the foot of man and the body and trunk of man do not support his own weight or the weight of the burden carried, is, I think, a carriage, and I do not think it matters that the man who is carried gives his own propulsion to the carriage. . . . I therefore come to the conclusion that a bicycle or tricycle is a "carriage" [within the meaning of a special Act which made carriages, etc, liable to tolls].' *Cannan v Abingdon (Earl)* [1900] 2 QB 66 at 71, DC, per Phillimore J

[The Customs and Inland Revenue Act 1888, s 4 (repealed), imposed duties on every 'carriage' as therein defined. The question on a case stated was whether a motor bicycle was a carriage within the Act.] 'I do not think that there is anything which could give rise to a reasonable doubt that a bicycle propelled by some mechanical means or other and carrying a person would be a carriage within the meaning of this Act. The definition of "carriage" in the Act includes "any carriage drawn or propelled upon a road or tramway, or elsewhere than upon a railway, by steam or electricity or any other mechanical power", and, having regard to the gradual extension of this Act and common knowledge of what is going on, it seems to me that a machine which carries a person along a road is none the less a "carriage" because it is a very uncomfortable thing and because the person on it is shaken very much when he is going along.' *O'Donoghue v Moon* (1904) 90 LT 843 at 844, per Lord Alverstone CJ

[The appellant, while pushing his pedal bicycle along a road, was drunk and incapable of having proper control over the bicycle. He was arrested without warrant and charged with 'being drunk in charge of a bicycle on a highway, contrary to s 12 of the Licensing Act 1872', which provides that 'every person . . . who is drunk while in charge on any highway or other public place of any carriage . . . may be apprehended', and shall be liable to a penalty.] 'I think a carriage can include any sort of vehicle, certainly a vehicle which is capable of carrying a person; and it may be, a vehicle capable of carrying goods. . . . I am clearly of opinion that the words of the Licensing Act are wide enough to embrace a bicycle under the expression "carriage". . . . whether it be a tradesman's bicycle or tricycle or the ordinary passenger bicycle . . . which was the case here.' *Corkery v Carpenter* [1951] 1 KB 102 at 105, 107, per Lord Goddard CJ

In bequest

'I am of opinion that this motor-car did not pass by the gift [in a will] of "all my carriages, horses, harness, and stable furniture and effects". I think that, having regard to the collocation of words in which the word "carriages" appears here, the testator meant to give only such carriages as were used in connection with horses, harness and stables. If I were to hold otherwise it might be contended that every means of travelling which came into use after the testator made his will was a carriage within the meaning of this gift.' *Re Hall, Watson v Hall* (1912) 107 LT 196 at 196, per Parker J

CARRIAGE OF GOODS   *See also*
CARRIER; COMMON CARRIER

'Carriage of goods' covers the period from the time when the goods are loaded on to the time when they are discharged from the ship. (Carriage of Goods by Sea Act 1971, Schedule (Hague Rules))

'Carriage of goods' includes the haulage of goods. (Road Traffic Act 1972, s 196)

'Counsel for the appellants . . . submits that "carry" means "transport from one place to another"; that art III, r 2 [of the Hague Rules] imposes a positive obligation on the carrier to carry the goods, and that the goods are not carried at all if they are loaded on the vessel and then discharged at the port of loading. . . . I incline to the view that a ship does "carry" goods, within the meaning of art III, r 2, from the moment when they are loaded on board; and I think that this view is supported by the definition of "carriage of goods" in art I(e): " 'Carriage of goods' covers the period from the time when the goods are loaded on to the time when they are discharged from the ship." The result is that counsel for the appellants has failed to establish his . . . point.' *Renton (GH) & Co Ltd v Palmyra Trading Corpn of Panama* [1956] 3 All ER 957 at 966, 967, HL, per Lord Morton of Henryton

' "Carriage", of course, is a very wide word, which can be used to cover an incidental carriage of goods as well as a whole cargo of goods. It need not convey the notion of something loaded on a vehicle, but anything so long

as it is carried on the vehicle.' *Customs and Excise Comrs v Jack Bradley (Accrington) Ltd* [1958] 3 All ER 487 at 489, per Lord Parker CJ; also reported in [1959] 1 QB 219 at 224

See, generally, 5 Halsbury's Laws (4th edn) paras 328–374.

CARRIAGEWAY

'Carriageway' means a way constituting or comprised in a highway, being a way (other than a cycle track) over which the public have a right of way for the passage of vehicles. (Highways Act 1980, s 329(1))

'A carriageway always includes a footway.' *Davies v Stephens* (1836) 7 C & P 570 at 571, per Lord Denman CJ

Made-up carriageway

'Made-up carriageway' means a carriageway, or a part thereof, which has been metalled or in any other way provided with a surface suitable for the passage of vehicles. (Highways Act 1980, s 329(1))

CARRIER   *See also* COMMON CARRIER

'Carrier' includes all persons carrying goods or passengers for hire by land or water. (Explosives Act 1875, s 108)

'Carrier' includes the owner or the charterer who enters into a contract of carriage with a shipper. (Carriage of Goods by Sea Act 1971, Sch (Hague Rules))

General carrier

New Zealand   'It is evident that the expression "general carrying" means something different from "carrying" . . . It must, however, like the words "general ship", have some reference to the business of a person who offers to carry for all and sundry whatever goods may lawfully be tendered to be carried. The term does not, however, necessarily include all that is covered by the term "common carrier", which refers generally to persons carrying between fixed points.' *Carter v Tapp* (1912) 32 NZLR 200 at 201, per Chapman J

Private carrier

' "A private carrier", which term includes every person carrying for hire who is not a common carrier, is defined [in Macnamara on Carriers by Land, 2nd edn, p 6] to be "a person whose trade is not that of conveying goods from one person or place to another, but who undertakes upon occasion to carry the goods of another and receives a reward for so doing."' *Watkins v Cottell* [1916] 1 KB 10 at 14, DC, per Avory J

See, generally, 5 Halsbury's Laws (4th edn) paras 301–327.

CARRY

Australia 'At the most, the meaning [of the phrase "carry at 8 per cent", which occurred in a client's instructions to a sharebroker to buy certain shares and "carry at 8 per cent",] is that the defendants . . . are to carry the shares, or the burden of the payment for the shares, until the plaintiff settle up, and are to charge him 8 per cent. on the purchase-money which they have paid for him. The natural and ordinary meaning of this request in natural and untechnical English is that the client takes the whole gain as well as any loss or risk resulting from the shares from the time that they are brought to him; and that the brokers take no loss, no risk, no gain, resulting from the purchase, but take the interest at 8 per cent on the purchase-money, in addition to their commission as brokers.' *Thornley v Tilley* (1925) 36 CLR 1 at 18, per Higgins J

CARRY ON BUSINESS

Carrying on business only exists where there is a joint relation of persons for the common purpose of performing jointly a succession of acts, and not where the relation exists for a purpose which is to be completed by the performance of one act. (7 Halsbury's Laws (4th edn) para 20)

The expression 'carries on business' refers to something of a permanent character. An individual who is personally attending to a business may carry it on in one county court district even though his office or place of business is in another district, and, similarly, a corporation can carry on business in more than one place. A person whose business within the court's district is conducted by means of an agent does not reside or carry on business within that district if he himself carries on business in a different place but, for the purposes of an action, a firm may carry on business at a branch establishment though the principal place of business is elsewhere. A temporary carrying on of business in a district by a person whose permanent place of business is elsewhere does not make the former locality his place of business for the purpose of being sued. The mere fact that a company carries on business in a certain district does not give the right to sue a director in that district. The term 'carries on business' implies something more than mere service, from which the person may be discharged at a moment's notice. Thus a clerk employed by a solicitor whose office is in the City of London does not 'carry on business' within the City. (10 Halsbury's Laws (4th edn) para 108)

'Business can only be said to be carried on where it is managed. No doubt there may be cases where a man carries on more businesses than one and in different places, but such cases are quite exceptional, and the place of business, in general, must be the place where the general superintendence and management take place. . . . A railway company carries on its business at the principal station only.' *Brown v London & North Western Rly Co* (1863) 32 LJQB 318 at 321, per Blackburn J

[The Companies Act 1862, s 4 (repealed; see now Companies Act 1985, s 716), enacted that no company, association or partnership consisting of more than twenty persons could be formed for the purpose of 'carrying on any business' (other than banking) that had for its object the acquisition of gain, unless it was registered.] 'The expression "carrying on" implies a repetition of acts, and excludes the case of an association formed for doing one particular act which is never to be repeated. That series of acts is to be a series of acts which constitute a business. Now, the word "business" might in a grammatical sense include things which no ordinary person would call a business, and inasmuch as the Legislature could not particularise every kind of business which they intended to include, they have, in order to confine the meaning of that large word "business", stated that it is to be a business "that has for its object the acquisition of gain". The association, then, must be formed in order to carry on a series of acts having the acquisition of gain for their object.' *Smith v Anderson* (1880) 15 Ch D 247 at 277, 278, CA, per Brett LJ

'I think that the expression "carry on business" is not ordinarily used in the sense of a person being busy or doing business merely. A butler employed to look after his master's plate and perform the other duties of his occupation may be a very busy man, but he could not be said to be carrying on business. A man who busies himself about science, the volunteer movement, or politics, though he may have a great deal of business to transact in respect of these matters, does not carry on business. I think that the expression has a narrower meaning than that of doing business or having business to do. In my opinion it imports that the person has control and direction with respect to the business, and also that it is a business carried on for some pecuniary gain.' *Graham v Lewis* (1888) 22 QBD 1 at 5, CA, per Fry LJ

'There would seem to be a presumption that a company continues to carry on business as long as it is engaged in collecting debts periodically falling due to it in the course of its former business. Business is not confined to being busy; in many businesses long intervals of inactivity occur.' *South Behar Rly Co v Inland Revenue Comrs* [1925] AC 476 at 488, per Lord Sumner

[The question was whether a company, disposing of its assets in the course of winding-up, was 'carrying on business' within the Companies Act 1948, s 332(1) (see now the Companies Act 1985, s 458)] 'I feel quite unable to say that the expression "carrying on any business" in the section is necessarily synonymous with actively carrying on trade or that the collection of assets acquired in the course of business and the distribution of the proceeds of those assets in the discharge of business liabilities cannot constitute the carrying on of "any business" for the purpose of the section. The decision of the House of Lords in *Theophile v Solicitor-General* [[1950] 1 All ER 405], and *Re Bird* [[1962] 2 All ER 406] appear to me to point very strongly in the opposite direction. Admittedly those cases were decided on s 4(1) of the Bankruptcy Act 1914 [repealed] where the expression used is "carried on business in England, personally or by means of an agent or manager", but they establish that, at least for the purpose of that section, a bankrupt carries on business until he has performed all the obligations that the fact of trade imposes on him. The instant case is really *a fortiori* because there was here not merely a passive suffering of undischarged liabilities but a continuous course of active conduct in the collection and distribution of the business assets.' *Re Sarflax Ltd* [1979] 1 All ER 529 at 534, 535, per Oliver J

Australia 'Just as residing connotes some fixed place in which a man personally lives, so carrying on business connotes a fixed place in which a man personally transacts his business, and . . . a grazier cannot be said to carry on business . . . in every place on which he has stock running.' *Nelson v Evans* [1923] St R Qd 158 at 161, per Shand J

CARRY OVER   *See* CONTINUATION

CART

[The grant of a right of way was expressed, in a conveyance, to be a right to go, pass and repass over the land in question with or without horses, 'carts' and agricultural machines and implements. It was contended that use by motor lorries was excessive user.] 'Counsel for the defendants . . . contends that . . . the word "carts" in this context should not be restricted to carts drawn by horses. He admits that the word "cart" is not a word apt in itself to describe a motor vehicle. For some reason or other, although the word "lorry" for instance, which was originally a word descriptive of a certain kind of horse-drawn vehicle, was adapted for use in connection with motor vehicles, and for a time the word "carriage" was so used in the old fashioned expression "horseless carriage", the word "cart" has never, if I may use the expression, been mechanised. Counsel for the defendants admits all that, but he says that, nevertheless, in this context one should not construe the reference to carts as excluding, if I may so describe them, carts propelled by mechanical means, or, in other words, either carts drawn behind a separate mechanical tractor or mechanical horse or carts propelled by a power unit carried on their own frame or chassis. In my judgment, the argument of counsel for the defendants on this point should prevail. It is unnecessary for me to decide that this is a right of way for all purposes. I propose to limit myself to the question whether the use of this way by motor lorries is an excessive user. In my judgment, it is not. I think that a reasonable construction should be placed on this grant, and that it should be construed as meaning that the grantee, his executors, assigns and so forth, and tenants can pass and repass over the way either on foot or with vehicles in the nature of carts or with agricultural machines or implements. A cart for this purpose, in my judgment, is primarily a vehicle adapted to carry materials, goods, and so forth, possibly in contradistinction to a vehicle adapted for carrying passengers, and I do not think the particular mode of propulsion of the cart or vehicle is for the present purpose of any materiality.' *Kain v Norfolk* [1949] 1 All ER 176 at 182, per Jenkins J

CARTRIDGE

Safety cartridge

'Safety cartridges' means cartridges for small arms of which the case can be extracted from the small arm after firing, and which are so closed as to prevent any explosion in one cartridge being communicated to other cartridges. (Explosives Act 1875, s 108)

CASE

'Case', in relation to dutiable alcoholic liquor, means 1 dozen units each consisting of a container holding not less than [65 nor more than 80 centilitres], or the equivalent of that number of such units made up wholly or partly of containers of a larger or smaller size. (Alcoholic Liquor Duties Act 1979, s 4(1))

[The words in square brackets were substituted by the Alcoholic Liquors (Amendment of Enactments Relating to Strength and to Units of Measurement) Order 1979, SI 1979 No 24.]

CASH   *See also* MONEY

'It was not . . . a mere coincidence that he [the testator, who had left his wife all 'cash' in house] had money orders in the house, but part of his mode of dealing with his property. Now, can the amount represented by the money orders be properly described as "cash in house"? . . . I think that the money orders in the house were just as much cash as Bank of England notes. I think they ought to be treated as "cash in house".' *Re Windsor, Public Trustee v Windsor* (1913) 108 LT 947 at 948, per Warrington J

[A testator, after making certain specific bequests, directed that 'cash' (if any) should go to his sisters or their children. The question was whether money deposited in the Post Office Savings Bank was included in the gift of 'cash'.] 'The will is home-made and badly expressed, and I cannot help thinking that to such a testator the word "cash" would mean something with which he could go to a shop and purchase goods, and not money obtainable on short notice. The phrase "cash in bank" and "ready money" have both been held not to include money on deposit. . . . The testator's deposit is in much the same category as deposits in ordinary banks and . . . is not included in the gift of "cash".' *Re Ashworth, Bent v Thomas* (1942) 86 Sol Jo 134 at 134, per Bennett V-C

'"Cash" . . . is a loose expression. Nowadays it does not mean mere cash in one's pocket, but it includes a chose in action like money on current or deposit account at the bank.' *Re Wellsted's Will Trusts, Wellsted v Hanson* [1949] Ch 296 at 314, per Lord Greene MR

Canada '"Cash" in the present case [of construction of will] may bear any meaning which that word is capable of bearing in ordinary usage, the context of the will as a whole being the key to the meaning which should be applied to it in this case. I would note, however, that the word has been held to include moneys on deposit in a bank in *Re Richardson* (1930) 39 OWN 208 (Ont HCJ) and to encompass a bequest to the testator in *Re Parker Estate* [1950] 2 WWR 1026 (Alta SC).

In the context of the present will, I have come to the conclusion that the meaning of the clause in question is that all property not specifically bequeathed is to be sold, the debts and estate costs are to be paid out of the money so derived, and that the balance remaining of that money should be divided among the three named beneficiaries. I say that because it does not appear that the deceased had, or expected to have, a significant amount of ordinary paper and coin currency, and the clause can most logically be explained by assuming that he believed he would have personal property other than that specifically disposed of, and that he intended that it be converted into a cash fund from which his debts and funeral and other expenses could be paid, leaving thereafter some "cash" balance.' *Re Parker* (1982) 139 DLR (3d) 292 at 295, BCSC, per Taylor J

South Africa 'The general rule is that (a) in a sale for cash ownership does not pass until the price is paid even if delivery has in the meantime been given; (b) in a sale on credit, ownership passes on delivery. This, however, is not an irrefrangible principle of law. It is basically a question of fact in each case. It depends whether the totality of the circumstances shows, by inference or otherwise, that the parties intended the ownership to pass or not to pass, as the case might be.' *Eriksen Motors (Welkam) Ltd v Protea Motors (Warrenton)* 1973 (3) SA 685 (A), per Holmes JA

Cash in hand

New Zealand 'The will thus speaks: "I give and bequeath . . . all cash in hand at my decease to be equally divided between" [certain beneficiaries]. . . . The testator was entitled to the income of certain property which was vested in trustees, and her trustees were in the habit of paying her the income when she asked for it. . . . "Cash in hand" is a phrase, and it cannot be literally interpreted, for when the will speaks the testatrix is dead, and it is inapt to speak of the money which she has left, as cash in her hands. It must mean cash under her immediate control, and must . . . be construed as "ready money". . . . "Ready money" means money over which the testator [*sic*] can exercise an immediate and direct control. . . . If these [the surrounding circumstances] are looked at the meaning of "cash in hand" would obviously be the cash under her control with the trustees, just as much as the cash in the bank, which was in the hands, in one sense, of the bank. . . . "In hand" may mean in the hands of another. . . . In this case the trustees acted as bankers, and the money was at call. That "ready money" means money in a bank at call is clear.' *Re Bloomfield, Bloomfield v Reay* (1914) 33 NZLR 1441 at 1443–1445, per Stout CJ; also reported 17 GLR 125 at 126

Cash with order

South Africa 'It is difficult for me to believe that a merchant who uses the expression "cash with order" can possibly mean anything except that the cash must be in his hands with the order, and that means, of course, that it must be in his hands at his place of business.' *Habib (Pty) Ltd Commercial Central Agency Co Ltd* 1948 NPD 256, per Hathorn JP

Cash receipts

Canada 'It seems to me, looking at the language of the Act [Bankruptcy Act (Can); RSC 1952, c 14], that as regards the trustee's commission on the "cash receipts" that these words mean cash received by a trustee from the assets belonging to a debtor, as it is to such assets the trustee must look for his remuneration. . . . "Cash receipts" means cash realised by a trustee from the debtor's assets for distribution in dividends to the unsecured creditors.' *Re Johnston* [1925] 4 DLR 226 at 227, Ont SC, per Fisher J

CASH PRICE

United States Except as the Administrator may otherwise prescribe by rule, the 'cash price' of goods, services, or an interest in land means the price at which the goods, services, or interest in land are offered for sale by the seller to cash buyers in the ordinary course of business, and may include (1) applicable sales, use, and excise and documentary stamp taxes, (2) the cash price of accessories or related services such as delivery, installation, servicing, repairs, alterations, and improvements, and (3) amounts actually paid or to be paid by the seller for registration, certificate of title, or license fees. The cash price stated by the seller to the buyer pursuant to the provisions on disclosure (Part 3) of this Article is presumed to be the cash price. (Uniform Consumer Credit Code 1969, s 2.110)

CASH PROCEEDS　　*See* PROCEEDS

CASUAL EMPLOYMENT　　*See* EMPLOYMENT

CASUAL PROFIT

'Casual profit' . . . means a revenue profit arising to a person from an activity or transaction entered into by him of a type which is outside the scope of his ordinary vocation or trade, and which by reason of its casual, isolated or non-recurring character does not in itself amount to a trade or vocation, but is nevertheless a profit or emolument accruing by virtue of a service or from property. (23 Halsbury's Laws (4th edn) para 625)

CASUAL VACANCY

'By the 72nd article [of a company's articles of association] any casual vacancy may be filled up by the board. "Any casual vacancy" means any vacancy not occurring by effluxion of time, that is, any vacancy occurring by death, resignation, or bankruptcy.' *York Tramways Co Ltd v Willows* (1882) 8 QBD 685 at 694, CA, per Lord Coleridge CJ

'What is the meaning of the expression "any casual vacancy"? "Any casual vacancy" in my judgment is any vacancy in the office of directors arising otherwise than by the retirement in rotation pointed out by the previous articles.'

Munster v Cammell Co (1882) 21 Ch D 183 at 187, per Fry J

CAT

'Cat' includes a kitten. (Protection of Animals Act 1911, s 15)

CATERING PREMISES

'Catering premises' means premises where, in the course of a business, food is prepared and supplied for immediate consumption on the premises. (Food Act 1984, s 132(1))

CATHEDRAL

Cathedral church

'Cathedral church' means any cathedral church in England existing at the passing of this Measure except the cathedral church of Christ in Oxford. (Cathedrals Measure 1963, s 52)

Cathedral corporation

The expression 'cathedral corporation' means any dean and chapter, and also any corporation of minor canons, or vicars choral, or any other subordinate corporation of or belonging to or connected with any cathedral or collegiate church in Wales. (Welsh Church Act 1914, s 38)

Cathedral preferment

In all cases where the term 'cathedral preferment' is used in this Act, it shall be construed to comprehend (unless it shall otherwise appear from the context) every deanery, archdeaconry, prebend, canonry, office of minor canon, priest vicar, or vicar choral, having any prebend or endowment belonging thereto, or belonging to any body corporate consisting of persons holding any such office, and also every precentorship, treasurership, sub-deanery, chancellorship of the church, and other dignity and office in any cathedral or collegiate church, and every mastership, wardenship, and fellowship in any collegiate church. (Pluralities Act 1838, s 124)

'Cathedral preferment' means the office of dean, provost, residentiary canon or stipendiary canon in any cathedral. (Pastoral Measure 1983, s 85(5))

Dean and chapter cathedral

'Dean and chapter cathedral' means any cathedral church in respect of which there is a corporate body known as the dean and chapter. (Cathedrals Measure 1963, s 52)

Parish church cathedral

'Parish church cathedral' means any cathedral church other than a dean and chapter cathedral. (Cathedrals Measure 1963, s 52)

CATTLE   *See also* LIVESTOCK

The word 'cattle' shall include horse, ass, mule, ram, ewe, wether, lamb, goat, kid, or swine. (Markets and Fairs Clauses Act 1847, s 3)

The word 'cattle' shall include horses, asses, mules, sheep, goats, and swine. (Town Police Clauses Act 1847, s 3; Towns Improvement Clauses Act 1847, s 3; Dogs Act 1906, s 7)

'Cattle' means bulls, cows, steers, heifers, and calves. (Animal Health Act 1981, s 89(1))

'By s 68 of the Railways Clauses Consolidation Act 1845, the railway company is bound to make a sufficient fence for the protection of the adjoining landowner. . . . The fence is to be sufficient for . . . "protecting such lands from trespass, or the cattle of the owners or occupiers thereof from straying thereout by reason of the railway". . . . I think the word "cattle" in this section is sufficiently comprehensive to include pigs.' *Child v Hearn* (1874) LR 9 Exch 176 at 181, per Bramwell B

'If one applies the ordinary canons of construction, there can be no doubt that a calf is cattle. . . . Dead meat is from animals, bovine as well as other. A calf is a young bovine animal. Cattle would include both parent and progeny, and I see no reason why progeny should be excluded.' *Williams v Davis* (1920) 89 LJKB 1164 at 1165, 1166, per Lord Reading CJ

'Cattle, in s 7 [of the Dogs Act 1906 (supra)], is said to include, "horses, mules, asses, sheep, goats, and swine". It seems to me clear that rabbits cannot possibly be said in that state of things to be included in that definition of "cattle". It only requires to be stated, I think, to be quite clear. Some things, which normally would not be cattle, are expressly included. If the legislature had intended to include a thing so remote from the ordinary definition of "cattle" as rabbits, it most certainly would have included them in the section about horses, mules, asses, sheep, goats and swine.' *Tallents v Bell & Goddard* [1944] 2 All ER 474 at 476, CA, per Finlay LJ

'I have had a number of cases cited to me in which the word "cattle" had to be construed, and in every one of them the narrow meaning [i.e. that the word merely referred to animals of the bovine class] was rejected and the wider meaning was adopted. I agree that they were all decisions on a particular Act, but they do establish that, in interpreting the word "cattle" in the Act, one has to look at what is the evil aimed at—what it is that the section wishes to deal with. If one finds that the word "cattle" must have been used in the wider sense, one must give effect to it. The conclusion to which I have come is that the word "cattle" in this section [Income Tax Act 1918, Sch D, Case III, r 4 (repealed)] does include pigs.' *Phillips (Inspector of Taxes) v Bourne* [1947] 1 All ER 374 at 377, per Atkinson J

CATTLE-GRID

'Cattle-grid' means a device designed to prevent the passage of animals, or animals of any particular description, but to allow the passage of all or some other traffic, and includes any fence or other works necessary for securing the efficient operation of the said device. (Highways Act 1980, s 82(6))

CAUSA CAUSANS

'[Counsel] has strenuously contended . . . that the master's action . . . was "*novus actus interveniens*", which broke the nexus or chain of causation, and reduced the unseaworthiness from "*causa causans*" to "*causa sine quâ non*". I cannot help deprecating the use of Latin or so-called Latin phrases in this way. They only distract the mind from the true problem which is to apply the principles of English law to the realities of the case. "*Causa causans*" is supposed to mean a cause which causes, while "*causa sine quâ non*" means, I suppose, a cause which does not, in the sense material to the particular case, cause, but is merely an incident which precedes in the history of narrative of events, but as a cause is not in at the death, and hence is irrelevant. . . . If tort, which may in some respects have its own rules, is put aside and the inquiry is limited to contract, the selection of the relevant cause or causes will generally vary with the nature of the contract. I say "cause or causes" because . . . causes may

be regarded not so much as a chain, but as a network. There is always a combination of cooperating causes, out of which the law, employing its empirical or common sense view of causation, will select the one or more which it finds material for its special purpose of deciding the particular case.' *Smith, Hogg & Co Ltd v Black Sea & Baltic General Insurance Co Ltd* [1940] AC 997 at 1003, 1004, per Lord Wright

'To cause a thing to be done is the same thing as to be its causa causans. "*Causa causans*" is the real effective cause as contrasted with the *causa sine quâ non* which is merely an incident which precedes in the history or narrative of events.' *Tophams Ltd v Sefton (Earl)* [1966] 1 All ER 1039 at 1044, HL, per Lord Guest

CAUSE (Legal action)

In this Act, unless the context otherwise requires . . . 'cause' means any action or any criminal proceedings. (Supreme Court Act 1981, s 151(1))

'I have no hesitation about the word "cause". It is not a technical word, . . . it is *causa jurisdictions*, any suit, action, matter or other similar proceeding competently brought before and litigated in a particular court.' *Green v Penzance (Lord)* (1881) 6 App Cas 657 at 671, per Lord Selborne LC

Australia [The Judiciary Act 1903–1986 (Cth), s 40(1), provides that 'any cause or part of a cause arising under the Constitution or involving its interpretation which is at any time pending in any Court of a State may at any stage . . . be removed into the High Court.'] 'It was said that a rule *nisi* for a *habeas corpus* was not a "cause" [within the meaning of s 40] because it was not an original proceeding. . . . The argument is disposed of in *Green v Penzance (Lord)* [supra] thus: "It"—the word "cause"—"is not a technical word signifying one kind or another, it is *causa jurisdictionis*, any suit, action, matter or other similar proceeding competently brought before and litigated in a particular Court". Nothing in the Judiciary Act . . . limits this wide ambit of the word.' *Re Yates ex p Walsh, Re Yates, ex p Johnson* (1925) 37 CLR 36 at 131, per Starke J

Cause of action

'The term "cause of action" means all those things necessary to give a right of action, whether they are to be done by the plaintiff or a third person.' *Hernaman v Smith* (1855) 10 Exch 659 at 666, per Parke B

'"Cause of action" has been held from the earliest time to mean every fact which is material to be proved to entitle the plaintiff to succeed—every fact which the defendant would have a right to traverse.' *Cooke v Gill* (1873) LR 8 CP 107 at 116, per Brett J

'If the word "action" is to embrace proceedings which are not actions in the true sense, it seems to me that for "cause of action" [in the Limitation Act 1980, s 9(1)], must be read "cause of proceeding".' *China v Harrow Urban District Council* [1953] 2 All ER 1296 at 1299, per Lord Goddard CJ

'"Causes of action" in the sub-section [the Law Reform (Miscellaneous Provisions) Act 1934, s 1(1)] means, I think, rights which can be enforced, or liabilities which can be redressed, by legal proceedings in the Queen's courts.' *Sugden v Sugden* [1957] 1 All ER 300 at 302, CA, per Denning LJ

Canada [An agreement with a provincial insurer preserved specified 'causes of action'.] 'The phrase "cause of action" . . . means what it has come to mean, that is, "right of action". "Cause of action" meant originally and is still defined at p 297 of Jowitt's Dictionary of English Law, 2nd edn, as meaning "the fact or combination of facts which give rise to a right to sue."' *Connolly v Royal Insurance Canada* (1985) 16 DLR (4th) 763 at 767, Ont SC, per Fitzpatrick J

New Zealand 'In an action for damages for breach of contract, the cause of action is the breach of contract. . . . There is . . . one class of cases in which the fact of damage is a necessary and essential ingredient in the "cause of action"—namely, actions for torts causing damage to person or property not actionable without special damage, or until damage is sustained.' *Dillon v Macdonald* (1902) 21 NZLR 375 at 392, per cur.; also reported 4 GLR 415 at 422

New Zealand 'In *Dillon v Macdonald* [supra], the Court of Appeal discussed the meaning of the phrase "cause of action" and referred with approval to the definition, enunciated in *Jackson v Spittall* [(1870) LR 5 CP 542], and subsequently approved by a conference of judges, that "a cause of action" is "the act on the part of the defendant which gives the plaintiff his cause of complaint".' *Bass v R* [1948] NZLR

777 at 781, per Gresson J; also reported [1948] GLR 305 at 306

New Zealand 'The contention now urged is that the applicant's right to claim for further provision out of the estate of the testator is a cause of action, which, by virtue of the provisions of the Law Reform Act 1936 (NZ), survives the death of the applicant and can be carried to completion for the benefit of his estate, modified of course by the circumstance of the applicant's death. . . . The expression "cause of action" [in s 3] is not defined, but it obviously means a right of action; and definitions . . . of a "cause of action" as meaning "the entire set of circumstances giving rise to an enforceable claim", are not completely applicable; it is the "enforceable claim" which survives, not "the set of circumstances".' *Re Hawke (decd), Hawke v Public Trustee* [1957] NZLR 152 at 154, per Stanton J

New Zealand 'What is meant [by the term "cause of action"] is all the facts and circumstances necessary to give rise to a right to relief in law or equity. The same facts and circumstances may give rise to a right to relief under more than one principle of law or equity and in such cases the causes of action are different, but if the same relief is claimed under two or more such causes of action they are alternative causes of action.' *Papps v Mahon* [1966] NZLR 288 at 292, per Wilson J

See, generally, 37 Halsbury's Laws (4th edn) para 20).

Cause shown

[The Companies Act 1862, s 141 (repealed; see now the Insolvency Act 1986, s 108(2)) enabled the court, on 'due cause shown', to remove a liquidator (the phrase now being 'on cause shown').] 'Now, what is the meaning of the words "on due cause shown" in the Companies Act 1862, s 141? . . . The words must have some meaning, but it is difficult to define the extent to which they distinguish a case from one in which the ordinary words "if the Court shall think fit" are used. I should say that, as a general rule, they point to some unfitness of the person—it may be from personal character, or from his connection with other parties, or from circumstances in which he is mixed up—some unfitness in a wide sense of the term.' *Re Sir John Moore Gold Mining Co* (1879) 12 Ch D 325 at 330, 331, CA, per Sir George Jessel MR

'In many cases, no doubt, and very likely, for anything I know in most cases, unfitness of the liquidator will be the general form which the cause will take upon which the court in this class of case [an application to remove a liquidator on 'due cause shown' pursuant to the Companies Act 1862 s 93 (repealed; see now the Insolvency Act 1986, s 108(2)] acts, but that is not the definition of due cause shown. In order to define "due cause shown" you must look wider afield, and see what is the purpose for which the liquidator is appointed. . . . The due cause is to be measured by reference to the real, substantial honest interests of the liquidation, and to the purpose for which the liquidator is appointed. Of course, fair play to the liquidator himself is not to be left out of sight, but the measure of due cause is the substantial and real interest of the liquidation.' *Re Adam Eyton Ltd, ex p Charlesworth* (1887) 36 Ch D 299 at 306, CA, per Bowen LJ

Canada [The Winding-up Act, RSC 1952, c 296, s 32 (repealed; see now RSC 1970, c W-10, s 32) provides that a liquidator may be removed by the court on 'due cause' shown.] 'I do not take the view that the words "on due cause shown" should be construed too narrowly, or that their meaning should be restricted to something amounting to a lack of integrity, incompetence or even mismanagement. The weight of authority favours the view that the Court may take all the circumstances into consideration and if it finds that it is, upon the whole, desirable that a liquidator should be removed it may in the exercise of its discretion remove him.' *Re United Fuel Investments Ltd and Deacon v Union Gas Co of Canada Ltd* [1966] 1 OR 165 at 173, per Schroeder JA

New Zealand 'This application is made under s 201 of the Companies Act 1882 [repealed; see now s 237(1) of the Companies Act 1955 (NZ)] which provides that the Court may, "on due cause shown", remove any liquidator and appoint another liquidator to act in the matter of a voluntary winding-up . . . (the phrase now being 'on cause shown'). "Due cause" is not confined to personal unfitness on the part of the liquidator. Whenever the Court is satisfied that it is for the general advantage of those interested in the assets of the company that a liquidator should be removed, it has power to remove him: *In re Adam Eyton (Limited), ex parte Charlesworth* [supra]; but undoubtedly it lies on those who claim that they have "due cause" for removing a liquidator

duly appointed by the company to show at least a prima facie case of advantage to the company by the removal. A mere conjectural or fishing case is not sufficient.' *Re Mercantile Finance & Agency Co Ltd* (1895) 13 NZLR 472 at 473, 474, per Denniston J

CAUSE (Verb)

'If a man who has a right to print a book stands back and allows some one else to do the printing, I do not think it can be said that he "causes" the book to be printed [within the Copyright Act 1842 s 15 (repealed; cf. now Copyright Act 1956, s 21(5))].' *Kelly's Directories Ltd v Gavin & Lloyds* [1902] 1 Ch 631 at 635, CA, per Vaughan Williams LJ

'The bye-law, No 14 [of a local authority], provides that the landlord shall in the first week of the month of April in every year cause every part of the premises to be cleansed. The use of the word "cause" partly creates the difficulty; if the word could be construed to mean "take reasonable steps", the same difficulty would not arise; but I think it means more than that—it means that the person upon whom the duty is cast must see that the work specified is done.' *Stiles v Galinski, Nokes v Islington Corpn* (No 2) [1904] 1 KB 615 at 622, DC, per Lord Alverstone CJ

[The Children Act 1908, s 17(3) (repealed; see now Sexual Offences Act 1956, s 28(1), (3)) provides that any person having custody of a girl under the age of sixteen, who 'causes' or encourages the seduction, etc, of her shall be guilty of a misdemeanour.] 'The Legislature . . . enacted that a person should be deemed to have caused or encouraged the seduction or prostitution—or . . . the unlawful carnal knowledge—of the girl, "if he has knowingly allowed the girl to consort with . . . any prostitute or person of known immoral character". . . . It is true that the offence may be proved without showing that the defendant took any active step to bring about the seduction, prostitution, or unlawful carnal knowledge. . . . If it was proved that a father, knowing that his daughter was consorting with persons of known immoral character, stood by and allowed such intimacies to continue when it was in his power to prevent them, that might furnish evidence of causing or encouraging her unlawful carnal knowledge. But there is a wide difference between allowing and "knowingly allowing" within the meaning of this enactment.' *R v Chainey* [1914] 1 KB 137 at 141, 142, CCA, per Isaacs CJ

'If a man intending to secure a particular result, does an act which brings that about, he causes that result. If he deliberately and intentionally does certain acts of which the natural consequence is that certain results ensue, may he not also be said to have caused those results even though they may not have been intended by him? I think he can, just as he can be said to cause the result if he is negligent, without intending that result.' *Alphacell Ltd v Woodward* [1972] 2 All ER 475 at 483, HL, per Viscount Dilhorne

Australia [The Police Offences Act 1953, s 35(1) [now Summary Offences Act 1953–1986 (SA)], makes it an offence to offer for sale, or 'cause' to be offered for sale a newspaper in which any report appears of legal proceedings or other matters concerned with sexual immorality, unnatural vice or indecent conduct, if the report occupies more than a given space or carries headlines exceeding given dimensions.] 'As the evidence stands we have a case of the retail sale of a newspaper, considered as an article of commerce, made by independent retailers, all parties alike being animated by every business motive to promote the sale of the article. On the state of the evidence the position of the newsagent is little different from any other retailer, except that he may return unsold copies to the supplier. No doubt before the end may be said to be "caused" within the meaning of s 35(1), it must appear that it was contemplated or desired. But preliminary or antecedent acts done in such contemplation or out of such a desire do not necessarily amount to a "causing".' *O'Sullivan v Truth and Sportsman Limited* (1957) 96 CLR 220 at 227, per Dixon CJ, Williams, Webb and Fullagar JJ

CAUSE OR PERMIT

[The Road Traffic Act 1930, s 35(1) (repealed; see now the Road Traffic Act 1972, s 140(3)) made it an offence for a person to use, or to 'cause or permit' to be used, an uninsured motor vehicle.] 'To "cause" the user involves some express or positive mandate from the person "causing" to the other person, or some authority from the former to the latter, arising in the circumstances of the case. To "permit" is a looser and vaguer term. It may denote an express permission, general or particular, as distinguished from a mandate. The other person is not told to use the vehicle in the particular way, but he is told that he may do so if he desires. However, the word also includes cases

in which permission is merely inferred. If the other person is given the control of the vehicle, permission may be inferred if the vehicle is left at the other person's disposal in such circumstances as to carry with it a reasonable implication of a discretion or liberty to use it in the manner in which it was used. In order to prove permission, it is not necessary to show knowledge or similar user in the past, or actual notice that the vehicle might be, or was likely to be, so used, or that the accused was guilty of a reckless disregard of the probabilities of the case, or a wilful closing of his eyes. He may not have thought at all of his duties under the section.' *McLeod (or Houston) v Buchanan* [1940] 2 All ER 179 at 187, HL, per Lord Wright

[The respondent was charged with unlawfully 'causing' a vehicle to be used on the road contrary to the Motor Vehicles (Construction & Use) Regulations 1951, regs 72(1) and 101 (revoked; see now the Motor Vehicles (Construction and Use) Regulations 1963, r 73(1)).] 'I think that, when one finds those two expressions "causes or permits" in contrast or juxtaposition, "permit" means giving leave and licence to somebody to use the vehicle, and "causes" involves a person, who has authority to do so, ordering or directing another person to use it. If I allow a friend of mine to use my motor car, I am permitting him to use it. If I tell my chauffeur to bring my car round and drive me to the courts, I am causing the car to be used.' *Shave v Rosner* [1954] 2 All ER 280 at 281, 282, per Lord Goddard CJ; see also [1954] 2 QB 113

'I think the words used by Lord Wright in *McLeod (or Houston) v Buchanan* [supra] apply where, speaking of the word "cause", he said that the man in question did not cause his brother to use the van on the road: "To 'cause' the user involves some express or positive mandate from the person 'causing' to the other person, or some authority from the former to the latter, arising in the circumstances of the case." Almost similar words were used—and, inferentially, at any rate, approved by the Court of Appeal in *Watkins v O'Shaughnessy* [[1939] 1 All ER 385]—in the judgment of the learned county court judge in that case, where he said: "There must, in my view, be something involving control, dominance or compulsion of B's movements by A to 'cause'." I respectfully agree with those expressions.' Ibid at 282, per Hilbery J

'"Permits" appears to suggest the giving of

leave and licence to somebody . . . importing a state of mind of the person permitting. . . . The word "causes" appears to me to involve a person possessing some degree of control or authority to order or direct the use [in this case, of a car] by another, and the giving of such an order or direction.' *Clark v Hunter* 1956 SLT 188 at 191, per Lord Russell

CAVEAT

'The defendant . . . entered a caveat against the probate of the will of the testator. A caveat is not a notice to any opponent in particular. It is a notice to the registrar or officer of the Court not to let anything be done by anybody in the matter of the will, or the goods of the deceased, without notice to the person who lodges the caveat. It is impossible to look at it as commencing any litigation. . . . When a caveat has been entered the person who wishes to prove the will has to warn the person who entered the caveat, and if such person, i.e. the caveator, intends to make any real objection, he enters an appearance. Then, if the litigation goes on, the person who wants to prove the will issues a writ and serves it on the caveator. Then, and not before, there is litigation between the person propounding the will on the one side, and the person opposing it on the other.' *Moran v Place* [1896] P 214 at 216, 217, CA, per Lindley LJ

CAVEAT EMPTOR   *See also* DEFECT

'*"Caveat emptor"* does not mean in law or Latin that the buyer must take a chance, it means that he must take care. It applies to the purchase of specific things, e.g. to a horse or a picture upon which the buyer can and usually does exercise his own judgment. It applies also whenever the buyer voluntarily chooses what he buys. It applies also whenever by usage or otherwise it is a term of the contract express or implied that the buyer shall not rely on the skill or judgment of the seller.' *Wallis v Russell* [1902] 2 IR 585 at 615, CA, per Fitzgibbon LJ

CAVITY

'A cavity cannot have attached to it a natural right to support: it is merely an empty space.' *Newcastle-under-Lyme Corpn v Wolstanton Ltd* [1947] 1 All ER 218 at 224, CA, per Evershed J

CENTRE

Of road

Canada 'It seems to me that in dealing with s 41(8) of the Highway Traffic Act, RSO 1950, c 167 [see now RSO 1980, c 198, s 127)], the words "centre of the road" must be taken in their commonly-accepted meaning, that is, that the "centre of the road" means the centre of that part of the roadbed prepared for the use of travelling vehicles and does not include the shoulder of the road which, while it may be travelled upon, is not intended to be ordinarily travelled upon. The width of a shoulder of a road may vary greatly, and if for instance the shoulder of a road on the right-hand side was 2 ft, and the shoulder of the road on the left-hand side was 6 ft, and the part in between, wrought by the authorities into a roadway to be travelled upon, was 18 ft, the centre of the road would not be the centre of the 26 ft, but would be the centre, in my view, of the 18 feet.' *Trinidad Leaseholds (Canada) Ltd v Gordon* [1953] 1 DLR 445 at 446, Ont Co Ct, per Anderson, Co Ct J

CEREMONY   *See also* RITE

'The terms rite and ceremony, as used in the first prayer-book, and from thence imported into our present prayer-book, are terms, so to speak, of ecclesiastical and ritual art, and must be construed with reference to their use in contemporaneous and other works of writers upon ritual, unless they receive a different meaning from a comparison of other passages or parts in the prayer-book or statute in which they are found. . . . On the whole, the result of this examination of authorities leads one to the conclusion that there is a legal distinction between a rite and a ceremony; the former consisting in services expressed in words, the latter in gestures or acts preceding, accompanying, or following the utterance of these words.' *Martin v Mackonochie* (1868) LR 2 A & E 116 at 130, 135, 136 (Ct of Arches) per Phillimore J; *on appeal* (1868) LR 2 PC 365

CERTAIN

'Now it is true that, if that which is agreed upon as the payment is uncertain, it is not a rent. It must be certain. But the rent is certain if, by calculation and upon the happening of certain events, it becomes certain, and . . . the mere fact of rent being fluctuating does not make it uncertain. If a lease be made for ten or twenty ears, at a rent increasing every two or every three years, there the rent fluctuates, no doubt, but it is not uncertain. It becomes certain as each year advances. And so in other cases. If the rent of a farm for one year, if you please in advance, is to be so much if a certain number of acres are ploughed up; then in the next year a different rent if so many acres are left in pasture or in crops; there the rent is fluctuating, but it becomes certain the moment the condition is fulfilled, and therefore, although a fluctuating, it is a certain rent.' *Re Knight, ex p Voisey* (1882) 21 Ch D 442 at 458, CA, per Brett LJ

CERTIFICATE

New Zealand 'The . . . requirement [in a building contract] is that "moneys shall be retained in hand until forty days after the work is satisfactorily completed and a certificate to that effect has been granted by the architect". I am asked to read in the words "in writing" after the word "certificate". I do not think I have any authority to do so, and therefore an oral certificate is all that is necessary.' *Meyer v Gilmer* (1899) 18 NZLR 129 at 139, per Stout CJ; also reported 2 GLR 33 at 38

Of title to securities

'Certificate of title to securities' means any document of title whereby a person recognises the title of another to securities issued or to be issued by the first-mentioned person, and in the case of any such document with coupons (whether attached or on separate coupon sheets) includes any coupons which have not been detached. (Exchange Control Act 1947, s 42)

CERTIFICATION MARK

United States The term 'certification mark' means a mark used upon or in connection with the products or services of one or more persons other than the owner of the mark to certify regional or other origin, material, mode of manufacture, quality, accuracy or other characteristics of such goods or services or that the work or labor on the goods or services was performed by members of a union or other organization. (Lanham Act 1946, s 45)

CERTIFY

'The words in this contract do not import that the architect is to certify in writing. The Recorder of London when he certifies to the Court the custom of the City does so by word of mouth, and it is plain that the usual meaning of "certify" does not require anything written: otherwise why should parties ever expressly stipulate as to certifying in writing?' *Roberts v Watkins* (1863) 32 LJCP 291 at 293, per Byles J

CERTIORARI

The order of certiorari is an order issuing out of the High Court and directed to the judge or officer of an inferior tribunal to bring proceedings in a cause or matter pending before the tribunal into the High Court to be dealt with in order to ensure that the applicant for the order may have the more sure and speedy justice. (11 Halsbury's Laws (4th edn) para 1521)

Certiorari lies to remove orders made by the Crown Court other than in matters relating to trial on indictment and all orders or commissions before justices of the peace in order to quash them. Certiorari also lies to bring up and quash an order of the county court where the judge of that court has acted without jurisdiction. Certiorari does not lie to quash a decision of an inferior court merely on the ground that fresh evidence which might have affected the result has come to light since the date of the hearing. (11 Halsbury's Laws (4th edn) para 1528)

'The writ [now order (see supra)] of certiorari is a very old and high prerogative writ drawn up for the purpose of enabling the Court of King's Bench to control the action of inferior courts and to make it certain that they shall not exceed their jurisdiction; and therefore the writ of certiorari is intended to bring into the High Court the decision of the inferior tribunal, in order that the High Court may be certified whether the decision is within the jurisdiction of the inferior court. There has been a great deal of discussion and a large number of cases extending the meaning of "court". It is not necessary that it should be a court in the sense in which this court is a court; it is enough if it is exercising, after hearing evidence, judicial functions in the sense that it has to decide on evidence between a proposal and an opposition; and it is not necessary to be strictly a court; if it is a tribunal which has to decide rights after hearing evidence and opposition it is amenable to the writ of certiorari.' *R v London County Council, ex p Entertainments Protection Assocn Ltd* [1931] 2 KB 215 at 233, per Scrutton LJ

'Of recent years the scope of certiorari seems to have been somewhat forgotten. It has been supposed to be confined to the correction of excess of jurisdiction, and not to extend to the correction of errors of law, and several learned judges have said as much. But the Lord Chief Justice has, in the present case, restored certiorari to its rightful position and shown that it can be used to correct errors of law which appear on the face of the record, even though they do not go to jurisdiction. I have looked into the history of the matter, and find that the old cases fully support all that the Lord Chief Justice says. Until about one hundred years ago, certiorari was regularly used to correct errors of law on the face of the record. It is only within the last century that it has fallen into disuse, and that is only because there has, until recently, been little occasion for its exercise. Now, with the advent of many new tribunals and the plain need for supervision over them, recourse must once again be had to this well-tried means of control.' *R v Northumberland Compensation Appeal Tribunal, ex p Shaw* [1952] 1 All ER 122 at 128, CA, per Denning LJ; also reported in [1952] 1 KB 338 at 348

Canada 'The writ of certiorari, at common law, is a prerogative writ to which, notwithstanding any statutory provisions to the contrary, recourse may be had in order to control the action of inferior jurisdictions and bring them back within the limits assigned by law, whenever there has been a failure, or absence, or excess of jurisdiction.' *Re Town of Dauphin and Director of Public Welfare and Close* (1956) 17 WWR 628 at 631, Man QB, per Duval J; affd. 19 WWR 97, Man CA

CESSPOOL

'Cesspool' includes a settlement tank or other tank for the reception or disposal of foul matter from buildings. (Building Act 1984, s 126)

CHAIRMAN

For this purpose 'chairman' means the person elected by the directors to be chairman of their meetings and includes a person who, though not so elected, holds any office (however designated) which in accordance with the company's constitution carries with it functions substantially similar to those discharged by a person so elected. (Companies Act 1985, Sch 5, para 24(1))

CHALLENGE

On the trial of an indictment, before the jurors are sworn, the defendant and the Crown must be allowed the opportunity of challenging, i.e. of objecting to, the jurors who are called to serve. The defendant is informed of his right to challenge by the clerk of the court. There is no right to challenge jurors empanelled to try collateral issues such as the determination of fitness to be tried or the establishment of a special plea.

Challenges are of two kinds, challenges to the array, i.e. to the whole number of persons in the panel, and challenges to the polls, i.e. to individual jurors. Challenges to the polls are either peremptory or for cause. A challenge to the array must be made before any juror is sworn; a challenge to the polls must be made after the jurors's name has been drawn (unless the court has dispensed with balloting for him) and before he is sworn.

A challenge to the array is the taking of exception to the whole panel of persons returned by the summoning officer by reason of matter personal to himself, and is either a principal challenge (on the ground of any partiality in the officer concerned in the summoning and return of the jury, as, for instance, if such officer is biased or has acted improperly) or 'for favour', where the position of the summoning officer is not necessarily inconsistent with indifference, but may be suspected.

Peremptory challenges, for which no cause need be shown, are allowed to the defendant to the number of seven. The Crown has no peremptory challenge in any case, but may challenge by asking that the juror 'stand by for the Crown' as the names are called over, and is not bound to show the cause of challenge until the panel is gone through. A defendant whose peremptory challenges have been exhausted, may be allowed to follow the same course, but has no right to do so.

A peremptory challenge, once exercised, cannot be withdrawn in order to be used against another juror; but a defendant who has challenged for cause which has been disallowed, may challenge the same juror peremptorily.

The causes for challenge are that the juror called is an alien or is not qualified to serve as a juror, or has some personal defect which renders him incapable of discharging the duty of a member of the jury, or that he is not impartial, or that he has served on the coroner's jury which inquired into the same matter.

If the cause for challenge is allowed, the juror is ordered to stand down and a fresh juror is called. Such challenges are unlimited.

A defendant is bound, however, to conclude his challenges, whether peremptory or for cause, before the Crown can be required to justify its challenges. (11 Halsbury's Laws (4th edn) paras 455, 456, 457, 458)

CHAMBERS

'A judge sitting in chambers does not mean that he is sitting in any particular room, but that he is not sitting in open Court.' *Hartmont v Foster* (1881) 8 QBD 82 at 84, CA, per Brett LJ

CHAMPERTY

'Champerty' is a particular kind of maintenance, namely maintenance of an action in consideration of a promise to give the maintainer a share in the proceeds or subject matter of the action.

Since 1967 both criminal and tortious liability for maintenance and champerty have been abolished [by the Criminal Law Act 1967, s 13]; but the abolition of these forms of liability does not affect any rule of law as to the cases in which a contract involving maintenance or champerty is to be treated as contrary to public policy or otherwise illegal. Accordingly, it continues to be necessary to treat maintenance and champerty in detail, notwithstanding that most of the cases involve the now defunct tortious liability. (9 Halsbury's Laws (4th edn) para 400)

Australia 'Champerty implies a bargain of some sort between the plaintiff or the defendant in a cause and another person who has no interest in the subject in dispute to divide the property sued for between them if they prevail, in consideration of that other person carrying on the suit at his own expense.' *Hayes v Levinson* (1890) 16 VLR 305 at 307, per Hood J

CHANCE   *See* GAME OF CHANCE; GAMING

CHANCELLOR

Of diocese

The judge of the [consistory] court is styled the chancellor of the diocese. As judge of the consistory court the chancellor acts in the capacity of official principal of the bishop, who appoints

him to the office by letters patent. Although the power of nomination and appointment resides in the bishop, the chancellor's authority is derived from the law. He is a Queen's judge, in one of the Queen's courts. He acts in the court as an Ordinary, that is to say, as an independent judge, uncontrolled by the bishop, and with no special instructions from him. There is no appeal from the chancellor to the bishop. The chancellor, being a judge independent of the bishop, may hear and determine in the consistory court a cause in which the bishop is himself interested. (14 Halsbury's Laws (4th edn) paras 1274, 1275)

'Chancellor of the diocese' means the judge of the consistory or commissary court of the Bishop of the diocese. (Interpretation Measure 1925, s 3)

CHANGE

Of voyage

(1) Where, after the commencement of the risk, the destination of the ship is voluntarily changed from the destination contemplated by the policy, there is said to be a change of voyage.

(2) Unless the policy otherwise provides, where there is a change of voyage, the insurer is discharged from liability as from the time of change, that is to say, as from the time when the determination to change it is manifested; and it is immaterial that the ship may not in fact have left the course of voyage contemplated when the loss occurs.

(Marine Insurance Act 1906, s 45)

New Zealand 'The distinction between a deviation and a change of voyage is thus dealt with in Joyce's Treatise on Insurance: "... herein lies the distinction between a deviation and a change or abandonment of the voyage insured. In the latter case the terminus *ad quem* of the voyage insured is absolutely lost sight of and given up".' *Union SS Co of New Zealand v Jakins & Bower* (1901) 19 NZLR 780 at 792, per Stout CJ; also reported 3 GLR 338 at 343

CHANNEL

New Zealand 'One ... has two quite different situations provided for in [the Soil Conservation and Rivers Control Act 1941];

the obstruction of existing flood channels and the obstruction of land containing no flood channel yet upon which flood waters might encroach or flow and I believe the difference is to be found in applying the popular meaning of "channel" as being something that at least has confining banks and an identifiable course where the river flows when it floods, with the condition of the land affording convincing evidence of it.' *Tassell v Bennett* [1962] NZLR 500 at 504, per Hardie Boys J

Narrow channel

[The Merchant Shipping Act 1854, s 297 (repealed; see now Collision Regulations (Ships and Seaplanes on the Water) and Signals of Distress (Ships) Order 1965, reg 25), provided that every steamship, in navigating a 'narrow channel', should, whenever it was safe and practicable, keep to that side of the fairway or mid-channel which lay on the starboard side of such steamship.] 'My notion of a narrow channel is this: where a channel is bounded on either side by land prima facie so that it is impossible under the circumstances that you can navigate at any great width between the two banks. Now, if you should be of opinion, without regard to what is stated in any boat, or anything of that kind, that the channel had ended, that is to say, that the place of collision was in the open sea, where there is a wide depth of water—an expanse of water on both sides—where ships may safely navigate, then I should come to the conclusion that it is not a narrow channel.' *The Florence Nightingale, The Meander* (1863) 8 LT 34 at 35, 36, PC, per Dr Lushington

[The Regulations for Preventing Collisions at Sea 1897, art 25 (revoked; see now Collision Regulations (Ships and Seaplanes on the Water) and Signals of Distress (Ships) Order 1965, reg 25), provided that in 'narrow channels' every vessel should, when safe and practicable, keep to that side of the fairway or mid-channel which lay on the starboard side of such vessel.] 'I have come to the conclusion which accords with that of the President and of the Elder Brethren below, . . . that the western entrance to the harbour of Cherbourg is a narrow channel within the meaning of that rule. Counsel for the appellants have strenuously argued that art 25 did not apply, on the ground that this was what they called an entrance or opening, and not a narrow channel. . . . It is said that "channel" imports or denotes length of channel as well as breadth, narrow or wide. That may be true, but it seems

to me that it is going very much further to say that if the channel is very short the article does not apply.' *The Kaiser Wilhelm der Grosse* [1907] P 259 at 263, 264, CA, per Lord Alverstone CJ

'The word "channel" denotes a depression between two banks or ridges having a definite boundary on each side, and a narrow channel is a channel in which the two boundaries are close to one another.' *The Treherbert* [1934] P 31 at 46, 47, CA, per Lawrence LJ

See, generally, 43 Halsbury's Laws (4th edn) para 890.

CHAPEL

The word 'chapel' is commonly applied to a sanctuary or place of Christian worship, whether or not in connection with the Church of England, not being the church of a parish or the cathedral church of a diocese, but in strict legal parlance a chapel is a building consecrated for the purposes of divine worship in accordance with the tenets of the Church of England, other than the church of a parish or the cathedral church of a diocese.

A chapel may have a district attached to it called a chapelry, or it may be built for the convenience in prayer and preaching only of parishioners who live far from the parish church, in which case it is called a chapel of ease. A chapel which has an ancient division of a parish attached to it by immemorial custom with the parochial rights of christening and burying, is a parochial chapel. (14 Halsbury's Laws (4th edn) para 1225)

'The legal meaning of the term "chapel" is a chapel of the Church of England.' *Caiger v St Mary, Islington, Vestry* (1881) 50 LJMC 59 at 64, DC, per Grove J

CHAPLAIN   *See also* ARMY CHAPLAIN

'I use the word "chaplain" because it is the plainest word to use if it is intended to signify clergymen employed upon religious duties.' *R v Haslehurst* (1884) 53 LJMC 127 at 131, per Stephen J

CHAPTER

A chapter is a congregation of canons of a cathedral or collegiate church, usually (but not necessarily) including a dean, who is chief and head of the chapter. (14 Halsbury's Laws (4th edn) para 638)

CHARACTER

[The Education Act 1944, s 8 requires that schools in an area must be sufficient in number, 'character', and equipment to afford variety in education.] 'The plaintiff's contention is, as I understand it, that the use of the words in s 8, "sufficient in . . . character", mean that the local authority must ensure that there are in their area at least some schools where the pupils are selected on academic merit or some schools of smaller size albeit of comprehensive nature if they are to comply with the terms of the Act. I respectfully agree with Megarry V-C that this contention is untenable. "Character" in this context means the intangible attributes of a school. For example, the type of pupil: girls, boys or mixed; the type of instruction available: religious, academic or practical; and so on. What it does *not* mean is the size or method of selection adopted for any particular institution. Provided that the authority make available for the school children in their area a sufficient variety of educational opportunity in the various subjects which should properly be taught, it matters not whether the schools are small or large, or whether the bright pupils are taught in a separate school from the less bright or whether all pupils are taught in the same school under one roof. It follows that the authority are lawfully entitled to have and to implement the comprehensive policy, and within the ambit of that policy to take such reasonable steps as they think fit.' *Smith v Inner London Education Authority* [1978] 1 All ER 411 at 424, 425, CA, per Geoffrey Lane LJ

Character and antecedents

[Under the Magistrates' Courts Act 1980, s 38 justices may consider the 'character and antecedents' of a person and in appropriate cases commit such person in custody to the Crown Court for sentence.]
'It is not necessary to enter into a discussion whether "character" [in Criminal Justice Act 1948, s 29(1) (repealed; see now Magistrates' Courts Act 1980, s 38, supra)] means general reputation. It certainly, in my opinion, relates to something more than the fact that a person has been previously convicted, and the word "antecedents" [see supra] is as wide as can be conceived.' *R v Vallett* [1951] 1 All ER 231 at 231, CCA, per cur.

'As I see it, speaking for myself, the expression "character and antecedents" [in the Magistrates' Courts Act 1980, s 38 (supra)] being as wide as it possibly can be, justices are entitled

to take into consideration in deciding whether or not to commit, not merely previous convictions, not merely offences which they are asked to take into consideration, but matters revealed in the course of the case connected with the offence charged which reflects in any way on the accused's character.' *R v King's Lynn JJ, ex p Carter* [1968] 3 All ER 858 at 862, per Lord Parker CJ

Good or bad character

'Good or bad character does not depend upon what a man knows of himself; it means his general reputation in the estimation of his neighbours.' *Leader v Yell* (1864) 16 CBNS 584 at 593, 594, per Erle CJ

[The Criminal Evidence Act 1898, s 1(f), provides that a person charged and called as a witness shall not be asked questions tending to show that he is of bad character unless he has attempted to establish, or given evidence of, his own 'good character'.] 'There is perhaps some vagueness in the use of the term "good character" in this connexion. Does it refer to the good reputation which a man may bear in his own circle, or does it refer to the man's real disposition as distinct from what his friends and neighbours may think of him? In *R v Rowton* [(1865) 10 Cox CC 25], on a re-hearing before the full court, it was held by the majority that evidence for or against a prisoner's good character must be confined to the prisoner's general reputation, but Erle CJ and Willes J thought that the meaning of the phrase extended to include actual moral disposition as known to an individual witness, though no evidence could be given of concrete examples of conduct. In the later case of *R v Dunkley* [[1927] 1 KB 323], the question was further discussed in the light of the language of the section, but not explicitly decided. I am disposed to think that in para (f) (where the word "character" occurs four times) both conceptions are combined.' *Stirland v Director of Public Prosecutions* [1944] AC 315 at 324, 325, HL, per Lord Simon LC

'The second matter of principle turns on this point, . . . whether evidence of a plaintiff's bad character is to be understood as meaning the character which he bears in public estimation, by which I mean his reputation, or the character which might be attributed to him on a nice assessment of all his actions, if not his thoughts and desires, by which I mean his disposition. In my opinion, character in this context [a libel action] ought to mean the former conception exclusively. . . . I do not believe that "the character that a man ought to have" or to enjoy has any intelligible meaning. It is not possible for a jury, learning, perhaps long after the event, of this or that discreditable action in a man's life, to remake the current public estimation of him by some ideal piece of analysis. The materials themselves could not be available. Moreover, any rule that made it possible for a defendant to put in evidence by way of mitigation some discreditable action of the plaintiff, irrespective of whether it was publicly known or not and so contributed to his reputation, would be a rule so inherently unfair that it ought not to be accepted.' *Plato Films Ltd v Speidel* [1961] 1 All ER 876 at 883, HL, per Lord Radcliffe; also reported [1961] AC 1090 at 1128, 1129

'A man's "character", it is sometimes said, is *what he in fact is*, whereas his "reputation" is *what other people think he is*. If this be the sense in which the words are being used, then a libel action is concerned only with a man's reputation, that is, with what people think of him; and it is for damage to his reputation, that is, to his esteem in the eyes of others, that he can sue, and not for damage to his own personality or disposition. . . . But there is another sense in which the word "character" is used, and quite properly used, when it overlaps the word "reputation". Thus, when I say of a man that "He has always borne a good character", I mean that he has always been thought well of *by others*; and when I want to know what his "character" is, I write, not to him, but to *others* who know something about him. In short, his "character" is the esteem in which he is held by others who know him and are in a position to judge his worth. A man can sue for damage to his character in this sense, even though he is so little known to the outside world that he has no "reputation" in the ordinary sense of that word. If it were said of Robinson Crusoe that he murdered Man Friday, he would have a cause of action, even though no one had ever heard of him before. But a man's "character", so understood, may become known to others beyond his immediate circle. In so far as this estimate spreads outwards from those who know him and circulates among people generally in an increasing range it becomes his "reputation" which is entitled to the protection of the law just as much as his character. But here I speak only of a reputation which is built on the estimate of those who know him. No other reputation is of any worth. The law can take no notice of a reputation which has no

foundation except the gossip and rumour of busybodies who do not know the man. Test it this way. Suppose an honourable man becomes the victim of groundless rumour. He should be entitled to damages without having this wounding gossip dragged up against him. He can call people who know him to give guidance of his good character. On the other hand, suppose a "notorious rogue" manages to conceal his dishonesty from the world at large. He should not be entitled to damages on the basis that he is a man of unblemished reputation. There must, one would think, be people who know him and can come and speak to his bad character. This leads me to the conclusion that, in order to arrive at a man's character and reputation, one should call those who know him and have had dealings with him; for they provide the only sound foundation on which to build.' Ibid at 889, per Lord Denning

Australia   [The Crimes Act 1958–1986 (Vic), s 399(e) [see now s 399(5)], which relates to questions that may be asked of a witness who is called upon the trial or hearing of a criminal charge against him, imposes a restriction upon asking questions tending to show (inter alia) that such witness is of 'bad character'.] 'The expression "bad character" in relation to a witness has no technical or legal meaning. The expression "good character" has, of course, a known significance in relation to evidence upon criminal trials; for it denotes a description of evidence in disproof of guilt which an accused person may adduce. He may adduce evidence of the favourable character he bears as a fact or matter, making it unlikely that he committed the crime charged. . . . "Bad character" may be regarded as the contrary of "good character".' *Attwood v R* [1960] ALR 321 at 323, 324, per cur.

Australia   ' "Good character" is not a summation of acts alone but relates rather to the quality of a person. The quality is to be judged by acts and motives, that is to say, behaviour and the mental and emotional situations accompanying that behaviour. However, character cannot always be estimated by one act or one class of act. As much about a person as is known will form the evidence from which the inference of good character or not of good character is drawn.' *Ex p Tziniolis* [1967] 1 NSWR 357 at 377, per Holmes JA

CHARGE (Accusation)

'I am of opinion that the word "charged" [in

the Metropolitan Police Courts Act 1839, s 29 (repealed; see now Police (Property) Act 1897, s 1(1))] must be read in its known legal sense, namely, the solemn act of calling before a magistrate an accused person and stating, in his hearing, in order that he may defend himself, what is the accusation against him.' *R v D'Eyncourt* (1888) 21 QBD 109 at 119, DC, per Field J

'In para (f) of s 1 of the [Criminal Evidence] Act of 1898 the word [charged] appears five times and it is plain that its meaning in the section is "accused before a court" and not merely "suspected or accused without prosecution". When the appellant denied that he had ever been "charged", he may fairly be understood to use the word in the sense it bears in the statute and to mean that he had never previously been brought before a criminal court.' *Stirland v Director of Public Prosecutions* [1944] AC 315 at 323, 324, HL, per Lord Simon LC

'"The person charged" has various different meanings, and, in my opinion, it may include the case of a person who has been arrested on a charge, as he might be in a case of felony, or that of a person who has been arrested on a warrant granted by a magistrate, or even that of a person who has been summoned, that being another form of bringing a person before a court to appear and answer a charge, but I think that the section [the Summary Jurisdiction Act 1879, s 44 (repealed; see now the Magistrates' Courts Act 1980, s 48)] must be confined to cases where the person is at least accused, and in that sense charged, with some felony or misdemeanour.' *Arnell v Harris* [1945] KB 60 at 63, per Humphreys J

[The distinction between felony and misdemeanour has been abolished; see the Criminal Law Act 1967, s 1.]

'In a sense a prisoner may be charged at the moment when a policeman arrests him without warrant on suspicion of felony and there is some obligation to inform the arrested person for what he is being arrested. There may be further action taken by the police at the police station, but it does not follow that what happens at those earlier stages makes the person arrested charged in the relevant and material sense, which I should have thought means that an information has been laid against him so that the proceedings against him have at that stage been started. I am not satisfied that he can be said to be charged [within the Indictable Offences Act 1848, s 17] . . . until an informa-

tion has been laid.' *R v Norfolk Quarter Sessions, ex p Brunson* [1953] 1 All ER 346 at 349, per Pearson J; also reported in [1953] 1 QB 503 at 510, 511

Canada [A person 'charged' with an offence has the right to be tried within a reasonable time; Canadian Charter of Rights and Freedoms, s 11(b).] 'I adopt the more prevalent view that the word "charged" in s 11 of the Charter refers to the laying of an information, or the preferment of a direct indictment where no information has been laid. In consequence, the time-frame to be considered in computing trial within a reasonable time only runs from the laying of a charge.' *R v Boron* (1983) 3 DLR (4th) 238 at 243, Ont SC, per Ewaschuk J

Canada [Person charged with an offence has the right to be informed without unreasonable delay of the specific offence; Canadian Charter of Rights and Freedoms, s 11(a).] 'A straightforward reading of this statutory provision makes it clear that the right attaches only when a person is "charged with an offence". On its face, the protection of this subsection is activated only when this step has taken place and affords no protection to a person not yet charged. The words "charged with an offence" cannot be equated with "when the authorities are or may be in a position to commence proceedings". Nor do the words mean "or *to be* charged with an offence".' *R v Heit* (1984) 7 DLR (4th) 656 at 659, Sask CA, per Tallis JA

CHARGE (Liability)   *See also* EQUITY, EQUITABLE; FLOATING CHARGE

'There is a distinction to be drawn between a charge upon premises and a charge upon a person, as the former would be binding upon the realty, whilst the latter would be a mere personal liability for expenses incurred in respect of the premises; but in this case it may be said that there was a charge upon the premises and a charge upon a person, viz. upon the plaintiff as owner of the premises. . . . These [paving] expenses paid by the plaintiff were incurred in respect of the demised premises. . . . The fact of the plaintiff paying them because he was compellable by law to do so, does not make them any the less a charge on the premises within the meaning of the covenant. . . . The plaintiff is also entitled to recover because these expenses were a charge upon "a person in respect of the premises," i.e. they were a debt payable by the plaintiff in respect thereof.' *Hartley v Hudson* (1879) 4 CPD 367 at 367–369, per Lindley J

'A charge differs altogether from a mortgage. By a charge the title is not transferred, but the person creating the charge merely says that out of a particular fund he will discharge a particular debt. But a charge differs from an assignment. A charge on a debt confers rights on the person to whom the charge is given to have it enforced by assignment—not by action against the debtor, but by proceedings against the person who created the charge to assign the debt.' *Burlinson v Hall* (1884) 12 QBD 347 at 350, DC, per Day J

'The word "charge" may well be used to describe a burden imposed upon land, and if a payment has to be made in respect of land, and it can only be enjoyed subject to the liability for that payment, I cannot think that there would be any great straining of language if it were spoken of as charged upon the land.' *Payne v Esdaile* (1888) 13 App Cas 613 at 623, 624, per Lord Herschell LC

[The Judicature Act 1873, s 25(6) (repealed; see now Law of Property Act 1925, s 136), contained provisions relating to any absolute assignment in writing, not purporting to be by way of 'charge' only, of any debt or other chose in action.] 'The document in this case does not appear to us to purport to be "by way of charge only", either expressly or by necessary inference from its provisions, within the meaning of the section; it is an absolute assignment of the debt; a document given "by way of charge" is not one which absolutely transfers the property with a condition for reconveyance, but is a document which only gives a right to payment out of a particular fund or particular property, without transferring that fund or property.' *Tancred v Delagoa Bay & East Africa Rly Co* (1889) 23 QBD 239 at 242, per Denman J

'The plaintiff's debenture contained the not unusual provision that the company should not be at liberty to create any mortgage or charge upon any property in priority to the debenture. . . . Garnishee proceedings are only a form of execution and do not lead to any "charge" in the true sense being created by the company on the debt garnished. The word "charge" in a provision of this class is construed strictly.' *Robson v Smith* [1895] 2 Ch 118 at 126, per Romer J

Australia 'The words "charge" and "lien" are often interchangeable. The quality of each . . . is that, so far as is necessary, it appro-

priates or sets aside some particular property, real or personal, by making a deduction from the absolute ownership of it, in favour of someone who is given by law, or by agreement, will, or otherwise, the right to resort to the property to satisfy or discharge some obligation. They add to the right *in personam* a limited right *in rem.*' *Re Price, ex p Tinning* (1931) 26 Tas LR 158 at 160, per Nicholls CJ

Australia 'An ordinary meaning of the word "charge" is a liability to pay money. It is not limited to such a liability when it is imposed on property but is also applicable to such a liability imposed on a person. It was in this sense that the word was held to have been used in the lease which fell to be construed in *Hartley v Hudson,* supra. The word is frequently used in the Local Government Act [Local Government Act 1919–1986 (NSW) as amended, s 615] in the sense of a liability to pay money laid upon real property. However, there is a cognate but distinct meaning of the word in the sense of cost or the price demanded for services or goods. These meanings are given separately in the Shorter Oxford English Dictionary. We have come to the conclusion that, when the word "charge" is in the Local Government Act used in conjunction with the word "fee", it is used in the latter sense, namely, as the price demanded for services or goods.' *Davison v Bathurst City Council* [1966] 1 NSWR 61 at 64

CHARGE (Responsibility) *See also* IN CHARGE OF

New Zealand 'The word "charge" has a meaning perhaps distinct from "control" or "custody". "Charge", according to Webster's and to Latham's Johnson's Dictionaries, means the exercise of "custody or care" over a person or thing. It is a responsibility.' *Thompson v Grey* (1904) 24 NZLR 457 at 465, per Stout CJ; also reported 7 GLR 136 at 143

CHARGES

'Charges' includes fares, rates, tolls and dues of every description. (London Regional Transport Act 1984, s 68)

'Although costs are costs when they are incurred, the moment you come to ask that they shall be borne as expenses by a particular fund, or by persons not parties to the proceedings in which they were incurred, they become, not costs, but charges and expenses.' *Re Beddoe, Downes v Cottam* [1893] 1 Ch 547 at 554, CA, per Lindley LJ

[A testator by his will directed the charges of the execution of his will to be paid out of personal estate and if that were insufficient, out of real estate.] ' "Charges of the execution of this my will" is an unusual expression. . . . In substance the direction in this will amounts to a direction to pay testamentary expenses out of residue. . . . The costs of the summons and the inquiries directed thereon, together with costs, charges and expenses properly incurred by the trustees, including costs of inquiries before summons, are payable out of residue.' *Re Townend, Knowles v Jessop* [1914] WN 145 at 145, per Eve J

[By a policy of marine insurance any 'charges' of the assured upon the cargo or any portion thereof were included among the things insured.] 'The question is, is the term "charges" or "any charges" used in this document sufficient to cover and include freight? In my opinion it is.' *Gulf & Southern SS Co (Incorporated) v British Traders Insurance Co Ltd* [1930] 1 KB 451 at 458, per Roche J

CHARITY—CHARITABLE PURPOSES

General meaning

To be charitable a purpose must satisfy certain tests: it must either fall within the list of purposes enumerated in the preamble to the ancient statute of Elizabeth I (sometimes referred to as the Statute of Charitable Uses or the Charitable Uses Act 1601) or within one of the four categories of charitable purposes laid down by Lord Macnaghten and derived from the preamble, and in the case of the fourth of those categories it must be within the spirit and intendment of the ancient statute, either directly or by analogy with decided cases on the same point, or it must have been declared to be charitable by some other statute. In addition, it must be for the public benefit, that is to say it must be both beneficial and available to a sufficient section of the community. (5 Halsbury's Laws (4th edn) para 502)

'Charitable purpose' means any charitable benevolent or philanthropic purpose, whether or not the purpose is charitable within the meaning of any rule of law. (House to House Collections Act 1939, s 11)

'Charity' means any institution, corporate or not, which is established for charitable pur-

poses and is subject to the control of the High Court in the exercise of the court's jurisdiction with respect to charities. (Charities Act 1960, s 45(1))

'Charitable purposes' means purposes which are exclusively charitable according to the law of England and Wales. (Charities Act 1960, s 46)

In this section [which deals with the reduction and remission of rates] 'charity' means an institution or other organisation established for charitable purposes only and 'organisation' includes any persons administering a trust; and a hereditament an interest in which belongs to a charity or any ecclesiastical corporation and in which (in right of that interest)—
(a) the persons from time to time holding any full-time office as clergyman or minister of any religious denomination, or
(b) any particular person holding such an office,
have or has a residence from which to perform the duties of the office, or in which (in right of the said interest) accommodation is being held available to provide such a residence for such a person, shall be treated for the purposes of this section as occupied by a charity and wholly or mainly used for charitable purposes, whether or not it would be so treated apart from this provision. (General Rate Act 1967, s 40(9))

'That according to the law of England a technical meaning is attached to the word "charity" and to the word "charitable" in such expressions as "charitable uses", "charitable trusts", or "charitable purposes", cannot, I think, be denied. . . . Charitable uses or trusts form a distinct head of equity. . . . Whatever may have been the foundation of the jurisdiction of the Court over this class of trusts, and whatever may have been the origin of the title by which these trusts are still known, no one I think who takes the trouble to investigate the question can doubt that the title was recognised and the jurisdiction established before the Act of 43 Eliz [Stat (1601) 43 Eliz c 4 (repealed)] and quite independently of that Act. The object of that statute was merely to provide new machinery for the reformation of abuses in regard to charities. . . . But by a singular construction it was held to authorise certain gifts to charity which otherwise would have been void. And it contained in the preamble a list of charities so varied and comprehensive that it became the practice of the Court to refer to it as a sort of index or chart. At the same time it has never been forgotten that the "objects there enumerated", as Lord Chancellor Cranworth observes [in *London University v Yarrow* (1857) 1 De G & J 72 at 79], "are not to be taken as the only objects of charity but are given as instances". . . . No doubt the popular meaning of the words "charity" and "charitable" does not coincide with their legal meaning . . . but it is difficult to fix the point of divergence, and no one as yet has succeeded in defining the popular meaning of the word "charity". . . . How far . . . does the popular meaning of the word "charity" correspond with its legal meaning? "Charity" in its legal sense comprises four principal divisions: trusts for the relief of poverty; trusts for the advancement of education; trusts for the advancement of religion; and trusts for other purposes beneficial to the community, not falling under any of the preceding heads. The trusts last referred to are not the less charitable in the eye of the law, because incidentally they benefit the rich as well as the poor, as indeed, every charity that deserves the name must do either directly or indirectly.' *Income Tax Special Purposes Comrs v Pemsel* [1891] AC 531 at 580, 581, 583, per Lord Macnaghten

'There are hospitals where patients pay something according to their means, but that does not prevent such a hospital from being a charity in the legal sense; nor do I think that a school would be prevented from being a charity because the boys who received its benefit paid for their education a moderate sum proportionate to their means.' *Re Webster, Pearson v Webster* [1912] 1 Ch 106 at 109, per Joyce J

'A society formed for the purpose merely of benefiting its own members, though it may be to the public advantage that its members should be benefited by being educated or having their æsthetic tastes improved or whatever the object may be, would not be for a charitable purpose, and if it were a substantial part of the object that it should benefit its members, I should think that it would not be established for a charitable purpose only. But, on the other hand, if the benefit given to its members is only given to them with a view of giving encouragement and carrying out the main purpose which is a charitable purpose, then I think the mere fact that the members are benefited in the course of promoting the charitable purpose would not prevent the society being established for charitable purposes only.' *Inland Revenue Comrs v Yorkshire Agricultural Society* [1928] 1 KB 611 at 631, CA, per Atkin LJ

'It is a common thing for a charitable institution to offer all kinds of privileges and benefits which are in no sense charitable in order to obtain funds for the purpose of carrying out its objects. As an instance I might mention the giving of dinners, dances, and theatrical entertainments, all of which entail an expenditure of money on non-charitable objects incurred for the purpose of obtaining funds to be applied for the charitable objects of the institution. Many charitable institutions, in return for annual subscriptions or donations, offer special benefits to the persons who become their members. None of the operations of this kind results in making the purposes of the institution non-charitable. So here the fact that members obtain privileges in no way militates against the proposition that the purpose of the Society was a charitable purpose only.' Ibid at 637, 638, per Lawrence LJ

'The difficult question whether or not a particular purpose not coming within the first three divisions of Lord Macnaghten's classification [see *Income Tax Special Purposes Comrs v Pemsel* (supra)] is a charitable purpose in the legal sense on the ground that it is beneficial to the community has been dealt with in numerous reported cases. It has been pointed out in several of these cases that Lord Macnaghten in describing the fourth class of charities did not mean that every purpose beneficial to the community was necessarily charitable, but that what he really meant was that besides the purposes mentioned in the first three classes there were other miscellaneous charitable purposes which could conveniently be classed under the head of "other purposes beneficial to the community not falling under any of the preceding heads"; see for example, *Re Macduff* [*Macduff v Macduff* [1896] 2 Ch 451 at 467, CA], in which case Lindley LJ stated the rule applicable to this kind of case as follows: "We must fall back upon the Statute of Elizabeth, not upon the strict or narrow words of it, but upon what has been called the spirit of it, or the intention of it. As Lord Eldon says, this Court has taken great liberties with charities; but the liberty is always restricted by falling back upon . . . the Statute of Elizabeth."' *Keren Kayemeth Le Jisroel Ltd v Inland Revenue Comrs* [1931] 2 KB 465 at 485, 486, CA, per Lawrence LJ, approved on appeal [1932] AC 650

'Where a society is instituted for a charitable purpose, it is obvious that the membership of the society may confer upon its holder personal advantages of considerable value to him in his profession or in his social standing. He may, for instance, have an exclusive right to affix to his name a certain designation, and will be known to the public as a person belonging to the society. He may have to observe disciplinary rules laid down with a view to ensuring that he does not bring discredit upon other members of the society. But in such cases, although the securing of such advantages to the members may in a sense be regarded as one of the objects of the society, such object is merely concomitant or incidental to the real object of the society; and if that real object be charitable the society is established for charitable purposes only.' *Institution of Civil Engineers v Inland Revenue Comrs* [1932] 1 KB 149 at 172, 173, CA, per Romer LJ

'A charitable purpose is not made non-charitable by indicating that one of the places where it may be performed or achieved is within the four walls of a non-charitable institution.' *Re Diplock, Wintle v Diplock* [1941] 1 Ch 253 at 260, 262, 264, CA, per Greene MR; affd sub nom. *Chichester Diocesan Fund and Board of Finance (Incorp) v Simpson* [1944] AC 341, HL

'There are, I think, two propositions which must ever be borne in mind in any case in which the question is whether a trust is charitable. The first is that it is still the general law that a trust is not charitable and entitled to the privileges which charity confers unless it is within the spirit and intendment of the preamble to 43 Eliz c 4, which is expressly preserved by s 13(2) of the Mortmain and Charitable Uses Act 1888 [repealed; cf. now the Charities Act 1960, s 38(4)]. The second is that the classification of charity in its legal sense into four principle divisions by Lord Macnaghten in *Pemsel's* case [supra] must always be read subject to the qualification appearing in the judgment of Lindley LJ in *Re Macduff* [[1896] 2 Ch 451]. Now Sir Samuel Romilly did not mean, and I am certain that Lord Macnaghten did not mean to say, that every object of public general utility must necessarily be a charity. Some may be and some may not be. Lord Macnaghten did not mean that all trades beneficial to the community are "charitable", but that there were certain beneficial trusts which fall within that category: and accordingly to argue that because a trust is for a purpose beneficial to the community it is therefore a charitable trust is to turn round his sentence and to give it a different meaning. So here it is not enough to say that the trust in question is for public purposes beneficial to the community or is for the public welfare: you must also show it to be a charitable trust, But it is just because the purpose of the trust deed in this case is said to be beneficial to the community or a section of the community and for no other reason that its "charitable" character is asserted. It is not alleged that the trust is (a) for the benefit of the community and (b) beneficial in a way which the law regards as charitable. Therefore, as it seems to me, in its mere statement the claim is imperfect and must fail.' *Williams' Trustees v Inland Revenue Comrs* [1947] 1 All ER 513 at 518, 519, HL, per Lord Simonds

'It is, no doubt, true that the advancement of religion is, generally speaking, one of the heads of charity. But it does not follow from this that the court must accept as proved whatever a particular church believes. The faithful must embrace their faith believing where they cannot prove; the court can act only on proof. A gift to two or ten or a hundred cloistered nuns in the belief that their prayers will benefit the world at large does not from that belief alone derive validity any more than does the belief of any other donor for any other purpose.' *Gilmour v Coats* [1949] AC 426 at 446, HL, per Lord Simonds

'Activities which do not in any way affect the public or any section of it are not charitable. Pious contemplation and prayer are, no doubt, good for the soul, and may be of benefit by some intercessory process, of which the law takes no notice, but they are not charitable activities.' *Re Warre's Will Trusts, Wort v Salisbury Diocesan Board of Finance* [1953] 2 All ER 99 at 101, per Harman J

'To my mind, the words "charities" or "charitable institutions" in an ordinary context in an English Act of Parliament or any English document must (prima facie at least) mean institutions regulated by, and subject to the jurisdiction of the laws or the courts of the United Kingdom and constituted for the carrying out of objects or purposes which, in the courts of the United Kingdom and nowhere else, would be held to be charitable. In my judgment, the two aspects of characteristics are almost inseparable. The law relating to charities or charitable trusts is a peculiar and highly complex part of our legal system. An Act of Parliament which uses the words "charity" or "charitable" must be intending to refer to that special and characteristic, if not in some respects artificial, part of our law.' *Camille Dreyfus Foundation Inc v Inland Reve-*

nue Comrs [1954] 2 All ER 466 at 470, CA, per Evershed MR; see also [1954] Ch 672

'The meaning of "charitable" in the legal sense is clear though its application is often difficult. Except in the case of the relief of poverty, the object or purpose to be charitable must involve some benefit to the community or a section of the community as opposed to benefit to individuals by reason of some private qualification.' *Trustees of National Friendly Deposit Society v Skegness Urban District Council* [1957] 3 All ER 199 at 201, CA, per cur.; also reported in [1957] 2 QB 573 at 580, 581

'I conclude by saying that the authorities show that the "spirit and intendment" of the preamble to the statute of Elizabeth have been stretched almost to breaking point. In the nineteenth and early twentieth century this was often due to a desire on the part of the courts to save the intentions of the settlor or testator from failure from some technical rule of law. Now that it is used so frequently to avoid the common man's liability to rates or taxes this generous trend of the law may one day require reconsideration.' *Scottish Burial Reform & Cremation Society Ltd v Glasgow City Corpn* [1967] 3 All ER 215 at 222, HL, per Lord Upjohn

[The General Rate Act 1967, s 40(1) provides for rating relief on any hereditament occupied by a charity and wholly or mainly used for 'charitable purposes'.] 'The wording of s 40(1) of the 1967 Act shows that the legislature did not consider that the mere fact that the hereditament in question is occupied by a charity justifies any relief from rates. That is only justified if the hereditament is being used for "charitable purposes" of the charity. So the first question which arises is: what are "charitable purposes" of a charity as distinct from its other purposes? The answer must be, I think, those purposes or objects the pursuit of which make it a charity—that is to say in this case the relief of poverty, suffering and distress.' *Oxfam v City of Birmingham District Council* [1975] 2 All ER 289 at 293, HL, per Lord Cross of Chelsea

Australia 'The word "charitable", as used in the Court of Equity, is a word of limited meaning, and in order that a purpose may be a charitable purpose, as the phrase is understood in this Court, it must be one of those within either the letter or the spirit of the stat. 43 Eliz. c 4. If the words used are so wide that the objects are not necessarily within the letter or

spirit of that Act the objects are not charitable purposes as understood in this Court.' *Re Tyson, Tyson v Webb* (1906) 7 NSWSR 91 at 94, per Street J

Australia ' "The method employed by the Court", said Chitty J in *Re Foveaux* [[1895] 2 Ch 501 at 504] "is to consider the enumeration of charities in the Statute of Elizabeth, bearing in mind that the enumeration is not exhaustive. Institutions whose objects are analogous to those mentioned in the statute are admitted to be charities; and, again, institutions which are analogous to those already admitted by reported decisions are held to be charities. The pursuit of these analogies obviously requires caution and circumspection. After all, the best that can be done is to consider each case as it arises, upon its own special circumstances." This is a safe but unenlightening conclusion. But the Courts seem now to have ventured from its dark security so far as to risk the modest generality that when, from motives which are altruistic, benevolent or philanthropic, purposes are put in execution for the benefit of the community, or of a considerable section or class, which do in fact tend to the amelioration of mind, manners or morals, or the relief of misfortune and are of a nature allowed by law and consonant with the received notions of morality, then these objects will be considered "charitable". The occasion for determining what purposes are charitable has, of course, arisen in the administration of the law of property. But once the view is adopted that the word "charitable" has itself a legal meaning there seems little difficulty in transferring it from the description of the purposes to which property is devoted, and understanding it as a description of the object for which an institution exists.' *Hobart Savings Bank & Launceston Bank for Savings v Federal Comr of Taxation* (1930) 43 CLR 364 at 374, 375, per Dixon J

New Zealand 'A distinction between health services carried on within hospital and those within other lawful institutions is no longer valid today in assessing the charitable nature of a purpose. In *Reschs Will Trust* [[1969] 1 AC 514] Lord Wilberforce . . . said ". . . the provision of medical care for the sick is, in modern times, accepted as a public benefit suitable to attract the privileges given to charitable institutions". Hospitals not run for private commercial gain are charitable because they provide for the "relief of the sick". It is my judgment that "relief of the sick" is today used n the broad sense of those requiring medical treatment . . . The provision of medical services within hospital is prima facie a charitable purpose.' *Auckland Medical Aid Trust v Inland Revenue Comr* [1979] 1 NZLR 382 at 389, per Chilwell J

'Charitable and benevolent'

The judgment which is appealed from is based upon the view that "charitable and benevolent" really mean such charitable gifts as are benevolent, and there is a considerable body of authority . . . to show not only that such a construction is possible, but that, in the absence of words to the contrary, it is the one which ought to be adopted. . . . I see no reason why a word which has a perfectly plain meaning, and should ordinarily be read as signifying something conjoined with what has gone before, should have its meaning altered in order that a gift which, upon the face of it, would be good should be made bad by severing two things which the testator had himself joined together.' *Caldwell v Caldwell* (1921) 91 LJPC 95 at 96, per cur.

New Zealand 'A gift for benevolent purposes is bad, because such purposes go beyond the legal definition of charities—a word which in the construction of wills, has always possessed a limited and technical meaning. . . . From this it follows that a gift for charitable or benevolent purposes is void for uncertainty because it is impossible to divide the gift between the two objects, or to determine to which it should be given, and consequently the good cannot be separated from the bad, and the gift fails.' *A-G for New Zealand v Brown* [1917] AC 393 at 395, 396, PC, per cur.

'Charitable and deserving'

'To my mind the words "charitable and deserving objects" mean only one class of objects, and the word "charitable" governs the whole sentence. It means objects which are at once charitable and deserving. If you were to treat the word "deserving" as standing alone it would be so vague that I do not know what meaning could be attached to it. Almost any object might be said to be a "deserving" object. But, to my mind, the testatrix has coupled the two words together. The objects of her bounty were "charitable" objects, and, as there are a great number of charitable objects, she draws the line a little closer by adding the words "and deserving". . . . I agree with the Master of the Rolls that, "benevolent, charit-

able, and religious" means that the gift may be applied in any one of those three ways. But when, as in the present case, the copulative conjunction connects the words "charitable" and "deserving", to my mind it changes the grammatical meaning altogether. The objects are to be at once charitable and deserving, and the testatrix shows that the class of objects which she wished to be chosen was to include those which should be both charitable and deserving.' *Re Sutton, Stone v A-G* (1885) 28 Ch D 464 at 465–467, per Pearson J

Charitable gift

'A gift to a charity may be of such a character as not to be in itself a charitable gift. On the other hand . . . in considering whether a gift is charitable or not one must not confine oneself to the character of the gift itself, but must pay regard also to the character and objects of the charity who are the intended recipients of the gift.' *Re Mariette, Mariette v Aldenham School Governing Body* [1915] 2 Ch 284 at 288, per Eve J

'The fundamental requirement of a charitable gift is, in my opinion, correctly stated in the following passage in Tudor on Charities (5th edn), p 11: "In the first place it may be laid down as a universal rule that the law recognises no purpose as charitable unless it is of a public character. That is to say, a purpose must, in order to be charitable, be directed to the benefit of the community or a section of the community." . . . The proposition is true of all charitable gifts and is not confined to the fourth class in Lord Macnaghten's well-known statement in *Pemsel's* case [*Pemsel v Inland Revenue Comrs* (supra)]. It does not, of course, mean that every gift that tends to the public benefit is necessarily charitable. What it does mean is that no gift can be charitable in the legal sense unless it is of the necessary public character.' *Re Compton, Powell v Compton* [1945] Ch 123 at 128, 129, CA, per Lord Greene MR

Ecclesiastical charity

The expression 'ecclesiastical charity' includes a charity, the endowment whereof is held for some one or more of the following purposes:—
(a) for any spiritual purpose which is a legal purpose; or
(b) for the benefit of any spiritual person or ecclesiastical officer as such; or
(c) for use, if a building, as a church, chapel, mission room, or Sunday school, or other-

wise by any particular church or denomination; or

(d) for the maintenance, repair, or improvement of any such building as aforesaid, or for the maintenance of divine service therein; or

(e) otherwise for the benefit of any particular church or denomination or of any members thereof as such.

Provided that where any endowment of a charity, other than a building held for any of the purposes aforesaid, is held in part only for some of the purposes aforesaid, the charity, so far as that endowment is concerned, shall be an ecclesiastical charity within the meaning of this Act; and the Charity Commissioners shall, on application by any person interested, make such provision for the apportionment and management of that endowment as seems to them necessary or expedient for giving effect to this Act.

The expression shall also include any building which in the opinion of the Charity Commissioners has been erected or provided within forty years before the passing of this Act mainly by or at the cost of members of any particular church or denomination. (Local Government Act 1894, s 75)

Local charity

'Local charity' means, in relation to any area, a charity established for purposes which are by their nature or by the trusts of the charity directed wholly or mainly to the benefit of that area or of part of it. (Charities Act 1960, s 45(1))

Parochial charity

'Parochial charity' means, in relation to any parish, a charity the benefits of which are, or the separate distribution of the benefits of which is, confined to inhabitants of the parish, or of a single ancient ecclesiastical parish which included that parish or part of it, or of an area consisting of that parish with not more than four neighbouring parishes. (Charities Act 1960, s 45(1))

Public charity

'I am rather of opinion that the word publick was meant only by way of description of the nature of them, and not by way of distinguishing one charity from another; for it would be almost impossible to say which are publick and which are private in their nature. The charter of the crown cannot make a charity more or less publick, but only more permanent than it would otherwise be, but it is the extensiveness which will constitute it a publick one. A devise to the poor of a parish is a publick charity. Where testators have not any particular person in their contemplation, but leave it to the discretion of a trustee to chuse out the objects, though such person is private, and each particular object may be said to be private, yet in the extensiveness of the benefit accruing from them they may very properly be called publick charities. A sum to be disposed of by AB and his executors, at their discretion, among poor housekeepers, is of this kind.' *A-G v Pearce* (1740) 2 Atk 87 at 88, per Lord Hardwicke LC

Scottish law

'There is no doubt that the English law has attached a wide and somewhat artificial meaning to the words "charity" and "charitable". . . . In the law of Scotland there is no such technical meaning attached to the words. . . . The words "charitable purposes" . . . include a wider range of objects than such as are of a merely eleemosynary character.' *Blair v Duncan* [1902] AC 37 at 43, per Lord Davey

'The words of bequest are:—"To divide the same as he shall think fit amongst such educational, charitable, and religious purposes within the city of Aberdeen as he shall select to be the recipients thereof." I find it impossible myself to read this as meaning that he is to select certain purposes which are combinedly educational, charitable and religious. I take it that the only reasonable meaning of it is that the trustee shall select certain purposes . . . which are educational or charitable or religious.' *M'Conochie's Trustees v M'Conochie* 1909 SC 1046 at 1048, per the Lord Justice-Clerk

'The Finance Act [1921] being an imperial taxing statute . . . the meaning of the word "charity" must be taken to be that which it bears as an English law-term. . . . That being so, it seems to follow that "charity" includes the advancement of education—why not, then, of technical education? . . . Instruction in the principles of a trade, and in the applications of science to its practice—which are the subjects taught in a technical college such as this— seems to me to be plainly educational in the proper sense.' *Scottish Woollen Technical College v Inland Revenue Comrs* 1926 SC 934 at 940, per the Lord President

CHARTERED FREIGHT   *See* FREIGHT

CHARTERPARTY

A contract by charterparty is a contract by which an entire ship or some principal part of her is let to a merchant, called 'the charterer', for the conveyance of goods on a determined voyage to one or more places, or until the expiration of a specified period. In the first case it is called a 'voyage charterparty', and in the second a 'time charterparty'. Such a contract may operate as a demise of the ship herself, to which the services of the master and crew may or may not be added, or it may confer on the charterer nothing more than the right to have his goods conveyed by a particular ship, and, as subsidiary to it, to have the use of the ship and the services of the master and crew. . . .

Charterparties by way of demise are of two kinds: (1) charter without master or crew, or bareboat charter', where the hull is the subject matter of the charterparty, and (2) charter with master and crew, under which the ship passes to the charterer in a state fit for the purposes of mercantile adventure. In both cases the charterer becomes for the time being the owner of the ship; the master and crew are, or become to all intents and purposes, his employees, and through them the possession of the ship is in him. The owner, on the other hand, has divested himself of all control either over the ship or over the master and crew, his sole right being to receive the stipulated hire and to take back the ship when the charterparty comes to an end. During the currency of the charterparty, therefore, the owner is under no liability to third persons whose goods may have been conveyed upon the demised ship or who may have done work or supplied stores for her, and those persons must look only to the charterer who has taken his place.

Although a charterparty which does not operate as a demise confers on the charterer the temporary right to have his goods loaded and conveyed in the ship, the ownership remains in the original owner, and through the master and crew, who continue to be his employees, the possession of the ship also remains in him. Therefore, the existence of the charterparty does not necessarily divest the owner of liability to third persons whose goods may have been conveyed on the ship, nor does it deprive him of his rights as owner. (43 Halsbury's Laws (4th edn) paras 402, 403, 404)

'Charterparty *est charta partita*, and is all one in the civil law, as an indenture is in the common law.' *Leighton v Green & Garret* (1613) Godb 204 at 204, per Coke CJ

'A charterparty is not a lease—it is a chattel that is being dealt with, a chattel that is essentially a mere subject of contract; and although rights of ownership or rights akin to ownership may be given under it prima facie it is a contract for the hiring or use of the vessel. Under these circumstances it is in accordance with ordinary business commonsense and custom that charterers should be able to contract as agents for undisclosed principals who may come in and take the benefit of the charterparty.' *Drughorn (Fred) Ltd v Rederiaktiebolaget Trans-Atlantic* [1919] AC 203 at 207, per Lord Haldane

Time charterparty

'A time charterparty is, in fact, a document which is of a very misleading nature, because the real nature of what is undertaken by the shipowner is disguised by the use of language dating from a century or more ago—language which was then appropriate to a contract of a totally different character. A century ago a time charterparty, then known as a demise charterparty, was an agreement under which the charterer was handed over the possession of the ship of the shipowner to put his servants and crew upon her and to sail her for his own benefit. That form of charterparty, which, as I say, was called a demise charterparty, has long since been obsolete. The modern form of time charterparty is, in essence, one under which the shipowner agrees with the time charterer that, during a certain named period, the shipowner will render service as a carrier by his servants and crew to carry the goods which are put on board his ship by the time charterer. Certain phrases surviving in the printed form now used are only pertinent to the older form of demise charterparty. Those phrases are, as in the present case, "The owners agree to let the steamer" and "The charterers agree to hire the steamer". There is no "letting" or "hiring" of the steamer, or anything of the sort, here. Then, at the end of the period, it was solemnly provided that the vessel should be redelivered by the time charterers to the shipowners. "Redelivery" is only a pertinent expression if there has been a delivery or handing over by the shipowners to the charterers. There never has been anything of that sort here. The ship has at all times been in the possession of the shipowners, and they simply undertook to do services with their crew in carrying the goods of the charterers. As I ventured to suggest in the course of the argument, in the two forms of contract there is all the difference between hiring a boat in which to row yourself about, in which case the boat is handed over to you, and contracting with a man on the beach that he shall take you for a row, in which case he merely renders the services to you in rowing you about. Now, having that in mind, the essential nature of this contract is that the shipowners, during a certain period of time, agree to perform certain services for the charterers.' *Re an arbitration between Sea & Land Securities Ltd & Dickinson & Co Ltd, The Arlesford* [1942] 1 All ER 503 at 503, 504, CA, per MacKinnon LJ

CHASE (Pursue)

[By the Dogs (Protection of Livestock) Act 1953, s 1(1), it is an offence for a dog to worry sheep. By s 1(2), worrying livestock includes 'chasing' them in such a way as may reasonably be expected to cause injury, etc.] ' "Chasing" is a word of varying meaning, and the real question comes to be whether the dog's activities amounted to chasing. . . . It was maintained that chasing means "pursuing or following with a view to capturing" and there was no finding that anything of this sort was taking place so far as the collie dog was concerned. [The dog had been running through the sheep scaring them and causing them to dash about the field.] But, although in one sense of the word chasing involves pursuing, there are wider meanings of that word, and, in my view, if the sheep were put to flight that would equally constitute chasing of the sheep within the meaning of the section.' *Stephen v Milne* 1960 SLT 276 at 278, per the Lord Justice-General (Clyde)

CHATTEL PAPER

United States 'Chattel paper' means a writing or writings which evidence both a monetary obligation and a security interest in or a lease of specific goods, but a charter or other contract involving the use or hire of a vessel is not chattel paper. When a transaction is evidenced both by such a security agreement or a lease and by an instrument or a series of instruments, the group of writings taken together constitutes chattel paper. . . . (Uniform Commercial Code 1978, s 9–105(1)(b))

CHATTELS   *See also* FIXTURES; GOODS AND CHATTELS

Corporeal and incorporeal

Property in chattels personal may be in possession or in action. It is in possession where the possessor has not only the right to enjoy, but the actual enjoyment of, the chattels, the chattels being in that case sometimes called 'corporeal chattels'. Where only a bare right to enjoy exists, the property is said to be 'in action', and the chattels are called 'incorporeal'. Personal property may also be partly in possession and partly in action, as, for example bills of exchange and promissory notes. The debt thereby secured is a chose in action, but the actual document is a chose in possession. (35 Halsbury's Laws (4th edn) para 1105)

Canada 'Chattels [in a chattel mortgage] is wide enough to include both chattels real and personal: *Blackstone Commentaries*, 14th edn (1803), vol 2, p 386 ff. Chattels real cannot be the subject-matter of a chattel mortgage: *Frazer v Lazier* (1852) 9 UCQB 679. Chattels personal include corporeal and incorporeal chattels, but it is only corporeal chattels which can be the subject of a chattel mortgage. "Corporeal chattels" are chattels in possession where the possessor has not only the right to enjoy, but the actual enjoyment of the chattels. . . . In my opinion the word "goods" or "chattels" in their ordinary usage are both equally apt to describe corporeal chattels.' *Re Goverde* (1972) 26 DLR (3d) 71 at 72, Ont SC, per Houlden J

Personal

Chattels personal are, strictly speaking, things movable, but in modern times the expression is used to denote any kind of property other than real property and chattels real. (35 Halsbury's Laws (4th edn) para 1104)

The expression 'personal chattels' shall mean goods, furniture, and other articles capable of complete transfer by delivery, and (when separately assigned or charged) fixtures and growing crops, but shall not include chattel interests in real estate, nor fixtures (except trade machinery as herein-after defined), when assigned together with a freehold or leasehold interest in any land or building to which they are affixed, nor growing crops when assigned together with any interest in the land on which they grow, nor shares or interests in the stock, funds, or securities of any government, or in the capital or property of incorporated or joint stock companies, nor choses in action, nor any stock or produce upon any farm or lands which by virtue of any covenant or agreement or of the custom of the country ought not to be removed from any farm where the same are at the time of making or giving of such bill of sale. (Bills of Sale Act 1878, s 4)

'Personal chattels' means carriages, horses, stable furniture and effects (not used for business purposes), motor cars and accessories (not used for business purposes), garden effects, domestic animals, plate, plated articles, linen, china, glass, books, pictures, prints, furniture, jewellery, articles of household or personal use or ornament, musical and scientific instruments and apparatus, wines, liquors and consumable stores, but do not include any chattels used at the death of the intestate for business purposes nor money or securities for money. (Administration of Estates Act 1925, s 55(1))

[The Bills of Sale Act 1854, s 7 (repealed; see Bills of Sale Act 1878, s 4, supra), enacted that the expression 'personal chattels' should include fixtures capable of complete transfer by delivery.] 'The defendant . . . has contended that the machinery and other things comprised in this deed were not personal chattels within the meaning of this statute, being fixtures annexed to the freehold and passing therewith. But it appears to us that, although, they were in one sense fixtures, being affixed to the soil, yet they were within the statute, which by s 7, interprets personal chattels to mean fixtures capable of complete transfer by delivery. . . . We hold this machinery to have been a personal chattel within the statute, notwithstanding the annexation to the soil.' *Waterfall v Penistone* (1856) 6 E & B 876 at 888, 889, per cur.

'The definition of personal chattels [in the Bills of Sale Act 1878, s 4 (supra)] may be said to divide "fixtures" roughly into fixtures separately assigned . . . and fixtures which are not separately assigned. That is not a complete division, because, curiously enough, "fixtures" are only excepted from the expression "personal chattels" when assigned together with a freehold or leasehold interest in any land or building to which they are affixed. . . . I think one may treat the definition as roughly dividing fixtures into two classes, those separately assigned, and those assigned together with the land or buildings to which they are affixed. In

the former case they are "personal chattels"; in the latter they are not.' *Topham v Greenside Glazed Fire-Brick Co* (1887) 37 Ch D 281 at 293, per North J

Real

Chattels real are interests concerning or savouring of realty, such as a term of years in land, an annuity issuing out of a term of years, or the next presentation to a church, which have the quality of immobility which makes them akin to realty, but lack indeterminate duration. In some respects they are subject, like other chattels, to the law of personal property, in others, to the law of real property. (35 Halsbury's Laws (4th edn) para 1103)

Personal estate is divided into chattels real and chattels personal. Terms of years are chattels real; chattels because they devolve at common law, with chattels in the proper sense, on the personal representatives; real because they are derived out of real estate.

The chief differences between real estate and chattels real were with regard to legal remedies the mode of devolution on death and the rights of succession on intestacy. These differences have now disappeared, and the distinction is mainly of historic interest. (39 Halsbury's Laws (4th edn) para 303)

CHEAT

['Cheat' means an offence under the Theft Act 1968, s 15 (ibid, s 25(5)). That section provides that a person who by any deception dishonestly obtains property belonging to another, with the intention of permanently depriving the other of it, shall on conviction on indictment be liable to imprisonment.]

'To cheat and defraud is to act with deliberate dishonesty to the prejudice of another person's proprietary right.' *R v Sinclair* [1968] 3 All ER 241 at 246, CA, per cur.

CHECK-WEIGH

'Check-weighed', in relation to any vehicle, means weighed with its load by means of the nearest suitable and available weighing equipment, and weighed again after it has been unloaded by means of the same or other suitable weighing equipment. (Weights and Measures Act 1985, s 94(1))

CHEESE

'Cheese' means the substance usually known as cheese, containing no fat other than fat derived from milk. (Food Act 1984, s 132(1))

CHEMICAL PROCESS

Canada [Validity of certain claims of patent depended on whether chemical process was used.] 'One must not find a "chemical process" merely because the trappings of a chemistry laboratory are employed in a simple, non-technical undertaking, but, conversely, one must be wary of failing to find a chemical process because the process employs commonplace items such as water or heat. The question whether a particular invention relates to substances produced by chemical processes is essentially one of fact.' *Dairy Foods Inc v Cooperative Agricole de Granby* [1976] 2 SCR 651 at 667, SCC, per Dickson J

CHEQUE

A cheque is a bill of exchange drawn on a banker payable on demand. (Bills of Exchange Act 1882, s 73)

'A cheque is in the nature of an inland bill of exchange payable to the bearer on demand. It has nearly all the incidents of an ordinary bill of exchange. In one thing it differs from a bill of exchange; it is an appropriation of so much money of the drawer's in the hands of the banker upon whom it is drawn, for the purpose of discharging a debt or liability of the drawer to a third person; whereas, it is not necessary that there should be money of the drawer's in the hands of the drawee of a bill of exchange. There is another difference between the two instruments—in the case of a bill of exchange, the drawer is discharged by default of a due presentment to the acceptor; but, in the case of a cheque, the drawer is not discharged by a delay in the presentment, unless it be shown that he has been prejudiced thereby, for instance, by the failure of the banker on whom it is drawn. In all other respects a cheque is precisely like an inland bill of exchange.' *Keene v Beard* (1860) 8 CBNS 372 at 381, per Byles J

'A cheque is clearly not an assignment of money in the hands of a banker; it is a bill of exchange payable at a banker's. The banker is bound by his contract with his customer to honour the cheque, when he has sufficient assets in his hands; if he does not fulfill his contract he is liable to an action by the drawer, in which heavy damages may be recovered if the drawer's credit has been injured.' *Hopkinson v Forster* (1874) LR 19 Eq 74 at 76, per Jessel MR

See, generally, 4 Halsbury's Laws (4th edn) paras 302–308.

Crossing of cheque

'A crossing is a direction to the paying bank to pay the money generally to a bank or to a particular bank, as the case may be, and when this has been done the whole purpose of the crossing has been served. The paying bank has nothing to do with the application of the money after it has once been paid to the proper receiving banker. The words "account AB" are a mere direction to the receiving bank as to how the money is to be dealt with after receipt.' *Akrokerri (Atlantic) Mines Ltd v Economic Bank* [1904] 2 KB 465 at 472, per Bigham J

'Pay cash or order'

[A cheque form, suitable for being filled in to make a cheque payable to order, was filled in so as to read: 'Pay cash or order'.] 'I think the four words "pay cash or order" cannot be read so as to give any sensible meaning to the whole four, and the result is that the printed words "or order" must be disregarded and we have a direction to pay cash—by necessary implication to pay it to the bearer of the document.' *North & South Insurance Corpn Ltd v National Provincial Bank Ltd* [1936] 1 KB 328 at 336, per Branson J

CHILD—CHILDREN

The general rule has been that in the absence of a contrary intention, express or implied, and unless it is more consonant with the object of the statute to include illegitimate children, all statutory provisions in respect of children refer exclusively to legitimate children. However, this rule has been altered extensively by statute; thus an illegitimate child may succeed on intestacy and may apply for provision out of the estate of a deceased parent; and for the purpose of a claim in respect of a wrongful act causing death for damages for the benefit of the deceased's dependants, 'dependant' includes a child or grandchild of the deceased, 'child' includes a stepchild, and an illegitimate person is to be treated as the legitimate child of his mother and reputed father. For the purposes of income tax child allowances, 'child' includes a stepchild and an illegitimate child whose parents have married each other after his birth. (24 Halsbury's Laws (4th edn) para 404)

'Child' means a person under the age of fourteen years. (Children and Young Persons Act 1933, s 107(1))

'Child' means a person who is not over compulsory school age. (Education Act 1944, s 114(1))

In this Act . . . 'child', in relation to one or both of the parties to a marriage, includes an illegitimate . . . child of that party or, as the case may be, of both parties. (Matrimonial Causes Act 1973, s 52(1) as repealed in part by the Children Act 1975, Sch 4)

'Child' includes an illegitimate child and a child *en ventre sa mère* at the death of the deceased. (Inheritance (Provision for Family and Dependants) Act 1975, s 25(1))

In the provisions of this Act relating to admissions to schools 'child' includes any person who has not attained the age of nineteen years. (Education Act 1980, s 38(4))

In this Part of this Act [Part I (protection of children living away from their parents)] . . . 'Child' means a person under the age of 18. (Foster Children Act 1980, s 22)

'The law does not contemplate illegitimacy. The proper description of a legitimate child is "child".' *R v Totley (Inhabitants)* (1845) 7 QB 596 at 600, per Lord Denman CJ

'As a general rule, it is certain the word "children" may mean "issue", and that we are to see whether the use of it in the particular will is such as to indicate that sense.' *Voller v Carter* (1854) 4 E & B 173 at 179, per Lord Campbell CJ

'This offence [concealment of birth of a "child"] cannot be committed unless the child had arrived at the stage of maturity at the time of birth, that it might have been a living child. It is not necessary that it should have been born alive, but it must have reached a period when, but for some accidental circumstances, such as disease on the part of itself or of its mother, it might have been born alive.' *R v Berriman* (1854) 6 Cox CC 388 at 390, per Erle J

'It must be taken as established by the rules of construction laid down in *Wild's* case [(1599) 6 Co Rep 16b], that where there is a devise of land to a man and his children, and he has at the time of the devise no child, then prima facie the word "children" shall be taken to be a word of limitation, and the first taker shall have an estate tail; but, on the other hand, if the first taker has children at the time of the devise, then the will shall prima facie be construed as giving a joint estate to the first taker and the children as purchasers.' *Byng v Byng* (1862) 10 HL Cas 171 at 178, per Lord Cranworth

'I see nothing to limit the word "child" in the statute [Offences against the Person Act 1861, s 60 (concealing the birth of a child)] to a child likely to live or likely to die. . . . As soon as the *fœtus* has the outward appearance of a child it is sufficient.' *R v Colmer* (1864) 9 Cox CC 506 at 507, per Martin B

'The term "children" in a will prima facie means legitimate children, and if there is nothing more in the will, the circumstance that the person whose children are referred to has illegitimate children will not entitle those illegitimate children to take. But there are two classes of cases in which that prima facie interpretation is departed from. One class of cases is where it is impossible from the circumstances of the parties that any legitimate children could take under the bequest. . . . The other class of cases is of this kind. Where there is upon the face of the will itself, and upon a just and proper construction and interpretation of the words used in it, an expression of the intention of the testator to use the term "children" not merely according to its prima facie meaning of legitimate children, but according to a meaning which will apply to and which will include illegitimate children.' *Hill v Crook* (1873) LR 6 HL 265 at 282, 283, per Lord Cairns

'I cannot substitute "issue" or "grandchildren" for "children" merely on the ground that at the date of the will or testator's death the named person has no child living, but only grandchildren; and . . . I can only alter the word "children" from its proper meaning if on a proper construction of the will itself it is found to have been intended to bear a larger signification.' *Re Kirk, Nicholson v Kirk* (1885) 52 LT 346 at 348, per Pearson J

'I do not see how I can avoid holding that where, in a gift to "children", there being both legitimate and illegitimate children, there is an exception of one of the illegitimate children, the word "children" is intended to include both classes.' *Re Lowe, Danily v Platt* (1892) 61 LJ Ch 415 at 417, per North J

'In order to determine the effect of a gift to the children of A and B, you must know something about A and B. The proper grammatical meaning of the expression "the children of A and B"—the preposition "of" not being repeated before "B", and A and B not having or being capable of having children together—is, the children of A and the individual B, not his or her children. But the expression "the children of A and B" may mean the children of A and the children of B; and in wills must have that meaning if B, to the knowledge of the testator, be dead leaving children still alive.' *Re Walbran, Milner v Walbran* (1905) 93 LT 745 at 745, per Joyce J

'It cannot, in my judgment, be true to say that the defendant Lionel Arthur Wicks was a child of the marriage; he is a legitimate child of the spouses, but he is not a child of the marriage because in fact he was born before his parents were married. . . . When one looks at this settlement, there can be, in my view, only one answer to the question raised. Lionel Arthur Wicks was not a child of the marriage and, therefore, is not an object of the power. The fact that he has now become a legitimate child does not make him an object of the power, he not being in fact a child of the marriage although he no doubt is a child of the two spouses.' *Re Wicks' Marriage Settlement, Public Trustee v Wicks* [1940] Ch 475 at 477, 478, 480, per Farwell J

'The Court is entitled to construe these words "child or children" in a case of this sort [where land is devised to A absolutely subject to a gift over in the event of A dying leaving no "child or children"] as meaning "issue" if, as a matter of construction of the will as a whole, the Court comes to the conclusion that that was what was intended. . . . Prima facie the words "child or children" mean what they say: but, as a matter of construction of a particular will . . . . it is open to the Court, if it thinks fit to do so, to give them a wider meaning.' *Re Milward's Estate, ex p Midland Rly Co* [1940] Ch 698 at 703–705, per Farwell J

'An illegitimate child, according to the old common law, was a child of nobody: so that, if the mother died without making a will, or the grandmother or grandfather died without making a will, none of their property would ever go to the illegitimate child, because it was no relation in law to them. It was of no kin to anyone. If money was left to children by will, it never went to an illegitimate child since the word "children" was always construed as referring only to legitimate children. That old law has been altered in part, but only in a very small part, by s 9 of the Legitimacy Act 1926

[repealed; see now the Legitimacy Act 1976, s 5]. Now, if the mother of an illegitimate child dies without leaving a will, and has no legitimate children, then the illegitimate child can take as next of kin of the mother. That is the only alteration. In all other respects the old law remains. If the mother of an illegitimate child marries and has legitimate children, the illegitimate child is still excluded on an intestacy; whereas, if an adoption order is made, the illegitimate child ranks equally with the other legitimate children. Again, if the mother dies before the grandmother and the grandmother dies intestate, the illegitimate grandchild is excluded from any benefit in the grandmother's estate: whereas if an adoption order is made, it will be entitled to a share. Again, if the mother, or anyone else, leaves a will leaving money to the "children" of this mother, the illegitimate child will take nothing: whereas, if an adoption order is made, the illegitimate child will rank as a child in the full sense of the law.' *Re D (an infant)* [1958] 3 All ER 716 at 717, 718, CA, per Lord Denning; also reported [1959] 1 QB 229 at 235, 236

[As to the law regarding acquisition and succession by or to illegitimate persons, see 1 Halsbury's Laws (4th edn) paras 616–620.]

Australia 'There is nothing on the face of this will to indicate that the word "children" is used in other than its ordinary and primary sense. . . . The word "children", said Lord O'Hogan, in *Dorin v Dorin* (1875) LR 7 HL, p 576, "*per se* points confessedly only to legitimates; the operation of law writes 'legitimate' before it; and before the word so impliedly inverted can be elided or lose its effect, enough should appear upon the face of the will to demonstrate conclusively that its bounty must be extended to another class of children.". . . It has been decided again and again that where no legitimate children could possibly take under the bequest the word "child" or "children" may be interpreted to extend to illegitimates.' *Re Goodes* [1902] SALR 86 at 89, 90, per Way CJ

Canada 'A "child" may be of any age. We are all the children of our parents, for instance, no matter what age we have attained, but in a particular sense a "child" means a young person. There are statutes which refer to "child" or "children" and these words in their usual application mean persons under twenty-one years of age. . . . The words used in the Wives' and Children's Maintenance Act [RSBC 1960, c 409] are "child" or "infant child". It is a statute for the maintenance of children and consequently is to have a generous interpretation for children, in my respectful opinion. "Infant child" in my respectful opinion can only mean a child under twenty-one years of age.' *Re Drysdale and Drysdale* (1967) 65 DLR (2d) 237 at 239, per Wootton J

Canada [A testator, with a step-child but with no natural children, left the residue of his estate 'equally among all my children'.] 'The word "child" itself is not one of restrictive technical meaning. Beyond any doubt it is not restricted to the meaning that it designates an infant born of the union of a man and woman lawfully married to each other. Indeed such a meaning is not even set out in the Oxford English Dictionary. The definitions employed by that authority, in dealing with the word as correlative to parents, are: "1. The offspring male or female of human parents; 2. In biblical and derived uses: descendants, members of the tribe or clan; 3. Applied to disciples of a Teacher; 4. Expressing origin, extraction, dependence, attachment, or natural relation to a place, time, circumstance of birth, ruling quality." Precisely the same definitions in more expanded form are to be found in Murray's English Dictionary. In the present case, the will to be construed was made, as I have said, within a week of the testator having undertaken responsibility for the care and support of a wife who came to him as a young widow with a seven-year-old child. Although he may well have contemplated fathering children, of whom his wife would be the mother, at the time of making his will he had dependent upon him for his daily support, guidance and direction, a little boy of very tender years whose natural father had died months before he was born. He brought this child into his very family—his household.' *Re Hendrie* [1969] 1 OR 673 at 688, 689, Ont SC, per Keith J
[It was held that the step-child was entitled to take the whole of the residue.]

Canada 'In the clause in the will, in making the devises to "my children", the testator specifically named those he intended to include in that designation, among whom was the respondent, his grandson. By so doing, in my opinion, he indicated at the time he made his will that he considered the grandson as one of his children. It appears to me, therefore, that the testator, when speaking of "my children" in the residuary clause, intended that expres-

sion to mean those he had so designated in the previous clause of his will. This view is strengthened by the use of the word "aforementioned", which could have referred only to "my children" as named in the preceding part of the will. As the only clause, other than the residuary clause, in which the testator speaks of "my children" is the one to which I have referred, that expression would include the respondent. While this conclusion does not give to the words "my children" their literal or natural meaning, it is, I believe, the meaning which gives effect to the intention of the testator as indicated by the terms of his will as a whole.' *Heinbigner v Heinbigner* [1972] 2 WWR 71 at 73, Sask CA, per Culliton CJS

New Zealand 'The word "children" [in a will] without any such limitation [as "living" or "born"] must be held to include a child en ventre sa mère at the period of distribution, when to include such child would be for its benefit.' *Re Brown, Brown v Brown* [1933] NZLR 115 at 118, per Reed J

United States A person's 'children' are that person's immediate offspring, whether legitimate or not, and any children legally adopted by that person. (Copyright Act of 1976, s 101)

CHIMNEY

In this Part of this Act the expression 'chimney' includes structures and openings of any kind from or through which smoke may be emitted. (Public Health Act 1936, s 110)

'Chimney' includes structures and openings of any kind from or through which smoke or (where the reference is to the chimney serving an oven) grit or dust may be emitted, and references to a chimney of a building include references to a chimney which serves the whole or a part of a building but is structurally separate therefrom. (Clean Air Act 1956, s 34(1))

CHIVALRY   *See* ARMS

CHOOSE

Australia 'In common parlance "to choose" means no more than to make a selection between different things to alternatives submitted, to take by preference out of all that are available.' *Judd v McKeon* (1926) 38 CLR 380 at 383, per Knox CJ, Gavan Duffy and Starke JJ

CHORAL WORKS

[A society was established to form and maintain a choir in order to promote the practice and performance of 'choral works'.] ' "Choral works" must not be regarded as works written for a chorus, or normally sung by what is normally called "a chorus". They are words well-known to mean works which are written for or are sung by a choir, which is a very different thing from what is commonly called a chorus. The type of music which is written for a choir or which is performed by a choir is a special type of music which requires a choir and a trained choir, for its adequate performance. Examples of the sort of works meant by "choral works" may be found from the actual practice of the society. Familiar names which occur to one, and which appear in the cases are, The Messiah, Beethoven's Mass in D, The Elijah and cantatas and oratorios, and so forth. It does not exclude choir singing of other kinds.' *Royal Choral Society v Inland Revenue Comrs* [1943] 2 All ER 101 at 104, CA, per Lord Greene MR

CHOSE IN ACTION   *See also* SHARES

The expression 'chose in action' or 'thing in action' in the literal sense means a thing recoverable by action, as contrasted with a chose in possession which is a thing of which a person has not only ownership, but also actual physical possession. The meaning of the expression 'chose in action' has varied from time to time, but it is now used to describe all personal rights of property which can only be claimed or enforced by action, and not by taking physical possession. It is used in respect of both corporeal and incorporeal personal property which is not in possession. (6 Halsbury's Laws (4th edn) para 1)

The expression 'choses in action' or 'things in action' in the literal sense means things recoverable by suit or action at law as contrasted with things or choses in actual physical possession. For general purposes, however, the expression 'choses in action' is now used in order to distinguish those chattel interests which, unlike choses in possession, are incapable of transfer by delivery of the subject matter. (35 Halsbury's Laws (4th edn) para 1105)

'A legal chose in action is something which is not in possession, but which must be sued for in order to recover possession of it. It does not include a right of action, such as, for instance, a right to recover damages for breach of a contract, or a legal right to recover damages arising out of an assault.' *May v Lane* (1894) 64 LJQB 236 at 238, CA, per Rigby LJ

' "Chose in action" is a known legal expression used to describe all personal rights of property which can only be claimed or enforced by action, and not by taking physical possession.' *Torkington v Magee* [1902] 2 KB 427 at 429, DC, per Channell J

CHOSE IN POSSESSION

Choses or things in possession include all things which are at once tangible, movable, and visible, and of which possession can be taken, as, for example animals, household articles, money, jewels, corn, garments, and everything else that can properly be put in motion and transferred from place to place. (35 Halsbury's Laws (4th edn) para 1105)

CHRISTIAN FAITH

' "Christian faith" . . . is an all-embracing term which includes many possible varieties— Roman Catholic, Anglican, Presbyterian, Lutheran and others. There are many mansions, but they are all included in one house. I should not be disposed to regard "Christian faith" as a phrase lacking in clearness and distinctness.' *Clayton v Ramsden* [1943] AC 320 at 331, HL, per Lord Wright

CHRISTMAS BREAK

'Christmas break' means the period beginning with the last week day before Christmas Day and ending with the first week day after Christmas Day which is not a bank holiday. (Local Government Act 1972, s 270(1); Representation of the People Act 1983, s 40)

CHURCH   *See also* CATHEDRAL; CHAPEL

In ecclesiastical law 'church', when used in relation to a religious body, has two distinct meanings: it may mean either the aggregate of the individual members of the church or it may mean the quasi-corporate institution which carries on the religious work of the denomination whose name it bears. (14 Halsbury's Laws (4th edn) para 302)

'Church' shall mean and include any chapel where there is no church. (Inclosure Act 1845, s 167)

The expression 'church' includes cathedral and other churches, chapels of ease, and other public chapels of the Church in Wales and in the case of a cathedral church includes the chapter house and cloisters and other precincts of the cathedral church. (Welsh Church Act 1914, s 38)

The expression 'church' means any church or chapel which has been consecrated for the purpose of public worship according to the rites and ceremonies of the Church of England. (Interpretation Measure 1925, s 3)

'Church' means a church or chapel which has been consecrated for the purpose of public worship according to the rites and ceremonies of the Church of England, and includes a building used or intended to be used partly for the purpose of such public worship and partly for the purpose of a church hall, whether the whole building is consecrated or only such part thereof as is used as intended to be used for the purpose of such public worship, and any reference to the consecration of a church shall, in the case of such a building, be construed as including a reference to the consecration of the part of the building used or intended to be used for the purpose of such worship as aforesaid. (Pastoral Measure 1983, s 87(1))

'Section 75 [of the Local Government Act 1894] . . . says that unless the context otherwise requires the expression ecclesiastical charity shall include various things, and (inter alia) a charity the endowment of which is held "for the benefit of any particular Church or denomination, or of any members thereof as such". The word "Church" here clearly does not mean building; it means a religious society of some sort.' *Re Perry Almshouses, Re Ross' Charity* [1899] 1 Ch 21 at 29, per Lindley MR

'Speaking generally, one would say that the identity of a religious community described as a Church must consist in the unity of its doctrines. Its creeds, confessions, formularies, tests, and so forth are apparently intended to ensure the unity of the faith which its adherents profess, and certainly among all Christian Churches the essential idea of a creed or confession of faith appears to be the public acknowledgment of such and such religious views as the bond of union which binds them together as one Christian community.' *Free Church of Scotland (General Assembly) v Overtoun (Lord), Macalister v Young* [1904] AC 515 at 612, 613, per Lord Halsbury LC

[A testatrix by her will made a residuary bequest to the vicar of St Alban's Church, Holborn, for such objects connected with the 'church' as he should think fit.] 'The bequest is to the Vicar as the Vicar of St Alban's Church and not St Alban's Parish for objects connected with the church. . . . It appears to me that the words "such objects connected with the Church" . . . are to be interpreted narrowly or rather, perhaps, as relating to the church in contradistinction to relating to the parish; and it is not disputed that if the objects were confined to the support of the church, its fabric and its services, that would be a good charitable bequest. . . . It is because we have got the church as the centre of this bequest and not the parish that I think we are right in rejecting outside considerations and in saying that this is a good bequest to the Vicar as a trustee for the purposes of his church, that is, for the fabric and for the services which are conducted therein.' *Re Bain, Public Trustee v Ross* [1930] 1 Ch 224 at 232, CA, per Lord Hanworth MR

New Zealand 'As I understand the term "church" it means a building for public worship, and in many Christian denominations a church is called the Lord's House. The size of the building or the grandeur of its architecture does not make a church; many Churches use buildings of the humblest description. It is the sacerdotal element in a building that makes it a church. . . . User by way of holding services is what converts what otherwise is an ordinary building into a church, so that there must be both occupancy and user for the specified purpose to give a building its sacerdotal character.' *Thames Borough Council v Congretional Church Trustees* [1929] NZLR 525 at 527, per Blair J; also reported [1929] GLR 134 at 135

Church of England

The term 'Church of England' has sometimes been loosely used to refer to the Anglican Communion and to include churches which, though not part of the Church of England, are in communion with it and accept the same standards of faith and doctrine. This is, however, incorrect, and in Church Assembly or General Synod Measures 'Church of England' does not include the Church in Wales. (14 Halsbury's Laws (4th edn) para 302)

The Church of England, established according to the laws of the realm under the Queen's Majesty, is declared to belong to the true and apostolic Church of Christ, being regarded as the branch of the Church which was founded in

England when the English were gradually converted to Christianity between the years 597 and 687. It contains the two provinces of Canterbury and York. The expression 'England' in this connection includes the town of Berwick-upon-Tweed, but not any part of England or Wales to which the Welsh Church Act 1914 applies. The Church of England has bishops and ecclesiastical organisations in certain foreign parts. (14 Halsbury's Laws (4th edn) para 345)

'Church of England' shall not include the Church in Wales. (Interpretation Measure 1925, s 2)

'Whatever difficulty there may be in giving a strict legal definition of what constitutes membership of the Church of England, I think that a person who has been baptised, has been confirmed, or is ready and desirous to be confirmed, and is an actual communicant, does hold the status of a member of that Church, and would be ordinarily regarded and spoken of as such.' *Re Perry Almshouses* [1898] 1 Ch 391 at 400, per Stirling J

Guild church

'Guild church' means a church in the City of London designated and established as a guild church under the City of London (Guild Churches) Acts 1952 and 1960. (Church of England (Worship and Doctrine) Measure 1974, s 5)

Parish church   *See* PARISH

CHURCH SCHOOL   *See* SCHOOL

CHURCHWARDEN   *See also*
PARISHIONER

Churchwardens are the guardians or keepers of the church, and representatives of the body of the parish. They are sometimes appointed by the minister, sometimes by the parish, sometimes by both together, as custom directs. They are taken, in favour of the church, to be for some purposes a kind of corporation at the common law; that is, they are enabled by that name to have a property in goods and chattels, and to bring actions for them, for the use and profit of the parish. Yet they may not waste the church goods, but may be removed by the parish, and then called to account by action at the common law: but there is no method of calling them to account, but by first removing them;

for none can legally do it, but those who are put in their place. (1 Bl Com 382)

'Churchwardens' shall mean also chapelwardens, or other persons discharging the duties of churchwardens. (Burial Act 1852, s 52)

CHURCHWAY

A right of way may exist by custom for parishioners to go to and from their parish church. Such a way is known as a churchway. It is distinguished from a highway insofar as no-one but a parishioner can be legally entitled to use a churchway, whereas every member of the public has the right to use a highway. A way leading to a church as its point of destination may be a highway, and so may a way across a churchyard. Such ways will be highways where dedication by the landowner is inferred from the facts. (21 Halsbury's Laws (4th edn) para 6)

A customary churchway is a quasi easement. . . . It is a right of way in favour of the parishioners to go to and from the parish church over the land of a private individual owner, and is enjoyed by the parishioners as a means of access to the parish church. Such a way can only exist by custom, and no landowner can dedicate a road with only such rights as the public would have over a churchway. Such a way arises from user from time immemorial and cannot now be created anew. A right of way to a parish church, however, is not necessarily a customary right of way belonging to the parishioners, but may be a public highway. Prima facie a custom in reference to a way to a parish church is a parochial custom in favour of the parishioners; and a customary churchway not for the use and benefit of the parishioners at large would be rare. (12 Halsbury's Laws (4th edn) para 437)

'A churchway is a way the rights over which exist by custom in favour of a limited class of the public, and no landowner can dedicate a road with only such rights as the public would have over a churchway.' *Farquhar v Newbury Rural Council* [1909] 1 Ch 12 at 16, CA, per Cozens-Hardy MR

CHURCHYARD

'Churchyard' includes a closed churchyard. (Cathedrals Measure 1963, s 52)

CIDER

'Cider' means cider (or perry) of a strength less than 8.7 per cent . . . obtained from fermentation of apple or pear juice without the addition at any time of any alcoholic liquor or of any liquor or substance which communicates colour or flavour other than such as the Commissioners [of Customs and Excise] may allow as appearing to them to be necessary to make cider (or perry). (Alcoholic Liquor Duties Act 1979, s 1(6))

[The words omitted were deleted by the Alcoholic Liquors (Amendment of Enactments Relating to Strength and to Units of Measurement) Order 1979, SI 1979/241.]

CINEMATOGRAPH FILM *See also* FILM

'Cinematograph film' means any film containing celluloid which is intended for use in a cinematograph or any similar apparatus. (Celluloid and Cinematograph Film Act 1922, s 9)

'Cinematograph film' means any sequence of visual images recorded on material of any description (whether translucent or not) so as to be capable, by the use of that material,—
(a) of being shown as a moving picture, or
(b) of being recorded on other material (whether translucent or not), by the use of which it can be so shown.
(Copyright Act 1956, s 13(10))

'Cinematograph film' means any print, negative, tape or other article on which a performance of a dramatic or musical work or part thereof is recorded for the purposes of visual reproduction. (Dramatic and Musical Performers' Protection Act 1958, s 8(1))

'Cinematograph film' means any print, negative, tape or other article on which a performance of a play or any part of such a performance is recorded for the purposes of visual reproduction. (Theatres Act 1968, s 7(3))

CIRCULAR

'In order that a document may be a circular, the various copies must be practically identical in form. . . . The document must also be intended for several persons. . . . The question whether advertising is the main and not merely an ancillary purpose is, in my opinion, really a question of fact. One has to see what was the object of despatching the circular. That may be ascertained partly from the document

and partly from other evidence.' *Cashmore v Smith* (1919) 83 JP 157 at 159, per Bray J

CIRCULATING CAPITAL *See* CAPITAL

CIRCULATION

'A bank-note in circulation ordinarily means a note which is passing from hand to hand as a negotiable instrument representing a certain value. When it is returned to the bank from which it was issued it ceases to circulate.' *Bank of Africa Ltd v Colonial Government* (1888) 13 App Cas 215 at 220, PC, per cur.

CIRCUS

'Circus' means a place where animals are kept or introduced wholly or mainly for the purpose of performing tricks or manoeuvres at that place. (Zoo Licensing Act 1981, s 21(1))

CITY

Australia 'A city is a more or less permanent, and highly diversified and organised, centre of occupation by men, women and children, which is greater, in size, complexity, and importance, than a town or village. Although very many of a city's buildings are dwelling-houses in one form or another, it is wholly compatible with urban living that many industrial and commercial buildings are to be found that lie at the heart of the business (including manufacturing business) sectors of a city. A city, in short, represents a small cross-section of the civilised world, excluding those areas that are dedicated to exclusively rural states or pursuits.' *Spic-n-span Corpn Pty Ltd v Fredericks* (1982) 50 LGRA 46 at 50, per Wells J

CIVIL COMMOTION *See also* RIOT

A civil commotion has been described as an insurrection of the people for general purposes, though not amounting to rebellion, but it probably cannot be precisely defined. Turbulence or tumult is essential; and an organised conspiracy to commit acts where there is no tumult or disturbance until after the acts does not amount to civil commotion. However, it is not necessary to show the existence of any outside organisation at whose instigation the acts were done. It therefore expresses a stage intermediate between riot and civil war, and although technically it probably includes a riot, once fighting begins matters have got beyond a mere civil commotion. (25 Halsbury's Laws (4th edn) para 623)

'But what is a civil commotion? It is something else [than rebellion]. The present was an insurrection of the people, resisting all law, setting the protection of the government at naught, taking from every man who was the object of their resentment that protection. . . . The Fleet prison was burnt down; Newgate was burnt down the night before. The King's Bench Prison is burnt and all the prisoners set at liberty. The new Bridewell is burnt; the Bank attacked. . . . Military resistance and an extraordinary stretch were ready made, and justified by necessity. There was a great deal of firing, many men were killed. . . . What is this but a civil commotion?' *Langdale v Mason* (1780) 2 Park's Law of Marine Insurances, 8th edn, p 965 at 967, 968, per Lord Mansfield CJ

'I think that a civil commotion, without making any attempt to define it, must at least involve that the acts which constitute the commotion should be acts done by the agents together and not merely acts which are done in preconcert and simultaneously and in proximity to one another, and where there has been no tumult and no disturbance until after the acts, those acts themselves cannot constitute civil commotion, though the subsequent uproar might or might not in itself be a civil commotion.' *London & Manchester Plate Glass Co Ltd v Heath* [1913] 3 KB 411 at 421, CA, per Hamilton LJ

CIVIL LIST

Since the accession of George III it has been customary for each succeeding Sovereign to surrender the hereditary revenues to the nation for the term of his life, in return for a fixed annual income. known as the Civil List. (8 Halsbury's Laws (4th edn) para 1413)

CIVIL OFFENCE

In this Act the expression 'civil offence' means any act or omission punishable by the law of England or which, if committed in England, would be punishable by that law. (Army Act 1955, s 70(2); Air Force Act 1955, s 70(2))

CIVIL PRISON *See* PRISON

CIVIL PROCEEDINGS *See* PROCEEDINGS

CIVIL SERVANT

'Let me now consider the nature of the employment of an established civil servant. The terms "servant" and "service" are convenient expressions and in common use relating to civil employment under the Crown, but I have to consider the true legal relationship. In Bacon's Abridgement sub. tit. "Prerogative" it is stated that ". . . the King hath an interest in all his subjects and is entitled to their services and may employ them in such offices as the public good and the nature of our constitution require." It was also said in *R v Dr Burnell* [(1698) Carth 478] that ". . . every man is a publick officer who hath any duty concerning the publick, and he is not less a publick officer where his authority is confined to narrow limits, because 'tis the duty of his office, and the nature of that duty, which makes him a publick officer, and not the extent of his authority". . . . An established civil servant, whatever his grade, is more properly described as an officer in the civil employment of Her Majesty and I can see no ground on which different rules of law in respect of his employment can be applied according to the grade or position he may occupy.' *Inland Revenue Comrs v Hambrook* [1956] 1 All ER 807 at 810, 811, per Lord Goddard CJ; affd., [1956] 3 All ER 338, CA

CLAIM

[The Workmen's Compensation Act 1906, s 2(1) (a) (repealed), required a 'claim' for compensation to be made within six months from the occurrence of the accident.] 'I think there can be no question that a claim cannot be said to be made unless it is communicated to the employers. In the present case the claim being in the form of a letter, is not "made" unless the letter is delivered.' *Watts v Vickers Ltd* (1916) 86 LJKB 177 at 181, CA, per Warrington LJ

'I think that the primary meaning of the word "claim"—whether used in a popular sense or in a strict legal sense—is such as to attach it to the object that is claimed; and is not the same thing as the cause of action by which the claim may be supported or as the grounds on which it may be based.' *West Wake Price & Co v Ching* [1956] 3 All ER 821 at 829, per Devlin J

'In my view, the allegation by the defendant that the covenant sued on is void owing to the libellous or defamatory allegations by the plaintiff does not bring this action within the words of s 6(1)(b) of the Administration of Justice (Miscellaneous Provisions) Act 1933 [repealed; see now the Supreme Court Act 1981, s 69(1)(b)], "A claim" in that subsection means the assertion of a cause of action.' *Shordiche-Churchward v Cordle* [1959] 1 All ER 599 at 601, CA, per Pearce LJ

[The Limitation Act 1939, s 23(4) [repealed; see now the Limitation Act 1980, s 29(5)], provides that where any right of action has accrued to recover any debt or other liquidated pecuniary claim and the person liable or accountable therefore acknowledges the 'claim', etc, the right shall be deemed to have accrued on and not before the date of the acknowledgment or last payment.] 'The words "the claim" are not, perhaps, very happy. A person may acknowledge that a claim has been made against him without acknowledging any indebtedness. It is clear that what the Limitation Act 1939, means is "acknowledges the debt or other liquidated pecuniary amount".' *Good v Parry* [1963] 2 All ER 59 at 61, CA, per Lord Denning MR; also reported in [1963] 2 QB 418 at 423

Australia 'I think that where the phrase "claim for compensation" is used in the same Act as the words "claim compensation", both mean the same thing—make a claim for compensation. Atkin LJ in *Bennett v L and W Whitehead Ltd* [[1926] 2 KB 380 at 407], has expressly stated they do mean the same thing; and I feel that I should follow that decision. All the cases to which Mr Rapke [counsel for the plaintiff] has referred have been concerned with the use of the word "proceed", and the New South Wales legislation showed, by the use of that word, that the worker would have to take some steps to bring the case before the Court other than merely giving notice. I do not think that the Victorian Legislature can be taken to have used these words, "claim compensation", as meaning that a proceeding before the Court had to be initiated in some way.' *Hardman v Lyall & Sons Pty Ltd* [1945] VLR 71 at 72, 73, per Martin J

Canada [The Sale of Goods Act 1920 (Ont), s 45(1) (repealed; see now RSO 1980, c 462, s 44(1)), enabled an unpaid seller to exercise his right of stoppage *in transitu* either by taking actual possession of the goods or by giving

notice of his 'claim' to the common carrier or other bailee in whose possession the goods were.] 'The defendants contend that there is no notice of their "claim" by the plaintiffs—as what the statute, s 45(1) means is notice of his claim against the vendee or of the nature of his claim. But such is not the meaning: "Claim" here means "claim to stop delivery".' *New Ontario Colonization Co Ltd v Grand Trunk Rly* (1925) 57 OLR 244 at 247, per Riddell J; affd (1926) 58 OLR 249

Canada [Insurer under liability policy was liable for 'claims made or suits brought in policy period.] 'The words "claims made" are not synonymous with "writs issued" or "suits brought". In my view the words "claims made" include but are broader than the words "writs issued" or "suits brought". Claims may be made against an insured without the institution of legal process whether by way of writ of summons or otherwise.' *Re St Paul Fire & Marine Insurance Co and Guardian Insurance Co of Canada* (1983) 1 DLR (4th) 342 at 349, Ont CA, per Goodman JA

Canada [Pursuant to the terms of a lease, a tenant agreed to indemnify her landlord against any 'claims'. The issue arose as to what the word 'claim' encompassed.] 'There do not appear to be Canadian cases of definition but American jurisprudence is replete with them. *Corpus Juris Secundum*, vol 14, p 115 et seq, defines "claim" as: '. . . embracing every species of legal demand, not necessarily limited to money demands; and, particularly when used in connection with property, 'claim' has been used to signify a demand and nothing more. The term has been specifically defined as meaning a demand of a right, or of an alleged or supposed right; a calling on another for something due or supposed to be due; an active assertion of right and the demand for its recognition; an assertion, demand, or challenge, of something as a right . . .".' *Re Prudential Assurance Co Ltd and Walwyn, Stodgell, Cochran, Murray Ltd* (1985) 50 OR (2d) 609 at 612, 613, Ont CA, per Grange JA

In bankruptcy proceedings

United States '[C]laim' means—
(A) right to payment, whether or not such right is reduced to judgment, liquidated, unliquidated, fixed, contingent, matured, unmatured, disputed, undisputed, legal, equitable, secured, or unsecured;
(B) right to an equitable remedy for breach of

performance if such breach gives rise to a right to payment, whether or not such right to an equitable remedy is reduced to judgment, fixed, contingent, matured, unmatured, disputed, undisputed, secured, or unsecured. . . .
(Bankruptcy Act 1978, s 101(4))

CLASS

Gift to

Prima facie a class gift is a gift to a class of persons included and comprehended under some general description and bearing a certain relation to the testator or another person or united by some common tie. Thus, where a testator divides his residue into as many equal shares as he shall have children surviving him, or predeceasing him leaving issue, and gives a share to or in trust for each such child, the gift is to a class. There may also be a class compounded of persons answering one or other of alternative descriptions, for example 'the children of A and the children of B', or 'the children of A who attain twenty-one and the issue of such as die under that age'. (50 Halsbury's Laws (4th edn) para 362)

'A gift to a class . . . is a gift to a set of persons all filling one common character, or holding some definite position, and a gift to a number of residuary legatees does not thereby constitute them a class. Where there is a gift to children as tenants in common this is a gift to a class as tenants in common, the members of the class not being ascertained until the death of the testator. In the same way a gift to executors as such, being made to them in that capacity, is a gift to them as a class, and on the death of one of the persons named in the testator's lifetime, his share will not lapse, but go to the survivors.'
Re Chaplin's Trust (1863) 12 WR 147 at 148, per Page Wood V-C

'Where the testator leaves to a class, we do not think he can be taken to contemplate the numbers, or to have in his mind the individuals of the class who may be living at the time of his death; he gives the whole or a portion, as the case may be, of his property to a portion or division of his family, or to others who as a class form an entity and come within the terms of his devise—a given portion to a given class.' *Fell v Biddolph* (1875) LR 10 CP 701 at 709, per cur.

'A gift is said to be to a "class" of persons, when it is to all those who shall come within a certain category or description defined by a

general or collective formula, and who, if they take at all, are to take one divisible subject in certain proportionate shares; and the rule is, that the vice of remoteness affects the class as a whole, if it may affect an unascertained number of its members.' *Pearks v Moseley* (1880) 5 App Cas 714 at 723, per Lord Selborne LC.

'Prima facie a class gift is a gift to a class, consisting of persons who are included and comprehended under some general description and bear a certain relation to the testator. . . . But it may be none the less a class because some of the individuals of the class are named. For example if a gift is made "to all my nephews and nieces including A", or if a gift is made "to C and all my other nephews and nieces", each of those would be a class gift. . . . There may also be a composite class, such as, for instance, children of A and children of B: that would be a good class. On the other hand a gift to A, and all the children of B, is, in my opinion, prima facie not a class gift.' *Kingsbury v Walter* [1901] AC 187 at 192, 193, per Lord Davey

Of creditors

'The word "class" is vague, and to find out what is meant by it we must look at the scope of the section [the Joint Stock Companies Arrangement Act 1870, s 2 (repealed; see now Companies Act 1985, s 425)], which is a section enabling the Court to order a meeting of a class of creditors to be called [where an arrangement is proposed between a company being wound up and its creditors]. It seems plain that we must give such a meaning to the term "class" as will prevent the section being so worked as to result in confiscation and injustice, and that it must be confined to those persons whose rights are not so dissimilar as to make it impossible for them to consult together with a view to their common interest.' *Sovereign Life Assurance Co v Dodd* [1892] 2 QB 573 at 583, CA, per Bowen LJ

Australia 'If one finds a group of creditors whose claims against the company are of precisely similar legal character then, prima facie, they should be regarded as a class [within the Companies Act (NSW) 1961–1986, s 181 as amended]. It is similarity of rights that underlies the test enunciated by Bowen LJ [*in Sovereign Life Assurance Co v Dodd* [supra] His Lordship's test is the guide for drawing the line at which rights become so dissimilar as to prevent them constituting a single class.' *Re Jax*

Marine Pty Ltd [1967] 1 NSWR 145 at 149, per
Street J

Of employment

'The phrase "class of employment" in the
subsection [the Workmen's Compensation Act
1925, s 11(3) (repealed)] is, I think, equivalent
to a description of the kind of trade or industry
in which a workman is engaged and receives his
remuneration. There are many such "classes"
of employment in such industry. There are
many classes of engineers. Each of the various
"trades" in engineering would no doubt constitute "a class of employment". But if a man is
still carrying on his same trade or profession
the fact that greater risks are at one time
involved in it than at another does not take him
out of the "class of employment" in which he
was previously spending his professional or
trade life. I, therefore, think that an increase of
risk is no distinction of "class".' *Shirley v
Fisher Renwick Ltd* [1943] 1 All ER 262 at 264,
CA, per Scott LJ

CLAUSE

'It has been suggested that a clause must mean
something self-contained and independent,
which when presented on paper would have a
meaning by itself, without reference to the
context. I do not know any law which says that
that is the necessary meaning of the word
"clause". When I read an enactment speaking
of a devise, that is to say, speaking of a will or
any clause in a will, I naturally infer that the
word "clause" there means some collocation of
words in the will which, when removed out of
the will, will leave the rest of the will intelligible. I know no rule which says that the clause
itself must be capable of being read as a document by itself if taken alone.' *Swinton v Bailey*
(1878) 4 App Cas 70 at 77, per Lord Cairns LC

CLEAN

[The Factory and Workshop Act 1901, s 13
(repealed; see now the Factories Act 1961,
s 20), restricted the employment of certain
persons in 'cleaning' machinery in motion.]
'Unless the fluff is removed—necessarily while
the machinery is in motion by the aid of mechanical power—the rollers become choked and
the process stops. . . . It is removed because if
it remains it will stop the machine. Now to
remove that which, if not removed, will stop
the machine and prove detrimental to it, is in

my opinion to clean the machine.' *Taylor v
Dawson (Mark) & Son Ltd* [1911] 1 KB 145 at
148, DC, per Darling J

CLEAN BILL OF LADING   *See* BILL OF
LADING

CLEANSE

[The Public Health Act 1875, s 42 (repealed),
dealt with the power and duty of a local
authority to undertake or to contract for the
'cleansing' of earth-closets, privies, ashpits and
cesspools.] 'He [counsel] says that
"cleansing", in s 42 does not cover disinfect-
ing. But the word "cleansing", as there
applied, has, in my judgment, a wide meaning
and includes removal of all matter which
causes the nuisance and it is admitted in the
case that . . . bacteria form a nuisance.'
Barnett v Laskey (1898) 68 LJQB 55 at 57, DC,
per Lord Russell of Killowen CJ

CLEAR

[A testator by his will devised to trustees a sum
of money to be laid out in the purchase of an
annuity 'clear' for A.] 'I must direct the
trustees to lay it out in the purchase of an
annuity free from taxes, which is the proper
meaning of the word "clear".' *Hodgworth v
Crawley* (1742) 2 Atk 376 at 376, per Lord
Hardwicke LC

'The words of the will are "one annuity or clear
yearly sum" and the argument is that the word
"annuity" is equivalent to "clear yearly sum";
but if it be so, which is to govern? Is it the word
"annuity"? It appears to me that any ambiguity
that there is in this expression is to be explained
by the word "clear"; and that the words "one
annuity or clear yearly sum" are equivalent to
the words "one clear annuity", the word
"clear" meaning "clear of all deductions".'
Gude v Mumford (1837) 2 Y & C Ex 445 at 457,
per Alderson B

[A testatrix by her will exercised a general
power of appointment by making gifts of so
much and such part of the trust fund as should
be of the 'clear' value of £1,000, these gifts
being followed by a gift of residue.] 'The question is, what is the meaning of the words "clear
value"? . . . I must treat the word "clear" as
expressing an intention that each of the
appointed shares in respect of which she has
used the word should come to the respective

appointees clear of any outgoings not merely under the settlement, but to which it might otherwise be subject under the appointment in her will, and that would of course include testamentary expenses.' *Re Currie, Bjorkman v Kimberley (Lord)* (1888) 57 LJ Ch 743 at 744, 745, per Kay J

'The question raised . . . is whether . . . the gift to the wife of a clear annuity of £2,000 amounts to a gift to her of that sum free of income tax. . . . Where there is a gift of an annuity or a clear annuity, or an annuity free from deduction or abatement, the annuitant has to bear the income tax, and the annuity is not given free of income tax; or in other words, the will is not to be read and construed as if it contained a gift of the annuity and of an additional sum equivalent to the income tax payable on it.' *Re Loveless, Farrer v Loveless* [1918] 2 Ch 1 at 3, 4, CA, per Swinfen Eady LJ

[A testator by his will bequeathed to the vicar and churchwardens of a church a sum to produce, after payment of tax and all other deductions, a 'clear yearly sum' of £60.] 'I thought at one time that the words "payment of tax" might be an incorrect reference to payment of death duties, but when one looks at the framework of the sentence, I think that cannot be right and that the "clear yearly sum" is intended to be a sum which is clear in the sense that tax and other deductions normally to be made from income as such have been provided for.' *Re Powell, Neale v Roberts* [1945] Ch 69 at 70, per Vaisey J

[A testator by his will gave certain annuities 'clear of all death duties and income tax up to but not exceeding 5s 6d in the pound but not sur-tax'.] 'In my opinion there is nothing in the language of the gift itself or in any other part of the will to justify an inference that the testator, in using the words "clear of income tax", meant "income tax at the standard rate". I am accordingly of opinion that the principle of *In re Pettit* [*Le Fevre v Pettit* [1922] 2 Ch 765] applies and that the annuitants cannot retain for themselves the whole of the proportion of the reliefs and allowances, referable to the annuities, to which from time to time they become entitled.' *Re Bates, Jenks v Bates* [1946] Ch 83 at 86, per Romer J

Australia 'The Shorter Oxford Dictionary gives as meanings of "clear", "distinct", "free from confusion" and "evident, plain". Wests, Words and Phrases, vol 7, p 635 et seq shows that the word "clearly" has been frequently

used in United States legislation in a variety of contexts, including "clearly appear", "clearly ascertainable", "clearly establish" and "clearly expressed". Again and again the courts have gone back to Webster's definition, viz: "in a clear manner; without entanglement or confusion; without uncertainty".' *Papadopoulos v Goodwin* [1982] 1 NSWLR 413 at 417, per Wooten J

Canada 'The adjective "clear" is defined in Murray's New English Dictionary, inter alia, as meaning "free from doubt". If a matter therefore is "free from doubt" it comes perilously near to indicating that a degree of proof is required not far removed from "beyond reasonable doubt".' *R v Gibbons* [1946] OR 464 at 490, Ont CA, per Hope JA

New Zealand 'By agreement for a lease . . . the plaintiff agreed to lease to the defendants certain premises . . . the defendants agreeing to pay to the plaintiff a clear rental of £1 10*s* weekly. There is no agreement on the part of the tenant in express terms to pay the rates on the property. . . . The plaintiff contends that an agreement to pay these rates is contained in the agreement to pay a "clear rental". I think the decision in *Henderson v Gurr* [(1913) 32 NZLR 785] is sufficient authority for this. . . . The defendants have contracted with the plaintiff to pay the rates on the premises included in the agreement for lease.' *Hanson v Wright* [1922] NZLR 856 at 856, 857, per Adams J

New Zealand [The testator, by his will, which was made in New Zealand, bequeathed annuities to each of two persons, who were at all material times resident and domiciled in the United Kingdom. He declared the annuities to be 'clear of income tax'.] 'There seems to be no authority which lays it down as a rule that a reference to income-tax in a New Zealand will necessarily means only New Zealand income-tax. . . . I conclude . . . that both New Zealand and British income-tax on both those annuities are to be borne and paid by the trustees and not by the annuitants or either of them.' *Re Edmiston (Deceased), New Zealand Insurance Co Ltd v I'Anson* [1954] NZLR 844 at 846, 850, per Stanton J

CLEAR (Period)

In many statutes, statutory rules and byelaws the intention to exclude [the first and the last] days and to give the person affected a clear interval of time between the two is put beyond ll doubt by the insertion of words such as clear days' or so many days 'at least'. (45 Halsbury's Laws (4th edn) para 1133)

The Bastardy Act 1809 (repealed) required hat a person aggrieved by an order thereunder should give notice ten 'clear' days before the quarter sessions, of his intention to appeal, and he cause and matter thereof.] 'Ten clear days means ten perfect intervening days between the act done and the first day of the sessions.' *R v Herefordshire JJ* (1820) 3 B & Ald 581 at 582, per cur.

Where so many "clear days" must elapse before some act is done, not merely the first but the last day is excluded.' *McMillan v HM Advocate* 1982 SCCR 309 at 311, quoting Dunedin Encyclopaedia of the Laws of Scotland (1933), vol 14, p 449

Australia 'The term "clear days" may be regarded as a well-known term in law with a well-known interpretation which has existed for more than half a century. When reference is made to "clear days" in a rule for the protection of another party, it is a minimum. When the rule is for the advantage of the party who is to take action, it may be a maximum. In either case it denotes a limit. When it is a minimum, two days, one before and after the period, are determined by it. But, when you talk of doing a thing within a period of a certain number of days, it is quite clear that the end of the last day is the furthest limit. It is impossible to say that a thing required to be done within seven days is done within seven days if done on the eighth day, and it is impossible to make any alteration of the limit by adding the word "clear".' *Armstrong v Great Southern Gold Mining Co* (1911) 12 CLR 382 at 388, per Griffith CJ

CLEARANCE

'Now "clearance" in my opinion has a well-known and definite meaning. It is a certificate issued by the Customs showing that the vessel named in it has complied with the Customs requirements and is authorised to proceed to sea; and the acts which have to be done at the Customs to procure such a certificate constitute the process of "clearing" the vessel.' *Thalmann Frères & Co v Texas Star Flour Mills* (1899) 15 TLR 471 at 472, per Bigham J; affd (1900) 82 LT 833, CA

Australia '"Clearance" is variously used. In the more general sense it indicates the ship's satisfying the proper local authorities that the law of the port has been complied with, so as to entitle the vessel to depart. Sometimes it is employed to denote the authorisation for departure; and, again, it sometimes designates the documents, such as a certificate or other papers . . . which evidence the right to depart. . . . The ship's papers, supposing them to be conclusive as to destination, could not determine whether the voyage came within s 5 [of the Commonwealth of Australia Constitution Act] because they could never settle what is the "first port of clearance". That first port might be the one named in the papers, or the immediately previous port, or a prior port in some foreign country, and that at once breaks the possibility of ship's papers—past or present, for they are all open to the same difficulty—being the absolute legal test of the voyage. There remains then no test but that of actuality—of which, of course, papers may be some evidence.' *Merchant Service Guild of Australasia v Commonwealth (Owners) Assocn* (1913) 16 CLR 664 at 696, per Isaacs J

CLEARANCE AREA

(1) A clearance area is an area which is to be cleared of all buildings in accordance with the following provisions of this Part.
(2) The local housing authority shall declare an area to be a clearance area if they are satisfied—
   (a) that the houses in the area are unfit for human habitation or are by reason of their bad arrangement, or the narrowness or bad arrangement of the streets, dangerous or injurious to the health of the inhabitants of the area, and
   (b) that the other buildings, if any, in the area are for a like reason dangerous or injurious to the health of the inhabitants of the area.
   and that the most satisfactory method of dealing with the conditions in the area is the demolition of all the buildings in the area.
(3) If the authority are so satisfied they shall—
   (a) cause the area to be defined on a map in such manner as to exclude from the area any building which is not unfit for human habitation or dangerous or injurious to health, and
   (b) pass a resolution declaring the area so defined to be a clearance area.
(Housing Act 1985, s 289)

CLEARING

'Clearing', in relation to land, means the removal of buildings or materials from the land, the levelling of the surface of the land, and the carrying out of such other operations in relation thereto as may be prescribed. (Town and Country Planning Act 1971, s 290(1))

CLEARING HOUSE

United States 'Clearing house' means any association of banks or other payors regularly clearing items. . . . (Uniform Commercial Code 1978, s 4–104(1)(d))

CLERGYMAN

'Clergyman' means a clerk in Holy Orders of the Church of England. (Marriage Act 1949, s 78)

Regular clergyman *See* REGULAR

CLERICAL ERROR

'It was suggested in the course of argument that . . . "clerical error" in s 20(1)(a) [of the Administration of Justice Act 1982] suggests a clerk. I do not accept this. A testator writing out or typing his own will can make a clerical error just as much as someone else writing out or typing a will for him.' *Re Williams (decd), Wiles v Madgin* [1985] 1 All ER 964 at 969, per Nicholls J

Australia 'In the New Oxford Dictionary one meaning attributed to the word "clerical" is "Of or pertaining to a clerk or penman: esp. in 'clerical error', an error made in writing anything out". According to Webster, one meaning of the word "clerical" is "of or relating to a clerk or copyist", and an example given is "clerical error, an error made in copying or writing". Probably no one would deny that a clerical error may produce a significant, and even profound, effect as for example, in a case in which a writer or typist inadvertently omits the small word "not". But the characteristic of a clerical error is not that it is in itself trivial or unimportant, but that it arises in the mechanical process of writing or transcribing.' *R v Comr of Patents, ex p Martin* (1953) 89 CLR 381 at 406, per Fullager J

Canada 'I accept that a clerical error is an error that arises in the mechanical process of writing or transcribing and that its characteristic does not depend at all on its relative obviousness or the relative gravity or triviality of its consequences.' *Bayer AG v Commissioner of Patents* [1981] 1 FCR 656 at 660, Fed Ct TD, per Mahoney J

CLERICAL WORK

'Clerical work' includes writing, bookkeeping, sorting papers, filing, typing, duplicating, machine calculating, drawing and the editorial preparation of matter for publication. (Offices, Shops and Railway Premises Act 1963, s 1)

'Clerical work' includes writing, bookkeeping, sorting papers, filing, typing, duplicating, punching cards or tapes, machine calculating, drawing and the editorial preparation of matter for publication. (General Rate Act 1967, s 32)

Australia 'Clerical work in industry has long since moved from the Dickensian era of the high stool and the quill pen. The voice and the mind are now part of clerical stock-in-trade. So is the acceptance of responsibility and the exercise of discretion. The conception is fluid and progressive and recourse to a dictionary gives only partial help. It is impossible, and in any event it would be undesirable, to attempt to devise a code as to what in the setting of industry today can fairly be regarded as clerical work. But too fine a toothcomb should not be used in solving this question in particular cases. . . . The salient point is that for years clerical work has been regarded for industrial purposes as including more than mere recording and covers work of different kinds which no doubt leads to or results from recording but in fact is part of the general office administration system. That is why I deprecate dividing office functions too strictly by attempting to quantify the recording done by different members of the team and using this as the test.' *Federated Clerks Union of Australia, NSW Branch v Australian Workers Union* (1971) AR 419 at 421, per Sheldon J

CLERK *See also* CLERICAL WORK; SERVANT

'Clerk', in relation to any authority or body, includes any officer of the authority or body authorised by them to act on their behalf either generally or in relation to any particular matter. (General Rate Act 1967, s 115)

CLIENT

'Client' includes—
(a) in relation to contentious business, any person who as principal or on behalf of another person retains or employs, or is about to retain or employ, a solicitor, and any person who is or may be liable to pay a solicitor's costs;
(b) in relation to non-contentious business, any person who, as a principal or on behalf of another, or as a trustee or executor, or in any other capacity, has power, express or implied, to retain or employ, and retains or employs or is about to retain or employ, a solicitor, and any person for the time being liable to pay to a solicitor for his services any costs.
(Solicitors Act 1974, s 87(1))

CLINICAL TRIAL

In this Act 'clinical trial' means an investigation or series of investigations consisting of the administration of one or more medicinal products of a particular description—
(a) by, or under the direction of, a doctor or dentist to one or more patients of his, or
(b) by, or under the direction of, two or more doctors or dentists, each product being administered by, or under the direction of, one or other of those doctors or dentists to one or more patients of his,
where (in any such case) there is evidence that medicinal products of that description have effects which may be beneficial to the patient or patients in question and the administration of the product or products is for the purpose of ascertaining whether, or to what extent, the product has, or the products have, those or any other effects, whether beneficial or harmful.
(Medicines Act 1968, s 31(1))

CLOG   *See also* FETTER; MORTGAGE

On equity of redemption

'Any provision inserted to prevent redemption on payment or performance of the debt or obligation for which the security was given is what is meant by a clog or fetter on the equity of redemption and is therefore void. It follows from this, that "once a mortgage, always a mortgage"; but I do not understand that this principle involves the further proposition that the amount or nature of the further debt or obligation the payment or performance of which is to be secured is a clog or fetter within

the rule. . . . A "clog" or "fetter" is something which is inconsistent with the idea of "security": a clog or fetter is in the nature of a repugnant condition. . . . If I give a mortgage on a condition that I shall not redeem, that is a repugnant condition. The Courts of Equity have fought for years to maintain the doctrine that a security is redeemable. But when and under what circumstances? On the performance of the obligations for which it was given.' *Santley v Wilde* [1899] 2 Ch 474 at 474, 475, CA, per Lindley MR

See, generally, 32 Halsbury's Laws (4th edn) para 585.

CLOSE

'Neither side relied on any dictionary for the meaning of the words "close", "curtilage" or "precincts" [in the Factories Act 1937, s 151(1) (repealed; see now the Factories Act 1961, s 175(1))], or on any case defining those words with precision. It was conceded that the words "close" and "precincts" import the notion of a boundary surrounding an inclosure, but that the boundary might be a line or notional surround. The first meaning of "precinct" given in the Shorter Oxford English Dictionary is: "The space enclosed by the walls or other boundaries of a particular place or building, or by an imaginary line drawn around it; esp. the ground immediately surrounding a religious house or place of worship". The word can also be used to mean "the environs".' *Walsh v Allweather Mechanical Grouting Co Ltd* [1959] 2 All ER 588 at 592, CA, per cur.; also reported in [1959] 2 QB 300.

CLOSE COMPANY   *See* COMPANY

CLOSE TO   *See also* ADJACENT

Canada [A city charter required certificate prior to construction upon or 'close to' street line.] 'The act extends also to buildings that are close to the street line, although not upon it. "Close to" is an approximate term and admits of more or less separation between the line of the building and the true line of the street. The object of the act is to provide that the street line may be authoritatively and conclusively settled by the city engineer, who in such matter acts as on a judicial inquiry.' *City of Halifax v Reeves* (1894) 23 SCR 340 at 342, SCC, per King J

CLOSING COSTS

United States 'Closing costs' with respect to a debt secured by an interest in land includes:
(a) fees or premiums for title examination, title insurance, or similar purposes including surveys,
(b) fees for preparation of a deed, settlement statement, or other documents,
(c) escrows for future payments of taxes and insurance,
(d) fees for notarizing deeds and other documents,
(e) appraisal fees, and
(f) credit reports.
(Uniform Consumer Credit Code 1969, s 1.301(5))

CLOSING ORDER

(1) An order (in this Act referred to as 'a closing order') made by a local authority, and confirmed by the Secretary of State in manner provided by this Act, may fix the hours on the several days of the week at which, either throughout the area of the local authority or in any specified part thereof, all shops or shops of any specified class are to be closed for serving customers.
(2) The hour fixed by a closing order shall not be earlier than seven o'clock in the evening on any day of the week.
(3) The order may—
    (a) define the shops and trades to which the order applies; and
    (b) authorise sales after the closing hour fixed by the order in cases of emergency and in such other circumstances as may be specified or indicated in the order; and
    (c) contain any incidental, supplemental, or consequential provisions which may appear necessary or proper.
(Shops Act 1950, s 8, amended by the Local Government Planning and Land Act 1980, s 194, Sch 34, Part IV)

A closing order is an order prohibiting the use of the premises to which it relates for any purpose not approved by the local housing authority. (Housing Act 1985, s 267(2))

CLOTHING

'Clothing' includes boots and other footwear. (Education Act 1944, s 114(1))

CLUB

A club, except a proprietary club or an investment club, may be defined as a society of persons associated together, not for the purposes of trade, but for social reasons, the promotion of politics, sport, art, science, or literature, or for any other lawful purpose; but trading activities will not destroy the nature of a club if they are merely incidental to the club's purposes. The association must be private and have some element of permanence. The purposes for which a club exists may be altered or modified, and there is no rule of law which requires a club to fulfil each and every separate purpose for which it was originally formed. Once the mutual assent of the members has been secured, the doctrine of ultra vires has no place with respect to the activities of such an association. (6 Halsbury's Laws (4th edn) para 201)

'Clubs . . . are societies the members of which are perpetually changing. They are not partnerships; they are not associations for gain; and the feature which distinguishes them from other societies is that no member as such becomes liable to pay to the funds of the society or to anyone else any money beyond the subscriptions required by the rules of the club to be paid so long as he remains a member. It is upon this fundamental condition, not usually expressed but understood by everyone, that clubs are formed; and this distinguishing feature has been often judicially recognised. It has been so recognised in actions by creditors and in winding-up proceedings.' *Wise v Perpetual Trustee Co* [1903] AC 139 at 149, PC, per Lord Lindley

'The word "club" is not defined in the Act [Gaming Act 1968], nor in any other Act, so far as I know. But it has a meaning well understood in the law. It denotes a society of persons associated together for the promotion of some common object or objects, such as social intercourse, art, science, literature, politics or sport. In law it is also well known that a "club" may be one of two kinds: a members' club or a proprietary club. In a members' club, the members are themselves the owners, probably through trustees or a committee, of the premises and the food and drink. They conduct it for their own benefit, not with a view to profit. In a proprietary club, the proprietor owns the premises and the food and drink. He conducts it with a view to profit, but he entrusts a good deal of the organising of it to the members or a committee of members.' *Tehrani*

Rostron [1971] 3 All ER 790 at 794, 795, CA, per Lord Denning

Australia 'Apart from any enactment affecting the matter, the position at law appears to be as follows: A club "is not a juristic entity: it is not even a partnership, it is simply a voluntary association of a number of persons for the purpose of affording its members and their friends facilities for social intercourse and recreation, and the usual privileges, advantages and accommodation of a club. The property acquired for or arising from the conduct of the club, though vested in trustees, belongs to the general body of members". (*Watson v J & A G Johnson Ltd* (1936) 55 CLR 63, 68).' *Ex p Turner, Re Hardy* (1948) 48 NSWSR 133 at 149, per Street J

Australia 'There is no precise legal definition of the word "club". The description of a club contained in Wertheimer on Clubs applies to most clubs: "A club may be defined to be a voluntary association of a number of persons meeting together for purposes mainly social, each contributing a certain sum either to a common fund for the benefit of the members or to a particular individual for his own benefit". But it is possible for a voluntary association to be a club though there are no pecuniary contributions or the contributions are uncertain in amount. A club may be a members' club where contributions are paid to a common fund, or a proprietary club where they are paid to an individual or a corporation, and a club may be unincorporated or incorporated. Clubs are voluntary, non-profit making associations but they vary almost indefinitely in other characteristics.' *Bennett v Cooper* (1948) 76 CLR 570 at 575, 576, per Latham CJ

New Zealand 'In my view s 162 [of the Sale of Liquor Act 1962] was not intended to include a sporting club simpliciter although there may be circumstances where a sporting club may qualify as a club for a charter under the Sale of Liquor Act where it can truly be said to be a "voluntary association of persons . . . combined for promoting the common object of private social intercourse, convenience, and comfort. . .".' *Re an appeal by Donsonby Old Boys Club* [1979] 2 NZAR 149 at 155, per McMullin J. Upheld in *Taumarunui Cosmopolitan Club (Inc) v Taumarunui Hotel Ltd and Others* [1984] 4 NZAR 323

Incorporated club

A members' club incorporated under the Companies Act 1948 [repealed; see now the Companies Act 1985], or earlier Companies Acts, enjoys the advantages incidental to incorporation as a company, especially that of suing and being sued as a legal entity. The company may be limited by shares or by guarantee, and in either case the liability may be merely nominal in amount. The most convenient method, when a members' club is incorporated, is to register it as a company limited by guarantee, the members of the club for the time being constituting the company. (6 Halsbury's Laws (4th edn) para 206

Members' club

An unincorporated members' club is a society of persons each of whom contributes to the funds out of which the expenses of conducting the society are paid. The contribution is generally made by means of entrance fees or subscriptions, or both. The society is not a partnership, because the members are not associated with a view to profit, nor, for the same reason, is it an association requiring registration as a company. It is not recognised as having any legal existence apart from the members of which it is composed. (6 Halsbury's Laws (4th edn) para 205)

'A club is the most anomalous group of human beings that is known to the law. It is a union of persons for social intercourse or for the promotion of certain pursuits, which are closely allied to social intercourse, and the members usually regulate their conduct in accordance with bye-laws or regulations to which they subscribe. A club has no existence apart from its members. It differs from a corporation in that respect. It differs from those statutory bodies like Friendly Societies which have a sort of pseudo-corporate existence by virtue of the statute-law which regulates their activities, and even a trading partnership, regulated by the code of 1890, has a position and an existence which is superior to those of a club.' *Feeney v MacManus* [1937] IR 23, per Johnston J
[Applied by Pennycuik J in *Abbat v Treasury Solicitor* [1969] 1 All ER 52 at 58.]

Proprietary club

A proprietary club is of an entirely different nature from a members' club. The property and funds of the club belong to the proprietor, who usually conducts it with a view to profit. The members, in consideration of the payment by them to the proprietor of entrance fees and subscriptions, are entitled to make such use of the premises and property, and to exercise such other rights and privileges, as the contract between them and the proprietor justifies.

The management of a proprietary club is usually given wholly or in part to a committee of the members.

In the case of an incorporated proprietary club, the relations between the members of the club and the company are governed by the same rules as those which govern the relations between the members and proprietor of an unincorporated proprietary club. An incorporated proprietary club, provided it is able to comply with the statutory requirements, may be registered as a limited liability company without use of the word 'limited'. (6 Halsbury's Laws (4th edn) paras 208, 209)

Shop club

The expression 'shop club' or 'thrift fund' means every club and society for providing benefits to workmen in connection with a workshop, factory, dock, shop or warehouse. (Shop Clubs Act 1902, s 7)

COAL MINING INDUSTRY

Australia 'In my opinion the coal mining industry is the industry which produces coal as the consequence of mining operations. Coal mining operations include, not only the actual excavation of the coal from the seam, but also the removal of it from the pit to the surface and placing it upon the surface in a disposable form. All those operations would, according to the ordinary use of the language, properly be included within coal mining operations and would be conducted as part of the coal mining industry. The subsequent treatment of coal, however, by turning it into gas or petrol or into dyes, or other products, would not, in my opinion, be part of the coal mining industry.' *R v Drake-Brockmann, ex p National Oil Pty Ltd* (1943) 68 CLR 51, per Latham CJ

COAST

'The coast is, properly, not the sea, but the land which bounds the sea; it is the limit of the land jurisdiction, and of the parishes and manors—bordering on the sea—which are part of the land of the county. This limit, however, and its character, varies according to the state of the tide: when the tide is in, and covers the

land, it is sea; when the tide is out, it is land as far as low-water mark; between high- and low-water mark, it must therefore be considered as *divisum imperium*.' *R v Forty Nine Casks of Brandy* (1836) 3 Hag Adm 257 at 275, per Sir John Nicholl

Canada [Fishing was regulated within specified distance from the 'coast' of Canada.] 'The argument on behalf of the appellant is expressed thus in his factum: That "coast" means the general coast line of the mainland at low water and that by the operation of the rule *noscitur a sociis* the word "coast" should be held in this context to have no application to a shore of such limited magnitude as to have no bays, harbours or creeks. I have no hesitation in rejecting this contention. I have no doubt the word "coasts" in this statute embraces the coast of any part of the territory of Canada.' *Schooner John J Fallon v The King* (1917) 55 SCR 348 at 356, SCC, per Duff J

COAST PROTECTION

'Coast protection work' means any work of construction, alteration, improvement, repair, maintenance, demolition or removal for the purpose of the protection of any land, and includes the sowing or planting of vegetation for the said purpose. (Coast Protection Act 1949, s 49)

COASTAL SHIPPING

'Coastal shipping' means the carrying of goods or passengers in ships by sea to or from any point in Great Britain from or to any point in the United Kingdom, the Isle of Man, the Channel Islands or the Republic of Ireland, but does not include the carrying of goods or passengers in the exercise of a right of ferry legally established whether by Act of Parliament or otherwise. (Transport Act 1962, s 92)

COASTAL WATERS

'Coastal waters' means waters within a distance of three nautical miles from any point on the coast measured from low-water mark of ordinary spring tides. (Public Health (Control of Disease) Act 1984, s 74)

'Coastal waters' means—
(a) in relation to the United Kingdom, the Channel Islands and the Isle of Man, so much of the waters adjoining those coun-

tries respectively as is within British fishery limits; and

(b) in relation to any other country, so much of the waters adjoining that country as is within the distance to which provisions of the law of that country corresponding to the provisions of this Act extend.

(Whaling Industry (Regulation) Act 1934, s 17, substituted by Fishery Limits Act 1964, s 3(3), Sch 1 and amended by the Fishery Limits Act 1976, s 9(1), Sch 2)

COASTING SHIP

'The Customs Consolidation Act 1876, s 142 [repealed; see now the Customs and Excise Management Act 1979, s 74], enacts that "no goods shall be carried in any coasting ship, except such as shall be laden to be carried coastwise at some port or place in the United Kingdom". . . . I do not think that the Legislature can have contemplated that the phrase "coasting ship", in the Customs Consolidation Act, should have a different meaning from the words "ships employed in the coasting trade", used in the Merchant Shipping Act 1854 [repealed]. I think that the words "ships employed in the coasting trade" are used in contradistinction to ships employed in foreign trade, and that "employed in the coasting trade" means, employed for the time, at least only in the coasting trade, and not a foreign trade. A ship which loads cargo at a port in England for a foreign port, and sails with that cargo to a foreign port, cannot, I consider, be said to become a coaster merely because, in the course of her voyage to the foreign port, she touches at an English port to discharge ballast and complete her cargo.' *The Winestead* [1895] P 170 at 173, 174, per Bruce J

COASTWISE

'"Coastwise" in the expression "beyond the seas or coastwise" has . . . its ordinary meaning, its ordinary meaning being a voyage between places on the coasts of the United Kingdom when used, as it is in this context, in contrast to "beyond the seas".' *British Oil & Cake Mills Ltd v Port of London Authority* [1914] 3 KB 1201 at 1219, CA, per Kennedy LJ; affirmed on appeal sub nom. *Port of London Authority v British Oil & Cake Mills Ltd* [1915] AC 993

COCA LEAF

'Coca leaf' means the leaf of any plant of the genus *Erythroxylon* from whose leaves cocaine can be extracted either directly or by chemical transformation. (Misuse of Drugs Act 1971, Sch 2, Part IV)

CODICIL

A codicil is of similar nature to a will as regards both its purposes and the formalities relating to it, but in general it is supplemental to and considered as annexed to a will previously made, being executed for the purpose of adding to, varying or revoking the provisions of that will. A codicil is nevertheless capable of independent existence, so that the revocation of a will does not necessarily effect the revocation of a codicil to it. (50 Halsbury's Laws (4th edn) para 201)

'The character of a codicil is very peculiar. Its nature is not substantive but adjective. It is as Mr Justice Blackstone describes it [2 Bl Cm 450, Kerr's Ed], "a supplement to a will, or an addition made by the testator, and annexed to and to be taken as part of a testament". A reference to the will therefore in itself carries with it a reference to that which is merely a supplement to or annexed to the will itself; and the mere fact that the testator describes the will by a reference to its original date, does not seem to me sufficient to exclude the inference that the will referred to is the will as modified by the codicils.' *Green v Tribe* (1878) 9 Ch D 231 at 238, per Fry J

COERCION *See also* THREAT; UNDUE INFLUENCE

'Coercion takes an infinite number of forms, but it may properly be thus defined:—the moment that the person who influences the other does so by the threat of taking away from that other something he then possesses, or of preventing him from obtaining an advantage he would otherwise have obtained, then it becomes coercion and it ceases to be persuasion or consideration.' *Ellis v Barker* (1871) 40 LJ Ch 603 at 607, per Lord Romilly MR

'"Coercion" is a word of ambiguous import. In one sense anyone is coerced who under pressure does that which he would prefer not to do; but a reluctant debtor who pays under stress of proceedings is not coerced within the legal meaning of the word. . . . "Coercion" involves something in the nature of the negation of choice. . . . An employer cannot properly be said to be coerced if, having two alternative courses presented to him, he follows that course which he considers conducive to his own interests.' *Hodges v Webb* [1920] 2 Ch 70 at 85–87, per Peterson J

COGNIZANCE

Australia [Under the Bankruptcy Act 1966 (Cth), s 30(1) 'the Court':—has full power to decide all questions, whether of law or of fact, in any case of bankruptcy or any matter under Part X or Part XI coming within the 'cognizance' of the court.] ' "Cognizance" has the general meaning of "knowledge, especially knowledge as attained by observation or information", and the specialized "legal" meaning of "the hearing and trying of a cause", and "the right of dealing with any matter judicially; jurisdiction".' *Re Amadio* (1978) 24 ALR 455 at 469, per Rogerson J

COHABITATION

'Cohabitation may be of two sorts, one continuous, the other intermittent. The parties may reside together constantly, or there may be only occasional intercourse between them, which may, nevertheless, amount to cohabitation in the legal sense of the term. Such cohabitation may indeed exist together with an agreement to live apart. . . . The circumstances of life, such as business duties, domestic service, and other things, may separate husband and wife, and yet notwithstanding, there may be cohabitation.' *Huxtable v Huxtable* (1899) 68 LJP 83 at 85, DC, per Jeune P

'I doubt whether any judge could give a completely exhaustive definition of cohabitation, and certainly I am not going to attempt to do so. At least a resumption of cohabitation must mean resuming a state of things—that is to say, setting up a matrimonial home together. That involves, so it seems to me, a bilateral intention on the part of both spouses so to do. The question then, is: Does coming together for a single night raise an irrebuttable presumption that the parties have resumed cohabitation even for that short time? . . . I am bound to say that I think that it would lead to an absurd state of things if one were bound to hold that that is so.' *Mummery v Mummery* [1942] 1 All ER 553 at 555, per Lord Merriman P

'Cohabitation does not necessarily depend upon whether there is sexual intercourse between husband and wife. "Cohabitation" means living together as husband and wife; and as I endeavoured to point out in *Evans v Evans* [[1948] 1 KB 175], cohabitation consists in the husband acting as a husband towards the wife and the wife acting as a wife towards the husband, the wife rendering housewifely duties to the husband and the husband cherishing and supporting his wife as a husband should. Of course, sexual intercourse usually takes place between parties of moderate age if they are cohabiting, and if there is sexual intercourse it is very strong evidence—in fact it may be conclusive evidence—that they are cohabiting; but it does not follow that because they do not have sexual intercourse they are not cohabiting. "Cohabiting", as I have said, means the husband and wife living together as husband and wife.' *Thomas v Thomas* [1948] 2 KB 294 at 297, per Lord Goddard CJ

'The cohabitation of two people as husband and wife means that they are living together as husband and wife, the wife rendering wifely services to her husband; the husband rendering husbandlike services to his wife. They must live together not merely as two people living in one house, but as husband and wife.' *Wheatley v Wheatley* [1950] 1 KB 39 at 43, per Lord Goddard CJ

Australia ' "Cohabitation" means, literally "living together", or, when used in such a context as a statute dealing with matrimonial relationships, "living together as man and wife". Although sexual intercourse between the parties is an important, and often significant, incident in "living together as man and wife", it is neither essential to that relationship, nor does it necessarily establish that relationship. Indeed, although my judgment in this suit is neither the time nor the place for such a study, a study of the views—as reflected in the law, the teachings of the Church, and the social outlook of the people—current in the community from time to time over a long period may well show that the importance and significance of sexual intercourse as an ingredient of "living together as man and wife" has considerably diminished. Indeed the extent of that diminution may well be one of the factors underlying the recent changes (both actual and mooted) in the Australian laws relating to sex in marriage.' *Clift v Clift* (1976) 2 Fam LR 11369 at 11372, per Sangster J

Canada 'The Century Dictionary, Vol II, defines "cohabitation" as: "The state of dwelling or living together as husband and wife, often with reference to persons who are not legally married, and usually but not always implying sexual intercourse." It is most generally used for the purpose of implying intercourse and is even commonly used as such in the Courts on examination of witnesses and is taken to include actual sexual intercourse.' *Mitchell v Mitchell* [1941] 3 WWR 152 at 153, Man KB, per McPherson CJKB

Canada [The Family Law Reform Act 1978 (Ont), c 2 (now RSO 1980, c 152), s 14(b)(i) defines a spouse as either of a man or woman not being married to each other who have 'cohabited' continuously for a period of not less than five years or in a relationship of some permanence where there is a child born of whom they are the natural parents.] 'It is my view that unmarried persons cannot be found to be cohabiting within the meaning of s 14(b)(i) unless it can be determined that their relationship is such that they have each assumed an obligation to support and provide for the other in the same manner that married spouses are obliged to do under s 15 of the Act. . . . In my view, the applicant has never cohabited with the respondent within the meaning of s 14(b)(i) of the Family Law Reform Act 1978. The evidence is clear that although from time to time the parties were intimate, their economic life was on an arm's length basis. Any household services that the applicant provided to the respondent were in satisfaction of a portion of the rent. Neither of the parties looked to each other for support or assistance outside of their unusual rental arrangement. Accordingly, the applicant's claim for spousal maintenance is dismissed.' *Re Stoikiewicz* (1978) 21 OR (2d) 717 at 720–721, Ont UFC, per Steinberg, UFCJ

COIN

'Coin' means coin which is current and legal tender in the United Kingdom. (Currency and Bank Notes Act 1928, s 13)

[As to the standards of gold and silver coins, see now the Coinage Act 1971, s 1, amended by the Currency Act 1983, s 1.]

'Exchange control [under the Exchange Control Act 1947] does not involve the exchange or bartering of copies or imitations of what would otherwise be coins. They are in no sense articles of monetary exchange and like Lord Parker CJ, I find that at the end of the day the answer to the questions which counsel for the respondent put: to be a coin does it mean a coin

issued by authority as a means of currency, to which I answer yes, or does it mean gold in the form of coins closely resembling a genuine old coin to which I answer no. I see very great difficulty in applying that last suggestion, and if indeed Parliament had intended to extend the meaning of gold coins to cover that type of article, then I would have expected the definition [coin which is current and legal tender in the United Kingdom] so to provide.' *Freed v Director of Public Prosecutions* [1969] 1 All ER 428 at 432, per Ashworth J

COINCIDE

[A testator by his will made certain provisions in the event of the decease of his wife preceding or 'coinciding' with his own decease.] 'It is in my judgment quite plain that "coinciding" in the context of "preceding" means coinciding in point of time; its natural and normal meaning in that context is not coincidence in any other respect, such as type or cause of death, though coincidence in time would normally require coincidence in type or cause. The process of dying may take even an unconscionable time: but the event of death, to which the testator referred, is the matter of a moment, the moment when life is gone for ever. I see no room, therefore, for "coinciding", in its normal and natural meaning, to involve some broad conception of overlapping or of occurring within a particular period. In my judgment the normal and natural meaning of "coinciding with" in relation to deaths occurring is the same as "simultaneous"—the word in [*Re Pringle, Baker v Matheson* [1946] 1 All ER 88]. It is possible in theory for two persons to die precisely coincidentally in time, though it would not be susceptible of absolute proof. If that was what was intended by the testator, his references to preceding and coinciding would indeed be merely a verbose reference to "not surviving".' *Re Rowland (decd), Smith v Russell* [1962] 2 All ER 837 at 844, CA, per Russell LJ; also reported in [1963] Ch 1 at 15

COLLAPSE

'The policy covers the assured . . . "against loss or damage caused by subsidence and/or collapse . . ." in respect of a building. . . . The plaintiffs have undoubtedly lost their building . . . in consequence of a dangerous structure notice . . . it has been demolished. . . . "Collapse" in its primary meaning denotes falling or shrinking together or breaking down or giving way through external pressure or loss of rigidity or support, and I am unable to take the view that in this policy the word covers the intentional destruction or demolition of a building by housebreakers.' *Allen (David) & Sons Billposting Ltd v Drysdale* [1939] 4 All ER 113 at 113, 114, per Lewis J

[The Building (Safety, Health and Welfare) Regulations 1948, reg 79(7) (revoked; see now the Construction (Working Places) Regulations 1966) required precautions to be taken, where necessary to prevent the accidental 'collapse' of part of a building.] 'In my opinion, the word "collapse" in this regulation must be given its ordinary meaning, which is the action of falling together, or a sudden shrinking together, or a giving-way through external pressure or loss of rigidity or loss of support. When one has to consider the words "collapse of part of the building", I do not think that it is necessary to delimit precisely the size of the part so long as that part is sufficient to allow the action described in my definition to operate.' *Mortimer v Allison (Samuel B) Ltd* [1959] 1 All ER 567 at 570, HL, per Viscount Kilmuir LC

COLLATERAL

'There may be a contract the consideration for which is the making of some other contract. "If you will make such and such a contract I will give you one hundred pounds", is in every sense of the word a complete legal contract. It is collateral to the main contract, but each has an independent existence. . . . But such collateral contracts must from their very nature be rare . . . [their] sole effect . . . is to vary or add to the terms of the principal contract, [and they] are therefore viewed with suspicion by the law. They must be proved strictly. Not only the terms of such contracts but the existence of an *animus contrahendi* on the part of all the parties to them must be clearly shown.' *Heilbut, Symons & Co v Buckleton* [1913] AC 30 at 47, per Lord Moulton

Canada ' "Collateral" means literally situated at the side, hence parallel or additional, and not, if the nature of the transaction does not require it, secondary: *In re Athill*, 16 Ch D 211. Collateral security is any property which is assigned or pledged to secure the performance of an obligation and as additional thereto, and which upon the performance of the obligation is to be surrendered

or discharged: *In re Wiggins Ltd* [1931] OR 337.' *Royal Bank of Canada v Slack* [1958] OR 262 at 273, Ont CA, per Schroeder JA

United States 'Collateral' means the property subject to a security interest, and includes accounts and chattel paper which have been sold . . . . (Uniform Commercial Code 1978, s 9–105(1)(c))

COLLATION

Admission of a presentee to the cure of souls and spiritualities of a rectory or vicarage is by institution by the bishop or, if he is for some grave and urgent cause unable to give institution himself, by his commissary. This act, which admits the clergyman to his office, may be performed either within or outside the diocese, and the particular seal used for the instrument of institution is immaterial. . . .

Where the bishop is himself patron of the rectory or vicarage, he institutes without a previous presentation; but although the act is in the same form (as where the person instituted has been presented by any other patron) it is commonly called collation. (14 Halsbury's Laws (4th edn) paras 845, 846)

COLLECTION

'Collection' means an appeal to the public made by means of visits from house to house, to give, whether for consideration or not, money or other property; and 'collector' means, in relation to a collection, a person who makes the appeal in the course of such visits as aforesaid. (House to House Collections Act 1939, s 11)

'A collection is not confined to an appeal by way of house to house visits "to give", but extends to such an appeal "to give, whether for a consideration or not"; and, if a person is induced to purchase an article on the representation that part of those proceeds will go to a charitable purpose, then, as it seems to me, the activity is plainly a collection within the meaning of the Act [House to House Collections Act] of 1939.' *Emanuel v Smith* [1968] 2 All ER 529 at 532, per Lord Parker CJ

Canada 'The key words in R 29 [providing for a commission in lieu of costs on the collection of accounts or claims] are "collection of accounts or claims" and the most significant of these words is the word collection . . . for a lawyer the word "collection" or "collections"

ad and I think still has a well-known meaning. That meaning was and I think still is this: The collection of accounts and claims on a contingency basis effected primarily by writing letters and arranging with debtors for payment. Because "collections" has a well-known meaning in the practice of law I think it is not unreasonable to infer from the use of the words 'collection of accounts or accounts or claims' in the Rule that the object of the Rule was to provide a tariff of charges for the collection of accounts and claims, primarily trade accounts, which would, having in mind successes and failures in collecting, when the client and solicitor had made no special agreement as to costs, provide a percentage tariff of charges fair and reasonable to both. I am not of the opinion that the wording of the Rule may be broadly construed to apply where a solicitor's engagement is to sue even though the purpose of suing is to recover on a claim or account and this purpose is achieved. The Rule only applies where the solicitor's engagement is to collect an account or claim and there is no special agreement as to costs.' *Re Harper* (1967) 60 WWR 658 at 662–663, BCSC, per Aikins J; affd (1968) 63 WWR 705, BCCA

COLLECTION GUARANTEED

Commercial paper

United States 'Collection guaranteed' or equivalent words added to a signature mean that the signer engages that if the instrument is not paid when due he will pay it according to its tenor, but only after the holder has reduced his claim against the maker or acceptor to judgment and execution has been returned unsatisfied, or after the maker or acceptor has become insolvent or it is otherwise apparent that it is useless to proceed against him. (Uniform Commercial Code 1978, s 3–416(2))

COLLECTIVE AGREEMENT

For purposes of this section [collective agreements and pay structures] 'collective agreement' means any agreement as to terms and conditions of employment, being an agreement between—

(a) parties who are to represent employers or organisations of employers or associations of such organisations; and

(b) parties who are or represent organisations of employees or associations of such organisations;

but includes also any award modifying or supplementing such an agreement. (Equal Pay Act 1970, s 3(5))

In this Act . . . 'collective agreement' means any agreement or arrangement made by or on behalf of one or more trade unions and one or more employers or employers' associations and relating to one or more of the matters mentioned in section 29(1). (Trade Union and Labour Relations Act 1974, s 30(1))

[The matters mentioned in section 29(1) of the Act are those matters which may be the subject of a trade dispute, *viz.* (a) terms and conditions of employment, or the physical conditions in which any workers are required to work; (b) engagement or non-engagement, or termination or suspension of employment or the duties of employment, of one or more workers; (c) allocation of work or the duties of employment as between workers or groups of workers; (d) matters of discipline; (e) the membership or non-membership of a trade union on the part of a worker; (f) facilities for officials of trade unions; and (g) machinery for negotiation or consultation, and other procedures, relating to any of the foregoing matters, including the recognition by employers or employers' associations of the right of a trade union to represent workers in any such negotiation or consultation or in the carrying out of such procedures.]

[See also the Dock Work Regulation Act 1976, s 15(1).]

United States 'A collective bargaining agreement is not an ordinary contract for the purchase of goods and services, nor is it governed by the same old common-law concepts which control such private contracts. . . . "[I]t is a generalized code to govern a myriad of cases which the draftsmen cannot wholly anticipate. . . . The collective bargaining agreement covers the whole employment relationship. It calls into being a new common law—the common law of a particular industry or of a particular plant.". . . In order to interpret such an agreement it is necessary to consider the scope of other related collective bargaining agreements, as well as the practice, usage and custom pertaining to all such agreements.' *Transportation-Communication Employees Union v Union Pacific Railroad Co* (1966) 385 US 157 at 160–61, per Black J

COLLECTIVE MARK

United States The term 'collective mark' means a trade-mark or service mark used by the members of a cooperative, an association or other collective group or organization and includes marks used to indicate membership in a union, an association or other organization. (Lanham Act 1946, s 45)

COLLECTIVE WORK

Copyright

United States A 'collective work' is a work, such as a periodical issue, anthology, or encyclopedia, in which a number of contributions, constituting separate and independent works in themselves, are assembled into a collective whole. (Copyright Act of 1976, s 101)

COLLEGE

New Zealand [A testator by his will authorised his executors to pay a sum out of principal for 'college' and university education of his sons.] 'Having regard to the context, the term "college education" appears to be used by the testator as meaning something other than university education, and ought to be construed . . . as covering education at institutions giving secondary education, such as Christ's College, the Waitaki Boys' High School, and the Otago Boys' High School.' *Re Darling, Darling v Darling* [1921] NZLR 542 at 551, per Sim ACJ; also reported [1921] GLR 454 at 456

COLLEGE OF ARMS *See* ARMS

COLLIERY

'Colliery' includes or may include all contiguous and connected veins and seams of coal which are worked as one concern, together with the workings and machinery necessary for working the minerals, and the business of selling the coal worked. (31 Halsbury's Laws (4th edn) para 13)

'Colliery activities' means searching or boring for, winning, working or getting, coal, bringing it to the surface, treating it and rendering it saleable, and includes depositing spoil arising from working coal or from any other of the activities mentioned in this definition. (Coal Industry Nationalisation Act 1946, s 6)

'Colliery concern' means a company whose business includes, or at any time on or after the first day of January, nineteen hundred and forty-six, included, the working of coal (excluding working undertaken for the purpose of digging or carrying away coal in the course of activities other than colliery activities, and working undertaken only as ancillary to the working of minerals other than coal) and any other person whose business includes, or at any such time included, such working of coal as aforesaid. (Coal Industry Nationalisation Act 1946, s 63)

Australia 'The term "colliery" connotes something more than a mere area of land; it has overtones of an activity or operation of an economic nature, as does the term "mine".' *Fox v A-G* [1969] 1 NSWR 444 at 447, 448, per McLelland J

COLLISION

'In common understanding, and as understood in the Court of Admiralty, damage by collision is damage sustained by a ship from another ship coming in contact with it.' *Everard v Kendall* (1870) LR 5 CP 428 at 432, per Montague Smith J

'The breakwater in question was made by the deposit of a number of large boulders, forming the toe of the breakwater, behind which the wall of the breakwater itself is built. I am of opinion that the words "pier", "breakwater", and "toe" all denote one and the same structure, and therefore that the expression "collision with piers . . . or stages or similar structures" covers the present case. I cannot distinguish "collision with" from striking against.' *Union Marine Insurance Co v Borwick* [1895] 2 QB 279 at 281, per Mathew J

' "Collision", when used alone without other words means two navigable things coming into contact.' *Chandler v Blogg* [1898] 1 QB 32 at 35, 36, per Bigham J

'As a matter of ordinary English I do not think any one would say that coming into collision with the end of a net a mile away from the ship is coming into collision with the ship.' *Bennett SS Co Ltd v Hull Mutual Steamship Protecting Society Ltd* [1913] 3 KB 372 at 376, 377, per Pickford J

[A policy of marine insurance included damage received by 'collision with any object' (ice included) other than water.] 'For many purposes, both in Acts of Parliament and in many documents, "collision' has a sense much narrower than is necessary to include this casualty . . . Gorell Barnes J in *The Normandy* [[1904] P 187 at 198] said . . . "the true meaning of collision is not a mere striking against, but a striking together; and to me it seems more correct to speak of a vessel stranding, or running, or striking upon or against rocks or the shore, than colliding therewith". From these observations . . . I should not venture or desire to dissent; but that is not quite the question which I have to decide. . . . It is quite obvious that the context in which the word occurs may make all the difference. It may be true to say that in some circumstances it *must* make all the difference. In Arnould on Marine Insurance, 11th ed, s 826, the matter is put thus: "Sometimes, however, the clause is wider, so as to include the risk of striking against, not merely floating or navigable objects, but also structures such as harbours, wharves, piers and the like, or obstructions such as ice or wreck.". . . [In] *Union Marine Insurance Co v Borwick* [supra] . . . I do not find anything to show that . . . "stranding" and "collision" were regarded by the learned judge as mutually exclusive terms. He says . . . . "I cannot distinguish collision with from striking against," and those words must be read in strict regard to the clause he was considering [which referred to collision with objects some of which were mobile, others immobile]. . . . The ultimate question in [this] case depends upon the test: Is contact with an ordinary natural feature a collision within the meaning of this policy or is it not? In my judgment it is, and my main reason for so holding is that the words are very general: "collision with any object".' *Mancomunidad Del Vapor Frumiz v Royal Exchange Assurance* [1927] 1 KB 567 at 571–574, 576, per Roche J

Collision clause in marine policy

Where two vessels come into collision and it is found that both are to blame, then, according to maritime law as administered by the English admiralty courts since the passing of the Maritime Conventions Act 1911, the damage done to each vessel is added together and is treated as a common loss to be divided in proportion to the degree of blame attributable to each vessel. If it is not possible to establish different degrees of blame the liability is apportioned equally between the two shipowners. (25 Halsbury's Laws (4th edn) para 169)

COLLUSION

Divorce proceedings

[In the UK collusion is no longer an absolute bar to divorce. The provisions of the Matrimonial Causes Act 1965, relating to collusion, were repealed by the Divorce Reform Act 1969, itself repealed and replaced by the Matrimonial Causes Act 1973.]

Canada 'In my opinion . . . collusion may be: (a) Any agreement or conspiracy to which the petitioner is a party which . . . tends to pervert or obstruct the course of justice; (b) Any agreement or conspiracy to which the petitioner is a party to obtain a divorce by means of manufactured evidence; (c) Any agreement or conspiracy to which the petitioner is a party to obtain a divorce by some fraud or deceit practised on the court.' *Johnson v Johnson* (1960) 31 WWR 403 at 415, BCSC, per Norris J

Canada 'The difficulty experienced by trial judges [in divorce proceedings] in deciding whether a particular agreement is a collusive one, arises when it is sought to apply the law to the facts of a specific case. One asks oneself, is there a test or criterion, a legal touchstone, to be found from a consideration of the numerous decisions, which, when applied to a particular agreement or bargain, will disclose whether such is collusive or not? . . . A study of four decisions of the court of appeal of this province leads me to the conclusion that in this jurisdiction [Saskatchewan] the law likewise requires as an essential element in a collusive bargain or agreement an attempt by adverse parties in the action to pervert the course of justice, by entering into such bargain or agreement with an improper, corrupt or dishonest purpose in view. This is the touchstone which, when applied, will distinguish between collusive and non-collusive bargains.' *Peel v Peel* (1965) 55 WWR 202 at 207–208, Sask QB, per Disbery J

South Africa 'In my view collusion consists in our law in an agreement between the parties to a suit to suppress facts, or to put false evidence before the court, or to manufacture evidence, in order to make it appear to the court that one of the parties has a cause of action, or a ground of defence, which in fact he has not.' *Kuhn v Karp* 1948 (4) SA 825 (T) per Roper J

In sale of land

Australia 'To be a "collusive" sale it must

have some secret term or aspect designed for the purpose of deceiving or imposing upon the mortgagor, or other the person entitled to redeem, and defeating his interests in some way. Cf. *Brine v Brine* [[1924] SASR 433]. Under other legal systems "collusion" has been defined as "a fraudulent arrangement between two or more persons to give a false or deceptive appearance to a transaction in which they engage" (Black's Law Dictionary).' *Conlon v Biggs* [1943] SASR 103 at 122, per Mayo J

Interpleader proceedings

It is difficult to draw a clear line between interest and collusion and the modern interpretation is that there must be no identification of interest between the applicant and the claimant. Collusion does not here necessarily entail anything morally wrong; it means that the applicant must not 'play on the same side' as one of the claimants. (25 Halsbury's Laws (4th edn) para 1019)

'Collusion, in the sense in which it is used in this Order [RSC (1883) Ord LVII, r 2(b) (revoked; see now RSC 1965, Ord 17, r 3(4)(b)), under which an applicant for relief by way of interpleader had to satisfy the court that he did not collude with any of the claimants], does not necessarily entail anything morally wrong, although the word has acquired a meaning generally associated with something morally wrong. . . . The word in the interpleader order has its logical signification, that the applicant . . . must not play the same game as one of the parties.' *Murietta v South American etc Co Ltd & Dever* (1893) 62 LJQB 396 at 398, DC, per Charles J

COLONIAL LAW

'Colonial law' means any Act, ordinance, or other law having the force of legislative enactment in a British possession and made by any authority, other than the Imperial Parliament or Her Majesty in Council, competent to make laws for such possession, (Colonial Courts of Admiralty Act 1890, s 15)

COLONY

'Colony' means any part of Her Majesty's dominions outside the British Islands except—
(a) countries having full responsible status within the Commonwealth;
(b) territories for whose external relations a country other than the United Kingdom is responsible;
(c) associated states;
and where parts of such dominions are under both a central and a local legislature, all parts under the central legislature are deemed for the purposes of this definition to be one colony. (Interpretation Act 1978, Sch 1)

[By a bequest in his will a testator gave to B. his collection of stamps of Great Britain and of the British 'colonies' except Malta.] There is in use among philatelists a convenient phrase, 'British Colonials', and that phrase is taken by philatelists to include the stamps of all countries in the British Commonwealth and mandated territories and even such countries as those which are now the Republic of Eire, Egypt and the Sudan. The phrase is clearly wide enough to cover the whole of the stamps in dispute in this matter. . . . In my judgment, on consideration, the phrase "the stamps of Great Britain and . . . of the British Colonies" is a paraphrase and equivalent to the phrase "British Colonials" as used by philatelists. Therefore in this case I propose to give that meaning to the phrase "British Colonies" in . . . the will.' *Re Van Lessen (decd), National Provincial Bank Ltd v Beaumont* [1955] 3 All ER 691 at 693, 694, per Wynn-Parry J

COLOUR OF RIGHT

New Zealand 'Then follow the words "and without colour of right" [see now the Crimes Act 1961 (NZ), s 293(2)]. This means . . . an honest belief in a state of facts which, if it existed, would be a legal justification or excuse. This would not be an answer to a civil action, but it is properly made an answer to a criminal charge, because it takes away from the act its criminal character. Less than this . . . cannot be held to be "colour of right".' *R v Fetzer* (1900) 19 NZLR 438 at 443, 444, per Edwards J; also reported 3 GLR 82 at 84

COLOURABLE

[The question of colourable imitation of, or colourable variation from, a trade mark is a test of infringement or non-infringement.] 'The defendants' trade mark is certainly not the same as that used by the appellants. But is it only colourably different? I think it is so different as to make it impossible to say that it is substantially the same. No general rule can be laid down as to what is or is not a mere colourable variation. All which can be done is to ascertain in every case, as it occurs, whether here is such a resemblance as to deceive a purchaser using ordinary caution. Here the differences are so palpable that no one can be deceived.' *Leather Cloth Co v American Leather Cloth Co* (1865) 11 HL Cas 523 at 535, per Lord Cranworth

United States The term 'colorable imitation' includes any mark which so resembles a registered mark as to be likely to cause confusion or mistake or to deceive. (Lanham Act 1946, s 45)

COMBINATION

'A combination . . . is . . . where parts are not claimed by themselves (as the subject of a patent], but only in combination with other parts with which they co-operate. . . . If what you have claimed, and the monopoly which you have obtained, is for a combination, that combination is the novelty, and you have no obligation beyond accurately defining it.' *British United Shoe Machinery Co Ltd v Fussell (A) & Sons Ltd* (1908) 25 RPC 631 at 649, 656, CA, per Fletcher Moulton LJ

COMMAND

Under command

'Vessel not under command' means a vessel which through some exceptional circumstance is unable to manoeuvre as required by the rules and is therefore unable to keep out of the way of another vessel. (43 Halsbury's Laws (4th edn) para 884).

'Article 4(a) [of the Regulations for Preventing Collisions at Sea 1897 (see now Collision Regulations, etc. Order 1953, Sch I, r 4)] . . . is applicable in its terms to "a vessel which from any accident is not under command", and, in my opinion, those words do not apply to a vessel which is fast aground. They apply to a vessel which is afloat.' *The Carlotta* [1899] P 223 at 227, per Gorell Barnes J

'This vessel, according to the view the Elder Brethren take, was under command; she was moving, and capable of doing what she wanted to do, and had, in the course of three-quarters of an hour, moved three-quarters of a mile; she was only hampered by the fact that she was dragging through the mud. . . . It seems to me doubtful whether she was "from any accident" not under command.' *The Bellanoch* [1907] P 170 at 174, CA, per Gorell Barnes P

'A reasonable interpretation of "under command" would seem to me to be that the ship is capable of performing the ordinary manœuvres which would be expected of such a ship, and I have doubts as to whether a steamer that can only go ahead, and that very slowly, by repeated reversals of her engines, and can only imperfectly obey her helm by reason that she is on the ground, can be said to be "under command".' Ibid at 187, per Fletcher Moulton LJ

'If a vessel is in such a condition owing to an accident that she can only get out of the way of another after great and unusual delay, I think she must be considered as "not under command" for the purpose of art 4.' *Mendip Range SS v Radcliffe* [1921] 1 AC 556 at 571, per Lord Finlay

COMMANDEER

'Service of a notice that a ship will be commandeered does not necessarily amount to commandeering her. But in this case the facts show that the Greek Government had the ship under their control from the date of the notice, and therefore, in my opinion, it was commandeered from that date.' *Capel v Soulidi* [1916] 2 KB 365 at 369, CA, per Lush J

COMMANDER

'Commander', in relation to an aircraft, means the member of the flight crew designated as commander of that aircraft by the operator thereof, or, failing such a person, the person who is for the time being the pilot in command of the aircraft. (Dumping at Sea Act 1974, s 12(1))

'Commander' in relation to an aircraft means the member of the crew designated as commander of that aircraft by the operator thereof, or, failing such a person, the person who is for the time being the pilot in command of the aircraft. (Civil Aviation Act 1982, s 94(7))

COMMENCE

New Zealand 'To "commence business" [in an agreement not to commence business again in a specified district] would certainly be ordinarily understood to mean to begin business on a man's own account, and not to take employment as a servant to a person carrying on a similar business.' *Dispatch Foundry Co*

Ltd v Kilgour (1896) 14 NZLR 652 at 659, per Conolly J

COMMENCEMENT

Of Act of Parliament

An Act or provision of an Act comes into force—
(a) where provision is made for it to come into force on a particular day, at the beginning of that day;
(b) where no provision is made for its coming into force, at the beginning of the day on which the Act receives the Royal Assent. (Interpretation Act 1978, s 4).

'Commencement', in relation to an Act or enactment, means the time when the Act or enactment comes into force. (Interpretation Act 1978, s 5, Sch I)

Of action or proceedings

[Proceedings under the Maritime Conventions Act 1911, s 8, in cases of collision and salvage must be commenced within two years of the cause of action.] 'The next contention was that the proceedings were not commenced within two years under s 8, because that section contemplates that proceedings should be commenced not by issuing a writ but by arrest [of the ship]. I do not agree. Section 8 relates to proceedings *in personam* as well as to proceedings *in rem*. . . . The Rules of the Supreme Court, show that an action in the Admiralty Division, like an action in any other Division, is commenced by the issue of a writ, and I can see no reason at all for giving a different meaning to the commencement of proceedings under s 8 from that which obtains in every other action.' *The Espanoleto* [1920] P 223 at 225, 226, per Hill J

COMMENT   *See also* FAIR COMMENT

Australia 'A statement may be held to be comment if it appears to be a deduction or conclusion come to by the writer or speaker from facts stated or referred to by him or in the common knowledge of the person writing or speaking and those to whom the words are addressed, and from which his conclusion may reasonably be inferred.' *Clarke v Norton* [1910] VLR 494 at 506, per Cussen J

COMMERCE

United States 'Commerce' means trade, traffic, commerce, transportation, transmission, or communication among the several States or between any State and any place outside thereof. (Labor Management Reporting and Disclosure Act of 1959, s 3(a))

United States The term 'commerce' means trade, traffic, commerce, or transportation—
(A) between a place in a State and any place outside thereof, or
(B) which affects trade, traffic, commerce, or transportation described in subparagraph (A).
(Consumer Product Safety Act 1972, s 3(a)(12))

Affecting commerce

United States The term 'affecting commerce' means in commerce, or burdening or obstructing commerce or the free flow of commerce, or having led or tending to lead to a labor dispute burdening or obstructing commerce or the free flow of commerce. (Labor Management Relations Act of 1947, s 2(7))

Distribution in commerce

United States The terms 'to distribute in commerce' and 'distribution in commerce' mean to sell in commerce, to introduce or deliver for introduction into commerce, or to hold for sale or distribution after introduction into commerce. (Consumer Product Safety Act 1972, s 3(a)(11))

Industry affecting commerce

United States 'Industry affecting commerce' means any activity, business, or industry in commerce or in which a labor dispute would hinder or obstruct commerce or the free flow of commerce and includes any activity of industry 'affecting commerce' within the meaning of the Labor Management Relations Act, 1947, as amended, or the Railway Labor Act, as amended. (Labor-Management Reporting and Disclosure Act of 1959, s 3(c))

United States The term 'industry affecting commerce' means any industry or activity in commerce or in which a labor dispute would burden or obstruct commerce or the free flow of commerce (Labor Management Relations Act of 1947, s 501(1))

interstate commerce *See* INTERSTATE
COMMERCE

Trademarks and tradenames

United States The word 'commerce' means
all commerce which may lawfully be regulated
by Congress. (Lanham Act 1946, s 45)

Used in commerce

United States For the purposes of this chapter
, mark shall be deemed to be used in
commerce (a) on goods when it is placed in any
manner on the goods or their containers or the
displays associated therewith or on the tags or
labels affixed thereto and the goods are sold or
transported in commerce and (b) on services
when it is used or displayed in the sale or
advertising of services and the services are
rendered in commerce, or the services are
rendered in more than one State or in this and a
foreign country and the person rendering the
services is engaged in commerce in connection
therewith. (Lanham Act 1946, s 45).

COMMERCIAL NAME *See* TRADE
NAME

COMMERCIAL PURPOSE

Canada [Assessment provision included
trailers used for commercial purposes.] 'While
the word "commercial" is susceptible of
various meanings, in only one of the above-
mentioned definitions is there any reference to
industry or to the activities and relationships of
industry and trade. The Act being a taxing
statute should be construed strictly in favour of
the subject, with the consequence that the
words "used for any commercial purpose"
should be given its ordinary rather than its
more extended meaning, that is, used for a
purpose relating to trade and the buying,
selling and exchange of commodities for
profit.' *Re Ashley Colter (1961) Ltd and
Minister of Municipal Affairs* (1970) 10 DLR
(3d) 502 at 505, NBCA, per Hughes JA

COMMERCIAL TRAVELLER

'A "commercial traveller" in the ordinary use
of the English tongue . . . is a person who goes
round soliciting and booking orders on behalf
of an employer, who, upon transmission to him
of such orders, is to supply them. But the char-

acter and scope of the appellants' sole selling
agency is obviously very much wider than that.
The most that can be said is that their agency
includes an element which is in the nature of
"commercial travelling". Now, if a business
includes an element or department which is in
the nature of soliciting and booking orders for
the goods of a principal or employer—which,
in other words, is in the nature of "commercial
travelling"—the question whether the business, as a whole, can be regarded as the business of a "commercial traveller" must, I think,
depend on whether that element or department is so predominating as to entitle one to
regard the whole business as substantially of
that character. But that is a question of fact and
nothing else.' *Findlay & Co v Inland Revenue
Comrs* 1928 SC 218 at 223, per the Lord
President

COMMERCIAL UNIT

United States 'Commercial unit' means such
a unit of goods as by commercial usage is a
single whole for purposes of sale and division
of which materially impairs its character or
value on the market or in use. A commercial
unit may be a single article (as a machine) or a
set of articles (as a suite of furniture or an
assortment of sizes) or a quantity (as a bale,
gross, or carload) or any other unit treated in
use or in the relevant market as a single whole.
(Uniform Commercial Code 1978, s 2–105(6))

COMMERCIAL WOODLANDS *See*
WOODLANDS

COMMISSION

Exercise of authority

'The word *commission* is one of equivocal
meaning. It is used either to denote a trust or
authority exercised, or the instrument by
which the authority is exercised, or the persons
by whom the trust or authority is exercised.' *R
v Dudman* (1825) 4 B & C 850 at 854, per
Abbott CJ

New Zealand [The question was whether an
artistic work was 'commissioned' in terms of
the Copyright Act 1962, s 9(3).] 'It does not
seem to me to be necessary to apply strict
contractual conceptions to the interpretation
of s 9(3) of the Act. The verb "commission" is

defined in the Shorter Oxford English Dictionary as follows: "(1) To furnish with a commission or legal warrant. (2) To empower; to entrust with an office or duty. (3) To send on a mission. (4) To give a commission or order to or for". The evidence is as plain as can be that [the plaintiff], acting for his company, placed an order for the product drawing: the company accordingly commissioned it. The company also quite definitely paid for it. The product drawing was made in pursuance of that commission.' *P S Johnson & Associates Ltd v Bucko Enterprises Ltd* [1975] 1 NZLR 311 at 317, per Chilwell J

Remuneration

'An auctioneer who is employed to sell . . . is acting as an agent; and if you take the remuneration of the agent to be what is generally meant by the word "commission", everything you pay him for his services in the course of his agency comes within the expression of the word "commission".' *Drielsma v Manifold* [1894] 3 Ch 100 at 104, CA, per Lindley LJ

'Commission is prima facie the payment made to an agent for agency work, usually according to a scale—it may be an ad valorem scale, but not necessarily an ad valorem scale. It is . . . the most general word that can be used to describe the remuneration paid to an agent for an agency work other than a salary.' Ibid at 107, per Davey LJ

'When one finds a clause in a charterparty providing for the payment of commission, without any words extending or limiting it, the inference is, in the absence of evidence of custom, that the commission is upon the sum payable on the performance of the contract, and not upon any sums which become payable as compensation for its non-performance.' *Moor Line Ltd v Dreyfus (Louis) & Co* [1918] 1 KB 89 at 93, CA, per Bankes LJ

COMMIT

For trial

'Committed for trial' means—
(a) in relation to England and Wales, committed in custody or on bail by a magistrates' court pursuant to section 6 of the Magistrates' Courts Act 1980, or by any judge or other authority having power to do so, with a view to trial before a judge and jury.

(Interpretation Act 1978, Sch 1, as amended by the Magistrates' Courts Act 1980, s 154, Sch 7)

Australia 'The question, in our opinion, turns upon the meaning of the words in s 3 of the Poor Persons Legal Assistance Act—"committed for trial". Those are words which have come to have, we think, a popular meaning. It was suggested by Mr Greenwood for the applicant that they are capable of meaning when a person has been committed to gaol to await his trial and have no wider meaning than that. We think to give the words that meaning under this section would be quite wrong. We think they clearly cover the case of a person who has been directed to be tried as a result of an investigation in a court of petty sessions, or before a justice of the peace, and who, having been directed to be tried, is either committed to prison to await his trial or admitted to bail pending his trial. . . . We think the words are clearly wide enough to cover, as they are used in the popular and well-established sense, a case where there has been a decision adverse to the accused person and where the justices or the court of petty sessions have determined that he shall stand his trial by judge and jury upon a charge on an indictable offence.' *R v Pierce* [1961] VR 496 at 497, 498, per O'Bryan J

To prison

'The first question . . . is this, whether the expression "committed to prison" [in the Prison Act 1877 (repealed; see now the Prison Act 1952)] refers to the granting of a warrant for the incarceration of the prisoner, or to the delivery of his person into the custody of the gaoler within the prison walls. . . . "Commitment" or "committal", for I take these words to be synonymous, express the act of the magistrate, who alone has power to commit to prison, whether pending further inquiry, for trial, or for punishment. His exercise of that power is complete whenever the warrant of commitment has been duly signed and delivered.' *Mullins v Surrey County Treasurer* (1881) 7 App Cas 1 at 11, per Lord Watson

'The question turns upon the meaning of the words "committed to prison" in art 10 of the Extradition Treaty of 1876 with France. That article provides that "if the fugitive criminal who has been committed to prison be not surrendered and conveyed away within two months after such committal, or within two months after the decision of the Court upon the return to a writ of habeas corpus in the United Kingdom, he shall be discharged from custody, unless sufficient cause be shown to the contrary.". . . It is contended on behalf of the prisoner that the words "committed to prison" mean committed to prison upon his arrest under the warrant for the purpose of being brought before a magistrate. It is contended on the other hand that the words mean the committal to prison, after the magistrate has heard the evidence in the case, to await the prisoner's surrender to the officer of the French Government. In my opinion the latter is the true meaning of the words.' *R v Brixton Prison (Governor), ex p Mehamed Ben Romdan* [1912] 3 KB 190 at 194, 195, DC, per Darling J

Traffic offence

[The Road Traffic Act 1960, s 6(4) (repealed; see now the Road Traffic Act 1972, s 5(5), substituted by the Transport Act 1981, s 25(2)) empowers the police to arrest without warrant a person 'committing' the offence of driving on a road while unfit to drive through drink.] 'I am of the opinion . . . that the word "committing" in s 6(4) must in the context . . . be read as "apparently committing", so that, if a police officer by reason of the conduct of the suspected person presently before him, whether evidenced by speech, actions, smell, general bearing or condition, comes reasonably to the conclusion that there is an offence, he may arrest. He may not arrest, however, for an offence antecedent by any substantial period of time to the moment of the arrest or on information or belief not based on facts directly observed by himself.' *Wiltshire v Barrett* [1965] 2 All ER 271 at 279, CA, per Davies LJ

COMMITTAL   *See* ATTACHMENT

COMMITTAL PROCEEDINGS

In this Part of this Act . . . 'committal proceedings' means proceedings before a magistrates' court acting as examining justices. (Criminal Justice Act 1967, s 36(1); Magistrates' Courts Act 1980, s 150(1))

COMMITTEE

'The term "committee" means an individual or a body to which others have committed or delegated a particular duty, or who have taken on themselves to perform it in the expectation

of their act being confirmed by the body they profess to represent or act for.' *Reynell v Lewis, Wyld v Hopkins* (1846) 15 M & W 517 at 529, per Pollock CB

'I observed in the argument, according to one's ordinary idea of the meaning of the word, a committee consists of more persons than one. But I was not right in saying that, because that is not *ex vi termini* the necessary meaning of the word "committee", which simply means a person or persons to whom anything is committed.' *Re Scottish Petroleum Co, Maclagan's Case* (1882) 51 LJ Ch 841 at 845, per Kay J

COMMITTEE ROOM

'Committee room' does not include any house or room occupied by a candidate as a dwelling by reason only of the candidate transacting business there with his agents in relation to the election, and no room or building shall be deemed to be a committee room by reason only of the candidate addressing in it electors, committee members or others. (Representation of the People Act 1983, s 118)

COMMODITY

'The advowson did not pass by . . . the said words. The words are four: commodities, emoluments, profits and advantages to the prebend belonging; all which four words are of one sense and nature, implying things gainful.' *London v Southwell Collegiate Church (Chapter)* (1618) Hob 303 at 304, per cur.

'The word "commodity" is one of extensive meaning, denoting anything that is useful, convenient, or serviceable.' *The Frederick VIII* [1917] P 43 at 44–46, per Evans P

Canada   'A "commodity" is anything that is usable for a purpose.' *R v Robert Simpson Co Ltd* (1964) 43 CR 366 at 371, Ont SC, per Landreville J

COMMON

The term 'common' in the old writers and reports usually refers to rights of common which are exercisable over land rather than to the place on which those rights are exercised, whereas at the present time, unless accompanied by some reference to a particular kind of right of common such as common of pasture or common of piscary, it usually denotes the land where rights of common are exercised, namely, open and uncultivated ground over which owners and occupiers of enclosed land in the vicinity (known as commoners) have certain rights, although they are not the owners of such ground. (6 Halsbury's Laws (4th edn) para 505)

The term 'common' means land subject at the passing of this Act to any right of common [and any land subject to be included under the provisions of the Inclosure Act 1845]. (Metropolitan Commons Act 1866, s 3, amended by the Metropolitan Commons Amendment Act 1869, s 2)

'Common land' means—

(a) land subject to rights of common whether those rights are exercisable at all times or only during limited periods;

(b) waste land of a manor not subject to rights of common;

but does not include a town or village green or any land which forms part of a highway. (Commons Registration Act 1965, s 22(1))

Australia 'The word "common" . . . has a technical meaning in England and in New South Wales; though what kind of enjoyment it may indicate, and for what persons, cannot be understood without something more. Standing alone it is an ambiguous term which requires explanation, and which may be explained by circumstances. But further it is very often used, though inexactly and in popular parlance, to denote land devoted to the enjoyment of the public or of large numbers of people.' *Sydney Municipal Council, New South Wales Agricultural Society & Sydney Driving Park Club Ltd v A-G of New South Wales & Milroy* (1894) 63 LJPC 116 at 120, 121, per cur.

Commonable lands

The lands to which rights of common attach may be divided into 'common lands', which are uncultivated wastes, to which no severalty rights attach, and 'commonable lands', which are held in severalty during a portion of the year, but which become commonable after the severalty crop has been removed, and in many cases during the whole of the year in which they lie fallow. Common lands as a rule are waste of a manor; commonable lands as a rule are not, the ownership of the soil being in the severalty owners. (6 Halsbury's Laws (4th edn) para 506)

Right of common pur vicinage

'Paragraph 507 of 6 Halsbury's Laws (4th edn) sets out the classification of rights of common

and says: "Rights of common are either (1) appendant, (2) appurtenant, (3) in gross, or (4) by reason of vicinage". Paragraph 566 says: "Common of pasture by reason of vicinage exists where the commonable beasts belonging to the inhabitants of one town or manor have been accustomed time out of mind to stray into the fields or wastes of an adjoining town or manor without molestation. The right must have existed from time immemorial, or for a period which the law accepts as proof that it has so existed." The beginning of the next sub-paragraph reads: "It has been said not to be a right, but only an excuse for trespass". . . . The earliest authority on vicinage is contained in Blackstone's *Commentaries* (23rd edn, 1854, bk 2, ch 3, pp 34–35): "Common *because of vicinage*, or neighbourhood, is where the inhabitants of two townships which lie contiguous to each other, have usually intercommoned with one another; the beasts of the one straying mutually into the other's fields, without any molestation from either. This is indeed only a permissive right, intended to excuse what in strictness is a trespass in both, and to prevent a multiplicity of suits . . ." There it was being described as a right, albeit a permissive right. . . . In my opinion, the authors of Halsbury in the paragraph which I read at the beginning correctly divide the rights of common in the way in which they did, that is to say as appendant, appurtenant, in gross or by reason of vicinage. While it may be useful as a shield against trespass (and in the cases to which counsel for the appellant referred the argument was always a defence to the distress, the animals being seized), it is still a right of common, though limited in character because it is determinable. It can be determined by fencing off, and however impracticable that might be in the present case, it is a theoretical possibility.' *Newman v Bennett* [1980] 3 All ER 449 at 452, 454, per Waller LJ

Rights of common

Rights of common are either (1) appendant, (2) appurtenant, (3) in gross, or (4) by reason of vicinage.

Right of common appendant is a right by common law incident to the grant to certain tenants of arable land before the Statute of Quia Emptores, by which the tenant is entitled to the use of the manorial waste for such purposes as are necessary to the maintenance of his husbandry.

Right of common appurtenant is a right

depending upon a grant, or upon a prescription which supposes a grant, annexing to particular lands a right of user of another piece of land.

Right of common in gross is a right depending upon a grant or prescription entitling the possessor to some user of a particular piece of land without reference to the ownership of land.

Right of common by reason of vicinage is the right which the commoners of certain adjoining lands have of letting their cattle stray over the dividing boundary. (6 Halsbury's Laws (4th edn) para 507)

'Rights of common' includes cattlegates or beastgates (by whatever name known) and rights of sole or several vesture or herbage or of sole or several pasture, but does not include rights held for a term of years or from year to year. (Commons Registration Act 1965, s 22(1))

COMMON (Usual)

[Under the Patents, Designs and Trade Marks Act 1883 s 74(1)(b) (repealed; see now Trade Marks Act 1938, s 9), an addition to any trade mark might be entered on the register, if it consisted of any distinctive word or combination of words, though the same were 'common' to the trade.] 'The phrase "common to the trade" is not to be interpreted otherwise than according to the ordinary rules of grammar, and I think "common to the trade" means exactly what it says. I cannot really make use of a better term; but I can make use of a term which I think exactly corresponds with the meaning—that it is "open to the trade".' *Burland v Broxburn Oil Co* (1889) 42 Ch D 274 at 280, per Chitty J

COMMON ASSAULT *See* ASSAULT

COMMON CARRIER

A common carrier is one who exercises the public profession of carrying the goods of all persons wishing to use his services or of carrying passengers whoever they may be. His rights and liabilities are determined by the common law for reasons of public policy, although they may be varied by contract, and stem from his status as a common carrier rather than from contract, express or implied. . . . Although their duties and liabilities are different, it would seem that there is no distinction to be drawn between what constitutes a common

carrier of goods and a common carrier of persons. (5 Halsbury's Laws (4th edn) para 302)

'A common carrier is one who, in the language of Lord Holt in *Coggs v Bernard* [(1703) 2 Lord Raym 909], exercises a public employment; and the law charges him "to carry goods against all events, but acts of God, and of the enemies of the King".' *Crouch v London & North Western Rly Co* (1854) 14 CB 255 at 296, per Cresswell J

'A common carrier is a person who professes to carry for whosoever is willing to employ him, and is responsible for any damage to the goods in his possession though guilty of no negligence, unless such damage is caused by certain expected things.' *Tamvaco v Timothy & Green* (1882) Cab & El 1 at 2, per Cave J

'I think it well to state what I understand by the term "common carrier". The following definition which I take from a well-known textbook [Macnamara on Carriers by Land, 2nd edn, p 11], seems to me to be accurate: "A common carrier is a person who undertakes for hire to transport from a place within the realm to a place within or without the realm the goods or money of all such persons as think fit to employ him. To render a person liable as a common carrier he must exercise the business of carrying as a public employment, and must undertake to carry goods for all persons indiscriminately, and hold himself out, either expressly or by course of conduct, as ready to engage in the transportation of goods for hire as a business, not merely as a casual occupation *pro hav vice*.". . . If a man exercises his employment in such a way as to incur the liability of a common carrier he is a common carrier.' *Watkins v Cottell* [1916] 1 KB 10 at 14, 15, per Avory J

'The liability of the defendant depends solely upon whether he was a common carrier or not. The question whether a man is a common carrier or not is one of fact. A man may be a common carrier without so styling himself. . . . To make a man a common carrier he must carry as a public employment; he must carry for all indifferently; he must hold himself out as ready to carry for hire as a business and not as a casual occupation *pro hac vice*. He is sometimes described as a person who undertakes for reward to carry the goods of such as choose to employ him from place to place. To this I think it would be safe to add the words "at a reasonable rate". All other carriers by land are private carriers. . . . For the purposes of my present decision I fall back upon this question: Did the defendant, while inviting all and sundry to employ him, reserve to himself the right of accepting or rejecting their offers of goods for carriage whether his lorries were full or empty, being guided in his decision by the attractiveness or otherwise of the particular offer and not by his ability or inability to carry having regard to his other engagements? Upon the facts as found by me I answer that question in the affirmative, and in my opinion that answer shows that he is not a common carrier.' *Belfast Ropewalk Co Ltd v Bushell* [1918] 1 KB 210 at 212, 215, per Bailhache J

COMMON FISHERY *See* FISHERY

COMMON FORM BUSINESS

'Non-contentious or common form probate business' means the business of obtaining probate and administration where there is no contention as to the right thereto, including—
(a) the passing of probates and administrations through the High Court in contentious cases where the contest has been terminated,
(b) all business of a non-contentious nature in matters of testacy and intestacy not being proceedings in any action, and
(c) the business of lodging caveats against the grant of probate or administration.
(Supreme Court Act 1981, s 128)

COMMON GAMING HOUSE *See* GAMING HOUSE

COMMON GOOD

'I have considered the evidence . . . and I think I have a reasonably clear apprehension of what the Common Good means in Scotland. I am satisfied that it is a fund, or possibly a collection of properties, or perhaps to put it in another way, it is an asset which is held under the control of the municipal authorities of the borough in question for the benefit of that borough or of its inhabitants. I think that we have here the counterpart of a trust for the benefit of the inhabitants of a defined area within the kingdom of Scotland.' *Re Baynes, Public Trustee v Leven Corpn* [1944] 2 All ER 597 at 598, per Vaisey J

COMMON KNOWLEDGE

'The knowledge which is known in patent law as "common knowledge" may be referred to by judges as "common knowledge" or "general public knowledge" . . . and by such common knowledge is meant the information which at the date of the patent in question is common knowledge in the art or science to which the alleged invention relates, so as to be known to duly qualified persons engaged in that art or science.' *British Thomson-Houston Co Ltd v Stonebridge Electrical Co Ltd* (1916) 33 RPC 166 at 171, per Younger J

COMMON LAW

The municipal law of England, or the rule of civil conduct prescribed to the inhabitants of this kingdom, may with sufficient propriety be divided into two kinds; the *lex non scripta*, the unwritten, or common law; and the *lex scripta*, the written, or statute law.

The *lex non scripta* or unwritten law, includes not only *general customs*, or the common law properly so called; but also the *particular customs* of certain parts of the kingdom; and likewise those *particular laws*, that are by custom observed only in certain courts and jurisdictions. . . .

This unwritten, or common, law is properly distinguishable into three kinds: 1. General customs; which are the universal rule of the whole kingdom, and form the common law, in its stricter and more usual signification. 2. Particular customs; which for the most part affect only the inhabitants of particular districts. 3. Certain particular laws; which by custom are adopted and used by some particular courts, of pretty general and extensive jurisdiction. (4 Bl Com 63, 67)

Australia 'Both Fleming . . . and Glanville . . . take it as clear that the phrase "the common law" in section 59(2) [Sale of Goods Act 1895 (SA)] is meant to include equity. Grunfeld in the Modern Law Review, vol 21 (1958) 661 puts it even more pithily: "Common Law" in section 61(2) [i.e. our section 59(2)] plainly includes equity.' *Graham v Freer* (1984) 35 SASR 424 at 435, per Zelling J

Ecclesiastical law

The laws of England may be divided into two kinds, the unwritten (or common) law, and the written (or statute) law. The ecclesiastical law which forms part of the law of England is not a foreign law, and naturally falls into the same divisions. It consists of statute law and common law. . . . The common law of the realm (which is none other than the common custom of the realm) must not be confused with the common law (jus commune) of the Church of Rome. When used by canonists 'common law' means the law common to the Church of Rome generally and universally, as opposed to the special customs and privileges of any provincial church. (14 Halsbury's Laws (4th edn) para 303)

COMMON LAW NUISANCE *See*
NUISANCE

COMMON LAW WIFE

'"Battered wives" is a telling phrase. It was invented so as to call the attention of the public to an evil. Few were aware of it. It arose when a woman suffered serious or repeated physical injury from the man with whom she lived. She might be a wife properly married to her husband; or she might only be a woman called, falsely, a "common law wife". No such woman was known to the common law, but it means a woman who is living with a man in the same household as if she were his wife. She is to be distinguished from a "mistress" where the relationship may be casual, impermanent and secret.' *Davis v Johnson* [1978] 1 All ER 841 at 846, CA, per Lord Denning MR

Canada 'A common law wife is a woman who is united to a man by marriage which though informal is such as was recognized as valid by the common law.' *Blanchett v Hansell* [1943] 3 WWR 275 at 280, Man KB, per Dysart J; affd. [1944] 1 WWR 432, Man CA

COMMON LODGING HOUSE *See*
also LODGING-HOUSE

In this Part of this Act the expression 'common lodging-house' means a house (other than a public assistance institution) provided for the purpose of accommodating by night poor persons, not being members of the same family, who resort thereto and are allowed to occupy one common room for the purpose of sleeping or eating, and includes, where part only of a house is so used, the part so used. (Public Health Act 1936, s 235; Public Health (Control of Disease) Act 1984, s 74)

'A common lodging house, in its ordinary sense, means a lodging house kept by somebody for the purpose of profit, and open to all

comers whether of a certain class or not.' *Booth v Ferret* (1890) 25 QBD 87 at 89, per Mathew J

COMMON PROSTITUTE *See*
PROSTITUTE

COMMONABLE LANDS *See* COMMON

COMMONWEALTH

Australia 'It may be granted that the word "Commonwealth" is used in the Constitution [Commonwealth of Australia Constitution Act 1900] sometimes geographically, as in part of covering clause 5 where it speaks of "every part of the Commonwealth", and sometimes as a reference to the political entity which the Constitution created, as in other parts of that covering clause. It may also be granted that the powers which were given to the Commonwealth were of different orders, some federal, limited by subject-matter, some complete and given expressly, and some no doubt derived by implication from the very creation or existence of the body politic. Consequently, the need to observe the nature of the powers sought to be exercised at any time by the Commonwealth is ever present. But the Constitution brought into existence but one Commonwealth which was, in turn, destined to become the nation. The difference in the quality and extent of the powers given to it introduced no duality in the Commonwealth itself. The undoubted fact that the Commonwealth emerged from a federal compact or that that compact is reflected in the limitations placed upon some of the powers of the Commonwealth or that the new political entity derived from a union of the peoples of the former colonies, does not deny the essential unity and singleness of the Commonwealth. Consequently, in my opinion, the expression 'law of the Commonwealth' embraces every law made by the Parliament whatever the constitutional power under or by reference to which that law is made or supported: see per Dixon CJ, *Lamshed v Lake* (99 CLR) at p 148. Although the territories may not be included in the federal system in the sense that the powers of the Commonwealth with respect to them are not federally circumscribed, they are, in my opinion, clearly included in the expression "The Commonwealth", e.g. throughout Chapter I of the Constitution. I see no occasion for contrasting a

Commonwealth which contains or embraces only the constituent elements of a federation with a Commonwealth which includes all the areas over which it can by one power or another legislate. If the fundamental concept of a single Commonwealth is accepted, there would seem to be no need to entertain any distinction between territories which originally contained people who were members of a colony at the point of federation and other territories or to seek to find significance in the presence within a territory of the seat of government.' *Spratt v Hermes* [1966] ALR 597 at 604, 605, per Barwick CJ

COMMOTION   *See* CIVIL COMMOTION

COMMUNICANT

'Communicant' means a person who has received communion according to the use of the Church of England or of a church in communion therewith at least once within the twelve months preceding the date of his declaration that he fulfils that requirement, or if a declaration is not required of him, at least once within the twelve months preceding the date upon which he is offered the appointment or requested to act in a capacity for which that qualification is required. (Ecclesiastical Jurisdiction Measure 1963, s 66)

[An ecclesiastical terrier contained a statement of rights belonging to the parish church of Batley:—'Easter offerings—Every communicant, 2*d*.'] 'What is the proper meaning to be put on the term "communicant": does it mean every person whom the Church in ancient times regarded as under an obligation to commune, and who was therefore virtually a "communicant", or only those who actually communed? Agreeing, as we do, that the word is capable of the wider sense, we are of opinion that the evidence fails to show that that is the sense in which it is used in the terriers, and that, in the absence of such evidence, we must attribute to the word "communicant" its proper and primary meaning, and hold that it is confined to those who actually communed.' *R v Hall* (1866) 35 LJMC 251 at 254, 255, per cur.

COMMUNICATE

The expression 'to be communicated' means to be delivered at the address of the person to whom the communication is directed. (Uniform Laws on International Sales Act 1967, Sch 2)

New Zealand   [The Labour Department Act 1954, s 13(1) provides that no information obtained by the Minister or by any officer or employee of the Department under any of the powers conferred by the Act shall be 'communicated' to any person or made use of except for the purposes of the Act. The question was whether this provision prevented the giving of evidence before the court concerning information obtained by an officer of the Labour Department in the course of his duties.] 'In a section as wide as this, set in the context of powers as wide as those of this department in the general field of employment, I do not think that a reference to the communicating or making use of information should be interpreted as extending to testimony.' *Bonner v Karamea Shipping Co Ltd* [1973] 2 NZLR 374 at 378, per Cooke J

COMMUNICATION

Debt collection

United States   The term 'communication' means the conveying of information regarding a debt directly or indirectly to any person through any medium. (Fair Debt Collection Practices Act 1977, s 803(2))

COMMUNICATIONS PROCEDURES

Canada   'The phrase "communications procedures" [as relating to aircraft] is a general one. Appellants admit that speech and vocabulary are communications procedures. Since this is the case, I fail to see how they can deny that when language is used for communicating it also is communications procedure.' *Association des Gens de l'Air du Quebec Inc v Lang* (1978) 89 DLR (3d) 495 at 499, Fed CA, per Pratte J

COMMUNION TABLE   *See also* ALTAR

'Their Lordships have already declared their opinion that the Communion Table intended by the Canon [82nd Canon of 1604] was a table in the ordinary sense of the word, flat and moveable, capable of being covered with a cloth, at which, or around which, the communicants might be placed in order to partake of the Lord's Supper, and the question is, whether the existence of a cross attached to the Table is consistent either with the spirit or with the letter of those regulations. Their Lordships are clearly of opinion that it is not.' *Liddell v Westerton* (1857) Brod & F 117 at 152, PC, per cur.

COMMUNITY

Australia 'The word "community" in my opinion has a much wider significance than the word "locality". In its widest sense, of course, it could embrace the entire South Australian community; and I do not say that there may not be cases in which the interests of the community as a whole in South Australia might not be relevant. But it can also apply to a community of a lesser purview than the entire State. For example, I should think it would be entirely consistent . . . to speak of the northern primary production areas of the State as a community. I should think it would be proper to speak of the farmers on Eyre Peninsula as a community. I think it would be quite possible to speak of the grazing community in the Southeast and so on. "Community", I repeat, seems to me to have a much wider signification than just "locality" and correspondingly a much wider range of interests to consider.' *Hollow & Kaye v State Planning Authority* (1983) 45 LGRA 39 at 45, per Wells J

Australia 'Examination of dictionary definitions of "community" is not rewarding, e.g. "the people of a district as a whole", "a body of people organized into a political, municipal, or social unity" (Oxford Dictionary). In today's society we find many groups ordinarily called communities living in towns or districts, e.g. the Greek community, the Vietnamese community, the Aboriginal community. Thus in determining the community whose wishes and needs require consideration, the Commission must embrace all groups.' *R v Liquor Commission of the Northern Territory, ex p Pitjantjatjara Council Inc* (1984) 31 NTR 13 at 19

Canada 'The word "community" has been applied in a variety of ways. It has been used to apply to the quality of holding goods in common; to society or the social state where life is in association with others; to a body of individuals having common or equal rank; to those members of a civil community, who have certain circumstances of nativity, religion, or pursuit common to them, such as religious communities; to a socialistic or communist society; and to a body of persons living in the same locality, "those little communities which

we express by the word neighbourhood". "The community" is an expression generally applied to the people of a country or district as a whole, the general body to which all alike belong, the public.' *National Council of Jewish Women of Canada, Toronto Section v Township of N York* [1962] OR 1 at 3, Ont CA, per Porter CJO

Canada [Municipal tax exemption was available for land used for benefit of the 'community'.] 'I consider that the word "community" must be looked at in its geographical or physical sense, in addition to its human sense, for the section refers to the community "in which" the land is "situate", and in my view those words give the matter a physical or geographical connotation as well.' *Re Piers Island Association and Area Assessor for Saanich and the Islands* (1976) DLR (3d) 270 at 273, BCSC, per Fulton J

COMMUNITY SERVICE ORDER

Where a person of over seventeen years of age is convicted of an offence punishable with imprisonment, the court by or before which he is convicted may, instead of dealing with him in any other way . . . make an order (in this Act referred to as 'a community service order') requiring him to perform unpaid work . . . for such number of hours (being in the aggregate not less than forty nor more than two hundred and forty) as may be specified in the order. . . . (Powers of Criminal Courts Act 1973, s 14(1))

COMPANIES COURT

'The phrase "Companies Court" is a modern term introduced into the forms made pursuant to the Companies Act 1929 [repealed], in place of the phrase in the previous forms "Companies Winding-up", in order to soothe the susceptibilities of those who desired to apply to the court for some relief in the case of entirely solvent companies (as, for instance, confirmation of the reduction of the capital of a company by the return of surplus capital to its members) and who disliked that the title to the necessary proceedings should contain a reference to winding-up. There is in fact no Companies Court separate and distinct from the court, viz., the High Court, on which jurisdiction in winding-up matters is conferred by the Companies Act 1948 [repealed; see now the Companies Act 1985]. The phrase is only a convenient way of describing the relevant division of the High Court when exercising a particular jurisdiction, viz., the jurisdiction conferred on it by the Companies Act 1948.' *Re Wool Textile Employers' Mutual Insurance Co Ltd* [1955] 2 All ER 827 at 831, per Wynn-Parry J

COMPANY

The word 'company' imports an association of a number of individuals formed for some common purpose. Such an association may be incorporated (that is, a body corporate with perpetual succession and a common seal) or it may be unincorporated. An incorporated company is a legal person separate and distinct from the individual members of the company, whereas an unincorporated company has no such separate existence and is not in law distinguishable from its members. (7 Halsbury's Laws (4th edn) para 1)

' "Company" denotes . . . a legal entity, the validity of which and the effect of which depends on the law of the country in which it is established.' *Colquhoun v Heddon* (1890) 6 TLR 153 at 154, per Pollock B

'The word "company" has no strictly technical meaning. It involves, I think, two ideas—namely, first that the association is of persons so numerous as not to be aptly described as a firm; and, secondly, that the consent of all the other members is not required to the transfer of a member's interest.' *Re Stanley, Tennant v Stanley* [1906] 1 Ch 131 at 134, per Buckley J

'The word "company" clearly is, or may be, one of considerable legal significance. Following on the names of individuals and preceded by the word "and" it would probably denote a partnership. Without the word "and" it might (where the concern was an English one) denote either an unlimited company or an unregistered company or (in the case of a foreign enterprise) a body possessing under the law of its domicil a legal entity of its own resembling that of a limited liability company in England. I think that one or other of these interpretations would be quite likely to appeal to the ordinary business man or banker, and I cannot think that the common sense view of the matter is that the word "company" adds nothing of significance to the individual names which precede it. In my opinion, the average person would assume that the addition of the word "company" to, e.g., "John & James Smith", was intended to have some meaning, and he would visualise from its presence something in

the nature of a corporate entity, or, at all events, some juridical conception which would not have occurred to him had the individual names stood alone.' *Arab Bank Ltd v Ross* [1952] 1 All ER 709 at 718 CA, per Romer LJ (also reported in [1952] 2 QB 216 at 234)

Abbreviation of name

' "Ltd," using my ordinary knowledge of commerce, is such a constant abbreviation that every commercial man of intelligence would know that by "Ltd", "Limited" was meant. The English way of abbreviating "Limited" is just as common as the whole word "Limited" itself, and with every sympathy for the intelligent foreigner whom counsel for the plaintiffs referred to, I think he must be taken to have the same knowledge as an ordinary Englishman would have of the way in which the English word is expressed in print.' *Stacy & Co Ltd v Wallis* (1912) 106 LT 544 at 547, per Scrutton J

'An ampersand is an abbreviation, it is a symbolic abbreviation of the word "and", and is used simply because it is shorter to write or print than to write out or print out the full word "and".' *Banque de L'Indochine et de Suez SA v Euroseas Group Finance Co Ltd* [1981] 3 All ER 198 at 201, per Goff J

[*See* further the Companies Act 1985, s 27(4).]

Affairs of company   *See* AFFAIRS

Articles of association   *See* ARTICLES

Associated company

For the purposes of this Chapter . . ., a company is to be treated as another's 'associated company' at a given time if at that time, or at any time within one year previously, one of the two has control of the other, or both are under the control of the same person or persons. (Income and Corporation Taxes Act 1970, s 302(1))

Close company

(1) For the purposes of the Corporation Tax Acts, a 'close company' is one which is under the control of five or fewer participators, or of participators who are directors, except that the expression does not apply—
  (a) to a company not resident in the United Kingdom, or
  (b) to a registered industrial and provident society within the meaning of

s 340(9) of this Act, or to a building society within the meaning of s 343 of this Act or any other company to which the said s 343 applies, or

(c) to a company controlled by or on behalf of the Crown, and not otherwise a close company, or

(d) to a company falling within sub-s (4) or s 283 below.

(2) Subject to section 283 below, a company resident in the United Kingdom (but not falling within subsection (1)(b) above) is also a close company if—

(a) on the assumption that it is so, or

(b) on the assumption that it and any other such company or companies are so,

more than half of any amount falling to be apportioned under Schedule 16 to the Finance Act 1972 in the case of the company (including any sum which has been apportioned to it, or could on either of these assumptions be apportioned to it, under that Schedule) could be apportioned among five or fewer participators, or among participators who are directors. . . .

(3) For the purposes of this section—

(a) a company is to be treated as controlled by or on behalf of the Crown if, but only if, it is under the control of the Crown or of persons acting on behalf of the Crown, independently of any other person, and

(b) where a company is so controlled, it shall not be treated as being otherwise a close company unless it can be treated as a close company as being under the control of persons acting independently of the Crown.

(4) A company is not to be treated as a close company—

(a) if—

(i) it is controlled by a company which is not a close company, or by two or more companies none of which is a close company; and

(ii) it cannot be treated as a close company except by taking as one of the five or fewer participators requisite for its being so treated a company which is not a close company;

(b) if it cannot be treated as a close company except by virtue of paragraph (c) of section 302(2) of this Act and it would not be a close company if the reference in that paragraph to parti-

cipators did not include loan creditors who are companies other than close companies.

(Income and Corporation Taxes Act 1970, s 282, amended by the Finance Act 1972, s 94(2), Sch 17).

[Section 283 of the above Act excepts certain companies with quoted shares; s 340(9) defines 'registered industrial and provident society'; and s 343 deals with the business of building societies.]

Co-operative company

Australia 'Whatever characteristics may be required in order to bring a company within that expression [i.e. 'co-operative company' in the Income Tax Assessment Act 1922 to 1928, s 4(c) (see now Income Tax Assessment Act 1936 (Cth), s 120(2)), which provides that 'income' does not include any rebate received by a member of a 'co-operative company' based on his purchases from that company where the Commissioner is satisfied that 90 per cent of its sales is made to its own members], it seems reasonably clear that the company must possess them by virtue of its constitution. It is not enough that a company may in fact conduct a series of transactions or a business upon principles which justify the title "co-operative". The company itself must be a union for "co-operation". To render the company co-operative by its constitution it is at least necessary that the contract *inter socios* shall be "co-operative".' *Shelley v Federal Comr of Taxation* (1929) 43 CLR 208 at 231, per Dixon J

Family company

'Family company' means, in relation to an individual, a company the voting rights in which are—

(a) as to not less than 25 per cent., exercisable by the individual, or

(b) as to not less than 51 per cent., exercisable by the individual or a member of his family, and, as to not less than 5 per cent., exercisable by the individual himself.

(Capital Gains Tax Act 1979, s 124)

Investment company

(1) In section 265 [distributions to investment companies] 'investment company' means a public company which has given notice in the prescribed forms (which has not been revoked) to the registrar of companies of its intention to carry on business as an

investment company, and has since the date of that notice complied with the requirements specified below.

(2) Those requirements are—

   (a) that the business of the company consists of investing its funds mainly in securities, with the aim of spreading investment risk and giving members of the company the benefit of the results of the management of its funds,

   (b) that none of the company's holdings in companies (other than those which are for the time being in investment companies) represents more than 15 per cent by value of the investing company's investments,

   (c) that distribution of the company's capital profits is prohibited by its memorandum or articles of association,

   (d) that the company has not retained, otherwise that in compliance with this Part [Part VIII: distribution of profits and assets], in respect of any accounting reference period more than 15 per cent of the income it derives from securities.

(Companies Act 1985, s 266(1), (2))

Joint stock company

For the purposes of this Chapter [Chapter II: companies not formed under companies legislation but authorized to register], as far as relates to companies limited by shares, 'joint stock company' means a company—

(a) having a permanent paid-up or nominal share capital of fixed amount divided into shares, also of fixed amount, or held and transferable as stock, or divided and held partly in one way and partly in the other, and

(b) formed on the principle of having for its members the holders of those shares or that stock, and no other persons.

(Companies Act 1985, s 683(1))

Limited and unlimited companies

(1) Any two or more persons associated for lawful purpose may, by subscribing their names to a memorandum of association and otherwise complying with the requirements of this Act in respect of registration, form an incorporated company, with or without limited liability.

(2) A company so formed may be either—

   (a) a company having the liability of its members limited by the memorandum to the amount, if any, unpaid on the shares respectively held by them ('a company limited by shares');

   (b) a company having the liability of its members limited by the memorandum to such amount as the members may respectively thereby undertake to contribute to the assets of the company in the event of its being wound up ('a company limited by guarantee'); or

   (c) a company not having any limit on the liability of its members ('an unlimited company').

(Companies Act 1985, s 1)

Oversea company

'Oversea company' means—

(a) a company incorporated elsewhere than in Great Britain which, after the commencement of this Act, established a place of business in Great Britain, and

(b) a company so incorporated which has, before that commencement, established a place of business and continues to have an established place of business in Great Britain at that commencement.

(Companies Act 1985, s 744)

Partnership distinguished

'An ordinary partnership is a partnership composed of definite individuals bound together by contract between themselves to continue combined for some joint object, either during pleasure or during a limited time, and is essentially composed of the persons originally entering into the contract with one another. A company or association (which I take to be synonymous terms) is the result of an arrangement by which parties intend to form a partnership which is constantly changing, a partnership to-day consisting of certain members and to-morrow consisting of some only of those members along with others who have come in, so that there will be a constant shifting of the partnership, a determination of the old and a creation of a new partnership, and with the intention that, so far as the partners can by agreement between themselves bring about such a result, the new partnership shall succeed to the assets and liabilities of the old partnership.' *Smith v Anderson* (1880) 15 Ch D 247 at 273, 274, CA, per James LJ

'I understand by a company—an unincorporated company—some association of members the shares of which are transferable. As distinguished from a partnership, I know of nothing else except the transferability of shares.' *R v Joint Stock Companies Registrar, ex p Johnston* [1891] 2 QB 598 at 610, 611, CA, per Lindley LJ

Public company

A 'public company' is a company limited by shares or limited by guarantee and having a share capital, being a company—
(a) the memorandum of which states that it is to be a public company, and
(b) in relation to which the provisions of this Act or the former Companies Acts as to the registration or re-registration of a company as a public company have been complied with on or after 23rd December 1980,
and a 'private company' is a company that is not a public company. (Companies Act 1985, s 1(3))

[The Judgments Act 1838, s 14, enacts that if any person against whom any judgment shall have been entered up in any superior court shall have any shares in any 'public company' in England (whether incorporated or not) standing in his name, it shall be lawful for a judge of one of the superior courts to order that such shares shall stand charged with the payment of the amount for which the judgment shall have been recovered.] 'I do not . . . think I can hold the Union Bank of London to be a public company within the meaning of the [Act], merely, because its capital is divided into shares. In my opinion, it would have been a public company if its capital had not been so divided; because the attributes of publicity would exist, namely, the return of the names and places of abode of the members from time to time, and of the officers appointed to sue and be sued on behalf of the company.' *Macintyre v Connell* (1851)1 Sim NS 225 at 239, per Lord Cranworth V-C

[A clause in a will empowered trustees to invest in the debentures or securities of any railway or other 'public company' carrying on business in the United Kingdom.] 'I think it is clear that all these companies are public companies within the clause. They are incorporated by public statute; the instruments which form their constitution are accessible to the public; and their shares are transferable to the public. I do not say that all these things are necessary to constitute a public company; but where they are all present, I think the company is clearly a public

company within this investment clause.' *Re Sharp, Rickett v Sharp* (1890) 45 Ch D 286 at 290, CA, per Fry LJ

'I thought that the meaning of a public company was settled as long ago as *Macintyre v Connell* [supra], and I take it that any company registered under the Companies Act 1862 [repealed; see now Companies Act 1985], is a public company within the meaning of that expression in the Apportionment Act [1870].' *Re Lysaght, Lysaght v Lysaght* [1898] 1 Ch 115 at 122, CA, per Lindley MR

'The will is one of an English testatrix, it is in all respects an English will, and where she speaks of the "public funds" or "Government securities" I think she means the public funds of the United Kingdom, and the securities of the British Government. . . . Then we come to the particular words "stocks, shares, and securities of any railway of public company", the word "public" being repeated. . . . Reading these words, therefore, in connection with the preceding words of this clause, I think, the testatrix must clearly have intended to confine these investments to shares in public companies in the United Kingdom.' *Re Castlehow, Lamonby v Carter* [1903] 1 Ch 352 at 355, per Byrne J

Statutory company

'Statutory company' means any railway company, canal company, dock company, water company, or other company incorporated by special Act, who are for the time being authorised under such an Act to construct, work, own, or carry on any railway, canal, dock, water, or other public undertaking, and includes any person or body of persons so authorised. (Statutory Companies (Redeemable Stock) Act 1915, s 2)

Subsidiary company

(1) For the purposes of this Act, a company is deemed to be a subsidiary of another if (but only if)—
(a) that other either—
   (i) is a member of it and controls the composition of its board of directors, or
   (ii) holds more than half in nominal value of its equity share capital, or
(b) the first-mentioned company is a subsidiary of any company which is that other's subsidiary.
(Companies Act 1985, s 736(1))

Trading company

For the purposes of this Schedule, a 'trading company' is any company which exists wholly or mainly for the purpose of carrying on a trade, and any other company whose income does not consist wholly or mainly of investment income, that is to say income which, if the company were an individual, would not be earned income; but for this purpose any amount which is apportioned to a company [apportionment between participators in a close company] shall be deemed to be income of the company and to be investment income. (Finance Act 1972, Sch 16, para 11(1)

Unregistered company

For the purposes of this Part [Part V: winding up of unregistered companies] the expression 'unregistered company' includes any association and any company, with the following exceptions—

(a) a railway company incorporated by Act of Parliament;
(b) a company registered in any part of the United Kingdom under the Joint Stock Companies Acts or under the legislation (past or present) relating to companies in Great Britain.

(Insolvency Act 1986, s 220)

COMPENSATION

'Compensation which is directed to be paid by the employer to a workman who is injured by accident arising out of and in the course of his employment under s 1 of the Workmen's Compensation Act [1906 (repealed)] has its natural meaning—that is to say, something that is to be paid which makes up for the loss that the man has sustained.' *Great Western Rly Co v Helps* [1918] AC 141 at 144, 145, per Lord Dunedin

Australia 'Compensation is a very well understood expression. It is true that its meaning has been developed in relation to the compulsory acquisition of land. But the purpose of compensation is the same, whether the property taken is real or personal. It is to place in the hands of the owner expropriated the full money equivalent of the thing of which he has been deprived. Compensation prima facie means recompense for loss, and when an owner is to receive compensation for being deprived of real or personal property his

pecuniary loss must be ascertained by determining the value to him of the property taken from him. As the object is to find the money equivalent for the loss or, in other words, the pecuniary value to the owner contained in the asset, it cannot be less than the money value into which he might have converted his property had the law not deprived him of it. You do not give him any enhanced value that may attach to his property because it has been compulsorily acquired by the governmental authority for its purposes. . . . Equally you exclude any diminution of the value arising from the same cause. The hypothesis upon which the inquiry into value must proceed is that the owner had not been deprived by the exercise of compulsory powers of his ownership and of his consequent rights of disposition existing under the general law at the time of acquisition.' *Nelungaloo Pty Ltd v Commonwealth* (1948) 75 CLR 495 at 571, per Dixon J

Australia 'Compensation paid under the Workers' Compensation Act is not "earnings" in the popular sense or in any other sense of which I am aware. The worker, indeed, is compensated because he has lost his ability to earn.' *Hardie v Hardie* [1947] VLR 79 at 81, per Gavan Duffy J

Canada ' "Due compensation" simply means a full indemnity in respect of all pecuniary loss by reason of the exercise of the powers of the corporation.' *Re Macdonald & Toronto* (1912) 27 OLR 179 at 182, per Garrow JA

Damages distinguished

'The question turns on the 14th section of the Conveyancing Act [(1881) (repealed; see now the Law of Property Act 1925, s 146)]. That provides that "a right of re-entry under any stipulation in a lease for breach of any covenant shall not be enforceable unless and until the lessor serve on the lessee a notice specifying the particular breach complained of, and, if the breach is capable of remedy, requiring the lessee to remedy the breach, and in any case requiring the lessee to make compensation in money for the breach, and the lessee fails within a reasonable time thereafter to remedy the breach, if it is capable of remedy, and to make reasonable compensation in money to the satisfaction of the lessor for the breach.". . . The section creates some diffiulty, because it seems to contemplate compensation as payment in every case of a breach, and because it uses, not the familiar word "damages" for a breach, but "compensation". But it is evident that many cases may occur in which, where the breach has been perfectly made good and no expense or loss incurred, there may be nothing for which to make compensation, and we are therefore of opinion that, notwithstanding the general terms of the notice required by the statute, the lessee is bound to make compensation, not absolutely in every case, but only when there is something to compensate. With regard to the word "compensation", we incline to the view that the word "damages" was not used because that is more appropriate to the compensation for a breach when ascertained by the verdict of a jury or the judgment of a Court; but that compensation under the section in question is to be measured by the same rule as damages in an action for the breach.' *Skinners' Co v Knight* [1891] 2 QB 542 at 544, 545, CA, per cur.

[The Merchant Shipping Act 1876, s 10 (repealed; see now s 460(1) of Merchant Shipping Act 1894), enacted that if it appeared that there was not reasonable and probable cause for the provisional detention of a ship under s 6 of the Act, the Board of Trade should be liable to pay to the shipowner 'compensation' for any loss or damage sustained by him by reason of the detention.] 'What is compensation? The expression "compensation" is not ordinarily used as an equivalent for "damages". It is used in such Acts as these in relation to a lawful act which has caused injury. Therefore that word would not . . . include damages at large.' *Dixon v Calcraft* [1892] 1 QB 458 at 463, 464, CA, per Lord Esher MR

New Zealand [The Property Law Act 1952 (NZ), s 118(1), provides that a right of re-entry or forfeiture under a lease shall not be enforceable unless the lessor first serves on the lessee a notice specifying the particular breach complained of and requiring the lessee to remedy it, and also requiring the lessee to make 'compensation' in money for the breach.] 'The word compensation, as used in the section, does not denote damage in lieu of remedial measures required by the notice in respect of defaults capable of remedy. It denotes rather the supplementary compensation which a lessor still regards as reasonably due to him, after the defaults have been faithfully remedied, as far as they are capable of remedy, within the time

given. . . . If the matters complained of are capable of being fully remedied, and are required in the notice to be fully remedied, no compensation will generally be claimed since there will be no supplementary damage in respect of which it could be claimed.' *Lowe v Ellbogen* [1959] NZLR 103 at 105, 106, per Turner J

COMPETENT   *See also* DISPOSITION

[The Quarries (General) Regulations 1956, SI 1956/1780, reg 41, requires the manager of a quarry to make and ensure the efficient carrying out of arrangements to secure that every inspection is carried out or done by a 'competent' person.] 'There is no definition of "competent" in the regulations. I am not prepared to hold either that "competent" means the most competent person available to the owners of the quarry or their manager, or that it means that he shall be so competent that he never makes a mistake. In my judgment, it means a man who, on a fair assessment of the requirements of the task, the factors involved, the problems to be studied and the degree of risk danger implicit, can fairly, as well as reasonably, be regarded by the manager, and in fact is regarded at the time by the manager, as competent to perform such an inspection.' *Brazier v Skipton Rock Co Ltd* [1962] 1 All ER 955 at 957, per Winn J

'Who is "a competent person" for the purpose of such an inspection [of lifting gear under the Docks Regulations 1934]? This phrase is not defined. I think that it is obviously to be taken to have its ordinary meaning of a person who is competent for the task. I think that a competent person for this task is a person who is a practical and reasonable man, who knows what to look for and knows how to recognise it when he sees it.' *Gibson v Skibs A/S Marina* [1966] 2 All ER 476 at 478, per Cantley J

To dispose

Australia 'I agree with the view expressed by Lord Greene MR in *Re Parsons* [[1943] Ch 12 at 15] that a person is competent to dispose of property which he can make his own, since the deceased could, by her act, have made . . . property pass to herself immediately before her death, she was competent to dispose of it . . . the competency spoken of must, I think, be legal competency to dispose and does not involve the question of possession at the relevant time of a practical ability then and there to make an effective disposition. Physical remoteness of the deceased from her property, the lack of postal facilities, of legal advice or whatever else might be actually necessary to effect this position; all such considerations would be irrelevant to the question of possession of the relevant competencies.' *Equity Trustees v Probate Comr* (1976) 10 ALR 131 at 133, per Gibbs J

COMPETITION

[The question at issue was whether a football pool was a 'competition' in which prizes were offered for forecasts of the result of a future event within the Betting and Lotteries Act 1934, s 26(1) (repealed; see now the Lotteries and Amusements Act 1976, s 14).] 'It is contended for the respondent company that this scheme is not a prize competition within the section, but simply pool betting. . . . In *Elderton v United Kingdom Totalisator Co Ltd* [[1935] Ch 373, 381], Eve J held that it was not a competition, but a betting transaction, and so was not prohibited by the Act. He said: "One does not compete with a man with whom a bet is made, nor does the winner regard the money paid by the loser as a prize." While that may be true with regard to an ordinary bet we are unable to agree with the learned judge that this scheme is not a competition. With all respect, it seems to us that the entrants are obviously competing against each other for the pool, which all hope to win in whole or in part. If half a dozen people enter for a race, each paying one shilling, the winner to take three-quarters of the pool and the second one-quarter and in the event of a dead heat the pool to be divided, they are all competing one against the other and, if the unlikely result happened that all ran a dead heat, so that they would all only get their stake back, they would none the less be competitors.' *Bretherton v United Kingdom Totalisator Co Ltd* [1945] KB 555 at 559, 560, DC, per Lord Goddard

[The Lotteries and Amusements Act 1976, s 14 makes it unlawful to conduct in or through any newspaper, or in connection with any trade or business or the sale of any article to the public, any 'competition' in which prizes are offered for certain types of forecast, or in which success does not depend substantially on the exercise of skill.] 'As in the case of lotteries, so with competitions Parliament [in the above Act] has not seen fit to provide any definition. There are two meanings. The first is the passive "competition" between, for example, 50 people who enter a raffle when there is only one prize. In one sense of the word each of the 50 is competing with the other 49 for the prize. The second is the active exercise of skill, or strength or prowess of some sort, a striving to do better than other contestants in the hope of excelling them. That is the sense in which I believe the word "competition" is used in the 1976 Act. The mischief which s 14 . . . sought to meet was the evasion of the law relating to lotteries by the requirement that some small degree of skill should be exercised by the participants. If the first meaning is the true one then almost all lotteries would be competitions, a result which Parliament would be unlikely to intend.' *Imperial Tobacco Ltd v A-G* [1980] 1 All ER 866 at 882, HL, per Lord Lane

Competition for prizes

In this Act 'competition for prizes' means a competition for prizes where—
(a) the allocation of prizes depends upon the outcome of sporting events, and
(b) each competitor has the right to forecast the outcomes of those events, and
(c) prizes can be won both where a competitor forecasts the outcome of those events, and where he does not,
and 'competition' includes any scheme or arrangement for the distribution of prizes among persons who have paid to participate, and 'competitor' shall be construed accordingly. (Pool Competitions Act 1971, s 7(2))

COMPETITIVE BIDDING

In this Act 'sale of goods by way of competitive bidding' means any sale of goods at which the persons present, or some of them, are invited to buy articles by way of competitive bidding, and 'competitive bidding' includes any mode of sale whereby prospective purchasers may be enabled to compete for the purchase of articles, whether by way of increasing bids or by the offer of articles to be bid for at successively decreasing prices or otherwise. (Mock Auctions Act 1961, s 3)

'The phrase "competitive bidding" is given an extended meaning for the 1961 Act [supra] states: "competitive bidding" includes any mode of sale whereby prospective purchasers may be enabled to compete for the purchase of articles, whether by way of increasing bids or by the offer of articles to be bid for at successively decreasing prices or otherwise. Omitting the words which are not relevant for present purposes, it amounts to this. Competitive bidding includes any mode of sale whereby prosective purchasers may be enabled to compete or the purchase of articles in any way.' *Clements v Rydhead* [1978] 3 All ER 658 at 661, *per* Eveleigh J

COMPILATION

Copyright

United States A 'compilation' is a work formed by the collection and assembling of pre-existing materials or of data that are selected, coordinated, or arranged in such a way that the resulting work as a whole constitutes an original work of authorship. The term 'compilation' includes collective works. (Copyright Act of 1976, s 101)

COMPLETION

'I am of opinion that, where the nature of the transaction is an agreement for a loan payable *in præsenti*, upon certain securities, guaranteed by the solicitor, it is a contemplated transaction if in fact, within a reasonable time after the date of the actual signing of the memorandum, the sums are actually advanced—more especially where, as in this case, it is purely in the interests and at the bequest of the client that the making of the advance is withheld in order to save him interest and bankers' charges.' *Re Baker* [1912] 2 Ch 405 at 412, *per* Parker J

Of contract for sale of land

'The vendor sold the land for a price; completion was to take place on October 27th, 1924; one of the conditions of sale was that all rents and periodical outgoings should be apportioned up to—not the date fixed for completion—but "up to the completion", and should be added to or deducted from the purchase money, as the case might require. There was no provision about interest. The contract for sale was not in fact completed for nearly a year after the date named for completion and about a fortnight after the end of the tenancy. . . . In these circumstances was the purchaser a person entitled to receive the rents and profits of the land at the termination of the tenancy? That question turns upon the meaning of the condition that "All rents and periodical outgoings shall be apportioned up to the completion", and particularly upon the meaning of the words "the completion", and whether they mean the date fixed by the contract for completion or the date of actual

completion. In my opinion the words mean the date of actual completion.' *Richards v Pryse* [1927] 2 KB 76 at 88, 89, CA, *per* Scrutton LJ

[A contract for sale of land contained a clause which provided that if the property were destroyed prior to the date fixed for 'completion' the purchaser should have the right to rescind.] 'In my opinion, c 11 [of the contract] deals with a date—the date fixed for completion. Now, what is meant by "completion" in this clause? I adopt the words of Turner V-C [in *Lewis v South Wales Rly Co* infra] and, in my judgment, in this contract the words "completion of the contract" mean "the complete conveyance of the estate and final settlement of the business".' *Killner v France* [1946] 2 All ER 83 at 86, *per* Stable J

See, generally, 42 Halsbury's Laws (4th edn) para 191.

Of purchase

[An agreement provided that certain money should be and remain in the possession of a bank until the completion of the purchase, and that interest should be paid up to the day on which the purchase should be completed.] 'The question is, what is the meaning of the words "until the completion of the purchase". Those words may, no doubt, import, and generally perhaps would be construed to refer to, the complete conveyance of the estate and final settlement of the business; but I do not think this is the only or necessary meaning of the words. They may mean, until the completion of the purchase by the purchaser, as to whose part the purchase is completed by the payment of the purchase-money; and the question is, whether this is not the true meaning of the words as contained in this agreement. . . . Here the subject-matter of the contract is the possession and the payment of interest on the purchase-money. What then is the reasonable construction of the words with reference to this subject-matter. . . . My opinion . . . is, that the words "of the completion of the purchase", as used in the agreement, must be construed to mean the completion on the part of the purchaser by payment of purchase-money.' *Lewis v South Wales Rly Co* (1852) 10 Hare 113 at 119, 120, *per* Turner V-C

'What is the completion of the purchase [within the Finance Act 1895, s 12]? . . . The simple date to take as the completion of the purchase is the final payment of the price to the seller.' *Lord Advocate v Caledonian Rly Co* 1908 SC 566 at 575, *per* the Lord President

Australia 'The words "completion of the purchase" may mean completion in the strictest sense, that is, payment of the whole purchase-money and conveyance to the purchasers by the vendors. But they may also mean completion by the purchasers, that is, payment of so much of the purchase-money as has to be paid, and acceptance of the title.' *Sutton v Cary* (1916) 16 SR (NSW) 254 at 257, 258, per Simpson CJ in Eq

Australia 'Whilst it is true that "completion" may mean payment of the whole of the purchase money and a conveyance or transfer of the subject land to the purchasers by the vendor, the word "completion" may also mean, in an appropriate context, the payment of so much of the purchase money as according to the terms of the contract has to be paid upon acceptance and transfer of the title, leaving the outstanding balance of purchase money to be secured possibly by a vendor's lien or mortgage back according to the circumstances.' *De Leuil v Jeremy* [1964–5] NSWR 1939 at 1953, per Asprey J

Of work

[In the Locomotives Act 1898, s 12(1)(b) (repealed; see now the Highways Act 1980, s 59(5)), it was provided that proceedings for the recovery of expenses of extraordinary traffic, where the damage was caused by a building contract of work extending over a long period, were to be commenced not later than six months after the 'completion' of the contract of work.] 'This Court has already decided that the words of s 12(1)(b) . . . "after the completion of the contract of work" mean after the constructional completion of the contract to work to the exclusion of an obligation as between the employer and the contractor which may continue after the construction is completed.' *Reigate Rural District Council v Sutton District Water Co* (1909) 78 LJKB 315 at 319, CA, per Buckley LJ

COMPLEX

'A "complex" is, I think, modern jargon for something which is capable of being regarded as an integer or unit though composed of independent or semi-independent parts.' *Dixon (Inspector of Taxes) v Fitch's Garage*

Ltd [1975] 3 All ER 455 at 458, per Brightman J

COMPOSITION

A composition is an agreement between the compounding debtor and all or some of his creditors by which the compounding creditors agree with the debtor, and, expressly or impliedly, with each other, to accept from the debtor payment of less than the amounts due to them in full satisfaction of the whole of their claims. (3 Halsbury's Laws (4th edn) para 1000)

'Composition', in relation to a medicinal product, means the ingredients of which it consists and the proportions, and the degrees of strength, quality and purity, in which those ingredients are contained in it respectively. (Medicines Act 1968, s 132)

COMPOUND

Debt

'The question really turns on the word "compound". Mr Willes says, it means not merely entering into, but completing some arrangement, by which the creditor takes a part of the debt for the whole. I do not see why the word should be so limited. I read it as meaning "arranging with creditors to their satisfaction".' *Pennell v Rhodes* (1846) 15 LJQB 352 at 355, per Patteson J

'To "compound" a debt or claim, is to accept, in satisfaction of it, something less than, or something different from, that which may be claimed as of right—generally by way of compromise or agreement.' *Irish Land Commission v Grant* (1884) 10 App Cas 14 at 30, 31, per Lord Selborne LC

South Africa 'The words "compound" and "composition" are both derived from the Latin word *componere*, and the ordinary meaning of the word "compound" is "to enter into a composition". By current use of language . . . a composition is a different thing from an assignment, for a composition is an arrangement by which an insolvent debtor agrees to pay, and his creditors to accept, [so much] in the pound, the debtor usually retaining his estate; while an assignment is an arrangement by which an insolvent debtor transfers his estate to the creditors, for whatever it may be worth, in full satisfaction of his debts.' *Ochse v van Aardt* 1824 OPD 271, per de Villiers JP

Offence

'The offence of compounding a felony in short is *an agreement* not to prosecute a felon in consideration of the return of the goods or other reward; see 4 Blackstone's Commentaries, p 133, *R v Burgess* [(1885) 16 QBD 141]; whereas in misprision there need be no benefit.' *Sykes v Director of Public Prosecutions* [1961] 3 All ER 33 at 41, HL, per Lord Denning

[All distinctions between felonies and misdemeanours were abolished by the Criminal Law Act 1967, s 1(1). Section 5 of that Act enacted new provisions as to the compounding of offences.]

COMPROMISE

'In our older legal language the word "compromise" appears to have been used, in accordance with its etymology: to express the mutual promises of "persons at controversy" to submit to the arbitrament of a third person the matters in dispute between the two (see "A compromise defined", 2 West Symboleography, 163). In our present language it undoubtedly embraces an agreement between two or more persons for the ascertainment of their rights when there is some question in controversy between them or some difficulty in the enforcement to the uttermost farthing of the rights of the claimant. But . . . the word is applicable only where there is some such controversy or some such difficulty. . . . The power to compromise does not include the power to give up one chose in action, namely, a secured debenture, in exchange for another chose in action of a totally different kind, namely, a preference share, in the absence of all dispute as to the rights of the creditor, of all difficulty in enforcing those rights, and of any suggestion that the full fruits of these rights could not be obtained. Such a transaction might be described as an exchange, possibly as a barter . . . but it is . . . not a compromise.' *Mercantile Investment & General Trust Co v International Co of Mexico (1891)* [1893] 1 Ch 484 n at 491 n, CA, per Fry LJ

'A compromise presupposes some dispute about the rights compromised, or some difficulty in enforcing them if dispute there is none.' *Re Guardian Assurance Co* [1917] 1 Ch 431 at 442, CA, per Younger J.

[A reinsurance policy provided that the insurer would only be called upon for a total constructive 'compromised and/or arranged total loss']. '"Compromised and arranged" . . . mean that "arranged" is something different from "compromised". "Compromised or arranged" may mean that the words are the same, and you are simply using two ways of expressing the same idea, but the words in this case are "compromised and/or arranged". . . . The phrase . . . means not only, "We will pay on a compromise; we will pay on an arrangement", but it may be that the nature of the transaction is such that you can call it both "compromised" *and* "arranged". The phrase "compromised and arranged" appears to me to suggest that some kinds of transactions may be arrangements which are not compromises and vice versa.' *Gurney v Grimmer* (1932) 38 Com Cas 7 at 12, 13, CA, per Scrutton LJ

'"Compromised" . . . assumes that a mutual concession has been made by both parties and that each party has got something less than he claimed. The word "arranged" . . . is a wider word altogether. In certain cases, and . . . in this case . . . it is equivalent to "agreed".' Ibid at 18, per Lawrence LJ

'I understand "compromise" to mean an agreement to settle an action or threatened action. It may be an agreement to apply for a consent judgment, and effect is given to it by applying for and obtaining the consent judgment. Or it may be an agreement that the dispute shall be settled on certain terms and that application shall be made for an order that the action be stayed with liberty to apply and such order is applied for and made: in that case the action merely becomes dormant, and the stay may be removed if the terms are not carried out. Or it may be an agreement to avoid a threatened action, and, if the agreement is not carried out, the action may still be brought. The parties have not reached finality or fully disposed of the proceedings or intended proceedings when they make their compromise agreement: further steps are required to effectuate the compromise and to give it finality. On the other hand, a judgment has finality, fully and effectively terminating the action. I am not seeking to decide what costs may be charged in the case of a compromise, but only to point out the difference of principle between a compromise agreement and a judgment.' *Marshall (W F) Ltd v Barnes and Fitzpatrick* [1953] 1 All ER 970 at 977, per Pearson J

'A reasonable compromise must be a compromise which can, by reasonable people conversant with the subject, be regarded as beneficial to those on both sides who are making it.' *Re Alabama, New Orleans, Texas & Pacific Junction Rly Co* [1981] 1 Ch 213 at 243, per Bowen LJ

'The word "compromise" implies some element of accommodation on each side. It is not apt to describe total surrender. A claimant who abandons his claim is not compromising it.' *Re NFU Development Trust Ltd* [1973] 1 All ER 135 at 140, per Brightman J

COMPULSORY ACQUISITION

Where land or an interest in land is purchased or taken under statutory powers without the agreement of the owner it is said to have been compulsorily acquired, but where there is statutory power to take mere possession of the land without the acquisition of any estate or interest in it apart from the possession, it is said to have been requisitioned. (8 Halsbury's Laws (4th edn) para 1)

COMPULSORY PAYMENT

Where the plaintiff has been compelled by law to pay, or, being compellable by law, has paid, money which the defendant was ultimately liable to pay, so that the defendant obtains the benefit of the payment by the discharge of his liability, the defendant is held indebted to the plaintiff in the amount of the payment. (9 Halsbury's Laws (4th edn) para 642)

COMPULSORY PURCHASE   *See*
COMPULSORY ACQUISITION

COMPULSORY SCHOOL AGE

In this Act the expression 'compulsory school age' means any age between five years and sixteen years, and accordingly a person shall be deemed to be of compulsory school age if he has attained the age of five years and has not attained the age of sixteen years and a person shall be deemed to be over compulsory school age as soon as he has attained the age of sixteen years. . . . (Education Act 1944, s 35,

amended by the Raising of the School Leaving Age Order 1972, SI 1972/444)

[It should be noted that under the Education Act 1962, s 9, amended by the Education (School Leaving Date) Act 1976, s 1, a child cannot leave school immediately he reaches the uppermost limit if that happens in the middle of a term, but must wait until the end of a spring or summer term following his birthday.]

COMPUTER   *See also* DATA

In this Part [Part I: hearsay evidence] of this Act 'computer' means any device for storing and processing information, and any reference to information being derived from other information is a reference to its being derived therefrom by calculation, comparison or any other process. (Civil Evidence Act 1968, s 5(6))

Computer bureau

A person carries on a 'computer bureau' if he provides other persons with services in respect of data, and a person provides such services if—

(a) as agent for other persons he causes data held by them to be processed [automatically]; or
(b) he allows other persons the use of equipment in his possession for the processing [of such data].

(Data Protection Act 1984, s 1(6))

CONCEALMENT

'If a man purposely avoids answering a question, and thereby does not state a fact which it is his duty to communicate, that is concealment. Concealment properly so called means non-disclosure of a fact which it is a man's duty to disclose, and [in a contract of insurance] it was his duty to disclose the fact if it was a material fact.' *London Assurance v Mansel* (1879) 11 Ch D 363 at 370, per Jessel MR

Australia [The Hire Purchase Act 1960 (NSW), s 32(1) provides that in any proceedings arising out of a hire purchase agreement where it appears to the court that the hirer was induced to enter into the hire purchase agreement by reason of the 'concealment' of the owner of any material facts the court may re-open the transaction.] ' "Concealment" in the context seems to me to mean more than simply "not communicate". To my mind it means a

conscious or deliberate keeping back of material facts.' *Clark v Esanda Ltd* [1984] 3 NSWLR
1 at 4–5, per Priestly JA

Concealed fraud

'Firstly, what is meant by concealed fraud? [in
the Real Property Limitation Act 1833, s 26
[repealed; see now Limitation Act 1980, s 32].
It does not mean the case of a party entering
wrongfully into possession; it means a case of
designed fraud, by which a party, knowing to
whom the right belongs, conceals the circumstances giving the right, and by means of such
concealment enables himself to enter and
hold.' *Petre v Petre* (1851) 1 Drew 371 at 397,
398, per Kindersley V-C

Of birth

'A final disposition is not necessary, but . . . a
temporary disposition is sufficient to constitute
the offence [of concealment of birth.]' *R v
Perry* (1855) Dears CC 471 at 473, CCR, per
Parke B

'It is an essential part of the statute [Offences
against the Person Act 1861, s 60] that there
should . . . be a secret disposition of the dead
body of the child. There must be a concealment
of the fact of the birth, and that concealment
must be carried out by the secret disposition of
the dead body. That secret disposition must be
of such a nature that anyone coming into the
room [where the body was] would not be likely
to see the body.' *R v Rosenberg* (1906) 70 JP
264 at 264, per Jelf J

To defraud creditors

Canada [Concealment of property to
defraud creditors is an offence under Criminal
Code, RSC 1970, c C-34, s 350(a)(ii).] 'I have
no doubt, however, that the word "conceals"
may, depending on the context, include the
non-disclosure of the existence of tangible
things when there is a duty to disclose their
existence. For example, s 343 of the Code
makes it an offence for a vendor or mortgagor
of property who is served with a written
demand for an abstract of title by or on behalf
of the purchaser or mortgagee to conceal from
him with intent to defraud any instrument
material to the title or any encumbrance on the
title. It seems clear that a vendor or mortgagor
of property who, in the circumstances mentioned in s 343, deliberately with intent to
defraud fails to disclose the existence of a
material instrument, is caught by the section. I
share, however, the view of the learned trial

judge that the word "conceals" as used in
s 350(a)(ii) contemplates some positive conduct on the part of the debtor as opposed to a
mere failure to disclose the existence of the
property, even though under a duty to do so.' *R
v Goulis* (1981) 125 DLR (3d) 138 at 140, 141,
142, Ont CA, per Martin JA

CONCERN

'Looked at apart from the Finance Act 1926
[repealed], the question whether an undertaking constitutes a "concern" does not
depend on the particular way in which the produce is disposed of, but upon the character of
the undertaking viewed as a whole. Just as
occasional and disconnected sales of gravel
won at a gravel pit by a landowner would not
result in that being a concern, so in my view the
absence of any sales would not deprive the
gravel pit of the character of a "concern" if
taken as a whole there is carried on at the
gravel pit a commercial undertaking.' *Mosley v
Wimpey (George) & Co Ltd* [1945] 1 All ER
674 at 682, CA. per Uthwatt J

'"Concern" is a very wide word, and appears
to imply an adequate degree of business organisation for the purpose of carrying on the
undertaking.' *Russell v Scott* [1948] AC 422 at
429, per Viscount Simon

CONCERNED IN

'The plaintiffs sue on a covenant, that the
defendant will not, so long as the plaintiffs
carry on their business, "engage in, or be in any
way concerned or interested in any similar
business within ten miles of the Royal
Exchange". The defence is, that the defendant
is only a servant at weekly wages, and therefore is not "engaged in or in any way concerned
or interested in" the business of his
employers. . . . It is not necessary to say
whether he is "engaged or interested in" the
business, "interested" meaning, in commercial
language, "entitled to profits"; but . . . the
words "concerned in" were intended to cover
this exact case, and I must regard them as
meaning "having something to do with" a similar business.' *Hill (George) & Co v Hill* (1886)
55 LT 769 at 771, per Kekewich J

'It would be absolutely impossible . . . to lay
down with precision what is or is not
comprehended in such words as "interested or
concerned in". You must look at the facts of
the particular case and look at the business

meaning of the words. That is the question to be determined. What was the business meaning of these words? . . . When you are dealing with the carrying on of a business and endeavouring to prevent the carrying on of that business directly or indirectly, or the having any part or concern in that business, I think every business man would quite comprehend that the mere fact of being a creditor of the firm is not being "concerned or interested in" it.' *Cory (William) & Son Ltd v Harrison* [1906] AC 274 at 275, 276, per Lord Halsbury LC

'A person may be "concerned in" a contract even though he does not participate in the profits. . . . A man is . . . "concerned" in a contract if he is in any way a party to it, whether as a sole contractor or as a partner or as an undisclosed principal. A concealed interest is as much an interest as an open interest. The Court will always look at the substance and not at the colourable externals.' *Everett v Griffiths* [1924] 1 KB 941 at 946, 949, per McCardie J

[The respondent had for a number of years carried on a quarry business. In 1935 he sold the business, covenanting with the purchasers not to be 'concerned in' the business of a quarry within a certain distance of that sold. In 1938 his sons decided to start a quarry business on adjacent land, and the respondent put up capital and took part in the negotiations.] 'In my view, in doing what he did, the father was "concerned in" the sons' business. The word "concerned" is of quite general import. Clearly it cannot be limited to "concerned" in the sense of financial interest or of being an employee of the business. Again, I can see no more effective way of being concerned in a business than by providing the capital necessary to establish it, and the word "concerned" seems also to cover the assistance given by the father in the course of the negotiations.' *Batts Combe Quarry Ltd v Ford* [1943] Ch 51 at 53, per Lord Greene MR

CONCILIATION

Australia [By the Constitution (63 & 64 Vict c 12) (Commonwealth of Australia Constitution Act 1900), s 51 (xxxv), Parliament has power to make laws with respect to 'conciliation and arbitration for the prevention and settlement of industrial disputes extending beyond the limits of any one State.'] 'The Commonwealth power of arbitration must be exercised by award "so as to settle" the dispute. But "conciliation" may not be so limited. We have not to decide it now. It may possibly be—we observe only to guard against misapprehension—that the constitutional power of conciliation may, on fuller examination than it has yet received, be found to extend to cases where persuasive reasoning, as distinguished from compulsive order, may induce industrial combatants to come to terms and end or avert a public danger even though the cause of quarrel is not one to be granted by either disputant.' *Federated Clothing Trades of Australian Commonwealth v Archer* (1919) 27 CLR 207 at 213, per Isaacs and Rich JJ

CONCLUDE

A contract of marine insurance is deemed to be concluded when the proposal of the assured is accepted by the insurer, whether the policy be then issued or not; and, for the purpose of showing when the proposal was accepted, reference may be made to the slip or covering note or other customary memorandum of the contract, although it be unstamped. (Marine Insurance Act 1906, s 21)

'A concluded contract is one which settles everything that is necessary to be settled and leaves nothing to be settled by agreement between the parties. Of course it may leave something which still has to be determined, but then that determination must be a determination which does not depend upon the agreement between the parties. . . . You may very well agree that a certain part of the contract of sale, such as price, may be settled by someone else. As a matter of the general law of contract all the essentials have to be settled. What are the essentials may vary according to the particular contract under consideration. We are here dealing with sale, and undoubtedly price is one of the essentials of sale, and if it is left still to be agreed between the parties, then there is no contract.' *May & Butcher Ltd v R* [1934] 2 KB 17 n at 21 n, HL, per Lord Dunedin

CONCLUSIVE

'The first point raises a serious question under s 51 of the Companies Act 1862 [repealed; see now Companies Act 1985 and the Companies (Tables A–F) Regulations 1985, SI 1985/805, art 47], whether after the declaration of the chairman it is competent for the court to receive evidence to impeach that declaration. Treating the matter apart from authority, it seems to me that this question must be answered in the negative. Section 51 enacts that "unless a poll is demanded by at least five [now two; see 1985 regs, supra] members a declaration of the chairman that the resolution has been carried shall be deemed conclusive evidence of the fact without proof of the number or proportion of the votes recorded in favour of or against the same." "Conclusive" seems to me to be a clear word. . . . I cannot regard "conclusive" as equivalent to "sufficient". I think the Legislature intended . . . that the chairman's declaration should be conclusive unless challenged by means of a poll demanded by five [two] members.' *Re Hadleigh Castle Gold Mines Ltd* [1900] 2 Ch 419 at 421–423, per Cozens-Hardy J

[The articles of a company provided that the minutes of meetings of the company and of directors if purporting to be signed by the chairman of the next succeeding meeting should be 'conclusive evidence' without any further proof of the facts therein stated. A shareholder in an action against the company proposed to call evidence challenging the accuracy of minutes so signed.] 'I have no doubt that the words "conclusive evidence" mean what they say; that they are to be a bar to any evidence being tendered to show that the statements in the minutes are not correct.' *Kerr v Mottram (John) Ltd* [1940] Ch 657 at 660, per Simonds J

CONCOURSE

[The definition given by Chatterton V-C in *Downshire [Marquis] v O'Brien* (1887) 19 LR Ir 380, describes a market as a franchise right of having a 'concourse' of buyers and sellers.] 'So far as I have observed from the cases, the phrase "a concourse of buyers and sellers" seems to be used as a coming together of buyers and sellers, a concourse of both, not separate concourses of each. "Concourse", in any event, does not seem to me to be an apt word to apply to persons who are not gathered together in one place for a common purpose, but who come independently and at their own convenience to particular premises with the object of buying from, or selling to, the occupier of these premises.' *Scottish Co-Operative Wholesale Society Ltd v Ulster Farmers Mart Co Ltd* [1959] 2 All ER 486 at 495, HL, per Lord Keith of Avonholm

CONCURRENT

'The appellant urged . . . that there were not concurrent findings in the courts below. . . . It is not necessary that the decision of a judge on any question of fact should be couched in any particular form of words. It appears to me quite enough if he uses language which clearly conveys the meaning that he decides the question one way or the other; and in my view a judge equally finds upon an issue of fact if he clearly expresses his concurrence with the decision of another judge who has decided that issue.' *Mendip Range SS v Radcliffe* [1921] 1 AC 556 at 573, 574, per Lord Atkinson

Australia [An insurance policy contained the following clause—'Additional insurances— Other insurance concurrent herewith is declared and allowed as hereunder and in event of loss this company will only contribute thereto rateably, viz.'] 'The "additional insurances" clause in the policy is only a reference to the insurance mentioned in the proposal with introduction of the word "concurrent" and addition of the company's stipulation as to rateable liability. "Policies are said to be 'concurrent' when they both apply to the same property or groups of property, every group being insured separately in each policy for equal or different amounts"; so Welford and Otter Barry Fire Insurance, 339. . . . The word "concurrent" is, I have no doubt, a very convenient word for the use of insurance companies, but I do not think that a special use among insurers has become generally or much known among persons insured. And when a company introduces the word to refer to insurance about which the proponent has told the company all that it apparently wanted to know, I cannot hold the insured bound to recognise, as a fact, that the company has given his answer a meaning different from his intention.' *Goldman v Southern Union General Insurance Co of Australasia Ltd* [1930] SASR 274 at 278, 279, per Piper J

CONDITION (State)

'While in reference to some things and to some defects in them "condition" and "quality" may mean the same thing, yet . . . they do not either necessarily or even usually do so. . . . "Condition" refers to external and apparent condition, and "quality" to something which is usually not apparent, at all events to an unskilled person. . . . A captain is expected to notice the apparent condition of the goods, though not the quality. He may qualify . . . the words "good order and condition"; but if he leaves them in he does not . . . get rid of the admission as to condition (meaning thereby apparent condition) by saying that the quality is unknown.' *Compania Naviera Vasconzada v Churchill & Sim, Compania Naviera Vasconzada v Burton & Co* [1906] 1 KB 237 at 244, 245, per Channell J

[A policy of insurance exempted the insurers from liability where the insured car was being driven in an unsafe or unroadworthy 'condition'.] 'It is true that there was nothing wrong with the intrinsic character of the vehicle; it was properly designed and manufactured and (so far as we know) maintained. But there was on this journey something wrong with its condition; it was in an overloaded condition. There are other "conditions" of a car which do not affect its intrinsic character. To take a very simple example, it may be in a clean condition or in a dirty condition. Similarly, it may be in a properly loaded or an overloaded condition. A condition does not have to be permanent; it may be a temporary state in which the car is.' *Clarke v National Insurance and Guarantee Corpn Ltd* [1963] 3 All ER 375 at 379, 380, CA, per Pearson LJ; also reported in [1964] 1 QB 199 at 210

Canada 'The word "condition" is a word of flexible meaning, and when applied to a person it is a broad word of indefinite application. It includes, inter alia, within its ambit the social standing or position of the person in the community, and also the person's physical, mental and moral condition.' *Schartner v Schartner* (1970) 10 DLR (3d) 61 at 67, Sask QB, per Disbery J

CONDITION (Stipulation) *See also*
WARRANTY

'There are three meanings of "condition" open to us. The first is the proper meaning, which is given pride of place in the Oxford English Dictionary: "Something demanded or required as a prerequisite to the granting or performance of something else"; and which is carried over into the law in this way: "In a legal instrument, e.g. a . . . contract, a provision on which its legal force or effect is made to depend". . . . The second meaning of "condition" is the common meaning which receives little attention in the Oxford English Dictionary: "a provision, a stipulation". The word is frequently used by laymen and lawyers in this sense. When an agreement is made for the sale of land, it is always subject to "conditions of sale". The Law Society's "Conditions of Sale" are in everyday use. When a building contract

is made, it is usually subject to the RIBA conditions. Whenever a quotation is given or invoice sent, the printed form invariably says it is subject to the "conditions" on the back. In all these cases the word "conditions" simply means *terms* of the contract. . . . I must turn to the third meaning of "condition". It is the meaning given to it by lawyers as a term of art. A "condition" in this sense is a stipulation in a contract which carries with it this consequence: if the promisor breaks a "condition" in any respect, however slight, it gives the other party a right to be quit of his future obligations and to sue for damages unless he, by his conduct, waives the condition, in which case he is bound to perform his future obligations, but can sue for the damages he has suffered. A "condition" in this sense is used in contrast to a "warranty". If a promisor breaks a warranty in any respect, however serious, the other party is not quit of his future obligations. He has to perform them. His only remedy is to sue for damages. . . . Where a word like this word "condition" is capable of two meanings, one of which gives a reasonable result, and the other a most unreasonable one, the court should adopt the reasonable one. In addition, if one of the meanings is an ordinary meaning, and the other is a term of art, then it should be given its ordinary meaning, unless there is evidence from the surrounding circumstances that it was used by both parties as a term of art.' *Wickman Machine Tool Sales Ltd v Schuler (L) AG* [1972] 2 All ER 1173, CA, per Lord Denning MR

In bill of lading

'The bill of lading, in so far as it refers to the charterparty, contains only the ordinary term "all other conditions as per charterparty". That reference . . . does not incorporate, as against the person who acquires title under the bill of lading, and who is not the shipper of the goods but who has bought from the shipper, a clause in the charterparty between the shipper and the shipowner, which would relieve the shipowner from the consequences, in regard to the carriage of the goods, of the negligence of his servants.' *The Draupner* [1909] P 219 at 228, CA, per Kennedy LJ; reversed on a question of fact, [1910] AC 450

'It [the bill of lading] contains the clause "freight and all other conditions and exceptions as per charter". Whatever view one might take of the word "conditions" in the absence of authority, there is now a long line of decisions binding on this Court, and acted on for years by commercial men, that the word "conditions" usually only incorporates "conditions" to be performed by the consignee of the bill of lading, including therein obligations on the shipowner, qualifying or relevant to such conditions.' *Hogarth Shipping Co Ltd v Blyth, Greene, Jourdain & Co Ltd* [1917] 2 KB 534 at 551, CA, per Scrutton LJ

In contract

'In Comyns's Digest, "Condition", where the subject of conditions properly so called is discussed, a case is put in which no condition under seal exists. It is unnecessary, however, to discuss that, because any event on the happening of which another event is to take place is a condition. "I sell you my horse for £10" makes the payment of the £10 as much a condition as if it were contained in an instrument under seal.' *Hayne v Cummings* (1864) 16 CBNS 421 at 427, per Willes J

'A party to a contract who has performed, or is ready and willing to perform, his obligations under that contract is entitled to the performance by the other contracting party of all the obligations which rest upon him. But . . . such obligations are not all of equal importance. There are some which go so directly to the substance of the contract or, in other words, are so essential to its very nature that their non-performance may fairly be considered by the other party as a substantial failure to perform the contract at all. On the other hand there are other obligations which . . . are not so vital that a failure to perform them goes to the substance of the contract. Both classes are equally obligations under the contract, and the breach of any one of them entitles the other party to damages. But in the case of the former class he has the alternative of treating the contract as being completely broken by the non-performance and . . . he can refuse to perform any of the obligations resting upon himself and sue the other party for a total failure to perform the contract. . . . Later usage has consecrated the term "condition" to describe an obligation of the former class and "warranty" to describe an obligation of the latter class. I do not think that the choice of terms is happy, especially so far as regards the word "condition", for it is a word which is used in many other connections and has considerable variety of meaning. But its use with regard to the obligations under a contract is well known and recognised, and no confusion need arise if proper regard be had to the context.' *Wallis, Son & Wells v Pratt & Haynes* [1910] 2 KB 1003 at 1012, CA, per

Fletcher Moulton LJ; approved on appeal, [1911] AC 394

In lease

A condition is a quality annexed to an estate, by virtue of which it may be defeated, enlarged or created upon an uncertain event. A condition may be express or implied. The words 'provided always' or 'upon condition' are suitable for introducing an express condition, but no precise form of words is necessary; it is sufficient if the words used were intended to have the effect of creating a condition, and a clause may operate as a condition, although it includes also words of covenant. If the clause constitutes only an agreement on the part of the lessee to do or not to do a specific act, it will not be construed as a condition, but as a covenant. The conditions in a lease commonly include a power of re-entry on non-payment of rent or breach of covenant. (27 Halsbury's Laws (4th edn) para 320)

In will

[A condition attached in a will to a bequest may amount to a trust.] 'The testator . . . used these words: "I give and bequeath unto . . . Mrs Ada Taylor all my money . . . on condition that she adopts my daughter Alma . . . and also gives to my daughters Jessie . . . and May . . . the sum of £5 each and a like sum of £5 to my son Alexander". . . . The question is what those words mean. . . . The word "condition" is not used in its strict legal sense. It is a gift to Mrs Taylor on condition, in the sense of on the terms or on the trust that she does certain things. . . . A devise, or bequest, on condition that the devisee or legatee makes certain payments does not import a condition in the strict sense of the word, but a trust, so that, though the devisee or legatee dies before the testator and the gift does not take effect, yet the payments must be made; for it is a trust, and no trust fails for want of trustees. When I come to look at the condition, it seems clear that what the testator intended was that Mrs Taylor should receive certain moneys on the term that she performed certain acts.' *Re Frame, Edwards v Taylor* [1939] Ch 700 at 703, 704, per Simonds J

Conditions precedent and subsequent

According to the construction of the will, a condition is either a condition precedent, that is to say such that there is no gift intended at all unless and until the condition is fulfilled, or a condition subsequent, that is to say such that non-compliance with the condition is intended to put an end to the gift. Subject to the terms of the will, the date at which a condition precedent must be fulfilled is the date at which the interest, if any, vests in possession. Where it is doubtful whether a condition is precedent or subsequent, the court prima facie treats it as subsequent, for there is a presumption in favour of early vesting. (50 Halsbury's Laws (4th edn) para 317)

CONDITIONAL SALE AGREEMENT

'Conditional sale agreement' means an agreement for the sale of goods under which the purchase price or part of it is payable by instalments, and the property in the goods is to remain in the seller (notwithstanding that the buyer is to be in possession of the goods) until such conditions as to the payment of instalments or otherwise as may be specified in the agreement are fulfilled. (Health and Safety at Work etc Act 1974, s 53(1). See also the similar definitions in the Consumer Credit Act 1974, s 189(1) and the Sale of Goods Act 1979, s 25(2)(b).)

CONDONATION

Australia 'The verb "condone", as ordinarily used, means to overlook an offence by acting as if it had not been committed. . . . Not only is this the ordinary modern meaning of the English verb, but it is the only relevant sense of the Latin *condonus*. . . . the word "condone" was never, we think, and is not now, used in the . . . purely subjective sense which the word "forgive" is clearly capable of bearing.' *Hemsworth v Hemsworth* [1947] VLR 292 at 303, per cur.

Canada 'The most common definition of condonation is that it is a complete forgiveness of a past offence or offences with full knowledge that such offences have been committed and with the condition implied that a similar offence shall not be repeated and that no similar further matrimonial offences will occur.' *Lovett v Lovett* [1944] 3 WWR 17 at 22, Alta SC, per Howson JA; affd. [1944] 3 WWR 607, Alta CA

Canada 'In *Cramp v Cramp & Freeman* [1920] P 158, McCardie J, gives an illuminative and comprehensive dissertation on the doctrine of condonation. At p 165 he makes a very

significant prediction: ". . . there can be no condonation without something in the nature of reinstatement of the offending spouse". . . . There was nothing in the case at bar "in the nature of reinstatement of the offending spouse". The plaintiff never forgave him for his adultery with the female defendant. She did not submit herself to him from choice, she did so under duress and threat for the sake of her children—a forced submission. There was no condonation.' *Williams v Williams* [1946] 3 WWR 555 at 555, 556, Sask KB, per Anderson J

CONDUCT (Noun)   *See also*
DISORDERLY CONDUCT

'The question raised depends upon what is the true construction of s 28 of the Bankruptcy Act 1883 [which provided that on a bankrupt's application for discharge 'the Court shall take into consideration a report of the official receiver as to the bankrupt's conduct and affairs'; see now the Insolvency Act 1986, s 289]. Does that section give the Court power, when it has to determine whether a discharge shall or shall not be granted to a bankrupt, to take into consideration any other facts than those which are mentioned in the proviso [specifying certain offences] to that section? May the Court consider other conduct and affairs of the bankrupt than what is mentioned in the proviso? . . . If he [the judge] may act upon other conduct and upon the state of the bankrupt's affairs other than the matters mentioned in sub-s (3) of s 28, is there any restriction with regard to the conduct and affairs which he may consider? . . . Now, as to the point whether the judge may consider other conduct and other affairs than those mentioned in sub-s (3), it seems to me perfectly clear upon the construction of s 28 that he may. . . . Does it follow that the judge may take into consideration . . . everything which has been done by the bankrupt during his past life? It seems to me that there must be some limit; and I think the judge ought not to take into his consideration conduct which could not have had anything to do with the bankruptcy; either in producing it or in affecting it in any way after its commencement. . . . Only such conduct or affairs as may or can have had some effect upon the bankruptcy itself ought to be taken into consideration.' *Re Barker, ex p Constable, Re Jones, ex p Jones* (1890) 25 QBD 285 at 291–293, CA, per Lord Esher MR

Australia [By the Bankruptcy Act 1924–59

Cth), s 68 (repealed; see now Bankruptcy Act 1966–1986, s 69(1)), a bankrupt on his public examination can be examined as to his 'conduct', trade dealings, property and affairs.] 'The object of the public examination of a bankrupt is to obtain a full disclosure of his assets and of facts relating to his bankruptcy, but it has the further object of affording protection to the public. A bankrupt cannot refuse to answer relevant questions put to him on the ground that the answers may incriminate him. The word "conduct" in s 68 is ordinarily a word of wide import but this word must, in my opinion, be subject to some restriction. It should, I think, be construed as meaning conduct which could or might have something to do in bringing about the bankruptcy of a debtor or affecting the bankruptcy in any way after its commencement. If the word "conduct" in s 68 of the Bankruptcy Act has an unqualified meaning, a bankrupt on his public examination might be asked and compelled to answer damaging questions which have no bearing on his bankruptcy.' *Re Smith, a Bankrupt* [1960] ALR 740 at 740, 741, per Clyne J

CONDUCT (Of proceedings)

The Prosecution of Offences Act 1979, s 4 provides that nothing in the Act shall preclude any person from instituting or carrying on any criminal proceedings; but the Director of Public Prosecutions may undertake the 'conduct' of those proceedings.] 'It may be observed that while any person may institute or "carry on" any criminal proceedings the director may undertake, at any stage, the "conduct" of those proceedings. The word "conduct" appears to us to be wider than the phrase "carry on" and suggests to our minds that when the director intervenes in a prosecution which has been privately instituted he may do so not exclusively for the purpose of pursuing it by carrying it on, but also with the object of aborting it, that is to say he may "conduct" the proceedings in whatever manner may appear expedient in the public interest. The director will thus intervene in a private prosecution where the issues in the public interest are so grave that the expertise and the resources of the director's office should be brought to bear in order to ensure that the proceedings are properly conducted from the point of view of the prosecution.' *Raymond v A-G* [1982] 2 All ER 487 at 491, per cur.

CONDUCT (Verb)

'A regulation having statutory force which provides that a ship is to be conducted by a pilot does not mean that she is to be navigated under his advice; it means that she must be conducted by him, and that makes pilotage compulsory.' *The Mickleham* [1918] P 166 at 169, CA, per Pickford LJ

'In my view "conduct" means something very like "control" or "manage", so that a man may conduct [a] business without personally undertaking or carrying out every item that is done in the business.' *Pharmaceutical Society of Great Britain (Council of) v Fuller* (1932) 96 JP 422 at 424, CA, per Scrutton LJ

[A local Act required that a sewage disposal works should be 'conducted' so as not to be a nuisance.] 'Counsel for the corporation tried to persuade the court that the word "conducted" was one of narrow significance—narrower, for example, than the words "use and keep" in the Public Health Acts. I cannot so construe it. The word "conduct" seems to me to mean "manage" or "operate".' *Pride of Derby v British Celanese Ltd* [1953] 1 All ER 179 at 189, CA, per Evershed MR; also reported in [1953] Ch 149 at 167

CONFECTIONERY

[The question was whether honey in pots was 'confectionery' within the meaning of that word in the Shops Act 1912 (repealed; see now Shops Act 1950, Sch 1), and therefore exempted from the operation of the Act.] 'The word "confectionery" in the Schedule . . . requires some process in the making of it.' *London County Council v Welford's Surrey Dairies Co Ltd* [1913] 2 KB 529 at 536, DC, per Pickford J

'Run honey means honey run from the comb without admixture of any other substance and without being submitted to any process other than that of extracting it from the comb. . . . Honey in that state is not confectionery. That word in its natural meaning indicates an article prepared from different ingredients by means of some process.' Ibid at 537, per Avory J

'The question turns upon the words of an order which extends the provisions of s 4 of the Shops Act 1912 [repealed; see supra] to the sale by retail of "confectionery (including sweets and chocolates)". . . . The magistrates held that the words of the order, "confectionery (including sweets and chocolates)", referred only to shops in which the sale of confectionary (i.e. pastry) and sweets and chocolates was carried on, and did not apply to shops in which only sweets and chocolates were sold. . . . That is an erroneous interpretation of the words. The sale of confectionery in fact includes the sale of sweets and chocolates, for it is impossible to contend that they are not confectionery. If the words "including sweets and chocolates" were omitted from this order, it would still apply to them.' *Gee v Davies* (1916) 114 LT 1132 at 1133, per Ridley J

'I adjudge that the word "confectionery" as used in the first part of Group 24 [of Part I of Sch 1 to the Purchase Tax Act 1963 (repealed)] means any form of food normally eaten with the fingers and made by a cooking process, other than baking, which contains a substantial amount of sweetening matter. That is the characteristic of both chocolates and sweets; they are normally eaten with the fingers; they are not made by baking, and they have substantial amounts of sweetening matter in them.' *Customs and Excise Comrs v Popcorn House Ltd* [1968] 3 All ER 782 at 784, per Lawton J

CONFER

Australia [The Local Government Act 1919 (NSW), s 342 U (1A) refers to an order 'conferring' on the council powers, authorities, duties and functions with respect to permitting, regulating, restricting or prohibiting, interim development on any land.] 'There can be no doubt that in that context the word "conferring" when it refers to "duties" includes "imposing". [The order] imposes a duty on the council.' *Liverpool City Council v Weir* (1984) 51 LGRA 250 at 254 (H Ct of A, Full Ct)

CONFESSION

'Confession' includes any statement wholly or partly adverse to the person who made it, whether made to a person in authority or not and whether made in words or otherwise. (Police and Criminal Evidence Act 1984, s 82(1))

CONFINEMENT

In this Chapter [Part II: Chapter I— contributory benefits] (a) 'confinement' means labour resulting in the issue of a living child, or labour after 28 weeks of pregnancy resulting in the issue of a child whether alive or dead, and

'confined' shall be construed accordingly; and (b) references to the date of the confinement shall be taken as referring, where labour begun on one day results in the issue of a child on another, to the date of the issue of the child, or if the woman is confined of twins or a greater number of children, to the date of the issue of the last of them. (Social Security Act 1975, s 23(1))

'Confinement' means the birth of a living child or the birth of a child whether living or dead after twenty-eight weeks of pregnancy. (Employment Protection (Consolidation) Act 1978, s 153(1))

CONFIRMATION

Of estate

'I find it difficult to understand how an estate that is expressly limited in restoration and in confirmation of an estate of exactly the same quality can be regarded as defeating that estate and creating a new one. The word "restoration", though it might suggest that the original life estate had suffered some change, to my mind amounts to no more than saying that it must be treated as still on foot, and the word "confirmation" has no real meaning if it once be assumed that the estate has been destroyed. It must be remembered that these words have for many years been used by learned conveyancers whose preciseness of language had often been the subject of undeserved reproach, and it is to my mind impossible to assume that they meant the opposite of what they say, for you cannot "confirm" what does not exist.' *Parr v A-G* [1926] AC 239 at 265, 266, per Lord Buckmaster

Of order

[By the Municipal Corporations Act 1837, s 38 (repealed by the Municipal Corporations Act 1882), certain orders by the justices for the payment of money had to be 'confirmed' by the borough council.] ' "Confirmed" is a word, the natural meaning of which is more than "indorsed" or "verified". It is equivalent to "approved"; and it is here to be construed in its natural sense.' *R v York Corpn* (1853) 1 E & B 588 at 596, per Wightman J

Of will

[By a later codicil a testator confirmed an earlier will, which included an intermediate codicil revoking a particular bequest.] 'The anguage of the statute which regulates these matters in the Colony [Nova Scotia] as well as n this country, so far as it is necessary in this ase to state it, is this: "No will or codicil shall ᴇe revived otherwise than by a codicil . . . howing an intention to revive the same." . . . Their Lordships are of opinion . . . that if the ᴍeaning be, as they consider it is, that he [the ᴇstator] confirms the will, . . . that is in itself a estoration of the . . . bequest . . . and their ᴌordships are also of opinion that the word 'confirm" is an apt word, and expresses the ᴍeaning . . . of the word "revive", which is ᴜsed in the statute.' *McLeod v McNab* [1891] ᴀC 471 at 474–476, per cur.

It is settled by authority that the effect of such ᴀ phrase as "I confirm my will in other ᴇespects" is a republication of the will.' *Re Champion, Dudley v Champion* [1893] 1 Ch ᴌ01 at 109, per North J; affd. [1893] 1 Ch 115, ᴄA

Canada 'The word "confirm" in English has many and varied meanings. In respect to wills it usually means that the will confirmed is republished. As regards minutes of meetings, confirmation verifies the accuracy of the minutes. It sometimes implies a knowledge of a defect in the act to be confirmed and the right to reject or ratify it. Confirmation has been defined as the action of making firm or sure, strengthening, settling, establishing institutions, opinions, etc and where by-laws are required to be confirmed by shareholders, by their confirmation the shareholders make the by-law their own act.' *R v Jasperson, ex p Knights* [1958] OWN 360 at 362, 363, Ont SC, per Ferguson J; revsd [1959] OR 63, Ont CA, without affecting definition

CONFIRMED CREDIT *See* LETTER OF
  CREDIT

CONFLICT OF INTEREST
  TRANSACTION

United States A conflict of interest transaction is a transaction with the corporation in which a director of the corporation has a direct or indirect interest. (Revised Model Business Corporation Act 1984, s 8.31(a))

CONFLICT OF LAWS

The branch of English law known as the conflict of laws, or private international law, in contradistinction to the ordinary local or domestic law of England, is concerned with cases having a foreign element. By a 'foreign element' is meant a contract with some system of law other than English law. Such a contract may exist, for example, because a contract was made or to be performed in a foreign country, or because a tort was committed there, or because property was situated there, or because the parties are not English. In the conflict of laws, 'foreign element' and 'foreign country' mean a non-English element and a country other than England. From the point of view of the conflict of laws, Scotland or Northern Ireland is for most purposes as much a foreign country as France or Germany. (8 Halsbury's Laws (4th edn) para 401)

CONFUSION

Ownership of goods may be acquired by confusion or intermixture if the goods, when mixed, are indistinguishable. If the goods are mixed by agreement or consent, the proprietors have an interest in common in proportion to their respective shares; if mixed by accident, or the act of a third party, for which neither owner is responsible, the proprietors become owners in common of the mixed property in proportion of the amounts contributed. Where, however, one man wilfully mixes his goods with those of another without the approbation or knowledge of the other, the whole belongs to that other person. (35 Halsbury's Laws (4th edn) para 1139)

CONGREGATION

'What is necessary to constitute a congregation has not been very strictly defined: but it has been commonly considered that "where two or three are gathered there together" there is a sufficient number to constitute a congregation.' *Barnes v Shore* (1846) 1 Rob Eccl 382 at 396, 397, per Sir Herbert Jenner Fust

'It was contended that . . . three ladies and one other person do not constitute a congregation. It is no doubt a small congregation, but I am unaware of any authority which makes a large multitude of persons essential to the constitution of a congregation.' *Re Hutchinson's Trusts* [1914] 1 IR 271 at 282, 283, per O'Connor MR

CONJOINTLY

[Under a will an estate was devised to a person and after her death to her two daughters and niece 'conjointly'.] 'The word "conjointly" is not inapplicable to a gift of property in equal shares so long as the property remains undivided.' *De Hertel v Goddard* (1896) 66 LJPC 90 at 91, per cur.

CONJURATION

'The conspiracy of which the appellants were found guilty was a conspiracy to contravene s 4 of the Witchcraft Act 1735 [repealed by the Fraudulent Mediums Act 1951] and the material words in count 1 of the indictment were: "To pretend to exercise or use a kind of conjuration, to wit, that through the agency of the said Helen Duncan spirits of deceased persons should appear to be present in fact in such place as the said Helen Duncan then was in, and that the said spirits were communicating with living persons then and there present.". . . The point submitted by Mr Loseby [counsel for the appellants] is that the word "conjuration" in the Act of 1735 has only one meaning, and the meaning has been well defined and crystallised in law. He says it bears the meaning in the language of Cowel's Interpreter (a publication of 1672) as contained in the following passage: "It is especially used for such as have personal conference with the Devil or evil spirits.". . . We must be allowed to doubt whether Cowel's Interpreter possesses the authority claimed for it by Mr Loseby, and we certainly do not think that this meaning or interpretation is to be given to the words "any kind of conjuration" in the Act of 1735. Indeed, the express alteration from the statute of James I [Stat (1603–4) 1 Jac I, c 12], which is being repealed, and the use of the words "any kind of conjuration" without reference to spirits, evil or otherwise, would seem to indicate the contrary. In the sixteenth and seventeenth centuries the word "conjuration" was commonly used with reference to traffic with spirits. In those centuries the minds of men were greatly concerned with evils which they believed arose from such conference, and as a result of the teaching of the Church, based possibly on passages in the Bible, all such spirits were regarded as, and were apt to be described as, evil spirits. Conjuration of these evil spirits was an offence, it was said, against God and religion and was usually linked with witchcraft, enchantment, invocation and sorcery, the punishment for which, as for heresy, was burning in early times. But "conjuration" was not a word which was to be taken to mean only "conjuration of evil and wicked spirits.' That was an express meaning given to it by the

inclusion of the words in the statutes where such words appear. The Oxford English Dictionary gives examples of its use in different ages right down to modern times. Coke's Institutes, third part, ch 6, associates the word "conjuration" with "invocation" and seems to suggest that the two words have the same meaning. . . . In our judgment, the words of the section with which we are concerned in this case are all-important. What was aimed at, as shown by the language of the statute itself, was that ignorant persons should not be deluded or defrauded by the pretence to exercise or use any kind of conjuration. The reference to "evil spirits" is omitted, and the words "any kind of" were added, and in our opinion, these words are wide enough to cover the conspiracy alleged.' *R v Duncan* [1944] KB 713, CCA, per cur.

CONNECT

'Do not the words "make a connection" between two things mean connect the two things, and nothing more or less than that? "Make a connection" does not seem to me to mean "make or construct a particular tube or tunnel or conduit", nor is that one physical thing what alone is referred to. I think it means physically to connect.' *Battersea Borough Council v County of London Electric Supply Co Ltd* [1913] 2 Ch 248 at 255, CA, per Cozens-Hardy MR

CONNECTED WITH   *See also* IN CONNECTION WITH

CONNECTION

Canada 'One of the very generally accepted meanings of "connection" is relation between things one of which is bound up with or involved in another; or again "having to do with".' *Re Nanaimo Community Hotel Ltd* [1944] 4 DLR 638 at 639, BCSC, per Macfarlane J; affd. [1945] 3 DLR 225, BCCA

CONNUBIAL INTERCOURSE

Australia 'In reading the earlier cases, it is necessary to remember that the expression "connubial intercourse" and several similar expressions are not used as meaning mere sexual intercourse as such, but as denoting the general relationship of husband and wife, the *onsortium vitæ* or "conjugal cohabitation" or *matrimonial relations" of which Cussen J peaks in *Tulk v Tulk* ((1907) VLR 64 at 5–66).' *Dobson v Dobson* [1947] VLR 244 at 251, per Fullager J

CONQUEST

By an ante-nuptial Scots settlement the wife assigned and conveyed whatever property she might 'conquest' or acquire during the marriage.] 'The word "conquest" is a word of technical signification, and, according to Mr Bell, in § 1974 of his Principles of the Law of Scotland, "when used substantively in marriage contracts, comprehends whatever is acquired, whether heritable or moveable, during the marriage by industry, economy, purchase, or donation; but not what comes by succession, or legacy, or accession to a subject already acquired". The ordinary provision of conquest inserted in marriage contracts applies only to the husband's acquisitions during the marriage. Lord Cowan, in his judgment in this case says, "A provision made by a wife of her conquest during the marriage is unprecedented.". . . . The word in the present case is not used substantively, but as a verb. . . . I understand that the word "conquest" when used as a verb is more flexible than when used as a substantive. . . . From the nature of the deed in its constitution of this trust, and from the character of its provisions, I am satisfied that the words "conquest" and "acquire" were not used in a strict and technical sense, but were meant to comprehend everything which might fall to the possession of the wife during the marriage.' *Diggens v Gordon* (1867) LR 1 Sc & Div 136 at 138–140, per Lord Chelmsford LC

CONSCIENTIOUS OBJECTOR

'A true conscientious objector . . . is one who on religious grounds thinks it wrong to kill and to resist force by force. He thinks that that is the teaching of Christ. The true conscientious objector remembers other undoubted teachings of Christ—namely, to help the injured, the suffering and the helpless—and remembers that there is such a thing as duty. The true conscientious objector is ready to do ambulance work, rescue work, ARP work and work among the helpless in shelters. There are many conscientious objectors who have proved the genuineness of their belief by that which they have done. This plaintiff likened himself to Quakers. Everybody knows the fine

work done by Quakers, particularly in the last war. One remembers the work they did on mine-sweepers, probably the most dangerous work there is. They were logical in their views. They recognised their duty to do all they could except to kill if need be. The true conscientious objector is loyal to his country. . . . He does not scoff at what other people do, and he is not a defeatist.' *Newell v Gillingham Corpn* [1941] 1 All ER 552 at 553, 554, per Atkinson J

CONSCRIPTION

Australia 'The word "conscription", in the sense that seems to be most apposite for the present purposes, means the compulsory enlistment of men (or women) for military (including naval or air force) service. The expression "civil conscription" appears to mean the calling up of persons for compulsory service other than military service.' *General Practitioners Society in Australia v Commonwealth of Australia* (1980) 31 ALR 369 at 387, per Gibbs J

CONSECRATION *See* CHURCH

CONSECUTIVE

Canada [While serving a term of life imprisonment, the accused escaped custody and was sentenced to two years 'consecutive' to life term to be served before he began to serve life imprisonment again pursuant to s 137(1) of the Criminal Code [RSC 1970, c C-34]. On appeal to Ontario Court of Appeal against the imposition of a consecutive sentence in these circumstances, the appeal was allowed.] 'In our respectful view, the language of the present s 137(1) is such that it is not open to a court to impose a sentence that, in effect, interrupts the sentence being served at the time of the escape. We construe "consecutively" as meaning, in its context and in accordance with its standard dictionary definition, "following immediately upon" the serving of the balance of the sentence being served at the time of the escape.' *Caddedu v R* (1980) 19 CR 93 at 96, Ont CA, per Morden JA

CONSENT

'The words used in the Act [Bankruptcy Act 1869 (repealed)] are "consent and permission". Those words imply knowledge. You cannot consent to a thing unless you have knowledge of it.' *Re Caughey, ex p Ford* (1876) 1 Ch D 521 at 528, CA, per Jessel MR

'I think it could hardly be disputed that although in the strict technical etymology of the word, "consent" as well as "agreement" implies two parties, yet "consent", used in the ordinary way in which that term is used, is satisfied when it is found that one person has given what is popularly known as consent.' *Bewley v Atkinson* (1879) 13 Ch D 283 at 298, 299, CA, per Thesiger LJ

[The Landlord and Tenant Act 1954, s 23(4) is concerned with a situation where an immediate landlord or his predecessor in title has 'consented' to a breach of covenant, or the immediate landlord has acquiesced in it.] 'I agree . . . that in the context of s 23(4) of the Act, whatever consent or acquiescence may mean in different contexts, in that context "consent" is put in plain antithesis to "acquiescence", and that, therefore, if something falls within the description "acquiescence", it is not consent. The difference which is pointed out between the two in this context is that "consent" involves some affirmative acceptance, not merely a standing by and absence of objection. The affirmative acceptance may be in writing, which is the clearest obviously; it may be oral; it may conceivably even be by conduct, such as nodding the head in a specific way in response to an express request for consent. But it must be something more than merely standing by and not objecting.' *Bell v Alfred Franks & Bartlett Co Ltd* [1980] 1 All ER 356 at 362, 363, CA, per Megaw LJ

'I am wholly satisfied that as a matter of English law a consent is not vitiated by a failure on the part of [a] doctor to give the patient sufficient information before the consent [to treatment] is given. It is only if the consent is obtained by fraud or by misrepresentation of the nature of what is to be done that it can be said that an apparent consent is not a true consent.' *Sidaway v Bethlem Royal Hospital Governors* [1984] 1 All ER 1018 at 1028, CA, per Sir John Donaldson MR

Canada   'I should think that, where one of two persons has opium in his custody or possession, another who knows that fact, even though he has no measure of control over it, but nevertheless co-operates with the person who has such custody in an effort to prevent detection, thereby "consents" within s 5(2) [of the Criminal Code RSC, 1927, c 36 (see now

RSC 1970, c C-34, s 3).' *R v Lou Hay Hung* [1946] OR 187 at 201, Ont CA, per Roach JA

New Zealand   'Section 7(1) [of the Adoption Act 1955] expressly requires that "consents to the adoption by all persons (if any) whose consents are required in accordance with this section shall be filed in the court", and, of course, that is a requirement that the documents be so filed. Thus, for the purposes of the court the only means contemplated by the Act for signifying and communicating any such consent is the formal document itself.' *M v G* [1982] 2 NZLR 673 at 682, CA, per Roper CJ, per Woodhouse P

CONSENT ORDER

'There is a great deal of difference between a consent order in the technical sense and an order which embodies provisions to which neither party objects. The mere fact that one side submits to an order does not make that order a consent order within the technical meaning of that expression.' *Chandless-Chandless v Nicholson* [1942] 2 KB 321 at 324, CA, per Lord Greene MR

'The expression "a consent order" may suggest some compromise or arrangement which might be inconsistent with the provisions of the Acts [Rent Restrictions Acts]. When the defendant is agreeing to submit to judgment because he is satisfied that the plaintiff can establish his right to an order under the Acts, it might be advisable to avoid the use of the word "consent", which may have a wider meaning and cover cases where the "consent" was the result of an arrangement which could not properly be made the basis of an order.' *Thorne v Smith* [1947] 1 All ER 39 at 44, CA, per Somervell LJ

'We have had a discussion about "consent orders". It should be clearly understood by the profession that, when an order is expressed to be made "by consent", it is ambiguous. There are two meanings to the words "by consent". That was observed by Lord Greene MR in *Chandless-Chandless v Nicholson* [supra]. One meaning is this: the words "by consent" may evidence a real contract between the parties. In such a case the court will only interfere with such an order on the same grounds as it would with any other contract. The other meaning is this: the words "by consent" may mean "the parties hereto not objecting". In such a case there is no real contract between the parties. The order can be altered or varied by the court in the same circumstances as any other order

hat is made by the court without the consent of
he parties.' *Siebe Gorman & Co Ltd v
'neupac Ltd* [1982] 1 All ER 377 at 380, CA,
•er Lord Denning MR

CONSEQUENCES   *See also* IN
    CONSEQUENCE OF

Of hostilities or warlike operations

The material words [in a policy of marine
insurance] . . . are "Consequences of hosti-
ities or warlike operations" or more succinctly
'Consequences of warlike operations". The
natural starting point in considering these
words is *Ionides v Universal Marine Insurance
Co* [(1863) 14 CBNS 259]. . . . In that case the
words were construed as being subject to the
ordinary rule observed in marine insurance
that the proximate cause is what is material in
deciding if a loss is recoverable. "Consequences" is a compendious description of the
perils to be excepted (or included), not a
description relating to a loss. As Willes J said in
Ionides v Universal Marine Insurance Co [at
290]: "The words all consequences of hostilities refer to the totality of causes, not to their
sequence.". . . "Proximate" here means, not
latest in time, but predominant in effici-
ency. . . . Cause here means what a business
or seafaring man would take to be the cause
without too microscopic analysis but on a
broad view . . . The clause was, in the first
instance, deliberately phrased to cover all the
possible varieties of war-risk losses. The
words . . . postulate (i) loss or damage (ii) due
to perils which can be described as consequences of hostilities, to which was later added
warlike operations.' *Yorkshire Dale SS Co Ltd
v Minister of War Transport* [1942] AC 691 at
705–707, per Lord Wright

'It is so easy to slip unconsciously into treating
the word "consequences" in the phrase "consequences of hostilities and warlike operations" not as itself a named peril, but as the loss
or damage consequential on—i.e., caused
by—a named peril. It may be urged that this
criticism of the loose use in thought, and even
in judgments, of the word "consequences";
without distinguishing between its two insurance senses, is academic and of little legal
import; but I do not agree. Once the true interpretation is recognised, namely, that the word
"consequences", in the established phrase is
descriptive of perils and therefore that every
opening which arises out of hostilities or
warlike operations and every act or thing done

for those purposes constitutes a specific war
peril "consequential" on the generic perils
named, the causal nexus between peril and loss
becomes clearer, just because the particular
happening, or act, is nearer to the loss; the
cause is more obviously "proximate", in the
sense given to that word in the decided cases. If
so, the above interpretation does seem to me to
be helpful for the light it throws on the final
inquiry, namely, whether the loss or damage
claimed was proximately caused by an insured
peril. On the facts of the present case, there is I
think no doubt that one such "consequence" of
the warlike operation (in my sense of the
insured peril) was the stowage, for the purpose
of the warlike operation, on No 2 well deck, of
certain military cargo of a kind, and in a manner likely, on the intended voyage in North
Atlantic winter weather, to do damage to the
ship. That act of stowage and the consequential
carriage of that cargo in that position, were
both acts done by the assured in furtherance
and therefore, consequential on the admittedly
warlike operation undertaken by the assured.
Each was thus "a consequence of the warlike
operation" of the *Priam* and insured specifically *eo nomine*; and so far as that stowage
was the cause of the damage which resulted
therefrom to the ship, the assured's case is
thereby established. . . . All the various perils
insured against in a war risks policy, as of those
excepted by an f.c. and s. clause from an ordinary marine policy, are generically covered by
the one phrase "the consequences of hostilities
and warlike operations". "Hostilities" and
"warlike operations" are not introduced as
separate and specific perils: indeed it is only
their "consequences" which the policy
supports to insure; and the only task in any
particular dispute is to ascertain whether some
particular "consequence" of hostilities or
warlike operations was the proximate cause of
the loss; the word "consequence" in that context *ex hypothesi* in the policy not meaning
effect, but cause. Its use by the draftsman has,
however, naturally tended to obscure the
whole discussion, just because the word "consequence" usually means effect and not cause.
Even in the language of the noble Lords in the
relevant cases in their House, the word "consequence" is not infrequently quoted as referring
not to the peril, but to the result, caused by
their operation of the peril. I venture humbly
to think that if one keeps one's mind on the
true insurance interpretation, namely, that
"the consequences of warlike operations" is
just a description of one wide category of
perils, with particular aspects of them covered

by the word "consequences", contained in the full Lloyd's policy *pari passu* with perils of the seas, but excepted by the f.c. and s. clause, it helps to a clearer understanding of the contrast to be drawn between the causal effect of any one insured peril and a loss or damage received casually during, but not caused by, any one of the insured perils.' *Ocean Steamship Co Ltd v Liverpool & London War Risks Association, Ltd* [1946] KB 561 at 569, 570, 573, 574, CA, per Scott LJ; *varied sub nom. Liverpool and London War Risks Association Ltd v Ocean Steamship Co Ltd* [1948] AC 243, HL

CONSERVANCY

'Conservancy authority' means a person or body of persons (whether corporate or unincorporate) having a duty or power imposed or conferred by or under an enactment to conserve, maintain or improve the navigation of a tidal water, and not being a navigation authority or a harbour authority. (Water Resources Act 1963, s 135)

CONSERVATION

In subsection (1) above [section 1(1): establishment of Nature Conservancy Council] 'nature conservation' means the conservation of flora, fauna or geological or physiographical features. (Nature Conservancy Council Act 1973, s 1(2))

Soil conservation

New Zealand 'I think that Parliament has deliberately left "soil conservation" unrestricted by express definition and has deliberately conferred very wide rights of objection. "Soil conservation" in the Acts [Soil Conservation and Rivers Control Act 1941 and Water and Soil Conservation Act 1967] is not confined to, but does include, the retention of soil for the purposes of production.' *Metekingi v Rangitikei-Wanganui Regional Water Board*, [1975] 2 NZLR 150 at 160, per Cooke J

CONSIDER

Canada [Expropriating authority was required by Expropriations Act, RSO 1970, c 154, s 8 (see now RSO 1980, c 148, s 8) to consider report of inquiry officer.] 'What is involved in [the] duty to "consider" the report? Certainly, the board must have the report

before it, and the evidence shows that each member had a copy at least three days before the approval meeting. Although the word "consider" imports a time element, I do not think a Court can or should impose any arbitrary temporal standard any more than it can or should monitor the degree of required concentration upon the contents of the report. In the present case, the board was in session on the report in committee of the whole for about one hour and one-half, and had before it a critical set of opposing reasons which it ultimately accepted. I see nothing improper, in view of the independent power of the board as an approving authority, in its having a pre-packaged opinion before it prepared by its solicitor. Unless the good faith, indeed the honesty, of the members of the board is called in question, the fact that they are briefed or counselled in advance to a rejection of the report is not a ground for concluding that they did not "consider" it.' *Walters v Essex County Board of Education* (1973) 38 DLR (3d) 693 at 697, SCC, per Laskin J

CONSIDERABLE

Australia [The expressed consideration for a guarantee, as stated upon the face of it, was 'in consideration of your promise to do a considerable portion of your business with this company'.] 'A fair and reasonable interpretation of "a considerable portion of your business" is, I think, at least a half.' *Lindsay v Stevenson (L) & Sons Ltd* (1891) 17 VLR 112 at 115, per Webb J

CONSIDERATION   *See also* CONTRACT

'Valuable consideration' includes marriage, but does not include a nominal consideration in money. (Land Registration Act 1925, s 3)

'A valuable consideration, in the sense of the law, may consist either in some right, interest, profit, or benefit accruing to the one party, or some forbearance, detriment, loss or responsibility, given, suffered, or undertaken by the other.' *Currie v Misa* (1875) LR 10 Exch 153 at 162, per cur.; affd. sub nom. *Misa v Currie* (1876) 1 App Cas 554

'The definition of "consideration" given in Selwyn's Nisi Prius (8th edn) p 47, which is cited and adopted by Tindal CJ in the case of *Laythoarp v Bryant* [(1836) 3 Scott 238] is this: "Any act of the plaintiff from which the defendant derives a benefit or advantage, or any labour, detriment, or inconvenience sustained by the plaintiff, provided such act is performed or such inconvenience suffered by the plaintiff, with the consent, either express or implied, of the defendant".' *Carlill v Carbolic Smoke Ball Co* [1893] 1 QB 256 at 271, CA, per Bowen LJ

I am content to adopt from a work of Sir Frederick Pollock . . . the following words as to consideration: "An act or forbearance of one party, or the promise thereof, is the price for which the promise of the other is bought, and the promise thus given for value is enforceable" (Pollock on Contracts (8th edn) p 175).' *Dunlop Pneumatic Tyre Co Ltd v Selfridge & Co Ltd* [1915] AC 847 at 855, HL, per Lord Dunedin

Bill of sale

'The Act [Bills of Sale Act 1878, s 8] requires that the bill of sale shall state the consideration for which it is given, by which I understand that which the grantor receives for giving the bill of sale.' *Re Rogers, ex p Challinor* (1880) 16 Ch D 260 at 268, CA, per Lush LJ

Factor taken into account

'I confess that I think that confusion can arise from the multiplicity of words which have been used in this case as suggested criteria for the testing of the validity of the exercise of a statutory power. The words used have included "objects", "purposes", "motives", "motivation", "reasons", "grounds" and "considerations". In the end, it seems to me, the simplest and clearest way to state the matter is by reference to "considerations". A "consideration", I apprehend, is something which one takes into account as a factor in arriving at a decision.' *Hanks v Minister of Housing and Local Government* [1963] 1 All ER 47 at 55, per Megaw J; also reported in [1963] 1 QB 999 at 1020

CONSIGNMENT

'It is true that some difficulty and confusion arises through the use of the phrase "on consignment" which is ordinarily used in commercial transactions in reference to the delivery of goods to an agent for sale by him on behalf of the consignor as principal. But the phrase need not necessarily bear this meaning. It is frequently used where goods are delivered "on approval" or "on sale or return" where a sale *to* and not *by* the consignee is contemplated.'

Universal Guarantee Pty Ltd v Metters Ltd [1966] WAR 74 at 79, per Jackson J

Australia [The Carriage of Goods by Land (Carriers) Liabilities Act 1967–1986 (Qld), s 2 defines a 'consignment' to mean the quantity of goods carried at one and the same time in or on any one vehicle for any one consignor. Section 6 of the Act provides that a carrier shall not be liable for the loss of or injury to any goods entrusted to him under a contract of carriage in an amount greater than a certain sum per 'consignment'.] 'A coincidental identity of consignor under a number of contracts of carriage does not make the goods a single consignment simply because they happen to be carried at one and the same time in or on a vehicle. There remain as many different consignments as there are contracts of carriage provided all the goods are consigned under a contract of carriage which are carried in or on one vehicle at one and the same time. The purpose of the definition is to provide that there may be more consignments than there are contracts of carriage when goods consigned under any particular contract of carriage are carried by the carrier in more than one vehicle.' *Penn Elastic v Sadleirs* (1976) 10 ALR 185 at 189, per Stephen J

CONSOLIDATED FUND

To enable Parliament to control the expenditure of the revenue there is kept at the Bank of England an account entitled 'Her Majesty's Exchequer' into which is paid all revenue from whatever source, except money directed to be applied as an appropriation in aid of money for a particular service. Such receipts together constitute the Consolidated Fund, and issues from that fund are subject to control by the Comptroller and Auditor General, who is a permanent official, independent of the executive government. (34 Halsbury's Laws (4th edn) para 1442)

CONSOLIDATION

Of actions

'At common law, what was known as consolidation was in effect an order to stay several actions pending the trial of one, on the terms that the defendants in the actions that were stayed agreed that, in the event of judgment being given for the plaintiff in the action which was tried, they would consent to a similar judgment being entered in the other actions. But consolidation in Admiralty means that the several causes shall be tried together as one case.' *The Strathgarry* [1895] P 264 at 268, per Bruce J

'The term "consolidation" cannot, as it seems to me, have any application when the actions or suits are brought by different persons, one by A against B, and another by B against A. . . . The practice of trying at the same time petitions by a husband and a wife has been adopted merely for convenience, and does not operate to consolidate the two suits in the sense of constituting one suit out of the two.' *Forbes-Smith v Forbes-Smith & Chadwick* [1901] P 258 at 270, 271, CA, per Collins LJ

Of mortgages

'A mortgagee, who holds several distinct mortgages under the same mortgagor, redeemable, not by express contract, but only by virtue of the right which (in English jurisprudence) is called "equity of redemption", may, within certain limits, and against certain persons (entitled to redeem all or some of them), "consolidate" them, that is, treat them as one and decline to be redeemed as to any, unless he is redeemed as to all. This doctrine of consolidation is well established. . . . There is no difficulty in its application, when all the mortgages, whether originally made to the same mortgagee, or having come into a single hand by subsequent assignments, are redeemable at the same time by the same person. Its extension to a case in which, after that state of things has once existed, the equities of redemption have become separated by the act of the person in whom they had been combined, though it may, perhaps, be open to objection on some practical grounds, rests upon an intelligible principle. The purchaser of an equity of redemption must take it as it stood at the time of his purchase, subject to all other equities which then affected it in the hands of his vendor; of which the right of the mortgagee to consolidate his charge on that particular property with other charges then held by him on other property at the same time redeemable under the same mortgage was one. The mortgagee cannot lose that right, because the mortgagor thinks fit to separate the equities of redemption.' *Jennings v Jordan* (1881) 6 App Cas 698 at 700, 701, per Lord Selborne LC

Of statutes   *See also* STATUTE

'The discussion in *Farrell v Alexander* [[1976] 2 All ER 721, HL] as to the proper approach to the construction of consolidating Acts is valuable. I would, however, add two comments to the guidance there given. First, when construing a consolidating statute, it is particularly useful to have recourse to the legislative history if a real difficulty arises. Consolidation is, or is intended by Parliament to be, the re-enactment "in a more convenient, lucid and economical form" [ibid, per Lord Simon at 733] of existing statute law. It is, in its "pure" form . . . neither amendment nor reform nor codification, but re-enactment. Strictly, as draftsmen have always recognised, a pure consolidation must incorporate the law as it stands, including its difficulties and ambiguities. The earlier statute law, therefore, and judicial decisions as to its meaning and purpose are very relevant, if there by difficulty or ambiguity. Second, I would not think it correct to distinguish between the various types of consolidation. There are now three and more may be added in the future. They are: (1) "pure" consolidation, i.e. re-enactment; (2) consolidation with "corrections and minor improvements"; (3) consolidation with Law Commission amendments. I have discussed the first. The second was made possible by the Consolidation of Enactments (Procedure) Act 1949 which confines permissible amendment to very minor matters. Certainly that Act in no way changes the essential character of consolidation, which is re-enactment. It cannot make any less legitimate a reference to the legislative history where there is difficulty or ambiguity. The same observations apply to consolidation with Law Commission amendments. But here there is an added feature. The Law Commission publishes a report which specifies the particular mischief (or mischiefs) which its proposed amendments are intended to remove. It is, therefore, perfectly plain to what extent one may use legislative history in the interpretation of a Law Commission consolidation.' *R v Heron* [1982] 1 All ER 993 at 999, HL, per Lord Scarman

CONSORT

Australia [The Police Act 1936 (SA), s 85(1)(j) (now Summary Offences Act 1953–1986, s 13) provides that any person shall be an idle and disorderly person within the meaning of the Act who habitually 'consorts' with reputed thieves, prostitutes, or persons having no visible means of support.] ' "Consorting", in s 85(1)(j) requires, of course, some form of overt activity. The notion of "associations" by persons comprehends (inter alia) the grouping of two or more persons where the individuals enjoy, or at least tolerate, each other, whether they congregate for no more than a few moments or for longer periods. The congregating together may be merely upon an accidental meeting of the group and without any discoverable motive whatsoever. The idea implicit in "consorting", however, suggests a more or less close personal relationship: at least some degree of familiarity or intimacy with persons, or attraction from or an enjoyment of some feature in common, that results in a tendency towards companionship. Where there is consorting it may be expected to be in obedience to an inclination or impulse to gravitate into the presence of or, if accidentally in such presence, to remain in a group with some other person or persons. The fundamental ingredient is companionship. The fact that people meet (inter alia) to carry on some trade or occupation is not inconsistent with a fraternising contemporary therewith amounting to consorting.' *Dias v O'Sullivan* [1949] ALR 586 at 590, per Mayo J

Australia '"Consorting" [Police Offences Act 1935–1986 (Tas), s 6] denotes some seeking or acceptance of association.' *Brown v Bryan* [1963] Tas SR 1, per cur.

CONSORTIUM

'Companionship, love, affection, comfort, mutual services, sexual intercourse—all belong to the married state. Taken together, they make up the consortium; but I cannot think that the loss of one element, however grievous it may be . . . can be regarded as the loss of the consortium within the meaning of the decided cases. Still less could any impairment of one of the elements be so regarded. Consortium, I think, is one and indivisible. The law gives a remedy for its loss, but for nothing short of that.' *Best v Samuel Fox & Co Ltd* [1951] 2 KB 639 at 665, CA, per Birkett LJ; affd. [1952] 2 All ER 394, HL

[*See also* the summary of decisions on the meaning of 'consortium' given by Birkett LJ, ibid at 657–661.]

Australia 'The question of consortium is . . . a different matter from that of physical separation. Consortium has been defined as a partnership or association; but in the matrimonial sense it implies much more than these rather cold words suggest. It involves a sharing of two

lives, a sharing of the joys and sorrows of each party, of their successes and disappointments. In its fullest sense it implies a companionship between each of them, entertainment of mutual friends, sexual intercourse—all those elements which, when combined, justify the old common law dictum that a man and his wife are one person. It is not necessary that all these elements should be present to establish the existence of a matrimonial consortium; one or very few may exist and they may show that the matrimonial consortium has not been destroyed; that it is still alive although in a maimed and attentuated form.' *Crabtree v Crabtree (No 2)* [1964] ALR 820 at 821, per Selby J

CONSPICUOUS

New Zealand 'Admittedly, "clearly visible" is one accepted dictionary meaning of the word "conspicuous", but the meaning to be given to it in s 12(1)(d) [of the Hire Purchase Act 1971, s 12(1)(d)] must take its colour from the context in which the word is there used. Section 12(1)(d) contemplated that the exempting statement for which conspicuity is sought will appear in a hire purchase agreement containing a variety of terms and conditions. If the exempting statement is only as clearly visible as the rest of the document (but no more so) that will not suffice. Something more is required by the statutory provision. The exempting statement must stand out from the rest of the document. It must have a distinctiveness which would alert the hirer to its presence. The alternative dictionary meaning of "striking to the eye" meets the test. Therefore, to be "conspicuous" for this purpose a statement must be one which is striking to the eye, which attracts special attention to it against the background of the other printed material in the agreement which itself is likely to be clearly visible. There must therefore be a distinctiveness or conspicuity such as to make a statement stand out in a prominent way in the document in which it is used.' *Clyde Engineering v Russell Walker Ltd* [1984] 2 NZLR 343 at 347, per McMullin J

United States 'Conspicuous': A term or clause is conspicuous when it is so written that a reasonable person against whom it is to operate ought to have noticed it. Whether a term or clause is conspicuous or not is for decision by the court. (Uniform Consumer Credit Code 1969, s 1.301(6))

United States 'Conspicuous': A term or clause is conspicuous when it is so written that a reasonable person against whom it is to operate ought to have noticed it. A printed heading in capitals (as: NON-NEGOTIABLE BILL OF LADING) is conspicuous. Language in the body of a form is 'conspicuous' if it is in larger or other contrasting type or color. But in a telegram any stated term is 'conspicuous'. Whether a term or clause is 'conspicuous' or not is for decision by the court. (Uniform Commercial Code 1978, s 1–201(10))

United States 'Conspicuous' means so written that a reasonable person against whom the writing is to operate should have noticed it. For example, printing in italics or boldface or contrasting color, or typing in capitals or underlined, is conspicuous. (Revised Model Business Corporation Act 1984, s 1.40(3))

CONSPIRACY

Conspiracy consists in the agreement of two or more persons to do an unlawful act, or to do a lawful act by unlawful means. It is an indictable offence at common law, the punishment for which is imprisonment or fine or both in the discretion of the court.

The essence of the offence of conspiracy is the fact of combination by agreement. The agreement may be express or implied, or in part express and in part implied. The conspiracy arises and the offence is committed as soon as the agreement is made; and the offence continues to be committed so long as the combination persists, that is until the conspiratorial agreement is terminated by completion of its performance or by abandonment or frustration or however it may be. The actus reus in a conspiracy is the agreement to execute the illegal conduct, not the execution of it. It is not enough that two or more persons pursued the same unlawful object at the same time or in the same place; it is necessary to show a meeting of minds, a consensus to effect an unlawful purpose. It is not, however, necessary that each conspirator should have been in communication with every other. (11 Halsbury's Laws (4th edn) para 58)

Subject to the following provisions of this Part [Part I] of this Act, if a person agrees with any other person or persons that a course of conduct shall be pursued which, if the agreement is carried out in accordance with their intentions, either—

(a) will necessarily amount to or involve the commission of any offence or offences by one or more of the parties to the agreement, or

(b) would do so but for the existence of facts which render the commission of the offence or any of the offences impossible,

he is guilty of conspiracy to commit the offence or offences in question. (Criminal Law Act 1977, s 1(1) as substituted by s 5 of the Criminal Attempts Act 1981)

[Part I (ss 1–5) amends the law with respect to criminal conspiracy, restricting the ambit of the offence and limiting the penalties. Section 2 exempts certain persons (e.g. spouses) from liability, and s 5 abolishes (with some exceptions) the offence of conspiracy at common law.]

'A conspiracy consists not merely in the intention of two or more, but in the agreement of two or more to do an unlawful act, or to do a lawful act by unlawful means.' *Mulcahy v R* (1868) LR 3 HL 306, in the opinion of the Judge (Willes J) at 317

'Intimidation, violence, molestation, or the procuring of people to break their contracts, are all of them unlawful acts; and I entertain no doubt that a combination to procure people to do such acts is a conspiracy and unlawful.' *Mogul SS Co v McGregor, Gow & Co* [1892] AC 25 at 37, per Lord Halsbury LC

'A conspiracy exists when two or more combine to do an unlawful act or to do a lawful act by unlawful means. No conspiracy is, in my opinion, known to the law, which has not for its object the accomplishment of an unlawful act (not necessarily a criminal act) or which does not involve the use of unlawful means.' *Boots v Grundy* (1900) 82 LT 769 at 772, per Bigham J

'A conspiracy involves an agreement expressed or implied. A conspiratorial agreement is not a contract, not legally binding, because it is unlawful. But as an agreement it has three stages, namely (1) making or formation, (2) performance or implementation, (3) discharge or termination. When the conspiratorial agreement has been made, the offence of conspiracy is complete, it has been committed and the conspirators can be prosecuted even though no performance has taken place: *Aspinall* [(1876) 2 QBD 48 at 58, 59], per Brett JA. But the fact that the offence of conspiracy is complete at that stage does not mean that the conspiratorial agreement is finished with. It is not dead. If it is being performed, it is very much alive. So long as the performance continues, it is operating, it is being carried out by the conspirators, and it is governing or at any rate influencing their conduct. The conspiratorial agreement continues in operation and therefore in existence until it is discharged (terminated) by completion of its performance or by abandonment or frustration or however it may be.' *Director of Public Prosecutions v Doot* [1973] 1 All ER 940 at 951, HL, per Lord Pearson.

'In the *Poulterers' Case* [(1610) 9 Co Rep 55b] it seems to have been decided once and for all that the essence of the crime of conspiracy lay in the unlawful agreement and not in its execution, and the principle of this decision was taken over by the Court of King's Bench after it assumed whatever remained of the tattered mantle of the Court of Star Chamber, and the principle has ever after remained undisputed.' *Kamara v Director of Public Prosecutions* [1973] 2 All ER 1242 at 1253, HL, per Lord Hailsham of St Marylebone LC

'It must be a self-evident proposition that one man acting alone cannot conspire and therefore cannot be guilty of conspiracy. It is the very essence of a conspiracy that a person agrees with some other person or persons.' *R v Shannon* [1974] 2 All ER 1009 at 1029, HL, per Lord Morris of Borth-y-Gest

'Conspiracy as a criminal offence has a long history. It consists of "the agreement of two or more persons to effect any unlawful purpose, whether as their ultimate aim, or only as a means to it, and the crime is complete if there is such agreement, even though nothing is done in pursuance of it". I cite from Viscount Simon LC's now classic speech in *Crofter Hand Woven Harris Tweed Co Ltd v Veitch* [[1942] 1 All ER 142 at 146]. Regarded as a civil tort, however, conspiracy is a highly anomalous cause of action. The gist of the cause of action is damage to the plaintiff; so long as it remains unexecuted, the agreement, which alone constitutes the crime of conspiracy, causes no damage; it is only acts done in execution of the agreement that are capable of doing that. So the tort, unlike the crime, consists not of agreement but of concerted action taken pursuant to agreement.' *Lonrho Ltd v Shell Petroleum Co Ltd* [1981] 2 All ER 456 at 463, HL, per Lord Diplock

'Part I of the Criminal Law Act 1977 effected a radical amendment of the law of criminal conspiracy. Criminal conspiracies are now of four kinds only. (1) A conspiracy to commit one or more substantive criminal offences contrary to s 1 of the 1977 Act. The maximum penalty for such a conspiracy is the maximum appropriate to the substantive offence or, if more than one, the most serious of the substantive offences involved in the conspiracy: s 3. Proceedings under s 1 in respect of a conspiracy confined to summary offences may not be instituted except by or with the consent of the Director of Public Prosecutions: s 4(1). (2) A conspiracy made an offence as such by some other enactment, e.g. s 3(a) of the Explosive Substances Act 1883, which is expressly excluded from the scope of s 1 of the 1977 Act by s 5(6). (3) A common law conspiracy to defraud: s 5(2). (4) A common law conspiracy to corrupt public morals or outrage public decency: s 5(3). The surviving common law conspiracies are subject to no limit as to penalty and require no statutory consent to the institution of proceedings. . . . In the overwhelming majority of conspiracy cases it will be obvious that performance of the agreement which constitutes the conspiracy would necessarily involve, and frequently will in fact have already involved, the commission of one or more substantive offences by one or more of the conspirators. In such cases one or more counts of conspiracy, as appropriate, should be charged under s 1 of the 1977 Act. Only the exceptional fraudulent agreements will need to be charged as common law conspiracies to defraud, when either it is clear that performance of the agreement constituting the conspiracy would not have involved the commission by any conspirator of any substantive offence or it is uncertain whether or not it would do so. In case of doubt, it may be appropriate to include two counts in the indictment in the alternative. It would then be for the judge to decide how to leave the case to the jury at the conclusion of the evidence, bearing always in mind that the crucial issue is whether performance of the agreement constituting the conspiracy would necessarily involve the commission of a substantive offence by a conspirator. If it would, it is a s 1 conspiracy. If it would not, it is common law conspiracy to defraud.' *R v Ayres* [1984] 1 All ER 619 at 621, 625, 626, HL, per Lord Bridge of Harwich

'An essential ingredient in the crime of conspiring to commit a specific offence or offences under s 1(1) of the 1977 [Criminal Law] Act is that the accused should agree that a course of conduct be pursued which he knows must involve the commission by one or more of the parties to the agreement of that offence or those offences. But, beyond the mere fact of agreement, the necessary mens rea of the crime is, in my opinion, established if, and only if, it is shown that the accused, when he entered into the agreement, intended to play some part in the agreed course of conduct in furtherance of the criminal purpose which the agreed course of conduct was intended to achieve.' *R v Anderson* [1985] 2 All ER 961 at 965, per Lord Bridge

Canada 'The word "conspire" derives from two Latin words, "con" and "spirare", meaning "to breathe together". To conspire is to agree. The essence of criminal conspiracy is proof of agreement. On a charge of conspiracy the agreement itself is the gist of the offence: *Paradis v The King* (1933) 61 CCC 184 at 186, [1934] 2 DLR 88 at p 90, [1934] SCR 165 at p 168. The actus reus is the fact of agreement: *Director of Public Prosecutions v Nock* [1978] 3 WLR 57 at p 66 (HL). The agreement reached by the co-conspirators may contemplate a number of acts or offences. Any number of persons may be privy to it. Additional persons may join the ongoing scheme while others may drop out. So long as there is a continuing overall, dominant plan there may be changes in methods of operation, personnel, or victims, without bringing the conspiracy to an end. The important inquiry is not as to the acts done in pursuance of the agreement, but whether there was, in fact, a common agreement to which the acts are referable and to which all of the alleged offenders were privy.' *R v Cotroni; Papalia v R* (1979) 93 DLR (3d) 161 at 177, SCC, per Dickson J

New Zealand 'Viewed simply in conceptual terms we incline to the view that s 66(2) [of the Crimes Act] has no application to a conspiracy charge for the reason that the concept of probable consequence of a common purpose used in that provision is inconsistent with the concept of conspiracy. It is of the essence of a conspiracy that there must be a common design, a meeting of the minds directed to the crime which is to be committed. That points to a state of knowledge on the part of the accused at the time the agreement is made between the conspirators. Reference to an offence which is a probable consequence of the crime which the conspirators have actually agreed to commit is at odds with an agreed common design to commit an agreed particular crime. In the end, and whatever academic arguments may be advanced to the contrary, we think that in the interests of certainty and as a matter of policy, the Court ought to reject the application of s 66(2) to a charge of conspiracy under s 310. To accept its application would run counter to the whole settled principle that the minds of the conspirators must go to the single conspiracy charged.' *R v Gemmell* [1985] 2 NZLR 740 at 748, per McMullin J

CONSTABLE

'A constable is one of the most ancient officers in the realm for the conservation of the peace, and by his office he is a conservator of the peace.' *Anon* (1593) Poph 12 at 13, per Popham CJ

'In my opinion, it is true to say that every police officer in England and Wales, whether he be a member of the metropolitan police force or a member of the police force of a county, city or borough, holds the office of constable, and within his constablewick has all the duties and rights conferred by common law or statute upon the holders of that office. He is required to take an oath of office, and his primary duty is to preserve the King's Peace. It follows that a police officer is a person who holds office under His Majesty within the meaning of the Official Secrets Acts.' *Lewis v Cattle* [1938] 2 All ER 368 at 370, DC, per Lord Hewart CJ

CONSTITUENCY

In this Act, and, except where the context otherwise requires, in any other Act passed after the Representation of the People Act 1948, 'constituency' means an area having separate representation in the House of Commons. (Parliamentary Constituencies Act 1987, s 1(2))

CONSTITUTED

'The term "constituted" [as applied to a company] is not equivalent to "incorporated"; it is of wider import. It seems to be equivalent to "established".' *Re East & West India Dock Co* (1888) 38 Ch D 576 at 582, per Chitty J

CONSTITUTIONAL LAW

Constitutional law is that part of English law which relates to the system of government of the country. The United Kingdom has no comprehensive document or documents of particular sanctity that might be said to embody 'the constitution', but there is a framework of rules defining the functions, composition and inter-relationship of the institutions of government, and the rights and duties of the governed. These rules describe the location, conferment, distribution, exercise and limitation of political power among the instruments of the state and may be said to embody all the elements of a constitution.

Nevertheless the boundaries of constitutional law have never been satisfactorily defined, partly because there is no constitutional document possessing an extraordinary sanctity, partly because the constitutional rules are susceptible of change, and partly because there is no fundamental difference between public law and private law and it is not possible to assign exclusive provinces to each. Thus, generally speaking, the same courts of law have jurisdiction whether the case raises questions of public or private law. (8 Halsbury's Laws (4th edn) para 801)

CONSTRUCT   *See also* ADAPT

Construction and adaptation of vehicles

'By Sch I to the Road Traffic Act 1934 [repealed; see now Road Traffic Act 1960, s 253] . . . all vehicles are divided into three classes. . . . Passenger vehicles are "vehicles constructed solely for the carriage of passengers and their effects". Goods vehicles on the other hand are vehicles constructed or adapted for use for the conveyance of goods or burden of any description. . . . Those words "constructed or adapted" . . . are both past participles, and the words mean "originally constructed", or, notwithstanding the original construction, subsequently adapted for use for the conveyance of goods or burden of any description.' *Hubbard v Messenger* [1938] 1 KB 300 at 306, 307, DC, per Lord Hewart CJ

'It was his [the magistrate's] opinion that the word "constructed" in the definition of a light locomotive in s 2, sub-s 1(b) of the [Road Traffic] Act of 1930 [repealed; see now s 253(7) of the Road Traffic Act 1960] meant "originally constructed". . . . In my view, "constructed" in that Act means constructed at any material time. The fact that originally a vehicle was constructed as a heavy motor-car will not operate to prevent its being a light locomotive if thereafter a reconstruction takes place.' *Keeble v Miller* [1950] 1 KB 601 at 604, 605, per Lynskey J

[The definition of a goods vehicle in s 27(7) of the Vehicles (Excise) Act 1949 (repealed; see now the Road Traffic Regulation Act 1984, s 138(3)), was: a mechanically propelled vehicle 'constructed or adapted' for use and used for the conveyance of goods, etc.] 'For my part, I confess that the definition section (s 27(1)) of the Act does connote that the adaptation for use is the adapting of the structure. It seems to me that the conjunction of the words "constructed or adapted" are really saying "originally constructed or where the structure is subsequently altered".' *Taylor v Mead* [1961] 1 All ER 626 at 628, per Lord Parker CJ

New Zealand 'The duty imposed on the Commissioners is to construct such works as may be necessary. . . . When the [Taieri Land Drainage] Act of 1910 [NZ] was passed the Silverstream was an existing watercourse, and the works required to be done may not be all of the nature of construction. It is obvious, therefore, that the word "construct" is here used in the wider sense of "execute" or "carry out".' *Brodrick v Blackie* (1915) 34 NZLR 1113 at 1116, 1117, per Sim J; also reported [1916] GLR 35 at 36

CONSTRUCTION (Building)

'Construction', in relation to a camp or building, includes the making of any alterations and additions to any building to adapt it for use in connection with a camp. (Camps Act 1939, s 6)

Of street

'Construction' and 'improvement', in relation to a street, include the planting, laying out, maintenance and protection of trees, shrubs and grass verges in and beside the street. (Highways Act 1980, s 232(9))

CONSTRUCTION (Interpretation)

'The court has no power of its own motion to declare how the discretion conferred by a statute shall be exercised or to lay down rules about it. It derives its power from the statute itself according to the construction which it puts on it—"construction" being a word that embraces not only the interpretation of the words used but also the ascertainment of the true intent of the statute, considered in relation to the branch of the law with which it is dealing.' *Berry v British Transport Commission* [1961] 3 All ER 65 at 75, CA, per Devlin LJ; also reported [1962] 1 QB 306 at 326

CONSTRUCTION MORTGAGE *See*
MORTGAGE

CONSTRUCTIVE DESERTION *See*
DESERTION

CONSTRUCTIVE FRAUD *See* FRAUD

CONSTRUCTIVE MALICE *See*
MALICE

CONSTRUCTIVE NOTICE

'I must not part with this case without expressing my entire concurrence in what has on many occasions of late years fallen from judges of great eminence on the subject of constructive notice, namely, that it is highly inexpedient for Courts of Equity to extend the doctrine—to attempt to apply it to cases to which it has not hitherto been held applicable. Where a person has actual notice of any matter of fact, there can be no danger of doing injustice if he is held to be bound by all the consequences of that which he knows to exist. But where he has not actual notice, he ought not to be treated as if he had notice, unless the circumstances are such as enable the Court to say, not only that he might have acquired, but also, that he ought to have acquired, the notice with which it is sought to affect him—that he would have acquired it but for his gross negligence in the conduct of the business in question.' *Ware v Egmont (Lord)* (1854) 4 De GM & G 460 at 473, per Lord Cranworth LC

'Constructive notice, properly so called, is the knowledge which the Courts impute to a person upon a presumption so strong of the existence of the knowledge, that it cannot be allowed to be rebutted, either from his knowing something which ought to have put him upon further inquiry, or from his wilfully abstaining from inquiry, to avoid notice.' *Espin v Pemberton* (1859) 3 De G & J 547 at 554, per Lord Chelmsford LC

'The doctrine of constructive notice is wholly equitable; it is not known to the common law. . . . The doctrine is a dangerous one. It is contrary to the truth. It is wholly founded on the assumption that a man does not know the facts; and yet it is said that constructively he does know them.' *English & Scottish Mercantile Investment Co v Brunton* [1892] 2 QB 700 at 707, 708, CA, per Lord Esher MR

'As regards the extension of the equitable doctrines of constructive notice to commercial transactions, the Courts have always set their faces resolutely against it. The equitable doctrines of constructive notice are common enough in dealing with the land and estates, with which the Court is familiar; but there have been repeated protests against the introduction into commercial transactions of anything like an extension of those doctrines, and the protest is founded on perfect good sense. In dealing with estates in land title is everything, and it can be leisurely investigated; in commercial transactions possession is everything, and there is no time to investigate title; and if we were to extend the doctrine of constructive notice to commercial transactions we should be doing infinite mischief and paralysing the trade of the country.' *Manchester Trust v Furness* [1895] 2 QB 539 at 545, CA, per Lindley LJ

CONSTRUCTIVE TOTAL LOSS *See also* ABANDONMENT (of ship); LOSS

(1) Subject to any express provision in the policy, there is a constructive total loss where the subject-matter insured is reasonably abandoned on account of its actual total loss appearing to be unavoidable, or because it could not be preserved from actual total loss without an expenditure which would exceed its value when the expenditure had been incurred.

(2) In particular, there is a constructive total loss—
   (i) Where the assured is deprived of the possession of his ship or goods by a peril insured against, and (a) it is unlikely that he can recover the ship or goods, as the case may be, or (b) the cost of recovering the ship or goods, as the case may be, would exceed their value when recovered; or
   (ii) In the case of damage to a ship, where she is so damaged by a peril insured against that the cost of repairing the damage would exceed the value of the ship when repaired.
      In estimating the cost of repairs, no deduction is to be made in respect of general average contributions to those repairs payable to other interests, but account is to be taken of the expense of future salvage operations and of any future general average contributions to which the ship would be liable if repaired; or

(iii) In the case of damage to goods, where the cost of repairing the damage and forwarding the goods to their destination would exceed their value on arrival.
(Marine Insurance Act 1906, s 60)

'Where a ship is damaged by a peril insured against, if the cost of repairing the damage, including the cost of raising, would exceed the value of the ship when repaired, she is constructively lost within the meaning of s 21 [of the Merchant Shipping Act 1894]. . . . The learned judge below decided that for insurance purposes the ship was undoubtedly "constructively lost" . . . but that it did not follow that the same rules as are applied for insurance purposes were necessarily to be applied in determining whether a ship is constructively lost under s 21. In my opinion the judgment is erroneous on this point. The expression "constructively lost" has no meaning as applied to a ship, except in connection with marine insurance, and a vessel which is a constructive total loss within the meaning of the term in marine insurance is "constructively lost" within the meaning of s 21 of the Merchant Shipping Act 1894.' *Manchester Ship Canal Co v Horlock* [1914] 2 Ch 199 at 206, 208, CA, per Swinfen Eady LJ

'The expression "constructive total loss" . . . is a technical expression relating to the rights and liabilities of assured and underwriters under marine policies and is not proper to be employed in dealing with the position as between owner and charterer under a charterparty. . . . Constructive total loss is a conception with which, as such, the charterparty has nothing to do. . . . The question what facts will constitute constructive total loss under a hull policy where the vessel is damaged by a peril of the sea appears to me to be fundamentally different from the question what facts will discharge the contract contained in the charterparty when the vessel has been damaged by a peril of the sea. In each case the amount of expenditure required to repair the vessel (if she is repairable) is a vital consideration.' *Carras v London & Scottish Assurance Corpn Ltd* [1936] 1 KB 291 at 313, 314, per Greene LJ

'A constructive total loss is a device intended to subserve the purpose of indemnity by enabling the assured, when, by insured perils, the postulated danger of loss or deprivation is caused, to disentangle himself, subject to definite limits and conditions, from the danger and throw the burden on the underwriters. If the assured elects to avail himself of this option, he must do so by giving notice of abandonment within a reasonable time after the receipt of sufficient information. He is not allowed to await events to see how things turn out, or to decide what may best suit his interests. If he duly elects to abandon on good grounds, the risk is ended, because the assured can recover as for a total loss and the salvage vests in the underwriter.' *Rickards v Forestal Land Timber & Rlys Co Ltd, Robertson v Middows Ltd, Kahn v Howard (W H) Brothers & Co Ltd* [1942] AC 50 at 83, 84, 86, 87, per Lord Wright

CONSTRUCTIVE TRUST   *See* TRUST

CONSULTANT

'Counsel for the plaintiff pressed us with some observations in the cases concerning consultants. He said that the defendant was a part-time consultant, and that a consultant was in a different position from the staff of the hospital. I think that counsel for the defendant gave the correct answer when he said that, whatever may have been the position of a consultant in former times, nowadays, since the National Health Service Act 1946, the term "consultant" does not denote a particular relationship between a doctor and a hospital. It is simply a title denoting his place in the hierarchy of the hospital staff. He is a senior member of the staff, and is just as much a member of the staff as the house surgeon is. Whether he is called specialist or consultant makes no difference.' *Razzel v Snowball* [1954] 3 All ER 429 at 432, 433, CA, per Denning LJ

CONSULTATION

[The New Towns Act 1946, s 1(1) (repealed; see now the New Towns Act 1981, s 1(1)), provides that the Minister of Town and Country Planning (now the Secretary of State for the Environment) might make an order designating the site of a new town after 'consultation' with local authorities.] 'The word "consultation" is one that is in general use and that is well understood. No useful purpose would, in my view, be served by formulating words of definition. Nor would it be appropriate to seek to lay down the manner in which consultation must take place. The Act does not prescribe any particular form of consultation. If a complaint is made of failure to consult, it will be for the court to examine the facts and circumstances of the particular case and to decide whether consultation was, in fact, held. Consultation may often be a somewhat continuous process and the happenings at one meeting may form the background of a later one.' *Fletcher v Minister of Town and Country Planning* [1947] 2 All ER 496 at 500, per Morris J

'A certain amount has been said as to what consultation means. In my view . . . it means that, on the one side, the Minister must supply sufficient information to the local authority to enable them to tender advice and, on the other hand, a sufficient opportunity must be given to the local authority to tender that advice.' *Rollo v Minister of Town and Country Planning* [1948] 1 All ER 13 at 17, per Lord Greene MR

CONSUMABLE PRODUCE

'Consumable produce' means produce grown for consumption or other use after severance or separation from the land or other growing medium on or in which it is grown. (Rent (Agriculture) Act 1976, s 1(2))

CONSUME

'Speaking for myself, I think that the word "consume" in s 4 [of the Licensing Act 1921 (repealed; see now Licensing Act 1964, s 59)] is to be construed in its natural and ordinary sense, and that there is no reason why a different meaning should be sought for it unless the literal construction of the word would involve a result so unreasonable that the Legislature cannot have contemplated it; in other words, it is not necessary to torture the expression into meaning something artificial if its natural meaning is not repugnant to reason. Looking at the statute as a whole and the apparent object of the Legislature in securing that there should be an interval during the afternoon when intoxicating liquor is not to be sold or supplied, I can see nothing repugnant to that object in a provision which would prevent, for example, persons purchasing intoxicating liquor in one licensed house, shortly before the termination of the permitted hours, and proceeding to adjoining licensed premises and claiming to be entitled to consume the liquor there on the ground that it had not been sold or supplied in those premises. The word "consume" means what it says, and the fact that the intoxicating liquor being consumed on the licensed premises was not sold or supplied there is an irrelevant circumstance.' *Caldwell v*

Jones [1923] 2 KB 309 at 312, DC, per Lord Hewart CJ

CONSUMER

'The rights given by s 41 [of a special Act] . . . are given only to consumers of water. The appellants say that the expression "any consumer of water" in that section means any person who wishes or proposes to become a consumer of water . . . that is doing too great violence to the language . . . the expression "any consumer of water" must mean a person who is actually consuming water or who, at the least, is entitled to demand a supply of water for his consumption and is taking the necessary steps to obtain it.' *Cooke, Sons & Co v New River Governor & Co* (1899) 14 App Cas 698 at 706, per Lord Macnaghten

Australia 'If two or more persons share liquor from one glass or other container, I suppose each individual will be a separate consumer. The word "consumer" does not require that one person ingest the full contents of some glass or container: e.g. *Caldwell v Jones* [1923] 2 KB 309 at pp 312, 313.' *O'Sullivan v De Young* [1949] SASR 159 at 171, per Mayo J

Debt collection

United States The term 'consumer' means any natural person obligated or allegedly obligated to pay any debt. (Fair Debt Collection Practices Act 1977, s 803(3))

United States The adjective 'consumer', used with reference to a credit transaction, characterizes the transaction as one in which the party to whom credit is offered or extended is a natural person, and the money, property, or services which are the subject of the transaction are primarily for personal, family, or household purposes. (Truth in Lending Act 1968, s 103(h))

CONSUMER CREDIT SALE *See* SALE

CONSUMER DEBT

United States '[C]onsumer debt' means debt incurred by an individual primarily for personal, family, or household purposes. . . . (Bankruptcy Act 1978, s 101(7))

CONSUMER GOODS *See* GOODS

CONSUMER LEASE

United States
(1) 'Consumer lease' means a lease of goods
   (a) which a lessor regularly engaged in the business of leasing makes to a person, other than an organization, who takes under the lease primarily for a personal, family, household, or agricultural purpose,
   (b) in which the amount payable under the lease does not exceed $25,000, and
   (c) which is for a term exceeding four months.
(2) 'Consumer lease' does not include a lease made pursuant to a lender credit card or similar arrangement.
(3) The amount of $25,000 in subsection (1) is subject to change pursuant to the provisions on adjustment of dollar amounts (Section 1.106).
(Uniform Consumer Credit Code 1969, s 2.106)

CONSUMER LOAN

United States Except with respect to a loan primarily secured by an interest in land (Section 3.105), 'consumer loan' is a loan made by a person regularly engaged in the business of making loans in which
(a) the debtor is a person other than an organization;
(b) the debt is incurred primarily for a person, family, household, or agricultural purpose;
(c) either the debt is payable in instalments or a loan finance charge is made; and
(d) either the principal does not exceed $25,000 or the debt is secured by an interest in land.
(Uniform Consumer Credit Code 1969, s 3.104(1))

CONSUMER PRODUCT

United States The term 'consumer product' means any article, or component part thereof, produced or distributed (i) for sale to a consumer for use in or around a permanent or temporary household or residence, a school, in recreation, or otherwise, or (ii) for the personal use, consumption or enjoyment of a consumer in or around a permanent or temporary household or residence, a school, in recreation, or otherwise. . . . (Consumer Product Safety Act 1972, s 3(a)(1))

CONSUMER RELATED SALE

United States A 'consumer related sale' is a sale of goods, services, or an interest in land which is not subject to the provisions of this Act applying to consumer credit sales and in which the amount financed does not exceed $25,000 if
(a) the buyer is a person other than an organization, or
(b) the debt is secured primarily by a security interest in a one or two family dwelling occupied by a person related to the debtor.
(Uniform Consumer Credit Code 1969, s 2.602(1))

CONSUMER SALE

In this section 'consumer sale' means a sale of goods (other than a sale by auction or by competitive tender) by a seller in the course of a business where the goods (a) are of a type ordinarily bought for private use or consumption; and (b) are sold to a person who does not buy or hold himself out as buying them in the course of a business. (Sale of Goods Act 1979, Sch 1, para 11)

CONSUMER USE

Goods are to be regarded as 'in consumer use' when a person is using them, or has them in his possession for use, otherwise than exclusively for the purposes of a business. (Unfair Contract Terms Act 1977, s 5(2)(a))

CONSUMMATION

Canada ' "Consummation" of the marriage refers, then, to the demonstration by the parties to the union of the capacity of each of them to engage in mutual sexual intercourse, demonstrated, that is, by performance of the act itself while the marriage subsists, as to which their relationship before marriage is irrelevant.' *Goss v Goss* (1973) 41 DLR (3d) 742 at 745, Man QB, per Wilson J

CONTAMINANT

Canada [Accused was charged with offence of adding 'contaminant' to the environment by removing topsoil and exposing sand.] 'In my view, a substance may be a contaminant under the section, whenever man, by changing the natural state of that substance, causes it to be a substance which may cause injury or damage to property or to plant or animal life. . . . Sand blown by the wind from a naturally occurring beach would not be a contaminant, because neither its existence nor its condition in a state in which it is likely to be borne by the wind, are caused by the activities of man. But, where sand which in its natural state would remain stationary is moved by man, as by a blasting operation, or is exposed and made subject to movement by the winds, as in the circumstances of the case at bar, then the sand, in my judgment, falls within the definition of contaminant, because it is no longer in its natural state.' *R v Glen Leven Properties Ltd* (1977) 76 DLR (3d) 172 at 177, 178, Ont Div Ct, per Southey J

CONTAIN

Australia [The Public Health Act 1962 (Tas) provides in section 63(1)(ba) that an article of food is adulterated if it 'contains' a foreign substance.] 'The word "contain" in ordinary usage is defined by the Oxford English Dictionary, in the most apt for present purposes of the meanings given as: "to have in it, to hold; to compromise; enclose". But although in the case of a cake something wholly within it, such as some article which had got into the mixture before it was cooked, would undoubtedly be enclosed by the cake and therefore be contained in it when cooked, it does not seem to me that the ordinary meaning of the word "contain" necessarily excludes something found on or in the surface of the cake after it is cooked. I agree that to some extent it is a question of fact. For example, an article which had become partly embedded in the icing of a cake before the icing dried might be said to be contained in the cake; whereas an article which had been dropped on to the surface after it was cooked and the icing dried and was simply resting on the surface, would not I should think be said to be contained in it.' *Doyle v Maypole Bakery Pty Ltd* [1981] Tas R 376 at 377–378, per Neasey J

CONTAINER

'Container', in relation to a medicinal product, means the bottle, jar, box, packet or other receptacle which contains or is to contain it,

not being a capsule, cachet or other article in which the product is or is to be administered, and where any such receptacle is or is to be contained in another such receptacle, includes the former but does not include the latter receptacle. (Medicines Act 1968, s 132)

'Container or label' includes anything in, on or with which goods are supplied or offered to be supplied. (Trade Descriptions Act 1972, s 1(6))

'Container' means an article of equipment having a minimum volume of 8 cubic metres, designed and constructed for repeated use for the inter-nodal carriage of goods by road, rail and water and for interchange between these forms of transport. (International Carriage of Perishable Foodstuffs Act 1976, s 19(1))

'Container' includes any bundle or package and any box, cask or other receptacle whatsoever. (Customs and Excise Management Act 1979, s 1(1))

'Container' includes any basket, pail, tray, package or receptacle of any kind, whether open or closed. (Agriculture and Horticulture Act 1964, s 24; Food Act 1984, s 132(1))

'Container' . . . includes any form of packaging of goods for sale as a single item, whether by way of wholly or partly enclosing the goods or by way of attaching the goods to, or winding the goods round, some other article, and in particular includes a wrapper or confining band. (Weights and Measures Act 1985, s 94(1))

Australia [The Factories, Shops and Industries Act 1962–1986 (NSW), s 35(1)(a) provides that in every factory in which there is any molten metal or hot or corrosive substance there shall be provided and maintained 'containers' of such design, material and construction as to ensure safe storage, handling, transport and use of such metal or substance within the factory.] 'It seems to me that what the section requires is the provision of containers in the sense of reservoirs in which those substances may be contained and stored. This pipe [a means of transferring liquid from one part of the plant to another] was not a receptacle constructed to contain or store acid; it was a means of conveying acid from one part of the plant to another. Its function was essentially dynamic rather than static. The fact that it did contain acid, in the sense that there was acid in it, is insufficient to my mind to answer the particular meaning which the section requires to be given to the word "container".' *Moulang v CSR Chemicals Ltd* (1974) 2 NSWLR 38 at 42, per Samuel AJ

CONTANGO

'Contango' is used in two different senses. In one sense it is the consideration paid to the seller by a purchaser wishing to carry over a bargain, which consideration is usually reckoned either at a price per share or other security or as a percentage on the price of the security. In its other and more usual sense, it has a meaning synonymous with continuation or carrying-over. (45 Halsbury's Laws (4th edn) para 101)

'When a client directs a broker to buy stock for which the client is not himself finding the money to pay at the time, the money is provided by the broker, and he borrows the money for the purpose. This is done sometimes, no doubt, by a pure and simple loan; but in a very large majority of cases . . . the thing is done by the broker finding the money on "contango", and then what happens is this: he is treated, not as the mortgagee or pledgee of the shares for the money which he advances, but he becomes by contract the purchaser of the shares, out and out, and they become his own property. The shares are not yet transferred to him—he does not acquire any legal interest in them; but as between the client on whose account he has bought them on the one hand, and himself on the other, when he finds the money on "contango" he becomes the absolute owner of the property, subject, however, to a contract made at the same time, or part of the same contract, that he is to resell to the client a like amount, not the same identical shares, but a like amount of similar shares, usually on the next account day, although a later day may be fixed by arrangement, at a price larger than that for which he gave his client credit on the first occasion; because the enhanced price is to cover interest upon the money in the meantime.' *Bentinck v London Joint Stock Bank* [1893] 2 Ch 120 at 140, per North J

CONTEMPLATION

[A company prospectus stated that no further calls were 'contemplated' on certain of its shares.] 'It is impossible to interpret the words "no further calls are contemplated" into an assurance or pledge that no call shall at any time be made.' *Accidental & Marine Insurance Corpn Ltd v Davis* (1866) 15 LT 182 at 183, per Willes J

'I think that the words "made in contemplation of" are stronger than "made in expectation of". Prima facie it seems to me that an agreement is not made in contemplation of something being done under it unless there is power and obligation to do that very thing.' *Scene Estates Ltd v Amos* [1957] 2 All ER 325 at 329, CA, per Parker LJ; also reported in [1957] 2 QB 205 at 213

Of marriage

Canada [Provision for division of family assets applied to property already acquired in specific contemplation of marriage: Marital Property Act, CCSM, c M45.] 'Several meanings of the word "contemplation" are to be found in The Shorter Oxford English Dictionary. Among them are: "1. The action of beholding", "2. The action of mentally viewing; attentive consideration, study; meditation" . . . "5. The action of taking into account; consideration, regard; view", "6. Prospect, expectation; intention". An example given in Oxford of the use of the word "contemplation" is "in view (as a contingency, or an end)". In my opinion, definitions 5 and 6 are most closely applicable to the purpose and intent of the Act. The term "contemplation of marriage" is governed adjectively by the word "specific". That word must be given meaning. One of the meanings ascribed to "specific" in Oxford is "Precise or exact in respect of fulfilment, conditions, or terms; definite, explicit. Exactly named or indicated, or capable of being so; precise, particular." The conjunction of "specific" with "contemplation" in the Act leads me to the conclusion that the circumstances must show a direct relationship between the acquisition and the marriage even though it may not be necessary to show the relationship was causal.' *Rotzetter v Rotzetter* (1985) 20 DLR (4th) 66 at 69, 70, Man CA, per Matas JA

New Zealand [The Law Reform Act 1944 (NZ), s 7(1) (repealed; see now the Wills Amendment Act 1955 (NZ), s 13) which was identical in its terms with the Law of Property Act 1925 (Eng) s 177, provided that a will expressed to be made in 'contemplation of a marriage' should, notwithstanding anything expressed in the Wills Act 1837, s 18, or any other statutory provision or rule of law to the contrary, not be revoked by the solemnisation of the marriage contemplated.] 'The words "made in contemplation of a marriage" mean that the will was made in contemplation of the marriage in the sense that the testator contemplated and intended that the will should remain in operation notwithstanding the marriage. . . . It follows that what is to be sought, where a testator has not used explicit words, is an expression of such contemplation and intention; and if what the testator has said in the will is consistent with a possible intention that the will should not operate after the marriage, the will is not one "made in contemplation of" the marriage within the meaning of the section.' *Burton v McGregor* [1953] NZLR 487 at 492, per F B Adams J

CONTEMPLATION OR FURTHERANCE

Of trade dispute

[The Trade Disputes Act 1906, s 3 (repealed) protected acts done 'in contemplation or furtherance of a trade dispute' and provided that such acts should not be actionable on the ground only that they interfered with another person's business.] 'I come now to the meaning of the words "an act done in contemplation or furtherance of a trade dispute". These words are not new in an Act of Parliament; they appear in the Conspiracy and Protection of Property Act 1875 [s 3 (repealed)]. I think they mean that either a dispute is imminent and the act is done in expectation of and with a view to it, or that the dispute is already existing and the act is done in support of one side of it. In either case the act must be genuinely done as described, and the dispute must be a real thing imminent or existing.' *Conway v Wade* [1909] AC 506 at 512, per Lord Loreburn LC

' "Furtherance" is not a merely subjective concept. There is an objective element in it. The Shorter Oxford Dictionary defines "furtherance" as "the fact or state of being helped forward". It seems to me that, for an act to be done "in furtherance of" a trade dispute [within the Trade Union and Labour Relations Act 1974, s 13(1)] it must be reasonably capable of doing so, or have a reasonable prospect of it, in this way that it must help one side or the other to the dispute in a *practical* way by giving support to the one or bringing pressure to bear on the other. Such as in the common case where men, who are in dispute with their employer, withdraw their labour, or "black" materials coming to his factory, or are supported by pickets outside his gates. Those are practical measures which have an impact *in fact* on the employer. They directly damage the employer's business. Such acts have a different quality from those which do not directly damage the employer's business but serve only to improve the morale of the strikers or promote their confidence or encourage them in their efforts, or damage innocent people not parties to the dispute. If this is all they do, they are not "in furtherance of" the dispute. In ordinary speech we draw a distinction between giving moral support to a cause and practical support to it. To be "in furtherance of" a dispute, an act must give practical support to one side or the other and not merely moral support.' *Express Newspapers Ltd v McShane* [1979] 2 All ER 360 at 364, 365, CA, per Lord Denning MR

CONTEMPORANEOUS

New Zealand 'A payment made seven days before the execution [of a security] cannot . . . be said to be made "contemporaneously with" the execution.' *Reid v McCallum's Official Assignee* (1886) 5 NZLR 68 at 76, CA, per Prendergast CJ

CONTEMPT OF COURT *See also*
ABUSE OF PROCESS

Contempt of court may be classified either as (1) criminal contempt, consisting of words or acts obstructing, or tending to obstruct or interfere with the administration of justice, or (2) contempt in procedure, consisting of disobedience to the judgments, orders, or other process of the court, and involving a private injury. (9 Halsbury's Laws (4th edn) para 2)

'The phrase "contempt in the face of the court" has a quaint old-fashioned ring about it; but the importance of it is this: of all the places where law and order must be maintained, it is here in these courts. The course of justice must not be deflected or interfered with. Those who strike at it strike at the very foundations of our society. To maintain law and order, the judges have, and must have, power at once to deal with those who offend against it. It is a great power—a power instantly to imprison a person without trial—but it is a necessary power. So necessary indeed that until recently the judges exercised it without any appeal. There were previously no safeguards against a judge exercising his jurisdiction wrongly or unwisely. This was remedied in 1960 [by the Administration of Justice 1960]. An appeal now lies to this court; and, in a suitable case, from this court to the House of Lords. With these safeguards this jurisdiction can and should be maintained.' *Morris v Crown Office* [1970] 1 All ER 1079 at 1081, CA, per Lord Denning

'The archaic description of these proceedings as "contempt of court" is in my view unfortunate and misleading. It suggests that they are designed to buttress the dignity of the judges and to protect them from insult. Nothing could be further from the truth. No such protection is needed. The sole purpose of proceedings for contempt is to give our courts the power effectively to protect the rights of the public by ensuring that the administration of justice shall not be obstructed or prevented.' Ibid at 1087, per Salmon LJ

'"Contempt of court" is an unfortunate and misleading phrase. It suggests that it exists to protect the dignity of the judges. Nothing could be further from the truth. The power exists to ensure that justice shall be done. And solely to this end it prohibits acts and words tending to obstruct the administration of justice. The public at large, no less than the individual litigant, have an interest, and a very real interest, in justice being effectively administered. Unless it is so administered, the rights, and indeed the liberty, of the individual will perish. Contempt of court may take many forms. It may consist of what is somewhat archaically called contempt in the face of the court, e.g. by disrupting the proceedings of a court in session or by improperly refusing to answer questions when giving evidence. It may, in a criminal case, consist of prejudicing a fair trial by publishing material likely to influence a jury. It may, as in the present case, consist of refusing to obey an order of the court. These are only a few of the many examples, that could be given of contempt. Contempts have sometimes been classified as criminal and civil contempts. I think that, at any rate today, this is an unhelpful and almost meaningless classification.' *Jennison v Baker* [1972] 1 All ER 997 at 1001, 1002, CA, per Salmon LJ

'The phrase contempt of court is one which is compendious to include not only disobedience to orders of a court but also certain types of behaviour or varieties of publications in reference to proceedings before courts of law which overstep the bounds which liberty permits. In an ordered community courts are established for the pacific settlement of disputes and for the maintenance of law and order. In the general interests of the community it is imperative that the authority of the courts should not be imperilled and that recourse to them should not be subject to unjustifiable interference. When such unjustifiable interference is suppressed it is not because those charged with the responsibilities of administering justice are concerned for their own dignity: it is because the very structure of ordered life is at risk if the recognised courts of the land are so flouted that their authority wanes and is supplanted. But as the purpose and existence of courts of law is to preserve freedom within the law for all well disposed members of the community, it is manifest that the courts must never impose any limitations on free speech or free discussion or free criticism beyond those which are absolutely necessary. When therefore a court has to consider the propriety of some conduct or speech or writing decision will often depend on whether one aspect of the public interest definitely outweighs another aspect of the public interest. Certain aspects of the public interest will be relevant in deciding and assessing whether there has been contempt of court. But this does not mean that if some conduct ought to be stigmatised as being contempt of court it could receive absolution and be regarded as legitimate because it had been inspired by a desire to bring about a relief of some distress that was a matter of public sympathy and concern. There can be no such thing as a justifiable contempt of court.' *A-G v Times Newspapers Ltd* [1973] 3 All ER 54 at 66, HL, per Lord Morris of Borth-y-Gest

'"Contempt of court" is a generic term descriptive of conduct in relation to particular proceedings in a court of law which tends to undermine that system or to inhibit citizens from availing themselves of it for the settlement of their disputes. Contempt of court may thus take many forms. One may leave aside for the purposes of the present appeal the mere disobedience by a party to a civil action of a specific order of the court made on him in that action. This is classified as a "civil contempt". The order is made at the request and for the sole benefit of the other party to the civil action. There is an element of public policy in punishing civil contempt, since the administration of justice would be undermined if the order of any court of law could be disregarded with impunity; but no sufficient public interest is served by punishing the offender if the only person for whose benefit the order was made chooses not to insist on its enforcement. All other contempts of court are classified as "criminal contempts", whether the particular proceedings to which the conduct of the contemnor relates are themselves criminal proceedings or are civil litigation between individual citizens. This is because it is the public interest in the due administration of justice, civil as well as criminal, in the established courts of law that it is sought to protect by making those who commit criminal contempts of court subject to summary punishment. To constitute a contempt of court that attracts the summary remedy, the conduct complained of must relate to some specific case in which litigation in a court of law is actually proceeding or is known to be imminent. Conduct in relation to that case which tends to undermine the due administration of justice by the court in which the case will be disposed of, or which tends to inhibit litigants in general from seeking adjudication by the court as to their legal rights or obligations, will affect not only the public interest but also—and this more immediately—the particular interests of the parties to the case. In this respect criminal contempt of court resembles many ordinary criminal offences, such as theft or offences against the person or property by which the interests of the victim himself are prejudiced more immediately than those of the public at large.' Ibid at 71, per Lord Diplock

'I find nothing to tell us what is meant by "committed in the face of the court". It has never been defined. Its meaning is, I think, to be ascertained from the practice of the judges over the centuries. It was never confined to conduct which a judge saw with his own eyes. It covered all contempts for which a judge of his own motion could punish a man on the spot. So "contempt in the face of the court" is the same thing as "contempt which the court can punish of its own motion". It really means "contempt in the cognizance of the court".' *Balogh v Crown Court at St Albans* [1974] 3 All ER 283 at 287, CA, per Lord Denning MR

[In the above case, the Master of the Rolls concluded: 'The new Crown Courts are in being. The judges of them have not yet acquired the prestige of the Red Judge when he went on Assize. His robes and bearing made everyone alike stand in awe of him. Rarely did he need to exercise his great power of summary punishment. Yet there is just as much need for the Crown Court to maintain its dignity and authority. The judges of it should not hesitate to exercise the authority they inherit from the past. Insults are best treated with disdain—

save when they are gross and scandalous. Refusal to answer with admonishment—save where it is vital to know the answer. But disruption of the court or threats to witnesses or to jurors should be visited with immediate arrest.']

'Although criminal contempts of court may take a variety of forms they all share a common characteristic: they involve an interference with the due administration of justice either in a particular case or more generally as a continuing process. It is justice itself that is flouted by contempt of court, not the individual court or judge who is attempting to administer it.' *A-G v Leveller Magazine Ltd* [1979] 1 All ER 745 at 749, HL, per Lord Diplock

[See, generally, the Contempt of Court Act 1981, which amends and clarifies the law of contempt of court, primarily as it effects matter published in newspapers and broadcasts.]

Australia ' "Contempt of court", understood as a legal term, principally signifies disrespect for what is entitled to "legal regard". . . . "Criminal contempt" may be defined as contumelious or obstructive behaviour directed against the court and one example of this is contempt in the face of the court. Every contempt is in some respect an obstruction of justice, a sinning against the majesty of the law, and the time-honoured punitive jurisdiction over such offences is now undisputed. Contempt of court has been defined as a disobedience to the court, or an opposing or a despising of the authority, justice or dignity thereof. It commonly consists in a party's doing otherwise than he is enjoined to do, or not doing what he is commanded or required by the process, order, or decree of the court. Sometimes it arises by one or more; their opposing or disturbing the execution or service of the process of the court, or using force to the party that serves it; sometimes by using words importing scorn, reproach or diminution of the court, its process, orders, officers, or ministers, upon executing or serving such process or orders. It is also a contempt to abuse the process of the court by wilfully doing any wrong in executing it; or making use of it as a handle to do wrong; or to do anything under colour or pretence of process of the court without such process or authority. One kind of contempt is, of course, scandalising the court itself.' *Ex p Bellanto, Re His Honour Judge Jack Harvey Prior, CBE, and in the Matter of the Supreme Court and Circuit Courts Act 1900–1954* [1963] NSWR 1556 at 1564, 1565, per cur.

Canada 'It is my opinion that, whatever may be the case with respect to contempt outside of court, contempt in the face of the court consists of conduct which deliberately and in most cases publicly flouts the law and interferes with the due administration of justice. It has the characteristics of a criminal offence and constitutes a criminal matter.' *R v Cohn* (1984) 13 DLR (4th) 680 at 690, Ont CA, per Goodman JA

New Zealand 'Before an act can be deemed a contempt of court, it must lead or be likely to lead to an interference with the due administration of justice.' *A-G v Blomfield, A-G v Geddis* (1913) 33 NZLR 545 at 556, per Stout CJ; also reported 16 GLR 218 at 223

CONTENTION

[The Local Government Act 1948, s 48(4) (repealed; see now General Rate Act 1967, s 76(5)), provided that a local valuation court should give such directions as appear to be necessary to give effect to the 'contention' of an appellant against an assessment for rating purposes, where the contention appeared to be well founded.] 'In my judgment the word "contention" refers to the figure aimed at and not to the various legal or factual arguments on which the appellants base their case.' *Morecambe and Heysham Corpn v Robinson (Valuation Officer)* [1961] 1 All ER 721 at 724, CA, per Holroyd Pearce LJ

CONTENTIOUS BUSINESS

'Contentious business' means business done, whether as solicitor or advocate, in or for the purposes of proceedings begun before a court or before an arbitrator appointed under the Arbitration Act 1950, not being business which falls within the definition of non-contentious or common form probate business contained in subsection (1) of section 94 of the Supreme Court Act 1981. (Solicitors Act 1974, s 87(1))

'It seems to me that the expressions "non-contentious business" and "contentious business", when used in the Acts and the orders, are referring to the nature of the work. If the commencement of proceedings had been intended to be the determining factor, how easy it would have been to say so in the definition section of the Act of 1932 [repealed; see now Solicitors Act 1974, s 87(1)]. Moreover, it is to be observed that conveyancing matters are classed as non-contentious business, even if the work is done during proceedings . . . which

again points to the nature of the work being the test. Further, any contrary view would lead to the absurd result that the solicitor would be entitled to different remuneration for identically the same work, depending on whether the claim was settled the day before or the day after proceedings were launched.' *Re A Solicitor* [1955] 2 All ER 283 at 289, CA, per Parker LJ; see also [1955] 2 QB at p 265

CONTENTS

Gift in will

'I think if the goods are appropriated to the house, that is to say belonging to it, as furniture or the like, and are only removed for the purpose of repair, it is quite plain they would pass. That last consideration does not apply to the case before me [i.e jewellery in a box deposited with a bank for safe custody only from time to time]. The case before me I think depends on this—that the usual locality of the goods in question was the house, and they were only removed for a temporary purpose. It is a very significant fact that the goods were in the house at the time the lady made her will.' *Re Johnston, Cockerell v Essex (Earl)* (1884) 26 Ch D 538 at 554, per Chitty J

'I am of opinion that by this gift of the mahogany desk with the contents thereof the testator did intend to give whatever was found therein at the time of his death. If the security box had been given with the contents thereof it would have been absurd, to my mind, to take out all the valuable things which were found therein and to say in substance that an empty box with any chattel put there by the testator, a lead pencil or the like, was all that was intended to pass. I think that "with the contents thereof" does not mean the pens, ink and paper and is not confined to mere chattels within the chattel. There is a distinction between a gift of chattels in a house and a gift of the contents of a desk; a desk being the kind of thing in which men do usually keep valuable things.' *Re Robson, Robson v Hamilton* [1891] 2 Ch 559 at 562, 563, 565, 566, per Chitty J

New Zealand 'The expression [in a will] "my house and contents" is not one that can or should be defined in isolation; but in the absence of any qualification or enlargement by its context, it suggests those tangible assets and effects which normally are used or enjoyed in or in association with the home and daily living and which are kept in or about the house. . . .

When the words are considered in their ordinary and grammatical sense, a gift of the contents of a house would not include valuable securities or choses in action.' *Re Harvey (deceased), Jenkinson v McWatters* [1962] NZLR 524 at 526, per Woodhouse J

CONTEST

Canada 'The appellant was convicted . . . under s 235(1)(h) of the Criminal Code [see now RSC 1970, c C-34, s 186] for that he did aid or assist in giving notice of an invitation to guess or to foretell the result or contingency of or relating to a contest. . . . In my view . . . the offence charged does not come within the purview of s 235(1)(h) under which the charge is laid. We have here no contest nor any contingency relating thereto upon the result of which the subscribers are invited to bet. What we have is an invitation to join with other subscribers in a guessing competition among themselves. In my opinion the subsection in question has not prohibited any such competition.' *R v Hamm* (1941) 56 BCR 66 at 70, 73, CA, per McDonald JA

CONTIGUOUS *See also* ADJOIN

'The first question to be decided is, what is the meaning of the phrase, "Any of the premises adjoining or contiguous to the hereditaments hereby demised"? I think the word "contiguous" was used there by someone who did not fully understand its meaning. I do not think it is intended to have its strict meaning, viz. "touching", because the phrase is "such adjoining or contiguous premises", and I think the two words . . . were not intended to be merely synonymous, but were meant to be alternative and that the meaning really was "such adjoining or neighbouring premises". But even if the word is to be construed strictly, still I think the plaintiff's and defendant's premises are "adjoining or contiguous". They are situate on opposite sides of the street, and . . . the defendant's houses on the opposite side of the street, belonging to the same lessors, are premises adjoining or contiguous to the plaintiff's premises.' *Haynes v King* [1893] 3 Ch 439 at 448, per North J

'It is not necessary for the purposes of this case to decide whether the word "contiguous" in this subsection [s 3(3) of the Rating and Valuation (Apportionment) Act 1928 (repealed)] is to be construed in its precise significance of "touching", for upon any true construction of the words "within the same curtilage or contiguous", I am satisfied that premises which are 235 yards distant cannot be said to be contiguous within the meaning of this section.' *Southwark Revenue Officer v Hoe (R) & Co Ltd* (1930) 143 LT 544 at 545, per Avory J

'If there is a demise of one house in a street, and a covenant . . . as to "contiguous" houses, and if . . . at the date of the lease all the houses existed as detached and separate buildings, then the word "contiguous" may be rightly construed as "next adjacent" or "contiguous houses" as "houses on contiguous plots".' *Spillers Ltd v Cardiff (Borough) Assessment Committee, Pierce v Wirral Assessment Committee, Pinsent v Plymouth Assessment Committee, Blunt v West Derby Assessment Committee, Same v Same* [1931] 2 KB 21 at 43, per Lord Hewart CJ

New Zealand 'The word "contiguous" . . . is not a word of precise meaning. . . . The definition of the meaning of the word "contiguous" in standard dictionaries, and the mode in which that word has been used by the most eminent judges, as well as common usage, all warrant its being construed in the sense of near to, but not actually touching. This also is the case with the word "adjoining" which would . . . convey to most men the meaning of actual contact more clearly than the word "contiguous".' *Waihi Grand Junction Goldmining Co Ltd v Dudson* (1909) 29 NZLR 499 at 505, per Edwards J; also reported 12 GLR 369 at 371

CONTINGENCY

'A contingency is an event which may or may not happen. If there is no real possibility that it will not happen, so that it is as good as certain that it will, it is a contingency without reality and substance and no contingency at all. But a real possibility is not the same thing as a probability. It may be highly improbable that an event will happen, but there can still be a real possibility that it will. If there is that possibility, however remote it may be, the contingency is one of reality and substance.' *Inland Revenue Comrs v Trustees of Sir John Aird's Settlement* [1982] 2 All ER 929 at 940, per Nourse J

CONTINGENCY INSURANCE *See* INSURANCE

CONTINGENT CREDITOR

Australia 'A contingent creditor, like an elephant, is rather easier to recognize than to define. The following statement by Pennycuick J in *Re William Hockley Ltd* [1962] 1 WLR 555 at p 558; [1962] 2 All ER, is well known: "The expression 'contingent creditor' is not defined in the Companies Act, but must, I think, denote a person towards whom under an existing obligation, the company may or will become subject to a present liability upon the happening of some future event or at some future date." In *Re Gasbourne Pty Ltd* [1984] VR 801 at p 837, Nicholson J said that he did not regard that description as exhaustive, and with respect I would not disagree.' *Federal Commissioner of Taxation v Gosstray* [1986] VR 876 at 878, per Tadgell J

CONTINGENT LIABILITY

'It would seem that the phrase "contingent liability" may have no settled meaning in English law because in this case Danckwerts J [in the court below] thought it necessary to resort to a dictionary and in *Re Duffy, Lakeman v A-G* [[1948] 2 All ER 756] . . . the Court of Appeal regarded its meaning as an open question. But the Finance Acts are United Kingdom Acts and there is at least a strong presumption that they mean the same in Scotland as in England. A case precisely similar to this case could have come from Scotland and your Lordships would then have considered the meaning of this phrase in Scots law. So I need make no apology for reminding your Lordships of its meaning there. Perhaps the clearest statement is in Erskine's Institute of the Law of Scotland, Vol 2, when he says (Book III, title I, § 6): "Obligations are either pure, or to a certain day, or conditional. . . . Obligations *in diem* . . . are those in which the performance is referred to a determinate day. In this kind . . . a debt becomes properly due from the very date of the obligation, because it is certain that that day will exist; but its effect or execution is suspended till the day be elapsed. A conditional obligation, or an obligation granted under a condition the existence of which is uncertain, has no obligatory force till the condition be purified; because it is in that event only that the party declares his intention to be bound, and consequently no proper debt arises against him till it actually exist: so that the condition of an uncertain event suspends not only the execution of the obligation, but the obligation itself. . . . Such obligation is therefore said in Roman law to create only the hope of a debt. Yet the granter is in so far obliged that he hath no right to revoke or withdraw that hope from the creditor which he had once given him." So far as I am aware that statement has never been questioned during the two centuries since it was written and later authorities make it clear that conditional obligation and contingent liability have no different significance. I would, therefore, find it impossible to hold that in Scots law a contingent liability is merely a species of existing liability. It is a liability which, by reason of something done by the person bound, will necessarily arise or come into being if one or more of certain events occur or do not occur.' *Winter v Inland Revenue Comrs* [1961] 3 All ER 855 at 858, 859, HL, per Lord Reid

CONTINGENT REMAINDER

Contingent or executory remainders (whereby no present interest passes) are where the estate in remainder is limited to take effect, either to a dubious and uncertain person, or upon a dubious and uncertain event; so that the particular estate may chance to be determined, and the remainder never take effect. (2 Bl Com 169)

CONTINUATION

If a purchaser of securities during a dealing period does not wish to complete his purchase during the next following settlement period, he may arrange to resell for the current account the securities which he has agreed to buy for that account, and to purchase for the new account. Conversely, a seller of securities during a dealing period who does not wish to deliver during the next following settlement period may arrange to repurchase for the current account the securities which he has agreed to sell, and to sell for the new account. Such an arrangement is known as a 'continuation' or 'carrying over'. (45 Halsbury's Laws (4th edn) para 100)

'"To continue" is a technical term. . . . It means to sell and to agree to rebuy the same amount of stock at a future day at the same price and a sum for the accommodation. Such a transaction is not a loan, but a sale and repurchase. The true nature of a continuation will be best seen by stating its consequences in all possible events. These are as follows: (1) The original seller . . . may perform his contract to rebuy; then he is entitled to receive the amount of bonds agreed to be sold to him, and if they are delivered to him the transaction is closed. If they are not delivered, he is entitled to the damages he has sustained by not getting them. (2) The original seller . . . may make default—i.e. not pay the amount at which he has agreed to rebuy; he then himself becomes liable to an action for breach of contract. Then, if (a) the bonds have gone up, the person to deliver them suffers no damage, but gains on the transaction. There are no damages to pay, and the transaction is at an end. But if (b) the bonds have gone down, the person to deliver them sustains damage, and the amount is the difference between their market value at the time when the original seller . . . ought to have paid for them and the price which he agreed to pay for them. To ascertain the market price the person who has to deliver them . . . sells the amount he had to deliver, or he gets the price fixed by the official assignee of the Stock Exchange. In all and every of these cases the bonds originally sold by the person wanting to carry them over or to continue them . . . remain the property of the person who first bought them. . . . But it is obvious that a sale and contemporaneous agreement for repurchase at the same price, though not a loan in point of law, is, in a business point of view, so like a loan by the first buyer to the first seller as to be easily mistaken by business men for a loan.' *Bongiovanni v Société Générale* (1886) 54 LT 320 at 321, CA, per cur.

CONTINUE

[Under the terms of a lease, the tenant was given the option of 'continuing' for an extension of seven or fourteen years.] 'The plain meaning of "continuing" is "carrying on" or "not ceasing to be", and reading "carrying on" for "continuing", the clause reads, "the tenant has the choice of carrying on for an extension of fourteen years with a break at seven years"; or, reading "not ceasing to be", the clause reads, "the tenant has the choice of not ceasing to be the tenant for an extension of fourteen years with a break at seven years".' *Gardner v Blaxill* [1960] 2 All ER 457 at 460, per Paull J

Canada "The words [in the Real Estate Agents Act 1947 (Man), c 41, s 3 (repealed; see now Real Estate Brokers Act, RSM 1970, c R 20, s 41)] "in the course of continued and successive transactions" deserve considera-tion. . . . They qualify the phrase "an isolated transaction". Two different ideas, it seems to me, are connoted by the words "continued"

and "successive". The former appears to be concerned with number—it suggests repetition or plurality of acts. The latter has regard to time—the acts should be sufficiently close together to qualify as "successive".' *Zinman v Baldry* (1955) 62 Man R 528 at 533, Man QB, per Freedman J

Continuing cause of action

'A "continuing cause of action" is a cause of action which arises from the repetition of acts or omissions of the same kind as that for which the action was brought. In my opinion that is a continuing cause of action within the meaning of the rule [Ord 36, r 58]. . . . It is a repetition of acts of the same kind as those which had been investigated at the trial, and had been decided to constitute a nuisance.' *Hole v Chard Union* [1894] 1 Ch 293 at 295, 296, CA, per Lindley LJ

Continuing guarantee

'Counsel for the plaintiffs suggested a con-struction of the guarantee [a continuing guar-antee of moneys owing to the plaintiffs by a customer upon his current account with them] to which in the absence of authority in its favour I cannot assent. He sought to treat a guarantee as giving a fresh right of action from day to day, a construction which would render it impossible, so long as the debt remained recoverable from the principal debtor by the bank, for the guarantor to obtain the benefit of the Statute of Limitations. I do not think that the word "continuing" involves any such meaning. The effect of that word is to extend a guarantee beyond the first sum advanced to sums subsequently advanced, as long as the guarantee is continued.' *Parr's Banking Co v Yates* [1898] 2 QB 460 at 466, CA, per Rigby LJ

Continuing offence

Australia 'A continuous or continuing offence is a concept well known in the criminal law and is often used to describe two different kinds of crime. There is the crime which is constituted by conduct which goes on from day to day and and which constitutes a separate and distinct offence each day the conduct conti-nues. There is, on the other hand, the kind of conduct, generally of a passive character, which consists in the failure to perform a duty imposed by law. Such passive conduct may constitute a crime when first indulged in but if the obligation is continuous the breach though constituting one crime only continues day by day to be a crime until the obligation is performed. In such a case in measuring the period of limitation, if one is applicable, the right to lay an information is not barred if the breach was cured before the information was laid, time counts from the day when the obligation was satisfied. The question whether an offence is of a continuing or continuous nature generally arises in the case of statutory offences and the question is solved by ascertaining what is the precise nature of the offence.' *R v Industrial Appeals Court, ex p Barelli's Bakeries Pty Ltd* [1965] VR 615 at 620, per O'Bryan and Gillard JJ

In service

Australia 'Under a marine insurance policy the risk attaches if in consequence of an accident the vessel be prevented from "continuing in service". . . . "Continuing in service" means the prolongation of a service already existing. To begin a new and different service using the vessel as a fast ferry for passengers between Southport and Stradbroke Island at the Gold Coast is not to continue the vessel in service as before but to begin a new and different service.' *L & M Electrics Pty Ltd v SGIO Queensland* [1984] 2 Qld R 394 at 398, per McPherson J

CONTINUOUSLY

'The defendants with other consignees received goods which had been shipped under bills of lading containing the following clause: "Goods are to be received by the consignee immediately the vessel is ready to discharge and continuously at all such hours as the Custom House authorities may give permission for the ship to work." . . . The word "continuously" does not add to the obligation of the merchants, and afford no indication of an intention to fix a definite time or rate of discharge. It means no more than that the merchant bound himself to do his work in a reasonable time and with a reasonable amount of exertion. If it was intended that he was to be responsible for all extraordinary causes of delay, the language used in this bill of lading was not the right language to use.' *MacLay v Bakers & Spiller Ltd* (1900) 16 TLR 401 at 401, per Mathew J

CONTRABAND

'The phrase "contraband of war" is . . . naturally applicable to goods, and not to despatches or persons; but I should be prepared to consider the question whether it might not be used in a wider sense, if there were anything to show that such a use of it was common among commercial men, or in commercial documents, or was recognised in the courts of law. It has, however, been admitted that . . . there is no instance in any reported case in which the term has been applied otherwise than to goods. It appears to have been applied to persons by one or two text-book writers only, in passages where it is apparent from the context that it was not being used in a strict sense.' *Yangtsze Insurance Assocn v Indemnity Mutual Marine Assurance Co* [1908] 2 KB 504 at 508, 509, CA, per Fletcher Moulton LJ

CONTRACT   *See also* ASSIGNMENT; BARGAIN; BREACH OF CONTRACT; COLLATERAL; CONDITION; FORWARD CONTRACT; SUBJECT TO CONTRACT

Whilst it was probably impossible to give one absolute and universally correct definition of a contract, the most commonly accepted definition is 'a promise or set of promises which the law will enforce'. The expression 'contract' may, however, be used to describe any or all of the following: (1) that series of promises or acts themselves constituting the contract; (2) the document or documents constituting or evidencing that series of promises or acts, or their performance; (3) the legal relations resulting from that series. (9 Halsbury's Laws (4th edn) para 201)

'An agreement between two persons, A and B, that one of them will either immediately, or at some future time, or subject to the performance of some condition, enter into an agreement with the other is I think not enforceable, because it does not fall within the meaning of the term "contract" as defined by law. Definitions of "contract" are to be found in the textbooks. . . . They are all founded on, and many of them simply adopt, the definition given by Pother in Part I, Ch I, s 1, of his work on Contracts. This is his definition. . . . "An agreement by which two parties reciprocally promise and engage, or one of them singly promises and engages to the other to give some particular thing, or to do or abstain from doing some particular act." Mr Pollock's definition in his work on the same subject . . . is, in my opinion, more complete and more accurate. He defines a contract, or rather an agreement, to be "an act in the law whereby two or more persons declare their consent as to any act or thing to be done or forborne by some or one of those persons for the use of the others or other of them"; and in commencing on this definition he explains what is intended by an act in the law, saying that it must be on the face of the matter capable of having legal effect and concerned with duties and rights which can be dealt with by a Court of Justice.' *Foster v Wheeler* (1887) 36 Ch D 695 at 698, per Kekewich J

'There are agreements between parties which do not result in contracts within the meaning of that term in our law. The ordinary example is where two parties agree to take a walk together, or where there is an offer and an acceptance of hospitality. Nobody would suggest in ordinary circumstances that those agreements result in what we know as a contract, and one of the most usual forms of agreement which does not constitute a contract appears to me to be the arrangements which are made between husband and wife. It is quite common, and it is the natural and inevitable result of the relationship of husband and wife, that the two spouses should make arrangements between themselves—agreements such as are in dispute in this action—agreements for allowances, by which the husband agrees that he will pay to his wife a certain sum of money, per week, or per month, or per year, to cover either her own expenses or the necessary expenses of the household and of the children of the marriage, and in which the wife promises either expressly or impliedly to apply the allowance for the purpose for which it is given. To my mind those agreements, or many of them, do not result in contracts at all, and they do not result in contracts even though there may be what as between other parties would constitute consideration for the agreement. The consideration, as we know, may consist either in some right, interest, profit or benefit accruing to one party, or some forbearance, detriment, loss of responsibility given, suffered or undertaken by the other [*Currie v Misa* (1875) LR 10 Exch 153]. That is a well-known definition, and it constantly happens, I think, that such arrangements made between husband and wife are arrangements in which there are mutual promises, or in which there is consideration in form within the definition that I have mentioned. Nevertheless they are not contracts, and they are not contracts because the parties did not intend that they should be attended by legal consequences.' *Balfour v Balfour* [1919] 2 KB 571 at 578, 579, CA, per Atkin LJ

'In order to establish a contract, whether it be an express contract or a contract implied by law, there has to be shown a meeting of the minds of the parties, with a definition of the contractual terms reasonably clearly made out, with an intention to affect the legal relationship: that is that the agreement that is made is one which is properly to be regarded as being enforceable by the court if one or the other fails to comply with it; and it still remains a part of the law of this country, though many people think that it is time that it was changed to some other criterion, that there must be consideration moving in order to establish a contract.' *Horrock v Farray* [1976] 2 All ER 737 at 742, CA, per Megaw LJ

United States 'Contract' means the total legal obligation which results from the parties' agreement as affected by this Act and any other applicable rules of law. (Compare 'Agreement'). (Uniform Commercial Code 1978, s 1–201(11))

Contract by deed *See* DEED

Contract in writing

'As to the suggestion which was made that the words "contract in writing" import a contract made by means of a writing or writings signed by both parties, I do not think the words necessarily have that meaning. A document purporting to be an agreement may be an agreement in writing sufficient to satisfy the requirements of an Act of Parliament though it is only verified by the signature of one of the parties.' *Ruf (T A) & Co v Pauwels* [1919] 1 KB 660 at 670, CA, per Duke LJ

Contract of record

Contracts of record, . . . are judgments and recognisances which are enrolled in the record of the proceedings of a court of record, and in law imply a debt though the obligation arises from the entry on the record and not from any agreement between the parties. (9 Halsbury's Laws (4th edn) para 209)

Contract of service *See* SERVICE

Contract under seal

A contract under seal, or, as it is sometimes called, a contract by speciality, is a contract which is made by deed. The separate promises made in such a contract are frequently termed covenants. The fundamental difference between under seal and simple contracts lies in the doctrine of consideration. The ordinary rule is that the law will enforce an executory promise given for consideration, but not an imperfect gift. A promise under seal, however, derives its validity from its form alone; it is regarded as binding at common law even without consideration, except where void, for example as being in restraint of trade, or illegal. Equity, however, has always refused to aid the enforcement of contracts under seal without consideration. (9 Halsbury's Laws (4th edn) para 210)

Executed contract

[A contract is said to be] executed when it has been wholly performed by all parties. (9 Halsbury's Laws (4th edn) para 206)

Executory contract

A contract is said to be executory so long as anything remains to be done under it by any party. (9 Halsbury's Laws (4th edn) para 206)

Illegal contract

A distinction must be drawn between illegality at common law and illegality arising from statutory prohibition, express or implied, of the contract, though both may be relevant in an individual case. There are two general principles. The first is that a contract which is entered into with the object of committing an illegal act is unenforceable. The application of this principle depends upon proof of the intent, at the time the contract was made, to break the law; if the intent is mutual the contract is not enforceable at all, and, if unilateral, it is unenforceable at the suit of the party who is proved to have the intent. The second principle is that the court will not enforce a contract which is expressly or impliedly prohibited by statute. If the contract is of this class it does not matter what the intent of the parties is; if the statute prohibits the contract, it is unenforceable whether the parties meant to break the law or not. A significant distinction between the two classes is this: in the former class one has only to look and see what acts the statute prohibits; it does not matter whether it prohibits a contract; if a contract is deliberately made to do a prohibited act, that contract will be unenforceable. In the latter class, what has to be considered is not what acts the statute prohibits, but what contracts it prohibits, the intent of the parties is irrelevant; if the parties enter into a prohibited contract, that contract

is unenforceable. (9 Halsbury's Laws (4th edn) para 422)

'In *Bennett v Bennett* [[1952] 1 All ER 413] it was pointed out that there are two kinds of illegality of differing effect. The first is where illegality is criminal or *contra bonos mores*, and in those cases, which I will not attempt to enumerate or further classify, such a provision, if an ingredient in a contract, will invalidate the whole although it may contain many other provisions. There is a second kind of illegality which has no such taint, and the other terms in the contract stand if the illegal portion can be severed, the illegal portion being a provision which the court on grounds of public policy will not enforce.' *Goodinson v Goodinson* [1954] 2 All ER 255 at 256, CA, per Somervell LJ; see also [1954] 2 QB 118

'The effect of illegality on a contract may be threefold. If at the time of making the contract there is an intent to perform it in an unlawful way, the contract, although it remains alive, is unenforceable at the suit of the party having that intent; if the intent is held in common, it is not enforceable at all. Another effect of illegality is to prevent a plaintiff from recovering under a contract if in order to prove his rights under it he has to rely on his own illegal act; he may not do that even though he can show that at the time of making the contract he had no intent to break the law and that at the time of performance he did not know that what he was doing was illegal. The third effect of illegality is to avoid the contract *ab initio*, and that arises if the making of the contract is expressly or impliedly prohibited by statute or is otherwise contrary to public policy.' *Archbolds (Freightage) Ltd v S Spanglett Ltd* [1961] 1 All ER 417 at 424, CA, per Devlin J; also reported [1961] 1 QB 374

Instalment contract

United States An 'installment contract' is one which requires or authorizes the delivery of goods in separate lots to be separately accepted, even though the contract contains a clause 'each delivery is a separate contract' or its equivalent. (Uniform Commercial Code 1978, s 2–612(1))

Of carriage

'Contract of carriage' applies only to contracts of carriage covered by a bill of lading or any similar document of title, in so far as such document relates to the carriage of goods by sea, including any bill of lading or any similar document as aforesaid issued under or pursuant to a charter party from the moment at which such bill of lading or similar document of title regulates the relations between a carrier and a holder of the same. (Carriage of Goods by Sea Act 1971, Schedule (Hague Rules))

Of employment

'Contract of employment' means a contract of service or of apprenticeship, whether it is express or implied, and (if it is express) whether it is oral or in writing. (Trade Union and Labour Relations Act 1974, s 30(1)); cf. also the Health and Safety at Work etc Act 1974, s 53(1), and the Employment Protection (Consolidation) Act 1978, s 153(1))

Petroleum marketing

United States   The term 'contract' means any oral or written agreement. For supply purposes, delivery levels during the same month of the previous year shall be prima facie evidence of an agreement to deliver such levels. (Petroleum Marketing Practices Act 1978, s 101(10))

Simple contract

Simple contracts include all contracts which are not contracts of record or contracts under seal. Simple contracts may be express or implied, or partly express and partly implied. Contracts are express to the extent that their terms are set out distinctly either by word of mouth or in writing. They are implied to the extent, if any, to which their terms are a necessary inference from the words or conduct of the parties. Express contracts may, of course, besides the terms which are expressed contain additional terms which are implied, and in that case they are partly express and partly implied. (9 Halsbury's Laws (4th edn) para 212)

Void contract

The expression 'void contract' is a commonly used and convenient term for a contract which from the beginning has no legal effect. However, as the term 'contract' is always used so as to include some element of enforceability, the expression 'void contract' is a paradox because in reality there is never any contract at all. The term 'void agreement' more aptly describes the situation where an offer and acceptance does not result in legal relations; but it is also used to describe a purported acceptance of a legally operative offer which does not amount to an acceptance in

law. The appellation 'void' has also been inaccurately used to describe an initially valid contract which ceases to have effect before its expiry in normal course, either automatically, or by the election of one of the parties after breach. (9 Halsbury's Laws (4th edn) para 207)

Voidable contract

A 'voidable contract' is one which is initially valid, but where one or more of the parties has a right of election to avoid or to continue and so validate it. Unless and until a right of avoidance is exercised, a voidable contract remains valid; but whilst the right of avoidance remains, it may be exercised whether the contract is executory or executed. (9 Halsbury's Laws (4th edn) para 207)

CONTRAVENTION

'Contravention' includes, in relation to—
(a) a provision of this Act, of an order made thereunder or of regulations; or
(b) a direction, prohibition, restriction or requirement given or imposed by a notice served under or by virtue of this Act by the Health and Safety Executive; or
(c) a condition attached to an exemption, consent, approval or authority granted or given under or by virtue of this Act by the Health and Safety Executive or an inspector;
(d) a prohibition or requirement imposed by or under health and safety regulations which expressly apply to all mines or quarries, any class of mine or quarry or a particular mine or quarry;
a failure to comply with the provision, direction, prohibition, restriction, requirement or condition, and the expression 'contravene' shall be construed accordingly. (Mines and Quarries Act 1954, s 182, as amended)

[Many other statutes provide that 'contravention', in relation to any provision, shall include a failure to comply with such provision.]

Australia   'If it is a characteristic of any contravention that it could result in a penalty after conviction for a punishable offence, then *e converso* when there can be no penalty there can be no conviction because there is no punishable offence, no conviction.' *Dimella Constructions v Stocker* (1976) 14 SASR 215 at 222, per Bray CJ

CONTRIBUTION *See also* ANNUAL
VOLUNTARY CONTRIBUTION; ENDOWMENT

Although its extent may be modified by contract, contribution is not based on contract, but on principles of natural justice. Payment by one person liable releases the others from the principal demand, and they are required to contribute as a return for this benefit; but the principle does not apply unless all the parties are liable to a common demand, and such liability, therefore, is a condition of contribution. (16 Halsbury's Laws (4th edn) para 1252)

United States 'Contribution' means any cash, property, services rendered, or a promissory note or other binding obligation to contribute cash or property or to perform services, which a partner contributes to a limited partnership in his capacity as a partner. (Revised Uniform Limited Partnership Act 1976, s 101(2))

Insurance

'Contribution exists where the thing is done by the same person against the same loss, and to prevent a man first of all from recovering more than the whole loss, or if he recovers the whole loss from one which he could have recovered from the other, then to make the parties contribute rateably. But that only applies where there is the same person insuring the same interest with more than one office.' *North British & Mercantile Insurance Co v London, Liverpool & Globe Insurance Co* (1877) 5 Ch D 569 at 581, CA, per James LJ

See, generally 25 Halsbury's Laws (4th edn) para 538, 539.

CONTRIBUTORY

In this Act, the expression 'contributory' means every person liable to contribute to the assets of a company in the event of its being wound up, and for the purposes of all proceedings for determining, and all proceedings prior to the final determination of, the persons who are to be deemed contributories, includes any person alleged to be a contributory. (Companies Act 1985, s 507(1))

'All members of a company, and there can be no doubt that the holders of fully paid shares are members, ought to be held to fall within the description of contributories.' *Re Anglesea Colliery Co* (1866) 1 Ch App 555 at 559, per Turner LJ

'It is alleged . . . that a contributory in this section [Companies (Consolidation) Act 1908, s 165 (repealed); see now Companies Act 1985, s 552] means somebody who is liable to contribute to the assets of the company in respect of his shares; in other words, that it is limited to the definition as found in s 124 of the Act of 1908 [now s 507(1) of the Act of 1985 (supra)], which means that the term "contributory" means "every person liable to contribute to the assets of a company in the event of its being wound up, and, in all proceedings for determining and in all proceedings prior to the final determination of the persons who are to be deemed contributories, includes any person alleged to be a contributory". It is unfortunate that in this Act, and in the Acts which it supersedes, the term "contributory" is used in a large number of places, not as limited to holders of partly-paid shares, but as including holders of fully-paid shares in the company. In the series of sections, ss 123–128 [ss 507–510 of the Act of 1985], which are headed with the word "Contributories", I am of opinion that the word "contributories" is used in the narrow sense—namely, the holders of partly-paid shares; but when we pass from that series of sections to the later series, for instance those headed "Winding up by Court", those headed "Liquidators", those headed "Committee of Inspection", and finally, those headed "Ordinary Powers of Court" in which ss 164 and 165 [Act of 1985, ss 551, 552] are found, it is clear that the word "contributories" is really used as synonymous with the word "members". Turning . . . to ss 164 and 165 [Act of 1985, ss 551, 552] . . . the proper course there is to hold that "contributory" is not limited to the narrower meaning of persons who owe money to the company in respect of their shares.' *Re Aidall Ltd* [1933] Ch 323 at 328, 329, CA, per Maugham J

See, generally 7 Halsbury's Laws (4th edn) paras 1212–1251.

CONTRIBUTORY NEGLIGENCE *See* NEGLIGENCE

CONTROL *See also* CARE; CONTROLLING INTEREST

Generally

Australia 'The word "control" is wide enough to include many types of possession which are not commensurate with full ownership.' *Johnston Fear & Kingham v Commonwealth* (1943) 67 CLR 314 at 324, per Rich J

Australia 'An unfortunate word of such wide and ambiguous import that it has been taken to mean something weaker than "restraint", something equivalent to "regulation".' *Bank of New South Wales v Commonwealth* (1948) 76 CLR 1 at 385, per Dixon J

New Zealand [The Family Benefits (Home Ownership) Act 1964 provides for the Social Security Commission to exercise the powers conferred upon it by the Act under the general direction and 'control' of the Minister. The Minister purported to specify the manner in which certain applications should be determined by the Commission.] 'I am unable to agree that the words "general direction and control" were intended in the context of the Act to empower the Minister to compel the Commission to reach a particular decision. In my opinion, s 4 is not expressed in language which gives the Minister power to override in the sense of giving "binding instructions by a superior", which the direction in question undoubtedly purported to do. Had it been the intention of Parliament to give that power it could have been stated simply and specifically.' *Social Security Commission v McFarland* [1979] 2 NZLR 34 at 42, per White J

South Africa ' "Control" has a technical legal sense. We speak of a lessee having the "control" of the property which is leased to him; we speak of the depositee having the "control" of the property which is deposited with him; and we speak of a factor having the "control" of the property which has been handed over to him. In these cases the word "control" has a particular technical meaning. But it has also a more general meaning. The ordinary meaning of "control" is that the person who has the control of a thing has the possession of it, and that he has the management (to a limited extent, it may be) of it.' *R v Harvey* 1913 TPD 605 per Wessels J

Of company

'Control', in relation to a body corporate, means the power of a person to secure—
(a) by means of the holding of shares or the possession of voting power in or in relation to that or any other body corporate, or
(b) by virtue of any powers conferred by the articles of association or other document regulating that or any other body corporate,
that the affairs of the first-mentioned body corporate are conducted in accordance with the wishes of that person, and, in relation to a partnershp, means the right to a share of more than one-half of the assets, or of more than one-half of the income, of the partnership. (Income and Corporation Taxes Act 1970, s 534)

For the purposes of this Chapter, a person shall be taken to have control of a company if he exercises, or is able to exercise or is entitled to acquire, control, whether direct or indirect, over the company's affairs, and in particular, but without prejudice to the generality of the preceding words, if he possesses or is entitled to acquire—
(a) the greater part of the share capital or issued share capital of the company or of the voting power in the company; or
(b) such part of the issued share capital of the company as would, if the whole of the income of the company were in fact distributed among the participators (without regard to any rights which he or any other person has as a loan creditor), entitle him to receive the greater part of the amount so distributed; or
(c) such rights as would, in the event of the winding up of the company or in any other circumstances, entitle him to receive the greater part of the assets of the company which would then be available for distribution among the participators.'
(Income and Corporation Taxes Act 1970, s 302(2), substituted by the Finance Act 1972, s 94(2), Sch 17, para 5)

Australia [The Income Tax Assessment Act 1936 (Cth), s 136 provides that where any business carried on in Australia is 'controlled' principally by non-residents the person carrying on the business shall be liable to pay income tax on a taxable income of such amount of the total receipts of the business as the Commissioner of Taxation determines.] 'The word "controlled", when used passively, in its ordinary meaning refers to *de facto* control rather than to capacity to control'. *Federal Taxation Comr v Commonwealth Aluminium Corpn Ltd* (1980) 30 ALR 449 at 458, per Stephen, Mason and Wilson JJ

Of motor vehicle

Canada 'I take the meaning of "control of a motor vehicle" (in the Criminal Code s 285(4)

see now RSC 1970, c C-34, s 234] as to driving while intoxicated), to be having the means of setting the motor vehicle in motion, that is, being in such a position that he could make the motor vehicle move as he pleased. This pre-supposes that the motor vehicle is mechanically capable of being set in motion.' *R v Hyatt* [1945] OR 629 at 631, Ont SC, per Kelly J

Canada 'Control, contemplated from the point of view of the motorist, is the fact of being in a condition to make instantaneously the desired manoeuvre in opportune time, and also that of not making a move that would constitute a bad or a dangerous manoeuvre.' *Desbiens v R* (1951) 103 CCC 36 at 41, Que SC, per Bienvenue J

Of property

'All that he [the testator] gives is full and absolute control. One of the meanings of control is given in Johnson's dictionary as "superintendence". That means, it seems to me, that the property should be under the superintendence and management. These words simply give her [the defendant beneficiary] a wide power of management over the property destined by him to be enjoyed by the defendant for life, and after her death to pass to his brother. They do not affect any prior interests, and therefore it became incumbent on her to preserve the personal property in such a way as not to affect the relative rights of tenant for life and remainderman. . . . I do not think that those words were intended by the testator to permit her to commit waste.' *Pardoe v Pardoe* (1900) 82 LT 547 at 549, per Stirling J

Of servant

'Control includes the power of deciding the thing to be done, the way in which it shall be done, the means to be employed in doing it, the time when, and the place where it shall be done. All these aspects of control must be considered in deciding whether the right exists in a sufficient degree to make one party the master and the other his servant.' *Ready Mixed Concrete (South East) Ltd v Minister of Pensions and National Insurance* [1968] 1 All ER 433 at 440, per MacKenna J

Of society

'If matters are entrusted by the constitution of the society [a co-operative society] to the control of the committee, that committee is supreme and final in regard to them, otherwise

the word "control" would have little meaning.' *Alexander v Duddy* 1956 SLT 146 at 149, per the Lord President (Clyde)

CONTROLLED LAND

(1) In this Act the expression 'controlled land' means land abutting on a street which is a maintainable highway or is prospectively a maintainable highway (in whatsoever use the land is for the time being, not excepting use as or as part of a garden or pleasure ground or the curtilage of a building), being land which either—

    (a) belongs to the street authority and is for the time being held by them, or capable of being immediately appropriated by them, for road purposes; or

    (b) is the subject of a subsisting authorisation of compulsory acquisition by them given with a view to their holding it for road purposes; or

    (c) lies between the boundary of the street and an improvement line prescribed under section thirty-three of the Public Health Act 1925, or under that section as applied by any other enactment, or under any corresponding provision in a special enactment.

(2) Where a piece of land which would be controlled land within the definition in the preceding sub-paragraph contains any building, structure or erection other than fences, fence-walls, gates, posts, hoardings or other similar structures or erections, the controlled land shall be treated as consisting of the piece of land exclusive of the building, structure, or erection, and of strata under or above it:

Provided that the placing of a building, structure or erection in controlled land after apparatus has been placed in it by virtue of an authorisation under this Schedule shall not affect the right of the undertakers to keep the apparatus there and to execute any undertakers' works in relation thereto (including the placing of apparatus by way of renewal thereof and undertakers' works requisite therefor or incidental thereto), and references in this Act to works executed in controlled land shall extend to works executed in exercise of that right.

(3) Land falling within the definition of controlled land in this paragraph which or an interest in which is held by the Minister shall not be treated as excluded therefrom

by reason of its being held by him on behalf of the Crown.
(Public Utilities Street Works Act 1950, Sch 1)

CONTROLLED SCHOOL   *See* SCHOOL

CONTROLLING INTEREST   *See also* CONTROL; INTEREST

Australia   'It is now beyond question that company A has a controlling interest in company C if, having control of company B, it has the majority voting power in company C by means of the votes attaching to its shares in company C and those attaching to the shares held in company C by company B. It is consistent with this approach to say that a parent company has a controlling interest in another company, its sub-subsidiary, even though it holds no shares in the sub-subsidiary, provided that it controls the majority in voting power in its subsidiary which in turn controls the majority voting power in the sub-subsidiary.' *Kolotex Hosiery (Australia) Pty Ltd v Federal Taxation Comr* [1973] 1 ALR 213 at 225, per Mason J

CONVENIENCE

[An agreement for the sale of shares in certain ships provided that the balance of the purchase-money should be payable at the 'convenience' of the purchasers.] 'If by the word "convenience" had been meant will or pleasure, those words would have been used. The phrase means that the money shall be paid at the convenience of the purchasers, thereby meaning their mercantile convenience. The purchasers are to pay as soon as they have money sufficient and free from the ordinary purposes of business. When they have sufficient clear profit to pay the purchase money then it will be convenient for them to pay it.' *Crawshaw v Hornstedt* (1887) 3 TLR 426 at 427, per Lord Esher MR

CONVENIENT   *See also* FIT

[A bond contained a condition to allow the plaintiff to thresh corn and carry it away at all times 'convenient'.] 'Here you have bound yourselves, and the condition is "at time convenient" and if he will come in the night, or on the Sabbath day, this is no convenient time, but although he come in a long time after it may be

"at" time convenient, and the words are not "within" time convenient.' *Kent's (Earl) Case* (1588) Gouldsb 76 at 77, per cur.

'I think that the breach of a covenant, in not allowing the landlord to view, is not made out. He is to view at "convenient times"; and I think that he ought to give notice that he is coming; and if he does not give notice, it is not to be considered a "convenient time", as it cannot be expected that, where any business is carried on, they can allow the landlord to go all over the premises without they have previous notice of his coming.' *Doe* d *Wetherell v Bird* (1833) 6 C & P 195 at 200, per Lord Denman CJ

CONVERSION   *See also* TROVER

Equitable doctrine

The rule that equity considers that as done which ought to be done has given rise to the doctrine of conversion by means of which land may be impressed with the legal qualities of personal estate, and money may be impressed with the legal qualities of real estate, even though no actual sale or purchase, as the case may be, has taken place. This change of one kind of property into the other may follow from a direction contained in a will or settlement, from a contract, from a court order, or from land becoming subject to a trust for sale by virtue of statute. The general principle is that land directed or agreed to be sold and turned into money, or money directed or agreed to be laid out in the purchase of land is to be considered as that species of property into which it is directed or agreed to be converted: thus the owner of the property or the contracting parties may make land money, or money land. It follows that no change is effected where land is directed to be sold and the proceeds reinvested in the purchase of land. The Administration of Estates Act 1925, by establishing a uniform system of intestate succession for real and personal property, greatly diminished the importance of the doctrine of conversion, which is now concerned mainly with the competing claims of devisees of land and legatees of money. (16 Halsbury's Laws (4th edn) para 1372)

'Nothing is better established than this principle: that money directed to be employed in the purchase of land, and land directed to be sold and turned into money, are to be considered as that species of property into which they are directed to be converted; and this in whatever manner the direction is given; whether by will, by way of contract, marriage articles, settlement, or otherwise, and whether the money is actually deposited, or only covenanted to be paid, whether the land is actually conveyed, or only agreed to be conveyed. The owner of the fund, or the contracting parties, may make land money, or money land. The cases establish this rule universally. If any difficulty has arisen, it has arisen from special circumstances.' *Fletcher v Ashburner* (1779) 1 Bro CC 497 at 499, per Sewell MR

'It is an established principle in equity that when money is directed or agreed to be turned into land, or land agreed or directed to be turned into money, equity will treat that which is agreed to be, or which ought to be, done as done already, and impresses upon the property that species of character for the purpose of devolution and title into which it is bound ultimately to be converted. This doctrine of conversion necessarily affects partnerships.' *A-G v Hubbuck* (1884) 13 QBD 275 at 289, CA, per Bowen LJ

United States An instrument is converted when
(a) a drawee to whom it it delivered for acceptance refuses to return it on demand; or
(b) any person to whom it is delivered for payment refuses on demand either to pay or to return it; or
(c) it is paid on a forged indorsement.
(Uniform Commercial Code 1978, s 3–419(1))

Of goods

Conversion exists in three forms. To constitute the first form of conversion there must be a positive wrongful act of dealing with the goods in a manner inconsistent with the owner's rights, and an intention in so doing to deny the owner's rights or to assert a right inconsistent with them. This inconsistency is the gist of the action. There need not be any knowledge on the part of the person sued that the goods belong to someone else; nor need there be any positive intention to challenge the true owner's rights. The action is not one in which fraud is a necessary ingredient. Goods may be the subject of successive and independent conversions by persons dealing with them in such a manner and with such an intention. A second form of conversion is committed where goods are wrongfully detained by the defendant. A wrongful detention gave rise to an action for detinue before detinue was abolished and now

gives rise to an action in conversion. The normal method of establishing a wrongful detention is to show that the plaintiff made a demand for the return of the goods and that the defendant refused after a reasonable time to comply with that demand. In many cases this form of conversion will coincide with the first. The third form of conversion lies for loss or destruction of goods which a bailee has allowed to happen in breach of his duty to his bailor. This enables conversion to be brought in a case which would not have constituted conversion at common law, but which would have been detinue before detinue was abolished. (45 Halsbury's Laws (4th edn) para 1422)

'In order to constitute a conversion it is necessary either that the party taking the goods should intend some use to be made of them, by himself, or by those for whom he acts, or that, owing to his act, the goods are destroyed or consumed, to the prejudice of the lawful owner. . . . But it has never yet been held, that the single act of removal of a chattel, independent of any claim over it, either in favour of the party himself or any one else, amounts to a conversion of the chattel.' *Fouldes v Willoughby* (1841) 8 M & W 540 at 547, per Lord Abinger CB

'Any asportation of a chattel for the use of the defendant, or a third person, amounts to a conversion; for this simple reason, that it is an act inconsistent with the general right of dominion which the owner of the chattel has in it.' Ibid at 548, per Alderson B

'Where, as is the case here, there is no unlawful taking of possession or assertion of dominion over the goods, although the goods may be destroyed, there is no conversion, unless the bailee is a participator in the act which causes their destruction.' *Heald v Carey* (1852) 11 CB 977 at 993, per Maule J

'In order to constitute a conversion, there must be an intention of the defendant to take to himself the property in the goods, or to deprive the plaintiff of it. If the entire article is destroyed, as, for instance, by burning it, that would be a taking of the property from the plaintiff and depriving him of it, although the defendant might not be considered as appropriating it to his own use.' *Simmons v Lillystone* (1853) 8 Exch 431 at 442, per Parke B

'Any person who, however innocently, obtains possession of the goods of a person who has been fraudulently deprived of them, and disposes of them, whether for his own benefit or that of any other person, is guilty of a conversion.' *Hollins v Fowler* (1875) LR 7 HL 757 at 795, per Lord Chelmsford

'I agree that the language used by Kelly CB, in *England v Cowley* [(1873) LR 8 Ex 126 at 131] supports the view that even in a case where possession has not been taken by the defendant but all that has happened is that the defendant claims to exercise as against the plaintiff the rights of owner in respect of the goods that is sufficient to support an action for conversion.' *Oakley v Lyster* [1931] 1 KB 148 at 155, CA, per Greer LJ

'Conversion was defined by Atkin J as he then was, in *Lancashire & Yorkshire Ry Co v Mac-Nicoll* [(1918) 88 LJKB 601 at 605, DC]. "Dealing . . . with goods in a manner inconsistent with the right of the true owner amounts to a conversion, provided that it is also established that there is also an intention on the part of the defendant in so doing to deny the owner's right or to assert a right which is inconsistent with the owner's right." This definition was approved by Scrutton LJ in *Oakley v Lyster* [supra]. Atkin J goes on to point out that, where the act done is necessarily a denial of the owner's right of an assertion of a right inconsistent therewith, intention does not matter. Another way of reaching the same conclusion would be to say that conversion consists in an act intentionally done inconsistent with the owner's right, though the doer may not know of or intend to challenge the property or possession of the true owner.' *Caxton Publishing Co Ltd v Sutherland Publishing Co Ltd* [1939] AC 178 at 201, 202, per Lord Porter

'It would be rash, I think, to attempt a definition of the term "converts to his own use" which would cover every possible case. A sale of the property by the bailee, contrary to the terms of the bailment, and for his own benefit, is clearly such a conversion. The reason is that the bailee in such a case has usurped the rights of the owner for his, the bailee's benefit. Is the position any different in the case of an attempted sale? I think not. If I am lent property, and then determine in my own mind to sell it for my own benefit contrary to the terms of the bailment, I have determined that in relation to the property I will no longer be a borrower but an owner, and an owner who wishes to sell. When I proceed to carry that intention into effect by offering the property for sale, I am standing in the owner's shoes in relation to that property and exercising an owner's right. In these circumstances I have, in

my view, already converted the property to my own use whether the attempted sale takes place or not; and if I have acted dishonestly in the matter, as the respondent here is found to have done, then the offence of larceny is committed.' *Rogers v Arnott* [1960] 2 All ER 417 at 420, per Donovan J; also reported in [1960] 2 QB 244 at 251

Of securities

'Conversion of securities' includes—
(i) a conversion of securities of a company into shares in the company, and
(ii) a conversion at the option of the holder of the securities converted as an alternative to the redemption of those securities for cash, and
(iii) any exchange of securities effected in pursuance of any enactment (including an enactment passed after this Act) which provides for the compulsory acquisition of any shares or securities and the issue of securities or other securities instead.
(Capital Gains Tax Act 1979, s 82(3)(a))

CONVERT

[A will contained a forfeiture clause directed against any child becoming a 'convert' to the Roman Catholic religion.] 'A person becoming a convert to the Roman Catholic faith must do definite acts and must be admitted into the Roman Catholic Church. Before being admitted into the Roman Catholic Church, such a person must renounce the religion which he or she had before, and before becoming a convert, is baptised, perhaps conditionally, into the Roman Catholic Church and is given a name on that baptism. There is . . . in this case no difficulty in the Court's ascertaining for itself whether a person has become a convert or not. Once the person has been admitted into the Roman Catholic Church the forfeiture operates (assuming it to operate at all) and no change of mind or failure to continue to be a Roman Catholic can affect the forfeiture which has taken place once and for all by the definite act of being received into the Roman Catholic Church.' *Re Evans, Hewitt v Edwards* [1940] Ch 629 at 634, 635, per Farwell J

CONVEYANCE   *See also* DISPOSITION
AND CONVEYANCE

Conveyance, unless a contrary intention appears, includes assignment, appointment, lease, settlement, and other assurance, and covenant to surrender, made by deed, on a sale, mortgage, demise, or settlement of any property, or on any other dealing with or for any property; and convey, unless a contrary intention appears, has a meaning corresponding with that of conveyance. (Conveyancing Act 1881, s 2)

'Conveyance' includes a mortgage, charge, lease, assent, vesting declaration, vesting instrument, disclaimer, release and every other assurance of property or of an interest therein by any instrument, except a will; 'convey' has a corresponding meaning; and 'disposition' includes a conveyance and also a devise bequest, or an appointment of property contained in a will; and 'dispose of' has a corresponding meaning. (Law of Property Act 1925, s 205)

'Convey' and 'conveyance' as applied to any person include the execution by that person of every necessary or suitable assurance (including an assent) for conveying, assigning, appointing, surrendering, or otherwise transferring or disposing of land whereof he is seised or possessed, or wherein he is entitled to a contingent right, either for his whole estate or for any less estate, together with the performance of all formalities required by law for the validity of the conveyance. (Trustee Act 1925, s 68)

'Conveyance' includes a mortgage, charge by way of legal mortgage, lease, assent, vesting, declaration, vesting instrument, disclaimer, release and every other assurance of property or of an interest therein by any instrument, except a will, and 'convey' has a corresponding meaning, and 'disposition' includes a 'conveyance' also a devise bequest and an appointment of property contained in a will, and 'dispose of' has a corresponding meaning. (Administration of Estates Act 1925, s 55(1))

'Conveyance' includes a mortgage, charge, lease, assent, vesting declaration, vesting instrument, release and every other assurance of property, or of an interest in property by any instrument except a will, and 'convey' has a corresponding meaning. (Land Charges Act 1972, s 17(1))

'The term "conveyance" is well known to conveyancers as meaning an instrument which passes a freehold interest in real property. It may perhaps include other things, but I think that in its ordinary use it implies that the document is under seal.' *Rodger v Harrison* [1893] 1 QB 161 at 169, 170, CA, per Lopes LJ

'It cannot, I conceive, be at all in doubt that the words "conveyance" or "convey" will, to a lawyer at any rate, include prima facie, a lease or the grant of a lease. In modern times that construction may be said to be enshrined in the definition to be found in s 205(1), para (ii) of the Law of Property Act 1925 [supra] but it is indeed of much older significance.' *Littlewoods Mail Order Stores Ltd v Inland Revenue Comrs* [1961] 3 All ER 258 at 264, CA, per Lord Evershed MR; also reported [1961] Ch 597 at 622

'There is a known ambiguity in such words as "conveyance", since by themselves they are capable of referring either to the transaction itself or to the legal instrument that effects it. This is true of "conveyance", "mortgage" or "lease", but it is not true of "vesting declaration", which can refer only to the instrument itself; and when I find these and other words linked together in a definition of the word conveyance with a general reference at the end of the list to "every other assurance . . . by any instrument", I feel little doubt that apart from any special contexts, "conveyance" and "convey" in the Act [Law of Property Act 1925 (supra)] are intended to apply to instruments in writing only.' *Rye v Rye* [1962] 1 All ER 146 at 153, 154, HL, per Lord Radcliffe

Canada 'Reference is made to s 17 of the Devolution of Real Property Act, RSS 1940, c 108 [repealed; see now RSS 1978, C D-27, s 17] the pertinent portion of which is as follows: "Where there are two or more personal representatives a conveyance, mortgage, lease or other disposition of real property devolving under this Act shall not be made without the concurrence therein of all such representatives or an order of the court. . . ." A "conveyance" is not defined in the Act but from its use elsewhere in the same Act, as for instance in s 10, it seems to me it must be taken to mean an instrument in writing transferring title and does not include an agreement for sale. I am further of the opinion that an agreement for sale does not come within the words "or other disposition of real property" appearing in the section referred to, for the reason in that in the application of the *ejusdem generis* rule, which I think should be applied here, the general words employed must take their meaning from the specific words preceding them. I am fully aware that the English decisions give a very wide interpretation of "conveyance" as used in the English statutes, and that Lord Cairns LC in *Credland v Potter* (1875) LR 10 Ch 8, at p 12, stated: "There is no magical meaning in the word conveyance; it denotes an instrument which carries from one person to another an interest in land." At the same time I am mindful of the fact that the majority of the Court of Appeal in Alberta refused in *Nerland v Crossfield SD* [1929] 2 WWR 330, under our system of dealing with land, to go that far, and held that a mortgage is not a conveyance of land but only a charge upon it.' *Materi v Schlosser* [1945] 2 WWR 15 at 18, 19, Sask Dist Ct, per Hogarth DCJ

United States 'Conveyance' includes every assignment, lease, mortgage, or encumbrance. (Uniform Partnership Act 1914, s 2)

Conveyance on sale

For the purposes of this Act the expression 'conveyance on sale' includes every instrument, and every decree or order of any court or of any commissioners, whereby any property, or any estate or interest in any property, upon the sale thereof is transferred to or vested in a purchaser, or any other person on his behalf or by his direction. (Stamp Act 1891, s 54)

In this section the expressions 'conveyance on sale' and 'assignment on sale' mean an instrument made on sale by virtue whereof there is conferred or completed a title under which an application for registration as first proprietor of land may be made under this Act, and include a conveyance or assignment by way of exchange where money is paid for equality of exchange, but do not include an enfranchisement or extinguishment of manorial incidents, where under the Law of Property Act 1922, or otherwise, or an assignment or surrender of a lease to the owner of the immediate reversion containing a declaration that the term is to merge in such reversion. (Land Registration Act 1925, s 123)

Any instrument whereby property is conveyed or transferred to any person in contemplation of a sale of that property shall be treated for the purposes of the Stamp Act 1891 as a conveyance or transfer on sale of that property for a consideration equal to the value of that property. (Finance Act 1965, s 90(1))

'Turning to the Stamp Act [1891] the words used are "a conveyance on sale". Does that expression mean a conveyance where there is a definite contract of purchase and sale preceding it? Is that the way to construe the Stamp Act, or does it mean a conveyance the same as if it were upon a contract of purchase and sale?

The latter seems to me to be the meaning of the phrase as there used. The nature of the transaction being in substance what I have indicated, it comes within that interpretation of the language of the Stamp Act.' *Great Western Rly Co v Inland Revenue Comrs* [1894] 1 QB 507 at 512, 513, CA, per Lord Esher MR

'The word "sale" is a term of art. It takes place at the time when and the place where the property in the goods agreed to be sold is transferred from the buyer to the seller. In the case of a c.i.f. contract in the London Cattle Food Trade Association form, the time at which the transfer of the property in the goods agreed to be sold takes place is when the documents, and in particular the bill of lading, are transferred to the buyer by the seller with the intention of passing the property, and the place at which it takes place is where the goods, to which the documents relate, happen to be at that time.' *Draper (C E B) & Son Ltd v Turner (Edward) & Son Ltd* [1964] 3 All ER 148 at 152, CA, per Diplock J; also reported [1965] 1 QB 424

'The expression "conveyance on sale" includes every instrument whereby any property or any estate or interest in any property, upon the sale thereof is transferred to or vested in a purchaser. When the share transfers were executed . . . the shares had not been sold. There was no contract of sale. There was no one who was a purchaser. No sum of money was owing in respect of the shares. There was no transfer to a purchaser or vesting in a purchaser. In these circumstances, I do not consider that the transfers of the shares were "on sale" or "upon the sale thereof". The fact that there was the hope or the expectation or the strong probability of a sale serves merely to emphasise that there was no sale.' *William Cory & Son Ltd v Inland Revenue Comrs* [1965] 1 All ER 917 at 922, HL, per Lord Morris of Borth-y-Gest

CONVEYANCE (Vehicle)

[Section 12 of the Theft Act 1968 makes it an offence to take a motor vehicle or other 'conveyance' without authority.]

For purposes of this section—
(a) 'conveyance' means any conveyance constructed or adapted for the carriage of a person or persons whether by land, water or air, except that it does not include a conveyance constructed or adapted for use only under the control of a person not carried in or on it . . . (Theft Act 1968, s 12(7))

[The exception apparently excludes such vehicles as goods trailers and milk floats.]

Canada 'The word "conveyance" is not defined in the Act [Liquor Act, RSS 1965, c 382] but giving to it its ordinary and natural meaning, it would encompass a passenger automobile.' *R v Mojelski* (1968) 65 WWR 565 at 570, Sask CA, per Culliton CJS

CONVICTION

'Conviction' and 'convicted' do not include or refer to a conviction which under foreign law is a conviction for contumacy, but the term 'accused person' includes a person so convicted for contumacy. (Extradition Act 1870, s 26)

In this Act, unless the context otherwise requires, 'conviction' includes—
(a) a finding of guilt,
(b) a finding that a person is not guilty by reason of insanity,
(c) a finding under section 30(1) of the Magistrates' Courts Act 1980 (remand for medical examination) that the person in question did the act or made the omission charged, and
(d) a conviction of an offence for which an order is made placing the offender on probation or discharging him absolutely or conditionally.
(Bail Act 1976, s 2(1), amended by the Magistrates' Courts Act 1980, Sch 7, para 143)

'From the language [in the Coinage Offences Act 1861, ss 9 and 12 (repealed; see now Forgery and Counterfeiting Act 1982, ss 6, 22)] it is as clear as anything well can be that the intention of the Legislature in this section was that the finding of the jury that the accused was guilty should be treated as a conviction, "convicted" meant "found guilty", and the sentence was to follow on the conviction. And a plea of guilty would equally be a conviction.' *R v Blaby* [1894] 2 QB 170 at 172, CCR, per Hawkins J

'The jury came to the conclusion that the appellant committed the act complained of, but was insane at the time. . . . It is now quite clear that the special verdict amounts to an acquittal of the person tried; and that being so he is not a person who has been convicted. The exact point arose in *Felstead v R* [[1914] AC 534]'. *R v Taylor* [1915] 2 KB 709 at 712, CCA, per Lord Reading CJ

'A conviction is an act of a court of competent jurisdiction adjudging a person to be guilty of a punishable offence. . . . A conviction is none the less a conviction because the ensuing penalty is not imprisonment, nor fine, but the finding of sureties for good behaviour.' *R v London County Quarter Sessions, ex p Metropolitan Police Comr* [1948] 1 KB 670 at 679, 680, per Atkinson J

'The question is whether in subsection (2)(a) [of s 21 of the Criminal Justice (Scotland) Act 1949] the word "convicted" is used in the narrow sense as indicating merely that the accused has been made the subject of a finding of guilty . . . or whether on the other hand the word "convicted" is used in what is recognised as the wider connotation as including not merely a finding of guilt but the executive action that follows thereon. . . . Unless the word "convict" in subsection (2)(a) has the wider meaning, it seems to me inevitable that a number of not merely inconvenient, but almost disastrous, consequences would ensue.' *HM Advocate v Churchill* 1953 SLT 45 at 46, per the Lord Justice-General (Cooper)

'The primary meaning of the word "conviction" denotes the judicial determination of a case; it is a judgment which involves two matters, a finding of guilt or the acceptance of a plea of guilty followed by sentence. Until there is such a judicial determination the case is not concluded, the court is not *functus officio* and a plea of *autrefois convict* cannot be entertained. . . . But the word "conviction" is used also in a secondary sense, that is, to express a verdict of guilty or acceptance of a plea of guilty before the adjudication which is only completed by sentence. Not only is the word used frequently in this sense in many judgments but also in many places in statutes dealing with these matters. As Tindal CJ, said in *Burgess's case* [(1844) 7 Man & G at 504]: "The word 'conviction' is undoubtedly *verbum aequivocum*. It is sometimes used as meaning the verdict of a jury, and at other times, in its more strictly legal sense, for the sentence of the court".' *S (an infant) v Manchester City Recorder* [1969] 3 All ER 1230 at 1246, 1247, HL, per Lord Upjohn

[The Criminal Appeal Act 1968, s 2(1) makes provision for the Court of Appeal to allow an appeal against 'conviction'.] 'That the word "conviction" is capable of more than one meaning has been recognised by the courts over many years. In *R v Ireland* [[1970] 1 KB 654] this court . . . cited an earlier decision in which it had been pointed out that the word "conviction" was undoubtedly equivocal, sometimes used as meaning the verdict of the jury and at other times used in a more strictly legal sense for the sentence of the court, and continued thus: "It is perfectly obvious that these words 'convicted', 'conviction', are neither of them words of precise meaning." In the House of Lords in *S (an infant) v Manchester City Recorder* [supra] . . . Lord Reid said this: "Much of the difficulty has arisen from the fact that 'conviction' is commonly used with two different meanings. It often is used to mean final disposal of a case and it is not uncommon for it to be used as meaning a finding of guilt. It is proper to say that a plea cannot be changed after 'conviction' in the former sense. But it does not at all follow that a plea cannot be changed after 'conviction' in the latter sense." We have reached the conclusion that "conviction" in the 1968 Act may properly encompass the verdict of the jury finding the accused guilty.' *R v Drew* [1985] 2 All ER 1061 at 1064, CA, per Lord Lane CJ

Australia 'The expression "conviction" in itself is undoubtedly ambiguous, and for its interpretation in all the circumstances the only guide is to be found in the terms of the statute in which it appears. . . . Avery J, however, has said that "without proceeding to conviction" may mean without recording a conviction, or, in other words, an adjudication that the offence has been committed plus a judgment (*Oaten v Auty* (1919) 2 KB 278).' *Re Stubbs* (1947) 47 NSWSR 329 at 335, per Davidson J

Australia 'The review of the authorities which we have made satisfies us that a plea of guilty does not of its own force constitute a conviction. In our opinion it amounts to no more than a solemn confession of the ingredients of the crime alleged. A conviction is a determination of guilt, and a determination of guilt must be the act of the court or the arm of the court charged with deciding the guilt of the accused. It may be that even a determination of guilt will not in all cases amount to a "conviction", for the latter term may be used in a particular context as meaning not merely conviction by verdict where no judgment is given, but conviction by judgment (*vide, Burgess v Boetefeur* (1844) 7 Man & G 481, and Hale's Pleas of the Crown, vol 1, p 686); but there must at least be a determination of guilt before there can be a conviction. There can accordingly be no conviction on a count to which an accused pleads guilty until by some act on the part of the court it has indicated a determination of the question of guilt. And if there can be no conviction till then, neither can there be a successful plea of *autrefois convict*.' *R v Tonks* [1963] VR 121 at 127, 128, per cur.

Australia [The Justices Act 1902–1986 (NSW), s 112(1) provides that any person aggrieved by any summary 'conviction' or order of any justice or justices may commence proceedings in the Supreme Court for relief in accordance with the section.] 'I think it is clear that, in some sections of the Justices Act, the expression "conviction" refers to a final determination or judgment and the complete disposal of a case. On the other hand there are sections which clearly indicate that a finding of guilt only is denoted. In my opinion, the expression where it appears in s 112(1) refers to a finding of guilt, whether or not there has been imposed a consequential penalty.' *Dixon v McCarthy* [1975] 1 NSWLR 617 at 624, per Yeldham J

Canada 'The word "conviction" is not a term of art that is applicable only to Criminal Code offences punishable in the manner provided in the Code. When used in a statute, its meaning varies depending on the context in which it is found; it may or may not include the imposition of a penalty. Generally, however, a "conviction is where a person is found guilty of an offence" (Jowitt's Dictionary of English Law, 2nd ed, vol 1, "conviction"). The verb "to convict" is defined in the Oxford English Dictionary as follows: "To prove (a person) guilty of an offence which makes him liable to legal punishment".' *Morris v R* (1978) 91 DLR (3d) 161 at 182, SCC, per Pratte J

CONVOCATION

Each of the provinces of the Church of England has a representative assembly of the clergy, known as the convocation of the province. The history of these bodies goes back to the provincial synods of the mediaeval period. They continued in existence after the Reformation; but by a statute of Henry VIII it was enacted that the clergy must not assemble in convocation without the authority of the Sovereign's writ, nor make, promulge or execute canons without the royal assent and licence, or in contravention of the royal prerogative or of the customs, laws or statutes of the realm. Early in the eighteenth century the activity of the convocations was suspended, and they did not meet again for the transaction of business until the middle of the nineteenth century. In the present century the convocations have continued to exist side by side with a new legislative body which includes representatives of the laity, that is, the Church Assembly (now the General Synod). Their distinctive character and importance have, however, been much diminished, especially in consequence of the transfer (in 1970) of the power of making canons from the convocations to the General Synod. The Houses of Bishops and Clergy of the General Synod are constituted by the membership of the Upper and Lower Houses respectively of the two convocations. (14 Halsbury's Laws (4th edn) para 442)

CO-OPERATIVE

'Co-operative marketing business' means a business carried on by a co-operative association and consisting of, or so much of a larger business so carried on as consists of, the storage, preparation for market or marketing, for the sole or primary purpose of assisting members engaged in the production in the United Kingdom of agricultural or horticultural produce for sale, of agricultural or horticultural produce produced by members of the association. (Agriculture Act 1967, s 64). [See amendment made by the Agriculture (Amendment) Act 1984, s 1.]

New Zealand 'The inclusion in its title of the word "co-operative" implies that it [the society or company] is a joint-stock society established for the purpose of carrying on its business among its members . . . a co-operative company is generally understood to mean one in which the business is confined to the members of the society.' *McGregor v Pihama Co-operative Dairy Co Ltd* (1907) 26 NZLR 933 at 938, per Cooper J; also reported 9 GLR 373 at 376

Farmers' co-operative association

New Zealand 'I think a proper definition of a "farmers' co-operative association" would be (a) that its shareholders are farmers; (b) that it either deals in farm produce or in those goods that are requisite for farmers, such as farm machinery, implements, and, it may be, building material, stock, and food and clothing that farmers may require as farmers, or that it carries on farming operations; (c) that it is co-operative. This, I think, would be giving a wide meaning to the phrase "farmers' co-operative association", and would not limit it to a co-operative association for farming or for the distribution of farm produce.' *New Zealand Farmers' Co-operative Distributing Co Ltd v Stamps Comr* (1905) 24 NZLR 638 at 640, 641, per Stout CJ; also reported 7 GLR 117 at 118

COPARCENARY

Before 1926 land might be held in coparcenary. Coparcenary arose where two or more persons took hereditaments by the same title by descent. This might be at common law or by special custom. Coparcenary arose at common law where upon the death of a man seised in fee or in tail the land descended upon two or more females as heirs general or heirs in tail; it arose by custom where, according to the custom of gavelkind, the land descended upon two or more male persons. Such persons were called 'coparceners'; they constituted but one heir to their ancestor; they had a joint seisin, and they had equal rights in the land as regards each other. However, under a devise to the testator's right heirs, if the heirs were coheiresses, they took as joint tenants and not as coparceners. . . . Descent or coparceners, whether under the general law of descent or by the custom of gavelkind, has been abolished, and on the death intestate after 1925 of a person seised in fee simple no coparcenary can arise. However, the abolition of the rules of descent does not affect the descent of an entailed interest, and coparcenary may still arise where under an entail the land devolves upon female coheirs; the land will be held on trust for sale, and the interest of the coparceners will be equitable entailed interests in the procees of sale. Coparcenary may also arise on the death of a person who was mentally disordered and of full age on 1st January 1926 and who dies without recovering his testamentary capacity. The custom of gavelkind has been wholly abolished, so that coparcenary in these two cases will only arise in circumstances where it would have arisen under the general law before 1926. (39 Halsbury's Laws (4th edn) paras 565, 567)

COPARTNERSHIP   *See* PARTNERSHIP

COPY   *See also* DUPLICATING PROCESS

'Copy', in relation to a cinematograph film, means any print, negative, tape or other article on which the film or part of it is recorded. (Copyright Act 1956, s 13(10))

'A copy is that which comes so near to the original as to give every person seeing it the idea created by the original.' *West v Francis* (1822) 5 B & Ald 737 at 743, per Bayley J

'The copyright in the picture belongs to Mr G. . . ., he made an engraving of it, of which he sold copies; he had not given any right to others to multiply them, and the photographs for which the penalties were recovered were made by photographing the engraving, and not the original picture, and it has been argued that the photograph of the engraving, being a reproduction of a copy of the design of the painting, is not a copy of the painting itself. It seems to me that cannot be so. When the subject of a picture is copied, it is of no consequence whether that is done directly from the picture itself or through intervening copies; if in the result that which is copied be an imitation of the picture, then it is immaterial whether that be arrived at directly or by intermediate steps.' *Ex p Beal* (1868) LR 3 QB 387 at 393, 394, per Blackburn J

United States 'Copies' are material objects, other than phonorecords, in which a work is fixed by any method now known or later developed, and from which the work can be perceived, reproduced, or otherwise communicated, either directly or with the aid of a machine or device. The term 'copies' includes the material object, other than a phonorecord, in which the work is first fixed. (Copyright Act of 1976, s 101)

COPYRIGHT   *See also* AUTHOR; COPY

Copyright is the exclusive right to do, and to authorise others to do, in the United Kingdom or in any other country to which the relevant provision of the Copyright Act 1956 extends, certain acts in relation to literary, dramatic and musical works, in relation to artistic works and in relation to sound recordings, cinematograph films, sound and television broadcasts and published editions of works. The acts concerned vary according to the subject matter: in general, the existence of copyright protects the maker of a work or other subject matter from the appropriation of his labours by another. For this reason, it has been said to be a negative right. (9 Halsbury's Laws (4th edn) para 801)

In this Act 'copyright' in relation to a work (except where the context otherwise requires) means the exclusive right, by virtue and subject to the provisions of this Act, to do, and to authorise other persons to do, certain acts in relation to that work in the United Kingdom or in any other country to which the relevant provision of this Act extends.

The said acts, in relation to a work of any description, are those acts which, in the relevant provision of this Act, are designated as the acts restricted by the copyright in a work of that description.

In accordance with the preceding subsection, but subject to the following provisions of this Act, the copyright in a work is infringed by any person who, not being the owner of the copyright, and without the licence of the owner thereof, does, or authorises another person to do, any of the said acts in relation to the work in the United Kingdom or in any other country to which the relevant provision of this Act extends. (Copyright Act 1956, s 1(1), (2))

[As to copyright in cable programmes, see s 4A of the Copyright Act 1956, inserted by the Cable and Broadcasting Act 1984, s 22.]

'The term "copyright" may be understood in two different senses. The author of a literary composition which he commits to paper belonging to himself, has an undoubted right at common law to the piece of paper on which his composition is written, and to the copies which he chooses to make of it for himself or for others. If he lends a copy to another his right is not gone; if he sends it to another under an implied undertaking that he is not to part with it or publish it he has a right to enforce that undertaking. . . . The other sense of that word is, the exclusive right of multiplying copies: the right of preventing all others from copying, by printing or otherwise.' *Jefferys v Boosey* (1854) 4 HL Cas 815 at 919, 920, per Parke B

Period of copyright

In this paragraph [referring to works of joint authorship] 'the period of copyright' means whichever is the longer of the following periods, that is to say—
(a) The life of the author who died first and a term of fifty years after his death, and
(b) The life of the author who died last.
(Copyright Act 1956, Sch 7(10))

[In the case of a single author, copyright in his work subsists until the end of the period of fifty years from the end of the calendar year in which the author died, and then expires; or where the work had not been published, performed etc, in his lifetime, then for fifty years after the year of first publication, performance, etc. (Copyright Act 1956, ss 2(3), 3(4))

COPYRIGHT OWNER

United States 'Copyright owner', with respect to any one of the exclusive rights comprised in a copyright, refers to the owner of that particular right. (Copyright Act of 1976, s 101)

COROLLARY

Canada [Divorce court was empowered to grant 'corollary' relief.] 'The use of the term "corollary" as an adjective is now rare but must, in the way it is used in the statute, be defined to mean "of the nature of a corollary". The relief sought must be of such nature. Several definitions of "corollary" as a noun are contained in the Oxford Concise English Dictionary. That dictionary offers four meanings. . . . None of these are of much assistance. There are two dominant themes—*consequential* and *additional*. It is obvious that a corollary is something bound by some tie to a principal matter. In this case the relief must be consequential or additional to the divorce relief. The legislation creates a nexus between the one and the other.' *Cook v Cook* (1981) 120 DLR (3d) 216 at 230, Nfld SC, per Goodridge J

CORONER

The coroner's is . . . a very ancient office at the common law. He is called a coroner, *coronator*, because he hath principally to do with pleas of the crown, or such wherein the king is more immediately concerned. And in this light the lord chief justice of the king's bench is the principal coroner in the kingdom, and may (if he pleases) exercise the jurisdiction of a coroner in any part of the realm. But there are also particular coroners for every county of England. . . . (1 Bl Com 335)

Franchise coroner

The expression 'franchise coroner' means any of the following coroners, that is to say, the coroner of the Queen's household, a coroner or deputy coroner for the jurisdiction of the Admiralty, a coroner appointed by Her Majesty the Queen in right of Her Duchy of Lancaster, and a coroner appointed for a town corporate, liberty, lordship, manor, university or other place, the coroner for which has heretofore been appointed by any lord, or otherwise than by election of the freeholders of a county, or of any part of a county, or by the council of a borough, and the expression, "franchise" means the area within which the franchise coroner exercises jurisdiction. (Coroners Act 1887, s 42)

CORPORATION

As all personal rights die with the person; and, as the necessary forms of investing a series of individuals, one after another, with the same identical rights, would be very inconvenient, if not impracticable; it has been found necessary, when it is for the advantage of the public to have any particular rights kept on foot and continued, to constitute artificial persons, who may maintain a perpetual succession, and enjoy a kind of legal immortality. These artificial persons are called bodies politic, bodies corporate (*corpora corporata*), or corporations: of which there is a great variety subsisting, for the advancement of religion, of learning, and of commerce; in order to preserve entire and for ever those rights and immunities, which, if they were granted only to those individuals of which the body corporate is composed, would upon their death be utterly lost and extinct. (1 Bl Com 455)

'Now it is to be seen what things are of the essence of a corporation. 1. Lawful authority of incorporation; and that may be by four means; by the common law, as the King himself, etc; by authority of parliament; by the King's charter (as in this case); and by prescription. The 2nd which is of the essence of the incorporation, are persons to be incorporated, and that in two manners, persons natural or bodies incorporate and political. 3. A name by which they are incorporated; as in this case governors of the lands, etc. 4. Of a place, for without a place no incorporation can be made. . . . 5. By words sufficient in law, but not restrained to any certain, legal, and prescript form of words.' *Sutton's Hospital Case* (1612) 10 Co Rep 1a at 29b, per cur.

'The City of London cannot make a corporation for that can only be created by the Crown; but this [the company and fellowship of porters] is only a fraternity, not a corporation, and a corporation may make a fraternity. A corporation is properly an investing the people of the place with the local government thereof, and therefore their law shall bind strangers; but a fraternity is some people of a place united together, in respect of a mystery and business, into a company, and their laws and ordinances cannot bind strangers, for they have not a local power or government.' *Cuddon v Eastwick* (1704) 1 Salk 192 at 193, per cur.

Australia 'In English law it has always been of the essence of the legal conception of a corporation that there should be a person in the case of a corporation sole or persons in the case of a corporation aggregate to be incorporated.' *Bank of New South Wales v*

Commonwealth [1948] 76 CLR 1 at 266, per Rich and Williams JJ

United States 'Corporation' or 'domestic corporation' means a corporation for profit, which is not a foreign corporation, incorporated under or subject to the provisions of this Act. (Revised Model Business Corporation Act 1984, s 1.40(4))

Bankruptcy

United States '[C]orporation'—
(A) includes—
   (i) association having a power or privilege that a private corporation, but not an individual or partnership, possesses;
   (ii) partnership association organized under a law that makes only the capital subscribed responsible for the debts of such association;
   (iii) joint-stock company;
   (iv) unincorporated company or association; or
   (v) business trust; but
(B) does not include limited partnership. . . . (Bankruptcy Act 1978, s 101(8))

Cathedral corporation *See* CATHEDRAL

City corporation

'Corporation' means the mayor and commonalty and citizens of the city acting by the common council. (City of London (Various Powers) Act 1967, s 3(1))

Corporation aggregate

A corporation aggregate has been defined as a collection of individuals united into one body under a special denomination, having perpetual succession under an artificial form, and vested by the policy of the law with the capacity of acting in several respects as an individual, particularly of taking and granting property, of contracting obligations and of suing and being sued, of enjoying privileges and immunities in common, and of exercising a variety of political rights, more or less extensive, according to the design of its institution, or the powers conferred upon it, either at the time of its creation or at any subsequent period of its existence. (9 Halsbury's Laws (4th edn) para 1204)

Corporation sole

A corporation sole is a body politic having perpetual succession, constituted in a single person, who, in right of some office or function, has a capacity to take, purchase, hold, and demise (and in some particular instances, under qualifications and restrictions introduced by statute, power to alienate) lands, tenements, and hereditaments, and now, it would seem, also to take and hold personal property, to him and his successors in such office for ever, the succession being perpetual, but not always uninterruptedly continuous; that is, there may be, and often are, periods in the duration of a corporation sole, occurring irregularly, in which there is a vacancy, or no one in existence in whom the corporation resides and is visibly represented. (9 Halsbury's Laws (4th edn) para 1206)

Ecclesiastical corporation *See* ECCLESIASTICAL CORPORATION

Municipal corporation *See* MUNICIPAL CORPORATION

CORPOREAL HEREDITAMENT *See* HEREDITAMENT

CORRESPOND

' "To correspond", does not usually, or properly, mean "to be identical with", but "to harmonise with", or "to be suitable to".' *Sackville-West v Holmesdale (Viscount)* (1870) LR 4 HL 543 at 576, per Lord Cairns

CORRESPONDENCE

'I disagree . . . with the proposition that the phrase "contract by correspondence" is apt to describe a contract resulting from the oral acceptance of an offer made by letter or from the acceptance by letter of an offer made orally. I do not think that a single letter can constitute "correspondence". I think that for there to be "correspondence" there has to be at least an exchange of letters. It is noteworthy that the definition of "correspondence" in the Oxford English Dictionary refers to "letters" in the plural. I leave aside and say nothing about cases where telegrams or telexes are used.' *Stearn v Twitchell* [1985] 1 All ER 631 at 634, per Warner J

CORRESPONDING

New Zealand 'Roper J in the Court below . . . relied on s 20A(1) of the Acts Interpretation Act 1924, to keep the old notices alive. This section, introduced into the Act by amendment in 1962, is as follows: "20A(1). Without limiting any other provision of this Act, it is hereby declared that the repeal or revocation of any provision by any Act, Order in Council, notice, regulations, or rules shall not affect any document made or any thing whatsoever done under the provision so repealed or revoked or under any corresponding former provision, and every such document or thing, so far as it is subsisting or in force at the time of the repeal or revocation and could have been made or done under that Act, Order in Council, or notice, or under those regulations or rules, shall continue and have effect as if it had been made or done under the corresponding provision of that Act, Order in Council, or notice, or of those regulations or rules, and as if that provision had been in force when the document was made or the thing was done." . . . We read "corresponding" in s 20A as including a new section dealing with the same subject matter as the old one, in a manner or with a result not so far different from the old as to strain the accepted meaning of the word "corresponding" as given in the Shorter Oxford English Dictionary— "answering to in character and function; similar to". The new [section] answers to the old one . . . in character and function; it is similar in purpose, prescribes the same thing to be done, and is designed to produce the same result. We hold it to be a "corresponding section".' *Winter v Ministry of Transport* [1972] NZLR 539 at 540, CA, per cur.

CORROBORATION

'Evidence which is admissible, relevant to the evidence requiring corroboration and (if believed) confirmatory of that evidence in a material particular, is capable of being corroborative and, when believed, is corroboration. The word 'corroboration' is not a technical term of art; it means by itself no more than evidence tending to confirm, support or strengthen other evidence. (11 Halsbury's Laws (4th edn) para 454)

'There is, I apprehend, a great difference between evidence of probability and evidence corroborative of a fact. . . . Evidence proving the probability of any transaction, but not going to the transaction or act itself, is *not* corroborative evidence in the sense in which I must use the term. . . . Where there is no rule as to the number of witnesses required, evi-

dence as to probability may have great weight and be justly considered in forming a conclusion; but when two witnesses are required by law, either together to one overt act, or separately to two overt acts, I conceive that evidence to mere probability, not applying to the act, cannot be received as corroborative. I think so for this reason, that, unless this distinction be adhered to, the rule of two witnesses must vanish into air, for there scarcely ever was a case in which some circumstance, in some degree tending to prove probability, might not be found.' *Simmons v Simmons* (1847) 1 Rob Eccl 566 at 572, 573, 575, per Dr Lushington

'Corroborative evidence is evidence which shows or tends to show that the story of the accomplice that the accused committed the crime is true, not merely that the crime has been committed, but that it was committed by the accused.' *R v Baskerville* [1916] 2 KB 658 at 667, CCA, per cur.

'The word "corroboration" in itself has no special legal meaning; it is connected with the Latin word *robur* and the English word "robust" and it means "strengthen": perhaps the best synonym is "support".' *Director of Public Prosecutions v Hester* [1972] 3 All ER 1056 at 1070, HL, per Lord Pearson

'There is, without doubt, some confusion in the authorities as to the extent to which lies may in some circumstances provide corroboration and it was this confusion which probably and understandably led the judge astray in the present case. In our judgment the position is as follows. Statements made out of court, for example statements to the police, which are proved or admitted to be false may in certain circumstances amount to corroboration. . . . To be capable of amounting to corroboration the lie told out of court must first of all be deliberate. Secondly it must relate to a material issue. Thirdly the motive for the lie must be a realisation of guilt and a fear of the truth. The jury should in appropriate cases be reminded that people sometimes lie, for example, in an attempt to bolster up a just cause, or out of shame or out of a wish to conceal disgraceful behaviour from their family. Fourthly the statement must be clearly shown to be a lie by evidence other than that of the accomplice who is to be corroborated, that is to say by admission or by evidence from an independent witness.' *R v Lucas* [1981] 2 All ER 1008 at 1011, CA, per cur.

'The leading case on the subject of corroboration remains *R v Baskerville* [supra] in which Lord Reading CJ said that it must be "independent testimony which affects the accused by connecting or tending to connect him with the crime. In other words, it must be evidence which implicates him—that is, which confirms in some material particular not only the evidence that the crime has been committed but also that the prisoner committed it." The other case to which reference must be made is *R v Mullins* [(1848) 3 Cox CC 526] in which it was said (by Maule J summing up to the jury), in our judgment correctly, that corroboration does not mean that there should be independent evidence of that which the accomplice relates, otherwise his testimony would be unnecessary, as it would merely be confirmatory of other independent testimony. These principles are indorsed by the textbooks.' *R v Beck* [1982] 1 All ER 807 at 815, per cur.

Australia 'Corroboration does not mean merely evidence which supports evidence of a complainant. It must also support that evidence in a material particular, and it must be evidence which *itself* implicates the accused—that is, shows or tends to show guilt of the offence charged.' *R v Witham* [1962] Qd R 49 at 53, per Hanger J

CORRUPT   See also DEPRAVE OR
   CORRUPT

'"Corrupt" is a strong word. The Book of Common Prayer, following the Gospel, has ". . . where rust and moth doth corrupt". The words "corrupt public morals" suggest conduct which a jury might find to be destructive of the very fabric of society.' *Knuller (Publishing, Printing & Promotions) Ltd v Director of Public Prosecutions* [1972] 2 All ER 898 at 932, HL, per Lord Simon

Australia 'The question has arisen of the direction to be given regarding the meaning of the expression "corruptly" on charges under para (b) of s 176(1) and (2) of the Crimes Act 1958 (Vic) . . . In my view, an agent does act corruptly if he receives a benefit in the belief that the giver intends that it shall influence him to show favour in relation to the principal's affairs. If he accepts a benefit which be believes is being given to him because the donor hopes for an act of favouritism in return, even though he does not intend to perform that act, he is, by the mere act of receiving the benefit with his belief as to the intention with which it is given,

knowingly encouraging the donor in an act of bribery or attempted bribery, knowingly profiting from his position of agent by reason of his supposed ability and willingness, in return for some reward, to show favouritism in his principal's affairs and knowingly putting himself in a position of temptation as regards the impartial discharge of his duties in consequence of the acceptance of a benefit.' *R v Dillon and Riach* [1982] VR 434 at 436, per Brooking J

Canada [By the Criminal Code, RSC 1927, c 36, s 504(2)(b) (see now RSC 1970, c C-34, s 383) it is an offence 'corruptly' to give any gift to an agent as an inducement for showing favour with relation to his principal's affairs.] 'The word "corruptly" in the section sounds the keynote to the conduct at which the section is aimed. The evil is the giving of a gift or consideration, not bona fide but mala fide, and designedly, wholly or partially, for the purpose of bringing about the effect forbidden by the section. It need not necessarily amount to a bribe to do some specific act, or a reward for having done it.' *R v Gross* [1946] OR 1 at 9, Ont CA, per Roach JA

CORRUPT PRACTICE

The following are corrupt practices [at elections]: (1) bribery; (2) treating; (3) undue influence; (4) personation; (5) making a false declaration as to election expenses; (5) incurring certain expenses without the authorisation of the election agent. (15 Halsbury's Laws (4th edn) para 687)

'First, as regards treating, which is specially dealt with by the [Corrupt Practices Prevention Act 1854], s 4 [repealed; see now Representation of the People Act 1983, ss 113–115]. Those who framed the Act appear to have intended that it should comprehend almost everything that can by any possibility happen in this way at an election, but they have governed it all by the word "corruptly". The interpretation of this word, as explained, and in my opinion rightly explained, by Mr Justice Willes, is not "wickedly", "immorally" or anything of the sort, but embraces such conduct as it was evidently the intention of the Legislature to discountenance.' *Bewdley Case* (1869) 19 LT 676 at 678, per Blackburn J

'Now what is the exact meaning of that word "corruptly"? It is difficult to tell; but I am satisfied it means a thing done with an evil mind—done with an evil intention; and except there be an evil mind or an evil intention accompanying the act it is not corruptly done. And thus when the word corruptly is used it means an act done by a man knowing that he is doing what is wrong, and doing so with evil feelings and evil intentions. I think it may be safely said that that is the meaning of the word "corruptly".' *Bradford Election Petition No 2* (1869) 19 LT 723 at 727, per Martin B

'The words of the Corrupt Practices Prevention Act [1854 (repealed; see supra)] are these: "Every person who shall directly or indirectly, by himself or by any other person on his behalf, give or procure, or agree to give or procure, or offer, promise, or promise to procure or to endeavour to procure, any office, place, or employment to or for any voter, or to or for any person on behalf of any voter, or to or for any other person, in order to induce such voter to vote or refrain from voting, or shall corruptly do any such act as aforesaid, on account of any voter having voted or refrained from voting at any election." Now the word "corruptly" has been several times under the consideration of the judges, and, as far as I know, they all agree. My brother Blackburn, certainly on two occasions, has laid down the law. . . . He says "What is the exact meaning of the word 'corruptly'?" This was undoubtedly upon the 4th section, and not upon this section which prohibits treating. "The word 'corruptly' means contrary to the intention of this Act, with motive or intention by means of it to produce an effect upon an election, not going so far as bribery, but going so far as to produce an effect upon the election." Now I construe that, and expressions of a similar character, as meaning that where the motive is, not a bona fide one of giving a privilege to a tenant, where the landlord expects nothing in return, and to have no influence upon his conduct—it is not that; but it is where the motive is to produce an effect upon an election.' *Launceston Case* (1874) 30 LT 823 at 831, per Mellor J

[The Public Bodies Corrupt Practices Act 1889, s 1(1) makes it a misdemeanour 'corruptly' to solicit or receive any gift, reward, etc, as a bribe in connection with a matter or transaction in which a public body is concerned.] 'The sole question, for the purposes of this case, is whether the word "corruptly" in its context means deliberately offering money, or whatever it may be, with the intention that it should operate on the mind of the person to whom the offer is made so as to make him enter into what I may call a corrupt bargain, or whether it means that the intention must be

that the transaction should go right through and that the offeror should obtain the favour for which he sought. It seems to this court that the word "corruptly" here used (and it is a word which appears throughout the Act of 1889 and other Acts dealing with corruption) is used in the former sense, namely, that it denotes that the person making the offer does so deliberately and with the intention that the person to whom it is addressed should enter into a corrupt bargain.' *R v Smith* [1960] 1 All ER 256 at 258, CCA, per cur.

COST

[The Public Service Vehicles (Travel Concessions) Act 1955, s 1(4) (repealed; cf the Transport Act 1985, s 94) provides that the council of a county borough or county district in whose area another local authority runs public service vehicles may contribute to any 'cost' in granting travel concessions.] 'There is a formal sense of the word "cost" which involves no expenditure: it is the cost of something done. If something is done free of charge, it will have cost the person doing it what might have been paid for it. But I do not think that "cost" here can mean that. I think that it must mean expenditure.' *Litherland Urban District Council v Liverpool Corpn* [1958] 2 All ER 489 at 492, per Harman J

Australia 'The word "cost" may be used in various senses. It may, in the case of manufacture, be used to mean the price paid for the raw material plus the wages paid for turning it into finished articles; and, in the case of trading, the price paid for what is re-sold. Or, in either case, it may include all the other expenses incurred in bringing into existence, or obtaining, and then selling a vendible article—what are generally described as "overheads".' *Ex p Brierley, Re Elvidge* (1947) 47 NSWSR 423 at 427, per Jordan CJ

Canada [An insurance policy provided for recovery of the 'cost' of restoration of damaged goods.] 'The word "cost" is capable of variable meanings and of longer or narrower construction according to the subject-matter and circumstances of the particular case. Often, the meaning intended is indicated or suggested by an associated word or phrase, such as "direct cost", "indirect cost", "cost of manufacture", "cost plus". And while the price of a commodity or service is sometimes said to be the "cost" of same, the words "cost" and "price" are not synonymous and where it appears in the "Limits of Liability" section [of the policy] the word "cost" is not to be read as meaning simply the amount charged, the "price", of repair.' *PM Scientific Fur Cleaners Ltd v Home Insurance Co* (1970) 12 DLR (3d) 177 at 184, 185, Man QB, per Wilson J; revsd 17 DLR (3d) 444, without affecting definition. Appeal quashed and application for leave to appeal dismissed 24 DLR (3d) 248n, SCC.

COST BOOK COMPANY

The term 'cost book' includes all books and papers relating to the business of a mine which are for the time being kept by a purser, or which, according to law or the custom of the stannaries, ought to be kept by him. (Stannaries Act 1887, s 2)

'A mining company, conducted on the cost-book principle, is somewhat in the nature of a joint-stock company, of which the essence is that the new partner comes in, not as a new partner, but in the place of the others.' *Geake v Jackson* (1867) 36 LJCP 108 at 109, per Montague Smith J

COST, INSURANCE AND FREIGHT   *See* c.i.f.

COST OF LIVING INDEX

Canada   [A lease provided for adjustment of rent pursuant to a formula based on the 'cost of living index.'] 'The governing principle must be to ascertain the intentions of the parties through the words they have used. In the Gage Canadian Dictionary, at p 263, "cost of living index" is defined as "a comparative study of the cost of living in a country or area, in Canada, especially that made monthly by the Dominion Bureau of Statistics". In the Canadian Living Webster Encyclopaedia Dictionary of The English Language, at p 230, cost of living index is defined as "an index indicating the weighted average of prices of 296 commodities purchased by consumers used to adjust wages to compensate for changes in the purchasing power of money. Also consumer price index". . . . It seems clear from the above dictionary definitions that the phrase, "cost of living index", is used in Canada commonly and interchangeably for the phrase, "consumer price index", and especially for the index published by the Dominion Bureau of Statistics. Judicial notice may be taken of the

fact that this Government Department is now known as Statistics Canada. We would be prepared to find, on this basis alone, that the proper interpretation of the phrase, "cost of living index", as used in para 24, is that it is synonymous with the "consumer price index" determined by Statistics Canada.' *Re Collins Cartage & Storage Co Ltd and McDonald* (1980) 116 DLR (3d) 570 at 572, 573, Ont CA, per Goodman JA

COSTS

'Costs' signifies the sum of money which the court orders one party to pay to another party in respect of the expense of litigation incurred. Except where specially provided by statute or by rule of court, the costs of proceedings are in the court's discretion. They normally follow the event so that the successful party will, in the absence of factors justifying some special order, be awarded his costs of suit to be agreed or taxed on a party and party basis. Such costs rarely provide complete reimbursement of expenses, and the principle of restitutio in integrum, which is applicable to damages, does not apply. (12 Halsbury's Laws (4th edn) para 1108)

'Costs' includes fees, charges, disbursements, expenses and remuneration. In relation to interlocutory proceedings, 'costs in the cause' means that the costs of those proceedings are to be awarded according to the final award of costs in the action; 'plaintiff's costs' (or 'defendant's costs') means that the plaintiff (or defendant) is to have the costs of the interlocutory proceedings without waiting for a final decision in the action; and 'plaintiff's (or defendant's) costs in any event' means that, no matter who wins or loses when the case is finally decided or settled, the plaintiff (or defendant) is to have the costs of those interlocutory proceedings, although it does not confer upon him a right to tax the costs until the event is finally decided or settled.

'No order as to costs' means that each party must bear his own costs. 'Reserved costs' are costs which will not be allowed on taxation unless the court makes a specific order dealing with them, and are not included in the costs of the action.

'Taxed costs' means costs taxed in accordance with the taxation provisions of the Rules of the Supreme Court. 'Fixed costs' are costs determined in relation to particular proceedings in accordance with prescribed scales.

'Party and party costs' are such costs as are

necessary or proper for the attainment of justice or for enforcing or defending the rights of the party whose costs are being taxed, and are designed, in theory at any rate, to indemnify that party against the expense to which he has been put by the litigation; they include only the bare costs necessarily incurred. 'Costs on the common fund basis' are more generous than party and party costs, and include a reasonable allowance in respect of all costs reasonably incurred. 'Solicitor and own client costs' are costs allowed on the taxation of a solicitor's bill to his own client, except one to be paid out of the legal aid fund or a bill with respect to non-contentious business, and include all costs except insofar as they are of an unreasonable amount or have been unreasonably incurred. (37 Halsbury's Laws (4th edn) para 1712)

'Costs' includes fees, charges, disbursements, expenses and remuneration. (Solicitors Act 1974, s 87(1))

'Costs' includes fees, charges, disbursements (including stamp duty), expenses and remuneration. (Costs of Leases Act 1958, s 2)

'A great principle, which underlies the administration of the English law, is that the courts are open to everyone, and that no complaint can be entertained of trouble and anxiety caused by an action begun maliciously and without reasonable or probable cause; but as a guard and protection against unjust litigation costs are rendered recoverable from an unsuccessful opponent. Costs are the creation of statute. The first enactment is the Statute of Gloucester, 6 Edw 1, c 1, which gave the costs of the "writ purchased". There is a passage in Lord Coke's Commentary, 2 Inst, 288, which it is worth while to examine, as it affords a key to the true view of the law of costs. That passage is as follows: "Here is express mention made but of the costs of his writ, but it extendeth to all the legal cost of the suit, but not to the costs and expenses of his travel and loss of time, and therefore 'costages' cometh of the verb 'conster', and that again of the verb 'constare', for these 'costages' must 'constare' to the court to be legal costs and expenses." What does Lord Coke mean by these words? His meaning seems to be that only legal costs which the court can measure are to be allowed, and that such legal costs are to be treated as expenses necessarily arising from the litigation and necessarily caused by the course which it takes. Professional skill and labour are recognised and can be measured by the law; private expenditure of labour and trouble by a layman cannot be measured. It depends on the zeal, and assiduity, or the nervousness of the individual. Professional skill, when it is bestowed, is accordingly allowed for in taxing a bill of costs; and it would be absurd to permit a solicitor to charge for the same work when it is done by another solicitor, and not to permit him to charge for it when it is done by his own clerk.' *London Scottish Benefit Society v Chorley* (1884) 13 QBD 872 at 876, CA, per Bowen LJ

Due to solicitor

[The 'costs' for payment of which a solicitor may obtain a charging order on property recovered in an action, include counsel's fees incurred, though not paid at the time of taxation.] 'The words [in the Solicitors Act 1860 s 28 (repealed; see now Solicitors Act 1974, s 73, which refers simply to "costs")] are "costs, charges and expenses". The Act is intended as a protection to the solicitor; and the charge covers costs, charges and expenses [e.g. counsel's fees] to be incurred, as well as those actually incurred at the date of the order [for taxation].' *Re Eden, Watkins v Eden* [1920] 2 KB 333 at 341, CA, per Bankes LJ

'Having regard to the definition [of the word "costs"; see now Solicitors Act 1974, s 87(1), supra], the phrase "costs due to a solicitor" must in the case of disbursements be interpreted as meaning disbursements due from the client to the solicitor. . . . A "disbursement" charged by a solicitor against his client for counsel's fees must always have meant a disbursement actually made—money paid out of the pocket of the solicitor— . . . and since the words "costs due to a solicitor" . . . have the same meaning, a solicitor is still prohibited from putting into his "bill thereof" any "disbursement" in respect of counsel's fees which he has not already paid, or at any rate unless at latest he pays it before delivering his bill to his client.' *Re Taxation of Costs, Re A Solicitor* [1936] 1 KB 523 at 530, CA, per Scott LJ

Following event

'Where the plaintiff succeeds on his claim and the defendant succeeds on his counterclaim costs follow the event in this way—the plaintiff is entitled to the costs of the action other than the counterclaim; the defendant is entitled to the costs of the counterclaim. . . . The costs must follow the two events.' *Shrapnel v Laing* (1888) 20 QBD 334 at 340, CA, per Fry LJ

'The words "the costs shall follow the event" [see now RSC 1965, Ord 62, r 3] mean that the costs are to be distributed according to the results of the several issues, while the party who is successful on the whole gets the general costs.' *Reid, Hewitt & Co v Joseph* [1918] AC 717 at 733, per Lord Finlay LC

Of appeal

' "Costs of the appeal" [in an order that the unsuccessful appellant should pay the costs of the appeal] mean additional expenses first incurred in the litigation which is started by the notice of appeal—extra expense incurred by reason of the appeal being taken.' *Kevans v Joyce* [1897] 1 IR 1 at 5, CA, per FitzGibbon LJ

See, generally, 10 Halsbury's Laws (4th edn) paras 827–829.

Of execution

[By the Bankruptcy Act 1890, s 11(1) (repealed; see now the Insolvency Act 1986, s 346), where a debtor's goods were taken in execution, and, before the sale or completion of the execution, the sheriff, on receiving notice that a receiving order had been made against the debtor, delivered the goods or money to the official receiver, the 'costs of the execution' were to be a first charge on the goods or money so delivered]. 'It is plain that the words in the subsection "the costs of the execution", mean the costs of the execution up to the time of the service on the sheriff of notice of a receiving order.' *Re Harrison, ex p Essex Sheriff* [1893] 2 QB 111 at 112, 113, DC, per Vaughan Williams J

'It is clear that under the subsection, the sheriff is not entitled to costs for any time for which he remains in possession after notice of a receiving order. I also think that, after notice of a receiving order, it ceases to be his duty to remain in possession.' Ibid at 113, per Bruce J

[A sheriff levied execution on the goods of a debtor and, at the latter's request, he remained in possession for fifteen months.] 'That section [the Bankruptcy Act 1890, s 11 (repealed; see supra] says that the costs of the execution shall be a first charge on the goods or money delivered up to the official receiver, and the only question really that we have to decide in the present case is, what costs are covered by or included in those words in this section, "costs of the execution"? . . . I do not see a word in the section to lead one to suppose that the words "costs of the execution" there mean

anything else than the costs of execution to which the sheriff would have been entitled apart from the bankruptcy. . . . The costs of execution cover all the ordinary costs which a sheriff would be entitled to if such costs were bona fide incurred in the course of execution.' *Re Beeston, ex p Board of Trade* (1899) 68 LJQB 344 at 349, CA, per Vaughan Williams LJ

'The costs of keeping possession, after the proper time for sale or other completion of the execution, are not costs of the execution [within the Bankruptcy Act 1890, s 11 (repealed; see supra] as against a creditor unless the creditor has consented to the prolongation of the possession.' *Re English & Ayling, ex p Murray & Co* [1903] 1 KB 680 at 682, per Wright J

Of reference to arbitration

'What are the costs of the reference? Those costs which are incidental to the reference and incurred in bringing it about—costs of arrangements, meetings, discussions, consultations, conferences, and all that are necessary to bring the parties *ad idem*—to the point on which they agree, but up to which there must be preliminary steps.' *Re Autothreptic Steam Boiler Co Ltd & Townsend, Hook & Co* (1888) 21 QBD 182 at 183, 184, per Huddleston B

'The costs of the submission are properly costs of the reference.' Ibid at 184, per Charles J

See, generally, 2 Halsbury's Laws (4th edn) paras 606–608.

COTTAGE

'A large dwelling-house or cottage may be divided into two or more distinct dwelling-houses or cottages, and each part may be so described . . . any small dwelling place may without impropriety of language be described as a cottage.' *Doe* d *Hubbard v Hubbard* (1850) 15 QB 227 at 239, 240, per Wightman J

'I conceive that there may be two cottages under the same roof, divided from each other by an internal partition, and that one cottage may be divided into two by such an internal partition, and by opening a new outer door. The definition of "cottage" contended for by the defendant [that a cottage necessarily means the whole interior of a small house under its roof and within its four walls] receives some countenance from that in Co Litt 56 b; "Cottage *cotagium*, is a little house without land to it"; and from stat 31 Eliz c 7 [repealed], respecting the erection and occupation of cottages, which seems to consider the whole building as one cottage, though occupied by several families. But we must suppose the word to be used by the testator in its common and familiar acceptation; and Dr Johnson in his dictionary defines cottage to be a "hut; a mean habitation; a cot; a little house". In Domesday Book *cotmanni* are often mentioned; and their dwellings were probably called cots or cottages, of whatever size or howsoever constructed.' Ibid at 244, per Lord Campbell CJ

COTTAGE GARDEN   *See*
AGRICULTURAL LAND

COTTAGER

'The term "cottager" is well known in the vernacular, and is used in common parlance to denote a man occupying a cottage as distinguished from a farm or mansion-house. It is often used to mean something more. . . . A cottager is often understood to mean a labourer who resides in a cottage on the estate on which he works, and which he rents from the landlord or farmer on easy terms.' *Foljambe v Smith's Tadcaster Brewery Co* (1904) 73 LJ Ch 722 at 724, per Kekewich J

COUNSEL

'Counsel' in this Act shall be construed to apply to attorneys in all cases where attorneys are allowed by law or by the practice of any court to appear as advocates. (Criminal Procedure Act 1865, s 9)

COUNTERCLAIM

When A has a claim of any kind against B and brings an action to enforce that claim, and B has a cross-claim of any kind against A which by the law he is entitled to raise and have disposed of in the action brought by A, then B is said to have a right of counterclaim (42 Halsbury's Laws (4th edn) para 407)

'A counterclaim is equivalent to a cross-action, and is instituted as a cross-action; there is the closest analogy between raising a counterclaim and instituting an action.' *Hood Barrs v Cathcart* [1895] 1 QB 873 at 875, DC, per Mathew J

COUNTERFEIT

For the purposes of this Part of this Act [Part II: counterfeiting and kindred offences] a thing is a counterfeit of a currency note or of a protected coin—
(a) if it is not a currency note or a protected coin but resembles a currency note or protected coin (whether on one side only or on both) to such an extent that it is reasonably capable of passing for a currency note or protected coin of that description; or
(b) if it is a currency note or protected coin which has been so altered that it is reasonably capable of passing for a currency note or protected coin of some other description.
(Forgery and Counterfeiting Act 1981, s 28(1))

[For the meaning of 'currency note' and 'protected coin', see ibid, s 27.]

'The coins were counterfeit in the strict and grammatical sense of the word, they were made other than that they ought to be, they were made to resemble that which they were not. They were not perfect and whole sovereigns; they were imperfect coin, milled so as to conceal their imperfections. . . . If the word "counterfeit" is to be taken in its ordinary or popular sense these coins seem to me to be counterfeit. In the ordinary sense of this word the idea of imitation is conveyed.' *R v Hermann* (1879) 4 QBD 284 at 288, CCR, per Lord Coleridge CJ

Trademark or tradename

United States A 'counterfeit' is a spurious mark which is identical with, or substantially indistinguishable from, a registered mark. (Lanham Act 1946, s 45)

COUNTING-HOUSE

'The description of "counting-house", in the absence of anything in the subject-matter or in the context to restrain it to any particular sort of counting-house, must be held to include anything that is a counting-house in the largest ordinary sense. That is the rule which has been constantly acted upon by this Court in construing the statutes which relate to the franchise. There can be no doubt that, in ordinary understanding, a counting-house is a part of a house which is devoted to the purposes of commercial business. It never has been suggested that it must be an entire house.' *Piercy v Maclean* (1870) LR 5 CP 252 at 260, 261, per Willes J

COUNTRY   *See also* OPEN COUNTRY

'Country' includes any territory. (Fugitive Offenders Act 1967, s 19).

Except where the context otherwise requires, in any provision of this Act to which this section applies a reference to a country or territory or to the territorial limits of any country shall be construed as including a reference to the territorial waters of the country or territory. . . . (Civil Aviation Act 1982, s 106(1))

COUNTRY OF ORIGIN

Canada 'It will be seen . . . that a prerequisite to registration [of a word or a group of words as a trade mark] in Canada, under s 28 (1)(d) of the Unfair Competition Act [see now Trade Marks Act RSC 1970, c T-10, ss 2.16] is that the appellant has already caused its trade mark to be validly registered in the "country of origin of such registration". Sub-s (2) of s 28 defines, for the purpose of that section, the expression "country of origin" to mean any country of the Union other than Canada, and "Country of the Union" is defined by s 2(b) of the Act to mean any country which has acceded to the Union for the Protection of Industrial Property under the Convention defined in s 2(a) of the Act, now known as the Convention of the Hague (1925) to which Convention both Canada and the United States are signatories. . . . Turning now to the words "country of origin" . . . there can be no doubt but that those words have reference to a country, other than Canada, which has acceded to the Convention of the Hague, and in which a person has registered a trade mark, which he now seeks to register in Canada, under s 28(1)(d) and (2) of the Act.' *Albany Packing Co Inc v Registrar of Trade Marks* [1940] Exch CR 256 at 263, 264, Ex Ct, per Maclean J

COUNTY BRIDGE   *See* BRIDGE

COUNTY COURT

(1) For the purposes of this Act, England and Wales shall be divided into districts, and a court shall be held under this Act for each district; at one or more places in it and throughout the whole of each district the court so held for the district shall have such jurisdiction and powers as are conferred by this Act and any other enactment for the time being in force.

(2) Every court so held shall be called a county court and shall be a court of record and shall have a seal.
(County Courts Act 1984, s 1)

COUNTY PALATINE

The prerogatives relating to the distribution of justice are, in general, inherent in and inseparable from the Crown, and although they formerly passed by way of franchise, along with the full jura regalia, to the grantees of the counties palatine of Durham, Chester and Lancaster, the prerogative rights relating to justice within those counties palatine are now in general revested in the Crown. The Courts of Chancery of the counties palatine of Durham and Lancaster have been merged with the High Court, and the jurisdiction of the Chester palatine courts has been abolished. It seems that grants of a like nature would now require the authority of an Act of Parliament. (8 Halsbury's Laws (4th edn) para 945)

COUPON

In this Part [Part V: Schedule C] of this Act . . . 'coupons' and 'coupons for any overseas public revenue dividends' include warrants for or bills of exchange purporting to be drawn or made in payment of any overseas public revenue dividends. (Income and Corporation Taxes Act 1970, s 107)

'A coupon [for payment of interest on a bond issued by a foreign government] is a security of the highest value; it is a security which when issued by such a government as this is held in the commercial world to be "as good as gold". It passes from hand to hand, as we all know, before and after it becomes payable, and is regarded as cash. In other words, the government undertakes with those who lend money to it that there will be, at the time when the interest becomes payable, money in the hands of their bankers or their agents at these different places [named in the coupon] to pay the amount of interest.' *Rothschild & Sons v Inland Revenue Comrs* [1894] 2 QB 142 at 146, DC, per Mathew J

COURSE OF DEALING

United States A course of dealing is a sequence of previous conduct between the parties to a particular transaction which is fairly to be regarded as establishing a common basis of understanding for interpreting their expressions and other conduct. (Uniform Commercial Code 1978, s 1–205(1))

COURSE OF EMPLOYMENT

'A workman is acting in the course of his employment when he is engaged "in doing something he was employed to do" or what is, in other and I think better words, in effect the same thing—namely, when he is doing something in discharge of a duty to his employer, directly or indirectly, imposed upon him by his contract of service. The true ground upon which the test should be based is a duty to the employer arising out of the contract of employment, but it is to be borne in mind that the word "employment" as here used covers and includes things belonging to or arising out of it.' *St Helens Colliery Co Ltd v Hewitson* [1924] AC 59 at 71, per Lord Atkinson

'The words "and in the course of" are not equivalent to "during". The accident must occur during the employment, but more than that, it must occur "in the course of the employment". The employment may be by the year. The accident must, of course, be one which happens during the year, but more than that, it must be in the course of the employment during the year. The employment may be to do some defined manual work, say, hewing coal, but the accident need not arise when the man is actually using his pick. He may be going down in the cage. He may be resting between shifts. He may be taking a meal. He may be merely standing by, waiting for the next job. All these and such as these, are not "the employment" but are incidental to the employment. The man is in the course of his employment—is engaged in his employment in all such cases. "They also serve who only stand and wait." In every case the facts have to be ascertained and discrimination made between the time during which or the place at which the employment is and those during or at which it is not being carried on. . . . The man is not in the course of his employment unless the facts are such that it is in the course of his employment, and in performance of a duty under his contract of service that he is found in the place where the accident occurs. If there is only a right and there is no obligation binding on the man in the matter of his employment there is no liability.' Ibid at 91, 92, 95, per Lord Wrenbury

'There can be no doubt that the course of employment cannot be limited to the time or place of the specific work which the workman is

employed to do. It does not necessarily end when the "down tools" signal is given, or when the actual workshop where he is working is left. In other words, the employment may run on its course by its own momentum beyond the actual stopping-place. . . . It is well-established that the workman, while leaving his employer's premises by one of alternative routes, is—at any rate, while on the premises—in the course of the employment, and it would surely be remarkable that, if, at the end of one of those permitted routes, the employers had provided by licence from third parties a route over such third parties' land for the very object of making the permitted route on the employer's premises an effective means of entrance or egress, the course of employment ceased on the employer's boundary.' *Weaver v Tredegar Iron & Coal Co Ltd* [1940] 3 All ER 157 at 164–166, HL, per Lord Atkin

'The words injury "arising out of and in the course of his employment" were used in the old Workmen's Compensation Acts from 1897 to 1945. The selfsame words have been used in the Road Traffic Acts 1930 and 1960. They have also been used in employer's liability policies. In my opinion they should receive the same interpretation in all three places for they are all so closely connected that they ought, as matter of common sense, to receive the same interpretation in each. The words were construed and applied in thousands of cases under the Workmen's Compensation Acts and I think we should follow those cases. The two leading cases, most apposite for present purposes, are *St Helen's Colliery Co Ltd v Hewitson* [supra] and *Weaver v Tredegar Iron and Coal Co Ltd* [supra]. They shew, to my mind quite conclusively, that when a man is going to or coming from work, along a public road, as a passenger in a vehicle provided by his employer, he is not then in the course of his employment—unless he is *obliged* by the terms of his employment to travel in that vehicle. It is not enough that he should have the right to travel in the vehicle, or be permitted to travel in it. He must have an *obligation* to travel in it. Else he is not in the course of his employment. That distinction must be maintained, for otherwise there would be no certainty in this branch of the law.' *Vandyke v Fender* [1970] 2 All ER 335 at 340, CA, per Lord Denning MR

Australia 'The proper construction of these words is now fairly well settled. The words "out of" require that the injury had its origin in the employment, whilst the words "in the course of" are not equivalent to "during"; the injury must occur in the course of the employment, that is, whilst the worker is doing something which is part of his service to his employer or master or incidental to the employment.' *South Maitland Railways Pty Ltd v James* (1943) 67 CLR 496 at 502, per Starke J

Australia 'It has been held in many cases that the words "course of employment" do not mark a period beginning and ending with the actual hours of work. A man may be in the course of his employment when he is on his way to his work or leaving his work. A plain case is where he is necessarily walking through one part of a factory in order to reach or to leave the part of the factory where his actual work lies. The course of employment may continue with break where a worker, with the permission of his employer, takes meals on the employer's premises.' *Davidson v Mould* (1944) 69 CLR 96 at 105, per Latham CJ

Australia 'In the Supreme Court, Jordan CJ, after referring to numerous authorities which establish that a workman injured while taking refreshment on the premises at a permitted hour may suffer an injury in the course of his employment, summed up the present state of the law as follows: "I think that if a worker is using part of his employer's premises for his own purposes during a rest period, it is immaterial, in this connection, whether he is doing so by the mere permission of his employer or in the exercise of a legal right conferred by the contract of employment. In the light of these authorities, if the terms of the contract of employment provide that the worker, during the course of the stipulated working day, may cease work for one or more short periods for the purposes of resting or refreshing himself, and he (the employer not objecting) on such an occasion occupies the period between the cessation of one period of work and the commencement of another by remaining in his workroom, it is, to say the least of it, possible to regard him as being in the course of his employment during the whole of the period that he so remains—as still doing something which can be regarded as being incidental to his employment. Nor would his position be bettered or worsened in this respect if he spent part of the time in eating and the remainder in dozing or all of it in resting. No doubt if in such a case he left his employer's premises altogether he would (prima facie at any rate) necessarily cease to be in the course of his employment whilst so absent. Between

these two extremes there is an infinite variety of possibilities, where the question is essentially one of degree and of fact. "I wish to express my entire concurrence with this summary. . . . But whereas the expression "out of the employment" denotes a certain degree of causal connection between the accident and the employment, the expression "in the course of employment" points to a period of time conditional by the workman's service . . . so that if the luncheon interval is included in that period, an injury received by the respondent during his lunch would not be an inquiry outside the course of his employment merely because in the course of having lunch he did something in an extremely negligent, rash or foolish way.' Ibid at 117, 119, per Williams J

Australia [An employee was shot outside his place of employment after having retreated into the street to escape an armed third party who had threatened him on the respondent company's premises. The quarrel which led to the threats and shooting had no connexion with the employment. The issue was whether the bullet wounds were an injury suffered in the 'course of employment' within the meaning of the Workers' Compensation Act 1926 (NSW), s 6.] 'The "course of employment" covers not only the performance of duties and the pursuit of ends laid down for the employee, but also activities which are adjuncts or incidents growing out of the employment. Certainly it must be correct to say that the avoidance of a risk of a personal injury arising from a danger at the place of employment, is something which the employee would be expected or authorized, if not required, to do by his employer, not only because it is in the interest of the employer that his servant should not sustain injury, but also because the employer would expect his servant to take reasonable steps for his own safety.' *Williams v Bill Williams Pty Ltd* [1971] 1 NSWLR 547 at 555, CA, per Mason JA

Canada 'The words "arising out of", in the Act [Workmen's Compensation Act, RSS 1902 (repealed; see now RSS 1978, c W-17 s 2)], suggest that the employment or the discharge of his duties by the workman must be the cause of the accident, and the words "in the course of employment" mean, that the workman in order to recover must be engaged at the time of the accident in the discharge of the duties he owes the employer under his contract of service.' *Kilgren v Browning Rural Municipality* (1928) 23 Sask LR 223 at 226, CA, per Martin JA

COURSE OF SHIP

'The whistling rule [now r 28 of the Collision Regulations 1965] . . . is limited. . . . Vessels must be . . . "taking any course authorised or required by these rules". It is not easy to put a clear interpretation upon the . . . limitation. . . . The word "required" is clear enough. There are certain things required by the rules to be done. The word "authorised" is, however, very much larger, and I am inclined to think that . . . it includes any course which, for the safety of the vessels, good seamanship requires to be taken with reference to the other vessel then in sight—although it is quite true that there are certain cases where you may say a more distinct authorisation arises. For instance, an overtaking vessel, which has to keep out of the way of the overtaken vessel, would be authorised in going to port or starboard, according as the circumstances of the case might require, and, under the crossing rule, the vessel which has to keep out of the way must be considered authorised to do so by one of several means, as the case may seem to require. I do not think the matter ought to be tied down to any narrow interpretation of the rule.' *The Uskmoor* [1902] P 250 at 253, 254, per Jeune P

' "Course and speed" in art 21 [of the Regulations for Preventing Collisions at Sea 1897; see now rule 21 of the Collision Regulations 1965] mean course and speed in following the nautical manœuvre in which, to the knowledge of the other vessel, the vessel is at the time engaged. . . . The "course" . . . does not mean the actual compass direction of the heading of the vessel at the time the other is sighted.' *The Roanoke* [1908] P 231 at 239, CA, per Lord Alverstone CJ

'We do not think that the words "taking any course authorised or required by these rules" [in art 28 of the Regulations for Preventing Collisions at Sea 1897; see now rule 28 of the Collision Regulations 1965] limited the application of the rule to the case of a course which, at the trial of a collision action, is found by the Court to have been authorised or required by the rules. We ought . . . to interpret the words as including any course alleged to have been taken by a vessel acting, whether under art 27 or art 29, or under the other articles, so as to avoid immediate danger. So that where . . . a vessel charged in an action with having taken—in acting for the other vessel—an improper course, causing or contributing to a collision, asserts in that action . . . that the

manœuvre was a proper course under the rules, she cannot successfully contend that because the Court holds that her story of the facts is an untrue story, and that upon the true facts the course taken by her was neither a course required nor authorised by the rules, she thereby gains exemption from liability from statutory blame for not sounding the signal appropriate to that course. It was a course which those in charge of the vessel professed at the time to take, and the owners of the vessel sought to justify in the action, as a course either authorised or required by the rules.' *The Hero* [1911] P 128 at 159, 160, CA, per cur.; affd. sub nom. *Hero (Owners) v Admiralty Comrs* [1912] AC 300

COURSING

'It cannot be held that the mere fact that . . . rabbits have no chance of escape prevents their chasing and worrying from being coursing. Whether the size of the enclosure was sufficient, or whether the way in which the rabbits were chased and worried was coursing, seems to me to be clearly a question of fact. If it took place in a room or other very small enclosure I can understand that it might be found as a fact not to be coursing at all, because it could not possibly afford a test of the coursing abilities of the dogs. The object is to test the coursing abilities of the two dogs which are slipped.' *Waters v Meakin* [1916] 2 KB 111 at 117, 118, per Bray J

'The mere fact of a rabbit being let loose in the view of dogs who chase it does not amount to coursing.' Ibid at 120, per Avory J

'The respondent was prosecuted for unlawfully killing a hare when he had no licence to kill game, contrary to the Game Licences Act 1860, s 4. . . . One of the exceptions in s 5 of the Act of 1860 . . . is "The pursuing and killing of hares respectively by coursing with greyhounds". . . . The contention on behalf of the appellant was that . . . the exception applied only to organised coursing meetings. On the part of the respondent it was contended that coursing meant any hunting of hares with greyhounds and was the sport of hunting with greyhounds by sight, and that the coursing need not be at an organised meeting to be within the meaning of the exception. . . . I find it a little difficult to perceive why this . . . exception should be restricted to a well-known sport. . . . If the Legislature had intended to limit the coursing which was excepted to a coursing in an organised way, nothing would have been easier than to say so.' *Dolby v Halmshaw* [1937] 1 KB 196 at 198–200, per Lord Hewart CJ

COURT

Originally the term 'court' meant, among other things, the Sovereign's palace. It has acquired the meaning of the place where justice is administered and, further, has come to mean the persons who exercise judicial functions under authority derived either directly or indirectly from the Sovereign. All tribunals, however, are not courts, in the sense in which the term is here employed. Courts are tribunals which exercise jurisdiction over persons by reason of the sanction of the law, and not merely by reason of voluntary submission to their jurisdiction. Thus, arbitrators, committees of clubs and the like, although they may be tribunals exercising judicial functions, are not 'courts' in this sense of that term. On the other hand, a tribunal may be a court in the strict sense of the term even though the chief part of its duties is not judicial. Parliament is a court. Its duties are mainly deliberative and legislative; the judicial duties are only part of its functions. A coroner's court is a true court although its essential function is investigation. (10 Halsbury's Laws (4th edn) para 701)

'Court' includes any tribunal or body exercising the judicial power of the State . . . (Contempt of Court Act 1981, s 19)

'I do not desire to attempt any definition of a "court". It is obvious that, according to our law, a court may perform various functions. Parliament is a court. Its duties as a whole are deliberative and legislative; the duties of a part of it only are judicial. It is nevertheless a court. There are many other courts which, though not courts of justice, are nevertheless courts according to our law. There are, for instance, courts of investigation, like the coroner's court. In my judgment, therefore, the existence of the immunity claimed [that defamatory statements made in proceedings before a 'court' are absolutely privileged] does not depend upon the question whether the subject-matter of consideration is a court of justice, but whether it is a court in law.' *Royal Aquarium & Summer & Winter Garden Society Ltd v Parkinson* [1892] 1 QB 431 at 446, 447, CA, per Fry LJ

'There are tribunals with many of the trappings of a court which, nevertheless, are not courts in the strict sense of exercising judicial

power. . . . It may be useful to enumerate some negative propositions on this subject: 1. A tribunal is not necessarily a court in this strict sense because it gives a final decision. 2. Nor because it hears witnesses on oath. 3. Nor because two or more contending parties appear before it between whom it has to decide. 4. Nor because it gives decisions which affect the rights of subjects. 5. Nor because there is an appeal to a court. 6. Nor because it is a body to which a matter is referred by another body. . . . The Board of Review [constituted to review the decisions of the Commissioner of Taxation] is an administrative as distinguished from a judicial tribunal.' *Shell Co of Australia Ltd v Federal Comr of Taxation* [1931] AC 275 at 296, 297, 299, PC, per cur.

'In my judgment, not every court is a court of judicature, i.e. a court in law. Nor am I prepared to assume that Parliament intends to establish a court as part of the country's judicial system whenever it constitutes a court. The word "court" does, in modern English usage, emphasise that the body so described has judicial functions to exercise; but it is frequently used to describe bodies which, though they exercise judicial functions, are not part of the judicial system of the kingdom. . . . When, therefore, Parliament entrusts a body with a judicial function, it is necessary to examine the legislation to discover its purpose. The mere application of the "court" label does not determine the question; nor, I would add, does the absence of the label conclude the question the other way. . . . Though the United Kingdom has no written constitution comparable with that of Australia, both are common law countries, and in both judicial power is an exercise of sovereign power. I would identify a court in (or "of") law, i.e. a court of judicature, as a body established by law to exercise, either generally or subject to defined limits, the judicial power of the state. In this context judicial power is to be contrasted with legislative and executive (i.e. administrative) power. If the body under review is established for a purely legislative or administrative purpose, it is part of the legislative or administrative system of the state, even though it has to perform duties which are judicial in character. Though the ubiquitous presence of the state makes itself felt in all sorts of situations never envisaged when our law was in its formative stage, the judicial power of the state exercised through judges appointed by the state remains an independent, and recognisably separate function of government. Unless a body exercising judicial functions can be demonstrated to be part of this judicial system, it is not, in my judgment a court in law. I would add that the judicial system is not limited to the courts of the civil power. Courts-martial and consistory courts (the latter since 1540) are as truly entrusted with the exercise of the judicial power of the state as are the civil courts.' *A-G v British Broadcasting Corpn* [1980] 3 All ER 161 at 180, 181, 182, HL, per Lord Scarman

Australia [The Criminal Code Act 1983 (NT) s 357 provides that when an accused person is called upon to plead to the indictment or during the trial it appears to be uncertain whether he is capable of understanding the proceedings at the trial so as to be able to make a proper response, the 'court' shall inquire into the question of whether he is capable or not. The question was whether 'court' means the court constituted by a judge and jury.] 'The distinction between the expression "the Court" and the expression "the jury" throughout the Code is clear cut and leaves little doubt that the expression "the Court" means the judge and not "the Judge and the jury": see, for example, ss 331(1), 334(1) and (2), and generally the reference to the court in Pt 9, Div 4.' *R v Bradley* (1986) 40 NTR 6 at 12, per Asche J

New Zealand 'Where the term "court" is used in contradistinction to the jury it means invariably the judge.' *R v George* (1890) 9 NZLR 541 at 543, CA, per Williams J

Court of record

'Wherever a statute gives a power to fine and imprison, the persons to whom such power is given are judges of record and their court is a court record.' *Groenvelt v Burnell* (1699) Carth 491 at 494, per cur.

Australia 'The term "court of record" is one of well-accepted legal connotation, and any court which has power to fine or imprison for contempt or for any other offence is at common law a court of record.' *Ex p Power, Re Devereaux* [1957] SR (NSW) 253 at 260, per Brereton J

Court of summary jurisdiction

'A court of summary jurisdiction must, of course, be a court, and the words "summary jurisdiction" appear to me to refer to a procedure primarily, at all events, criminal, wherein the court does not proceed in the finding of a grand jury or information by the Attorney-General, but has the power to deal with an offence without those provisions which the original constitution of this country enforced as a security for the subject against criminal procedure. . . . It seems to me that neither popularly nor technically would a licensing meeting be a court of summary jurisdiction.' *Boulter v Kent JJ* [1897] AC 556 at 563, 564, per Lord Halsbury LC

'The fact that at some time a body is a court of summary jurisdiction does not make it always a court of summary jurisdiction; it must be a body which is exercising a judicial, as distinguished from an administrative, function.' *Huish v Liverpool JJ* [1914] 1 KB 109 at 116, DC, per Scrutton J

Court or judge

'"A court or a judge" [in the Rules of the Supreme Court] means the court sitting *in banc* or a judge at chambers representing the court *in banc*. It has never been held that such a phrase comprised a judge, who was neither the court nor acting at chambers, merely because he was the judge at the trial.' *Baker v Oakes* (1877) 2 QBD 171 at 175, CA, per Brett JA

'When the rules [of the Supreme Court] say "the court or a judge", it is understood that "the court" means a judge or judges in open court, and "a judge" means a judge sitting in chambers.' *Re B—— (An Alleged Lunatic)* [1892] 1 Ch 459 at 463, CA, per Kay LJ

'So far as I know, it is neither the legal nor the common practice to speak of magistrates or justices as "judges". No doubt they have important judicial functions to perform, but they have been called "justices" for centuries; and prima facie when the Legislature uses the words "a court or a judge thereof" it is intended to exclude those Courts.' *Re Jones* [1896] 1 Ch 222 at 227, CA, per Rigby LJ

'In the Chancery Division . . . all orders made in chambers are orders of the judge, though taken without the parties actually going before him. . . . All orders in the Chancery Division are made by the court or by a judge, either personally or through a master.' *Lloyd's Bank v Princess Royal Colliery Co* (1900) 82 LT 559 at 560, per Byrne J

'The word "court" can clearly in ordinary language bear different meanings according to the context. Considering the matter apart from authority, it is obvious, for example, that the words "an application to the court" may, in certain contexts, clearly mean an application in chambers. In other contexts it might as clearly mean an application to the judge at the trial or otherwise in open court. . . . In recent years, the expression "the court or a judge" has been frequently used, and, in this expression, the "court" means a judge or judges in open court, and "a judge" means a judge sitting in chambers. We are, however, clear, both on authority and in principle, that there is no rigid rule which compels us to construe the word "court" as excluding jurisdiction exercised in chambers.' *Friend v Wallman* [1946] 1 KB 493 at 498, 499, CA, per cur.

Inferior court

'One of the matters most in controversy, both in the Divisional Court and here, was the question whether the ecclesiastical courts were and are inferior courts. And the more this matter was investigated the clearer it became that the word "inferior" as applied to courts of law in England had been used with at least two very different meanings. If, as some assert, the question of inferiority is determined by ascertaining whether the court in question can be stopped from exceeding its jurisdiction by a writ of prohibition issuing from the King's Bench, then not only the ecclesiastical courts, but also Palatine courts and Admiralty courts are inferior courts. But there is another test, well recognised by lawyers, by which to distinguish a superior from an inferior court, namely, whether in its proceedings, and in particular in its judgments, it must appear that the court was acting within its jurisdiction. This is the characteristic of an inferior court, whereas in the proceedings of a superior court it will be presumed that it acted within its jurisdiction unless the contrary should appear either on the face of the proceedings or *aliunde.' R v St Edmundsbury and Ipswich Diocese (Chancellor), ex p White* [1948] 1 KB 195 at 205, 206, CA, per Wrottesley LJ

COURT MARTIAL

Serious offences against military or air force law are tried by court-martial. There are three types of courts-martial:—(1) general, (2) district, and (3) field general. The composition of these courts varies, and their competence to try officers, and the amount of punishment which they can impose, differ; but their jurisdiction is not expressly limited by the exclusion of certain offences. (41 Halsbury's Laws (4th edn) para 479)

Air force and army courts-martial

A general court-martial under the Army Act 1955 or the Air Force Act 1955 must consist of the president and not less than four other officers belonging to Her Majesty's military or air forces and subject to military or air force law, as the case may be, each of whom has held a commission in any of Her Majesty's naval, military or air forces for not less than three years in the aggregate, and of whom not less than four must be of a rank not below that of captain or flight lieutenant, as the case may be. A district court-martial must consist of the president and not less than two other officers belonging to Her Majesty's military or air forces and subject to military or air force law, each of whom has held a commission in any of Her Majesty's naval, military or air forces for not less than two years in the aggregate. A field general court-martial must consist of the president and not less than two other officers or, if the convening officer is of the opinion that three officers having suitable qualifications are not available without serious detriment to the public service, of the president and one other officer belonging to Her Majesty's military or air forces and subject to military or air force law, as the case may be. It is not permissible to add an officer to any kind of court-martial after the accused has been arraigned.

A judge advocate must be appointed to officiate at every general court-martial, and may be appointed to officiate at a district or field general court-martial. (41 Halsbury's Laws (4th edn) para 481)

Naval courts-martial

The procedure and practice of naval courts-martial is regulated by the Naval Discipline Act 1957 and by general orders which the Secretary of State has made under that Act. The general orders which the Secretary of State is empowered by the Naval Discipline Act 1957 to make have no effect so far as they are inconsistent with any provisions of that Act. Such general orders must be made by statutory instruments which are subject to annulment by either House of Parliament.

Courts-martial must sit in open court and in the presence of the accused, and must be held on board one of Her Majesty's ships or vessels, or at such premises on shore, whether within or out of the United Kingdom, as the authority which ordered the court may direct. Courts must sit from day to day, except Sundays, until a finding is reached or, in the event of conviction, until sentence is given, unless prevented by weather or other unavoidable cause. However, a court may be adjourned if it appears to it that an adjournment is desirable, but the adjournment may not exceed six days unless the prosecutor and the accused consent.

A court-martial must consist of not less than five and not more than nine officers of Her Majesty's naval forces not below the rank of lieutenant who are subject to the Naval Discipline Act 1957, and who have held a commission in any of the armed forces or have been an officer in the Queen Alexandra's Royal Naval Nursing Service or the Women's Royal Naval Service or in any reserve of either of those forces for not less than three years or for periods amounting in aggregate to not less than three years. The officer who orders a court-martial must not sit as a member of the court, and the members of a court must not all belong to the same ship or naval establishment. For the trial of a flag officer the president of the court must be a flag officer and the other members not under the rank of captain; for the trial of a commodore or captain the president must not be under the rank of captain, and the other members not under the rank of commander; in other cases the president must not be below the rank of captain, and if the person to be tried is of the rank of commander at least two members, in addition to the president, must not be below the rank of commander. The captain and executive officer of the accused's ship cannot sit on the court. The members of a court-martial, and such spare members as may be required to fill vacancies, are nominated by the authority which orders the court. (41 Halsbury's Laws (4th edn) paras 445, 446)

COURT OF CHIVALRY *See* ARMS

COUSIN

'The testator intended to use the two expressions, "first cousins or cousins german", in the same sense; the one as explanatory of the other. What then is the meaning of a first cousin? Obviously, the relation first in degree to whom that appellation is given; that is, the child of an uncle or aunt; and to no other does the appellation belong; for though the child of such first cousin is called a first cousin once removed, it is not known by the appellation of first cousin; and, in fact, it is a cousin in the second degree, though not called a second cousin, as being the second class of persons to whom the appellation of cousins is given. . . . I

have looked into several dictionaries, and I find that in them all the two terms are treated as synonymous, and in some both are explained as meaning children of a brother or sister; thus, in Chambers' edition of Johnson, it is said, "the children of brothers and sisters are called cousins german, the only sense in which the word is now used". So in Boniface's French Dictionary, I find, "first cousin—cousin german—children of brothers and sisters". So in Ainsworth, under "Patruelis"—"a cousin german by the father's side, a father's brother's son"; "*frater patruelis*, the father's brother's son or cousin german".' *Sanderson v Bayley* (1838) 4 My & Cr 56 at 59, 60, per Lord Cottenham LC

'If a testator says no more than that he gives to "cousins", he must be taken to mean first cousins. That will be a practical construction, and one by which the parties entitled will be easily ascertained: it coincides too with ordinary experience, for when a person speaks of cousins he generally means first cousins, the children of an uncle or aunt.' *Stoddart v Nelson, Stanger v Nelson* (1855) 6 De GM & G 68 at 73, per Lord Cranworth LC

'The question is, the meaning of the word "cousins". I think this is governed by the old cases, which I have followed. Prima facie the word "cousin" means first cousin, and not a first cousin once or more times removed; still less does it mean a second or third cousin, which might go on indefinitely.' *Stevenson v Abingdon* (1862) 31 Beav 305 at 308, per Romilly MR

'The term "cousin" [is] . . . one in which the dominant idea is consanguinity. . . . It is not accurate to say that a lady who marries a cousin of the testatrix is a cousin. As regards the terms "nephew" and "niece", popular language has attached a meaning which includes nephews and nieces by marriage; but I do not think there is any such popular usage with regard to the term "cousin".' *Re Taylor, Cloak v Hammond* (1886) 56 LJ Ch 171 at 173, CA, per Bowen LJ

'I agree with Lord Justice Bowen in what he has said about the proper meaning of the word "cousin"—namely, that it imports consanguinity. But it is sometimes used in a sense which does not import consanguinity, as when Her Majesty addresses a nobleman or a member of her Privy Council as her "cousin", or when we speak of "country cousins".' Ibid at 173, per Fry LJ

'The word "cousins" when occurring in a

testamentary writing ought to be held to signify "first cousins", unless there is something in the context of the deed or in the circumstances of the case to show that it was intended to designate more remote relatives.' *Copland's Executors v Milne* 1908 SC 426 at 430, per Lord Ardwall

'This is a summons which raises the question as to who are included under a gift to the testatrix's cousins and half cousins. . . . The contest is between a first cousin—who undoubtedly takes as a cousin . . . second cousins, and first cousins twice removed. . . . There is nothing to show that the testatrix is employing the words "cousins" and "half cousins" in any special local signification. . . . On the whole it is safer for me to give a meaning to the word such as it bears in the English language, ordinarily speaking, as used in ordinary life, without attempting to give the term any particular local signification. Now, what is that meaning? In Sir James Murray's Oxford English Dictionary . . . "half cousin" is defined as: "The child of one's father's or mother's cousin; a second cousin. Sometimes applied to the child of one's own cousin, or to the cousin of one's father or mother." In the English Dialect Dictionary the definition of "half cousin" is: "A first cousin once removed". An interpretation . . . that "half cousins" might mean cousins by the half blood, must be rejected, because . . . the testatrix had no cousins by the half blood. On the whole, I think I must hold that there are included in the gift first cousins, first cousins once removed, and second cousins.' *Re Chester, Servant v Hills* [1914] 2 Ch 580 at 582, 583, per Sargant J

Australia 'The word "cousin" is capable of bearing and may properly bear a wider meaning than "first cousin". The furthest, I think, the learned judges (in the cases cited) were prepared to go was that the primary use of the word "cousin" is first cousin.' *Re Cullen deceased* [1946] VLR 47 at 50, per Herring CJ

COVENANT

A covenant is an agreement under seal whereby the parties, or some or one of them, are or is bound to do or not to do a specified thing, as covenants in a lease under seal to pay rent or not to carry on certain trades; or whereby they undertake that a certain state of affairs exists, as a covenant in a conveyance that the grantor is entitled or that he has not incumbered. The word will, however, be construed to cover stipulations in an agreement under hand if otherwise it would have no effect, as where a document refers to the 'covenants' contained in a lease which is not under seal. The words of a covenant are to be taken most strongly against the covenantor; but this must be qualified by the observation that due regard must be paid to the intentions of the parties as collected from the whole context of the instrument. (12 Halsbury's Laws (4th edn) para 1539)

A covenant is an agreement under seal, whereby one or more of the parties to the deed stipulates for the truth of certain facts, or is bound to do or not to do a specified thing. 'Covenant' will, however, be construed to cover a stipulation in an agreement under hand if otherwise it would have no effect, as where a document refers to the 'covenants' contained in a lease which is not under seal. A covenant may be express or implied. An express covenant is an agreement which is framed in express terms, or is inferred on the construction of the entire instrument. An implied covenant, or covenant in law, is one which the law implies either from the nature of the transaction or from the use of certain technical words. There is a variety of circumstances in which the court will supply what is not expressed in a lease, but in general no covenant ought to be implied unless there is such a necessary implication that the court can have no doubt what covenant or undertaking it ought to write into the agreement. An express covenant in a lease excludes an implied covenant dealing with the same subject. . . . Covenants by a landlord commonly provide for quiet enjoyment, and for payment of rates and taxes, and for the maintenance of the premises, so far as these obligations are to be borne by him. If an agreement for a lease does not specify what covenants are to be inserted in the lease, the parties can require the insertion of the usual covenants. (27 Halsbury's Laws (4th edn) para 320)

'Covenants . . . are either covenants by express words or covenants in law. . . . A covenant in law, properly speaking, is an agreement which the law infers or implies from the use of certain words having a known legal operation in the creation of an estate: so that, after they have had their primary operation in creating the estate, the law gives them a secondary force, by implying an agreement on the part of the grantor to protect and preserve the estate so by those words already created: as, if a man by deed demise land for years, covenant lies upon the word "demise", which imports, or makes, a covenant in law for quiet enjoyment; or, if he grant land by feoffment covenant will lie upon the word "*dedi*".' *Williams v Burrell* (1845) 1 CB 402 at 429, 430, per cur.

'No particular form of words is necessary to form a covenant: but, wherever the court can collect from the instrument an engagement on the one side to do or not to do something, it amounts to a covenant, whether it is in the recital or in any other part of the instrument.' *Great Northern Rly Co v Harrison* (1852) 12 CB 576 at 609, per Parke B

'It is urged that the word "covenant" is inapplicable to anything but an instrument under seal. It is true that the word in strictness does not apply otherwise than to such agreements as are executed under the solemnity of a seal. But, in common parlance, it is applied to any agreement whether under seal or not.' *Hayne v Cummings* (1864) 16 CBNS 421 at 426, per Willes J

''Any words in a deed which show an agreement to do a thing make a covenant . . .": Com. Dig. *Covenant* (A 1). Again, "If the words are introduced by words of condition, as, if a lease be upon condition that the lessee shall keep and leave the house in as good plight, etc; or with proviso that, if the lessee dies within forty years, his executor shall have it for so many years, this is a covenant by the lessor that the executor shall have it": Com. Dig. *Covenant* (A 2). . . . So, in Sheppard's Touchstone, p 162, it is laid down that "there needs not formal and orderly words, as covenant, promise, and the like, to make a covenant on which to ground an action of covenant, for a covenant may be had by any other words": and the following instance is put: "If these words be inserted in a deed, amongst other covenants, 'that the lessee shall repair, provided always that the lessor shall allow timber', or 'that the lessee shall scour ditches, provided always that the lessor do carry away the earth', these are good covenants on both sides." There neither the word "covenant" nor the word "agreed" is used.' *Brookes v Drysdale* (1877) 3 CPD 52 at 57, 58, per Grove J

'The Act of Parliament [Settled Estates Act 1877, s 46 (repealed see now Settled Land Act 1925, s 42(1)(iii))] requires "that such a demise do contain a covenant for payment of the rent, and such other usual and proper covenants as the lessor shall think fit." . . . When the Act of Parliament mentions "covenant" it means a legal covenant which can be sued upon at law,

and not some right which might, or might not, arise from equitable considerations.' *Boyce v Edbrooke* [1903] 1 Ch 836 at 841, 842, per Farwell J

For freedom from incumbrances

In the covenants for title implied by statute on a conveyance for valuable consideration as beneficial owner, the covenant against incumbrances follows the covenant for quiet enjoyment [infra] as part of it. The covenant against incumbrances is consequently a future covenant, like the covenant for quiet enjoyment, and the two are in effect a single covenant that the covenantee shall enjoy free from incumbrances. The mere existence of an incumbrance does not give the right to sue on the covenant against incumbrances; there must be interruption of enjoyment by a claim or demand on the purchaser. An incumbrance has been said to be every right to or interest in the land which may subsist in third persons to the diminution in the value of the land, but consistent with the passing of the fee in the conveyance. It will include a mortgage, charge or lien capable of being enforced against the purchaser, an easement and a subsisting term, unless, in the case of a term, the real subject of the purchase was the reversion on the term, and probably also a restrictive covenant enforceable against the purchaser. Apart from the effect of the statutory provisions as to the registration of local land charges or of any relevant conditions contained in the contract for sale, the question whether expenses payable to a local authority in respect of work done under statutory power constitute an incumbrance depends upon whether the expenses are merely a liability of the landowner personally or are charged upon the land and whether, if they are a charge upon the land, the charge attached before completion. (42 Halsbury's Laws (4th edn) para 355)

For further assurance

Under the covenant for further assurance the vendor is bound to do such further acts for the purpose of perfecting the purchaser's title as the purchaser may reasonably require and the vendor can properly do. The purchaser should tender a draft of the further conveyance to which he considers that he is entitled, and should tender or offer to pay the vendor's costs. The vendor is entitled to a reasonable time to procure professional assistance. If the conveyance is proper and he declines to execute it or to do any act which the purchaser can properly require this constitutes a breach of the covenant. The purchaser cannot by means of the covenant for further assurance, obtain a greater estate than that which was the subject of the original conveyance, although if the vendor's title was defective, the vendor may be required to assure an estate which he has got in since, whether by devise, or by purchase. (42 Halsbury's Laws (4th edn) para 356)

For quiet enjoyment

The covenant for quiet enjoyment is a future covenant. Consequently there is no breach of the covenant until the covenantee is disturbed in his enjoyment. The implied covenant for quiet enjoyment extends to lawful interruption or disturbance by the person who conveys or any person conveying by his direction, or rightfully claiming by, through, under, or in trust for the person who conveys or any person conveying by his direction, or by, through, or under anyone (not being a person claiming in respect of an estate or interest subject whereto the conveyance is expressly made) through whom the person who conveys derives title, otherwise than by purchase for value. A covenant for quiet enjoyment limited to lawful disturbance by the covenantor or any person claiming under or in trust for him is not broken by claims under title paramount to that of the covenantor, or by tortious acts other than those of the covenantor himself. Since the covenant is a future covenant, the damages seem to be measured by the loss to the covenantee when the disturbance takes place. Thus, in case of eviction the damages include the value of improvements which he has made. (42 Halsbury's Laws (4th edn) para 354)

For right to convey

The covenant for right to convey is a covenant for title, but the covenant for quiet enjoyment [supra] is a covenant relating to possession. This distinction affects both the date when the covenant is broken and the measure of damages. A covenant for title is an assurance to the purchaser that the grantor has the very estate in quantity and quality which he purports to convey, and it is broken by the existence of an adverse right such as a right of way, or any outstanding interest, charge, or claim which may prevent the purchaser from enjoying this estate. There is also a breach where, by the vendor's omission to prevent the acquisition of an adverse title by possession, he has no title to part of the land he purports to convey. Hence the covenant for right to convey

is not a continuing covenant, but is broken once and for all at the time of the conveyance if there is then a defect in title which prevents the vendor from conveying the estate which he purports to convey. Consequently time begins to run forthwith against an action for breach of the covenant. The purchaser can sue on the covenant, notwithstanding that the defect in title is disclosed by a recital in the conveyance. (42 Halsbury's Laws (4th edn) para 352)

Implied covenant

'The term "implied covenant" is often used in a two-fold sense; first, as denoting a covenant which is to be gathered from the four corners of the instrument, or from words or phrases not generally used in law to express a covenant, and in this sense an implied covenant is for all legal purposes the same as an express covenant; but, secondly it is also used to denote a covenant in law—that is, a covenant attached by the law—apart from any expressed intention of the parties—by reason of the use of some particular words, for example, "demise"; or by reason of a particular relation, for example, that of landlord and tenant.' *Baynes & Co v Lloyd & Sons* [1895] 1 QB 820 at 823, 824, per Lord Russell of Killowen CJ

Restrictive covenant

'The equitable doctrine was brought to a focus in *Tulk v Moxhay* [(1848) 2 Ph 774], which is the leading case on this subject. It seems to me that that case decided that an assignee taking land subject to a certain class of covenants is bound by such covenants if he has notice of them, and that the class of covenants comprehended within the rule is that covenants restricting the mode of using the land only will be enforced. It may be also, but it is not necessary to decide here, that all covenants also which impose such a burden on the land as can be enforced against the land would be enforced. Be that as it may, a covenant to repair is not restrictive and could not be enforced against the land; therefore such a covenant is within neither rule.' *Haywood v Brunswick Permanent Benefit Building Society* (1881) 8 QBD 403 at 407, 408, CA, per Brett LJ

COVER

'"Cover" [in transactions between a stockbroker and his client] . . . means that . . . money is deposited by the client to secure the broker from loss in the event of the stock alling in value.' *Re Cronmire, ex p Waud* [1898] 2 QB 383 at 395, CA, per A L Smith LJ

United States After a breach within the preceding section [dealing with the failure of the seller to make delivery or repudiate or the buyer's rightful rejection or justifiable revocation of acceptance] the buyer may 'cover' by making in good faith and without unreasonable delay any reasonable purchase of or contract to purchase goods in substitution for those due from the seller. (Uniform Commercial Code 1978, s 2–712(1))

COVERING

'The [railway] company have power [under their special Act] to charge for covering; and on the question of what is to be understood by covering, we think it means not only the labour of unfolding and making fast the sheets over a loaded waggon, but also the use of the sheets.' *Hall & Co v London, Brighton & South Coast Rly Co* (1885) 15 QBD 505 at 517 n, DC, per Sir Frederick Peel

CRAFT

'I am . . . of opinion that the appellant has incurred no penalty; in other words, that he has not worked or navigated "any wherry, lighter, or other craft," within the meaning of sect 37 [of a private Act]. What he has done is, to navigate a steam tug in moving a vessel. And the question is, whether that is within the words of the section. All turns upon the wide term "craft". It is said that this may include a steam tug; and so it may: but it is a general rule that when a word of wide signification follows others of a signification less wide, it must be interpreted as having a meaning bringing it within the same class as those others. I think, therefore, that "craft" must be confined to vessels of the same kind as the wherries which are employed for passengers and the lighters which are employed for goods. In common understanding, a steam tug is a vessel of quite a different kind.' *Read v Ingham* (1854) 3 E & B 889 at 901, per Erle CJ

[A bill of lading provided that shipowners should at their option be entitled to discharge goods into 'craft' hired by them at consignee's risk and expense.] 'The word "craft" in the bill of lading includes any class of vessel that can reasonably be used for the purpose. Strictly speaking, anything that floats may be called a craft, but the word must be construed reason-

ably. . . . They [the shipowners] must begin with lighters, and if no lighters are available they must take the next thing in the scale of craft that can be obtained. . . . In the circumstances here sailing barges are the next thing in the scale above lighters, and as no lighters were available the [shipowners] . . . were justified in using sailing barges.' *United States Shipping Board v Vigers Brothers* (1924) 41 TLR 26 at 27, per Rowlatt J

CRAFTSMANSHIP

'"Craftsmanship", particularly when considered in its historical context, implies a manifestation of pride in sound workmanship—a rejection of the shoddy, the meretricious, the facile.' *Hensher (George) Ltd v Restawile Upholstery (Lancs) Ltd* [1974] 2 All ER 420 at 434, HL, per Lord Simon of Glaisdale

CREAM

'Cream' means that part of milk rich in fat which has been separated by skimming or otherwise. (Food Act 1984, s 132(1))

CREATE

New Zealand 'The meaning of the words "a trust has been created" has not been judicially considered. The dictionary meaning of the word "create" is "to make, form, constitute, or bring into legal existence"; see Shorter Oxford Dictionary. In my opinion the phrase "a trust has been created" . . . simply means "a trust has been brought into legal existence".' *Baldwin v Comr of Inland Revenue* [1965] NZLR 1 at 6, per Macarthur J

United States A work is 'created' when it is fixed in a copy or phonorecord for the first time; where a work is prepared over a period of time, the portion of it that has been fixed at any particular time constitutes the work as of that time, and where the work has been prepared in different versions, each version constitutes a separate work. (Copyright Act of 1976, s 101)

CREDIBLE WITNESS

'Under the statute [Licensing (Scotland) Act 1903, s 65 (repealed)] . . . it is distinctly provided that one credible witness is sufficient to prove the case. . . . A credible witness means a witness whose credibility commends itself to the presiding magistrate, whose duty it is to hear the evidence and to judge as to the trustworthiness of the evidence adduced before him; and, however bad the character of the witness may be, if the presiding magistrate, having seen her and heard and observed the evidence given, is satisfied, it is impossible . . . for this Court to say that that witness is not a credible witness.' *Manson v Macleod* 1918 SC(J) 60 at 66, per the Lord Justice-General

['Credible witness' was also interpreted in another connection in *R v Noakes* [1917] 1 KB 581, CCA. The Court did not actually define the term, but clearly intimated that a witness speaking from hearsay was not within the meaning of the phrase.]

Canada 'A "credible" witness [to a will within the meaning of the Statute of Frauds] means a witness not incapacitated by mental imbecility, interest or crime.' *Ryan v Devereux* (1866) 26 UCR 100 at 107, Ont CA, per cur.

CREDIT   *See also* LETTER OF CREDIT

[A guarantee stated that if a certain person was given 'credit', the guarantors would be responsible that his payments should be regularly made.] 'There is nothing in the words of the guarantee as to any particular terms of credit, but the language is, if you give him credit, not the usual credit, but credit generally, which means if you trust him. It is not to be a dealing on the terms of the trade, but on the terms to be settled between the parties. It must be a fair and reasonable credit, or it might operate as a fraud upon the sureties.' *Simpson v Manley* (1831) 2 Cr & J 12 at 13, 14, per Bayley B

'The words [in a guarantee] are,—"In consideration of Messrs. *Edwards, Ringer, & Co,* tobacco manufacturers, *Bristol,* giving credit to Mr *David Jevons,* grocer, *Tipton,* I hereby engage to be responsible, and to pay, any sum, not exceeding £120, due to the said *Edwards, Ringer* & Co by the said *David Jevons.*" It is objected that the words "giving credit" are ambiguous and uncertain,—they may refer to credit already given, or to future credit,—and therefore the guarantie is bad. . . . What . . . is the meaning of "giving credit"? The authorities clearly shew that it may mean the forebearance of a past or a future debt: and that the declaration shews it was future. It seems to me that the guarantie is not ambiguous upon the face of it. That which is applicable equally to two states of circumstances, cannot be called ambiguous. I think the guarantie is good.'

Edwards v Jevons (1849) 8 CB 436, per Wilde CJ

[An instrument addressed to the cashier of a corporation by the corporation's managing director directed the cashier, after the lapse of a specified period, to 'credit' a particular company in cash on account of the corporation.] 'As I understand the words "credit in cash" this is an order by one person on another, to hold to the use, or at the command, of a third party, a certain sum. That means "pay the money to him".' *Ellison v Collingridge* (1850) 9 CB 570 at 573, per Wilde CJ

[The Bankruptcy Act 1883, s 31 (repealed; see now Insolvency Act 1986, s 355), made it an offence for an undischarged bankrupt to 'obtain credit' to the extent of £20 or upwards from a person without informing such person that he was an undischarged bankrupt.] 'In Johnson "credit" is defined as being "correlative to debt"; and in the present case the debt was created by getting the horse and not paying for it; in other words, the creditor gave credit to the debtor. Webster defines it as "trust, the transfer of goods in confidence of future payment" a definition which is strictly applicable to the present case, where the man in Ireland delivered the horse relying on the credit and probity of the buyer. . . . If a person in the position of the prisoner obtains goods to the amount of £20 on credit without saying that he is an undischarged bankrupt, he comes not only within the words but within the mischief of the Act.' *R v Peters* (1886) 16 QBD 636 at 641, CCR, per Lord Coleridge CJ

'The obtaining of credit . . . means obtaining some benefit from another, without immediately giving the consideration in return for which that benefit is confirmed.' *R v Miller* [1977] 3 All ER 986 at 991, CA, per cur.

Australia 'In commercial and financial affairs the word "credit" may signify the financial arrangement in a transaction or the reputation for solvency and honesty which entitles a person desirous of incurring a debt or liability to do so on the terms that payment is to be deferred. In its former meaning it includes the delivery of goods or the advancing of money with the trust that the debtor will have the means to pay and will pay at a future date. The element of trust or confidence in the creditor is not eliminated by taking a promissory note for the debt. It is rather manifested by doing so.' *Herbert v R* [1941] 64 CLR 461 at 467, per McTiernan J

United States 'Credit' means the right granted by a creditor to a debtor to defer payment of debt or to incur debt and defer its payment. (Uniform Consumer Credit Code 1969, s 1.301(7))

Arranger of credit *See* ARRANGER OF CREDIT

Consumer credit sale *See* SALE

CREDIT-BROKER

'Credit-broker' means a person acting in the course of a business of credit brokerage carried on by him, that is a business of effecting introductions of individuals desiring to obtain credit (a) to persons carrying on any business so far as it relates to the provision of credit, or (b) to other persons engaged in credit brokerage. (Sale of Goods Act 1979, s 61(1))

CREDIT CARD

United States The term 'credit card' means any card, plate, coupon book or other credit device existing for the purpose of obtaining money, property, labor, or services on credit. (Truth in Lending Act 1968, s 103(k))

Accepted credit card

United States The term 'accepted credit card' means any credit card which the cardholder has requested and received or has signed or has used, or authorized another to use, for the purpose of obtaining money, property, labor, or services on credit. (Truth in Lending Act 1968, s 103(l))

Lender credit card

United States 'Lender credit card or similar arrangement' means an arrangement or loan agreement, other than a seller credit card, pursuant to which a lender gives a debtor the privilege of using a credit card, letter of credit, or other credit confirmation or identification in transactions out of which the debt arises
(a) by the lender's honoring a draft or similar order for the payment of money drawn or accepted by the debtor;
(b) by the lender's payment or agreement to pay the debtor's obligations; or
(c) by the lender's purchase from the obligee of the debtor's obligations.
(Uniform Consumer Credit Code 1969, s 1.301(9))

Seller credit card

United States 'Seller credit card' means an arrangement pursuant to which a person gives to a buyer or lessee the privilege of using a credit card, letter of credit, or other credit confirmation or identification primarily for the purpose of purchasing or leasing goods or services from that person, a person related to that person, or others licensed or franchised to do business under his business or trade name or designation. (Uniform Consumer Credit Code 1969, s 1.301(16))

CREDIT SALE

'Credit-sale agreement' means an agreement for the sale of goods, under which the purchase price or part of it is payable by instalments, but which is not a conditional sale agreement. (Health and Safety at Work etc Act 1974, s 53(1); Consumer Credit Act 1974, s 189(1))

United States The term 'credit sale' refers to any sale in which the seller is a creditor. The term includes any contract in the form of a bailment or lease if the bailee or lessee contracts to pay as compensation for use a sum substantially equivalent to or in excess of the aggregate value of the property and services involved and it is agreed that the bailee or lessee will become, or for no other or a nominal consideration has the option to become, the owner of the property upon full compliance with his obligations under the contract. (Truth in Lending Act 1968, s 103(g))

CREDIT SERVICE CHARGE

United States 'Credit service charge' means the sum of (1) all charges payable directly or indirectly by the buyer and imposed directly or indirectly by the seller as an incident to the extension of credit, including any of the following types of charges which are applicable: time price differential, service, carrying or other charge, however denominated, premium or other charge for any guarantee or insurance protecting the seller against the buyer's default or other credit loss; and (2) charges incurred for investigating the collateral or other creditworthiness of the buyer or for commissions or brokerage for obtaining the credit, irrespective of the person to whom the charges are paid or payable, unless the seller had no notice of the charges when the credit was granted. The term does not include charges as a result of default, additional charges (Section 2.202), delinquency charges (Section 2.203), or deferral charges (Section 2.204). (Uniform Consumer Credit Code 1969, s 2.109)

CREDIT UNION

[A 'credit union' may be registered under the Industrial and Provident Societies Act 1965 if (a) it is shown to the satisfaction of the appropriate registrar that certain specific conditions are fulfilled; (b) that the rules of the society comply with the statutory requirements; and (c) that the society's registered office is to be situated in Great Britain. The objects of a credit union are the promotion of thrift among members by the accumulation of their savings, the creation of sources of credit for the benefit of members at a reasonable rate of interest, the use and control of members' savings for their mutual benefit, and the training and education of members in the wise use of money and in the management of their financial affairs. *See* Credit Unions Act 1979, s 1.]

CREDITOR   *See also* JUDGMENT
CREDITOR

United States 'Creditor' includes a general creditor, a secured creditor, a lien creditor and any representative of creditors, including an assignee for the benefit of creditors, a trustee in bankruptcy, a receiver in equity and an executor or administrator of an insolvent debtor's or assignor's estate. (Uniform Commercial Code 1978, s 1–201(12))

Debt collection

United States   The term 'creditor' means any person who offers or extends credit creating a debt or to whom a debt is owed, but such term does not include any person to the extent that he receives an assignment or transfer of a debt in default solely for the purpose of facilitating collection of such debt for another. (Fair Debt Collection Practices Act 1977, s 803(4))

In bankruptcy

'Creditor'
(a) in relation to a bankrupt, means a person to whom any of the bankruptcy debts is owed . . ., and
(b) in relation to an individual to whom a bankruptcy petition relates, means a person who would be a creditor in the

bankruptcy if a bankruptcy order were made on that petition.
(Insolvency Act 1986, s 383(1))

Lien creditor   *See* LIEN CREDITOR

Of company

'The word "creditor" is used in the Act of 1870 [Joint Stock Companies Arrangement Act 1870, s 2 (repealed)] in the widest sense. . . . It includes all persons having any pecuniary claims against the company.' *Re Midland Coal, Coke & Iron Co, Craig's Claim* [1895] 1 Ch 267 at 277, CA, per cur.

'The question is, whether the holder of a bond who, upon the making of periodical payments, will at a future date become entitled to the payment of a sum of money by the company is a contingent or prospective creditor within the meaning of s 137 of the Companies (Consolidation) Act 1908 [see now the Insolvency Act 1986, s 124(1)], which includes any "contingent or prospective creditor or creditors". No doubt originally the Companies Acts did not allow of the presentation of a petition for winding-up by a contingent or prospective creditor, and that continued to be the law until the passing of the Act of 1907. . . . Then in the Companies Act 1907 [repealed], s 28, is introduced. . . . That s 28 provides, 'In determining whether a company is unable to pay its debts within the meaning of s 80 of the Companies Act 1862 [repealed], the Court shall take into account the contingent and prospective liabilities of the company, and any contingent or prospective creditor shall be a creditor entitled to present a petition for winding-up the company under s 82 of that Act". . . . Now those provisions of s 28 are to be found in the Act of 1908 [repealed] . . . and I have no doubt that the words "contingent or prospective creditor" in the Act of 1908 bear no other interpretation than that which would be applied to contingent or prospective creditor in the Act of 1907. . . . I think the contingent or prospective creditor mentioned in s 28 must be a creditor contingent or prospective in respect of the liabilities of the company mentioned in the previous lines; and that, secondly, "contingent or prospective creditor" includes such a person as a policy-holder and such a person as the petitioner in the present case, whose position does not seem to me distinguishable from that of the holder of a policy.' *Re British Equitable Bond & Mortgage Corpn Ltd* [1910] 1 Ch 574 at 578, 579, per Neville J

I am . . . of opinion that the word "creditor" in s 137 of the Companies (Consolidation) Act 1908 [see now Insolvency Act 1986, s 124(1)], includes a creditor in equity as well as a creditor at law and consequently that a creditor in equity can still petition for the winding-up of a company. . . . An assignee of a definite part of a debt is . . . a creditor in equity in respect of that part . . . and . . . is entitled to present a winding-up petition under s 137 without joining the persons interested in the remainder of the debt as co-petitioners.' *Re Steel Wing Co Ltd* [1921] 1 Ch 349 at 355, 357, per P O Lawrence J

CREEK

Australia 'It needs to be said . . . that the word "creek" has a meaning in Australian usage entirely different from that in Great Britain. . . . A "creek" in Great Britain means a small arm of the sea and in Australia it means a branch of a main river, a rivulet, brook or small stream (see Oxford English Dictionary 1933 edition).' *Errington v Jessop* (1982) 59 FLR 99 at 101, per Forster CJ

CREMATORIUM

'Crematorium' shall mean any building fitted with appliances for the purpose of burning human remains, and shall include everything incidental or ancillary thereto. (Cremation Act 1902, s 2)

Canada 'An "incinerator" is a plant for consuming refuse, rubbish, etc. . . . A "crematory" is a plant for reducing human bodies to ashes.' *Butler v Saskatoon City* (1918) 11 Sask LR 1 at 6, per Lamont J

CREW

'Crew', in relation to a ship or aircraft, means all persons actually employed in the working or service of the ship or aircraft, including the captain, and 'member of the crew' shall be construed accordingly. (Immigration Act 1971, s 33(1)

'The articles [between master and seaman] . . . contained the following provision, viz. "The crew (if required)] to be transferred to any other ship in the same employ". . . . It was further contended on the part of the plaintiff, that, assuming the articles to be valid, the provision for transferring "the crew" into any other ship applied only to a case where the whole crew were transferred together, and did not apply to the transfer of less than the whole. The articles constitute in all other respects an agreement between the owners and each of the crew for himself; and the expression "the crew" is used in other parts of the agreement to express the crew respectively; and in the clause under consideration it governs the stipulation "not to trade on their own account", which is clearly several as to each of the crew, and not merely joint as to all.' *Frazer v Hatton* (1857) 2 CBNS 512 at 523, 526, 527, per cur.

CREW ACCOMMODATION *See* ACCOMMODATION

CRIME *See also* GRAVE CRIME

There is no satisfactory definition of crime which will embrace the many acts and omissions which are criminal, and which will at the same time exclude all those acts and omissions which are not. Ordinarily a crime is a wrong which affects the security or well-being of the public generally so that the public has an interest in its suppression. A crime is frequently a moral wrong in that it amounts to conduct which is inimical to the general moral sense of the community. It is, however, possible to instance many crimes which exhibit neither of the foregoing characteristics. An act may be made criminal by Parliament simply because it is criminal process, rather than civil, which offers the more effective means of controlling the conduct in question. (11 Halsbury's Laws (4th edn) para 1)

A crime, or misdemesnor, is an act committed, or omitted, in violation of a public law, either forbidding or commanding it. This general definition comprehends both crimes and misdemesnors; which, properly speaking, are mere synonymous terms: though, in common usage, the word, 'crimes', is made to denote such offences as are of a deeper and more atrocious dye; while smaller faults, and omissions of less consequence, are comprised under the gentler name of 'misdemesnors' only.

The distinction of public wrongs from private, of crimes and misdemesnors from civil injuries, seems principally to consist in this: that private wrongs, or civil injuries, are an infringement or privation of the civil rights which belong to individuals, considered merely as individuals; public wrongs, or crimes and misdemesnors, are a breach and violation of the public rights and duties, due to the whole community, considered as a community, in its social aggregate capacity. As if I detain a field from another man, to which the law has given him a right, this is a civil injury, and not a crime; for here only the right of an individual is concerned, and it is immaterial to the public, which of us is in possession of the land: but treason, murder, and robbery are properly ranked among crimes; since, besides the injury done to individuals, they strike at the very being of society; which cannot possibly subsist, where actions of this sort are suffered to escape with impunity.

In all cases the crime includes an injury: every public offence is also a private wrong, and somewhat more; it affects the individual, and it likewise affects the community. Thus treason in imagining the king's death involves in it conspiracy against an individual, which is also a civil injury: but as this species of treason in its consequences principally tends to the dissolution of government, and the destruction thereby of the order and peace of society, this denominates it a crime of the highest magnitude. Murder is an injury to the life of an individual; but the law of society considers principally the loss which the state sustains by being deprived of a member, and the pernicious example thereby set, for others to do the like. Robbery may be considered in the same view: it is an injury to *private* property; but were that all, a civil satisfaction in damages might atone for it: the *public* mischief is the thing, for the prevention of which our laws have made it a capital offence. In these gross and atrocious injuries the private wrong is swallowed up in the public: we seldom hear any mention made of satisfaction to the individual; the satisfaction to the community being so very great. And indeed, as the public crime is not otherwise avenged than by forfeiture of life and property, it is impossible afterwards to make any reparation for the private wrong; which can only be had from the body or goods of the aggressor. But there are crimes of an inferior nature, in which the public punishment is not so severe, but it affords room for a private compensation also: and herein the distinction of crimes from civil injuries is very apparent. For instance; in the case of battery, or beating another, the aggressor may be indicted for this at the suit of the king, for disturbing the public peace, and be punished criminally by fine and imprisonment: and the party beaten may also have his private remedy by action of trespass for the injury, which he in particular sustains, and recover a civil satisfaction in damages. So also, in case of a public nuisance, as digging a ditch across a highway, this is punishable by indictment, as a common offence to the whole kingdom and all his majesty's subjects: but if any individual sustains any special damage thereby, as laming his horse, breaking his carriage, or the like, the offender may be compelled to make ample satisfaction, as well for the private injury, as for the public wrong.

Upon the whole we may observe, that in taking cognizance of all wrongs, or unlawful acts, the law has a double view: viz. not only to redress the party injured, by either restoring to him his right, if possible; or by giving him an equivalent; . . . but also to secure to the public the benefit of society, by preventing or punishing every breach and violation of those laws, which the sovereign power has thought proper to establish, for the government and tranquillity of the whole. (4 Bl Com 5–7)

'The proper definition of the word "crime" is an offence for which the law awards punishment.' *Mann v Owen* (1829) 9 B & C 595 at 602, per Littledale J

'If . . . an agreement is illegal because it is wrong to the public, it seems to me impossible to say that it is not indictable. An illegal act which is a wrong against the public welfare seems to have the necessary elements of a crime.' *Mogul SS Co Ltd v McGregor, Gow & Co* (1889) 23 QBD 598 at 605, 606, CA, per Lord Esher MR

'It seems to us that to hold that the very same acts which are expressly legalised by statute remain nevertheless crimes punishable by the common law is contrary to good sense and elementary principle.' *Connor v Kent, Gibson v Lawson, Curran v Treleaven* [1891] 2 QB 545 at 560, per cur.

'Criminal law is about the right of the state to punish persons for their conduct, generally where that conduct is undertaken with a wicked intent or without justificatory excuse. A code of criminal law defines offences, i.e. the kinds of conduct which render the person guilty of it liable to punishment. Conduct which constitutes a crime of a person's doing or, less frequently, omitting to do physical acts; and the definition of the crime always contains a description of physical acts or omissions though it may, and in English law generally does, also require that the physical acts or omissions which constitute the described conduct should be done with a particular intent either expressly stated in the definition or to be implied from the mere fact that Parliament has made the described conduct punishable.' *Treacy v Director of Public Prosecutions* [1971] 1 All ER 110 at 120, HL, per Lord Diplock

Australia 'What is a criminal offence? A criminal offence can be identified only in terms of its factual ingredients, or elements, and the criminal penalty which the combination of elements attracts. Littledale J, speaking of criminal offences in *Mann v Owen* [supra], said: "The proper definition of the word 'crime' is an offence for which the law awards punishment." That view accords with Sir James Fitzjames Stephen's definition of crime as "an act or omission in respect of which legal punishment may be inflicted on the person who is in default either by acting or omitting to act": *History of the Criminal Law of England* (1883), vol 1, p 1; see also Sir Samuel Griffith's Code definition of offence: "An act or omission which renders the person doing the act or making the omission liable to punishment" (Criminal Code (Q) s 2)'. *Kingswell v R* (1985) 159 CLR 264 at 292, per Brennan J

Canada 'Where the proceeding . . . is not simply for recovery of money payable to some individual informant but for the punishment of an offence against social order and where the punishment may be not only the imposition of a fine but imprisonment . . . the offence . . . is . . . a crime.' *R v Roddy* (1877) 41 UCR 291 at 302, UCBQ, per Harrison CJ

CRIME OF VIOLENCE

[The applicants, who were train drivers, suffered nervous shock, anxiety and depression as a result of trespassers jumping onto the railway line in front of trains they were driving and being killed. The applicants each applied for compensation under the Criminal Injuries Compensation Scheme claiming that they were victims of a 'crime of violence' within para 5 of the revised 1969 scheme and para 4(a) of the revised 1979 scheme.] 'The mere endangering of safety, without more, does not in itself import violence, whether in the railway or on the factory floor. . . . The trespasser who commits suicide on the railway may well be in breach of a duty of care owed to the driver of and the passengers on the train; his action may result in the driver suffering from depression and in passengers being injured. But it surely would be a startling result that the trespasser could properly be said to have committed a

crime of violence. . . . In conclusion, we feel bound to say that we find it highly unsatisfactory that there is no definition, nor even a reasoned explanation of what constitutes a crime of violence for the purposes of the scheme. If a definition is called for from us, we would suggest "any crime in respect of which the prosecution must prove as one of its ingredients that the defendant unlawfully and intentionally, or recklessly, inflicted or threatened to inflict personal injury upon another".' *R v Criminal Injuries Compensation Board, ex p Warner* [1985] 2 All ER 1069 at 1074, 1075, 1076, per cur.

CRIMINAL CAUSE OR MATTER

'The result of all the decided cases is to show that the words "criminal cause or matter" in s 47 [of the Judicature Act 1873 (repealed; see now the Supreme Court Act 1981, s 18(1))] . . . should receive the widest possible interpretation. The intention was that no appeal should lie in any "criminal matter" in the widest sense of the term, this Court [the Court of Appeal] being constituted for the hearing of appeals in civil causes and matters [but see now the Criminal Appeal Act 1968]. The meaning of the words "criminal cause or matter" was considered in various cases which have been cited, but the case which helps one most to the true construction is I think, *R v Fletcher* [(1876) 2 QBD 43, CA], following *R v Steel* [(1876) 2 QBD 37, CA]. In *R v Fletcher* . . . Mellish LJ said: "In *R v Steel* we held that the clause was not confined, as was contended, to the High Court when sitting as the Court to hear points reserved in criminal cases, but extended to all criminal cases in the High Court, and therefore to criminal cases in the Queen's Bench Division. . . . The intention of the Legislature appears to me clearly to have been to leave the procedure in criminal cases substantially unaltered." . . . I said . . . "I should read the clause as meaning 'no appeal shall lie from any decision of the High Court by way of judgment in any criminal cause or matter'." In the present case, I think I must try to express my meaning in other words. I think that the clause of s 47 in question applies to a decision by way of judicial determination of any question raised in or with regard to proceedings, the subject-matter of which is criminal, at whatever stage of the proceedings the question arises.' *Ex p Woodhall* (1888) 20 QBD 832 at 835, 836, CA, per Lord Esher MR

'It seems to me that the question [whether a

particular proceeding is a "criminal cause or matter" within s 47 of the Judicature Act 1873 (repealed; see supra)] is really one of procedure. . . . That it is a question of procedure may be easily seen by taking the case of an assault. An assault may be made the subject of civil procedure by action, in which case there may be an appeal to this Court; or it may be made the subject of criminal procedure by indictment.' *Seaman v Burley* [1896] 2 QB 344 at 346, CA, per Lord Esher MR

'In order that a matter may be a criminal cause or matter [for the purposes of determining whether an appeal therefrom is competent] it must, I think, fulfil two conditions which are connoted by and implied in the word "criminal". It must involve the consideration of some charge of crime, that is to say, of an offence against the public law (Imperial Dictionary, tit. "Crime" and "Criminal"); and that charge must have been preferred or be about to be preferred before some Court or judicial tribunal having or claiming jurisdiction to impose punishment for the offence or alleged offence. If these conditions are fulfilled, the matter may be criminal, even though it is held that no crime has been committed, or that the tribunal has no jurisdiction to deal with it . . . but there must be at least a charge of crime (in the wide sense of the word) and a claim to criminal jurisdiction.' *Re Clifford & O'Sullivan* [1921] 2 AC 579 at 580, per Lord Cave

Australia [The Supreme Court Civil Procedure Act 1932 (Tas) provides by s 9–(1) that except as provided in Part IX nothing in the Act or the Rules of Court shall affect the jurisdiction of the Court or any judge thereof, or the law to be applied, or the procedure or practice—[inter alia] in criminal causes, matters, or proceedings.] 'Section 46 of the Acts Interpretation Act 1931 defines "crime" as "an offence punishable upon indictment as provided by the Criminal Code" and by virtue of s 24 of that Act the derivative adjective "criminal" has a corresponding meaning. . . . I hold that the expression "criminal cause, matter or proceeding" appearing in s 9(2) of the Supreme Court Civil Procedure Act 1932 (Tas) is not confined to appeals from criminal proceedings as defined in the Acts Interpretation Act 1931 (Tas) but includes appeals from proceedings in a court of summary jurisdiction in respect of any offence. I am not purporting to exhaustively define the phrase.' *Pikor v Fletcher* [1980] Tas R 55 at 59 per Green CJ

CRIMINAL CONVERSATION

Canada ' "Criminal conversation" in its broad, comprehensive sense is synonymous with the term "adultery", but in actions of this character [alienation of affections] it signifies adultery in the aspect of a tort, and the right violated by the tortfeasor is the husband's prerogative to exclusive sexual intercourse with his wife which the law grants as a necessary consequence of the marriage relation.' *Kungl v Schiefer* [1961] OR 1 at 2, Ont CA, per Schroeder JA; varied, [1962] SCR 443, without affecting definition.

[In England the action for criminal conversation was in form abolished by s 59 of the Matrimonial Causes Act 1857].

CRIMINAL NEGLIGENCE *See* NEGLIGENCE

CRIMINAL PROCEEDING

'It seems to me that the true test is this, if the subject-matter be of a personal character, that is, if either money or goods are sought to be recovered by means of the proceeding—that is a civil proceeding; but, if the proceeding is one which may affect the defendant at once, by the imprisonment of his body, in the event of a verdict of guilty, so that he is liable as a public offender—that I consider a criminal proceeding. Undoubtedly informations by the Attorney-General for smuggling have not been deemed criminal proceedings, but rather in the nature of civil proceedings.' *A-G v Radloff* (1854) 10 Exch 84 at 101, 102, per Platt B

[The judges differed in this case, the Court being equally divided. Platt B's judgment was, however, confirmed in *A-G v Bradlaugh* (1885) 14 QBD 667.]

'Wherever a party aggrieved is suing for a penalty, where the proceeding can be treated as the suit of the party,—as, for instance, an application for an order in bastardy,—the proceeding is a civil one, and the defendant is a competent witness. But when a proceeding is treated by a statute as imposing a penalty for an offence against the public, the amount of which penalty is to be meted by the justices according to the magnitude of the offence, there can be no doubt that the proceeding is a criminal one.' *Parker v Green* (1862) 2 B & S 299 at 311, per Crompton J

Australia 'We think that the ill treatment complained of was habitual. It is conduct capable of causing danger to bodily or mental health and it qualifies as conduct amounting to ill treatment of a character recognised in the legal conception of cruelty.' *La Rovere v La Rovere* [1964] ALR 761 att 773, per cur.

Canada 'Over the years the courts have steadfastly refrained from attempting to formulate a general definition of cruelty. As used in ordinary parlance "cruelty" signifies a disposition to inflict suffering; to delight in or exhibit indifference to the pain or misery of others; mercilessness or hard-heartedness as exhibited in action. If in the marriage relationship one spouse by his conduct causes wanton, malicious or unnecessary infliction of pain or suffering upon the body, the feelings or emotions of the other, his conduct may well constitute cruelty which will entitle a petitioner to dissolution of the marriage if, in the court's opinion, it amounts to physical or mental cruelty "of such a kind as to render intolerable the continued cohabitation of the spouses". That is the standard which the courts are to apply, and in the context of s 3(d) of the Act [Divorce Act 1967–68 (Can) c 24 (now 1986 (Can) c 4, s 8(2)(b)(ii))] that standard is expressed in language which must be taken to exclude the qualifications laid down in *Russell v Russell* [[1897] AC 395], and the numerous other cases which have followed and applied the ancient ecclesiastical rule in matrimonial disputes.' *Knoll v Knoll* [1970] 2 OR 169 at 176, Ont CA, per Schroeder JA

To animals

'The prosecution was instituted under s 2 of 12 & 13 Vict c 92 [Cruelty to Animals Act 1849; replaced by Protection of Animals Act 1911, s 1(1)(a)] . . . which provides that if any person shall cruelly . . . ill-treat . . . any animal, he shall be liable to a penalty. . . . In this statute the word "cruelly" must refer to something done for no legitimate purpose. Cruelty must be something which cannot be justified, and which the person who practises it knows cannot be justified. . . . Cruelty means the infliction of grievous pain without a legitimate object, either existing in truth or honestly believed in.' *Lewis v Fermor* (1887) 18 QBD 532 at 534, per Day J

'The word "cruelly" in the statute . . . cannot apply to cases of merely inflicting pain, for many useful and necessary operations cause great pain. . . . There must be something of

the moral element of cruelty to bring a case within the section. . . . The question in the present case is whether the act [an operation on sows to increase their weight and development] was done for a lawful purpose; and not whether in point of fact, in the opinion of the tribunal that has to adjudicate, the practice is a good one.' Ibid at 535, per Wills J

'The expression "cruelly ill-treat" applies to a case where a person wilfully causes pain to an animal without justification for so doing.' *Barnard v Evans* [1925] 2 KB 794 at 797, 798, per Avory J

'The Protection of Animals Act 1911, s 1(a) . . . is directed against any person who "shall cruelly ill-treat". . . . One has to consider what is cruelty. I do not think it can be better defined than as "causing unnecessary suffering". It is necessary in some operations to cause suffering. . . . What the justices have to look at, when a man is charged with cruelly beating or illtreating, is whether he is doing something which it was not reasonably necessary to do.' Ibid at 798, per Shearman J

New Zealand 'I think it is clear from the definition of cruelty [in the Animals Protection Act 1960, s 2] that there must be an act accompanied by the will to inflict pain or suffering of the nature described in the definition [suffering that in its kind or degree, or in its object, or in the circumstances in which it is inflicted, is unreasonable or unnecessary].' *Hawker v Hammett* [1971] NZLR 830 at 831, per Wild CJ

CRUSH

[A workman claimed compensation in connection with silicosis arising from 'crushing' bricks.] 'I do not question that, in ordinary use of words, people distinguish "breaking" from "crushing". . . . The difference is in the degree to which the disintegration is carried. Wherever there are differences of degree, there must be cases where the one word becomes more applicable than the other, just as in the old problem of how many things constitute a heap. . . . The judge has held (with abundant evidence) that the work of the applicant exactly complied with the definition of crushing which he accepted and with which I agree: "He compressed the cemented bricks with violence so as to destroy their natural shape or condition: he broke them down into small pieces so as to constitute particles of dust".' *Forster v Llanelly Steel Co (1907) Ltd* [1941] 1 All ER 1 at 6, 7, HL, per Lord Wright

CRYSTALLISE

'The learned county court judge held that . . . the rights of the debenture-holders had not become "crystallised", the debentures not having become due, and no receiver for the debenture-holders having been appointed. . . . The second ground on which the learned county court judge proceeded was that the rights of the debenture-holders had not "crystallised", or, in other words, that the moneys secured by the debentures had not become payable. As to this, it is . . . to be observed that although this is so, yet by reason of the clause of the trust deed . . . the security constituted by that deed had become enforceable by reason of the fact that an execution had been sued out against the company. . . . The company as a going concern had come to an end, and although the due date of the debentures had not arrived, the holders were entitled to intervene to protect their security.' *Davey & Co v Williamson & Sons* [1898] 2 QB 194 at 199, 201, DC, per Lord Russell of Killowen CJ

'A floating security . . . is a floating mortgage applying to every item comprised in the security, but not specifically affecting any item until some event occurs or some act on the part of the mortgagee is done which causes it to crystallise into a fixed security. . . . [Counsel] argued that it was competent to the mortgagee to intervene at any moment and to say that he withdrew the licence as regards any particular item. That is not . . . the nature of the security; it is a mortgage presently affecting all the items expressed to be included in it, but not specifically affecting any item till the happening of the event which causes the security to crystallise as regards all the items. This crystallisation may be brought about in various ways. A receiver may be appointed, or the company may go into liquidation and a liquidator be appointed, or any event may happen which is defined as bringing to an end the licence to the company to carry on business.' *Evans v Rival Granite Quarries Ltd* [1910] 2 KB 979 at 999, 1000, CA, per Buckley LJ

[The term 'crystallise' is comparatively modern; see *Re Victoria Steamboats Ltd, Smith v Wilkinson* [1897] 1 Ch 158 at 161, where Kekewich J called it a 'newly-adopted' term.]

CUBICLE

'The ventilation and atmosphere of the dormitory are stated in the case to be common to all the cubicles [in the police station], and the window of each cubicle necessarily helps the natural lighting of the adjoining cubicle or cubicles. These are, it appears to me, matters essential to consider when the question is whether each cubicle can be regarded as part of a house capable of being separately occupied as a dwelling. As I have stated, we are not informed whether there are any and what arrangements for the artificial lighting and heating of the room in which these cubicles are situate; but, even assuming (against probabilities) that each cubicle had a separate arrangement for warming and lighting, it follows from the fact that the cubicles were open at the top that each of the occupants would to some extent share the warmth and light of the dormitory as a whole. Again, the arrangement of the cubicles precludes the idea of that complete or secure privacy implied in the separate occupation of a dwelling, and is probably adopted partly with a view to supervision and the maintenance of discipline generally in the room. It seems to me, therefore, that these men sharing as they do, so many things in the occupation of these cubicles, cannot be said to be separately occupying them as dwellings.' *Barnett v Hickmott* [1895] 1 QB 691 at 694, per Lord Russell of Killowen CJ

CUIUS EST SOLUM EIUS EST USQUE AD COELUM   *See also* LAND

'I can find no support in authority for the view that a landowner's rights in the air space above his property extend to an unlimited height. In *Wandsworth Board of Works v United Telephone Co* [(1884) 13 QBD 904] Bowen LJ described the maxim, *usque ad coelum*, as a fanciful phrase to which I would add that if applied literally it is a fanciful notion leading to the absurdity of a trespass at common law being committed by a satellite every time it passes over a suburban garden. The academic writers speak with one voice in rejecting the uncritical and literal application of the maxim. . . . The problem is to balance the rights of an owner to enjoy the use of his land against the rights of the general public to take advantage of all that science now offers in the use of air space. This balance is in my judgment best struck in our present society by restricting the rights of an owner in the air space above his land to such height as is necessary for the ordinary use and enjoyment of his land and the structures on it, and declaring that above that height he has no greater rights in the air space than any other members of the public.' *Lord Bernstein of Leigh v Skyviews & General Ltd* [1977] 2 All ER 902 at 907, per Griffiths J

CUL-DE-SAC   *See also* HIGHWAY

'An argument was put before us on the ground that this land [a lane leading only to a village] was a cul-de-sac, and that, therefore, following observations in some of the cases—such as in the Stonehenge case, *A-G v Antrobus* [[1905] 2 Ch 188], per Farwell J—it was a very important factor that no public money had ever been spent on it. I do not regard this lane as a cul-de-sac. A cul-de-sac, as I understand it, is a blind alley which this is not. There are innumerable villages and hamlets throughout the length and breadth of the land where the highway leads only to the one place, whether it be a hamlet underneath the downs or one beside a river, and the like. They are not culs-de-sac. So in this case. It must be determined according to the principles applicable to ways in general and not as a cul-de-sac.' *Huyton-with-Roby Urban District Council v Hunter* [1955] 2 All ER 398 at 401, CA, per Denning LJ

CULPABILITY

Australia   'In my view, the word "culpability" in s 19 [of the Crimes Act 1900 (NSW)] means . . . "blameworthiness" and not "deserving of punishment". The word *culpa*, after all, means blame; and . . . the Shorter Oxford English Dictionary gives "blameworthiness" as the preferable definition.' *R v Bell* (1985) 2 NSWLR 466 at 479, per Samuels JA

CULPABLE HOMICIDE   *See* HOMICIDE

CULPABLE NEGLIGENCE

Australia   [The Criminal Code (Tas) 1924–1986 provides, by s 156(2)(b), that homicide is culpable when it is caused by an omission amounting to 'culpable negligence' to perform a duty tending to the preservation of human life; and by s 159(1) that 'culpable' homicide not amounting to murder is manslaughter.] 'Culpable (i.e. criminal) negligence is the same under the Tasmanian Code as at common law

and includes inadvertent negligence.' *R v Holsness* [1970] Tas SR 74, per Burbury CJ

CULPRIT

'The word "culprit" appears to arise from an abbreviated entry which used to be made on the record of a criminal court engaged in trying a prisoner for felony or treason. The prisoner at the bar was asked how he pleaded to the indictment, and on his saying "not guilty", if the prosecutor joined issue, this was recorded in the words "culpabilis: prest", that is to say "the prosecution says you are guilty and is ready to prove it". The words were abbreviated in the form "cul. prit.". The clerk of the court then asked the prisoner "How wilt thou be tried?" and the prisoner replied "By God and the country", the last word meaning the jury. (In the old days the clerk of assize, when addressing the jury after it had been sworn and before trial commenced, told the jury that the prisoner had been arraigned and on his arraignment had pleaded not guilty "and for trial has put himself upon God and the country, which country you are", etc.) It has been suggested that the abbreviation "cul: prest", or "cul. prit", though really only a record of joinder of issue, came to be understood to be a word addressed to the prisoner, and hence the modern word "culprit". It is perhaps, some excuse for this excursus that the word "culprit" is undoubtedly sometimes used to mean the person guilty of a crime and sometimes (as in the illustration above) to mean the person accused of being guilty, and is, therefore, . . . a word of narrow or wider import according to the context in which it is found.' *Barnard v Gorman* [1941] AC 378 at 385, 386, HL, per Lord Simon LC

CULTIVATION   *See also* AGRICULTURE

Australia   [Section 130(2)(b) of the Health Act as amended provides that, save under and in accordance with the authority of a licence or other authorisation provided by or under the Act a person shall not 'cultivate' a prohibited plant or attempt to do so.] 'There is no definition of the word "cultivate" in the Act. In the Oxford English Dictionary a number of meanings are given, two of them relevant to the present question. The first is "to bestow labour and attention upon land in order to the raising of crops; to till; to improve render fertile by husbandry". The offence with which we are concerned, however, is not the cultivation of land, but the cultivation of a plant. The second meaning given in the Oxford English Dictionary is "to bestow labour and attention upon a plant so as to promote its growth; to produce or raise by tillage" . . . Other dictionaries to which we were referred were Webster's Third International Dictionary: "To protect and encourage the growth of", and Collins International Dictionary (1979): "to plant, tend, harvest or improve plants by labour or skill". An undefined word in a statute is to be construed according to its ordinary natural meaning. "Cultivate" is a word with a number of different meanings; not only does one cultivate the soil or cultivate a plant; one cultivates one's mind and one may cultivate a person in the sense of courting acquaintance or friendship with him. The last two meanings I have mentioned are of course entirely inappropriate to the notion of cultivating marihuana, but the first two are not. The offence is that of cultivating a plant, and while some means of cultivating a plant require a working of the soil, others do not, for example the application of liquid fertiliser. I do not understand why the application of water should not be regarded as cultivating the plant, in the sense of bestowing labour or attention upon it so as to promote its growth.' *R v Kirkwood* [1982] Qd R 158 at 159–161 per Lucas SPJ

Non-cultivation

'The particular states two positive acts that are alleged to amount to breaches of the defendant's covenant, and one act of a negative character. . . . The negative act charged in the particular is, "non-cultivation". The learned Baron declined under this particular to receive evidence of bad cultivation, as not falling within the natural meaning of non-cultivation. It appears to me that he did right.' *Doe* d *Winnall v Broad* (1841) 2 Scott NR 685 at 687, 688, per Tindal CJ

'"Non-cultivation" means leaving the land waste, which is not an uncommon thing in some parts of the country.' Ibid, at 688, per Bosanquet J

CUPBOARD

'"Cupboard" is a word of several meanings. No doubt, the common cupboard under the stairs is not a piece of furniture, nor is the cupboard which was once more commonly called a closet, but a cupboard fitted up for clothes may just as well be called a wardrobe and is certainly a piece of furniture.' *Gray v*

Fidler [1943] KB 694 at 709, 710, CA, per MacKinnon LJ

CURATE

Curates or ministers in charge include clergymen who are in charge of a parish either (1) during a vacancy in the benefice, including cases where the right of presentation is suspended; or (2) where a sequestration under a judgment against the incumbent or under his bankruptcy has been in force for six months; or (3) in certain cases where the incumbent is in breach of his duty of residence; or (4) where the incumbent is under a disability upon which the ministerial committee has reported; or (5) where a censure of suspension or inhibition has been pronounced against the incumbent. In these cases the clergyman is appointed as a stipendiary assistant curate and acquires his position of curate in charge by the incumbent's permitted or enforced withdrawal. An assistant curate may be also temporarily in charge of a parish during a short absence of the incumbent, but in that case acts as the representative of the incumbent and under his directions. (14 Halsbury's Laws (4th edn) para 704)

CURIOSITY

'I am quite prepared to accept the definition of "curiosity" in the Oxford English Dictionary; that is to say, a curiosity is an "object of interest: any object valued as curious, rare or strange". Mr Cunliffe has endeavoured to confine that definition, which I hold to be the ordinary meaning of the word "curiosity", to some kind of article not made by machinery; that is to say, an article which has an intrinsic value owing to its having been manufactured by an individual with his own hands; or, on the other hand, an article which is a natural curiosity, which has not been manufactured or made by any man. I cannot myself draw any such fine distinction.' *Re Zouche (Baroness), Dugdale v Zouche (Baroness)* [1919] 2 Ch 178 at 186, per Lawrence J

CURRENCY

Of insurance policy

'The policy [of insurance on a ship] contained the following provision: "Returning one guinea per cent. should the vessel be employed in the Eastern trade during the whole currency of this policy". The vessel was lost some time before the 12 months expired, and from April 1st, 1899, to the date of her loss she was employed only in the Eastern trade. . . . The question is as to the meaning to be put upon the expression, "the whole currency of the policy". The plaintiffs say the currency of the policy ends when the ship is lost; the defendant says the expression means the 12 months for which the vessel was insured. I think the plaintiffs' contention is the right one. The risk no longer exists after the ship is lost; the amount insured is immediately payable, and, being paid, the policy , and all obligations created by it, are at an end; the policy is no longer in any sense current.' *Gorsedd SS Co Ltd v Forbes* (1900) 16 TLR 566 at 566, per Bigham J

CURRENCY (Money)   *See also* FOREIGN CURRENCY

United States   An instrument payable in 'currency' or 'current funds' is payable in money. (Uniform Commercial Code 1978, s 3-107(1))

CURRENT

For the time being in force. (Social Security Act 1975, Sch 20)

'The word "current" necessarily speaks as at some point of time.' *Granby Consolidated Mining, Smelting & Power Co Ltd v A-G for British Columbia* [1923] AC 247 at 251, PC, per cur.

[A charterparty provided that the charterers should have the option of appointing the stevedores at loading places, the stevedores to be paid by the master at 'current rates'.] 'The umpire has adopted the construction . . . that the current rates must be the rates charged by the ring [i.e. a group of exporters]. . . . The expression "current rates" must mean the rates which the shipowner would have had to pay if he had had to make his own arrangements for loading.' *Britain SS Co Ltd v Bunge & Co Ltd* (1929) 46 TLR 40 at 41, per Roche J

Australia   [A charterparty provided that the charterer should appoint stevedores to load a cargo of wheat at a cost 'not exceeding the current rate for first class work' at the port of loading.] 'I can find no legal definition of current rate, and I adopt the meaning given in the New English Dictionary of the word "current" in the sense in which it is used in the charter, i.e. "generally accepted".' *Westralian Farmers Ltd v Federal Steam Navigation Co Ltd* (1930) 32 WAR 26 at 27, per Draper J

Australia   'As to whether "current" (in the clause [of a hire purchase agreement] providing that in the event of a seizure of the car by the company, promissory notes then current are to be delivered to the respondent [the hirer] and are to be void) refers to promissory notes unpaid though due, we think it refers to promissory notes which still have time to run—i.e. which are running—and not to those of which the due date for payment has arrived or passed. Mr Walsh, for the respondent contended that "current" meant "outstanding". That is not the ordinary meaning of the word "current", and there is no reason why the ordinary meaning should not be adhered to.' *Eager (E G) & Son Ltd v Jaenke* [1931] ST R Qd 257 at 263, per cur.

CURRENT PRICE   *See* PRICE

CURTILAGE

[A plot of land formed part of the unconsecrated churchyard of a church. The question was whether the plot formed part of the 'curtilage'. The court held that it was not, and so could be transferred to the local authority.] 'My conclusion is that for the purposes of s 7 of the 1964 Measure [Faculty Jurisdiction Measure 1964] curtilage is to be construed as meaning such small area of the churchyard which physically adjoins the church building and is required to serve some purpose of the church building in a necessary or useful way. It is in effect an integral part of the church. . . . It is enough if the two are in common occupation, not necessarily exclusive occupation. Its territorial extent will depend on the facts of the individual case and circumstances of the particular site. In the ordinary run of events the footpaths which may surround the church and the land which carries extended foundations, the drains and soakaways and supply services will obviously be part of the curtilage but beyond that one hesitates to express any general view as to the limits. If the churchyard happens to be quite small, it may well be that in such circumstances the churchyard and the curtilage of the church are coterminous in fact.' *Re St George's Church, Oakdale* [1975] 2 All ER 870 at 879, (Salisbury Consistory Court), per the Chancellor

'What . . . is meant by the curtilage of a

property? In my judgment it is not sufficient to constitute two pieces of land parts of one and the same curtilage that they should have been conveyed or demised together, for a single conveyance or lease can comprise more than one parcel of land, neither of which need be in any sense an appurtenance of the other or within the curtilage of the other. Nor is it sufficient that they have been occupied together. Nor is the test whether the enjoyment of one is advantageous or convenient or necessary for the full enjoyment of the other. A piece of land may fall clearly within the curtilage of a parcel conveyed without its contributing in any significant way to the convenience or value of the rest of the parcel. On the other hand, it may be very advantageous or convenient to the owner of one parcel of land also to own an adjoining parcel, although it may be clear from the facts that the two parcels are entirely distinct pieces of property. In my judgment, for one corporeal hereditament to fall within the curtilage of another, the former must be so intimately associated with the latter as to lead to the conclusion that the former in truth forms part and parcel of the latter. There can be very few houses indeed that do not have associated with them at least some few square yards of land, constituting a yard or a basement area or passageway or something of the kind, owned and enjoyed with the house, which on a reasonable view could only be regarded as part of the messuage and such small pieces of land would be held to fall within the curtilage of the messuage. This may extend to ancillary buildings, structures or areas such as outhouses, a garage, a driveway, a garden and so forth. How far it is appropriate to regard this identity as parts of one messuage or parcel of land as extending must depend on the character and the circumstances of the items under consideration. To the extent that it is reasonable to regard them as constituting one messuage or parcel of land, they will be properly regarded as all falling within one curtilage; they constitute an integral whole.' *Methuen-Campbell v Walters* [1979] 1 All ER 606 at 621, CA, per Buckley LJ

'"Curtilage" may well be smaller than "churchyard" and the greater includes the less.' *Re St Mary Magdalene, Paddington* [1980] 1 All ER 279 at 280 (Consistory Court), per the Chancellor

Australia [Section 66(13) was added to the Police Act 1892 (WA) in 1962. It makes it an offence for any person to be, or have been, without lawful excuse, in or upon any premises or the curtilage, whether enclosed or fenced or not, of any premises.] 'There is no doubt that, when the term "curtilage" is used without qualification, it is associated only with a dwelling house and not with any other building. The dictionary definitions are all to this effect. For example, the Oxford English Dictionary defines the term to mean "a small court, yard, garth, or piece of ground attached to a dwelling house, and forming one enclosure with it, or so regarded by the law; the area attached to and containing a dwelling house and its outbuildings. . . . [T]he Macquarie Dictionary as 'the area of land occupied by a dwelling and its yard and outbuildings, actually enclosed and considered as enclosed'." Jowitt's Dictionary of English Law (2nd ed) defines it as "a courtyard adjoining a messuage; a courtyard, garden, yard, field, backside, or piece of ground lying near and belonging to a dwelling house". For a recent judicial consideration of the term, reference may be made to *Methuen Campbell v Waters* [supra].' *Hislop v Spurr* [1983] WAR 180 at 181–182, per Kennedy J

CUSTODIAN

Bankruptcy

United States '[C]ustodian' means
(A) receiver or trustee of any of the property of the debtor, appointed in a case or proceeding not under this title;
(B) assignee under a general assignment for the benefit of the debtor's creditors; or
(C) trustee, receiver, or agent under applicable law, or under a contract, that is appointed or authorized to take charge of property of the debtor for the purpose of enforcing a lien against such property, or for the purpose of general administration of such property for the benefit of the debtor's creditors. . . .
(Bankruptcy Act 1978, s 101(10))

CUSTODIAN BANK

Investment securities

United States A 'custodian bank' is a bank or trust company that is supervised and examined by state or federal authority having supervision over banks and is acting as custodian for a clearing corporation. (Uniform Commercial Code 1978, s 8–102(4))

CUSTODY   *See also* CARE

Legal custody

'Commit to custody' means commit to prison or, where any enactment authorises or requires committal to some other place of detention instead of committal to prison, to that other place. (Magistrates' Courts Act 1980, s 150(1))

Of child

'Custody', in relation to a child, includes access to the child. (Matrimonial Causes Act 1973, s 57(1))

'Section 38(2) of the [Children] Act [1908 (repealed; see now Children and Young Persons Act 1933, s 17)] . . . distinguishes between the custody, charge, or care of a child. . . . Is it possible for a parent by a voluntary agreement, whether oral or in writing, to get rid of the legal presumption that he has the custody of the child which for the purposes of this Act is created by s 38(2)? . . . In my opinion it is not possible for parents by their own act to get rid of this legal presumption. . . . No separation agreement can rebut that presumption.' *Brooks v Blount* [1923] 1 KB 257 at 263, 265, 266, per Lord Hewart CJ

'The person who has the custody of a child cannot be heard to say that he has not the custody of the child unless he is deprived of the custody by the order of a competent Court.' Ibid at 267, per Salter J

[In the case of *Re Agar-Ellis, Agar-Ellis v Lascelles* (1883) 24 Ch D 317, Brett MR said: 'The law of England . . . is that the father has the control over the person, education and conduct of his children until they are twenty-one years of age. That is the law.'] 'I utterly reject the notion that an infant is, by law, in the custody of his father until he is twenty-one (repealed). These words "in the custody of a parent" were first used in the Limitation Act 1939. During the next year youngsters of eighteen and nineteen fought the Battle of Britain. Was each of them at that time still in the custody of his father? The next use of the words was in the Law Reform (Limitation of Actions, &c) Act 1954. Since which time pop singers of nineteen have made thousands a week, and revolutionaries of eighteen have broken up universities. Is each of them in the custody of his father? Of course not. Neither in law nor in fact. Counsel for the defendant realised the absurdity and sought to graft

exceptions on to the rule in *Re Agar-Ellis*. But he failed to provide any satisfactory definition of his exceptions. By the time he finished, it looked to me as if the exceptions would swallow up the rule. I would get rid of the rule in *Re Agar-Ellis* and of the suggested exceptions to it. That case was decided in the year 1883. It reflects the attitude of a Victorian parent towards his children. He expected unquestioning obedience to his commands. If a son disobeyed, his father would cut him off with 1s. If a daughter had an illegitimate child, he would turn her out of the house. His power only ceased when the child became twenty-one. I decline to accept a view so much out of date. The common law can, and should, keep pace with the times. It should declare, in conformity with the recent report on the Age of Majority, that the legal right of a parent to the custody of a child ends at the eighteenth birthday; and even up till then, it is a dwindling right which the courts will hesitate to enforce against the wishes of the child, the older he is. It starts with a right of control and ends with little more than advice. However, I will not pursue this legal concept further; because I am quite clear that in these Acts the words "in the custody of a parent" are used to denote a state of fact and not a state of law. The word "parent" is defined to include grandparents and stepparents. Whoever heard of an infant being, by operation of law, in their legal custody? And the Act [Limitation Act 1939] contemplates that a man of twenty-four, if of unsound mind, may be "in the custody of a parent". That may be if he is utterly dependent on him, but not otherwise. My conclusion is that an infant is "in the custody of a parent" if he is, in point of fact, in the effective care and control of a parent at the time of the accident.' *Hewer v Bryant* [1969] 3 All ER 578 at 582, CA, per Lord Denning MR

'The law relating to parent and child is concerned with the problems of the growth and maturity of the human personality. If the law should impose on the process of "growing up" fixed limits where nature knows only a continuous process, the price would be artificiality and a lack of realism in an area where the law must be sensitive to human development and social change. If certainty be thought desirable, it is better that the rigid demarcations necessary to achieve it should be laid down by legislation after a full consideration of all the relevant factors than by the courts, confined as they are by the forensic process to the evidence adduced by the parties and to whatever may properly fall within the judicial notice of judges. Unless and until Parliament should think fit to intervene, the courts should establish a principle flexible enough to enable justice to be achieved by its application to the particular circumstances proved by the evidence placed before them. The underlying principle of the law was exposed by Blackstone and can be seen to have been acknowledged in the case law. It is that parental right yields to the child's right to make his own decisions when he reaches a sufficient understanding and intelligence to be capable of making up his own mind on the matter requiring decision.' *Gillick v West Norfolk and Wisbech Area Health Authority* [1985] 3 All ER 402 at 421, 422, HL, per Lord Scarman

[*See* FULL AGE]

Australia '"Custody" is not necessarily co-extensive with "guardianship". Both words appear in the Guardianship of Infants Act and may have different significations. . . . It may be "guardianship" and "custody", when used in contrast, are several aspects of the same relationship. The former can very well be employed in a special context to denote duties concerning the child *ab extra*; that is, a warding off; the defence, protection and guarding of the child, or his property, from danger, harm or loss that may enure from without. Commonly, guardianship is used in a wider sense (*Neale v Colquhoun* [1944] SASR 119 at 129–130). Custody essentially concerns control, and the preservation and care of the child's person, physically, mentally and morally; responsibility for a child in regard to his needs, food, clothing, instruction, and the like.' *Wedd v Wedd* [1948] SASR 104 at 106, 107, per Mayo J

Australia [The Criminal Code 1899–1986 (Qld), s 352 deals with cases where a person unlawfully takes an unmarried girl under the age of 17 years out of the 'custody' or protection of her father or mother.] 'Section 352 strikes at a person who "takes" a girl "out of the custody of her father", etc. There is involved a physical removal of the girl, e.g. by force or enticement. If the word "custody" in the section means "tutela"—the status of guardianship—the words have no meaning since a girl cannot be physically taken or enticed out of a status. Some other reading for the word "custody" as used in the section must be sought. The root word "custos" means a

"keeper" and "custody" has a primary meaning according to the Oxford Dictionary of "safe-keeping: protection". Thus a prisoner in custody is in safe-keeping and a person who unlawfully takes him out of that custody is guilty of rescue. In my view the word "custody" in the section is used in the same sense.' *R v Johnson* [1957] St R Qd 594 at 597, per cur.

Australia 'I am strongly persuaded to the view . . . that in the present context [Limitation of Actions Act 1958, s 23(1) "custody" should be construed to denote a state of fact and not of law and that the test of "in the custody of a parent" is the existence of effective or actual care and control of a child by a parent. It is the exercise by a parent of the personal powers of care and physical control over a child which results in the child being in the custody of a parent—not some theoretically existing powers in a parent over a child regardless of any exercise thereof in fact.' *Verboon v McMahon* [1970] VR 282 at 291, per Adam J

Australia 'In its wider meaning the word "custody" is used as if it were almost the equivalent of "guardianship" in the fullest sense – whether the guardianship is by nature, by nurture, by testamentary disposition, or by order of a court. (I use the words "fullest sense" because guardianship may be limited to give control only over the person or only over the administration of the assets of an infant). Adapting, the convenient phraseology of counsel, such guardianship embraces a "bundle of rights", or to be more exact, a "bundle of powers", which continue until a male attains 21, or a female infant marries. These include power to control education, the choice of religion, and the administration of the infant's property. They include entitlement to veto the issue of a passport and to withhold consent to marriage. They include, also both the personal power physically to control the infant until the years of discretion and the right (originally only if some property was concerned) to apply to the courts to exercise the powers of the Crown as parens patriae. It is thus clear that somewhat confusingly one of the powers conferred by custody in its wide meaning is custody in its limited meaning, namely, such personal power of physical control as a parent or guardian may have.' *In the Marriage of Newbery* (1977) 2 Fam LR 11,652 at 11,654, per Demack J

CUSTODY OR POSSESSION

New Zealand ' "Possession" has been defined by s 17 of the Coinage Offences Act 1936 (UK), as follows: (*e*) A thing shall be deemed to be in the possession of any person, if he himself has it in his personal custody or possession, and also if he knowingly and wilfully has it in the actual custody or possession of some other person, or in some building or place (whether belonging to or occupied by himself or not), and whether he has it for his own use or benefit or for that of any other person. . . . In our opinion, this would be an apt definition of the words "custody or possession" in the section [s 52(1)(f)] of the Police Offences Act 1927 [repealed; see now the Summary Offences Act 1981, s 14] with which we are concerned; and constructive possession in appropriate circumstances can be sufficient to maintain a charge under the section.' *R v Rollo* [1956] NZLR 522 at 526, 527, CA, per cur.

CUSTOM   *See also* TIME IMMEMORIAL

A custom is a particular rule which has existed either actually or presumptively from time immemorial and obtained the force of law in a particular locality although contrary to, or not consistent with, the general common law of the realm. As regards the matter to which it relates, a custom takes the place of the general common law and, in respect of that matter, is the local common law within the particular locality where it obtains. Custom is unwritten law peculiar to particular localities. A custom exists in a particular locality only in respect of some particular matter or matters; other matters within the same locality are governed by the general common law.

Customs have several essential characteristics . . . but the essential characteristics which, taken in conjunction with one another, distinguish customs from all other legal concepts are, first, the necessity for the existence of the custom, actually and presumptively, from time immemorial, and secondly, the confinement of all customs to a definite limited locality. . . . [T]here is a well-defined rule that all customs must be local and confined to particular places. There cannot be a custom in one place to do something in another place. A custom must import some general right in a district. The land in a particular place and the inhabitants in respect of it may be charged by custom for matters within the place, but the custom will not apply to matters outside that place. A custom cannot extend to the whole realm, nor can it embrace every member of the public, for, in either case, it would then amount to the common law of the land. A custom which relates to the person or goods does not bind the Crown. The word 'custom' has been used to denote habits and usages not conforming to the essentials required by the foregoing definitions, but in its strict legal meaning it denotes exclusively an immemorial local custom. (12 Halsbury's Laws (4th edn) paras 401, 402)

'All customs are purely local, and confined to particular places. There cannot be a custom in one place to do something in another. The land in a particular place, and the inhabitants in respect thereof, may be charged by custom, for matters within the place; but custom will not apply to matters out of it.' *R v Ecclesfield (Inhabitants)* (1818) 1 B & Ald 348 at 360, per Lord Ellenborough CJ

'I believe the proper meaning of the word "custom" as applied to a matter of this description [custom for inhabitants of a parish to erect a maypole on the ground in certain land in the parish, and dance round and about the same, and otherwise enjoy any lawful and innocent recreation at any times in the year on such land] is something that has the effect of local law, but the general law puts a limit on that, and requires that it shall be reasonable and certain . . . Looking to the nature and origin of such customs, it would be unreasonable to expect any precise certainty as to what should be enjoyed as a matter of right. I cannot myself see, independently of authority, that there is anything so uncertain in this alleged custom that we are bound to reject it.' *Hall v Nottingham* (1875) 1 Ex D 1 at 3, 4, per Cleasby B

'Now, what is a custom? A custom, as I understand it, is local common law. It is common law because it is not statute law; it is local law because it is the law of a particular place as distinguished from the general common law. Now, what is the meaning of local common law? Local common law, like general common law, is the law of the country as it existed before the time of legal memory, which is generally considered the time of Richard I. Therefore, when people allege a custom they allege that which they call a custom as having been the law of the place before the time of legal memory. I say this because it appears to me that in some of the books custom has been confused with evidence of custom, which is quite a different thing. For instance, when we are told that custom must be certain, reasonable, and continuous—that all relates to the evidence of a custom. There is no such thing as law which is uncertain—the notion of law means a certain rule of some kind.' *Hammerton v Honey* (1876) 24 WR 603 at 603, per Jessel MR

Canada 'The term "custom" has more or less been identified as relating to practices going back to ancient times. The term "usage" seems more appropriate as describing a course of conduct which is recognized as being normal in various types of occupations and contractual relationships. In other words, usage is a question of fact and does not necessarily involve time immemorial.' *Re Gainers Ltd & Local 319 United Packinghouse Workers of America* (1964) 47 WWR 544 at 552, Alta SC, per Riley J

British custom

'The bill of lading . . . provides that "average, if any, is to be adjusted according to British custom". . . . The custom or usage prevailing among average staters in England is uniform and invariable that goods thus damaged or destroyed [by water thrown upon them to extinguish a fire] are not brought into account in an average adjustment. . . . The phrase "British custom" in this bill of lading was intended to refer, and, upon a true construction, does refer to this custom or usage, even if it be different from British law.' *Stewart v West India & Pacific SS Co* (1873) 28 LT 742 at 744, Ex Ch, per cur.

Of country

The custom of the country is the custom prevalent throughout the district, and is not proved by showing that it is the usage of a particular estate or of the property, however large, of a particular individual; and such usage will not be imported into the terms of a tenancy where it is not shown that the tenant was aware of it. The custom is to be collected, not from what witnesses say they think the custom is, but from what they depose to have been done publicly throughout the district. It must be proved by the party alleging it. (1 Halsbury's Laws (4th edn) para 1015)

'The jury have found a verdict for the defendant under an impression that the words in the declaration, "according to the custom of the country", required a more strict and specific proof in respect of the relative quantity of land allowed to be annually in tillage than I think they demanded. The words are, that the defendant promised to "use and occupy the premises in a good and husbandlike manner according to the custom of the country where the said premises lie". By which I understand the parties to have meant no more than this, that the tenant should conform to the prevalent usage of the country where the lands lie. From the subject-matter of the contract it is evident that the word custom, as here used, cannot mean a custom in the strict legal signification of the word; for that must be taken with reference to some defined limit or space which is essential to every custom properly so called. But no particular place is here assigned to it; nor is it capable here of being so applied. What shall be considered in farming as a good and husbandlike manner must vary exceedingly according to soil, climate, and situation. And therefore the custom of the country with reference to good husbandry must be applied to the approved habits of husbandry in the neighbourhood under circumstances of the like nature. That is the fair and natural meaning of the words of the contract as laid.' *Legh v Hewitt* (1803) 4 East 154 at 158, 159, per Lord Ellenborough CJ

Ordinary custom of port

'Prima facie the receiver is bound to receive the cargo as fast as the steamer can deliver; but this obligation is usually qualified by words, such as "customary steamship despatch" or "ordinary custom of the port", which mean, as explained judicially, the user of those facilities which the customary method of discharge at the port gives for the particular kind of cargo.' *Fawcett & Co v Baird & Co* (1900) 16 TLR 198 at 198, per Kennedy J

CUSTOMARY

New Zealand [An insurance policy provided that if the policy were terminated the company would retain the customary short-period rate for the time the policy had been in force.] 'The expression "the customary short-period rate" . . . in the absence of any indication of a contrary intention . . . ought to be construed . . . as meaning the rate which had been adopted by the [underwriters'] association and was in force at the date when the insurances were terminated.' *Lane, Walker, Rudkin Ltd v Yorkshire Insurance Co Ltd* [1928] NZLR 77 at 78, per Sim J; also reported [1927] GLR 450 at 451

CUSTOMARY STEAMSHIP DESPATCH   *See* CARGO

CUSTOMER

Of bank

It is true that there is no definition of customer in the Act [Bills of Exchange Act 1882], but it is a well-known expression, and I think that there must be some sort of account either a deposit or a current account or some similar relation, to make a man a customer of a banker.' *Great Western Rly Co v London & County Banking Co Ltd* [1901] AC 414 at 420, 421, per Lord Davey

'It is not necessary to say that the keeping of an ordinary banking account is essential to constitute a person a customer of a bank, for if it were shown that the cheques were habitually lodged with a bank for presentation on behalf of the person lodging them, and that when honoured the amount was credited and paid out to such person, whether with or without any profit to the bank for so presenting them, I would not say that such transactions might not constitute such person a customer within the meaning of s 82 [of the above Act; but see now Cheques Act 1957, s 1(2)(a)].' Ibid at 422, 423, per Lord Brampton

'The word "customer" [in s 88 of the Bills of Exchange Act 1909 (No 27 of 1909, Commonwealth) which is in the same terms as s 82 of the Bills of Exchange Act 1882 (repealed; see now Cheques Act 1957, s 1(2)(a)] signifies a relationship in which duration is not of the essence. A person whose money has been accepted by a bank on the footing that they undertake to honour cheques up to the amount standing to his credit is . . . a customer of the bank in the sense of the statute, irrespective of whether his connection is of short or long standing. The contract is not between an *habitué* and a newcomer, but between a person for whom the bank performs a casual service, such as, for instance, cashing a cheque for a person introduced by one of their customers, and a person who has an account of his own at the bank.' *Taxation Comrs v English, Scottish & Australian Bank Ltd* [1920] AC 683 at 687, PC, per cur.

'What does the expression "customer of a bank" cover? The most ordinary meaning, I suppose, is "a person who keeps an account at the bank". . . . But banks do various kinds of business, and in all those the individuals or the companies with whom they do the business may properly be called customers; and they can properly be so called, whether they are individuals or whether they are banks.' *Importers Co Ltd v Westminster Bank Ltd* [1927] 2 KB 297 at 305, per Bankes LJ

'If a non-clearing bank regularly employs a clearing bank to clear its cheques, the non-clearing bank is the "customer" of the clearing bank.' Ibid at 310, per Atkin LJ

United States   'Customer' means any person having an account with a bank or for whom a bank has agreed to collect items and includes a bank carrying an account with another bank. . . . (Uniform Commercial Code 1978, 4–104(1)(e))

Letters of credit

United States   A 'customer' is a buyer or other person who causes an issuer to issue a [letter of] credit. The term also includes a bank which procures issuance or confirmation on behalf of the bank's customer. (Uniform Commercial Code 1978, s 5–103(1)(g))

CUSTOMS DUTIES   *See also* EXCISE DUTIES

Duties of customs, or customs duties, in the strict sense are pecuniary charges or tolls payable upon goods exported from or imported into the country, as contrasted with excise duties which are payable upon goods produced and consumed within the country. (12 Halsbury's Laws (4th edn) para 501)

CYCLE   *See also* BICYCLE; MOTOR CYCLE

'Cycle' means a bicycle, tricycle, or cycle having four or more wheels, not being in any case a motor vehicle. (Road Traffic Act 1972, s 196(1))

CYCLE TRACK

'Cycle track' means a way constituting or comprised in a highway, being a way over which the public have the following, but no other, rights of way, that is to say, a right of way on pedal cycles (other than pedal cycles which are motor vehicles within the meaning of the Road Traffic Act 1972) with or without a right of way on foot. (Highways Act 1980, s 329, amended by Cycle Tracks Act 1984, s 1(1))

CY-PRES

Application to charity

Where a clear charitable intention is expressed, it will not be permitted to fail because the mode, if specified, cannot be executed, but the law will substitute another mode cy-près, that is, as near as possible to the mode specified by the donor.

An application cy-près results from the exercise of the court's ordinary jurisdiction to administer a charitable trust of which the particular mode of application has not been defined by the donor. When he has in fact prescribed a particular mode of application and that mode is incapable of being performed, but he had a charitable intention which transcended the particular mode of application prescribed, the court, in the exercise of this jurisdiction, can carry out the charitable intention as though the particular direction had not been expressed at all.

However, where the particular mode of application prescribed by the donor was the essence of his intention, which may be shown by a condition or by particularity of language, and that mode is incapable of being performed, there is nothing left upon which the court can found its jurisdiction, so that in such circumstances the court has no power to direct any other charitable application in place of that which has failed.

Where the particular mode of application does not exhaust a gift, these principles apply to the surplus.

There can be no question under English law of a cy-près application of property subject to trusts which are not charitable in law. (5 Halsbury's Laws (4th edn) para 696)

[See, further, as to the application of property cy-près, and assistance and supervision of charities by court and central authorities, Part III of the Charities Act 1960.]

South Africa 'That [cy-pres] doctrine only means this: that if there is a legacy or bequest to charitable uses, and it is impossible to apply the money exactly in the way prescribed because the institution to be benefitted has ceased to exist, or for some other good reason, the court may allow the money to be devoted to some other similar purpose.' *Ex p Wit Deep and Knights Central Joint Medical Society* 1918 WLD 13 per Wessels J

Application to power of appointment

Where there is not even substantial conformity in an appointment, the court may nevertheless interpose in favour of the general intention and execute the particular intention cy-près. This application of the cy-près doctrine which the courts will not extend further, but appears still to exist, applies only to testamentary appointments of realty, and not to appointments by deed or appointments of personalty or of blended realty and personalty. Under the doctrine, the court will construe an appointment to an object for life with remainder in tail to his first and other sons (who are not objects) as an estate tail in the appointee, provided that to do so will neither omit any object intended to be included nor include any object intended to be omitted. It is essential that the particular estate should be a freehold estate, and that the remainder should be in tail; but on a class gift the cy-près doctrine may be applied to some members of the class only, and not to others (36 Halsbury's Laws (4th edn) para 874)